WINE APPRECIATION

WINE APPRECIATION
A Comprehensive User's Guide
to the World's Wines and Vineyards

RICHARD P. VINE, Ph.D.

Coordinator—Enology and Viticulture
MISSISSIPPI STATE UNIVERSITY

Wine Consultant
AMERICAN AIRLINES

Drawings and Cartography
LARRY BOST

 Facts On File
New York · Oxford

Dedicated to:

THE BROTHERHOOD OF THE
KNIGHTS OF THE VINE

PER VITEM! AD VITAM!

WINE APPRECIATION:
A Comprehensive User's Guide to
the World's Wines and Vineyards

Library of Congress Cataloging-in-Publication Data

Vine, Richard P.
   Wine appreciation.

   Bibliography: p.
   Includes index.
   1. Wine and winemaking.   I. Title.
TP548.V484 1987   641.2′22   87-12831
ISBN 0-8160-1148-6

Printed in the United States of America

10 9 8 7 6 5 4 3 2 1

CONTENTS

LIST OF TABLES

FOREWORD

To find an American author who can write creatively and authoritatively not only about the American wine scene, but about the world of wine itself, is as exciting as discovering a new and rare vintage.

Who more apt to plumb the depths of wine than a writer named Richard P. Vine? The name alone bespeaks a special orientation toward all things vinous. Head of grape and wine research at Mississippi State University, as well as author of another great wine book, *Commercial Winemaking*, Dr. Vine offers in the present volume a vast store of wine knowledge to all who thirst for it. This book can also be credited with several firsts.

Wine Appreciation is possibly the first major work by an American author to meet the needs and desires of contemporary wine consumers, those who are seeking greater refinement and pleasure and for whom wine is one more way to enhance their enjoyment of life. This is also the first wine appreciation book to present the facts about wine and human physiology. In addition, it is the first to tackle the difficult but important topic of wine-consuming responsibility.

American wine educators and enthusiasts will be especially delighted with the American slant, American tone, and American English of *Wine Appreciation*. Many of us are sated with the highly judgmental pronouncements of European wine authorities who dictate, usually in British English, how, when, where, and which wines to enjoy, and who won't touch any wine unless it comes from Europe. Dr. Vine tips the balance toward American wines and the needs of American wine drinkers, and he does it in precise American-accented prose.

Wine Appreciation also traces the history of wine and its parallels with the development of Christianity and Western civilization. Dr. Vine here succeeds in being both comprehensive and entertaining.

We Americans have just begun to scratch the surface of wine appreciation. For too long we have been blinded by the notion that truly civilized pleasures were obtainable only abroad and especially in Western Europe. No one would deny the excellence of European wines and cuisine, and the necessity of educating the palate to their subtlety and variety, but we must not forget the wonderful bounty of foods and wines coming out of America right now.

For many, the words *wine* and *gourmet* and the associations they conjure up are quite frightening, but there's really no need to be intimidated. Being a gourmet simply means being able to appreciate the artful transformation of fresh, natural products into lovely, well-prepared meals. Enjoying and knowing about wine is just another part of this appreciation. Americans at last are waking up to how wonderful and rewarding wine can be. Civilized dining with wine may be an art form, but it is an art that appeals immediately, directly, and simply to the senses of sight, smell, and taste. It is also an art that the stomach can readily accept.

This volume conveys the scope of wine appreciation—the traditions, romance, and customs that have long surrounded wine—as well as the facts about human physiology, wine composition, production, and taste. For this we are indebted to Dr. Vine and those who assisted him in putting together this delightful and definitive book.

Norman Gates

Grand Commander,
Brotherhood of the Knights of the Vine

INTRODUCTION

Modern anthropological discoveries indicate that humans have appreciated wine for at least 8000 years and probably much longer. This seems entirely plausible when one considers that wine is essentially a natural beverage that requires no brewing or processing. Wine will, literally, make itself. The first vintners may have been cave people who discovered the "magic" of fermentation when they left some crushed grapes in a crude container for a few days. Long before the Stone Age, yeast cells have existed naturally on the outside of grape skins. Once these skins are broken the yeasts convert the sugars inside the grape into alcohol and carbon dioxide gas—hence, the bubbling "magic" of fermentation.

Wine today remains one of our most natural and simple foods. Yet wine as a subject has spawned a vast and complex body of knowledge. During the eighty centuries or more that wine has developed alongside Western civilization, humans have applied nearly every major academic discipline to advance the state of the art of wine.

We cannot and need not inquire too closely into the quality of wines made and consumed prior to the nineteenth century. Such products were often cloudy if drunk sooner and vinegar if drunk later. Nevertheless, people drank them for their taste, for their nutritive value, and because they provided a substitute for fouled water. There exist differing opinions as to the roles that wine has played in regard to agriculture, economics, medicine, nutrition, sociology, and theology throughout the history of Western civilization, but most experts agree that wine has had a significant impact on civilization. Indeed, Plato wrote: "Nothing more excellent or valuable than wine was ever granted by the gods to man."

In modern times wine growing has become a huge industry. Wine expert Hugh Johnson says that throughout the world one out of every one hundred persons is either a winegrower, a winemaker, or a wine merchant, and of every 130 acres of cultivated land, 1 is a vineyard. There are more than 25 million acres of vineyards spread over the Earth, and the annual world wine harvest is sufficient to supply every adult in the world with about twelve bottles of wine per year. Although Americans now consume more wine than spirits, they still drink less than one-tenth the per capita wine consumption of the French—and the French trail behind the Italians.

From simple beginnings have come thousands of different wines, and the range expands with each new vintage and each new vintner. The scientific findings and romantic fancies about wine have produced an overwhelming literature on every conceivable aspect of the subject. Indeed, a collection of all the different wine dictionaries, wine encyclopedias, wine textbooks, wine cookbooks, and other manifestos would fill a large library. There are hundreds of works addressing the topic of wine geography alone. All this information can perplex even the connoisseur—and persuade the neophyte that acquiring a true appreciation of wine is an impossible feat in one lifetime. Nonetheless, assisting the reader to become an educated wine consumer is the primary purpose of this book.

The overwhelming majority of comprehensive wine appreciation books offered in the American market are written by European authors, who, naturally, have European biases. Despite the fact that three out of every four bottles of wine consumed in America are from grapes grown in this country, we find our wines slighted in European books and consigned to brief sections of back chapters. *Wine Appreciation* is written for Americans, by an American, with American biases, and it considers American wines first. Being a born and bred easterner, from the Finger Lakes region of upstate New York, I may be guilty of giving eastern American grapes and wines more attention than their proportionate market shares would indicate. I accept such criticism without attempting to justify myself.

Alec Waugh, a noted English wine expert, recalls a time when a French lady asked him if he could tell the vintage year and district of a particular French wine by its taste. "Of course I can't," he replied, to which the woman retorted, "A Frenchman could." He politely responded with the tactful comment, "Some could, I know," although he did not add aloud what he was thinking, "but very few." A Frenchman may easily be able to recognize select vintages and/or vineyard sources in the wines that he tastes. A native Burgundian, for instance, may approach wine appreciation with blind passion (and even blinder prejudice) since wine is the very lifeblood of Burgundy. But while his expertise may be deep, it most likely will also be narrow. That same Frenchman would, in all likelihood, have great difficulty in making profound judgments upon wines from other countries. After studying this book carefully, the reader will still not be able to pick up every glass of wine and identify its precise source and vintage—no person, not even the greatest of experts, can do that. The philosophy herein aims to lead the reader toward a comprehensive knowledge of the wines of the world.

Dr. George Gale, professor, philosopher, vintner, and friend, relates two very important principles to consider when approaching one's first study of wine:

> Wine is an expression of the simple pleasures of geography, climate, winemaker's skill and, ultimately, the palate. But the wine snob typically uses it only as an expression of his or her wealth and supposed good taste. This is a perversion of one of the simple joys of our good green earth.
>
> And wine snobs often miss out on good wines. The most famous wines are not necessarily the best ones . . . . The wine snob knows about wine labels but doesn't necessarily know about wine. The only way to gain knowledge about wine is to drink it, studying and observing its many qualities and features.

Fragments of wine knowledge and mystical wine lore have turned many a wine bibber into an arrogant pseudo-expert. Some of the most common symptoms of this condition are name-dropping the great growths while turning up the nose at common wines, the praising of only dry wines while faulting all that have any detectable degree of sweetness, and a predilection for pitting classic European wines against their domestic counterparts. Unfortunately, this syndrome can often intimidate the bona fide wine student. The only "cure" is to experience many different kinds of wine. The true quality of the great growths may often be disappointingly similar to less noble vineyards; many of the truly fine white wines of the world are sweet, not dry; and American wines often outdo European counterparts, even in European competitions.

While both the quantity and quality of wine education in America has taken quantum leaps during the past several decades, wine still retains a certain mystique. Some perceive wine as a beverage reserved for the aristocracy, others fear using wine lest they commit a blunder of etiquette, yet others cling to some of the many wine myths that seem to pervade our country.

Dr. G. Hamilton Mowbray, winner of the American Wine Society Award of Merit for wine education, has made a fascinating study of wine myths, which has been published in the *American Wine Society Journal*. Among the many falsehoods that Dr. Mowbray reveals is, "Good wines must be expensive, or, expensive wines must be good."

He quotes the dean of American wine educators, Dr. Maynard A. Amerine, from a column in *The Friends of Wine* magazine:

> The concept that age per se is a guarantee of quality is unfortunately too common. It has led to some excessively inflated prices for old wines of ordinary quality. Perhaps in

many cases the high prices represent rarity, that is, the law of diminishing returns has been incorrectly applied.

Unfortunately, other such myths have somehow resisted debunking.

A significant share of the snobbery that continues to persist on the subject of wine has doubtless evolved from some of the more archaic literature. Prior to Pasteur writers traditionally adopted grandiose attitudes toward wine—perhaps understandably so—since wine answered so many human needs. The emergence of scientific explanations for the "magic" of wine, however, did less to curtail the flowery phraseology than one might have expected. It is, however, true that we hold wine in a reverence granted to no other human food. There are no international milk appreciation organizations, we do not have comparative tastings of orange juice, this years' production of beer is not given any special regard over that of last year, we do not collect and store different colas in our cellar, and we would have difficulty finding a syndicated column on the subject of coffee appreciation. Because wine commands a special attention and involvement, we can forgive those who have succumbed to the fancier notions of wine culture and refinement.

This book intends to be straightforward in debunking the snobbery, myth, and obscurity surrounding the enjoyment of wines.

The late André Simon, a great British wine writer of many volumes, once remarked that "there are all sorts of wine, young and old, good and bad, still and sparkling. There are times, moods and occasions when young wine will give us greater pleasure than the old; others when we shall enjoy the company of the old far more than that of the young." This thought establishes an ideal of wine appreciation—an understanding encompassing much more than just a casual list of acquired wine preferences, but, rather, one that is measured by the full extent of the pleasure with which wine rewards each individual.

It seems sensible to first define wine, and then explain how to classify and identify wines. Next comes the most important part of this work, the human physiological aspects of wine and wine enjoyment: How one selects, buys, stores, serves, and cooks with this remarkable beverage; how one goes about wine tasting and judging; and the tradition of wine toasts and sentiments. Then comes a full measure of wine history that not only sets roots deeply, but also "savoring a wine's historical associations along with what's in the glass can add even more to its interest," to borrow from the words of wine writer and historian Desmond Seward. Finally, we direct attention to the major wine-growing districts, subdistricts, villages, cellars, and, in some instances, even the individual vineyards, within the major wine-growing countries that form the immense world of wine. The apprentice is then left to plumb further and more pleasurable depths of wine appreciation.

Having discussed the seeds of reasoning behind this volume, I can find no adequate expression of gratitude to the many learned people who have contributed to its fruition. I would like to acknowledge my personal obligation to some of these individuals:

Some of us need more encouragement in such projects than others—this writer being one of those who needs full measures of such motivation. Those who were particularly inspiring were Dr. Gale Ammerman, Dr. Lanny Bateman, Dr. John Boyle, Mr. William Clifford, Dr. Warren Couvillion, Dr. Rodney Foil, Mr. John Grisanti, Father Thomas Hayes, Dr. James Heitz, Mr. David Levin, Father Bill Richter, Dr. Donald Robin, Mr. Thomas Storey, Mr. James Verges, Dr. Louis Wise, and Dr. Donald Zacharias.

There were, of course, many who contributed unselfishly in order to bring this work to realization. Dr. Peter Dahl, Mr. Jack Daniels, Dr. George Gale, Mr. Wilbur Garrett, Mr. Norman Gates, Mr. David Laskin, Dr. Hamilton Mowbray, Ms. Elizabeth Schwartz, Mr. Frank Stone, Dr. Douglas Stringer, and Mr. John Thornton each gave of their time and talent.

Special assistance, such as securing illustrations, searching out historical backgrounds, and other related information, were provided by Mr. Leon Adams, Mr. William Deutsch, Ms. Stacey Eaton, Ms. Mary Fetzer, Ms. Candace Frasher, Mr. Craig Goldwyn, Mr. Philip Hiaring, Sr., Mr. Morton Hochstein, Ms. Paula Kornell, Ms. Mary Lannin, Mr. R. deTreville Lawrence, Ms. Linda Jones McKee, Mr. Brian Moffett, Mr. Marcus Moller-Rocke, Mr. Kenneth Onish, Ms. Priscilla Price, Mr. William Shill, Ms. Barbara Shattuck, Mr. Michael Skurnik, Mr. Rodney Strong, Mr. William Stuht, Mr. Robert Theissen, Mr. Tracy Totten, Dr. Sergio Traverso, Ms. Gwen Watson, and Ms. Carolyn Wente.

The world of wine is blessed with many organizations that serve the needs of projects such as this. Eager cooperation was provided by the American Wine Society, Bordeaux Wine Information Bureau, Brotherhood of the Knights of the Vine, Bully Hill Wine Museum, Canadian Wine Institute, Centre for International Agricultural Development in Israel, Champagne News and Information Bureau, Chilean Trade Promotion Bureau, Comité Interprofessionel des Vin d'Alsace, Comité Interprofessionel des Vins des Côtes-du-Rhône, Deutsches Weininstitut, Food and Wines from France, German Wine Information Bureau, Italian Wine Promotion Center, KWV of South Africa, Les Amis du Vin, OPAV of Switzerland, Oregon Winegrowers Association, Rioja Wine Information Bureau, Sherry Institute of Spain, Society of Wine Educators, Vinos de España, Vins Vaudois of Switzerland, and the U.S. Wine Institute.

The contributions received from some periodicals were invaluable also: *The International Wine Review*, *New Zealand Wine and Food Annual*, *Vineyard and Winery Management*, *Vinifera Wine Growers Journal*, *Wine East*, and *Wine and Vines*.

The value of this effort was, at one time or another, critiqued and/or reviewed by Ruth Ellen Church, Dr. Frank Gadek, Mr. J. William Moffett, Ms. Lucy Taylor Morton Garrett, Mr. Victor Robilio, Messrs. Archie Smith, Jr., and III, Mr. Philip Wagner, and Mr. Bruce Zoecklein. Their comments and suggestions were extremely helpful in constructing this work.

The real work was performed by three wonderful ladies. Ms. Ruth Josey spent many hours, in addition to her regular duties as secretary, attending to the thousands of telephone calls and letters necessary in this project. Ms. Velma Jo Barham Miller contributed day after day on the keyboard, typing manuscript revisions. I lost track after we once counted up a total of 1,588 pages. Standing in for me in the classroom from time to time, and at meetings of the American Society for Enology and Viticulture, the American Wine Society, and for a number of other presentations that I could not attend personally, was Ms. Ellen Harkness, eno-microbiologist extraordinaire. Without these three remarkable women, this project could not have come to pass.

Most of all, there was the support from my family—each of whom, once more, sacrificed dearly in order that the time for this book could be provided. Thank you, wife Gaye, son Scott, and daughters Sabrina and Stacia. You are all terrific!

In vino veritas,
Richard P. Vine, Ph.D.

WINE APPRECIATION

Buena Vista

PRIVATE RESERVE

HARASZTHY

SONOMA VALLEY - CARNEROS

Chardonnay

ESTATE GROWN AND BOTTLED BY
BUENA VISTA WINERY, CARNEROS, SONOMA, CALIFORNIA, USA
Alcohol 12.9 % by Volume

1

THE STATE
OF THE ART

WINE—ORIGINS AND
DEFINITIONS OF THE TERM

Humans appreciated wine long before there was any word for it. Though experts disagree as to the exact origin of the term, many scholars now identify the Hittite script *wee-an* as the first "wine" word root recorded as early as 1,500 B.C. The *Oxford English Dictionary* traces the modern English word *wine* back to the Old English *win*, associated with the Latin *vinum*, which in turn is related to the Greek *oinos* and the archaic Greek *woinos*. The Greek *oinos logos* (wine knowledge) is the origin of our term *enology* (or *oenology*), the science of viniculture.

The common dictionary definition of wine is "an alcoholic beverage obtained by the fermentation of the juice of the fruit of the vine." The U.S. Bureau of Alcohol, Tobacco and Firearms (BATF) defines wine as "the product of the juice of sound, ripe grapes." One technical criticism of that statement is directed toward the phrase "sound, ripe grapes." There are several famous wines made from green grapes and even more made from overripe grapes. More importantly, the BATF definition overlooks the all-important fermentation process necessary to generate "the product."

Wine as the word used in this book is the product of fermenting and processing the grape juice or *must* (crushed grapes). Wine made from any other fruit would be qualified in the manner of "peach wine" or "blackberry wine" or "plum wine."

3

FERMENTATION

Fermentation is a natural process in which the grape sugars (e.g., sucrose, fructose, dextrose, and levulose) are transformed into alcohol (ethanol) and carbon dioxide gas. In 1810 the French chemist and physicist Joseph-Louis Gay-Lussac described this process in an equation:

$$C_6H_{12}O_6 \longrightarrow 2C_2H_5OH + 2CO_2$$
(grape sugars)   (alcohol + carbon dioxide)

This transformation is carried out by microscopic one-celled plants called *yeasts*, which produce enzymes—the catalysts of fermentation. Apart from the discovery of yeasts by Louis Pasteur, the only modification of the original Gay-Lussac equation has been the discovery that heat energy is released during fermentation:

$$C_6H_{12}O_6 \xrightarrow{\text{yeasts}} 2C_2H_5OH + 56 \text{ kilocalories of energy}$$
(grape sugars)   (alcohol + carbon dioxide + heat)

Consequently, we are dependent upon two very different plant forms for the making of wine: the grapevine and the yeast cell.

THE VINE

The leaves, stems, and roots of the grapevine classify it biologically as a higher-form plant. Such plants are able to use sunlight to make sugars from carbon dioxide and water through the process of photosynthesis. Some of these sugars are used in the metabolic processes of the plant's life system. Another portion of these precious sugar compounds is stored in the grapevine's roots until *veraison*—when the grape berries ripen and the stored sugars in the roots are transferred to the grape berries.

Taxonomically, the grapevine is classified as follows:

Group	*Spermatophyta*
Division	*Tracheophyta*
Subdivision	*Pteropsida*
Class	*Angiosperm*
Subclass	*Dicotyledoneae*
Order	*Ramnales*

Family	*Vitaceae (Ampelidaceae)*
Genus	*Vitis*
Subgenera	*Euvitis* and *Muscadinia*

There are fewer than sixty species of *Vitis* known, and many of these are indistinguishable to all but highly skilled viticulturists. Origins of the vine are largely limited to the Northern Hemisphere, and the North American continent is particularly abundant in native species.

Vitis is a deciduous plant that climbs by grasping supporting objects with outgrowths called *tendrils*. In the wild, vines may reach the tops of tall trees, but in viticulture the natural growth is generally controlled by annual spring pruning. Typically, vines in vineyards are trained onto post-and-wire trellises that are designed to optimize both the quality and the quantity of the grapes. Exposure of grape leaves to sunlight increases the production of grape sugars by allowing photosynthesis to transform carbon dioxide, which eventually will result in grapes of varying levels of sweetness. Generally, quality is closely linked to sweetness, and grape growers monitor sweetness levels carefully. Severe pruning is often practiced for smaller crops of higher quality; lesser pruning is generally used for larger-quantity, lower-quality fruit.

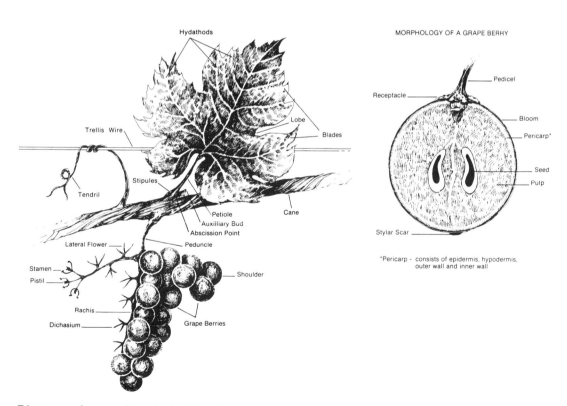

Diagram of grape bunch, leaf, and cane.

As a rule, two buds emerge from the axil of each leaf on the vine and are covered by a single cap, or *caliptra*. In many varieties a third bud is also found but rarely sprouts. Unless damaged by spring frost or some other malady, the primary buds and secondary buds develop and grow, and the secondary shoot normally falls with the leaves in autumn. When primary buds or shoots are damaged, secondary buds will then grow to produce a grape crop. Shoots that bear fruit will become "ripened" canes upon which buds are formed for the next year's crop. The flowers of the vine emerge on developing shoots—usually the finest wine grapes result from the primary bud shoots. At the perimeter of the flower, several male stamens produce pollen which, through wind, insect activity, or other mechanical means, finds its way to the central female pistil where fertilization takes place and formation of grape berries commences. All fruit results from the current season's growth. Bunches of grapes may be comprised of less than 10 berries each for some varieties, while others may exceed 300 berries per bunch. Shapes range from long, cylindrical forms (with or without "shoulders") to shorter conical structures. The grape is a true berry morphologically since it is a simple fruit which has a pulpy pericarp consisting of four skin layers: the epidermis, hypodermis, outer wall, and inner wall.

Generally, grapes are native to temperate zones, primarily between forty and fifty degrees south latitude, and are widely grown throughout the world.

The subgenus *Euvitis* includes all the world's grapevines that produce grapes in clusters—some fifty-odd species. The most important species of *Euvitis* is *Vitis vinifera*—the "Old World" grape which originated in Asia Minor. *Vinifera* is cultivated around the world today as the true noble wine grape. Among its many varieties are the famous Chardonnay, Sémillon, Sauvignon Blanc, Grenache, Cabernet Sauvignon, Gamay, and Pinot Noir widely grown in France, and Johannisberg Riesling and Sylvaner cultivated in Germany. *Vinifera* in Italy include the Barbera, Nebbiolo, Sangiovese, Trebbiano, and Verdicchio.

Vitis labrusca is the "fox" grape (so named for its strong "foxy" taste and aroma) that is native to northeastern America and southeastern Canada. Some varieties of *labrusca* are often called "slip-skin" grapes since the pulp is easily separated from the skin when squeezed. Isabella is one *labrusca* variety that was important in the early days of the New York State wine industry.

Vitis riparia is referred to as the "post-oak" or "frost" grape by some viticulturists. It is widely adapted to almost all of temperate North America, but mostly found east of the Rocky Mountains from Canada to the Gulf Coast. Because of its hardiness in cold weather, it is often used for grafting as a rootstock or in grape breeding by researchers.

Other grape species of note are

Vitis rupestris
Vitis cinerea   } North American
Vitis aestivalis
Vitis berlandieri

Vitis congentiae } Asiatic

Vitis sylvestris } European
Vitis sativa

The subgenus *Muscadinia* is more commonly known in America's Deep South as "muscadine"—the bronze-skinned varieties, collectively referred to as "scuppernongs," are actually one type of *Muscadinia*. The most widely cultivated species of *Muscadinia* is *Vitis rotundifolia*. Among the most commercially important of these are Carlos, Magnolia, Sterling, Noble, and Tarheel.

Note in the following table (table 1-1) that only about 3 percent of the total grape composition accounts for the difference between the very finest of grapes and the

TABLE 1-1   Composition of Grapes and Natural Table Wine

Componet Compound	Approx. % in Grapes	Approx. % in Wine
Water	75.0	86.0
Sugars (dextrose, levulose)	22.0	0.2
Alcohols (ethanol & higher)	.1	11.2
Organic Acids (tartaric, malic, lactic, oxalic, etc.)	.9	.6
Minerals (potassium, calcium, sodium, magnesium, etc.)	.5	.5
Tannins (catechin, gallocatechin, gallic acid, ellagic acid, chlorogenic acid, caffeic acid, etc.)	.2	.2
Nitrogenous compounds (protein, amino acids, humin, amide, ammonia, etc.)	.2	.1
Polyphenols (anthocyans, chlorophyll, xanthophyll, flavonols, etc.)	.1	.1
Total	99.0	99.9

Adapted from: M. A. Amerine et al. *The Technology of Wine Making*, 4th ed., Westport, CT: AVI, 1967, pp. 111 and 112 by permission of the publisher.

poorest (water and sugars, which account for 97 percent, will not significantly affect aroma and taste).

IMPORTANT GRAPE VARIETIES FOR WINEMAKING

Vitis vinifera (Old World Grapes)

White Wine Varieties

Chardonnay (shar-doe-NAY).   This classic grape is grown for both table wines and sparkling wines. It ripens late midseason to small clusters of medium compactness and typically yields small spherical berries arranged upon short cylindrical bunches. It is native to France. Chardonnay, which produces sparse crops even on fertile soils, is generally considered by experts to epitomize the vinous character. It is the principal variety grown in the Val de Marne of Champagne and is the grape for the white Burgundies of Chablis, Meursault, and Montrachet. It produces equally fine dry white wines in northern California, Wahington State, New York State, Pennsylvania, Virginia, and other eastern states.

Chenin Blanc (SHENEN blawn).   Chenin Blanc is grown primarily for table wines and is native to the Loire Valley Region of west central France. It is a vigorous and productive vine, yielding long, conical, compact bunches. Chenin Blanc typically has a delicate fruity flavor—somewhat figlike when properly vinified.

Gewürztraminer (ge-VOORTS-trah-meener).   Gewürztraminer is native to northern Italy, but is generally considered the grape of the Alsace in northeastern France. It is usually grown only for table wines and yields fair-sized crops of small cylindrical bunches replete with small, oval berries that are characteristically pinkish brown. Gewürztraminer is often referred to as "spicy," owing to the rather gingerlike aroma discernible in all well-made wines from the variety. Significant acreage of Gewürztraminer exists in California, with plantings in eastern America being gradually expanded.

Johannisberg Riesling (yo-HANNES-berg REEZ-ling).   This variety is often called *White Riesling* in western America. Native to Germany, it is the principal grape grown for the highest-quality table wines made in that country. It ripens in midseason to spherical, yellow-skinned berries dotted with characteristic russet spots. Bunches of Johannisberg Riesling are small, compact, and cylindrical in shape. Production is usually rather sparse. Wines from this classic variety are scented with a distinct flowery aroma when entrusted to the care of a skilled wine master. This variety is common in California, Washington State, and in several midwestern and northeastern states.

Muscat de Frontignan (MOOSkat dah frawn-teen-YAWN). One of many Muscat grape varieties that are prized for their bold, powerful aroma and flavor values, this variety is heavily grown in southern France. It produces elliptically shaped berries upon medium-sized, compact clusters. A close relative, Moscato, is grown in northern Italy for the famed Asti Spumante sparkling wines.

Palomino (pahl-o-MEEN-oh). Palomino is often referred to as *Golden Chasselas* in California and other viticultural locales. Palomino is the principal grape grown in Spain for the production of the finest sherry dessert and cocktail wine-types. It ripens late midseason to large, frequently shouldered bunches of greenish yellow, oblate (oblong or oval-shaped) berries. Vines of Palomino are generally rather vigorous and productive. While some vineyards of Palomino exist in California, the variety is not commercially planted anywhere in eastern America.

Sauvignon Blanc (so-veen-YOHN BLAWN). This classic table wine variety, native to France, is the principal grape grown in the eastern Loire Valley as well as in the Graves subdistrict of Bordeaux. Bunches of Sauvignon Blanc are rather small, with loosely clustered small whitish yellow berries. It is a vigorous vine and ripens its fruit during the early midseason. The fine wines from Sauvignon Blanc are characteristically smoky in aroma and finish with an aftertaste that may be grassy or earthy. Sauvignon Blanc is widely planted in northern California—yielding some of the fine *fumé* table wines that have become popular (sometimes labeled "Fumé Blanc"). The variety is sparsely planted in eastern America, but growing interest is encouraging new plantings.

Sémillon (SEM-mee-yohn). The Sémillon is most closely identified with the famed Sauternes table wines of Bordeaux, France. Sémillon ripens to spherical, golden, medium-sized berries rather compact in distribution upon short, conically shaped clusters. There is limited acreage devoted to Sémillon in California and Washington State, but very little is grown commercially in eastern America.

Sylvaner (sil-VAHN-ner). Sylvaner is native to Germany and can generally be found in the warmer, more southern wine-growing districts of that country. It matures to small, cylindrical, compact bunches of spherical yellow-green berries.

Sylvaner generally yields heavier crops than its sibling, Johannisberg Riesling, but its aroma and flavor are not nearly as intense as the prized Riesling. The Alsace in France is also a principal region for the cultivation of Sylvaner. Interest in the variety has never been widespread in California or eastern America.

Trebbiano (treb-bee-YAHN-oh).   This variety is grown in several regions of Italy and takes its name from the Trebbia Valley in Emilia-Romagna. It may yield either ordinary or fine whites, depending upon where it is grown and how it is vinified. Some of the better-known wines made from Trebbiano grapes include Soave, Orvieto, and Frascati. As a rule Trebbiano is made into table wine, but some is produced as Italian *frizzante*. In France the variety is known as *Ugni Blanc*. Trebbiano yields large, long, cylindrical bunches, usually shouldered or branched. Berries are medium-sized and oblate, with a greenish white color—occasionally blushed with pink. There is limited interest in Trebbiano in California, but it is rarely found in eastern American vineyards.

Red Wine Varieties

Barbera (bahr-BEHR-ah).   This variety is grown widely in the Piedmont and Lombardy regions of northern Italy. It is often very harsh as a young red wine, but mellows well with adequate wood aging. Barbera is a vigorous and productive vine that ripens its fruit in midseason. Clusters are medium in size and conical in shape, with heavily colored blue-skinned elliptical berries. It is popular in California both as a varietal table wine grape and as a blending wine used to enhance acidity levels. Few vines of Barbera are found in commercial eastern American vineyards.

Cabernet Sauvignon (cab-behr-NAY so-veen-YOHN).   The classic Cabernet Sauvignon is perhaps the most famous grape in the world. There are diverse opinions as to its origin, but it remains the principal variety grown for the renowned châteaux of Bordeaux in France. It has an aroma of bell peppers and a berry flavor reminiscent of black currants. The vine is vigorous and rather productive—yielding long, loose, conical clusters of small spherical blue/black-skinned berries. The deeply lobed leaves of Cabernet Sauvignon are often used as the models for vinicultural artwork. Cabernet Sauvignon is widely grown in northern California and Washington State by many of the finest vintners. The variety is also gradually finding growers in eastern America, although present acreage is comparatively small.

Gamay (gam-AY).   Gamay is the premier grape variety of the famous Beaujolais subdistrict of Burgundy in France. It is a vigorous vine that produces abundant medium-sized conical, compact clusters of large, slightly elliptical, blue-skinned berries. Gamay ripens in late midseason. The wine from Gamay is usually rather light-bodied, although the better vineyards can yield richer red table wines. In California it is widely grown for both red and rosé table wines. Some Gamay vineyards exist in eastern America, but the variety is not important there as yet.

Grenache (gren-AHSH).   This variety is native to Spain, where it is called Garnacha, but is widely grown in the Rhône Valley of France and in California for the production of red and rosé table wines. Grenache ripens in late midseason. Clusters are short and conical, often shouldered, with loosely arranged, medium-sized, slightly elliptical, reddish blue berries. Grenache is rarely found in eastern America.

Merlot (mair-LOH).   Next to Cabernet Sauvignon, Merlot is the most important grape variety in the blending of the great Bordeaux châteaux wines of southwestern France. It has long, large conical clusters of compact medium-sized berries that are spherical and blue-violet in color. In recent years the soft, but rich, full-bodied character of Merlot has gained this red wine increasing popularity throughout America. California and Washington State have responded with many new vineyards, and eastern winegrowers are also planting the variety.

Pinot Noir (PEENOH nwah).   This is the regal variety of the renowned "Slope of Gold"—The Côte d'Or of northern Burgundy in east central France. Pinot Noir does not seem to grow anywhere else in the world as well as in Burgundy. Few vintners in California can render much more than relatively ordinary wines from the variety although Oregon is gaining a good reputation with it. A few fine wines in eastern America are made from Pinot Noir, but they are rare. It is typified by a light-bodied and light-colored amber-red wine with a distinctive coffeelike bouquet when properly vinified. At maturity Pinot Noir clusters are small, cylindrical, and compact. It has small, oval, blue-black berries. The vine is usually not very vigorous and is shy to yield more than comparatively small quantities of fruit.

Nebbiolo (neb-BYO-loh).   Nebbiolo is the aristocrat among red wine grapes in the prestigious wine-growing regions of northern Italy, producing such highly esteemed wines as Barolo, Barbaresco, and Gattinara. It ripens late to long, conical clusters that are often shouldered. Berries are spherical, gray-blue in color, and medium-sized. On good soils Nebbiolo can be somewhat productive. Its wine is often tart, heavy, and, at its best, has a hint of raspberries in the bouquet. Nebbiolo is not very popular in California and is rarely found in eastern American vineyards.

Syrah (sear-RAH).   Most of the fine red table wines of the Rhône Valley in southern France are blends: While Grenache is the major base ingredient, the heavy richness of the blend comes from the thick, black-ruby wines from Syrah. Clusters of Syrah are comparatively short and conical, with slightly elliptical, black berries. Interest in the variety is growing among quality winegrowers both in California and eastern America.

Vitis Labrusca (Native American Grapes)

White Wine Varieties

Catawba (kah-TAW-bah).   Catawba was found growing in the wild near the Catawba River in North Carolina and was planted in Ohio vineyards to make America's first commercial sparkling wine. It ripens late, with medium-sized, conical bunches of large, pink-skinned spherical berries. The Catawba remains heavily planted in eastern American vineyards, but interest is gradually diminishing in the wake of newer selections. Catawba vines are rarely found in California.

Delaware.   The origin of Delaware is Delaware County, Ohio, where the variety was discovered in the early 1800s. It is the most widely grown native American-type planted in eastern America for the commercial production of white table wines and sparkling wines. It ripens rather early to small, cylindrical clusters of small, spherical, pink-skinned berries. Delaware has a tendency to yield only small crops, but its wines can exhibit a pleasant, fruity aroma that is often compared to some of the Teutonic varieties in Europe. Few Delaware vines are cultivated commercially in California.

Niagara.   Niagara is a *hybrid cultivar** developed by researchers in Niagara County, New York, during the 1860s. It is a vigorous and productive vine when grown in rich soils. Niagara is the standard-bearer for the rich, heavily scented wines that made New York a famous wine-growing state. It is used primarily for blending in table and sparkling wine production—and even more widely used in the sherry-type wines made by some of the larger eastern American vintners. At maturity, Niagara yields medium-sized bunches of large, greenish yellow, spherical berries. Like Catawba and Delaware, Niagara is practically nonexistent in commercial Californian vineyards.

---

*In viticultural terminology, *cultivars* are cultivated varieties resulting from hybridizing; grape types that occur in nature are termed simply *varieties*.

Red Wine Varieties

Concord.   Concord is better known for its juice and jelly production than for wine; taking all its various uses together, it is unquestionably the most widely grown cultivar in eastern America. Many food products labeled "grape flavored" borrow from the rich, fruity aroma characteristic of the Concord grape—often referred to as a "foxy" flavor. Concord was developed in Massachusetts in the 1840s and brought to New York State shortly thereafter to make dessert wines and, some years later, sparkling wines as well. A few Concord vineyards exist in California, but the acreage is not important there.

French-American Hybrid Grapes

White Wine Varieties

Aurora Blanc (ah-ROH-rah BLAWN).   This is one of the most widely planted of the French-American hybrids in eastern America. It was developed in France during the latter part of the ninetenth century and has the characteristic of ripening very early in the vintage season. Clusters of Aurora are long, cylindrical, often shouldered, and very compact. Berries, which vary in size, are spherical with a greenish white color—sometimes exhibiting a pink blush. Aurora Blanc is usually made into a slightly sweet white table wine, the best of which may be somewhat reminiscent of Barsac wines from Bordeaux in France. Only token plantings of Aurora Blanc are to be found in California.

Seyval Blanc (SAY-vahl BLAWN).   Seyval Blanc is considered by many to be the finest of the French-American hybrids. It ripens midseason to large, conical bunches of medium-sized, slightly elliptical berries that are greenish yellow in color. Well-made Seyval Blanc can compete favorably with some dry white wines made from Chardonnay, Pinot Blanc, and other fine white table wine varietals. Vines of Seyval Blanc are grown widely in eastern and midwestern states, but they are comparatively rare in California.

Vidal Blanc (VEE-dahl BLAWN).   This French-American hybrid cultivar is rather Teutonic in character, producing residually sweet white table wines that can rival the better Sylvaner varietals. It ripens in the latter part of midseason to very long, cylindrical clusters that are almost always shouldered. Berries are rather small, spherical, and often tightly compacted on the bunch. The color of Vidal Blanc fruit is greenish white and exhibits russet spots in a manner similar to Johannisberg Riesling.

Red Wine Varieties

Chancellor.   Chancellor ripens during the late midseason to rather large conical bunches of medium-sized, slightly elliptical, blue-black berries. It can yield fine, heavy-bodied, rich red table wines when properly aged in wood—often compared to the wines of Bordeaux in France. The susceptibility of Chancellor to mildew and other maladies in the vineyard has made winegrowers in eastern America a bit wary of it; the variety is rarely found in commercial California vineyards.

DeChaunac (dah-SHOW-nack).   This variety is one of the red French-American hybrid selections most widely planted in eastern America. It matures late during the midseason to very long, loosely clustered bunches of small, spherical, blue-skinned berries. It makes a good everyday red table wine—though in some years DeChaunac can be superior when handled by skilled wine masters. Some offerings of DeChaunac rosé can be found in the marketplace. As with most French-American hybrid cultivars, few are commercially grown in California.

Maréchal Foch (MAR-shall fowsh).   Mature fruit from Maréchal Foch is typified by very small, tight clusters of small, spherical, blue-black berries. It ripens early in the vintage season and may yield grapes with exceptionally high sugar content, but often only in small quantities. The finest vintners can make Maréchal Foch from a superior vintage into high-quality red table wines often favorably compared to some of the Burgundies of France. While little Maréchal Foch can be found commercially grown in California, there are some plantings of the cultivar in Burgundy and other regions in France. It is widely planted in eastern and midwestern America.

WINE MICROBIOLOGY

Yeasts

Yeasts are microscopic, egg-shaped cells which, because they lack stems, leaves, roots, and chlorophyll, are referred to as lower-form plants. They can reproduce once every half-hour or less—a rate that can generate a huge amount of yeasts in a relatively short period of time.

Yeasts are taxonomically classified as follows:

Phylum	*Thallophyta*
Subphylum	*Fungi*
Class	*Eumycetes*
Subclass	*Ascomycetes*
Order	*Endomycetales*
Family	*Saccharomycetaceae*
Subfamily	*Saccharomycoideae*
Genera	*Saccharomyces*

Saccharomyces cerevisiae is the species within which the most important fermentation yeasts are found. The variety *ellipsoideus* is a cultured wine yeast; some of the more popular strains are *Montrachet, Épernay, Champagne, Fermivin,* and *Steinberg.*

Saccharomyces genera *Apiculata* are often referred to as "apiculate" yeasts because the cells look pointed or irregularly shaped at one or both ends. These are the "wild" yeasts that collect on the outer skin of grapes and, until Pasteur developed microbiology, they were often the natural yeasts that performed the "magic" of fermentation. Today these organisms are known to cause undesirable flavors. Consequently, wine masters usually employ one or another strain of cultured *ellipsoideus* in their wine fermentations.

Most wine yeasts grow throughout the entire volume of fermenting juice or must. There are, however, also surface-growing yeasts called *Flor*, which transform alcohol into a compound that is often described as having a nutlike aroma and flavor characteristic of "maderized" wines such as sherry. *Saccharomyces beticus* is the Flor strain that is cultured for the famous Spanish sherries, but other surface-growing film yeasts such as the genera *Candida, Kloeckera,* and *Pichia* are spoilage microorganisms that cause "off" flavors.

Bacteria

The microbes most feared by wine masters are the vinegar bacteria—more properly known as *Acetobacter*, or acetic acid bacteria. Fortunately, we know that these bacteria require oxygen to grow, a condition that can be controlled in well-equipped wineries. The most common strain of vinegar bacteria is *Acetobacter aceti.*

Depending upon the wine type and wine master's intent, malolactic bacteria can be either beneficial or detrimental. The action of these microorganisms is, as their name suggests, to transform malic acid to lactic acid—the former an organic acid that tastes and smells rather applelike, while the latter is somewhat cheesy in nature. *Leuconostic oenos* is the most cultured strain of malolactic bacteria and is generally used for excessively heavy and tart red table wines.

Lactobacillus brevis may spoil wine with an infection known by some as *Tourne*—a malady that renders a wine insipid. Tourne is also typified by the formation of acetic acid, lactic acid, and carbon dioxide gas. These same compounds are also formed by *Lactobacillus buchneri* that are responsible for *Piqure lactique*, a condition that results in a harsh, pungent wine.

Pediococcus cerevisiae bacteria produce histamine in some wines, predominantly red table wines. Histamine is an organic compound that stimulates blood circulation. It also plays a major role in allergic reactions.

A wine spoilage that the French call *Vins Filant* or *Graisse* is often termed *Amertume* in America. This disorder results in wines that have developed acrolein—a very bitter compound that is highly irritating to the nasal passages. *Leuconostoc mesenteroides* is the bacterium that causes Amertume.

Molds

While the viticulturist may have to contend with such molds as black rot, brown rot, downy mildew, powdery mildew, and others in the vineyard from year to year, there are few molds that directly affect the finished wine in the well-managed winery. In general, such molds damage the fruit, and this, in turn, may seriously affect the quality of the wine.

The famous "noble mold," or more properly, *Botrytis cinerea*, is an exception. When desired and grown in optimal conditions, this fuzzy gray mold permeates the skin of grape berries and allows internal water to evaporate, resulting in lighter, sweeter fruit and sweeter and more intensely flavored wines. Such grapes, when harvested, make the renowned *pourriture noble* (noble mold) wines of Sauternes in Bordeaux, France, and "late harvest" wines in America and the Rheinland in Germany (where the noble mold is known as *Edelfäule*. Connoisseurs consider the noble mold wines some of the most exquisite white wines made, and they are usually expensive. Unless properly handled, though, the permeated berries may become infected with *Penicillium*, another mold that is often observed on moist surfaces in both vineyard and winery. *Penicillium* can render fruit worthless and can also be a problem on tank and equipment surfaces left moist in the winery.

WINE CLASSIFICATION AND PRODUCTION METHODS

Wine experts generally divide wine into five categories: table wines, sparkling wines, dessert wines, aperitif wines, and pop wines. The distinctions among the classes are based primarily on major differences in their manner of vinification.

Table Wines

The overwhelming majority of the wine produced in the world falls into the category of table wine. Table wines range from the obscure and ordinary to the most expensive and celebrated classics. As the name suggests, table wines are designed for use at the table as a complement to good food, and for this reason they also are often referred to as *dinner wines*. Table wines are usually dry, or nearly so, but a few, especially some of the whites, may be sweet or just residually sweet. Table wines range from bland to tart, from thin-bodied to heavy, and from pale white to deep ruby red. Virtually all, however, are fermented to contain less than 14 percent alcohol by volume.

Table wines may be either *generic* or *varietal*. Generic table wines are labeled for the area in which they are grown, such as Burgundy, Bordeaux, California, New York State, and the Rhein Valley. Varietal wines are labeled for the variety of grape principally used in their production, such as Cabernet Sauvignon, Catawba, Johannisberg Riesling, and Seyval Blanc.

Among the most widely enjoyed American wines are the "jug" wines that can be found in most markets. Unfortunately, these often have the worst reputations —perhaps owing to the old myth that "to be a truly good wine, it must necessarily be expensive."

Jug wines are defined as any wine commercially marketed in a container of 1.5-liters' capacity or larger. Most experts consider jug wines as California generic offerings, which is generally true, though varietals also can be found. There are also jug wines from eastern American and European vintners. Most jug wines are table wines, but a few jug dessert wines answer a comparatively small demand.

To some extent, jug wines epitomize the many advancements in wine-producing technology. Research has met consumer demands for freshness, flavor, and overall appeal with new techniques to make wine more quickly at less cost. To these specific ends, jug wines are primarily designed for immediate consumption and usually do not improve with bottle aging. One frequently hears that jug wines are "America's answer to the *ordinary* wines of Europe." In most cases jug wines are far superior.

In 1985 Americans consumed 377 million gallons of table wines, of which approximately 257 million gallons were produced in California; 112 million gallons were imported, primarily from Europe; and 8 million gallons were produced by the other forty-nine states.

White Table Wines

The basic principles of white winemaking are rather straightforward. However, capturing natural essences and flavors from fine white wine grapes can be an elusive and exasperating task for the vintner.

Across the world's range of white wine production one can find examples varying in color from very pale to medium gold, and in taste from bone dry to very sweet, and from bland to acidic and astringent. Vintners in America are free to produce white wines in almost any combination of these qualities they choose, providing, of course, that cellar treatments and label graphics meet the standards set by law. Foreign winegrowers, depending on their country and regional locale, often have far less freedom due to government regulations and traditional interpretations of what white wine qualities are desired.

White table wines are generally made from the juice pressed from white grapes and fermented at cold temperatures for several weeks. Red and blue grapes are also used, but not nearly to the extent of the whites. Most grapes have white juice regardless of color; pigmentation is contained almost entirely in the skins.

Vintage Season.   The winemaker carefully scrutinizes each container of grapes that arrives at the winery; then weighing, crushing, and stemming take place immediately. Stems, which contain tannins (complex polyphenols), can cause astringency in white wines and, therefore, the removal of stems is a common practice.

Typically, a small amount of sulfur dioxide is added to each container of grapes as it is being dumped into the crusher-stemmer. Sulfur dioxide will generally inhibit the action of natural microorganisms, but will not usually be concentrated at a high enough level to restrict the growth of cultured yeasts used to ferment the juice.

Unlike reds, white grapes are not normally fermented "on the skins" (skins in contact with the juice); this prevents pigments from being extracted. White grape pigments often contribute undesirable color and flavor values to wine. Hence, much of the flavor remains in the pomace (skins, pulp, and seeds) after the juice is pressed out. Some vintners choose to crush and stem white grapes, leaving the must intact for a period from several hours to as long as several days, in order to leach out additional flavor from the skins. This can greatly enhance flavor intensity, but also runs the risk of bacteria and mold growth, as well as the premature start of fermentation with undesirable natural yeasts.

Pressing.   The pressing of white grapes is yet another step that must be completed properly or else poor juice and, in turn, poor wine may result. A large amount of juice will run through the press before any pressure is applied. This is aptly called *free-run* juice and is often kept in a separate lot as a completely different wine from that made from the pressed juice. Some vintners feel that the free-run juice is superior to that which is yielded under pressure. However, there are probably just as many winemakers who feel that the juice obtained from lower pressures is every bit as good as free-run. In any event, most vintners agree that white grapes cannot be subjected to high pressure for the extraction of high-quality juice. For most of the best-known white wine cultivars, a yield of more than 175 gallons per ton would be considered excessive. For the native muscadine grapes of the Deep South, perhaps 140 gallons per ton would be the maximum. Higher pressures increase the amounts of solids, oils, and tannins in the press yield.

Pressing grapes in the Champagne region of France. (Source: Champagne News and Information Bureau.)

Cooling.   Immediately following pressing, the juice is cooled in settling tanks maintained at a cool fermentation temperature of about 55 degrees Fahrenheit. After several days, the juice is *racked* (decanted, see below) to a fermenting tank. The wine master will then carefully measure the volume of the juice and analyze its sugar content (expressed in degrees *Brix*, which is roughly a percentage of sugar solids in the juice) and total acidity. These analyses indicate whether adjustments in sugar and acidity levels are necessary (provided such adjustments are permitted by governing regulations).

Analysis.   Each degree Brix measured in white grape juice will ferment to about .535 percent alcohol by volume. In other words, in order to finish a fermentation with 12 percent alcohol, a beginning Brix of about 22.5 degrees is required. If sweetness is desired in the wine, the wine master may calculate how much additional sugar will be needed to attain that sweetness level. Higher sugar levels are achieved by allowing grapes to overmature in the vineyard or by the addition of grape juice concentrates or cane, beet, corn, and other types of approved sugars. Acid adjustments are made in much the same fashion, using tartaric and fumaric acids.

Typically, the grapes of California are high in sugar and low in acidity, while the reverse is true in eastern America. Consequently, sugar additions are prohibited in commercial California winemaking, and acid additions are tightly controlled in the East by BATF regulations.

Fermentation.   White wines of superior quality are dependent upon simple but precise fermentation procedures. A healthy yeast culture, free of bacteria and mold contamination, is carefully inoculated in the fermenter. It normally takes at least three weeks, at a temperature of 55 degrees Fahrenheit, to complete a white wine fermentation. Temperatures in excess of 55 degrees Fahrenheit may cause significant evaporation and loss of fruit aromas.

Racking.   During and after fermentation, pulp solids and yeast cells will precipitate to the bottom of the fermenter in the form of a sediment called *lees*. In order to prevent this sediment from decomposing and infecting the new wine with mousy flavors, several rackings are performed during the first two or three months of the young white wine's life: The wine is drawn off its lees, either by draining or pumping, and transferred to a new clean barrel or tank.

Blending.   Blending is a phase of wine production that has given rise to many different personal philosophies. It is an operation that may take place several months or several years after the vintage, depending upon the wine and the winemaker. For white wines, there are several factors that the wine master will be taking into account when blending wines from different vintage years.

First, blending will reduce positive qualities as well as negative qualities of separate wines unless, of course, the positive qualities predominate. Blending ensures consistency and uniformity. Often one year will yield wine of exceptional individual characteristics compared to normal vintages. Overpowering varietal flavors, especially those of the very distinctive varietal selections, may be improved with blending. Blending has limits set by the BATF for varietal and vintage labeling, and there are moral limits beyond those. Most of the world's great wines are made from grapes of a single vintage grown at one recognized locale: They may be blends of different grape *varieties*, but they are unlikely to be blended beyond that.

Clarification.   New wines are generally hazy or cloudy in appearance due to suspended particles of grape pulp, yeasts, and certain colloids. Within another several months after blending, if any blending is done, new white wines are usually ready for clarification using gelatin and clay materials in different orders. These clarifying agents combine to form a compound that precipitates and removes the suspended particles as *clarification lees*.

Stabilization.   New white table wines are almost always unstable. Undesirable by-products of fermentation should be removed before any further processing takes place. Normally, the smaller wineries use extended refrigeration for stabilizing young wines. Following clarification, the wines are transferred to casks or vats in a cellar and held at about 28 degrees Fahrenheit while stored there for at least one month. During this time tartar crystals and other by-products that make wine unstable crystallize and precipitate. The next step is filtration, in which the wine is poured through coarse filters into clean casks or vats.

Aging.   White wines will age in stainless-steel, glass, and other rather nonporous tanks, but aging will occur much faster in wooden vessels.

More and more vintners are turning to stainless-steel aging tanks for white wine processing and aging. These tanks are easier to maintain, yield more consistent results, and generally provide a more antiseptic atmosphere. Also, white wines of fine texture can be overpowered by the flavoring effects of wood storage.

Nevertheless, redwood continues to be a popular material for white wine storage tanks, especially in California. In Germany and the best white wine regions within France, various breeds of oak, principally *Limousin* and *Nevers*, are cherished for their aging effects.

The length of time for aging after filtration can vary from a few weeks to a few years depending upon the wine result desired; the size, type, and condition of the cooperage (wooden containers) used, the temperature of the aging cellar, and the particular demands of the wine types. Normally, delicately flavored wines such as those from Chenin Blanc, Delaware, Cayuga, Seyval Blanc, and Villard Blanc are not aged for long periods. There are circumstances that will give rise to exceptions, but as a rule, these white wines are more widely accepted as fresh, young, and free of the complexity added by significant wood aging.

Other types, such as Chardonnay and Pinot Blanc, may be improved with the vanilla flavor that some oak tanks can contribute. Redwood can offer some interesting grassy and herbaceous flavor values. Perhaps the most common examples of white wines that mature with aging are those from Johannisberg Riesling, Gewürztraminer, and Vidal Blanc grapes, principally those harvested at various stages of overripeness. Others include the wines made from the variety Sémillon. Some of the great dry whites from Chardonnay grown in America and France respond gracefully to extensive oak aging.

Bottling.   In large wineries bottling often depends on such factors as sales and inventory. In small wine cellars there are different barometers for determining bottling dates. In the best of these, it is a master's nose and palate that determine the bottling order. Even the best of laboratories can provide only indicators of the components of any given wine. Important as those indicators are, only a human expert with finely tuned sensory perceptions can really determine if that same wine is, or ever will be, worthy of its label.

Labeling.   There are many European generic names for different table wine types—each reflecting the geographic origin of the particular wine. The dry, crisp white wines from Chablis in northern Burgundy, for example, are made from the grape variety Chardonnay. Similar wines grown in California, Texas, Virginia, Washington State, and other states, however, are usually labeled as Chardonnay—the American varietal wine equivalent to the European generic. Following are a few other examples:

Generic Name	*Varietal Equivalent*
Alsace (French)	Gewürztraminer
Chardonnay	Sauvignon Blanc
Graves (French)	Sauvignon Blanc
Rheingau (German)	Johannisberg Riesling
Soave (Italian)	Trebbiano
Vouvray (French)	Chenin Blanc

Background and descriptions of these wines can be found in later chapters according to individual country of origin.

A topic of considerable controversy is the use of European generic wine terms on the labels of some American wines. Such startling marriages as "California Burgundy" and "New York State Rhine Wine" are but two of many examples. In more recent times BATF regulation has become more strict in limiting such practices and consumer pressure has caused many vintners to discontinue "generic labeling."

Red Table Wines

The traditional approach to making red table wines sounds rather romantic: violent beginnings mellowing to aged beauty. Actually, as with white table wines, the making of red wine is based upon a set of rather simple principles to which talented winemakers can contribute their individual variations.

RED WINE

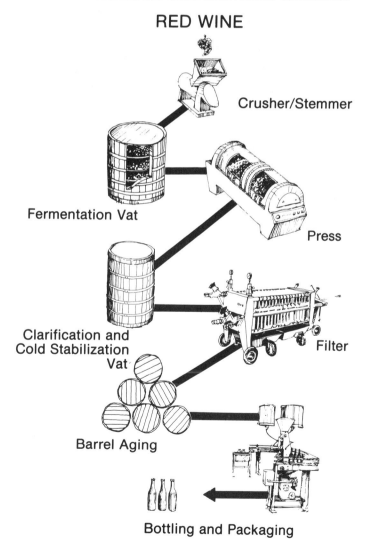

Crusher/Stemmer

Fermentation Vat

Press

Clarification and Cold Stabilization Vat

Filter

Barrel Aging

Bottling and Packaging

Most of the world's premium-quality red table wines are dry. Usually, skins are fermented along with the juice from red wine grapes in order to extract the natural color. From fermentations often exceeding 80 degrees Fahrenheit and with tumultuous "boiling"—red wines can be born from must in only several days. At some predetermined point wine will be pressed from the must and stored in settling tanks awaiting clarification and stabilization.

Some vintners, especially in Northeastern America, heat red grape must to 125 to 150 degrees Fahrenheit or so prior to pressing in order to extract the color pigments from the grape skins. This practice, known as *hot-pressing*, can save considerable time and effort if a vintner has grapes that can endure such rigors without significant damage to color and flavor. Such cultivars as Concord and Ives, in the native American *Vitis labrusca* species, are good examples of grapes that can be successfully hot-pressed.

Vintage Season.   Stems can contribute to the amount of tannins in red wines and, therefore, destemming is a common practice in good cellar procedure. Some wine masters leave various amounts of stems in the must during fermentation in order to extract some of this tannin. The presence of tannins will give longer life to wines. (However, tannin levels can be much more precisely controlled by adding food-grade tannic acid available from winery suppliers.) The must may require only several days at higher temperatures in order to ferment from 22.5 degrees Brix (the amount of sugar content needed to achieve 12 percent alcohol) down to 2.0 degrees *Balling*. (In simplest terms, Brix and Balling readings are calibrated to indicate sugar content in grape must—a reading of 22.5 degrees Brix means that the must has approximately 22.5 percent sugar by weight. Balling and Brix scales are calibrated identically, except a Balling reading indicates that there is alcohol present in the liquid being analyzed.)

The tops of red wine fermenting vats are left open in order that the *cap*, or the floating skins, can be "punched" down into the fermenting juice several times during each twenty-four-hour period. This maintains contact between skins and alcohol so that the wine attains the proper color from the grape skins.

Pressing.   Red grapes handled as white, that is, with the juice pressed from the grapes prior to a cold fermentation, will normally yield light red or blush wines—sometimes even white wines, if red pigments in the grape skins are unstable and/or in low concentrations.

In most red wine grape varieties the majority of stable color pigments will be extracted before the juice reaches a Balling of 2 degrees (about 70 percent complete).

Some vintners choose to keep "free-run" and "pressed" lots separate, discriminating against the lower quality of the latter. Judicious pressure on the wine press has made this distinction unnecessary in many cellars.

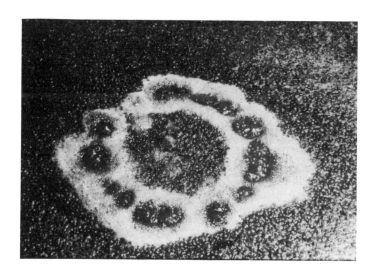

The "cap" that forms during red wine fermentation. (Source: Food and Wines from France.)

It can be easy to overpress fermented must, since it takes little exertion from pressing machinery to extract the wine. High pressure applied to fermented red must can add significant amounts of bitter tannins and oils (complex polyphenols) that are detrimental to a high-quality product. Unfortunately, the desire for efficient yields often overrides the desire for top-quality wine. Normally, about 175 gallons per ton is considered a good yield from the red wine press.

Blending.   The blending of red table wines has been practiced in Europe since the very beginnings of the wine industry there. In addition to blending different wines together, Europeans may also blend different grapes together at the vintage. For example, an Haut-Médoc château in Bordeaux may have vineyards totaling 100 acres, of which 60 acres are Cabernet Sauvignon, 25 acres Merlot, 10 acres Malbec, and the remaining 5 acres Cabernet Franc. Each year, all of these grapes may be combined to make up the vintage of that particular château. The blend, therefore, is generic; that is, it is identified by its origin and type.

Some reputable American vintners have followed suit and begun to blend, moving away from single varietal content. The back labels of some California varietal wines will actually list the blend components. For example:

77%	Cabernet Sauvignon
23%	Merlot
	or
78%	Pinot Noir
15%	Gamay
7%	Syrah

Perhaps only the wine master who created these blends knows the exact reasoning behind the components chosen and their percentages. In these examples the wine masters no doubt chose a predominance of Cabernet Sauvignon and Pinot Noir in order to satisfy BATF regulations that require certain minimum content of a single variety to qualify the bottle for varietal labeling. Perhaps the Merlot is included to soften the heavy, robust character of the Cabernet Sauvignon and also to create a product that competes more closely with a generic French Bordeaux of similar composition. The Gamay may be brought to the Pinot Noir blend in order to add some fruitlike character, while the Syrah is included to enhance color intensity that is typically deficient in Californian Pinot Noir wines. A significant part of the blender's judgment may have been based on the economics of grape cost, inventory, sales demands, and other such factors, as well.

Ordinary red table wines are often blends of wine from different regions or even different countries; for example, the strong, full reds of Algeria have been blended with the thinner reds of France's Midi region to produce balanced bulk wines.

Blending is part of the art of the master winemaker. Much of the in-depth knowledge needed to become a master blender must be acquired through years of experience.

Processing.   Racking, clarification, stabilization, and filtration of young red table wines are similar to the processing operations performed on white table wines (see above).

Aging.   The increasing popularity of Nouveau-type light red wines (the very young red wines typically produced in some areas of Beaujolais) has added a new twist to traditional American philosophies of red wine aging. In fact, some vintners are using aging programs for their red wines very similar to those used for their whites.

Oak barrel aging cellar in Bordeaux. (Source: Food and Wines from France.)

However, the vast majority of premium red table wines are still aged in wood. Red wines will age in stainless steel, glass, and other nonporous tanks, but the aging process will occur much faster in wooden vessels.

Some vintners like, in moderation, the flavor notes contributed to reds by new barrels and other containers made of American white oak. But most wine experts agree that the vanilla flavor imparted by French Limousin and Nevers oak cooperage are the most desirable for red wine aging. Unfortunately, the French oak can be several times more expensive than American white oak.

The length of time for aging after filtration can vary from a few weeks to a few years depending upon the wine result desired; the size, type, and condition of the cooperage employed; the temperature of the aging cellar; and the particular demands of the wine type. In general, aging will occur more rapidly in smaller wooden cooperage held in warmer cellars. Aging processes will be slower, therefore, in larger containers within cooler cellars.

Labeling. As with the white table wines, there are many European generic names for different red table wine types—each denoting a specific geographic region of origin. Heavy-bodied red wines from the Côte d'Or in northern Burgundy are made from the grape variety Pinot Noir. Similar wines grown in California and other American states are usually labeled as "Pinot Noir." As with whites, there are varietal equivalents for the major generic names for red wines. Following are a few other examples:

Generic Name	*Varietal Equivalent*
Barolo (Italian)	Nebbiolo
Bordeaux (French)	Cabernet Sauvignon (and/or Merlot)
Chianti (Italian)	Sangiovese
Chinon (French)	Cabernet Franc
Rhône (French)	Syrah
Valpolicella (Italian)	Molinara (and/or Corvina)

Background and descriptions of these wines can be found in later chapters according to country of origin.

Rosé Table Wines

Experts generally agree that the best rosé table wines are made by fermenting red or blue-black grapes just as one would for red table wines, except that there should be only a partial exposure "on the skins" until the desired amount of color has been attained. Rosés may also be made by blending white and red wines together—a practice that can give more consistent results.

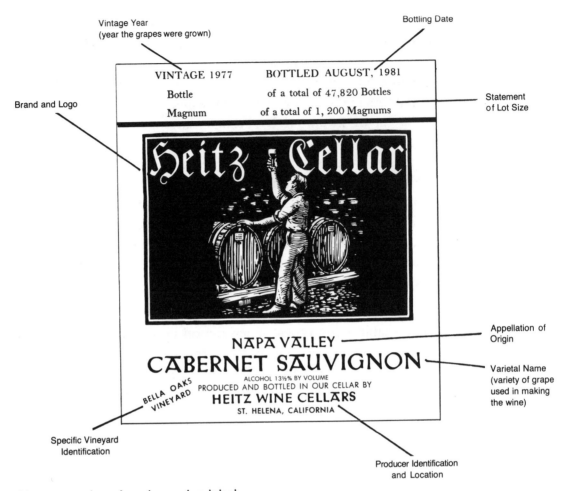

Vintage Year
(year the grapes were grown)

Bottling Date

Brand and Logo

Statement
of Lot Size

VINTAGE 1977   BOTTLED AUGUST, 1981

Bottle   of a total of 47,820 Bottles

Magnum   of a total of 1,200 Magnums

NAPA VALLEY

CABERNET SAUVIGNON

ALCOHOL 13½% BY VOLUME
BELLA OAKS VINEYARD   PRODUCED AND BOTTLED IN OUR CELLAR BY

HEITZ WINE CELLARS

ST. HELENA, CALIFORNIA

Appellation of
Origin

Varietal Name
(variety of grape
used in making
the wine)

Specific Vineyard
Identification

Producer Identification
and Location

How to read an American wine label.

Most rosé table wines are made to be sweet, although a few are dry and some are very sweet. Nearly all commercial rosés are released to the market before they are two years old and are seldom exposed to any form of wood aging.

The term *rosé* has a common international generic meaning and does not denote any specific geographical region. There are, however, some important regions for rosé table wines in Europe; here is a list of some of these along with their varietal wine equivalents:

Generic Name	*Varietal Equivalent*
Anjou (French)	Cabernet Franc
Chiaretto (Italian)	Molinara
Marsannay (French)	Pinot Noir
Tavel (French)	Grenache

Background and description of these wines can be found in later chapters according to country of origin.

Sparkling Wines

Sparkling wines were invented only several centuries ago in France and are, therefore, something of a child in the wine family. Legend has it that sparkling wine was "discovered" by Dom Pérignon, a blind Benedictine monk, during the latter portion of the seventeenth century. Actually, Pérignon was one of the first to use natural cork as a bottle stopper, a closure that was so effective that it trapped some of the carbon gas resulting from the last throes of fermentation inside the bottle. This trapped gas caused bubbles, or *effervescence*, in Dom Pérignon's wine and made his Abbey of Hautvilliers, near Épernay, in the département of Champagne, very famous.

The process has long since evolved to precise specifications, whereby selected table wines are made into a *cuvée* (pronounced koo-vay´) blend (see glossary) and fermented a second time in a closed container to capture the carbon dioxide gas resulting from the second fermentation. When the wine is properly processed, it will effervesce or "sparkle" as the carbon dioxide gas bubbles are released. Champagne has long been recognized as the royalty of the sparkling wines. While Champagne is always sparkling wine, not all sparkling wines are Champagne (though many claim to be). True Champagne comes from a specially designated region of France and must be made by the *méthode champenoise*, described below.

Sparkling wines are often served at festive events and special occasions. They are usually dry (*naturel*), or nearly so (*brut*). A bit less dry is *extra-sec* and a bit less dry than this is *sec*. Some have a discernible sweetness (*demi-sec*), and a few are made very sweet (*doux*). Most are white and range from bland to tart and from thin-bodied to rather heavy. Virtually all, however, are fermented to contain less than 14 percent alcohol by volume.

Of course, in order to make a good sparkling wine, one must begin with a good cuvée wine. Following are some of the more popular grape varieties used by American vintners for the two basic types of sparkling wine:

Vinous	*Fruity*
Chardonnay	Catawba
Pinot Blanc	Delaware
Ravat Blanc	Muscat
Seyval Blanc	Niagara
Pinot Noir	Johannisberg Riesling
	Vidal Blanc

The vinous types are typified by the dry Brut Champagnes of France and the super-premiums from America. Usually rather tart, these are expertly blended to marry fruit and acidity. Fruity types, the overwhelmingly popular choice of the American wine neophyte, offer a much broader range of styles.

Apart from flavor considerations, the most crucial factor in cuvée blending is acid balance. The wine master may standardize vinous-type sparkling wines to be rather crisp and tart. The enthusiasts of the fruitier products, however, generally find less acidity more appealing.

Méthode Champenoise

The *méthode champenoise*, the traditional method by which sparkling wines are made in France, is now used by makers of premium sparkling wines around the world. Cuvée wines are fermented in specially designed bottles that are strong enough to withstand pressure and undergo extensive processing.

Fill and Secondary Fermentation.   The process of filling and capping the special pressure-type sparkling wine bottles is called, aptly, the *fill*.

In France, the term *liqueur de tirage* refers to the dissolved sugars and other elements that are added to the wine so that yeast can create secondary fermentation in the bottle. The filled bottles are then laid on their sides in rows and stacked row upon row.

As secondary fermentation nears completion, yeast cells will break down and diffuse into the cuvée. This accounts for the fresh yeasty flavor that better examples of méthode champenoise sparkling wines feature. (See chapter 6, p. 389 for illustrations of the méthode champenoise.)

Riddling.   The dangerous task of shaking down the yeast sediment from the sides of the bottles (that have been laid horizontally) into the bottle neck is called the *remuage* (shaking) in France and *riddling* in America. Some people also call this simply "the clearing process."

Disgorging.   When the wine master has determined that the sparkling wine batch is ready for finishing, and the riddling operation is complete, the *disgorging* process starts.

Disgorging is the procedure by which sparkling wine bottles are chilled so that an ice plug is frozen in the neck of each bottle. All the sedimentation that gathered in the bottle neck during riddling is trapped in the ice plug. When the disgorger removes the temporary cap, the internal "head pressure" blows out the ice plug—carrying the sediment with it.

Dosage.   The disgorged bottle is then immediately transferred to the finishing *dosage* machine, which adds a precisely measured amount of perservative and sweetener. The volume of dosage is designed to replace the volume lost by the ice plug during disgorging.

Corking and Hooding.   The high cost of natural cork has led some sparkling wine producers to switch to plastic stoppers, but most of the vintners who care about quality and want to preserve their image continue to use corks. Immediately after the cork or stopper is driven in, a specially made wire hood is lashed to the bottle neck to prevent the *head pressure* from pushing out the cork. (By regulation, French sparkling wines must have at least four times the atmospheric pressure of carbon dioxide pressure, or about 58 pounds pressure per square inch at room temperature. Most commercial sparkling wines, however, are created with at least six atmospheres of carbon dioxide pressure.)

The most well-known sparkling white wine made by the méthode champenoise is unquestionably *Champagne*. Champagne is made from the white juice pressed from two black-skinned grapes, Pinot Noir and Pinot Meunier. Another version is made from the white-skinned Chardonnay grape and is called *blanc de blanc*.

Saumur, from the Loire Valley of France, is another popular sparkling wine—often simply referred to as *vin mousseux*. Saumur is made from the Chenin Blanc grape.

The increasingly popular *spumante* sparkling wines of Italy are made by the méthode champenoise, although virtually all of the famous Asti Spumante is made by the Charmat process, discussed below. The vast quantities of sparkling wines from Catalonia in northern Spain are also made by the traditional French method.

Producers of méthode champenoise sparkling wines in America label their wines with the statement, "Fermented in *this* bottle" (emphasis added).

Sparkling wines made in Germany are called *sekt*, and the finest of these are made by the méthode champenoise.

Sparkling red and rosé wines are rarely made by the méthode champenoise. Lesser quality *sekt* and some of the cheaper American sparkling wines are made by the transfer or Charmat processes, described below.

Transfer Method

The *transfer method* of sparkling wine production is similar to the méthode champenoise except that, after fermentation of the cuvée wine in the bottle is completed, the wine is removed, filtered, and rebottled mechanically. Such wines usually display the statement, "Fermented in *the* bottle" (emphasis added).

Charmat Process

This process is often called the *bulk* process, or the *tank* method. As the name implies, cuvée wines are fermented in bulk tanks that are specially constructed to withstand the pressure of fermentation. Once fermentation is completed, the wine is filtered and bottled in a fashion similar to that of the transfer method outlined above.

Vins Pétillant

Wines of this category are table wines that have just a small amount of effervescence (usually less than two times the atmospheric pressure [22 pounds per square inch at 72 degrees Fahrenheit]). Often this effervescence is the result of carbon dioxide gas remaining in the wine from fermentation.

The category as a whole is not very popular in America, though the French enjoy a number of vins pétillant, among them certain types of *Vouvray*. In Germany pétillant wines are known as *perlwein* and in Italy as *frizzante*.

Generic labeling of sparkling wines in the United States is widespread, with the vast majority of vintners offering their products as some type of "Champagne."

In 1985 American consumption of sparkling wines was in excess of 45 million gallons and, since 1975, consumption has increased by more than 100 percent.

Crackling Wines

The effervescent wines in this category are made by the addition of synthetic carbon dioxide gas—much like carbonated soft drinks.

Dessert Wines

Dessert wines, of which sherry and port are the two most famous examples, are made by adding grape brandy to wines to raise the alcohol level from about 12 percent by volume to 18 percent. The brandy may be added either after fermentation or before fermentation has been completed. In the latter case, the addition of brandy (known as the *fortification*) will raise the alcohol level and stop the yeast from fermenting whatever sugar remains in the wine. These unfermented sugars are what make the wine taste sweet.

For sherries, the addition of brandy takes place after fermentation is complete; ports are fortified before all the sugar in the wine has been converted to alcohol. In both cases, the addition of high-proof brandy (usually 185 to 192 proof) is customarily made prior to clarification and stabilization so that the entire blend can be stabilized as a unit.

While most fortified wines are sweet, there are a few exceptions, such as dry cocktail-type sherries.

Types of Sherry

There are three basic sherry-type wines commonly produced in America. Dry, or cocktail, sherry, usually very pale amber in color, is comparable to the Fino sherry from Spain. Very dark amber and sweet sherry types are labeled as cream sherry by most American vintners. These types are generally compared to the Oloroso sherry of Spanish production. Sherries of medium color and sweetness are referred to as Amontillado in the Jerez de la Frontera, the sherry district of Spain.

Because of similarities in vinification and the wine that results from it, Marsala wines from Italy and Madeira from the Portuguese island of the same name are often considered "sherry-type" wines. However, the wines are distinct. Further background and descriptions are offered in later chapters according to countries of origin.

Maderization of Sherries: Baking and Flor Yeasts.   The characteristic nutty or raisinlike taste and amber color of sherry are from a process known as *maderization* (named for the famous dessert wine from the island of Madeira).

Maderization may take place gradually under the influence of Flor (surface-growing) yeast or more rapidly through a "baking process." The most popular method for making sherry-type wines in America is by baking, while in Spain the surface-growing Flor yeasts are allowed to "bloom" on the wine. The Flor contributes a highly distinctive nutty taste and delicate aroma to true Spanish sherry. (See chapter 9.)

If the baking process is used, then the base wine *shermat* (material for sherry) should be composed only from grapes grown and processed expressly for this purpose. In eastern America, the cultivar Niagara is used extensively; while in California, Thompson seedless is a common shermat-base wine grape.

The baking process, generally performed after fortification with brandy, may be a simple aging of shermat in sun-exposed barrels, where oxidation may take years to produce the desired result; or it may consist of a highly technical procedure known as *Tressler* baking, in which the shermat is gently heated in carefully monitored tanks of a special design.

Flor yeasts, responsible for the delicate flavors of the finest Spanish sherries, grow on the surface of shermat made principally from Palomino and Pedro Ximénes (often referred to simply as PX) grapes, both varieties of *Vitis vinifera*. The Spanish sometimes like to "plaster" musts before pressing out the juice. This means they add gypsum to the wine, thereby increasing acidity and reducing the risk of bacteria spoilage. The different levels of color and sweetness achieved in sherries is obtained by blending in varying amounts of very dark and sweet *dulce pasa* wines.

The action of Flor yeasts on Spanish sherries brings about a similar general reaction as takes place in the baking process, but there are flavor differences that result from use of the Flor yeasts—most of them are minute, but very complex.

Flor yeasts, *Saccharomyces beticus*, must be carefully distinguished from other surface-growing yeasts such as *Candida, Kloeckera, Pichia,* and others, which are spoilage microorganisms.

In the Jerez de la Frontera, where sherries are the only commercial wines made, the Flor yeasts pose no threat to any other form of wine production. In small American wineries, on the other hand, where several types of wine may be made in close proximity, there is the potential for Flor infection. This is one of the major reasons that the baking of sherry-type wines is the method of maderization preferred by virtually all American vintners.

Solera Fractional Blending System for Sherry.   The Spanish solera fractional blending system contributes a great deal to the rich distinctive mellowness of traditional sherries.

The term *solera* describes an annual aging and blending process in which the sherry wines travel down through rows of barrels, called *criadera,* each graduated by age. Each criadera is always maintained at least half-full; whenever wine from a particular criadera is drawn off, it is immediately refilled with wine from criadera above it. The final criadera is termed the *solera*; this row contains the wines that are drawn off and bottled. Wines undergo complex blending as they pass from criadera to criadera so that newer wines mingle with older wines. Some of the wine from every vintage always remains—the average age of the solera becoming older and older with each vintage.

Port

The key difference between the production of port and sherry is that in port the grape brandy fortification is added *before* fermentation is complete. Because the fortification halts the fermentation process, unfermented grape sugar will remain in the wine. Thus, port is by definition sweet.

Ports are blends from up to a dozen or more different grape varieties. Genuine Portuguese port may by made only from grapes grown in a strictly defined region of the Douro River Valley east of the town of Oporto (whence the wine's name). There is also California port, made in a similar fashion. Port producers usually maintain their own distinctive styles from year to year by careful blending. However, in exceptionally fine years, vintage port will be produced—port wine made from the best grapes harvested in a single year. Vintage port ages in the cask for several years and is then aged for considerably longer periods in the bottle. Other types of port, known as "wood ports," receive much longer aging in the cask and are ready to drink when bottled.

For more detailed information on the true port wines of Portugal, see chapter 9.

Clarification and Stabilization. The procedure for clarification and stabilization of dessert wines is basically the same as for table wines. The most significant difference is that dessert wines do not usually need intense clarification treatments since, following stabilization, long periods of aging stabilize the wine naturally.

Aging. Most sherry- and port-type wines can be aged effectively in American white oak. European oaks, such as Limousin and Nevers, however, are ideal for dessert wine aging. The use of redwood casks has not gained acceptance among American vintners interested in highest-quality aging results.

Consumption

During the past two decades, Americans' taste for dessert wine has steadily declined. In 1985 American consumption of dessert wines was less than 35 million gallons and, since 1975, consumption has fallen more than 40 percent.

Port and sherry, the most notable of the world's dessert wines, are products of Portugal and Spain: However, both generic names find their way onto American wine labels for wines of similar types.

Aperitif Wines

Essentially, *aperitif wines* are dessert wines further processed by the addition of herbs, spices, and/or other flavorings and coloring. Fennel seed, citrus flavors, thyme, cinnamon bark, ginger root, and caramel are only a few of the ingredients infused into some aperitif wines. In the wine industry, aperitif wines are often referred to as *formula wines* because their formulation must be approved by the BATF prior to their manufacture and release onto the market.

Aperitif wines normally have an alcohol content from 16 to 19 percent by volume and may be either very dry or very sweet and very light to very dark. Most popular aperitif wines nowadays are used as mixers for cocktail beverages, although in years past they were often drunk as appetizer wines, hence the common term *aperitif* to denote the category.

Some of the most notable aperitif wines on the market today include dry vermouth, sometimes referred to as "French-type" vermouth—and sweet vermouth, sometimes referred to as "Italian-type" vermouth. Other popular types are "Dubonnet," "Pernod," and "Lillet."

In 1985 American consumption of aperitif wines totaled less than 7 million gallons and, since 1975, consumption has decreased by about 25 percent.

Pop Wines

There is some controversy as to whether pop wines get their name from being *pop*ular, or from their close kinship to soda*pop*. In any event, the category, though very new, has already begun to decline from its peak of consumer acceptance in America during the 1970s.

The alcohol content of pop wines may be either more or less than 14 percent. Virtually all pop wines are made by adding synthetic fruit flavorings, often citrus fruit extracts, to table wines in order to produce exotic results.

Perhaps the most notable pop wine is Sangria—originally a Spanish wine drink made with whole or segmented fruits and other ingredients. In its pop wine version, all the ingredients and flavors are premixed, bottled, and ready to serve.

In 1985 American consumption of pop wines totaled about 27 million gallons and, since 1975, consumption has decreased by some 50 percent.

Miscellaneous

It is unfortunate that the scope of this text cannot include the many delicious fruit wines that are again steadily gaining consumer acceptance in some American regional wine markets. Vegetable wines also exist that are primarily used in cooking. Mead, a wine made from honey, is also commercially produced by a number of vintners in America. Discovering these and other specialty wines is one of many pleasures of the pursuit of wine appreciation.

The most recent phenomenon on the American wine market is known as the *wine cooler*. These are wine products made with greatly reduced alcohol levels, often packaged in cans, and generally designed to compete with soft drinks and beer. It remains to be seen whether the initial great success of these types of wines will continue over the long run. If it does, the wine market will no doubt have to expand to include a sixth category.

THE COMMERCIAL WINE SCENE

The Industry

Louis Gomberg, a noted wine consultant from California, has studied the wine industry for many years, and observes that different types of wine-producing firms make up the industry. He classifies it into six categories, each characterized by a different size and/or organizational structure.

The Giants

To qualify as a giant, the wine production facilities must have storage capacities in excess of 100 million gallons, and there is only one at this level in America. The E. & J. Gallo Winery of Modesto, California, is the largest wine producer in the world, having a toal capacity in excess of 300 million gallons, spread among four separate winery facilities.

The Corporates

Wine production companies in the corporate category have been subject to much activity from public offerings and corporate mergers during the past twenty-five years or so. The Heublein Corporation is the largest of these, owning Almaden Vineyards, Inglenook Winery and Beaulieu Vineyard. Almaden, with a capacity exceeding 80 million gallons has been located in Los Gatos, California, for many years but shall soon be moved to Heublein's Madera facilities in the San Joaquin Valley. Inglenook and Beaulieu are classic old Napa Valley wineries, each having about 2 million gallons of capacity—although the Inglenook name has been used on jug wines made at the Madera winery. Vintners International Company is the second-largest corporate wine producer and owns Paul Masson Vineyards (38 million gallons), which has three operating locations in the Monterey, California, vicinity. Vintners International also owns Taylor, Great Western, and Gold Seal—all New York State wineries having a total capacity of about 30 million gallons. Next in size is the Sierra Wine Corporation, which is primarily a bulk wine producer (maker of blending wines for supply to other wineries). Some of the other important members of the category are M. LaMont, JFJ Bronco, Delicato, California Growers, and Giumarra, all in California, and Canandaigua in New York State.

The Cooperatives

There are only eight wine cooperatives in America remaining from the more than forty that had been established between 1934 and 1975. These firms primarily supply bulk wines to other wine producers for blending—a market that has eroded as a result of changing conditions and product demands. The most important wine-producing cooperative is Guild in California, which has a capacity of about 60 million gallons. Also in California are Gibson, Woodbridge, East-Side, and Delano—each with less than 10 million gallons of capacity.

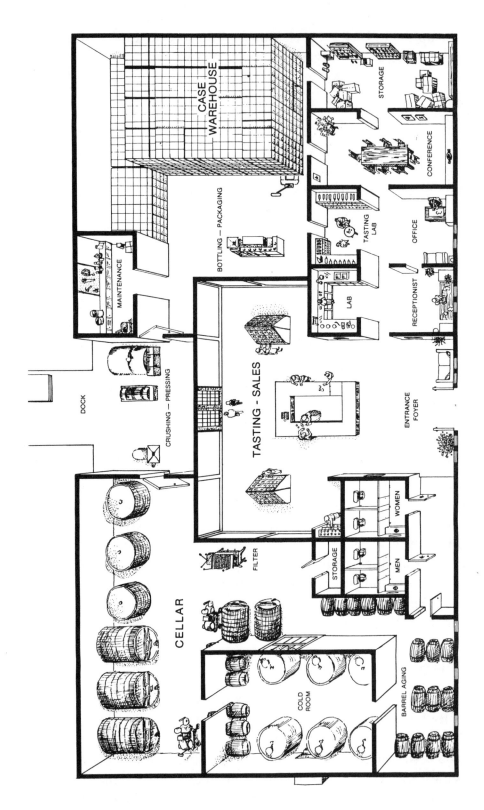

Anatomy of a winery.

The Family Firms

There are approximately 150 family-type vintners in this category; most of them have entered the wine business since the repeal of Prohibition in 1934. These firms are typically closely-held corporations with regional or national distribution networks. Products range in price from about $1.75 for generic wines to more than $20 per 3/4-liter bottle for vintage-dated "reserve" varietals. One of the oldest and largest of these wineries is the Charles Krug winery—operated by Peter Mondavi and sons in the Napa Valley of California. Another of the older and larger family firms is Sebastiani in the Sonoma Valley. Both Krug and Sebastiani have capacities of approximately 6 million gallons. A very well-known family wine producer is the Robert Mondavi Winery, having commenced operations in 1966 following a family dispute at the Krug winery. Among the other important California family wine producers are Heitz, Martini, Papagni, Turner, and Wente. A notable New York State family vintner is Fredonia, while Warner is an important family wine firm in Michigan.

The "Mom-and-Pop" Wineries

Wineries in this category are even smaller and more closely associated with a family, often one couple, than wine firms in the previous category. Most of the approximately 500 Mom-and-Pop wineries that entered the wine business since 1934 have either shut down their operations or been absorbed by other, larger concerns. Typically, these firms were established by individuals who had held onto their small vineyards during Prohibition. Having discovered that wine production and wine marketing were far more demanding than the grape business, some were forced to abandon the business. Filipi, founded in 1934, and Pedrizetti, in 1938, are typical Mom-and-Pop wineries still operating.

The Boutique Wineries

This is the newest concept and the most dynamic segment of premium wine production in America today: During the past fifteen years, hundreds of boutique wineries have sprung up all over the country, but principally in California. Typically, the goal of a boutique winery is to use state-of-the-art technology to produce small quantities of high-quality wines. These operations have captured a segment of the market that was once the exclusive domain of prestigious European wine estates. Boutique wines are usually varietals priced from about $5 per 3/4-liter bottle to more than $40 for rare selections. The following is a listing of just a few of the most highly regarded California boutique wineries that have entered the industry since 1970:

Acacia Winery
Alexander Valley Vineyards
Cakebread Cellars
Carneros Creek Winery
Caymus Vineyards
Clos du Bois
Clos du Val
Creston Manor Vineyards
Dehlinger Winery
Dry Creek Vineyard
Far Niente Winery
Firestone Vineyard
Grgich Hills
Jordan Vineyard and Winery
Lakespring Winery
Lambert Bridge

Leeward Winery
Lytton Springs Winery
Mount Palomar Winery
Niebaum-Coppola Estate
Pat Paulsen Vineyards
Preston Vineyards
San Pasqual Vineyards
Santa Barbara Winery
Santa Ynez Valley Winery
Shown & Sons Vineyards
Silver Oak Wine Cellars
Sonoma-Cutrer Vineyards
Stag's Leap Wine Cellars
Stonegate
Trefethen Vineyards
William Wheeler Winery
Whitehall Lane Winery

The following is, likewise, a listing of some of the most highly regarded boutique wineries that have entered the industry more recently in other states.

Adelsheim Vineyard (Oregon)
Alexis Bailly Vineyard (Minnesota)
Arbor Crest (Washington State)
Beachaven Winery (Tennessee)
Biltmore Estate (North Carolina)
Casa Larga Vineyards (New York)
Catoctin Vineyards (Maryland)
Château Grand Traverse (Michigan)
Château Montgolfier Vineyards (Texas)
Claiborne Vineyards (Mississippi)
Eyrie Vineyards (Oregon)
Fall Creek Vineyards (Texas)
Glenora Wine Cellars (New York)
Habersham Vineyards (Georgia)
Haight Vineyard (Connecticut)
Hinzerling (Washington State)

Hogue (Washington State)
Ingleside (Virginia)
Knudsen-Erath Winery (Oregon)
Lafayette Vineyards (Florida)
Llano Estacado (Texas)
Meredyth Vineyards (Virginia)
Nissley Vineyards (Pennsylvania)
Pheasant Ridge (Texas)
Pindar Vineyards (New York)
Prince Michel Vineyard (Virginia)
Tabor Hill (Michigan)
Tewksbury Wine Cellars (New Jersey)
Tualatin Vineyards (Oregon)
Vierthaler Winery (Washington State)
Wagner Vineyards (New York)
Wiemer Vineyard (New York)
Wollersheim Winery (Wisconsin)

The Market

Wine marketed in the United States is under strict control by the U.S. Bureau of Alcohol, Tobacco, and Firearms (BATF) as well as state and local regulatory authorities. The many regulations that restrict the sale and consumption of wine in America are beyond the scope of this book.

The classic three-tier marketing system of manufacturer, wholesaler, and retailer applies to the wine business as it is practiced throughout most of America. The wholesale segment includes négociants (merchant/shippers), jobbers and exporters, and the various government agencies that control them. Vintners also sell bulk wines "in bond" (excise taxes not paid) to processors, but this commerce is not generally considered part of wine-consumer product marketing. In all other cases, excise taxes are paid by the vintner upon shipping or by the foreign négociant at the U.S. port of entry.

Some areas in the country permit departures from the three-tier system. There are, for example, considerable retail wine sales made directly to consumers who visit and tour American wineries. Some vintners also operate as the wholesaler in market areas adjacent to their winery premises.

Monopolies

There are twelve states in which the wholesale marketing of wines is controlled, in whole or in part, by state monopolies: Alabama, Idaho, Iowa, Maine, Michigan, Mississippi, Montana, New Hampshire, Oregon, Pennsylvania, Utah, and Wyoming.

State and county monopolies purchase wine directly from vintners and négociants, usually from a listing that is approved and periodically updated by a board set up for this purpose. In some cases the governing authority warehouses and distributes wines to "state stores" for retail sale. In other cases only certain classes of wines are sold through state outlets, with the remaining classes offered to properly licensed retail entrepreneurs. Some states allow certain licensees to share the retail market with the state and, in still other instances, the state monopoly comprises only the wholesale channel, with all retail wine sales being made in privately owned outlets.

The Wholesale Channel

Wholesale activities in the remaining states are typically governed by various forms of licensing, with accompanying fees and/or taxes, that limit solicitation, shipping, and pricing practices. Wholesalers supply to wine shops, restaurants, and other types of retail establishments in franchised areas.

The Retail Channel

This channel is far more complex than the wholesale channel in current American wine marketing. There are hundreds of specific regulations governing how wine may be offered for sale to consumers. Sales are restricted on certain days of the week (election days, holidays, Sundays, etc.) and at certain times of day (after midnight or before noon, for example). There are age restrictions that qualify buyers. There are also limitations on the places where wines may be offered for sale, such as certain distances from churches, schools, and polling places.

Some of these rules date from legislation of the mid-1930s and reflect the social attitudes of the period following Prohibition. The great changes in American life styles during the past fifty years have rendered many of the old rulings unrealistic and, in some cases, difficult to enforce.

In virtually all locales in America, a prospective wine retailer must secure and maintain a valid license in order to market wines legally. Usually either an "off-premise" or "on-premise" license is issued; rarely are both allowed. An off-premise license permits the sale of wines in bottles or "packages" (whence the term "package store") for consumption off the retail premises. An on-premise license generally gives consent to the sale and service of wine to legal-age consumers on the premises, for example, restaurants, bars, and hotels. Normally such licenses also permit the sale of other alcoholic beverages as well.

The Consumer

One of the most in-depth studies of the American wine consumer was made in 1977 by Folwell and Baritelle of the U.S. Department of Agriculture. They surveyed 7,000 American households to learn what factors lead consumers to buy wine. It was found that American consumers rely heavily upon brand names and the advice of friends and/or relatives in wine purchase decisions. Pricing is another very important decision factor, as are label statements, wine origins, and the overall appeal of the wine to the senses. Wine critics' advice and display materials were found to have less influence in wine purchase decision making. The Folwell and Baritelle study, *The U.S. Wine Market*, is highly recommended to anyone interested in wine marketing in America.

The Winery of the Future

During the next several decades, progress will no doubt continue in winery design, operational philosophies, and the development of wine products.

What will the wineries of the twenty-first century look like? They will probably be forced to make much more use of "free" resources, such as solar power, air, and rainwater: The sun will generate energy for increasing percentages of winery electrical requirements; and rainwater may be efficiently collected, purified, and stored. After being used in the winery, water may be repurified and infused with nutritional and pesticidal compounds for vineyard irrigation applications in doses prescribed by automatic monitoring devices. Vine-training systems will provide automated pruning, while danger from frosts may be eliminated with trellises equipped with electrically heated support wires.

Wine production in the winery of the future may be restricted to only those products that can be maintained at minimal inventory levels and matched to maximal consumer demand as determined by precise projection forecasting updated perhaps weekly, or even daily, by automated electronic technology.

The handling of grapes may be synchronized, with vineyard harvest pinpointed down to the hour. Totally automated machinery may gather harvests at considerably more than the yield levels possible now. Processing may be aligned to highly technical cold-concentrating systems producing syrups and essences that will permit annual output to exceed total storage capacity by several times. Processing and preservation may employ techniques precisely controlled by computerized laboratory analyses.

Packaging may be limited to recyclable ceramic materials and renewable resources such as fibrous compounds and organic plastics.

Prices may be calculated at any chosen moment from dependency models programmed to reflect current costs, demand, supply, disposable consumer income, competitive activities, and other significant factors. Computerized "sales calls," order processing, shipment, invoice, and credit instruments may administer to market needs.

While these predictions seem to be farfetched, keep in mind that most of these functions have already been implemented in some industries or are under study in research projects.

FONDÉE EN 1859

BROUILLY

APPELLATION CONTROLÉE

MISE EN BOUTEILLES PAR

LOUIS JADOT

LOUIS JADOT, NÉGOCIANT-ÉLEVEUR A BEAUNE · COTE-D'OR · FRANCE

PRODUCE
OF FRANCE

ALC. BY VOL. 13,1%

750 ml (25.4 FL. OZ)

RED BURGUNDY
TABLE WINE

IMPORTED BY KOBRAND CORPORATION, N. Y., N. Y., SOLE U. S. IMPORTERS

2

WINE AND HUMAN PHYSIOLOGY

*E*ach of us carries around a well-set-up laboratory for wine evaluation in the form of primary sense organs: visual, olfactory (smell), and gustatory (taste). Certainly these sense organs are more perceptive and finely tuned in some individuals, but, for the most part, anyone can develop with time and practice truly impressive powers of wine discrimination. The foundation for these powers is discussed in this chapter, beginning with the fundamental questions of how people smell and taste and see: How does the human body evaluate the information gathered by the senses? Next is the subject of wine and how to judge it. The last portion of the chapter will deal with the metabolism of wine within the human body and the effects of wine on health. There is an examination of both the pleasant and enjoyable aspects of wine but also its potential dangers.

HOW HUMAN SENSES PERCEIVE WINE—SENSORY EVALUATIONS

The interaction of human sensory organs with the environment supplies the basic information by which the world is perceived. Nerves transmit this informa-

The author is indebted to Dr. Douglas L. Stringer for the initial draft of this chapter. Dr. Stringer is a neurosurgeon in Panama City, Florida, and, obviously, a learned enophile.

tion to the brain, where it is evaluated and interpreted. For any given sensation, there are specialized nerve endings and cells that can be trained to higher levels of acuity.

The sensory pathways involved in the evaluation of wine include the *visual, olfactory,* and *gustatory.* Each transmits messages to a different part of the brain. Thus, while information for vision is gathered in the eye; information for smell gathered in the nose; and information for taste gathered in the tongue and mouth—we actually see, smell, and taste in specialized areas of the brain called the *visual cortex, olfactory cortex,* and *gustatory cortex.*

Visual Perception

Sight is the dominant human sense. The sensory receivers (the rods and cones of the retinas) of the eyes comprise over 70 percent of the the total sensory receptors of the human body. The two physical factors affecting our visual perception are light, which is interpreted as brightness, and the colors of the spectrum (interpreted from varying wavelengths). During vision, our eyes and brain are actually performing several different functions at once:

1. discrimination between light and dark
2. perception of color
3. image reproduction, or form vision
4. visual acuity
5. spatial, or depth sense
6. perception of motion, or resolution of images in time
7. appreciation of brightness or intensities of light
8. recognition and comparisons of fresh images with previous images (This occurs in the frontal and temporal lobes of the brain.)

Anatomy of Vision (Visual Pathway)

Visual information is transported through the lens of the eye to the back of the eye, which is called the *retina,* where the rods and cones are located. The information is then projected through the optic nerve and optic tracts that go to both of the brain's occipital lobes, where the images are analyzed.

Visual interpretation of something seen at any given moment is a result of the comparison of that image to previous experiences of it. An analysis of an image takes place in the occipital lobe, but interpretation, comparison, and image storage take place in the frontal and temporal lobes of the brain. So, for example,

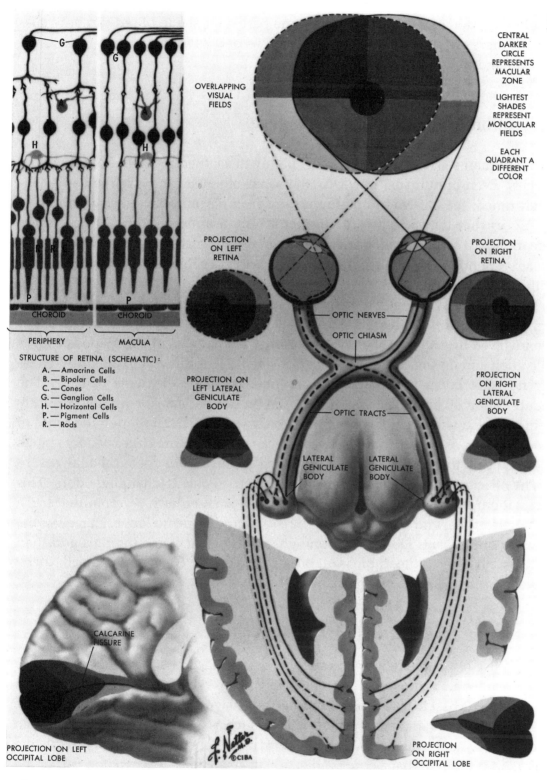

A diagram of the human visual system. (Photo by Linden Color Labs; Source: Ciba Pharmaceuticals.)

an identification of a wine's color as some particular shade of red can only take place if there are stored many previous visions of reds from which to make comparison and judgment.

Perception of Smell (Olfactory Sense)

The human sense of smell is not as highly developed as that of other animal species. Even in humans, however, the sense of smell can be refined and delicately tuned: Tea sniffers and perfumers, for example, may have such discriminating noses that they will be able to identify thousands of odors. People often remark how a certain smell brings with it images, associations, and memories of past experiences. The smell of freshly baked bread or cookies can conjure up one's entire childhood in a flash.

The olfactory system is very complex. In addition to perceiving odors and calling up associations with great immediacy, it stimulates other nerve systems that are involved in emotional behavior patterns. The aromas of many foods trigger salivation and lip smacking. The sense of smell also is difficult to quantify. There are no basic odors for comparison as there are basic elements of taste. The identification of smell, like vision, is based on comparisons of what is currently being smelled with what has been previously smelled. Even though the sense of smell in humans is comparatively weak, it can detect minute traces of odors much more quickly than most methods involving sophisticated chemical analyses.

The olfactory nerve cells become accustomed quickly to changing odors. This adaptation process can be seen, for example, when entering a room that has a distinctly unpleasant odor. After about two minutes one no longer perceives the odor as unpleasant. However, if one goes outside for a few minutes and then returns, once again the unpleasant odor is perceived. The sense of smell, therefore, is easily exhausted in humans.

Anatomy of Smell (Olfactory Pathway)

The olfactory nerve cells are located high up in each nostril. As one sniffs, the odor-bearing air is directed to the olfactory nerve cells. To perceive odors most intensely, it is best to take quick, deep sniffs so that odors can reach high up in the nose. With gentle, slow sniffs, subtle smells, such as wine bouquet, may not reach the olfactory nerve cells. Although it is not known how the entire olfactory system works, it is thought that a crude indication of smell takes place in one part of the brain (the olfactory bulb) while more subtle smell discriminations occur in another (the olfactory cortex). Some researchers believe that certain olfactory nerve cells

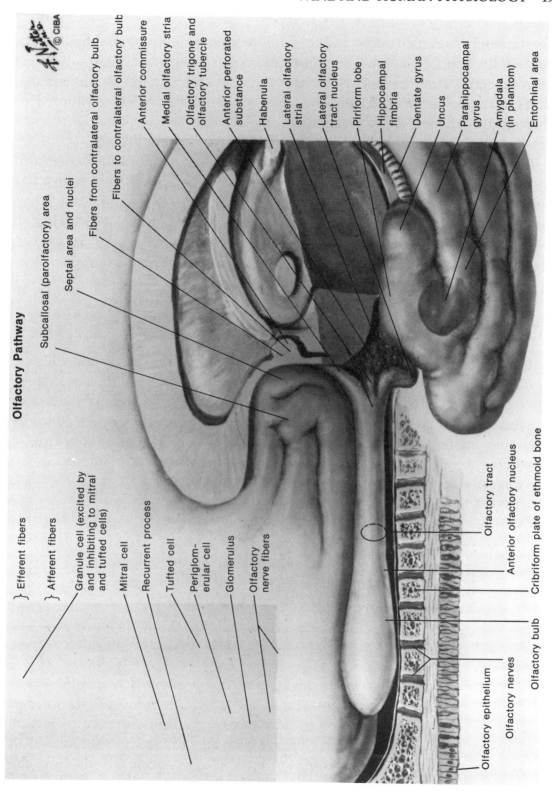

A diagram of the human olfactory system. (Photo by Linden Color Labs; Source: Ciba Pharmaceuticals.)

respond only to certain odors and that different odors are projected to different parts of the brain. (A unique phenomenon known as *cross-talk* occurs when one smells an odor. It seems that, as the odor stimulates the nerve cells, this stimulation can also be transmitted from one nerve cell to another. Scientists think that, through this sharing of information, people are able to interpret intensities of smell, probably from the number of nerve cells that are stimulated.)

The brain's response to odors is very rapid and its recovery from odors can also be rapid, depending on the intensity of the odor. Recovery can vary from a few seconds to several minutes. In most cases, a person can identify more than seventy odors in one hour if proper concentration is maintained. Human sensitivity to odor varies considerably with the intensity of the odor. People can detect a strong odor diffused at one-millionth the concentration of a weak odor.

Perception of Taste (Gustatory Sense)

Taste is usually equated with flavor, but flavor is actually a combination of taste and smell. True taste is a less finely shaded sensation than smell. It takes a much stronger stimulus to activate the taste buds than it does to stimulate olfactory nerve cells. It has been estimated that approximately twenty thousand times more molecules are needed to induce a taste sensation than a smell sensation. Thus, a stimulus strong enough to induce taste will also usually make an impression on the olfactory system.

Humans have four basic taste sensations:

1. *Salt*—perceived most intensely on the side of the tongue.
2. *Sour*—sensed most intensely partway back on the tongue.
3. *Sweet*—perceived most intensely on the tip of the tongue.
4. *Bitter*—tasted primarily on the back of the tongue.

Since the center of the tongue has only a few taste buds, it is considered "taste blind."

The ends of the nerve cells in the taste buds are in contact with the "taste nerves," which transmit taste messages to the brain. The taste buds are shaped rather like brandy snifters—dissolved substances enter through a pore in the taste bud to interact with the taste cells. The taste buds are grouped into *papillae*, which are distributed in different parts of the tongue. These papillae are what give the tongue a rough surface. Each papilla has about 250 taste buds and may contain taste buds that respond to different tastes. Many nuances of taste are the result of the different patterns of taste buds in the papillae. The intensity of taste is believed to be caused by how frequently each taste cell is stimulated. The sense of taste, like the sense of smell, can be easily exhausted, or *fatigued*. Taste may be further inhibited by *adaptation*, which is also a response to overstimulation. Usually there is rapid recovery from both adaptation and fatigue, but one must allow sufficient time before tasting results will be accurate again. In wine tasting, allow at least two minutes for recovery between wines. Adaptation and fatigue of the four major tastes vary considerably:

1. *Salt*—adaptation to salt does not affect sensitivity to salty tastes.
2. *Sour*—adaptation to one sour taste (acidic) reduces the taster's sensitivity to all others. However, recovery of sensitivity to sourness is rapid since most common acids are easily rinsed away by saliva.
3. *Sweet*—adaptation to one particular sugar may or may not reduce sensitivity to other sugars. Sugar and saccharin do not fatigue sensitivities to each other. Recovery of sensitivity to most sugars occurs more rapidly than the recovery to other sweeteners.
4. *Bitter*—this taste may last longer than the other three basic tastes. A bitter taste may persist for over a minute, even after rinsing the tongue (probably because bitter substances have an affinity, hence remain longer, for the skin).

There is a great variation in the concentrations needed to activate the nerve cells for the four basic tastes. *Threshold concentration* is the smallest amount of the taste needed to greatly stimulate the nerve cell. Threshold concentrations for sugar are greater than those for salt. Salt is greater than for sour, and sour is greater than for bitter. Or, to put it another way, it takes less of a bitter substance to stimulate the nerve cells than any of the other basic tastes. But the perception of tastes is relative. Practiced tasters may taste a substance at one-fiftieth the concentration needed to make an impression on a novice taster. Temperature also can significantly change sensitivity to taste for various substances. For example, sensitivity to salt increases greatly as temperature increases.

There is a decrease in the sensitivity to taste with age since the total number of taste buds declines markedly after forty. A human baby has more than 10,000 taste buds, including some on the palate and pharynx. This explains, in part, why babies dislike spicy food, whereas elderly people, who have fewer and duller taste buds, may prefer more spices and salt in their food.

Anatomy of Taste (Gustatory Pathway)

The sensation of taste travels from the mouth to the brain along specially adapted nerves. They enter the brain stem via the *chorda tympani* nerve, at the junction of the *pons* and *medulla*.

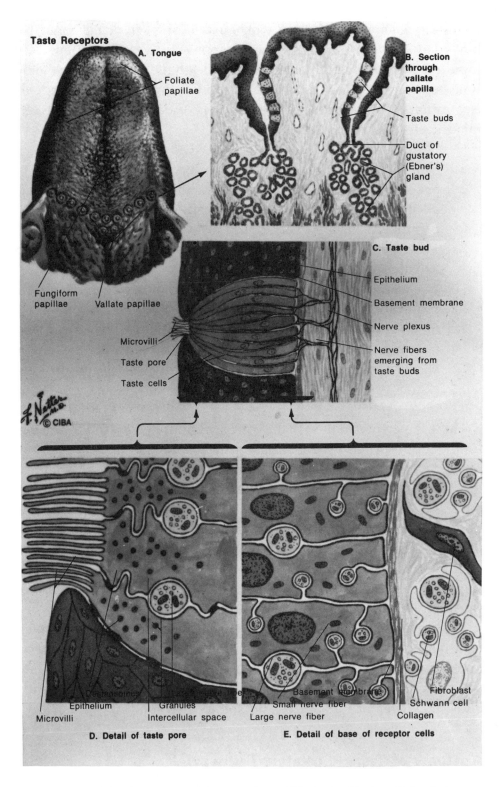

A diagram of the human gustatory system. (Photo by Linden Color Labs; Source: Ciba Pharmaceuticals.)

In summary, most of what is interpreted as taste is really flavor, and flavor is primarily olfactory (smell), rather than gustatory (taste). One is able to taste only four basic taste sensations, which are sweet, sour, salty and bitter. To adequately stimulate the human sensory system it is important that the stimulus be applied to the sensory system being stimulated in sufficient quantities and in close enough contact for a sufficient length of time to obtain maximal stimulation. It is important in a tasting process that sufficient time is allowed between wines for recovery from adaptation and fatigue (usually at least two minutes) and for conscious critical comparison to previous tasting experiences. Speed is not of the essence in wine tasting and may be inversely proportional to what will be retained from the experience since information hastily gathered may be unavailable for recall.

WINE JUDGING

It would be unfortunate if one has begun reading this book with this section—especially if one intends to scan the next few pages rapidly in the hopes of becoming an "instant expert." It just doesn't work that way. Becoming a proficient wine judge, like attaining mastery in most disciplines, requires dedication, patience, and practice.

Even with all the recent advances made in analyzing the chemistry of wine, no one has yet devised a method of accurately calculating "goodness" and "badness" in wines. In fact, such measurements will no doubt always remain an individual matter. Individual, yes—but not entirely subjective or haphazard. Wine evaluation has come a long way from the realm of snap judgments based on the hedonic scales, such as "like a lot," "like," "like a little," "dislike," etc. Over the years there have been a number of endeavors to standardize the personal evaluation procedure, and today we have a range of wine-judging methods from which to choose.

The following sections outline certain numerically ranked, or cardinal, scales and discuss how to use them in judging wine.

Developing Descriptive Terminology

Despite the fact that science can quantify virtually all wine components by chemical analysis, there still exists only a rudimentary language for communicating what wine actually tastes like. Taste values are exceedingly difficult to describe—nearly impossible, in fact, unless other familiar sensory values are employed as a point of reference. Consequently, the aspiring wine judge is encouraged to learn the basic sensations that wine produces on the eyes, nose, and tongue (organoleptic values). As expertise develops, more and more values and terms will be added to one's "vocabulary" of wine judging. It is hoped that a definitive terminology will be the result. Ambiguous descriptive words such as *luscious*, *racy*, and *supple*, among many others, should be avoided. Wine judging remains subjective enough without introducing further confusion with such meaningless terms.

Getting Ready to Judge

The beginning wine taster might find it helpful to isolate certain wine constituents in a water solution before actually sampling wine. Once these basic elements can be accurately detected from repeated "blind" taste testing, the student may wish to proceed with some components isolated in water and ethanol (ethyl alcohol) solutions (for this purpose alcohol from a neutral grain spirit such as vodka is recommended—unless, of course, a neutral brandy is available). These exercises will aid greatly in accustoming oneself to the subtle organoleptic characteristics of wine and in developing a good eye, nose, and palate. Some institutions of higher learning and correspondence courses offer this kind of instruction. See appendix III.

Blending together about 1 cup of water and 1/4 cup of neutral vodka provides a solution of about 10 to 12 percent alcohol by volume. This blend can then be used to sample as many different flavor essences as one has. A pinch of tartaric acid will produce a tart taste; a few drops of vinegar will illustrate acetic acidity; a pinch of tannic acid can portray the tannin sensation upon the palate. Cane sugar can, of course, reveal sweetness; a drop or two of bitters can represent bitterness. In much the same way, essences of fruit flavors, coffee, softened vegetables such as bell peppers and spinach, as well as other materials can be dissolved or suspended in alcohol/water solutions in order to train the senses to each individual taste.

Perhaps the best procedure would be to purchase one of the flavor "essence" kits to train the nose and palate to the distinctiveness of different fruit, vegetable, spice, and other nuances that can be found in wines. The Wine Ambiance Company in San Francisco markets several sizes of kits that are expressly designed for training neophyte wine tasters.

Cardinal (Numerically Ranked) Scales

There are many cardinal scales from which the taste tester may choose. One of the most common in America is the "Twenty-Point Scale" developed at the University of California at Davis. Here is how it's structured:

Criteria	Maximum Points
Clarity	2
Color	2
Aroma	4
Bouquet	2
Total Acidity	2
Tannin	2
Body	1
Sugar	1
General Flavor	2
Overall Impression	2
Total	20

The discussion below explains each category of the scale in detail and what criteria to use in assigning points. Most commercially sold wines score between nine and seventeen points. Wines that score less than nine are unmarketable; wines that rate higher than seventeen are quickly bought up. As a general rule, we can use the Twenty-Point Scale to break wines into three classes:

1. Scores of seventeen to twenty—high-quality wines of distinctive character and virtually faultless composition
2. Scores of thirteen to sixteen—good-quality wines of acceptable character, but without finesse and with detectable faults
3. Scores of nine to twelve—adequate wines of neutral character, with obvious faults, but drinkable as everyday table wines

The Twenty-Point Scale, while widely accepted, is not always used consistently. Some judges rearrange point values to suit their personal preferences. For example, they will reduce the "clarity" category to one point and upgrade "body" to two points. Sometimes the distinction between "aroma" and "bouquet" is dispensed with—making it a single category with a total of six points. Such reassignments should probably be avoided by the beginner.

The Twenty-Point Scale is simple to use, popular, and generally adequate, but, as do all scales, it has its faults. One major shortcoming is its failure to provide a *trueness-to-type* criterion—thus a wine may be judged near-faultless organoleptically, yet still fail miserably as a representative of its type or grape variety. Another criticism concerns the Twenty-Point total itself. The constraint of twenty points allows for little leeway in scoring, particularly in the single-point values assigned to the "body" and "sugar" categories. A 100-point scale provides much more flexibility and precision in scoring, greater ease in compiling results, and readier recognition since this is the scale used in most academic grading. For how a 100-point scale can be structured, see diagram p. 57. The "perfect" scale, of course, does not exist. We must, therefore, select or devise numerical scales that best serve our needs. In the discussion of wine judging below, the Twenty-Point Scale is used throughout because it remains the most widespread in the United States.

The Wine-Judging Environment

We cannot always expect to have perfect conditions in which to judge wine and, realistically, we may often find ourselves sampling fine wines in settings that dull our powers of perception. Nevertheless, it's good to know what the optimal wine-testing environment should be. The following is a suggested checklist:

1. *Wineglasses*—There should be an ample number of identical wineglasses available (differences in size, shape, and color make comparative wine judgment much more difficult). Glasses should be uncolored and free of adornment; preferably of the all-purpose tulip-shape; cleaned with hot water, but without the use of detergents; and stored in an environment free from cardboard, varnish, paint, or other odors.
2. *Tasting Area*—This should be sufficiently large so that tasters are not cramped and should be equipped with a solid, stark-white, Formica-type counter top or tabletop, along with comfortable stools or chairs. Ample spit buckets should be provided.
3. *Environment*—The wine-tasting area should be noiseless and odorless, preferably a room without distracting interferences. Temperatures should be in a range of 68-72 degrees Fahrenheit, with moderate humidity. Daylight or incandescent light of ample supply (fluorescent illumination and other types of light can interfere with the evaluation of wine color) should be provided.

WINE EVALUATION ANALYSIS

EXAMINATION SEGMENT	WINE NO 1	WINE NO 2	WINE NO 3	WINE NO 4	WINE NO 5	WINE NO 6
COLOR (20)						
Hue (5)						
Intensity (5)						
RTV* (10)						
CLARITY (20)						
Suspension (10)						
Precipitate (10)						
NOSE (25)						
Acescence** (10)						
Bouquet (8)						
RTV (7)						
TASTE (25)						
Tartness (3)						
Astringency (3)						
Sweetness (3)						
Balance (3)						
Body (3)						
Flavor						
Taste (3)						
Aftertaste (2)						
RTV (5)						
IMPRESSION (10)						
TOTAL (100)						

The 100-point scale for wine evaluation.

*Representative of Type or Variety
**Acetic Acid Formation

4. *Palate Clearers*—Salt-free soda crackers, mild cheese (such as Muenster), and room-temperature pure water (not chlorinated or fluoridated) should be provided to clear, or "neutralize," the palate between wine samples.
5. *Wine Samples*—There should be a good supply of bottles so that spares are on hand if needed. All bottles should be brought to cool room temperature and organized according to type, origin, color, sweetness, etc., as may be desired.
6. *Recording Materials*—Score sheets, pencils, etc., of sufficient quantity should be available.
7. *Ground Rules*—Guidelines—such as seating arrangements (separated so that each judge may keep his or her scores private), the prohibition of comments, gestures, and utterances that may bias other judges' opinions, etc.—should be laid down beforehand.
8. *Time*—Ample time is needed so that judging is not hurried (there can be, however, reasonable limits set in the ground rules).

Procedure

Wines to be judged together should be opened and poured at the same time. If there is a large number of samples, the wines should be divided up into "flights" (groups to be sampled separately). In most wine-judging competitions, no more than eight wines will be assigned to a single flight. Each glass should be clearly identified on the stem or base with a code so that no confusion arises about the content. Glasses should be carefully filled to about one-quarter or one-third capacity and presented to the judges simultaneously in a straightforward manner.

Visual

Clarity.   The visual character of a wine is divided into two categories: clarity and color. The common procedure in judging clarity is to hold the wineglass by the stem or base so that light from a source behind the glass can filter through the wine.

Wine with perfect clarity has no trace of suspended particles. There are four general classes of clarity usually referred to in wine judging: *cloudy, hazy, clear,* and *brilliant,* in ascending order of clarity value.

To replicate a *cloudy* condition, fill an 8-ounce wineglass halfway with pure water and add 2 drops of whole milk. One drop of milk creates *haziness.* Diluting the hazy mixture with 4 more ounces of water results in a *clear* condition and, of

The Visual Mode.

course, pure water with no addition of milk represents a *brilliant* or "bottle-bright" wine.

The surface of a wine, termed the *disc* by the French, appears absolutely brilliant when the wine is in good condition. A wine not yet completely processed in the winery could be dull. A "dusty" surface may indicate bacterial action, especially if the wine also exhibits an unpleasant, vinegary ordor. Bacteria can also make the disc appear iridescent, a condition the French call *vins filant*. An oily or shiny disc may result from careless use of lubricants or contaminants in the winery.

Using the Twenty-Point Scale, the judge may award the following points for clarity:

Brilliant = 2 points
Clear =   1 point
Hazy =   0 points

Color.   To examine the hue and intensity of color composition in wine, a wine judge usually sets the sample glass upon a stark-white counter top or tabletop. By looking downward through the glass, one can perceive variances in the color that go from lightest to darkest as one progresses from the outside edge to the center of the glass. Some judges prefer to make this examination by holding the glass at an angle and looking from side to side through the bowl of the glass. Whichever approach is adopted, the judge should remain consistent.

Wine color is often referred to as the *robe* by the French, or the *gown* by the British. Generally, all white wines fall into one of these categories: *water-white, pale straw, straw-gold, dark straw,* or *very dark gold,* in increasing order of color intensity. Each white wine has its appropriate color category. For example, dry French-type vermouth should be as near water-white as possible; anything darker would be grounds for deducting points. Aged French Sauternes vinified from "noble mold" grapes may be a dark straw or even very dark gold in color; anything lighter would lose points. White wines typically pale straw are Chablis wines from France and the Orvieto wines from Italy. Straw-gold wines include late-harvest, noble-mold German wines, such as Beerenauslese and Trockenbeerenauslese, and Sauternes from Bordeaux, France.

Red wines range from a light crimson hue, found typically in Beaujolais and American Pinot Noir wines, to a heavy ruby found in the Rhône wines of France and the Syrah wines of America. Pommard and Volnay wines from the Côte de Beaune in France are generally medium-range in color.

Rosé table wines run from the very pale "blush" wines found in northern California at the lightest to select vintages of Tavel rosé, which may exhibit a rich, heavy color concentration.

The colors of sherry and other maderized wines range from the very pale straw of the dry Fino sherries to the very dark amber of Oloroso or cream sherry-types.

Port wines come in a range of colors from white to tawny to ruby. White port should properly be medium straw in color; the tawny ports run more to a caramel-auburn hue; the color of ruby port is comparable to a heavy Haut-Médoc Bordeaux.

Sweet Italian vermouths are often a deep chocolate brown color.

Ideally, to gain familiarity with the proper colors of wines, one should acquire several good samples of all the wines mentioned above and study them carefully—though this would involve a considerable outlay of funds. Perhaps to ease the financial burden, several beginning wine tasters could pool their resources, or one could proceed gradually, studying one color at a time. Unfortunately, it's not really possible to replicate true wine colors by making solutions of food colorings and water. Photographs also fail to reproduce the complexity and richness of color in fine wines.

Typical faults of color in white wines are browning due to oxidation (the process of combining with oxygen; usually a result of defective wine production), yellowing due to excessive pigmentation, and tinting, which may occur in white wines made from red grapes. Rosé table wines often lose their attractive pink color, or light-redness, because of preservatives and/or aging, resulting in wine that is rather orange. This may or may not be a serious fault, depending upon the particular rosé wine-type being judged. Young red wines may have a pronounced purple hue that is almost always criticized, even for the celebrated Nouveau wines of Beaujolais in France. Good red table wine usually shows some browning about the edges of the wine in the tasting glass. However, except for intentionally overoxidized wines, such as the sherry-types and tawny port-types, excessive browning in red wines should be penalized in judging.

Using the Twenty-Point Scale, the judge may award the following points for color:

$$
\begin{array}{ll}
\text{Characteristic color} = & \text{2 points} \\
\text{Slight variance in color norm} = & \text{1 point} \\
\text{Browning, yellowing, or tinting} = & \text{0 points}
\end{array}
$$

Olfactory

Aroma.   Aroma is the single most-important (and heavily weighted) category in wine judging for the simple reason that it involves the most sensitive human organ of evaluation—the nose. There is a subtle, but crucial, distinction between a

The Olfactory Mode.

wine's aroma and its bouquet: the aroma derives from the grape from which the wine is made, whereas the bouquet results from the influences of the vintner, the person who makes the wine. The beginning wine taster should try to experience the aromas of as many different grape varieties as possible. One should also endeavor to learn basic descriptive terms employed in aroma judging, such as *character, flowery, fruity, spicy, varietal,* etc. (See glossary in appendix I for definitions of these terms.)

As mentioned in the previous section, the human brain, properly trained, has the capacity to classify, store, and recall a wide range of wine aromas. As one refines one's sniffing expertise with experience, one will be able to identify more and more specific odorous compounds. Some people are more sensitive than others to certain volatile substances, which may result in a keener ability to judge various wine odors.

The first examination of aroma should be made while the wine is at rest in the glass upon the counter top or tabletop. The judge will be smelling only the vapors that the wine gives off naturally. Insert the nose in the glass and inhale through it deeply, making a mental note of your reaction. Sometimes closing the eyes during this phase is of help.

The second aroma judgment may be taken immediately after the wine has been fully swirled around the inside walls of the glass. Grasp the glass stem and gently rotate the bowl. This significantly increases the surface area of wine from which vapors can arise and thus intensifies the aroma.

The third aroma examination is made by gently shaking the glass so that the wine splashes a little in the glass. This will aerate the sample and, like swirling, enhance the formation of aromatic vapors. It may take some practice to perfect one's swirling-and-shaking techniques to the point at which embarrassing untidiness can be avoided.

Using the Twenty-Point Scale, the judge may award the following points for aroma:

Very characteristic of grape variety, exceptional =   4 points
Characteristic of grape variety =   3 points
Distinct, but not varietal =   2 points
Clean and neutral =   1 point
Deficient, "off," uncharacteristic =   0 points

Bouquet.   Bouquet, as explained above, is largely determined by the vintner. Bouquet may be characterized by odors reminiscent of grass, wood, and yeast, among others. Bouquet also depends upon cellarage and bottle aging, which can contribute odors resembling herbs, mushrooms, tea, tobacco, vegetables, and other organic substances.

Aroma, deriving from natural sources, will vary little more than in its distinctiveness and intensity, unless there have been serious problems in the vineyard. Bouquet, on the other hand, arising from the deliberate manipulation of knowledge, machinery, and materials, offers a wide field for the development of different values—both good and bad.

The most common criticism of bouquet is that the wine has become *acetose* because of acetic acid, or vinegar, formation. This condition can be re-created by putting 4 ounces of pure water in an 8-ounce wineglass and adding about 1 teaspoon of red wine vinegar. Acetic acid in wines may become further compounded into ethyl acetate, which has an unmistakable paint-thinner odor.

Acetaldehyde formation in most table wines is a fault. It is detected as a rather nut-like aroma, resulting primarily from the oxidation of alcohol. However, high concentration of acetaldehyde is what gives sherry-type wines their distinctive character. Similarly, the caramel-like value of a compound called hydroxymethylfurfural is criticized in most table wines, but is an asset in maderized types such as Madeira, Marsala, and sherry.

Many vintners continue to add sulfur dioxide as a wine preservative. When used to excess it creates an odor similar to that of a freshly lighted match and causes a tingling sensation in the nose.

Infrequently, wines exhibit a very foul odor, perhaps best characterized as rotten eggs—the result of the formation of hydrogen sulfide. This can become even worse if the hydrogen sulfide is permitted to undergo conversion to mercaptans. Perhaps the best descriptive term one can use in characterizing the presence of mercaptans is *skunky*.

Certain bouquets can be regularly observed in wines made in particular ways from specific grapes. Chardonnay, for example, may exhibit a "buttery" nose from a chemical called *diacetyl*, which is inherent in the wines of Montrachet in Burgundy, France. Chardonnay grown in the Chablis region, however, exhibits more of a crisp apple character and less of a buttery impression. Johannisberg Riesling is often "floral," Gewürztraminer is "spicy," while Sauvignon Blanc (Fumé Blanc) is "grassy" or "smokey." Cabernet Sauvignon is regularly described as "bell pepper," "cigar box," and "black currant," while Pinot Noir has a distinctive coffee bouquet. Gamay has a "cherry" nose, and Nebbiolo is somewhat "raspberry" in character.

Researchers at the University of California at Davis have succeeded in formulating a standardized system of wine-aroma terminology. It uses a three-tier system of principal, secondary, and tertiary levels of aroma definition. While not yet perfect, it does establish a basis upon which people can communicate effectively in discussing the many, varied olfactory impressions that exist in the vast world of wine. The list that follows is adapted from the *American Journal of Enology and Viticulture*.

Principal or 1st Tier Term	2nd Tier Term	3rd Tier Term
I. Floral	A. Floral	1. Terpene
		2. Linalool
		3. Jasmine
		4. Rose
		5. Violet
		6. Geranium
II. Spicy	B. Spicy	7. Cinnamon
		8. Cloves
		9. Black pepper
		10. Licorice, Anise
		11. Mint
III. Fruity	C. Citrus	12. Grapefruit
		13. Lemon
		14. Orange
	D. Berry	15. Blackberry
		16. Raspberry
		17. Strawberry
		18. Black currant (Cassis)
	E. (Tree) Fruit	19. Cherry
		20. Apricot
		21. Peach
		22. Pear
		23. Apple
	F. (Tropical) Fruit	24. Pineapple
		25. Melon
		26. Banana
	G. Estery	27. Artificial fruit (Fruit essence)
	H. (Dried) Fruit	28. Strawberry jam
		29. Raisin
		30. Prune
		31. Fig
	I. Labrusca	32. Methyl anthranilate
	J. Muscat	
IV. Herbaceous/ Vegetative	K. Fresh	33. Stemmy
		34. Grass, cut green
		35. Bell pepper

Principal or 1st Tier Term	2nd Tier Term	3rd Tier Term
	L. Dried	36. Eucalyptus
		37. Hay/straw
		38. Tea
	M. Canned/cooked	39. Green beans
		40. Asparagus
		41. Green olive
		42. Black olive
		43. Artichoke
V. Earthy	N. Earthy	44. Dusty
		45. Mushroom
		46. Concrete
		47. Earthy
	O. Moldy	48. Musty
		49. Moldy cooperage
		50. Moldy cork
VI. Chemical	P. Petroleum	51. Tar
		52. Plastic
		53. Kerosene
		54. Diesel
	Q. Sulfur	55. Rubbery
		56. Hydrogen sulfide
		57. Mercaptan
		58. Onion
		59. Garlic
		60. Skunk
		61. Cabbage
		62. Burnt match
		63. Wet wool, wet dog
	R. Papery	64. Filter pad
		65. Wet cardboard
		66. Wet paper
	S. Pungent	67. Ethyl acetate
		68. Acetic acid
		69. Ethanol
		70. Sulfur dioxide
	T. Other	71. Fishy
		72. Soapy

Principal or 1st Tier Term	2nd Tier Term	3rd Tier Term
		73. Sorbate
		74. Fusel alcohol
VII. Oxidized	U. Oxidized	75. Acetaldehyde
VIII. Wood	V. Phenolic	76. Phenol
		77. Vanilla
	W. Resinous	78. Pine
		79. Cedar
		80. Oak
IX. Caramelized	X. Caramel	81. Honey
		82. Butterscotch
		83. Buttery (Diacetyl)
		84. Soy sauce
		85. Chocolate
		86. Molasses
	Y. Burned	87. Smoky
		88. Burnt toast/charred
X. Microbiological	Z. Yeasty	89. Flor-yeast
		90. Leesy
	AA. Lactic	91. Sauerkraut
		92. Butyric acid
		93. Sweaty
		94. Lactic acid
	BB. Other	95. Horsey

Adapted from: Nobel. A.C. et al., "Progress Towards a Standardized System of Wine Aroma Ternminology," *Am. J. Enol. Vitic.*, Vol. 35, No. 2, 1984.

The aromatic values of wines are made up of volatile acetals, acids, alcohols, amides, carbonyls, and esters. A complete list is lengthy and surpasses the scope of this text. Interested readers should seek out appropriate books on the subject by Maynard Amerine, V. L. Singleton, and other authorities.

The procedure for examining bouquet is identical to that of aroma described above. The wine judge may evaluate aroma and bouquet simultaneously upon becoming familiar with the specific values that separate the two criteria. Using the Twenty-Point Scale, the judge may award the following points for bouquet:

Characteristic of grape variety, age, and origin = 2 points
Characteristic, but faulted =   1 point
Faulted, vinegary =   0 points

Gustatory

We divide gustation from olfaction for convenience of discussion, but actually the discernment of flavor through taste is a complex process involving the tongue, the nose, the mouth, and even the throat. A taste sensation such as astringency from wine tannins, for example, leaves an impression not only on mouth and nose but on the pharyngeal passage as well. Other elements of wine's overall flavor, such as alcohol or carbon dioxide gas, are perceived as a burning or prickling sensation in the mouth but do not involve the gustatory or olfactory sense receptors (nerve cells). To properly evaluate a wine's flavor, we must be alert to all of these different sensations.

The Gustatory Mode.

In tasting wines, the following procedure is recommended: raise the tasting glass to the lips and take a sip. "Wash" the mouth with the wine and spit it out. Take another sip, hold it in the mouth, and "wash" the mouth again, so that all its sensitive surfaces are exposed. After spitting out the second sip, some judges find it helpful to close their eyes and/or to take a deep breath through the mouth. After ten to twenty seconds, a small portion of the wine may be swallowed, with the remainder spat out. The swallowed portion is exposed to the pharyngeal passage for aftertaste impressions. This procedure may be repeated if the judgment is not clear, or if some aspect of the wine was confusing at first exposure. After the tasting is completed, the taster should take a sip of pure, room-temperature water, and rinse the mouth fully several times, spitting out the rinse water each time. The taste values by which one judges wines are total acidity, tannin, body, and sugar. Discussions of each of these criteria follow below. After rinsing the mouth with water, one may wish to take a bite of neutral, salt-free cracker or some bland cheese, and then rinse with water again. The mouth should then be prepared for another evaluation. The judge will need to learn how to "pace" a series of such evaluations, since olfactory and gustatory receptors tire easily, diminishing one's abilities to detect and differentiate important values.

Wines to be critically evaluated and judged should be brought to cool room temperatures, as excessive cold inhibits the taste receptors. The ideal temperature for most whites and rosés is between 42 degrees and 50 degrees Fahrenheit, with the sweeter wines generally served colder than the dry ones. Serve reds at between 65 degrees and 68 degrees Fahrenheit.

Total Acidity.   Total acidity, as the term implies, is the sum total of acids present in wine, consisting primarily of *tartaric, malic, lactic,* and *acetic acids.* In most wines the total acidity can be measured between .5 and .75 percent of the entire wine composition. We perceive acidity on the tongue as a tartness; a wine that lacks sufficient acidity will taste bland, devoid of the tang of freshness characteristic of well-made wines. The acid balance differs for different wines. Wines from cool, northern regions—such as the white wines of Germany—usually have higher acid content than wines from hot climates with abundant sunshine, such as Sicily.

Sweetness can mask a wine's total acidity, and the beginning wine taster should devote some time to studying the interaction of these two qualities. A good way to experience acidity is to purchase wines of known dryness (absence of any detectable sweetness) and set up a scale of various acid contents by adding increasing amounts of ascorbic acid ("Fruit-Fresh") to small samples of the wine.

The control sample will have no added acid; the next will have a pinch of ascorbic acid; the next, two; the next, three, etc. Be sure the ascorbic acid is fully dissolved before performing the test. Taste the various samples you have prepared several times and then try it blind—perhaps by having a friend or relative administer the test.

Using the Twenty-Point Scale, the judge may award the following points for total acidity:

Balanced =	2 points
Slightly out of balance, high or low =	1 point
Markedly out of balance, high or low =	0 points

Tannin Compounds.   Tannins are complicated compounds that inhibit wine aging by reducing oxidation. Drawn from grape skins, seeds, and stems during fermentation, they contribute an astringency to the wine, to which the palate reacts by puckering. Some describe the taste sensation of tannins as leathery; others compare it to very strong tea.

Tannin is most often associated with young red table wines that are not yet ready for drinking. In traditional methods of vinification, some or all of the tannin-bearing grape stems were left with the red wine must. The higher tannin content gave the wine longer life, and its harshness mellowed with the years. Today, most vintners use precisely measured amounts of tannic acid to attain the tannin level they desire in the wine. Generally, red wines have much more tannin than whites. When the tannin has properly mellowed, it improves the wine's overall flavor; but a harsh tannic taste is a fault.

The mouth-puckering sensation produced by tannin can be experienced by mixing 1/4 of a tablespoon of wood tannin (available at pharmacies) with 8 ounces of water.

Bitterness is a fault in wines but a rather uncommon one in most commercial wines. Unlike the tartness from total acidity, bitterness is not masked significantly by sweetness. One of the most unfortunate forms of bitterness in wines results from an infection known as Amertune. It is caused by special strains of bacteria.

Using the Twenty-Point Scale the judge may award the following points for tannin:

Smooth, no harshness or bitterness =	2 points
Slightly harsh or bitter =	1 point
Distinctly harsh or bitter =	0 points

Body.   One judges a wine's body by whether it feels thin or full and heavy in the mouth. Heavy-bodiedness results from solids such as sugars and color pigments. *Glycerol* is a dense constituent of wine that can also greatly contribute to body.

Intuitively, sweet wines must have more body than dry wines, but it is the relative degree of body that is the judgment criterion.

Body is a rather difficult concept to teach and learn—let alone judge. There is a proper body for each wine type, and it takes time, experience, and a certain intuition to recognize what is right. Sweet white wines must have more body than dry whites, for example. The reader may wish to acquire a selection of dry white table wines, such as generic Chablis, Pinot Blanc, Seyval Blanc, and other selections in order to establish some reference points for thin-bodiedness. At the opposite end of the scale would be a selection of some of the very sweet French Sauternes, American and German late harvest white wines, which are the epitome of heavy-bodiedness. Lighter reds are typified by the lesser Beaujolais wines from France and Chianti from Italy. Good examples of heavier-bodied reds include varietal Cabernet Sauvignon, Syrah, and Zinfandel.

Using the Twenty-Point Scale, the judge may award the following points for body:

> Normal =   1 point
> Too heavy or light =   0 points

Sugar.   The sugar content (or sweetness) of a wine, like the acid level, must be in proper balance for the wine to taste right. Sweetness arises from natural or added dissolved sugar, but all sugars do not have the same sweetening effect. The capacity to generate sweetness ascends from glucose to sucrose to fructose, the sweetest sugar.

Glucuronic Acid.   This is another sweetening compound found in wines that have been made from grapes that were allowed to mature in the vineyard with the "noble mold," *Botrytis cinerea.* Background and descriptions of this phenomenon can be found in chapter 1, p. 16 and also in the Sauternes section of chapter 6.

Novice wine judges are encouraged to set up different levels of sweetness by adding increasing amounts of sugar to sample glasses of a dry wine in a fashion similar to the acidity scale described above in the "Total Acidity" section.

Wines that are labeled as being dry, or are traditionally so, will be penalized if determined to be sweet, as will supposedly sweet wines that taste dry. Nearly all red table wines are dry, but the dessert wine port is, by definition, sweet. Some wines, such as varietal Johannisberg Rieslings and Gewürztraminers, are not straightforward—their sweetness or dryness levels can be a subjective matter.

Using the Twenty-Point Scale, the judge may award the following points for sugar:

> Balanced = 1 point
> Slightly out of balance, high or low = 0 points

General Flavor

Perhaps it would be well to reiterate here that general flavor is not the same as taste. As discussed previously, we can perceive only four taste values: sour, bitter, salty, and sweet—none of which has much bearing on general flavor. General flavor values, like those of aroma and bouquet, will appeal most intensely to the nose.

The grape variety used in making the wine will contribute the most important values of general flavor. Some grape varieties yield subtle flavor values that must be conserved with extreme care by the vintner in order to produce superior products. Examples of such grapes are Chardonnay, Pinot Blanc, and Seyval Blanc. Other varieties, such as Delaware, Gewürztraminer, Johannisberg Riesling, and Vidal Blanc, may yield moderate flavor values. Varieties exhibiting powerful flavors include the native muscadines of the Deep South, the famous Old World Muscats, and most of the native northeastern American *Vitis labrusca* varieties such as Catawba, Concord, and Niagara. Some wine aficionados memorize and recall wine flavors by associating them with some other food—such as the bell-pepper character of Cabernet Sauvignon or the coffee character of Côte d'Or Burgundies. And, in some instances, the judge merely distinguishes between various values of "typical varietal flavor."

Another important general flavor is that of oakiness or woodiness. The great California vintner, Louis Martini, advises that "oak in wine is like garlic in cooking—if you can taste it, it's too much." Excessive redwood aging produces a grassy character, while overaging in oak can result in a distinctive vanilla value.

A sauerkraut flavor is probably due to acetic bacteria spoilage, which may, especially in Italian Chianti wines, be a positive constituent when held to subtle levels. Applelike flavors may be the result of high levels of malic acid. Cheesy wines are the result of *malolactic* fermentation by bacteria that convert malic acid to lactic acid. Wines that are strong upon the palate may have an excessively high alcohol content. Wines that are excessively tart may indicate that the grapes did not sufficiently mature during ripening, which sometimes occurs with wines grown in colder regions. Conversely, wines that are insipid, or too low in acidity, may emerge from overly matured fruit, which may happen in warmer regions.

Another aspect of general flavor is the *aftertaste*, the impression a wine leaves in the mouth and the back of the throat after it has been swallowed. A pleasant, lingering aftertaste is one sign of a well-made, complex wine.

Using the Twenty-Point Scale, the judge may award the following points for general flavor:

Well balanced, very distinctive, with ample aftertaste = 2 points
Balanced, distinctive, with aftertaste =   1 point
Neutral, but sound =   0 points

Overall Impression

Judges use this two-point category to rate the subjective impression that a wine has made on them. It is also a fudge-factor that allows the judge to add or subtract a point if the wine exhibited an exceptional value (either good or bad) in some other category. Sooner or later, wine judges encounter wines that scored rather well, but are just not that good—and conversely, wines that scored rather poorly, but are not that bad. The overall impression category allows for adjustments.

Using the Twenty-Point Scale, the judge may award the following points for overall impression:

Very enjoyable = 2 points
Enjoyable =   1 point
Unimpressed =   0 points

Summing the Results

Wine judgings are not without controversy. Vintners are subjected to the published opinions of wine writers in much the same way that actors and directors are subjected to theater reviews. Gatherings of wine critics at judging functions have been known to end up with unfair, and, therefore, unfortunate, results; the vintner's business suffers and the consumer is misled.

One major difficulty arises from the manner in which samples to be judged are obtained. Not all retailers and wholesalers employ optimal storage facilities: sometimes their less-popular wines remain in storage for extended periods or inventories are not rotated, with the result that samples are not really representative

Scoring wine at a competition.

of the wine-type. Wine-judging committee members charged with selecting samples should be highly qualified for this responsibility and carry it out with the greatest care.

There are many opinions as to the merit of judgings, and, of course, many complaints—with and without foundation. One school of thought holds that while gold medals shower great glory on winning entries, silver and bronze medals are actually deleterious. The vintners of these second- and third-place wines fear that nobody will buy their entries, worthy as they are. Other wine producers and enthusiasts feel that some wines that score poorly at a judging may actually be a better accompaniment to food than champion wines. The uncommonly distinctive wines, in their opinion, may overpower the meal, while lesser wines contribute to the total interplay of food and wine flavors.

But despite the controversies, such functions are sure to continue in the vast world of wine. Wine judging may never become totally fair or unbiased, but it is an integral part of the art of wine appreciation. The wine novice can learn a great deal from the evaluations of the experts, though, in the end, there is no substitute for personal experience.

WINE COMPONENTS, METABOLISM, AND NUTRITION

Wine and Its Component Parts

Wine is a complex, living substance that interacts with the human body to induce pleasure and health when used properly, but which can be harmful if abused. We know that wine is composed of ethyl alcohol in varying degrees, sugars, vitamins, minerals, acids, and other organic compounds. There have been studies of the pharmacological and physiological effects of each of these elements on our bodies.

According to *Wine and Medical Practice*, a Wine Institute publication, more than 300 chemical components of wine have been isolated and identified. There remain many others still to be isolated in future research. Wine derives its appearance, aroma, and flavor from the interplay of myriad chemical components (see table 2.1).

Wine Alcohols

Wine is an alcoholic beverage, containing, for the most part, water. Ethyl alcohol (ethanol) is present in concentrations varying from 10 to 14 percent of volume for a dry table wine and 17 to 22 percent for dessert wines. Other alcohols, such as isobutanol, present in wine in smaller amounts average approximately .03 percent in California wines, for example.

Physiologically, alcohol is a depressant, although in small quantities it may be more of a tranquilizer, that is, a relaxant, than a depressant. Alcohol has also been shown to increase gastric secretions, thus aiding digestion and stimulating appetite. The physiological effects of the alcohol contained in wine depend on the amount of wine that is absorbed from the gastrointestinal tract into the blood stream than on the total volume of wine consumed. It has been determined that the average person can completely metabolize approximately 1/4 bottle (187 ml) of table wine if it is drunk over a period of six hours.

The effect of alcohol on the body varies with the weight and sex of the individual, the presence or absence of food in the stomach, previous exposure of the individual to alcoholic beverages, and the type of beverage in which the alcohol is

TABLE 2-1   Chemical Components of Typical Table and Dessert Wines

	Units	Dry Red Table	Dry White Table	Medium Sweet Sherry	Port	Rosé	Champagne
Calcium	ppm*	62	63	60	57	70	67
Copper	ppm	0.2	0.2	0.2	0.5	0.1	0.3
Iron	ppm	6.0	4.7	2.5	3.5	3.0	7.5
Potassium	ppm	794	780	757	939	673	740
Sodium	ppm	85	113	78	94	160	68
Ethyl alcohol	% (vol.)	12.2	11.9	19.9	19.8	12.2	12.5
Higher alcohols	ppm	298	254	401	384	249	246
Acetaldehyde	ppm	46	91	55	68	80	83
pH	——	3.7	3.5	3.7	3.8	3.45	3.20
Acetic acid	%	0.047	0.029	0.004	0.033	0.029	0.005
Tartaric acid	%	0.6	0.6	0.4	0.4	0.6	0.7
Hexoses	%	0.2	0.3	3.1	11.7	1.12	1.50
Total esters	ppm	280	244	419	305	260	191
Tannins	%	0.18	0.03	0.03	0.10	0.05	0.04

*Parts per million.
Adapted from *Wine and Your Well-Being*, by Salvatore Pablo Lucia, M.D.

consumed. With wine (and beer), the rise in blood alcohol per ounce consumed is much smaller than with spirits, and there is more of a plateau in the level of increase than a sharply rising peak and fall. The amount of alcohol absorbed from the gastrointestinal tract to the blood and subsequently to the brain is important not only physiologically but from a medicolegal aspect. Most states have specific blood alcohol levels allowable for drivers (usually below .10 gm/cc). Alcohol, if taken on an empty stomach, reaches the bloodstream in fifteen to twenty minutes, and, if taken on a full stomach, reaches the blood stream in one to three hours. Research has shown that when wine is taken with food there is a much slower elevation of blood alcohol levels.

Wine Sugars

The sugar content of wine varies from less than 1 percent in dry red and white wines to as high as 15 percent in sweet dessert wines. Fructose is present in the highest concentration in wine, and it has been shown that fructose hastens the body's rate of metabolism of alcohol.

Blood-Alcohol Curves

The combined rates of alcohol absorption, distribution, metabolic breakdown and excretion are reflected in the blood-alcohol concentration.

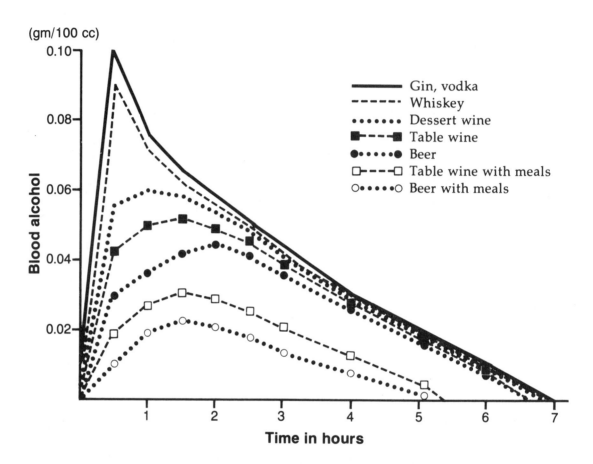

Typical blood-alcohol curves resulting from ingestion of various spirits, wines and beer, each at amounts equivalent to 0.6 gm of alcohol per kilogram of body weight. (Compiled from data of Goldberg: Haggard, Goldberg and Cohen; Loill; Newman and Abramson, and others, and presented here to illustrate relative effects.)

Adapted from: WINE, HEALTH & SOCIETY, A Symposium
Jointly Sponsored by: University of California, San Francisco
Society of Medical Friends Of Wine
Wine Institute, San Francisco

GRT Book Printing Oakland, California

Acids

There are two groups of acids that naturally occur in wine: (1) acids obtained from the grapes: citric, malic, phosphoric, tannic, and tartaric; and (2) acids produced by fermentation, acetic, phenylacetic, carbonic, formic, lactic, and succinic. Other acids occur in small quantities.

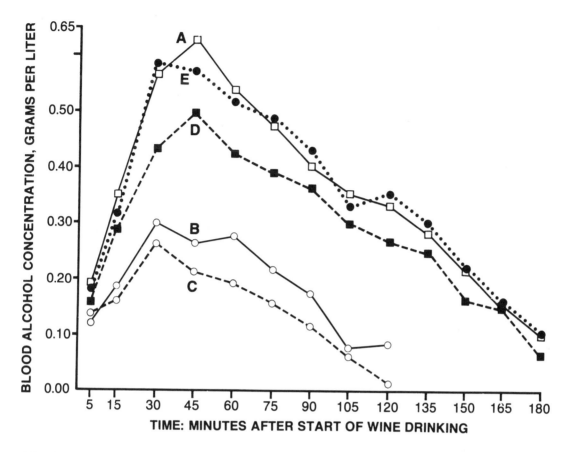

Blood Alcohol Concentrations after Wine Drinking in a Single Dose. A: fasting. B: during meal.   C: 2 hours after meal.   D: 4 hours after meal.   E: 6 hours after meal.

Adapted from: WINE, HEALTH & SOCIETY, A Symposium
          Jointly Sponsored by: University of California, San Francisco
                                Society of Medical Friends Of Wine
                                Wine Institute, San Francisco

GRT Book Printing Oakland, California

Nutritional Aspects of Wine

Studies have shown the presence of minerals and vitamins in wine, which are thought to reflect both the soil in which the grapes were grown and the vinification techniques used. Wine is known to be an effective iron supplement, and 80 percent of the iron in wine is present in the ferrous form that is readily available for use in the human body. Dry red wines contain about 6 milligrams per liter of iron, as compared to about 4.7 for dry white table wines and 3.5 for port. The sodium content of wine may be a concern to people on low-salt diets. The average concentration of sodium is 7 milligrams per 100 ml of Champagne; 8 milligrams per

100 ml for red table wines and sherry; 9 milligrams per 100 ml for port; 10 milligrams per 100 ml for sweet wines; 16 milligrams per 100 ml for rosé table wines; and 14 milligrams per 100 ml for muscatel. The vinification technique may have an impact here, since some methods may create significantly higher levels of sodium. Tests have shown that wine enhances the absorption of nutrients in a diet: people who drank wine absorbed significantly larger amounts of calcium, iron, magnesium, phosphorus, and zinc from their food. This same effect was not noted when other alcohol solutions were taken.

It is of considerable interest to scientists that wine is much more than the sum of its individual parts or components, namely, there remain many mysterious and as yet not understood interactions of wine with the human body.

Caloric Content of Wines

Most of the caloric content of dry wines comes from its alcohol content. Seventy to seventy-five percent of the calories from the alcohol in wine are available to the human metabolic system. Alcohol can replace fats and carbohydrates in a diet on a basis of a one-for-one caloric trade. However, a reasonable proportion of wine alcohol in the diet would be 10 percent of the total caloric intake (see table 2-2).

WINE AND MEDICAL THERAPEUTICS

Use of wine in moderation has long been an accepted part of medical therapeutics. In fact, a compilation of all the medicinal therapeutic properties of wine that have been handed down through the centuries, both in folklore and medical literature, would fill many volumes. This discussion is limited to some of the more well-known and accepted beneficial effects of wine—specifically its use in treating some diseases and in helping people accept and enjoy the inevitable aging process. Most would agree that wine is far preferable to stimulants, tranquilizers, and supplemental digestive enzymes for alleviating anxieties, soothing tempers, and making uninteresting meals more palatable.

Wine and Appetite

Wine can have the effect of both stimulating and depressing the appetite. Many people drink a glass of wine before a meal as an aperitif—but, somewhat

TABLE 2-2   Caloric Content of Major Wine Types

Wine	Cals./100 ml	Cals./Oz.	Typical Serving (Oz.)	Cals./ Typical Serving
Red Table Wines				
Barbera	81.3	24.4	4	97.6
Burgundy—Pinot Noir	80.2	24.1	4	96.4
Cabernet Sauvignon	82.8	24.8	4	99.2
Chianti	81.8	24.5	4	98.0
Zinfandel	81.8	24.5	4	98.0
Rosé Table Wines	78.3	23.5	4	94.0
White Table Wines				
Chablis—Chardonnay	73.8	22.1	4	88.4
Rhein Wine—Johannisberg Riesling	82.5	24.8	4	99.2
Sauternes	77.2	23.2	4	92.8
Dessert and Aperitif Wines				
Red Port	161.3	48.4	2	96.8
White Port	150.0	45.0	2	90.0
Muscatel	163.2	49.0	2	98.0
Dry Sherry	130.1	39.0	2	78.0
Sweet Sherry	152.7	45.8	2	91.6
Dry Vermouth	113.2	34.0	2	102.0
Sweet Vermouth	150.4	45.1	2	135.3

Adapted from *Wine and Your Well-Being*, by Salvatore Pablo Lucia, M.D.

paradoxically, wine taken thirty to forty-five minutes prior to a meal may help some people control compulsive eating through its tranquilizing properties. Wine has also been used in treatment of hypochlorohydria (lack of sufficient gastric acid in the stomach to digest food), since it stimulates gastric secretions. No alcoholic beverage, however, including wine, should be used by people who have an active stomach ulcer or pancreas disease.

Wine and Alcoholic Liver Disease

Cirrhosis is a liver disease that causes loss of liver cells and damage to the liver's supporting network, blood vessels, and ability to be healed.

Research has shown that cirrhosis of the liver is caused more by malnutrition and lack of adequate caloric intake than by any direct toxic effects of alcohol.

Wine in the Treatment of Maladies of Increasing Age

Galen, a physician and writer in ancient Rome (c. 130-c. 200 A.D.), has been credited with describing wine as "the nurse of old age." Increasing age impairs human abilities to deal with day-to-day emotional stress and basic health and well-being. Old age also affects the bowels and urinary tract. In addition, lack of appetite and insomnia are frequent complaints of the elderly. Obviously, wine taken in a moderate amount will not remedy all the changes that inevitably occur with age. However, it can do a lot to make the later years of life more tolerable. Certainly a glass of port taken at bedtime is preferable to sleeping medication. And wine has many more subtle benefits as well that cannot be calculated through an analysis of its individual components. Wine drinkers frequently seem to have a better outlook on life; a more robust, energetic feeling; a more pleasant, congenial attitude. Wine encourages and enhances cooperation, conversation, and laughter. In fact, wine is now being prescribed as part of the daily diet in many nursing homes throughout the United States and in the geriatric wards of major hospitals. It is important to note that these beneficial effects are not due entirely to the alcohol content of wine—other alcoholic beverages do not have such therapeutic properties.

Wine and Cardiovascular Disease

The alcohol in wine increases blood flow through the blood vessels, such as arteries and veins, both in organs such as the kidneys, liver, heart, and brain, and also in the skin. Because of this, wine has been prescribed in the treatment of certain disorders of blood circulation, such as Raynaud's disease and Buerger's disease. Wine has also been used to reduce the anxiety component of hypertension, although care must be taken to prescribe wines that are low in sodium. Significantly, many of the beneficial effects of wine on the heart and blood vessels are thought to be related to the nonalcoholic components of wine (particularly the *aldehydes* and *phenols*). There has been some evidence indicating that a fortified wine taken after a heavy meal may reduce the level of fat in the blood. (Some of these properties are attributed to such complex substances in wine as *isoquercitroside*, *leucocyanidin*, and *epicatechin* that occur in significant levels in brandy.) There is no evidence to support the notion that moderate amounts of alcohol produce increased levels of cholesterol. Recent articles published in the *Journal of the American Medical Association* have shown that coronary artery disease was less likely to develop in men who drank alcoholic beverages in moderation than those who abstained or were heavy drinkers. This finding proved to be remarkably constant for beer, wine, and liquor after adjusting for the different alcoholic content of each of these types of beverages. Therefore, it seems probable that this particular effect is due to the alcohol itself rather than the other substances found in each type of drink. It also has been shown that levels of substances that are protective against coronary heart disease are elevated with alcohol consumption, and that substances that cause coronary heart disease are lowered by alcohol consumption.

Wine and Diabetes

Dry wines with low-sugar content can be an excellent and regular energy source for those on diabetic diets. Wine may also be substituted for fat in diabetic diets without producing *ketosis* (the accumulation of excessive ketones in the body). The feeling of well-being that wine induces can help the diabetic accept the need for a strict diet. Alcohol, with the possible exception of sugar, is the most easily digestible food substance, but, unlike sugar, it is readily metabolized without insulin. However, we should note that immediately following the intake of wine, blood sugar levels rise slightly; this brief hyperglycemic (high-glucose level in blood) period is followed by a period of hypoglycemia (low-glucose level), which may last in excess of four hours. Although marked ketosis has been noticed in some diabetic patients who drink alcohol, no such effect has occurred when the alcohol consumed is a dry table wine. However, people on a diabetic diet who take oral medication for control of diabetes, such as tolbutamide, sometimes experience flushing, profuse sweating, and a moderate drop in blood pressure after drinking wine—or any other alcoholic beverage—on an empty stomach. If one suffers from diabetes, consult with a physician before making wine a regular part of the diet.

Wine and Epilepsy

In some patients with epilepsy, alcohol has been shown to raise the potential for seizures, and thus increase their susceptibility to seizures. There is no direct evidence that alcohol itself causes seizures, but rather that it may decrease the protective effect of seizure medication or decrease the brain's built-in seizure prevention mechanism. An epileptic may not be able to metabolize Dilantin (a drug commonly prescribed for seizure control) after drinking. It is important to note, however, that many more seizures occur after the abrupt withdrawal of high levels of alcohol than with mild-to-moderate alcohol consumption, particularly in the form of wine.

Wine and Pregnancy

Considerable concern has arisen in the past few years regarding possible adverse effects of alcohol on pregnancy. In the 1970s the term *fetal alcohol syndrome* was coined to describe a group of congenital defects seen in the children of alcoholic mothers. Babies who suffered from this syndrome had low birth weights; problems with head and face development such as *microcephaly* (a smaller-than-average head size at birth); mental retardation; and delayed nervous system development. Though current research has described the full fetal alcohol syndrome only in the offspring of heavy drinkers, some scientists feel that the syndrome could occur with the exposure of the fetus to *any* level of alcohol. The bulletin of the Federal Drug Administration in July 1981 stated that even the smallest amount of alcohol might be dangerous to the fetuses of pregnant women. The full-blown fetal alcohol syndrome has, to this date, been reported only in women suffering from chronic alcoholism who, in one study, drank as much as one and one-half gallons of liquor per day. It is also significant that 75 percent of the chronic alcoholic women who delivered children with fetal alcohol syndrome died within five years of their children's birth. The definition of heavy, moderate, and mild drinking is somewhat hazy: some put the numbers at 1.6 ounces of absolute (almost 100-proof) alcohol a day for heavy drinkers and 1 ounce a day for an average drinker. The chronic alcoholics who delivered children with fetal alcohol syndrome consumed an average of 5.9 ounces of absolute alcohol a day. For the most part, research has shown that it is the exposure of the developing fetus to high levels of alcohol that is the potential cause of the birth defects. (The blood alcohol of the mother is transmitted through the womb to the fetus quickly and without alteration). The fetal alcohol syndrome has been seen both in chronic alcoholics who consumed high levels of alcohol on a regular basis and in binge drinkers. It has been shown conclusively that the alcohol in distilled spirits produces almost twice the blood alcohol levels as beer and wine when equivalent alcohol amounts are consumed. Also, when beer and wine are consumed with food the rise in the blood alcohol level is much slower. In addition to the fetal alcohol syndrome, there has been a correlation of stillbirths in women who consumed high levels of alcohol: women who drank 400 to 600 milliliters of wine per day had double the normal stillbirth rate of nondrinkers, and those who drank over 600 milliliters a day had triple the stillbirth rate (a full bottle of wine is 750 milliliters).

To put the fetal alcohol syndrome in perspective, it is important to note that only approximately 500 cases of fetal alcohol syndrome to date have been described in medical literature. Most physicians advocate a commonsense approach to alcohol intake during pregnancy. Wine taken with meals produces by far the smallest rise in blood alcohol levels in the mother and thus in the fetus. We should also note that it is somewhat misleading to attribute all the effects of the fetal alcohol syndrome solely to the amount of alcohol consumed, since many of these women were also heavy smokers, some used "hard" drugs, and many had poor diets.

Wine and Drug Interactions

Most of the research undertaken regarding the interactions of alcoholic beverages and drugs has focused on the impact of alcohol on drug metabolism and the effects of the drugs. Very little research, however, has been conducted specifically on wine. Three possible types of drug and alcohol interactions may occur:

1. The alcohol may have a direct impact on the drug, increasing or inhibiting its action.
2. The metabolism of the alcohol may affect the metabolism of the drug.
3. Most importantly, the alcohol may alter the effects of the drug within the human body.

Alcohol is known to increase the effects of such drugs as sedatives, tranquilizers, and antihistamines. In many cases drug overdoses are due to the augmenting effects of alcohol on drugs. Marijuana has been shown to delay the effects of alcohol for a short period of time; then the effects of high blood alcohol will occur suddenly. Certain drugs, such as some of the oral drugs used for the treatment of diabetes and a drug used to treat a vaginal infection will produce a reaction similar to a drug (Antabuse) given to alcoholics to make the effects of alcohol unpleasant: flushing of the skin and face, increased heart rate, nausea, and vomiting. Some work has also shown that some of the components of wine may adversely affect certain blood pressure medications—thus, if wine is taken, the patient's blood pressure may become elevated in spite of the continuation of the appropriate dose of medication.

Wine and Neurological Disorders

Many of the neurological disorders and deficiencies attributed to the abuse of alcohol can also be seen in nutritional disorders, and in most cases are actually due to nutritional deficiencies rather than any direct toxic effect of alcohol. Alcoholics notoriously have diets low in calories other than alcohol and deficient in vitamins and minerals. Except for acute intoxication and alcoholic seizures, the neurological disorders discussed below arise primarily from nutritional deficiencies and are secondary effects of alcoholism.

Acute Intoxication

The first effect of acute alcohol intoxication is the inhibition of higher brain functions beginning with a feeling of relaxation and followed closely by loss of judgment; personality changes, varying from placidity to combativeness; and impaired coordination. Delirium tremens (D.T.'s) is a serious complication of alcoholism seen most often with abrupt withdrawal of alcohol and concurrently abrupt withdrawal of the sedative effects of alcohol. There is a marked neurological activity and irritability. The first symptoms of delirium tremens are usually restlessness, irritability, loss of appetite, elevated temperature, agitation, nightmares, hallucinations (usually in the form of insects or animals), and seizures. Respiration and heartbeat rates become rapid. Unless treated quickly and appropriately, death can occur.

Wernicke's Encephalopathy and Korsakoff's Psychosis

This syndrome, which is associated with chronic alcoholism, begins with difficulties of eye movement, difficulty in walking, and dementia. The onset can be sudden. The syndrome, once identified, is treated with thiamine (vitamin B_1). The eye and walking difficulties respond quickly, although the mental symptoms may not improve.

Changes Within the Brain due to Chronic Alcoholism (Nutritional Deficiency)

Several changes within the structure of the brain have been described in people with nutritional deficiency and/or alcoholism. One is marked by symptoms that include abnormalities of eye movement, facial weakness, difficulty with speech, and difficulty with swallowing. These are thought to be related to the dehydration that may accompany alcoholism and malnutrition.

Marchiafava-Bignami's Disease

This disease was originally identified in Italian men who drank large quantities of red wine. For many years the disease was linked with excessive consumption of Italian red wine. However, throughout the years there have been sporadic cases of the disease reported in other countries and suffered by people who drank other forms of alcoholic beverages. More recent evidence indicates that this is a nutritional deficiency seen in alcoholics rather than a toxic effect of alcoholism. The symptoms include psychic and emotional disorders, intellectual deterioration, convulsive seizures, and varying degrees of tremor, rigidity, and paralysis, among other neurological disorders. The duration ranges from several weeks to months, and recovery is possible in varying degrees if abstinence from alcohol and adherence to good nutrition are established and maintained.

Peripheral Neuropathy (Neuritic beriberi)

Most of the cases of peripheral neuropathy (impaired peripheral nerve function) seen in alcoholics are identical to those caused by nutritional deficiencies. The disease results from a deficiency of B-complex vitamins, particularly B_1.

Alcoholic Cerebellar Degeneration

This form of brain degeneration, brought on by nutritional deficiencies, is seen in alcoholics as well as nonalcoholics who suffer from nutritional disorders. There is marked atrophy of certain brain centers that may result in an acute difficulty with walking and can be cured with an early prognosis and prompt withdrawal of alcohol and treatment with B-complex vitamins. The chronic form develops over a period of many weeks or months and may progress to the point where the patient is confined to a wheelchair. Recovery from the chronic form is much less likely.

Myopathy (Muscle Changes in Chronic Alcoholism)

Scientists are still uncertain whether the chronic muscle wasting and muscle tenderness seen in alcoholics is due to the effects on the nerves of malnutrition or a direct toxic effect of the alcohol on muscle.

Carcinogenicity

The recent publicity given to *ethyl carbamate* (urethane) in wines by the "Center for Science in the Public Interest" has been a vehicle for their well-known special interest in neo-prohibition. It is true that all wines, as well as all fermented foods (bread, cheese, sauerkraut, soy sauce, vinegar, yogurt—to name only a very few), contain some urethane—typically a few parts per billion in table wines. While the U.S. Food and Drug Administration and several major universities continue to study the situation, Canada has exacted legal limits for urethane in wines—and most U.S.-made wines easily pass tests for Canadian importation. There is no question that urethane can cause cancer—but the minute levels of the compound found in wines makes this a common-sense issue.

In summary, the major indications and contraindications for the clinical use of wine are:

Major Indications

1. Wine can be used as a mild tranquilizing agent to counter emotional tension and anxiety, as long as low-blood-alcohol levels can be maintained over extended periods.

2. Wine may be a useful component of the normal diet, providing energy and aiding digestive processes.

3. Since alcohol is metabolized without insulin, dry (nonsweet) wine may serve both as a useful source of energy and as a valuable psychological adjunct to the diabetic diet.

4. Dry wines have been used effectively to stimulate appetite in such eating disorders as anorexia nervosa.

5. Presumably because of their tranquilizing action, both table and dessert wines (in moderation) have helped obese patients maintain prescribed weight-reducing diets.

6. In cardiovascular diseases, wine has been found beneficial as a tranquilizing agent. It may also prove useful where there is a need to dilate (open) blood vessels and improve dull or monotonous diets. Recent epidemiological studies, provocative even if inconclusive, have suggested that wine in the diet may actually help protect against coronary disease. The fact that naturally-made wine is low in harmful salt (sodium) and high in beneficial salt (potassium) suits it to the dietary needs of many cardiac patients who are avoiding sodium, taking diuretics, and supplementing dietary potassium.

7. In the care of convalescent patients and especially in geriatrics, wine may be

an ideal way to improve nutrition, relieve emotional tension, and supply mild sedation.

8. Finally—and not least important—wine, used as a food with other foods at mealtimes, may play a vital role in developing a cultural or sociological protective pattern against excessive drinking.

Major Contraindications

1. The most important contraindication to the use of wine is the inability of some patients to use alcohol in any form without becoming dependent on it.

2. Wine is usually not recommended in the presence of inflammation, irritation, or ulceration of the mouth, throat, esophagus, or stomach. As with all other alcoholic beverages, it is contraindicated in gastritis, any condition that causes excessive gastric secretions, gastric cancer, or bleeding in the upper digestive tract.

3. In healing duodenal ulcers, wine may be helpful for some patients, but not for others.

4. All alcoholic beverages are clearly contraindicated in disease of the pancreas and should be used with caution in the presence of proved or suspected liver disease.

5. Use of alcoholic beverages is to be avoided in the presence of acute kidney infection, although they may be considered in selected cases of chronic kidney disease.

6. Persons with severe heart muscle damage and chronic congestive heart failure should probably not drink alcoholic beverages at all. Other cardiac patients should limit their use of alcohol. Patients with coronary disease should refrain from activity that could induce angina (pain) for two hours after drinking.

7. All alcoholic beverages should be used cautiously or not at all in people suffering from epilepsy.

8. Alcohol in any form may react to increase the effects of such drugs as barbituates, tranquilizers, narcotics, and similar medications. When these drugs are prescribed, the use of wine must be carefully supervised and controlled.

9. The link between maternal alcohol abuse and undesirable outcomes of pregnancy has been recognized since ancient times. Growth retardation in the baby, congenital defects, and reduced intellectual function can occur with excessive alcohol intake.

10. Wine and other alcoholic beverages are usually contraindicated in diseases of the prostate or diseases in the genitourinary tract.

WINE AND ALCOHOL DEPENDENCY

Wine in moderation continues to be an inexhaustible source of pleasure. The key word here is *moderation*, for wine or any form of alcohol in excess can be a serious danger both to the drinker and other people. Anyone who writes about the pleasures and benefits of alcoholic beverages also has a responsibility to discuss the risks of alcohol dependency and alcoholism.

Modern medicine has come to recognize alcoholism as a medical problem, and much money and research is being devoted to identifying the hereditary, cultural, and emotional factors associated with it. We know that people who drink beverages high in alcohol content (such as whiskey, brandy, and vodka) are more prone to alcoholism than those who drink beer and wine. This accounts in part for the high levels of alcoholism in countries such as Switzerland, Poland, and Russia, where high-alcohol spirits predominate. In Italy, Greece, southern France, Denmark, and southern Russia, the most popular alcoholic beverages are beer and wine, and the risk of alcoholism is considerably lower. Leon Adams, an authority who has spent much of his life studying and writing about wine, asserts that there are no chronic alcoholics who became alcoholics by drinking wine. Most of the "winos" drink wine only because it is cheaper: they started out on distilled spirits.

Research has demonstrated that the drinking patterns of low-risk and high-risk groups are marked by significantly different sociological and cultural influences. In the low-risk group there is an early, unemotional initiation to the drinking of alcoholic beverages, usually occurring in a family group and with meals. There also is a social stigma attached to excessive consumption of alcoholic beverages and drunkenness. In groups that are prone to alcoholism, high levels of alcohol are consumed, often before meals, for the purpose of getting drunk, and there is a cultural acceptance of drunkenness. The initiation to alcoholic beverages usually occurs during adolescence, usually away from home, and the first experience often involves drinking to excess. Drinking to excess is not only tolerated in high-risk groups, but there is often an assumption that heavy drinking and even drunkenness are somehow "macho."

Alcoholism or alcohol addiction is a complex problem, difficult to identify and difficult to cure. Genetic, biological, social, and psychological factors may all contribute to it. It is known that alcoholism or alcohol addiction runs in families, and that children of alcoholic parents constitute a high-risk group that should be targeted for prevention efforts. It is also known that reinforcement of positive cultural and social drinking patterns will reduce the incidence of drinking problems.

The problem must be attacked at the community level. Researchers Leake and Silverman have coined the phrase "the social pharmacology of alcoholic beverages" to focus attention on the complex nature of drinking problems.

Also, a study by Benos concluded that only negative social attitudes toward intoxication and alcohol abuse will enable a society to solve the problems of alcoholism. He reported that in Greece, where the yearly alcohol consumption is about 13 liters of absolute alcohol per capita population age 15 and over, there is the lowest number of alcoholics in all of Europe. He attributed this to the aversion of Greek society to public drunkenness and alcohol excess. The consumption of alcohol in the United States is about 11 liters per capita population age fifteen and over.

Articles published in medical literature in 1983 have estimated that about 35 percent of all United States adolescents are experiencing alcohol problems, consuming two to five drinks at least once a week. It was also found that more boys than girls drink. In a 1978 survey, it was found that alcohol was the most popular substance among school students, with 87 percent reporting some use of alcohol; marijuana was the second most-popular drug, with 68 percent reporting some use of marijuana. A recent article in the *American Medical News* reports that the College of American Pathologists estimates as many as nine out of every ten fatal traffic accidents involve drunk drivers. Much of the problem in the United States is thought to be due to the large quantities of distilled spirits consumed in this country. The popularity of the "happy hour" in bars and the social cocktail party encourages drinking to excess. Wine and beer, though available at many cocktail parties and lounges, are seldom pushed on drinkers to the same degree as distilled spirits.

In conclusion, here are four approaches that may contribute to a decline in alcoholism and alcohol dependency:

1. study of societies where alcoholism is rare, identification of social and cultural norms that discourage alcohol abuse, and incorporation of as many of these as possible into our society and social structure;
2. education of children to help them develop positive attitudes toward drinking in moderation and intolerance of alcohol excess and drunkenness;
3. discouragement of the use of alcoholic beverages for self-medication to alleviate stress, physical distress, or emotional problems;
4. identification and education of high-risk groups.

Wine has traditionally been associated with pleasure. If consumed in moderation, as it should be, wine can be a joy to the human senses as well as a valuable nutritional adjunct.

CHATEAU MONTELENA

ESTABLISHED 1882

NAPA VALLEY

Chardonnay
1981

PRODUCED AND BOTTLED BY CHATEAU MONTELENA
WINERY • CALISTOGA, NAPA VALLEY, CALIFORNIA

ALCOHOL 13.0% BY VOLUME

3

THE ENJOYMENT
OF WINE

The enjoyment of wine means different things to different people, as it has meant different things to different cultures throughout the ages. The ancients probably appreciated wine most as relief from thirst and pain. Some ancient cultures valued wine as a cosmetic base, while others prized it as a medicine. The Hellenic Greeks enjoyed many of their wines only after they were mixed with seawater, or herbs, spices, and resins. In Rome mealtime conversations were often devoted to in-depth wine evaluations. Although wine was used as a religious symbol by cultures earlier than Egyptian civilization, such as in the ancient Near East, it was Christ at the Last Supper who made wine the symbol of His blood, a symbol that is now recognized the world over. Monks dispensed wine as a staple of the diet to local peoples and travelers during the Middle Ages. During the Renaissance, wine became an article of trade, taxation, and economic leverage. And, naturally, artists and writers throughout all ages have found countless ways to portray the enjoyment of wine.

As the state of the wine-growing arts has improved with advances in science, the quality of wine has improved as well. Consequently, there is more opportunity to enjoy wine in America than ever before. The larger cities in the United States offer wine selections that are unrivaled, even in Europe. The largest wholesalers of wine in America maintain thousands of different items in inventory.

In contemporary America, some people enjoy wine virtually every day, while others prefer to drink only at special events or occasions. To whatever degree it is incorporated in a life-style, one will be able to enjoy it more if one knows how to select, buy, store, serve, and evaluate it. Most enophiles feel that these functions are all part of the enjoyment of wine—even the wine buying! This chapter covers the most important ways to enhance wine enjoyment.

WINE SELECTION

Knowing how to select the right wine for the occasion, be it a meal, a toast, or a party, surely ranks among the most valuable social graces. Properly matching wine to food, company, and mood can turn a simple gathering into a memorable event. Many people, however, find the prospect of wine selection so intimidating that they forgo the pleasures of wine altogether. This is needless. Selecting the right wine requires neither vast erudition nor initiation into an arcane mystery. It is, above all, a matter of common sense.

There are, of course, certain rules and traditions governing the selection of wine; but, in recent years, especially in America, there has been a trend toward innovation and experimentation in matching wine, food, and occasion. There are those who refuse to acknowledge any guidelines for serving wine as well as those who are fully acquainted with wine heritage but enjoy adding a personal touch to age-old traditions. More and more people are experimenting with new and different combinations of wine and food. Departing in small ways from convention, discoveries can be made that become personal favorites and even establish new conventions of our own. Like an expert chef improving freely on a classic recipe, seasoned enophiles know exactly how unorthodox to be. They also know that experimenting at home with close friends or relatives is usually the most enjoyable way to make new discoveries. Using the boss and the boss's spouse as guinea pigs for a latest brainstorm, say, warm Champagne and bananas, should probably be avoided. Experiments with wine have their time and place. Common sense again should be the guide.

Most people will want to know the basic rules and try them out first before attempting to improve on them. The suggestions in this chapter should be enough to get one started. Try them first, and, if they work out, a ready store of selections will be available to serve guests. One may want to make adjustments, either in the seasoning of the food or the selection of wine—substituting, for example, a heavier wine for a light wine recommended here. Once the right match is made to suit personal taste, there will be less worry and more fun preparing for social functions.

Perhaps the first criterion for wine and food matching should be dictated by the season. Most people prefer cold or iced drinks in the hot summer months: thus chilled dry white and rosé wines are natural choices and go perfectly with such summer fare as crab and shrimp as well as fresh salads. Avoid sweet wines in warm weather as these may raise body temperature. Dessert wines with higher alcohol content may make people feel even warmer. In colder weather, these warming effects may, of course, be welcome. Dry red table wines are frequent autumn and winter choices: they are drunk at room temperature and complement hearty winter foods, all beef entrees, and many Italian and Spanish dishes. These examples, necessarily brief and simple, are not meant to set down hard-and-fast rules but rather to alert one to the general seasonal preferences of most wine drinkers.

THE ENEMIES OF WINE

Before plunging into a discussion of which foods go with which wines, it should be mentioned which foods and seasonings simply don't lend themselves to wine matchmaking. Vinegar, for example, kills the taste of wine; thus any dressing that is vinegar-based should not be considered for wine accompaniment. In France this causes little problem since the salad is often the last course served—after all the wine has been consumed. In America, however, the salad is usually served first, or just after the appetizer or soup, or sometimes along with the entrée. In each case, one can cleanse the palate of the vinegar taste by eating a bit of bread or potato, or sipping some water.

Some of the worst enemies of wine are, unfortunately, also holiday favorites. Cranberries, molasses, onions, tomatoes, and pineapple top the list. Asparagus fights with wine, as do candied and creamed vegetables. Though most people avoid serving red wine with fish under any circumstance, it should be noted that oily fish dishes and mackerel, in particular, are especially inimical to red wine. Foods that are heavily citrus flavored are also difficult to match with wines gracefully—especially lemon appetizers and desserts. Strong spices such as chili, curry, and garlic do not lend themselves well to wine matchmaking unless such seasonings are carefully limited and/or very hearty red wines are chosen. Matching white wines and egg dishes may be difficult, and chocolate finds few wine friends.

MATCHMAKING

The following sections provide basic lists of suggestions for specific wine types with foods served for a variety of occasions. These lists, by no means comprehensive, are designed to serve as initial guides. Background and descriptions of the wines listed can be found in later chapters according to country of origin.

Luncheon

Most people prefer their luncheon wines to be inexpensive and informal—often jug wines that are light, fresh, and fruity. Also, most people nowadays have neither the time, money, or inclination to linger and enjoy full pleasures over lunch and savor the richness of fine wines. Luncheon fare for most is rather simple and is complemented suitably by *vin ordinaire*. And, of course, afternoon work yet to be done usually limits the quantity of wine consumed.

It is common to find only one wine at luncheon, and it may be poured before the luncheon dish is served as sort of a "mini-cocktail" and again during the meal itself. If the luncheon is formal, perhaps two wine selections may be made—one served before the meal and the other with the entrée. There are still those whose luncheon menus may require several wine selections, including a dessert wine—but such midday dining is becoming rare.

Here are some luncheon wine suggestions to add to white, rosé, and red jug wines:

Beef casserole	Gamay, Maréchal Foch, Beaujolais
Bratwurst	Johannisberg Riesling (slightly sweet), Vidal Blanc, Rheingau
Broiled salmon	Verdicchio, Chardonnay, Puligny-Montrachet, Seyval Blanc
Burgers	Gamay, Maréchal Foch, Beaujolais
Chef salad (without vinegar-based dressings)	Pinot Blanc, Vignoles, Mâcon Blanc, Neuchâtel
Chicken	Gewürztraminer, Vidal Blanc, Alsace
Cioppino	Madeira, Dry Sherry, Dry Marsala
Cold cuts	Gewürztraminer, Vidal Blanc, Alsace
Corned beef	Pinot Noir, Maréchal Foch, Rhône
Eggs benedict	Chenin Blanc, Vidal Blanc, Barsac

Filet of sole	Pinot Blanc, Aurora Blanc, Mâcon Blanc
Goulash	Zinfandel, Egri Bikavér
Meat loaf	Pinot Noir, Maréchal Foch, Volnay, Pommard
Omelets	Grenache Rosé, Crackling Rosé, Tavel
Pasta dishes (cheese sauces)	Sauvignon Blanc, Soave, Vidal Blanc, Barsac
Pasta dishes (tomato sauces)	Barbera, De Chaunac, Valpolicella
Seafood casserole	Johannisberg Riesling (not sweet), Vidal Blanc, Mosel
Tuna	Pinot Blanc, Aurora Blanc, Muscadet
Vegetable casserole	Barbera, Baco Noir, Bardolino

Appetizer and Cocktail Wine Selections

Serving wines as cocktails is a rather new notion in American dining—and it's an ideal innovation for wine bibbers since most cocktail drinks made with distilled spirits can dull the taste buds for fine food and wine served later on. The preference for aperitif wines, such as dry vermouth or sweet vermouth, either neat, on the rocks, or as mixers in classic martini or manhattan cocktail recipes, is giving way to the universal popularity of simple white table wines. Sparkling wines are also excellent cocktail wines if they are crisp and dry, and dry sherry refreshes the palate before dinner. A wine cocktail hour offers the host an opportunity for creativity in devising fresh and original ideas for food and wine selections. Here are some suggestions for matching canapés and hors d'oeuvres with wines:

Anchovy	Pinot Blanc, Vignoles, Graves, Muscadet
Avocado	Fino Sherry, Dry Marsala, Madeira
Capers	Vidal Blanc, Soave, Verdicchio, Trebbiano
Caviar	fine Champagne
Chicken	Gewürztraminer, Vidal Blanc, Alsace
Cream cheese	Merlot, Chancellor Noir, St.-Émilion
Dried beef	Gamay, Maréchal Foch, Beaujolais
Eggs	Sauvignon Blanc, Vidal Blanc, Pouilly-Fumé
Ham	Grenache Rosé, Anjou, Tavel
Herring	Pinot Blanc, Vignoles, Graves, Muscadet

Mushroom	Fino Sherry, Dry Marsala, Madeira
Octopus	Sauvignon Blanc, Vidal Blanc, Barsac
Olives	Gewürztraminer, Vidal Blanc, Alsace
Paté	Chardonnay, Seyval Blanc, Chablis
Ribs	Grenache Rosé, Anjou, Tavel
Sardines	Sauvignon Blanc, Vignoles, Graves, Muscadet, Vouvray
Sausage	Gewürztraminer, Vidal Blanc, Alsace
Shellfish	Chardonnay, Villard Blanc, White Burgundy, Verdicchio
Smoked salmon	Chardonnay, Villard Blanc, White Burgundy, Verdicchio

Wine and Soup

The soup course allows for a range of options in wine matchmaking. Thin broths such as chicken soup are often served with a dry sherry, even though this is technically considered a dessert wine. Heavy chowders go well with fresh, light, dry, or near-dry, white jug wines. Some people omit the wine altogether, feeling that the soup, being a liquid, doesn't need it. If you are not of this persuasion, consider these wine selections to serve with soups:

Borsch	Gamay, Maréchal Foch, Beaujolais
Bouillabaise	Sauvignon Blanc, Vidal Blanc, Barsac
Clam	Johannisberg Riesling, Vidal Blanc, Mosel
Consommé	Dry Sherry, Dry Marsala, Madeira
Gumbo (beef)	Gamay
Gumbo (chicken)	Sauvignon Blanc
Gumbo (seafood)	Gewürztraminer
Minestrone	Barbera, Baco Noir, Valpolicella
Mushroom	Sauvignon Blanc, Vidal Blanc, Barsac
Onion	Dry Sherry, Dry Marsala, Madeira
Oxtail	Dry Sherry, Dry Marsala, Madeira
Oyster	Johannisberg Riesling, Vidal Blanc, Rheingau
Vegetable	Barbera, Baco Noir, Valpolicella

Wine Selections for Entrées

The entrée wine is, of course, the most important selection made for any dining occasion—whether simple or formal. Most important, and to many, the most difficult. Gone are the days when one could apply the simple rule of white wine with white meats, red wines with red meats, and rosé with anything. It's not that the rule is wrong, but rather that wine selecting is rarely this simple anymore in households where wine is truly appreciated.

Personal tastes, styles, and moods make for extremely varied choices, and the situation is further complicated by fluctuations in availability. With all the new and different types of entrées and all the wonderful wines available, how can one begin to bring together all these variables in the best possible combinations?

There are no simple answers; as one gains more and more experience, specific tastes and associations can be filed away in the memory to be used as a basis of comparison for new suggestions or ideas. For instance, lightly sautéed shellfish dishes are accompanied nicely by drier selections of Mosel or Johannisberg Riesling. This preference may lead to discoveries that creamed shellfish entrées call for a crisp, dry Chablis or Chardonnay. Filets of sole or halibut delicately poached are enhanced by a Rheingau, Johannisberg Riesling, or Vidal Blanc that have a hint of residual sweetness; while baked salmon or trout are more often served with Barsac or the fumé wines made from Sauvignon Blanc. Barbequed chicken can be perfect with a spicy Alsatian white or Gewürztraminer. Roast duckling, curiously, does not take to white wine very well, and one may wish to choose instead a hearty Pommard, Pinot Noir, or Maréchal Foch. Prime ribs of beef are usually rather delicate as red meat entrées go, and, therefore, lighter Bordeaux-types such as St.-Émilion are in order—perhaps also a Merlot or Chancellor Noir. At the other end of the beef flavor scale may be a fine filet mignon wrapped in a strip of bacon and served with a nicely seasoned Bearnaise sauce. This rich and pungent dish calls for the complex flavor of a Chambertin or Rhône, or else a full-bodied Pinot Noir or Barolo. Breaded veal cutlets and pork roasts find difficulty with red wines; heavily flowered Rheingau or Johannisberg Riesling wines may be far more compatible companions.

There are many more examples that could further give to illustrate how sophisticated matching wines to entrées has become these days. Ultimately, this new sophistication makes for lots of creative fun and serves to expand one's appreciation of wine. The following suggestions represent a small portion of the state of the art:

Baked ham	Gewürztraminer, Grenache Rosé, Vidal Blanc, Alsace, Tavel
Beef Bourguignon	Pinot Noir, Maréchal Foch, Burgundy
Beef pot roast	Pinot Noir, Maréchal Foch, Rhône, Burgundy
Beef stew	Pinot Noir, Maréchal Foch, Rhone, Burgundy
Beef stir fry	Pinot Noir, Maréchal Foch, Burgundy
Beef Strogonoff	Zinfandel, Egri Bikavér
Beef Wellington	Pinot Noir, Chambertin

Broiled flounder	Chardonnay, Chenin Blanc, Seyval Blanc, Chablis, White Burgundy, Muscadet
Broiled pork chops	Sauvignon Blanc, Johannisberg Riesling, Vidal Blanc, Barsac, Rheingau
Broiled red snapper	Chardonnay, Chenin Blanc, Seyval Blanc, Chablis, White Burgundy, Muscadet
Broiled spareribs	Sauvignon Blanc, Johannisberg Riesling, Vidal Blanc, Barsac, Rheingau
Broiled steak	Cabernet Sauvignon, fine Bordeaux
Broiled swordfish	Chardonnay, Chenin Blanc, Seyval Blanc, Chablis, White Burgundy, Muscadet
Broiled whitefish	Chardonnay, Chenin Blanc, Seyval Blanc, Chablis, White Burgundy, Muscadet
Brunswick stew	Gamay, Barbera, Maréchal Foch, Beaujolais, Valpolicella
Châteaubriand	Pinot Noir, Chambertin, Brunello
Chicken almond	Gewürztraminer, Vidal Blanc, Alsace
Coq au vin	Gewürztraminer, Vidal Blanc, Alsace
Crawfish étouffée	Chardonnay, Seyval Blanc, Pouilly-Fuissé
Crown roast	Cabernet Sauvignon, Barbera, Zinfandel
Filet of beef	Pinot Noir, Chambertin
Fried smelt	Gewürztraminer, Sauvignon Blanc, Vidal Blanc, Alsace, Barsac
Jambalaya	Chardonnay, Seyval Blanc, Pouilly-Fuissé
Lamb or veal stews	Pinot Blanc, Vignoles, Mâcon, Verdicchio
Lasagne	Barbera, Maréchal Foch, Valpolicella
Leg of lamb	Merlot, Gamay, Baco Noir, St.-Émilion, Beaujolais
Lobster Newburg	Chardonnay, Seyval Blanc, Meursault, Montrachet, fine Chablis
Lobster Thermidor	Chardonnay, Seyval Blanc, Meursault, Montrachet, fine Chablis
Pan-fried fish	Gewürztraminer, Sauvignon Blanc, Vidal Blanc, Alsace, Barsac
Roast beef	Cabernet Sauvignon, Barbera, Zinfandel, Bordeaux, Chianti Classico
Roast capon	Gewürztraminer, Johannisberg Riesling, Sauvignon Blanc or Vidal Blanc, Alsace, Mosel or Barsac
Roast chicken	Gewürztraminer, Johannisberg Riesling, Sauvignon Blanc or Vidal Blanc, Alsace, Mosel or Barsac

Roast duck	Pommard, Pinot Noir or Maréchal Foch, Burgundy or Valpolicella
Roast game hen	Gewrüztraminer, Johannisberg Riesling, Sauvignon Blanc or Vidal Blanc, Alsace, Mosel, or Barsac
Roast goose	Pinot Noir or Maréchal Foch, Burgundy, or Valpolicella
Roast pork	Johannisberg Riesling, Vidal Blanc, Rheingau
Roast turkey	Gewürztraminer, Johannisberg Riesling, Sauvignon Blanc or Vidal Blanc, Alsace, Mosel, or Barsac
Shish kebab	Pinot Noir, Maréchal Foch, Burgundy
Shrimp scampi	Chardonnay, Seyval Blanc, Meursault, Montrachet, fine Chablis
Spaghetti	Gewürztraminer, Sauvignon Blanc, Vidal Blanc, Alsace, Barsac
Standing rib	Cabernet Sauvignon, Barbera, Zinfandel, Bordeaux, Chianti Classico
Steak Diane	Pinot Noir, Maréchal Foch, Burgundy
Steak Tartare	Cabernet Sauvignon, fine Bordeaux
Swiss steak	Pinot Noir, Maréchal Foch, Burgundy
Tournedos of beef	Pinot Noir, Maréchal Foch, Burgundy
Trout almondine	Gewürztraminer, Vidal Blanc, Alsace
Veal Parmigiana	Barbera, Maréchal Foch, Valpolicella, Barolo
Veal roast	Cabernet Sauvignon, fine Bordeaux

Wine and Cheese

Someone once remarked that wine and cheese go together like love and marriage. Casanova believed that Chambertin and Roquefort together was an aphrodisiac. Truly, this is an extraordinary combination, but whether or not it will generate much desire must, of course, be left to each individual to judge. Not all wines and cheeses make such good partners, however, and some basic principles may help in making the right selections.

One common myth holds that white wines should never be served with cheese. There can be no question that the bold flavors of some classic cheeses, such as Boursault, Camembert, and Swiss, do best with rich red wines. On the other hand, there are some heavily flavored cheeses that can do well with both red and white wines. Good examples are Blarney with Sémillion and Limburger with Johannisberg Riesling. Some of the lighter cheeses, such as Fontina, Gouda, and

Havarti, are often overwhelmed by the heaviest red wines—in which case a fine white wine can be the best complement.

As a rule young wines call for rather new cheese, and, conversely, aged wines marry well with aged cheeses. Matching wines and cheeses from the same country of origin can be helpful in making good selections, too. For instance, a nicely ripened French Brie finds a good partner in a fine Burgundy—both are aged for only brief periods of time and both, of course, are French. Bel Paese is perfect with Valpolicella or Barbaresco; New York State Cheddar can match with a well-made Maréchal Foch; and Monterey Jack combines well with California Cabernet Sauvignon.

Some people offer cheeses and fancy crackers as canapés with wine before dinner, but such hors d'oeuvres can be so filling that they actually blunt the appetite. Consequently, wine and cheese best follow the main courses at dinner—often served along with fruits such as apples, grapes, and pears.

The following is a short list of some popular wine-and-cheese combinations:

Appenzeller	Pinot Noir, Maréchal Foch, Assmanshausen
Bel Paese	Barbera, Baco Noir, Valpolicella, Barbaresco
Blarney	Sémillon, Delaware, Sauternes
Bleu	Pinot Noir, Maréchal Foch, Burgundy
Bonbel	Sémillon, Delaware, Sauternes
Boursault	Cabernet Sauvignon, Chancellor Noir, Bordeaux
Brick	Sauvignon Blanc, Vidal Blanc, Barsac
Brie	Pinot Noir, Maréchal Foch, Burgundy
Camembert	Pinot Noir, Maréchal Foch, Burgundy
Cheddar	Pinot Noir, Maréchal Foch, Burgundy
Cheshire	Pinot Noir, Maréchal Foch, Burgundy
Edam	Gamay, Anjou, Cabernet Rosé, Beaujolais
Feta	Cabernet Sauvignon, Chancellor Noir, Bordeaux
Fontina	Chardonnay, Seyval Blanc, Chablis
Fontinella	Grenache Rosé, Tavel
Gjetost	Grenache Rosé, Tavel
Gorgonzola	Zinfandel, Chancellor Noir, Chianti Classico
Gouda	Johannisberg Riesling, Vidal Blanc, Rheingau
Gourmondise	Sémillon, Delaware, Sauternes
Gruyère	Gamay, Baco Noir, Beaujolais
Havarti	Sémillon, Delaware, Sauternes
Jarlsberg	Johannisberg Riesling, Vidal Blanc, Rheingau
Liederkranz	Johannisberg Riesling, Vidal Blanc, Rheingau
Limburger	Johannisberg Riesling, Vidal Blanc, Rheingau

Monterey Jack	Cabernet Sauvignon, Merlot, Chancellor Noir
Muenster	Johannisberg Riesling, Vidal Blanc, Mosel
Port du Salut	Cabernet Sauvignon, Chancellor Noir, Bordeaux
Provolone	Barbera, Baco Noir, Valpolicella, Barbaresco
Roquefort	Pinot Noir, Maréchal Foch
St.-Paulin	Cabernet Sauvignon, Chancellor Noir, Bordeaux
Stilton	Zinfandel, Chancellor Noir, Barolo
Swiss	Pinot Noir, Maréchal Foch, Burgundy
Tilsit	Chardonnay, Seyval Blanc, Chablis

For those who have a taste for dessert wines, port is a classic to serve at the end of the meal with cheese. A well-chosen combination of wine, cheese, and fresh fruit can be the perfect finish to luncheon and evening meals.

Dessert Wines

Nowadays many dinners end with coffee after the entrée and, perhaps, dessert. With the constraints of diets and food budgets, the popularity of dessert wine has receded considerably in recent years. However, we all still celebrate occasions when we may wish to enhance a special dessert or continue a nice mood with a good after-dinner wine selection.

A few things to keep in mind: First, wine and coffee do not go very well together, and, as mentioned earlier, neither do wine and chocolate. Coffee and chocolate, however, complement each other nicely in most instances.

Sometimes a sweeter sparkling wine such as Asti Spumante can serve as the dessert in itself, or as an accompaniment to fancy fruit dishes such as peach melba and strawberry shortcake. Here are a few more suggestions:

Angel food cake	Sauternes, late-harvest Riesling
Baked Alaska	sweet sparkling wine
Carrot cake	Sauternes, late-harvest Riesling
Cheesecake	Sauternes, late-harvest Riesling
Cherries jubilee	sweet sparkling wine
Cream puffs	Sauternes, late-harvest Riesling
Crêpes suzette	Oloroso, Cream Sherries
Dessert soufflé	sweet sparkling wine
Fruitcake	Port, Tawny Port
Maple torte	Oloroso, Cream Sherries
Mincemeat pie	Oloroso, Cream Sherries

Nut cake	Oloroso, Cream Sherries
Peach cobbler	sweet sparkling wine
Pecan pie	Oloroso, Cream Sherries
Zabaglione	Sweet Marsala

SELECTING WINE IN RESTAURANTS

Matching wine and food in a restaurant is governed by the same general principles as matchmaking at home—though the circumstances and resources may be quite different.

In some restaurants, the wine list may be limited, and selecting the right wine may be something of a challenge. Some eateries may also provide little care for their wine inventories. In such cases it is often best not to order any wine at all. In some locales the law permits brown-bagging, whereby the diners may bring their own wine selections and pay a "corkage" for the restaurant's service.

If a restaurant offers wine at all, chances are it has one or more "house wines." These are usually good ordinary jug wines sold by the glass or carafe. As a rule, these can be good values and offer an economical alternative to buying a whole bottle.

Sometimes selecting the wine becomes difficult because of varied entrée orders. If one guest orders poached fish, another orders shrimp scampi, yet another prefers lamb chops, and, finally, the host selects a steak, how can a satisfactory wine be selected? One solution is to consider a dry rosé that is only moderately chilled. Or choose two half-bottles, one a white for the fish and shrimp entrées, the other a red for the lamb and beef. Some restaurants have several house wine selections that may allow for even closer matching.

In fine restaurants a sommelier, the waiter in charge of wines, will be employed and she or he will have very specific suggestions for wine selection. This is not only fun, but often very enlightening as well. Don't, however, be bullied or intimidated. If the group agrees upon an unusual choice, see it through; maybe the sommelier will learn something, too.

Normally the host of the restaurant party has the final word on the wine to be selected. Usually she or he will poll the group beforehand to see what entrées are being considered. The host of a party of serious wine drinkers can often sway one or two members of the party from, say, a fish entrée to a red-meat dish so that a bottle of fine red wine may be enjoyed by all. After all, to many, the wine choice takes precedence over the food!

SERVING WINES

One of the most pervasive myths in winedom is that red wines should be opened well in advance of being served—perhaps an hour or so. There are several explanations given to support this practice. One is that stale gases collect in the head-space (space below the cork and above the wine) of the bottle and advance uncorking allows these to escape. Another is that exposure of the wine to the air allows it to "breathe," amplifying the fruit and mellowing tannins. A third is that opening a bottle in advance allows sulphur dioxide, sometimes used to excess as a preservative, to dissipate. There may be some truth in this last notion, but the others are marginal, at best. Opening a bottle actually introduces very little oxygen and may, in fact, serve to deteriorate older reds. The renowned wine writer Alexis Bespaloff conducted an experiment whereby he served prominent vintners their own wines—one set having been opened an hour before and another set just prior to serving. The vintners tasted from unmarked glasses, not knowing which wine was which, and acknowledged a "blind" preference for the wines that had been uncorked just prior to pouring.

During the last several decades wine connoisseurs, wine writers, and pseudo-experts have introduced a multitude of "right and wrong" wine-serving codes. Some of these rules are plain and others fancy, but, by and large, they have created complexity, contradiction, and confusion, especially for interested wine novices. Some people, perplexed, even intimidated, by the hype, avoid serving wine altogether rather than risk committing a social blunder.

There is no need for this. Wine should be as common at the table as bread or cheese; it's certainly as easy to serve. All it takes is a modest investment and a few basic guidelines. As with wine selecting, common sense can take one most of the way to serving wines correctly.

Temperature

The proper temperature for any wine is essentially a personal matter. There are those who argue that it is heresy to chill red wines, while others contend that a slightly chilled Beaujolais or Gamay makes for a better match with borscht and other dishes that call for such wines. One cannot know one's preferences until such combinations are tried. Experimentation—and even accident—may lead you to some wonderful discoveries. One may find, for example, that the Chardonnay that warmed to 61 degrees Fahrenheit (instead of the "optimal" 45 degrees Fahrenheit) when the picnic got delayed tastes *better* that way. On the other hand, another person may vow the next time to have a small cooler for their wine picnic service (a great gift idea).

White table wines are generally chilled to household-refrigerator temperature and held at that level until serving. In some cases the full bouquet and flavor of a particularly delicate or shy white wine may come forth with less chilling, or with no chilling at all. The colder a wine is, the less impression it makes on our organs of taste and smell. Super-cold wines, at less than 35 degrees Fahrenheit, may even seem rather tasteless. However, because chilled wines are so refreshing, especially in warmer weather, many people forgo the optimal conditions. Sometimes one may forget to chill a wine until the last few minutes before dinner and may be tempted to place the bottle in the freezer for a quick chill. This is not recommended because, if forgotten, the bottle will almost surely freeze and often explode. Again, keep in mind when chilling wines that the best temperature is the one that maximizes pleasure. There is simply no way that any wine writer can pinpoint a specific optimal temperature for every wine.

Red wines are often served at room temperature or "cool" room temperature—a range from about 65 degrees to 72 degrees Fahrenheit. One can approximate cool room temperatures by holding bottles for short periods of time in the refrigerator.

Rosé wines are almost always chilled and in much the same manner as described earlier for white wines.

Sparkling wines, whether white, red, or rosé, are traditionally chilled in an ice bucket; if left on ice for too long, the temperature will near 35 degrees F or so—which is perhaps too cold for some people. Experimentation will reveal the temperature that best suits your taste. An ice bucket is a nice touch and imparts a festive air; if silver, silver plate, or pewter exceeds the budget, one might consider a chrome or stainless steel bucket.

Dessert wines are generally served at ambient room temperature. A dry sherry may be served either chilled (sometimes even on the rocks as a cocktail) or at room temperature, depending on how it may best match the food (if any) that it accompanies. Aperitif wines are often served neat, or as mixers on the rocks, which precludes any concern with temperature.

Opening

The first time one attempts to open a bottle of wine can be a traumatic experience, especially if other people are watching. Perhaps it's better to try it alone

Rhône   Burgundy   Rheinland   Sherry   Loire   Franken
Champagne   Bordeaux

Traditional bottle shapes

a few times to develop a smooth technique. There really isn't much to it, so long as one has an adequate corkscrew. Two of the most common—and practical—corkscrews are the wing type (metal side wings rise as the "worm" spirals into the cork, and then, when the wings are pressed back down, the worm pulls the cork out of bottle neck), and the captain's knife (you screw the worm into the cork, affix the lever to the lip of the bottle opening, and then pull up on the other end of the lever until the cork emerges).

Virtually all wine bottles have a ring molded into the glass at the top of the bottleneck: it is just beneath this ring that the capsule covering the cork is cut. Some bottles these days come equipped with a plastic tab that is pulled to pop the capsule-top off. Start the corkscrew at an angle for about a full turn and then straighten it so as to go directly down through the center of the cork. This binds the cork with the corkscrew and allows for more effective removal of crumbly or otherwise unsound corks. Use only enough pressure to ease the cork out, and, if possible, remove the cork while the bottle is standing upright on a table: using the knees as a vice or wrestling with the bottle should be reserved only for particularly unruly corks.

After removal, the cork may be examined for any signs of failure and retained for a closer inspection later.

Opening a bottle of sparkling wine requires special attention. The pressure exerted by the gas is what makes the wine bubble—and it also makes the bottle potentially dangerous unless handled properly. First, cut the capsule of the bottle to expose the wire hood that is fitted over the cork. With one hand, grasp the butt (the bottom) of the bottle firmly, making sure that the top of the bottle is pointed away from everyone, including oneself. Now carefully undo the wire hood and remove it gently so as not to disturb the cork. Take the cork firmly in the free hand and hold it stationary while the hand grasping the butt slowly twists the bottle. The cork should ease out into the hand that's holding it and not fly across the room. With practice, one becomes able to regulate the loudness of the pop as the cork comes out.

Sedimentation and Decanting

Some wines, especially aged reds and dessert wines that were made without benefit of extensive clarification and filtration, will "throw" (precipitate) a sediment. Sedimentation of this type is common, and, in some cases, expected. Hundreds of vintners in Burgundy, for example, use time-honored processing techniques that yield fine wines that nonetheless throw sediment. Beware, however, of young white and rosé wines that exhibit a noticeable sediment—particularly when the wine is hazy or cloudy and has yellowed or browned. This may indicate that the wine has decomposed because of air leakage past the cork, or that the wine has degenerated in some other way. Some older whites, such as the German late-harvest specialties and Bordeaux Sauternes, perhaps even some of the older white Burgundies, may mature in the bottle with a bit of sediment and a golden hue. American vintners often go to great lengths to keep their wines free of any appreciable sedimentation. There is, unfortunately, something of a double standard in this area: sedimentation in European wines is excused, and even held up as evidence of Old World wine artistry; while American vintners are criticized if their wines show the least tendency to throw a sediment. Consequently, wine masters in the United States now lead the world in achieving wines whose clarity is considered the epitome.

Any wine, no matter its origin, should be decanted if it throws a heavy sediment. Sediment is bitter to the taste and can cause discomfort in much the same manner as grounds in coffee. There are other reasons for decanting. Among these are that the decanter itself may be a beautiful object to display on the table. The decanter can also nicely hide a jug wine's origin.

The wine to be decanted should be disturbed as little as possible beforehand. Several days prior to decanting, the bottle should be taken from its horizontal cellar-storage position and stood upright on the table or at an angle in a cradle. This allows any disturbed sediment to resettle. Some enthusiasts employ a *décantavin*, a wine cradle that can be precisely tipped for decanting by means of a geared crank (a wonderful gift idea).

Unless one has a wine-cellar storage area with a special table for decanting, the operation is usually performed upon a buffet or at a corner of the table. Reds are often uncorked (carefully) a few minutes or so before serving whether or not they are to be decanted; this is to allow any sediment stirred up in opening to resettle and to permit sulphur dioxide gas to dissipate. Whites are traditionally served right after uncorking and decanting. One should have a lighted candle to assist in seeing the sediment.

If one is right-handed take the opened bottle firmly in that hand and position it so that the candle is seen through the neck of the bottle as it is gently tipped for pouring. The decanter is held firmly in the left hand and angled so that the wine flowing from the bottle runs gently down the side of the decanter and does not splash. A fine silver funnel may also be employed for this purpose. Some delicate old wines develop aromatic nuances that are so fragile that rough handling may mute, disturb, or dissipate them altogether. If all goes well no sediment should appear in the neck until 90 to 95 percent of the wine has been decanted. Whenever the first signs of sediment show up in the candlelight, the decanting is stopped. If significant wine remains in the bottle it should be gently placed back upon the table or in the cradle and allowed to resettle. Sometimes a bit more wine can be recovered, although extremely heavy sedimentation may make this impractical. In any case, never serve wine with sediment suspended in it—most sediments are bitter and generally offensive to both the taster and the wine.

It is probably a good idea to develop a decanting technique by practicing before attempting a decanting display in front of guests. One may even want to enlist an accomplished enophile for basic instruction. It is not a difficult task, nor is it mystical—carving a roast turkey properly is far more involved. All it takes is a bit of patience and a little application.

Pouring

Before one can pour wine, one must, of course, have wineglasses in which to pour it. Unless there is the desire (and the means) for different shapes and styles of wine crystal, there is no real need for more than a single service of all-purpose, tulip-shaped stems. Serving wine in water tumblers or cocktail glassware is rather crass and should be avoided. A set of eight heavy-duty, 8-ounce, all-purpose wineglasses should not cost more than $20—often significantly less than that. These will generally have a rather heavy bead around the lip to help guard against chipping or cracking. Most service crystal will be made of somewhat heavy-weight glass; striking the fingernail against the bell may produce only a faint ringing sound. These are the glasses typically used in many restaurants. Fine leaded

Traditional wineglass shapes

crystal wineglasses of the same general shape will usually have a very thin lip and will be delicate; lightly striking the bell of such glasses with the fingernail will produce a resonant ring that may last for more than a minute. Such elegance, of course, is always expensive, and sometimes very expensive, depending on the brand of crystal. Steuben and Waterford, for instance, have single-stem offerings that are priced at several hundreds of dollars—complete services run several thousands of dollars.

The bowl of the glass allows for swirling—which, as discussed previously, increases the surface area of the wine and amplifies its bouquet. Most wine authorities recommend bowls without color, engraving, or other adornments because the wine is much easier to examine, judge, and appreciate in plain, clear glass or crystal.

Care should be taken in the proper cleaning and storage of wineglasses. An extra rinse cycle in the dishwasher will insure that *all* detergent residuals have been removed. Or wash and rinse them thoroughly by hand. Keep glasses in as neutral an environment as may be practical. Glasses housed in varnished cabinets or in the same cupboard as spices can pick up odors or tastes that will show up in the wine. Cardboard boxes are particularly notrious for a "papery" smell.

The all-purpose, tulip-shape wineglass can be used for cocktail wines, entrée wines, and dessert wines. They are not satisfactory for sparkling wines, however. Sparkling wines require special glasses, preferably tall, narrow champagne "flutes," that retain and display the precious effervescence. Some of the better-quality Champagne glasses have small rough surfaces set into the bottom of the bell that act as focal points from which the carbon dioxide bubbles are released and effervesce to the surface of the wine like tiny strings of pearls.

Some people offer dessert wines in a smaller 4- or 6-ounce version of the all-purpose, tulip shape or a sherry *copita*, similar in shape to the smaller tulip but somewhat taller and narrower. The copita is elegant, but many wine authorities prefer the all-purpose style.

There are, of course, a number of traditional wineglass shapes and styles that have evolved from Old World wine-growing regions. One of the most interesting is the German *roemer*, which some people refer to as *hock* glasses—from the English name for Rheinland wines shipped from Hochheim. The bowl of the Alsatian wineglass is reminiscent of the German roemer, but it has a slender green stem whereas the roemer's cylindrical stem flares out like a bell from bowl to base. The modern Loire wineglass also exhibits a thin graceful stem, but it is colorless. Also, the Loire bowl is straight-sided and flat-bottomed, which creates a "tumbler on a stem" effect. A Mosel wineglass is often ornately etched, sometimes even of cut-glass design, in a style that seems more French than German. The Mosel is similar in shape to our modern-day, all-purpose tulip style, but its bowl is somewhat wider and more shallow. Lovers of fine Bordeaux and Burgundy, both reds and whites, find the large "Paris goblets" appealing. These are reminiscent of brandy snifters but with a wider opening in the bowl and a taller stem. Paris goblets are fun but impractical. They take up lots of space on the table, are unbalanced and a bit awkward to handle, and they are difficult to wash and store. The traditional Italian wineglass has a capacity of about 6 ounces or so and is widest at the opening of the bowl, tapering gracefully to the stem.

A collection of wineglasses can add a great deal to the pleasures of wine, but it should be remembered that the appreciation of the wine must come from the wine itself, and for this even the simplest, plainest glass will suffice.

If one has only one service of glasses, it is perfectly all right to ask guests to bring their wine cocktail glasses with them to the table. Otherwise clean service should be already set at the table.

The wineglass is placed at the upper right of the place setting, about 2 or 3 inches from the plate. If more than one glass is to be used during the course of the meal, these may be appropriately lined up in the order in which they will be used—with the first nearest the plate. No more than three wineglasses should be set at each place. If more are needed, then the used stems should be removed and a new service made during the course of the meal.

The first pour of wine should properly be made in the hostess's or host's wine glass. This allows any bits of cork that may have dropped into the wine to be separated from the guests' portions. Also, it gives the host a chance to evaluate the wine first—rejecting it if it is not up to par. Perhaps this custom also alludes to the old romantic notion of the king's winetaster, though in this case the taster is also the host or hostess.

An all-purpose wineglass is usually filled only to about one-third full—certainly never more than one-half full. The decanter or bottle should not touch the lip of the glass while pouring; when the portion is dispensed the bottle may be twisted a quarter turn to help prevent dripping. Some prefer to wrap the bottle neck in a white towel, and this is also in good taste. There are also drip rings that fit over the necks of bottles. Dessert wines may be poured to fill the copita or other dessert wineglass; if a full-sized table wineglass is used for dessert wines, then fill to one-third full.

The only other wineglasses that may be served more than half-full are those used for sparkling wines. These may be carefully filled, guarding against foaming over, to about three-quarters or four-fifths full. The champagne flute-shape, in particular, can display an amazing dance of bubbles on the surface of a vigorously sparkling wine.

An offer of additional helpings may be made when the level in a guest's glass falls below one-quarter or one-fifth full. When the level of wine in someone's glass does not recede, it is usually a good sign that the person does not care for the wine. The host or hostess should not badger that person to take more—even when other guests are accepting additional helpings. Neither should that individual be embarrassed with an offer of some other kind of wine. Merely make a mental note that she or he does not enjoy that particular wine and that it is not a good future choice.

The best way to handle wine spilled on the tablecloth is to add a bit of milk to the spill so that the wine acidity will not have a chance to set a stain. Sponge up as much as possible and carry on with the dinner party without a lot of fuss. Do, however, launder the table cloth as soon as possible so the milk won't spoil in the fabric. If no pad is used under the tablecloth one should be sure that no moisture has seeped through to cloud the finish of a wooden tabletop. In this instance it may be a good idea to place a dry terry-cloth towel between the wet portion of the tablecloth and the table until after dinner is completed.

Dessert wines, like cordials, may be served either at the table after dinner or in some other area of the home, such as the living room or library. Guests may wish to stand and stretch a bit after lingering at the dinner table—and a glass of fine sherry or port can be the perfect final touch.

In a restaurant, there is, or should be, much less for the hostess or host to worry about in pouring the wine. The waiter, waitress, or sommelier should take care of such things. One's sole responsibility should be to examine the cork after it has been removed from the bottle and evaluate the first pour.

Another common myth is that the cork is presented to the hostess or host in a restaurant so that he or she can use it to judge the soundness of the wine. Some people respond by sniffing the cork and performing other fancy operations with it. In fact, the cork is offered so that the patron may insure that the waiter or sommelier has served the wine that was ordered. Also it is offered so that one can check that the wine has not leaked through between the cork and the bottle neck. One sign of a potentially bad bottle can be the telltale stain on the cork from end to end. More than just some loss of wine, such a stain can also mean that air (and therefore oxygen, as well) has entered the bottle, bringing oxidation and perhaps spoilage. Most vintners have their corks branded with logos and sometimes with the vintage year as well. All one really needs to do is read the cork. The sommelier, waitress, or waiter usually pours a small portion of the ordered wine into the hostess's or host's glass. A special guest may also be designated as the taster. The sample should be judged promptly—first with a brief examination of aroma and bouquet and then with a sip that is swallowed. With a nod of approval the service is made to the other guests. If the wine is unsatisfactory, the host or hostess may either opt for another bottle of the same kind of wine (in cases in which a defective cork is to blame) or make another selection. In either case, the rejected bottle should not be charged on the check.

Unfortunately, there are still restaurants in America that have marvelous food, superb coffee service, and attentive personnel, but pitiful wine offerings and inept service. Red wines will arrive ice cold while white wines are served from shelves in the dining room with no chilling whatsoever. The waiter may bring a bottle from the kitchen already uncorked and abruptly commence pouring without waiting for the host's or hostess's evaluation or approval. Even if you passionately object to such service, you should not do so in the presence of guests. A trip back to the restaurant the next day or so and a word to the manager may bring far more positive results than lost tempers.

COOKING WITH WINE

Though wine has been used in cooking for many centuries—even predating the ancient Greeks—French housewives probably should be credited with the first widespread use of wine in cooking. They learned that the cheaper, more ordinary cuts of fish and meat could be made much more palatable and interesting by using wine in their preparations. Rather quickly wine became an important part of French cuisine, considered by many to be the world's finest. Now, more and more Americans are making wine a part of their own cuisine.

All types of wine may be used regularly for cooking. Easiest and cheapest is to use leftover wines from dinner or cocktails: these can be recorked and stored in the refrigerator until needed for a recipe. When cooking with wine, one doesn't have to worry about children or people who don't drink because the alcohol of wine quickly evaporates when heated—in the same manner that the alcohol in vanilla extract disappears when a simmering temperature is reached. Wine enhances the natural flavors of many foods; it adds a subtle flavor of its own; and, in the case of red or amber wines, contributes color as well.

There are no specific rules for cooking with wine. Some chefs poach eggs and fish in red wine and others prepare red meat sauces with white wines. Wine is the most important ingredient in the making of certain celebrated sauces used for entrées in fine cuisine, such as Madeira sauce, beurre blanc, and sauce Bordelaise. It is generally added at the beginning of such preparations and allowed to diminish through simmering to a rich mellow essence.

Some noted chefs subscribe to the old adage that "wines unfit for drinking are unfit for cooking." This is certainly true as regards harsh, overly acidic wines because the acidity is amplified in cooking and may contribute an unpleasant taste to the food.

On the other hand, the moderate acidity of wine is essential in its use as a marinade to tenderize meats. And wine is indispensable in taming the excessively powerful flavors of wild game.

Most experienced cooks tend to avoid the wines specifically labeled "cooking wines" that are offered in some supermarkets. These are not made from wines of high quality, and frequently they have been infused with various herbs and salts. This makes it rather difficult to regulate one's own seasoning with any exactness. Cooking with your leftover table wines will not only save you money, but will produce more tasty results.

Karen and Richard Keehn, owners of famed McDowell Valley Vineyards in California's Mendocino County, are experts in the matching of wine with herbs, spices, and other food flavoring components. They believe that it is the choice of seasonings that links food to wine. By using a careful selection of one or two herbs and a spice in each recipe, there are certain patterns that are predictable in the best choice of a wine to accompany that dish—and vice-versa. One that may be helpful is to identify the wine's fruit flavor and select a traditional seasoning compatible with that wine's character. For example, Chenin Blanc usually has flavors reminiscent of apples, melons, and pears. These fruits are often teamed with citrus and spices having a sweet, licorice, or mint flavor. Therefore, pair Chenin Blanc with foods seasoned by lemon or thyme (citric), mint or basil (menthol), tarragon (licorice), and cinnamon/clove or allspice (sweet and spicy hot).

Following are some of the Keehn theories that can guide one in anticipating the results with greater success, saving anxiety, expense and time:

1. The more delicate the wine flavors, the more delicate the seasoning (for example, use a delicate Chenin Blanc with the more subtle flavors of dill, chervil, or parsley).

2. The stronger the wine flavors, the stronger the herb, spice, or flavoring (for example, a rich Chardonnay with sage or clove; a Syrah with rosemary or caraway).

3. Some wines have an inherent spiciness and can be combined with seasonings having spicy or hot properties (for example, a spicy Fumé Blanc with mustard or ginger; Zinfandel, Petite Sirah, or Syrah with peppers or allspice).

4. If a wine is made in a sweeter style, it usually complements seasonings that are sweet, tart, or salty (for example, sweet Chenin Blanc with the sweet licorice flavor of tarragon; a sweet White Zinfandel with tart seviche; a slightly sweet rosé with salty ham or prosciutto).

5. Excessive use of strong seasonings can overpower the taste and pleasure of wine. These strong seasonings include salt, garlic, vinegar, ginger, sugar, hot peppers, and cilantro. Do not avoid using them altogether, just use with some restraint or combine with milder ingredients or dairy products to diminish their impact.

6. Many vegetables have acids that compete with the pleasures of wine; in particular, artichokes, asparagus, spinach, and sorrel. We suggest diminishing the competitive effect of these acids by using sweet spices or sauces containing cheese, cream, mayonnaise, or other dairy products.

7. Use the beverage wine as a seasoning ingredient in sauces, etc. It really doesn't take much wine and it reinforces the same flavors in the food that are in the wine. If this sounds too inconvenient or expensive, use a wine of similar flavor, structure or style. Its flavors are at their best when added ten minutes or so prior to serving so as not to distort the original flavor components.

8. Serve more simply prepared foods with restrained seasoning when serving older wine vintages because the subtle, complex flavors so valued in older wines can be destroyed by strong food flavors or seasonings.

9. Try pairing a wine with an herb and a hot spice; the combination can often enhance the wine's flavors more than if only one of the seasonings is used (squash with sage and cracked pepper for Chardonnay; meats with mint and green pepper for Cabernet Sauvignon).

10. Most importantly, the quality of the result is directly proportional to the quality of the food, seasoning, and wine selected.

There are many dishes that depend upon wine for their very existence—Braised Beef Bourguignon, Chicken Amontillado, Coq au Vin, Lobster Newburg, and Sherry Chiffon Pie are a few examples among many others. The late Charles Fournier, French-born and French-trained master of Gold Seal Vineyards in upstate New York, was renowned for his accomplishments and inspirations in cooking with wine. The following is a list of some of his basic ideas:

TABLE 3-1   Cooking with Wine

	Foods	Amount	Wines
SOUPS	Cream Soups	1 tsp. per serving	Sauternes or Sherry
	Meat and Vegetable Soups	1 tsp. per serving	Burgundy or Sherry
SAUCES	Cream Sauce and Variations	1 tbsp. per cup	Sherry or Sauternes
	Brown Sauce and Variations	1 tbsp. per cup	Sherry or Burgundy
	Tomato Sauce	1 tbsp. per cup	Sherry or Burgundy
	Cheese Sauce	1 tbsp. per cup	Sherry or Sauternes
	Dessert Sauces	1 tbsp. per cup	Port
MEATS	Pot Roast—Beef	1/4 cup per lb.	Burgundy
	Pot Roast—Lamb and Veal	1/4 cup per lb.	Sauternes
	Gravy for Roasts	2 tbsps. per cup	Burgundy, Sauternes, or Sherry
	Stew—Beef	1/4 cup per lb.	Burgundy
	Stew—Lamb and Veal	1/4 cup per lb.	Sauternes
	Ham, Baked—Whole	2 cups (for basting)	Port
	Liver, Braised	1/4 cup per lb.	Burgundy or Sauternes
	Kidneys, Braised	1/4 cup per lb.	Sherry or Burgundy
	Tongue, Boiled	1/2 cup per lb.	Burgundy
FISH	Broiled, Baked, or Poached	1/2 cup per lb.	Sauternes
POULTRY & GAME	Chicken, Broiled or Sauté	1/4 cup per lb.	Sauternes or Burgundy
	Gravy for Roast or Fried Chicken and Turkey	2 tbsps. per cup	Sauternes, Burgundy, or Sherry
	Chicken, Fricassee	1/4 cup per lb.	Sauternes

Foods	Amount	Wines
Duck, Roast—Wild or Tame	1/4 cup per lb.	Burgundy
Venison, Roast, Pot Roast, or Stew	1/4 cup per lb.	Burgundy
Pheasant, Roast or Sauté	1/4 cup per lb.	Sauternes, Burgundy, or Sherry
FRUIT Cups and Compotes	1 tbsp. per serving	Port, Muscatel, Sherry, Rosé, Sauternes, or Burgundy

WINE BUYING

Buying Smart

Even the wealthiest wine bibber will want to pay the best (i.e., lowest) prices for the wines he or she buys. In large cities this may take some shopping around. The fact remains that the very same wine of the same vintage year can be found at different shops with significant variations in price. This is proof, if any were needed, that a high price is no guarantee of quality in wine. Then again, bargains are not always what they appear to be. Sometimes wines offered at greatly reduced prices are from poor years or past their prime. Vintage charts combined with the good advice of competent wine writers can help to avoid some mistakes. Even better is to cultivate a relationship with a reputable wine merchant. If a consumer shows an interest in learning more about wines, a good retailer will quickly return the interest. As the merchant gets to know individual tastes, he or she may begin setting aside bottles for special customers; soon they become the "privileged" customers who receive notices about special shipments, sales, and tastings. It's a good idea to buy early in the week when the merchant generally has more time to answer questions and discuss the wine.

Good wine buys can also be found by visiting the wineries themselves. Many vintners keep "reserve" wines sold only at the winery because the volume is too small to market them through wholesale and retail channels. If one likes a wine that is tasted at the winery and decides to order it, make sure the same wine is

The wine retailer at work. Courtesy: Skinflint's of Atlanta.

actually received. Most vintners are highly reputable, but there is the occasional operater who may try to pass off nonvintage wine on the unwary visitor who thought he or she was ordering the superb 1978 vintage that was tasted after the tour.

Also, think twice before ordering large quantities of wine that will need to be transported home from the winery. A case of wine weighs about thirty-five pounds: if traveling in the heat of summer, it will be necessary to haul it in and out of the motel room each night and figure out a way to keep it from overheating during the day. Make sure it's worth it before buying.

Wines for Everyday Drinking

For most people, price plays a significant role in the wines chosen for everyday drinking. Fortunately, America is a country where jug wines are plentiful, inexpensive, and often superb in quality. On a price-per-liter basis, there are American jug wines available at less than $2 per liter—as cheap as, or cheaper than, French *vin ordinaire*, and in most cases much better.

Jug wines will normally keep and lose very little of their freshness if they are reclosed securely and stored in the refrigerator. They can be used for cooking; and, of course, the 1.5-liter and 3-liter jugs offer excellent values.

There are dessert wines such as port and sherry available in jugs at jug-wine prices, though the regular 3/4-liter bottle size will probably suit most people's everyday needs more conveniently. If properly reclosed after use, these bottles will last for some time without needing any refrigeration.

Wines for Gifts

Buying wine as gifts can be a lot of fun, especially if one is familiar with the taste preferences of the recipient. With luck, wines can be discovered that she or he may enjoy and has not yet tried. This takes the agonizing out of gift giving. One can usually find wide ranges of prices on gift wines and many of the best products come with gift boxes. If the storekeeper doesn't have boxes, a simple ribbon or some foil around the bottle will do nicely. For large gifts or really special occasions, one may want to order a whole case. Most wine merchants offer a discount when the whole case is purchased.

Wines for Special Occasions

When deciding what wines to buy for special occasions, it helps to think both about the nature of the occasion and how many guests have been invited. These factors will help determine how much wine to buy.

The most special seasonal occasion in each year is, of course, New Year's Eve, and Americans traditionally have celebrated this event with sparkling wines. New Year's Eve parties can go on for hours and are often the scene of considerable consumption. Party givers should provide enough so that each guest may have at least four servings; this may mean about one bottle of sparkling wine for every two adult guests. Obviously, this could be very expensive if one chooses to serve fine Champagne. It makes good sense to find an economy, Charmat bulk-process sparkler that will serve. Be sure to have a designated driver.

At baptismals and christenings while there is, of course, no wine poured for the child, it is still traditional in America for a sparkling wine to be popped to create a festive mood. Just a glass or two is all that is necessary, and one should count on a maximum of about eight to ten servings per 3/4-liter bottle. If one is entertaining a dozen adults three bottles should do nicely. Again, one may wish to buy a whole case if the retailer makes it worthwhile—laying down the unused balance in the wine cellar or other wine-storage area.

The festive mood set off by sparkling wines is also traditional at wedding receptions, and it is a good idea to have enough on hand for three or four servings per adult. The retailer may be able to assist in arranging for a wine fountain and other nice touches that can help to make the reception even more special.

For baptismals, christenings, and wedding receptions, the sparkling wine purchased should be a premium. Some of the New York State brands or perhaps the premium California brands would do very well, as would nonvintage French and Italian sparklers.

A good bottle of deep dark heavy red wine is perfect for Valentine's Day—a Cabernet Sauvignon would be ideal. A lovely accompaniment to a hearty roast beef or steak, this wine suits both the day's romantic mood and the chilly winter season. One may want to splurge and get fine Napa Valley Cabernet Sauvignon from California or a classified-growth Bordeaux.

The Easter ham usually calls for a flavorful rosé. Since rosés frequently invite consumption from family members who ordinarily do not partake of wine, it's a good idea to buy one 3/4-liter for every six people. Rosés for the most part do not survive long storage very well, so one should also be careful not to buy an excessive amount; it would be better in most instances to get just the number of rosé bottles you need and let the quantity discount go.

When the Fourth of July is blistering hot, almost anything that is cold tastes good. Ribs on the charcoal pit slowly basted, a Fourth-of-July favorite, could be served with a cool, but not ice-cold, glass of dry, crisp Chardonnay or Seyval Blanc. At this sometimes-uproarious occasion figure one bottle for two to four people. When wine is purchased in the warmer months, don't let it suffer in the hot car; buy wine so that it spends as little time as possible in the heat.

Sooner or later most wine enthusiasts are "trick or treated" on Halloween by adults in funny costumes bearing empty wineglasses. This is usually after dinner, and in most parts of the country the weather is cool at the end of October. Nothing does the trick so well as a glass of medium-dry sherry or port. A little goes a long way, however, and one can figure to get twelve to sixteen servings from a 3/4-liter bottle.

Thanksgiving is usually a family affair, and the traditional turkey may be best set off by the gentle residual sweetness of a good Johannisberg Riesling or German Mosel or Rhinegau. With big families especially, conversations at the table can linger for an hour or more after dinner, during which time folks may consume three or four wine servings. It makes sense to buy one bottle for each four adults. Later a sweet sherry is perfect with the pecan or pumpkin pie. Normally, one bottle will suffice for eight to ten people. After the family has gone, the Thanksgiving hosts can sit down and relax with some fruit and cheese and a special glass or two of port or madeira.

At parties during the holiday season, when the occasion calls for a champagne punch, the economy brands offer the most fun for the least outlay of money. It's a good idea to buy in case lots to have plenty on hand for those impromptu parties that always seem to get going at this time of year. There may even be additional savings in buying two or three cases at once.

Christmas is, of course, another family gathering, and Christmas wine requirements will be similar to those of Easter or Thanksgiving. But whether one has ham, or turkey, or lasagne, remember that any wine needed for the holidays should be bought well ahead of time; generally discounts and case prices are not nearly as attractive in December as they are in September.

WINE STORAGE

Buying wines for stocking private wine cellars requires first, of course, that one has a proper place to lay them down. The term *laying down* refers to the practice of placing the wine bottle on its side so that the cork, always in contact with the wine, stays moist and supple. This will prevent the cork from drying out and shrinking, which may allow air to enter the bottle and harm the wine. The wine-storage cellar should be kept at an even, preferably cool, temperature that does not fluctuate radically. This is much more important for white and rosé wines than reds. Consequently, store the best whites nearest the floor where it is cooler, rosés above that, and red wines up to chest level. There should be minimal light, only whatever incandescent lighting is necessary to find one's way around and to read labels. Sunlight, especially, can have a devastating effect upon wine. When leaving the cellar, turn off the lights. It makes good sense to ask several local people who already have home wine cellars to assess your wine-cellar plans before any major investments are made.

It is a good idea to keep wine storage away from heating ducts, appliances, and drafts. The old rule that wine-storage cellars must be maintained at a constant 55 degrees Fahrenheit is not very practical for most people—a steady range of 50 to 70 degrees Fahrenheit is usually good enough. Modern wine-making methods succeed in producing wines that will accept most reasonably administered cellar temperatures.

Vibration should be minimized in order that corks are not loosened. Sedimentation can also be aggravated by severe vibration, and sediment already having precipitated in wine bottles can be agitated back into suspension. An area adjacent to a dishwasher or laundry is thus especially discouraged.

Humidity should be kept moderate. Wine storage facilities that are too dry (less than 15 percent relative humidity) can dry out corks, while excessive humidity (more than 75 percent) can cause molding of labels and capsules. Generally, humidity that is comfortable to people is also acceptable for wine storage.

Wine enthusiasts who don't have access to an environmentally controlled room or an underground wine cellar have engineered some ingenious and inexpensive structures for the storage of wine. Many people convert closets or cupboards into wine storage areas. Some just pile their wines on ordinary planks, using bricks to create space between the shelves. Others take simple cylindrical drainage tiles and lay them one upon another along a wall, inserting one bottle inside each tile. Old refrigerators, especially of institutional size, can also serve well when their thermostats are properly adjusted. Wooden crates are still used by some fine wine shippers, and these can make very fine storage containers. Cardboard wine cartons may be used temporarily, but they can mold from high humidity and deface bottle labels. Even worse, damp cases can collapse and the bottles can come crashing down. The major criteria remain stability of the rack or shelf and accessibility that allows for ease of handling and examining the bottles in storage.

Once the wine cellar is started, one should establish a cellar record so that one can keep track of purchases, dates, prices, and inventory. Tasting notes and scores, as well as those of friends, can also be noted in the cellar records. Some cellar keepers develop their own codes for quick reference. Dr. Philip Jackisch has published a definitive article on the subject of maintaining wine records in *The Friends of Wine* magazine.

Wines purchased for everyday drinking can be stored in the kitchen or dining room. Most jug wines can withstand any reasonable treatment for several weeks, but once they are opened, they should be properly resealed and stored in the refrigerator. Some people install attractive counter racks that can hold up to twelve bottles, which are fine so long as the inventory turns over rather quickly. In general, if wine is kept out in the open in the dining room or kitchen, just make sure not to allow the same bottles to remain there too long.

People buy wines for laying down for a number of reasons, among which are the following:

1. Wines purchased in larger lots are less expensive.
2. Promising vintages are usually much less expensive when purchased at an early age and allowed to mature in the home wine-cellar.
3. Wines layed down in the home wine-cellar are convenient to use.
4. Laying down wines allows one to observe the differences that take place as wines continue to age.
5. Collecting wines is a hobby.

If one is just beginning to lay down wines, it is best to start small, and, while experimenting, buy only several bottles at a time. Don't, however, buy half-bottles (the 3/8-liter size) in an effort to get just a sample taste. These small sizes are generally not very popular and they can often remain in a retail wine shop for months or years before resale, during which time the wine may have gone beyond its peak. Wines will age faster in the smaller bottles because there is less wine exposed to the headspace, which may cause oxidation. In any event, the small bottles will not be representative of a wine in full-sized 3/4-liter bottles.

Another good way to become familiarized with different wines to lay down in quantity is to go to wine-tasting parties. Sometimes retailers, wholesalers, and/or vintners sponsor such programs. There are also national and international wine appreciation organizations such as Les Amis du Vin (The Friends of Wine), the American Wine Society, the Knights of the Vine, and others that one may join. Finally, there are private gatherings and parties where one can enjoy good company and good wines at the same time.

From these sources the beginning wine enthusiast will develop lists of preferred wines that will be suitable for laying down. Once it is decided which to purchase, seek out the best price, which will probably be in case lots so that discounts can be maximized.

WINE-TASTING PARTIES

The wine-tasting party is one of faster growing social events in America. Wholesalers, retailers, restaurateurs, and importers hold many tastings in order to promote their wine offerings. Other organizations host wine-tasting gatherings for fund raising or just plain fun. In fact, committed enophiles will throw a wine tasting for any number of reasons.

Private Wine Tastings

While the wine neophyte may learn a lot about how to organize and administer a wine tasting by attending the large, commercially sponsored, and often rigidly regimented affairs, there's no question that a small private tasting can be more fun. The relaxed atmosphere at home and the intimacy of close friends and relatives make for more candid comments in wine judging and offer more opportunity for individual involvement.

A good-sized group is eight to twelve persons, a number that most living rooms will accommodate comfortably. A 3/4-liter bottle of wine can be stretched if you serve about 2 to 3 ounces per taster—which is plenty when a number of different wines are to be tasted.

It is common in many groups for each couple or individual participant to bring a bottle of wine that is appropriate to the tasting party. This, of course, helps considerably to reduce the expense for the party giver and also may be something of a "homework assignment" if each contributor prepares a short dissertation about the particular wine to be presented at the time it is served. Some groups prefer to have the hostess or host take her or his turn regularly providing all of the wines and all of the research.

Service for the wine-tasting party may be made casually in a living room or den, around a coffee table, or more formally with participants seated in the dining room. The kitchen, as a rule, does not serve well. It is mandatory that all refrain from smoking and wearing heavy perfumes. Out-of-doors may be fine as long as there are agreeable conditions: no insects or street noise, comfortable temperatures and calm winds, sufficient but not harsh or glaring sunlight. Inside there should also be adequate lighting and comfortable temperatures. Some groups develop a signal that is given to get everyone's attention so that comments and questions may be exchanged. Often, one or another of the participants may be asked by the host or hostess to "speak to the wine," that is, to discourse for a minute or two on his or her reactions to and evaluation of that particular wine.

Generally, the wine tasting either precedes the dinner or is designed to accompany dinner. Tastings held during cocktail hour should be provided with only limited canapés and hors d'oeuvres. Ideally, each wine being judged should be followed with just a simple unsalted cracker or piece of white bread, and perhaps a small chunk of bland cheese, in order to cleanse and neutralize the palate. Large offerings of fancy nibbles can spoil pre-dinner appetites.

Having score sheets and pencils handy is a good idea. Some of the more serious enophiles, however, may carry their own recording devices so that they can refer back to their own personal tasting notes.

The order of serving is generally drys first, progressing to the sweetest last, and whites first, progressing to the darkest red last. Dryness takes priority over color in ranking, so a sweet white, for example, would be served after *all* the dry wines, both red and white. Generally between four and eight wines are sampled at a tasting. Wine tastings can be organized in a number of ways, and a few examples are outlined below.

A "general" wine tasting might include the following selections:

Chardonnay		Chablis
Johannisberg Riesling		Rheingau
Pinot Noir	or	Red Burgundy
Barbera		Valpolicella
Cabernet Sauvignon		Red Bordeaux
Sherry		Sherry

Background and descriptions of these wines can be found in later chapters according to country of origin.

An "appellation," or "horizontal," wine tasting will include a number of wines from a given vintage and from a specific wine-growing area, such as the following from Bordeaux:

Château Calon-Ségur (St. Estèphe)
Château Lynch-Bages (Pauillac)
Château Léoville-Barton (St.-Julien)
Château Citran (Central Médoc)
Château Lascombes (Margaux)
Château La Mission-Haut-Brion (Graves)
Château Gazin (Pomerol)
Château Figeac (St.-Émilion)

This gathering of wines features some of the better red wines from each of the most important wine-growing subdistricts of Bordeaux and will cost a fair amount of money. It's smaller, however, when compared with the cost of such *Grand Cru* (First Growth) wines as Château Lafite-Rothschild, Château Margaux, Château Haut-Brion, or the great wines of Châteaux Pétrus and Cheval-Blanc. Such a tasting would be astronomical in price!

A "comparative" wine tasting assesses wines made from the same grape variety or wines of different origins made by a similar technique. If one chose to compare various wines made from Chardonnay grapes, for example, one might include:

Chablis Grand Cru (Chablis)
Puligny-Montrachet (Côte de Beaune)
Pouilly-Fuissé (Mâconnais)
Napa Valley Chardonnay (California)
New York State Chardonnay
Virginia or Ohio Chardonnay

Also popular is the "vertical" wine tasting, where the different vintages of one particular variety from a single vineyard or winery are evaluated. For example, Beaulieu Vineyard (Napa Valley, Rutherford, California):

1969 Cabernet Sauvignon
1971 Cabernet Sauvignon
1973 Cabernet Sauvignon
1974 Cabernet Sauvignon
1976 Cabernet Sauvignon
1978 Cabernet Sauvignon

There are, of course, many other ways of organizing wine-tasting parties. While the examples given here have been limited to superior (and rather costly) wines, such wines are not the only ones that should be considered for a wine tasting. On the contrary, for most people who live on a budget, part of the fun of a tasting lies in discovering inexpensive wines that give pleasure at good value. In fact, one of the best ways to discover such hidden jewels in the wine marketplace is at wine tastings.

WINE BOOKS, EDUCATION, ORGANIZATIONS, PARAPHERNALIA, PERIODICALS, AND TOURS

There are all sorts of supplemental materials and activities that are grape and wine oriented. Full consideration of these vast resources must be reserved for another text.

TOASTS AND SENTIMENTS

The touching of glasses following profound, moving, or jolly words is a tradition that has contributed greatly to enriching the history of Western civilization. Here are some of the finer moments:

Eat, drink and be merry,
For tomorrow we shall die!
—adapted from Isaiah 22:13

No thing more excellent nor more valuable than wine was ever granted mankind by God.
—Plato

Wine brings to light the hidden secrets of the soul, gives being to our hope, bids the coward fight, drives dull care away, and teaches new means for the accomplishments of our wishes.
—Horace

Wine was given by God, not that we might be drunken, but that we might be sober. It is the best medicine when it has the moderation to direct it. Wine was given to restore the body's weakness, not to overturn the soul's strength.
—St. Chrysostom

I feast on wine and bread, and feasts they are.
—Michelangelo

Wine is light, held together by water.
—Galileo

A meal without wine is like a day without sunshine.
—Brillat-Savarin

Old wood to burn! Old wine to drink!
Old friends to trust! Old authors to read!
—Bacon

Let's drink to our friend and host.
May his generous heart, like his good wine, only grow
mellower with the years.
—Unknown

And fill them high with generous juice,
As generous as your mind,
And pledge me in the Generous toast—
The whole of human kind!
—Robert Burns

While there's life on the lip,
while there's warmth in the wine,
One deep health I'll pledge,
and that health shall be thine.
—Unknown

A dinner, coffee and cigars,
Of friends, a half a score.
Each favorite vintage in its turn—
What man could wish for more?
—Unknown

Then here's to thee, old friend: and long
May thou and I thus meet,
To brighten still with wine and song
The short life ere it fleet.
—Unknown

Drink to me only with thine eyes,
And I will pledge with mine;
Or leave a kiss but in the cup,
And I'll not look for wine.
                              —Ben Jonson

A Book of Verses underneath the Bough,
A Jug of Wine, a Loaf of Bread—and Thou
Beside me singing in the Wilderness—
Oh, Wilderness were Paradise enow!
                              —Omar Khayyam

Come, love and health to all:
Then I'll sit down. Give me some wine, fill full,
I drink to the general joy o' the whole table.
                              —Shakespeare

Bacchus ever fair and young,
Drinking joys did first ordain;
Bacchus' blessings are a treasure,
Drinking is the soldier's pleasure:
Rich the treasure, Sweet the pleasure,—
Sweet is pleasure after pain.
                              —Dryden

'Tis mighty easy, o'er a glass of wine,
On vain refinements vainly to refine,
To laugh at poverty in plenty's reign,
To boast of apathy when out of pain.
                              —Charles Churchill

This bottle's the sun of our table,
His beams are rosy wine;
We planets that are not able
Without his help to shine.
                              —R. B. Sheridan

What though youth gave love and roses,
Age still leaves us friends and wine.
                              —Thomas Moore

O, for a draught of vintage! that hath been
Cooled a long age in the deep-delved earth,
Tasting of Flora and the country green,
Dance, and Provençal song, and sunburnt
mirth!
                              —John Keats

A glass of good wine is a gracious creature,
And reconciles poor mortality to itself,
And that is what few things can do.
                         —Sir Walter Scott

A glass of wine is a great refreshment after a hard day's work.
                         —Beethoven

My manner of living is plain and I do not mean to be put out of it.
A glass of wine and a bit of mutton are always ready.
                         —George Washington

I have lived temperately, eating little animal food.
Vegetables constitute my principal diet. I double, however,
the doctor's glass and a half of wine,
and even treble it with a friend!
                         —Thomas Jefferson

God in his goodness sent the grapes
To cheer both great and small;
Little fools will drink too much
And great fools none at all.
                         —Unknown

The flavor of wine is like delicate poetry.
                         —Louis Pasteur

My only regret in life is that I did not drink more Champagne.
                         —John Maynard Keynes

Wine is one of the most civilized things in the world . . . and it offers a greater range of
enjoyment and appreciation than, possibly, any other purely sensory thing which may be
purchased.
                         —Ernest Hemingway

APPELLATION CONTROLÉE

CHÂTEAU AUSONE
ST ÉMILION
⚜ 1937 ⚜

ÉDOUARD DUBOIS-CHALLON

Propriétaire

MIS EN BOUTEILLE AU CHÂTEAU

ROUSSEAU FRERES, Bᵈ

4

THE HISTORY OF
WINE

Fossilized leaf of *Vitis balbiani*, one of the earliest examples of grapevine. (Photo by Roger Viollet, Source: Sorbonne Geological Laboratory.)

The grapevine has existed since the infancy of plant life on the Earth. Fossils found in France and Germany reveal that a vigorous plant, which bears some resemblance to the rambling European *Ampelopsis*, existed some 500 million years ago. This was the prolific ancestor of the vine that now bears wine.

North American fossilized rocks indicate that grape seeds were borne by vines during the Tertiary period. *Vitis*, the genus of the grapevine, first appeared during the same geologic era, perhaps 50 million years ago.

One of the first distinct species to emerge was *Vitis sezannensis*, apparently named after Sézanne, the locale in the Champagne region of France where some of the earliest vine fossils were found. *Sezannensis* is strikingly similar to *Vitis rotundifolia*, the muscadine grape that is native to the southeastern United States. Later, between ten and fifteen million years ago, several more species of *Vitis* evolved, among which were *Vitis vinifera*, the renowned vine from which the hundreds of classic European wine varieties have been cultivated, and *Vitis labrusca*, the celebrated fox grape indigenous to the central and eastern portions of North America.

Paleontologists date the phenomenon of fermentation back more than 100 million years—to the Mesozoic era. And most authorities agree that crude fermented beverages made from fruit were familiar to early humans more than 100,000 years ago. There can be little doubt that the Cro-Magnons enjoyed some form of wine.

Fossilized seed packs from the mounds of the south central European lakes region have given archaeologists definite evidence that humans have consumed the grape since at least the Stone Age. In Neolithic times, about 8,000 years ago, the lake-city dwellers made wine and enjoyed it with a rather varied menu of bread, fish, meats, shellfish, and soups.

Though the precise point in time when humans introduced wine into their diet may never be determined, we know that it long pre-dates the history of recorded civilization.

THE CRADLE OF WINE GROWING

There is some doubt whether the culture of the vine began in Egypt or in Mesopotamia. Both were crucial centers of early civilization and early wine growing. Wine was cultivated about 6,000 years ago in the Tigris-Euphrates basin of Mesopotamia, in what is now known as Iraq. Some authorities extend this first vineyard region northwestward through modern-day eastern Turkey and into the Caucasus mountains of Georgian Russia. According to the Bible, Noah landed his ark in these mountains, on Mount Ararat specifically, subsequently planting a vineyard and making wine. In Genesis 9:20-21 it is written that "Noah was the first tiller of the soil. He planted a vineyard; and he drank of the wine and became drunk."

There are Sumero-Akkadian documents that affirm that the pre-Islamic Arabs drank wine in early Mesopotamia, and one archaic Persian poem rhapsodizes that "the wineskin is a kingdom to him who possesses it, and kingdom therein, though small, how great it is!"

As Mesopotamian civilization developed, so did wine growing. By 2250 B.C. wine had become a common article of commerce. Some of the first written references to grapes are dated at about 2100 B.C. Wine had its first religious application in the rites of the Persian god of light, Mithra: it was mixed with blood during the violent ceremonies of that cult.

The laws of the Babylonian King, Hammurabi, drafted in the eighteenth century B.C., threatened stern punishment for any who tried to pass off bad wines as good. There were, no doubt, many poor wines during those times, as the natural alcohol content would probably not have been sufficient to serve as a reliable preservative against vinegar-bacteria spoilage.

Sennacherib, King of Assyria (705-681 B.C.), and Nebuchadnezzar, King of Babylonia (circa 605-562 B.C.), planted extensive vineyards. Herodotus, the Greek historian, visited Persia and provided a colorful account of the importance of wine to the Persians in the fifth century B.C., but, unfortunately, nothing is mentioned about the precise beginnings of wine growing in the Mesopotamian valleys.

Mohammed conquered the Persians and converted them to the religion of Islam, which demanded total abstinence from fermented beverages, thereby consigning winegrowing to the Jews. This first Prohibition, however, had little effect since the Persians continued to drink wine heavily and maintained ample supplies.

ANCIENT PALESTINE

Hebrew law went into extraordinary detail about the selection and culture of the vine. Wine played both a ceremonial role in the Jewish religion and was an important part of everyday life. The Old Testament contains 155 direct references to wine, some richly descriptive and others giving practical advice about the best uses for wine. Along with a warm appreciation for wine, there are powerful warnings about excessive drinking.

Celebrations of wine as God's gift to man can found in Joel 2:23:

> Be glad then, ye children of Zion, and rejoice in the Lord your God for he hath given
> you the former rain moderately . . .
> and the latter rain in the first month. And the
> floors shall be full of wheat, and the vats shall overflow
> with wine and oil.

Proverbs 23:21 contains a stern admonition against drinking wine to excess:

> Hear thou, my son, and be wise, and guide thine heart in the way. Be not among
> winebibbers; among riotous eaters of flesh: for the drunkard and the glutton shall come
> to poverty; and drowsiness shall clothe a man with rags.

The celebrated Canaan grape was a legend even in biblical times when Moses
dispatched two envoys, Joshua and Caleb, into Palestine to learn more about this
great vine. The immense bunch of grapes that Joshua and Caleb brought back
became an enduring symbol of the Promised Land.

Sixteenth-century German woodcut, "Explorers of the Land of Canaan," showing Joshua
and Caleb carrying the celebrated Canaan grape. (Source: The Seagram Museum
Collection.)

EGYPT

As mentioned previously, the question of whether or not the Egyptians preceded the Mesopotamians as the first winegrowers in Western civilization remains unresolved. It is certain, however, that both cultures used wine to the fullest.

The ancient people of Egypt considered wine a gift from their most divine God, Osiris, the son of Heaven and Earth. Hieroglyphic inscriptions portray Osiris as the "Lord of the vine in flower." Tombs of the pharaohs contain art treasures that clearly portray scenes of gathering grapes and winemaking amidst the festivity of dance and song. One such relic at the burial site of Phtah-Hotep is estimated to be about 5,000 years old.

The importance of wine to the Egyptian monarchs is apparent by the numerous grape seeds that have been discovered in the crypts of the pyramids—suggesting a desire for bountiful wine crops in the hereafter. The hieroglyphic account of offerings made at the funeral of Pharaoh Pepi II mentions the wines of Letopolis and Pelusium. Other archaic writings admired the wines from the vineyards of Buto, Kakenie, Kenemen, Suanit, and Tjetje.

Ancient Egyptian viticulture, winemaking, and wine marketing—from the tomb of Khaemwaset, Eighteenth Dynasty. (Source: The British Museum.)

The Roman Pliny the Elder describes two Egyptian wines, *Ecbolada*, which according to his account was an aphrodisiac, and *Sebennytic*, one of the most choice selections. Perhaps most famous of all the old Egyptian wines was *Arp Hut*, the wine of Anthylla that Cleopatra poured for Antony. The vineyards of Anthylla flourished on the banks of Lake Mareotis and yielded grapes that made an impressive wine charmingly described by the Greek geographer Strabo: "Its color is white, its quality is excellent, and it is sweet and light, with a fragrant smell."

The Egyptians probably made mostly sweet wines, both red and white. They began the process by crushing the grapes with their feet, a romantic rite that lives on today as a joyful symbol of winemaking. Crushed grapes were pressed in sacks, the juice then collected and fermented in earthenware jars called *amphorae*. When the sediment settled, the new wine was decanted (racked) and kept in other amphorae closed with resin seals.

While a few of these wines enjoyed grand reputations, some were merely acceptable, and, most likely, many others were not even that. The best wines were consumed by the pharoahs and the members of their households, along with their priests and soldiers. The common people of Egypt received grape wine only on special occasions—everyday peasant fare was either a drink made from palms or a pomegranate wine mixed with water called *Shebdou*.

The Egyptians reserved some wines for special purposes, such as the alluring wine-based perfume used by Queen Nefertiti. According to Diodorus Siculus, Egyptian physicians often prescribed a compound of wine, stramony, and opium for treating colic and depression. A powder made from pulverized Memphis stone was mixed with wine or vinegar as a styptic for wounds. Wine was even used as a cleansing fluid in part of the embalming procedure before mummification.

Most of the great Egyptian vineyards were located along the banks of the Nile River, from Thebes to Memphis. Inscriptions in the pyramids of Saqqarah tell of the "Water of Rebirth"—the "Holy Water" that enriched the soil in the vineyards as the river flooded. The vineyards still required irrigation, however, a tedious task that involved carrying water from the Nile in animal skins. Trees were used as a trellis support upon which the vines were trained—a system that is still maintained in some of the Mediterranean vineyards. Demand for wine in ancient Egypt was, however, much greater than these vineyards could supply, and additional wines were imported from Ethiopia, Greece, Palestine, Phoenicia, and Syria.

GREECE

The Phoenician traders are credited with bringing both grapevines and wines across the eastern Mediterranean Sea from Egypt to Greece.

The first Greek grapevines were planted upon land that was already being used for pasture, barley crops, and olive groves. It was not until about the seventh century B.C. that Greek land was cleared exclusively for vineyards. Writing some seven centuries later, the Roman poet Virgil explained to the Greeks:

Plant your vines neatly, and let the neat rows crossed by regular alleyways form a perfectly symmetrical plot. They should be like a legion before a great battle where the cohorts are deployed and drawn up in the open countryside.

The Greeks used manure to fertilize their vineyards, and the Roman naturalist Pliny the Elder describes six methods for pruning the vines, each suited to different grape varieties and soil types. Both Virgil and Pliny claimed that there were too many separate varieties of the vine to distinguish them all. They do, however, recognize *Alopecis*, *Argitis*, *Basilica*, *Dracontios*, *Graecule*, *Mareotica* (perhaps named for the Mareotis vineyards in Egypt), and *Psitia* for white wines. Reds were made from *Amephystos* and *Helvennaca*. In the *Odyssey*, Homer spoke of the vineyard of Alcinous:

There flourishes a fertile and luxuriant vine,
Whose clusters in part are dried by the sun
In the more open and airy places, and elsewhere
They are gathered by hand from the leafy stalk,
Or pressed out by the feet in the great vats;
Sour are the grapes here, there fragrant are the blossoms,
And the grapes are purple and gold.

Homer relates that the crude wine made from the wild vines growing near the Cyclops was so bad that the monster preferred to wash down his meal of two of Odysseus' men with sheep's milk. The legend continues that Odysseus then gave Cyclops a Thracian wine from Ismarus, the birthplace of Dionysus, a wine properly made from cultivated vines. The beast found such great pleasure in this wine that he quaffed until he became drunk—giving Odysseus the opportunity to blind Cyclops' one eye.

The wine fermentation in classical Greece lasted for about nine days—the new wine being racked into amphorae and sealed with lids coated with pine pitch. The Greeks added various types of flavor compounds, such as gums, herbs, honey, pepper, and pine pitch resin, to their wines in order to make them more appetizing. There can be little doubt that this practice is the primordial root of aperitif wines, notably the French and Italian vermouth types that are commonplace today. Pine resin is still added by Greek vintners to make the famous *retsina* wine. The ancient Greeks also mixed their wines with seawater and considered those who drank their wine without such amelioration as barbarians.

Among the most fascinating of Greek relics are their wine amphorae—the two-handled jugs that were also used for honey and oil storage. Jugs with only one handle were called *oinochoe* (from the prefix, *oinos*, meaning "wine" in classic Greek). The Greeks drank their wines out of a large, two-handled cup known as a *skyphos*. The artistry of these beautiful vessels was superb, both in design and decoration. The Greeks painted abstract designs and scenes from daily life and mythology on their amphorae and oinochoe, unlike the Egyptians, who painted on their walls. While the Greeks took pride in the decoration of their wine vessels, the Egyptians used diverse materials in fabricating amphorae—including alabaster, bone porcelain, bronze, glass, gold, ivory, and stone, as well as earthen clay.

The Hellenic wine masters buried their amphorae, which may have been an early technique to protect the wine from the destructive effects of exposure to air and high temperatures. This practice may also indicate that wine cellars did not exist in Homeric Greece. There is, however, some evidence that wine may have been made and/or stored in special rooms—this is particularly apparent in excavations of the ancient *agora* (marketplace) in Athens.

As in Mesopotamia and Egypt before, wine became the principal beverage of Greece. At all periods of Greek literature, wine was called upon by the great chroniclers to express the color and feeling of their experiences. As Theognis explained, "Wine is wont to show the mind of man."

A Greek *skyphos* (drinking cup) of the fifth century B.C. (Source: Lowie Museum of Anthropology, University of California, Berkeley.)

As the earliest forms of Greek civilization ripened into Greece's Golden Age, wine took the place of blood as a sacrifice to the gods. Homer points to this when he describes the meeting of King Agamemnon and Odysseus in the *Iliad*: "They drew wine from the bowl in cups, and as they poured it on the ground they made their petition to the gods that have existed since time began."

Dionysus, the wine god and son of the Greek paternal deity, Zeus, was an extremely important expression of Hellenic culture. First portrayed as a beardless youth, Dionysus evolved into a strong young man with a full beard and was also depicted as a bull, a ram, a stag, an old man, as well as various other forms. He is also frequently depicted holding a pruning knife; a clear indication of the importance the Greeks placed on disciplining the vine—a viticultural practice known perhaps even in prehistoric times. The image of Dionysus as a fat, inebriated delinquent appeared mostly in pagan Rome, where he was renamed Bacchus.

Initial celebrations of the Dionysiac cult were drunken orgies, held under torchlights, that often became the scene of extreme violence. At one such celebration the mythic poet Orpheus was said to be dismembered for failing to honor Dionysus.

Although the Dionysian orgies persisted for some time at Delphi and Thebes, eventually the savagery softened into more humane festivities. The cult of Dionysus developed into seasonal reunions held four times a year.

The first festival, known as the "lesser Dionysia," was probably an assemblage for the first tasting of the new wines. The second gathering was named the "Lenaea," after the place where it was first located. This celebration honored the vintage at a "feast of winepresses" and often was the occasion for new plays to be staged by rival groups—laying the foundations for classic Greek theater. Patrons here enjoyed a wine called *ambrosia*, the fabled "food of the gods." The third Dionysiac festival lasted three days and was designated the "Anthesteria." This was considered perhaps the most joyous feast of all. It began when the wine amphorae were opened, and everyone, family and servants alike, joined in the celebration. The "greater Dionysia," the fourth festival, lasted for about a week and was held at Elaphebolion in March. Wealthy citizens would lavish food and wine on the populace while games and sideshows went on in much the same manner as at modern-day carnivals.

Concurrent with the development of the Dionysia was the "symposium," a gathering of artisans, scholars, and local squires for evenings of wine appreciation. Socrates once commented prior to such an evening that

> so far as drinking is concerned, gentlemen, you have my approval. Wine moistens the soul and lulls our grief to sleep while it also wakens kindly feelings. Yet I suspect that men's bodies react like those of growing plants. When a god gives plants too much

water to drink they can't stand up straight and the winds flatten them, but when they drink exactly what they require they grow straight and tall and bear abundant fruit, and so it is with us.

The symposium followed the evening meal's heavily salted or spiced desserts, such as cheese, figs, nuts, and dried olives. While Greeks were not known for gourmet cooking, they did know how to leave the palate thirsty and ready for more wine, which they genuinely enjoyed. Aristotle remarked that "The chief object of the dessert, besides the pleasure to the palate which its dainties afforded, was to keep up the desire of drinking."

Aristophanes, circa 448 B.C., wrote,

And dare you rail at wine's inventiveness:
I tell you nothing has such go as wine.
Why, look you now; 'tis when men drink they thrive,
Grow wealthy, speed their business, win their suits,
Make themselves happy, benefit their friends.
Go fetch me out a stoup of wine, and let me
Moisten my wits, and utter something bright.

Their wines were served both cold and warm in large drinking vessels called *kraters*.

The Greeks were probably the first to publicly advertise wine, using images of Dionysus on their coins as the medium. The prices of wine in Greece varied widely with the quality of the product. Five gallons of one wine from Chios was priced at one entire ox!

Despite some of the high prices, the Greeks consumed great quantities of wine—even the poor were provided for. Homer told of Odysseus being offered wine even though he was cloaked as a beggar. Though most Grecian women were allowed to drink wine, the Spartans forbade this and were most stern in enforcing this precept,

the husband is the judge and censor of his wife; there is no appeal from his decision; if she has acted wrongfully he punishes her; if she has drunk wine or if she has committed adultery, he kills her.

The Homeric works praised the wines from the beautiful vineyards of Arné in Boeotia and revealed that the wines from Heraea caused men to lose their sense of reason and increased the fertility of women; further, that the wines from Cyrene and Troezen induced abortions.

Hippocrates thought that tetanus was best treated with Cretan wine, while the mentally infirm were medicated with very aromatic wines. Wine was used also for snake bites, bee stings, fungal poisonings, as an antidote for hemlock, and, when steeped with herbs, as a treatment for wounds. Asclepiades, the god of the medical art, stated that "even the almighty power of the gods can scarcely equal the usefulness of wine."

One heavy red wine from the island of Cos was noted for precipitating a crystal sediment called *faecula coa*, which was gathered and used in cooking as a crude form of cream of tartar. The most famous wines were probably from the vineyards of Arvisian and Phanaean, which were acclaimed as the finest growths in Greece by Virgil. Pliny the Elder, the first-century A.D. Roman naturalist and writer, preferred the wines from Cyprus, Oenoe, and Samos. The wines from Phyrigia, mixed with honey, were favorites of the Romans, as were the wines of Miletus and Smyrna that were imported by Rome for centuries.

Many islands around Greece produced wine, including Euoea, Icaria, Mykonos, Naxos, Tenos, Thera, and others in addition to those already mentioned.

The Greeks were great innovators of the wine-growing art, pioneering such practices as pruning, the use of amphorae for storage, serving wine with meals, and mixing wine with seawater. Perhaps more importantly, they were authoritative teachers. The Grecian viniculturists took their wine culture with them as they colonized what is now the southeastern Mediterranean seaboard from Marseilles to Cadiz and eastward from the Crimea to the Caspian Sea. The Romans extended the knowledge of grapes and wine even farther.

ROME

The gift of wine was enjoyed in Italy long before the existence of the Roman Empire. In 753 B.C., several centuries before Romulus' name was taken for the imperial city of Rome, the Etruscans made wine in what are now the superb wine-growing regions of Lazio and Tuscany in central Italy.

Farther south, Greek colonists at Cumae, near Naples, made *Falernian,* a wine that had already become famous by the fourth century B.C. Falernian, the first wines from modern-day Campania, was a very heavy-bodied dark red wine with a remarkable capacity for aging.

In general, the earlier wines of Rome were more robust than the delicate wines of Greece, although the Greek selections were usually more aromatic. The common Romans probably preferred their wines to be sweetened with honey, regardless of where they were made.

Julius Caesar served the Grecian Chian and Lesbian wines, as well as the domestic Falernian. Caesar also enjoyed the honored *Mamertine* wine grown near the Messina area on the island of Sicily.

The wine-growing arts advanced during the Roman Empire to a high level of sophistication. Cato the Elder, born in 234 B.C., wrote a book on farming that described grape-growing and winemaking techniques in considerable detail. He also told of a potion made of myrtle berries and wine—myrtle being the sacred tree of Venus. This compound of divine liquids may have been thought of as an aphrodisiac, which perhaps accounts for its popularity among Rome's elderly senators.

Columella was a second-century B.C. Roman naturalist dedicated to the improvement of grape growing and winemaking. He took great care in the handling of his plant materials and despised the Greek method of adding flavorings and water to wine. He wrote that

> we judge to be best every kind of wine which can grow old without any treatment, nor should anything at all be mixed with it, which might dull its natural flavor. For that wine is immeasurably the best, which needs only its own nature to give pleasure.

Observing that the grapes gathered from vineyards of higher elevations make better wines, the poet Horace remarked that "Bacchus loves the hills." This may mark the beginning of the "struggling vine" concept; that vines growing on poor hillside soils yield fruit that has smaller berries with more concentrated sugar and flavor constituents. Richer land is thought to allow vines to grow lush with heavy bunches of grapes that are watery and dilute the essences needed for wines of fine quality.

The Bacchanalia, held in the sacred woods near Rome, reverted to the violence and brawling of the first Dionysiac rites. A special senate committee investigated following the infamous revelry of 186 B.C., and the Senatus Consultum de Bacchanalibus was passed, which made such celebrations illegal in all of Italy.

The favorite wine of Caesar Augustus was *Setine*. This must have delighted Virgil since the Setine wines were grown on the hillsides above Verona, not far from his birthplace in Mantua. Also made in this area was a white wine called *Rhaetic*, a distant forerunner of the popular contemporary *Soave* wine from the same locale. Rhaetic was particularly good with oysters, a favorite food of the ancient Romans.

The second *Georgic* by Virgil indicates that Romans distinguished among wines by how they best complemented different courses of their meals. The classical Roman defined wine types by geographical region in much the same fashion as twentieth-century wines are categorized by the viticultural district. White wines, such as the Rhaetic, were drunk young, while Falernian wines were often much older than those who were fortunate enough to drink them. Their wines were purchased, stored, and served with great care and skill similar to the meticulous attention afforded to fine wines today.

Some seventy years after the birth of Christ, Pliny the Elder, declaring Rome the wine capital of the world, provided detailed descriptions of more than ninety grape varieties along with precise data on how they were grown. Pliny also expounds on the medical properties of wine:

"Wine on its own is a remedy. It will improve the strength and the blood of a man! It settles the stomach, it allays unhappiness and worries." Pliny continues with advice that the wine of Alba was good for coughs, diarrhea, and fever.

Other well-known wines of Roman times were *Babia* from Calabria, and *Galea, Status, Trebellicum,* and *Veliternus,* among others, from the Naples area. The wines grown in the Brutia, namely *Consentia, Rhegium,* and *Tempsa,* were used by the peasants of that region to pay their taxes.

Many of the Roman wines were adulterated, primarily with honey in order to make up for deficiencies in natural grape sugar, but also with the traditional herbs, resins, spices, and water. The stately Falernian did not escape this hideous adulteration. Pliny stated that even Romans of nobility were served debased wine and that well-cared-for wine cellars were almost unknown.

Surrentinum, a wine from the Sorrentine Peninsula, was also rather big and hearty, requiring at least twenty-five years of aging according to the contemporary Roman experts. Nevertheless, it was still considered to be too thin by the emperors Caligula and Tiberius. Caligula rejected it as *nobilis vappa,* "wine that is good for nothing."

When Petronius, a notorious rake at the court of Nero and the author of the *Satyricon,* directed that guests be served the most expensive wine in Rome, the wine chosen was a 100-year-old Falernian. The poet Martial wrote sensuously that he "wanted not merely to drink the kisses left in the loved one's cup but to kiss lips moist with old Falernian." The Falernian wine became highly esteemed and placed in a class with the Epicurean wines imported from the Greek islands of Chios, Cos, and Lesbos. Greek wines in Rome were very expensive, and the political and military leader Lucullus recalled that his father never offered more than one glass of Greek wine, even at the most lavish dinners.

The Romans made and stored their wines in amphorae—again showing the influence of the Greek and Egyptian heritage. Many of the Roman wine vessels were, however, much larger than those of their eastern Mediterranean predecessors, the very largest of these amphorae being called *dolia.*

Roman wine masters heat-treated their wines in a type of kiln called a *fumaria,* hence the many references to "smoky" wines in the works of Latin writers. Amphorae were filled with wine and then protected with a thin surface layer of olive oil before being sealed with a plasterlike substance. The vessels were then placed in the fumaria and heated—a process which, apparently, helped to stabilize their wines against spoilage, still a mysterious process at that time. Ovid wrote that "he draws the wine which he had racked in his early years when stored in a smoky cask."

Many of the common Greek and Roman amphorae were fashioned with ungainly looking pointed bottoms: this feature allowed them to be slipped easily into leather and raffia slings hung from the mainstays inside wine shops, and it also facilitated tipping them for pouring and carrying them in harnesses. This system must surely be the forerunner of the raffia-covered fiasco bottles commonly used in more modern times for the wines from Chianti and Orvieto in Italy. Glass making was a well-known art form in classical Roman times, but few glass bottles were used for wine.

Vintage years were inscribed on Roman amphorae, but age was much more important than the particular year of the growth. Columella felt that nearly all wines improved in quality with aging. Wines were often dated by being named in honor of the reigning Roman emperor.

In bringing civilization to the barbarians of the western Mediterranean, the Greeks and Romans realized that wine was one of their most effective allies. Wherever a colony was founded they would plant a vineyard. These were the seeds that grew to become today's vast European wine industry.

GAUL

About seven centuries before the birth of Christ the first Greek expeditions landed in southern Gaul and colonized the port of Massilla, the city now known as Marseilles, France. Following the conquest of Asia Minor by the Persian Cyrus in 546 B.C., more Greeks carried their culture westward and founded the port colonies of Monoikos (Monaco) and Kikai (Nice).

The first cultivated French vines were planted by the Greeks on the hillsides near their seaport of Marseilles. Trading stations were established on the shores of Marseilles and to the west toward Spain. But the further development of wine growing there was impeded lest the colonial wines offer too much competition to those grown in Greece itself. According to the historian Diodorus Siculus, the international currency was slaves, and the price of one amphora of wine was one young boy.

The early French people, the Gauls, were originally beer drinkers, but a taste for Greek wines soon developed. The Gauls lacked the materials and skill to duplicate the Greek wine amphorae, however, and used instead wooden barrels for the storage of their wines. The staves of the barrels and casks were, of course, porous, which allowed wines to mature and spoil rather quickly—a dilemma that was overcome by consuming wines while they were still quite young.

When Rome supplanted Greece as the major Mediterranean power, the Greek colonists at Marseilles petitioned Rome for support against barbarians. Rome responded and occupied the province. To this day this wine-growing district is called *Provence.*

As they conquered Gaul, the Romans taught the native barbarians the ways of wine and how to establish vineyards along the banks of the rivers, in the forests, and on the valley slopes. These original vineyards have long since been replaced, but today vast tracts of vines still yield wines along the Rhône, Saône, and the other great French rivers.

By 125 B.C. there were two centers of commerce established by the Romans—one at Norbo Martius (Narbonne) and the other at Portus Veneris (Port-Vendres). Both were situated on a highway that had been constructed to link Italy with Spain. In a short time Narbonne evolved as the chief trading center, and the whole region became known as *Narbonensis*—the area known today as the Languedoc.

The Romans exported wine into the Narbonensis by large merchant ships that carried amphorae and other wine-storage vessels. One of the recent *Calypso* expeditions led by Jacques Cousteau was successful in locating one of these ships buried about 130-feet deep in the mud-bottomed sea just a few miles to the southwest of Marseilles. This ship had been commissioned by wealthy Roman merchant Marcus Sestius in the third century B.C. and carried Cycladic wines loaded at the Greek port of Delos, as well as Latium wines from Italy. A total of some 1,000 amphorae and about 800 vases were found, most of which remain sealed and intact! The wine was sampled but proved to be a disappointment, as it had become a pale lifeless liquid, quite unlike the flavorful wine the ancients drank more than twenty-two centuries ago.

Trade was expanded northward from the Narbonensis with depots for wine amphorae along several main routes. Some of these wines were carried overland by mule-train while other trade was carried up and down the Rhône and Saône rivers by flat-bottomed boats. Wine commerce also extended on into the Teutonic Rheinland, which required both land and water transportation. This business activity flourished until the Narbonensis became very affluent. Pliny the Elder described the colony as "not really a province but a part of Italy itself."

The Romans needed wheat, not wine, since most Italian soils were too poor to grow grain. Consequently, as the Roman Empire grew, an economy was planned that would have Provence, Spain, and North Africa become regions of wheat farms rather than grape vineyards. There was even a Roman edict prohibiting new vineyard plantings. However, clever provincial winegrowers in Narbonensis circumvented the law by arranging for a phony sale of land to either a Roman civil servant or soldier, both of whom were exempt from the planting restriction. The vineyard would be planted and tended by the native Narbonensian until the vines matured. Then the Roman would "sell" the tract back to the provincial. Vineyards that "existed" were not affected by the prohibition.

The large numbers of soldiers involved in Caesar's conquest of Gaul required large volumes of wines, most of which were grown in the Narbonensis and were probably of rather poor quality. The Roman fumaria were still used to heat the Gallic wines, and amelioration with herbs and spices was also practiced on them. In time, however, the quality of wine in Narbonensis did improve. With centuries of wine-growing experience behind them, the Roman colonists found new grape varieties and new methods to improve their craft. *Vitis biturica*, the Spanish grape called *Biturigia*, was probably grown in the Aquitaine, the province north and west of Narbonensis that corresponds with Bordeaux. This grape is thought to be the ancestor of Cabernet Sauvignon—perhaps the most celebrated vine now in existence.

To the northeast, near what is now Burgundy, the *Allobrogian* vine was discovered—a vine with small black grapes that ripened before the first autumn frost. This variety is almost certainly the progenitor of today's superb Pinot Noir that yields all of the precious red Burgundies. Other grape varieties that have survived into the present from early Gallic winegrowers are Carignan, Chasselas, and Muscat, but such cultivars as *Amethyston, Aminea, Bailic, Maronea,* and *Nomentum* from Greece and Italy seem to have disappeared.

The Narbonensian expansion in Gaul resulted in a huge production of wines, so immense that the imported Roman wines were totally replaced by domestic production. The Italian winegrowers appealed to the Emperor Domitian for relief from this loss of market for their exports, and, in 92 A.D. the Narbonensian consul ordered about half of the Gallic vineyards to be uprooted. This decree proved to be as much a blessing for the Narbonensians as it was for the Italian wine exporters. Wine growing had spread so profusely in Narbonensis that it threatened other critically needed agricultural produce. But the provincial governors enforced the Domitian law loosely, and, in 276 A.D., the Emperor Probus repealed the statute.

The *Pax Romana* was brought to Bordeaux by Crassus in 56 B.C. Caesar was not a part of wine-growing history in this region of the Aquitaine. Crassus found vineyards already flourishing there and, left undisturbed, they prospered without interruption for another four centuries. One of the most renowned figures on the early Bordeaux wine scene was Ausonius, a Bordeaux-born son of a Roman senator, who led a brilliant career as a lawyer and politician. Ausonius was also a poet and wine connoisseur—a combination that made him a favorite of the Roman court during the early fourth century A.D. He retired to his villa near the forerunner of the city of St.-Émilion in Bordeaux and eventually died there. The estate stands today as Château Ausone, one of the most prestigious vineyard growths in the St.-Émilion district.

Farther north, Roman soldiers were employed during the third century A.D. in clearing the woodland that covered the Montagne de Reims so that the land there could be worked and planted with vines. This was to become the famous Champagne district northeast of Paris. Many of these original vineyard plots still exist, although they are now planted with contemporary vines.

As a result of the original Narbonensian trade routes, wine growing reached the Rhône Valley in the first century A.D., while Burgundy was established as a viticultural area in the second century, and the Loire Valley had producing vineyards in the third century A.D. The spread of Roman viticulture ended another century later at the Rheinland of "Germania."

GERMANIA

Evidence of the Roman influence on wine in Germany: a Roman wine boat at Neumagen, Mosel, West Germany. (Source: German Wine Information Bureau.)

Grape vines grew wild in the Rheinland long before the arrival of the Roman legions. The first wine drunk there, however, was probably that brought from Italian vineyards by Caesar's armies. Some historians believe that Emperor Probus may have brought the first cultivated vines to Germany in the third century. A Roman glass bottle that contained traces of wine was recently discovered near Speyer; the relic is dated at about the time of Probus.

The desperate need for grain in Italy continued, but the steep banks of the rivers Mosel and Rhein were not adaptable to any serious agricultural use other than the cultivation of the grapevine. Consequently, the Romans set the Germanic natives to work on the establishment of vineyards.

In Roman times Trier was known as the *Augusta Trevisorum*—"the capital beyond the Alps." Roman emperors and other dignitaries often visited there, some even lived there, which contributed greatly to social activities and festivities that resulted in large amounts of wine being consumed.

According to Ausonius, the Roman proconsul from Bordeaux, there were many vineyards flourishing along the hillsides of the winding Mosel by the fourth century. As he says in one of his poems, "Oh Mosel, you have so much wine." Despite this great bounty of wine, there is evidence that the best wines of ancient Roman Germany were imported from Gaul or Italy—principally, of course, for the aristocracy who could afford such fare.

It was not for another several centuries that truly fine wines would be grown in the Mosel or the Rheinland.

SPAIN

Whether or not the grapevine is native to the Iberian peninsula remains open to question. It is thought, however, that the Phoenicians were the first to bring wine to Spain—perhaps as early as the seventh century B.C. Some of the earthenware wine vats used by the Phoenicians in Cyprus are very similar to those used in Aragón by contemporary Spaniards.

Roman forces first occupied Spain during the Second Punic War (218- 201 B.C.) with the great Carthaginian general Hannibal. But it was several hundred years more before the province of Hispania was totally secured for the Roman Empire.

Much the same as in Gaul, the Romans made great advancements in wine-growing technology in Spain. Spanish wines during Roman times were fermented and stored in large jars called *orcae*. These earthenware vessels are still used in La Mancha and Montilla.

Spanish wines were exported to Rome in large volumes. The discovery of amphorae near Rome, at Monte Testaccio, contained many wine seals of Spanish origin. This export market was relatively short-lived, however, as the edict of Emperor Domitian in the first century A.D., which limited vine plantings in Gaul, also curtailed the establishment of new vineyards in the Hispanic province.

As the Roman legions penetrated the interior of Spain, the need for wine outweighed the restrictions of Domitian's decree—and a number of important wine-growing centers were developed as a result. The contemporary traveler can still find a vineyard believed to be Roman near a Montserrat viaduct in Catalonia.

The sweet wines of Málaga were a favorite of the times and the Roman Columella, born in Spain, wrote of Málaga wines in both his *Agricultura* and *De Re Rustica*. Democritus, Pliny the Elder, and Virgil also praised the wines of Málaga.

CHRISTIANITY

Perhaps the vineyards on the slopes of Mt. Vesuvius best symbolize the beginnings of the fall of the Roman Empire. Here is how Martial describes the scene following the massive volcanic eruption of 79 A.D., when Pompeii and its vineyards were deluged:

> Here is Vesuvius, once covered with green pastures, whose prolific fruit used to fill our wine presses. Here were vineyards which Bacchus preferred to those of Nysa. In ancient times satyrs would have danced on these hills, the home of Venus and Hercules. The flames have destroyed it all, and everything is covered up by that mountain of cinder. Surely even the gods did not intend this.

Over the millenia, the influence of Christianity on wine has proved to be much more powerful and enduring than that of either Greece or Rome.

Wine played a symbolic role in many religions centuries before the advent of the Christian faith; since earliest history, humans have associated the red color of blood and wine and have used wine in religious ceremonies to create an aura of mystery and reverence. Christianity brought the religious symbolism of wine to its highest expression and most universal observance.

The Bible contains 165 direct references to wine, 155 of which are in the Old Testament. Wine played an important part in the everyday lives of the people in Biblical times. One can find rich descriptions of wine drinking and wine imagery in the Bible, along with much advice about the best uses for wine.

There can be no doubt that the Bible considers wine God's gift to man. One illustration of this comes in the following passage from Psalms 104:15:

> He causeth the grass to grow for the cattle, and herb for the service of man; that he may bring forth food out of the earth; and wine that maketh glad the heart of man.

The Old Testament also contains passages concerning winemaking, such as this one from Judges 9:27:

> And they went out into the fields, and gathered their vineyards, and trode the grapes, and made merry.

But the Old Testament does not only celebrate the vine. There are also warnings against drinking wine to excess, as here in Proverbs 23:29:

> Who hath woe? Who hath sorrow? Who hath contentions? Who hath babbling? Who hath wounds without cause? Who hath redness of eyes? They that tarry too long at wine; they that go to seek mixed wine.

Several important passages in the New Testament concern wine as well. Christ's first miracle, performed at the marriage feast of Cana in Galilee, was to turn water into wine. The passage occurs in John 2:6-9 and 11:

> Now six stone jars were standing there, for the Jewish rites of purification, each holding twenty or thirty gallons. Jesus said to them, "Fill the jars with water." And they filled them up to the brim. He said to them, "Now draw some out and take it to the steward of the feast." And they took it . . . the water now became wine . . . . This, the first of his signs, Jesus did at Cana in Galilee, and manifested his glory; and his disciples believed on him.

The New Testament also advised on winemaking practices, for example, in Matthew 9:17

> And no man putteth new wine into old bottles; else the new wine doth burst the bottles, and the wine is spilled, and the bottles will be marred; but new wine must be put into new bottles.

According to St. Luke, Christ observed that: "No man having drunk old wine straightaway desireth new: for he saith, The old is better." We read in Timothy 5:23, the very famous quotation of St. Paul, who surely must have known the value of wine as an aid to digestion: "Drink no longer water, but use a little wine for thy stomach's sake and thine often infirmities."

Perhaps it was the fact that wine is perpetually renewed each vintage that explains why Jesus Christ chose wine as the everlasting symbol of his blood. One frequently cited passage occurs in I Corinthians 11:25, where Christ says: "This cup is the new covenant of my blood. Do this as often as you drink it, in remembrance of me."

Wine thus became a crucial part of the Christian ritual. Wherever Christianity flourished, wine would become necessary.

THE MIDDLE AGES

Western civilization is greatly indebted to the Christian monks for the continuance of winemaking during the period of history following the destruction of the Roman Empire. Monks, of course, did more in preserving and restoring civilization than just make wine. They maintained hospitals, schools, and libraries; provided leadership for the church; distributed charity; and looked after cultural and social services. But their expertise in wine growing and making was unique. The monasteries were the only communities that had the resources for research and improvement of wine-growing skills. Monks used methods and devices in their wine cellars that were unknown to lay vintners. There can be no question that viticulture would have taken far longer to develop in Europe without the contributions made by the Catholic church.

St. Martin of Tours, the first viticulturist monk, was born about 316 A.D. in what today is Hungary. He was so popular locally that the people of Tours in France forced Martin to become their bishop—escorting him with an armed guard to their city. A successful evangelist who brought Christianity to the pagan countryfolk and built churches in many early French villages, Martin carried out his episcopal duties faithfully and found time to establish a community of hermits at Marmoutier, on the banks of the Loire River. The discovery of the now-famous Chenin Blanc grape variety in the Loire Valley is credited to St. Martin—and each year toward the end of January a festival is held in his honor. St. Martin died in 397; his red cloak became one of the most sacred relics in France.

Benedict of Nursia, the founder of Benedictine monasticism, played an extremely important role in the history of Western civilization. Born circa 480, St. Benedict studied in Rome and, feeling the call of the monastic life, spent several years in seclusion near the ruins of one of Nero's palaces. His worldly restraint impressed some neighboring monks who invited him to be their abbot. But St. Benedict's discipline was more severe than the monks had anticipated, and they decided to get him out of the way by poisoning his wine. Witnesses attest that when he raised the cup and made the sign of the cross, it shattered, saving his life.

St. Benedict established another monastery at Monte Cassino, with a dozen or so monks of a more obedient nature. The rule of St. Benedict emphasized agricultural work, particularly a triad of staples—grain, oil, and wine—which assured that Benedictines would cultivate vineyards. Nevertheless, St. Benedict drank wine only occasionally and was strict about the moderate amounts of wine allowed his monks.

The lofty reputation of St. Benedict won for his monks a measure of peace from the violence and pillaging that swept Europe after the fall of Rome, and the vineyards could be tended without harassment. Lay workers in search of sanctuary soon joined the *vigneron* work forces in the monastery.

Benedictine monasticism still lives on as a significant force in the culture and development of European vineyards.

Following the death of St. Benedict circa 543 the Italian abbeys were sacked by the Byzantines who held them for only a short time before they were, in turn, overcome by the Lombard conquest. During the latter part of the sixth century, bloodshed and turmoil engulfed much of Europe—dynastic wars among the Franks, Teutons, and Visigoths wreaked havoc in Gaul. In Spain religious battles between Arian and Catholic Visigoths brought chaos and destruction. Among all agricultural endeavors, viticulture suffered most.

International trade was not significantly affected by the wars until the seventh century when the Moslems gained control of the Mediterranean, and maritime wine traffic was ended.

Despite the devastation, the monks survived, as did most of their abbeys. Under the direction of Pope Gregory the Great, new monasteries were developed during the early seventh century, mostly in the Benedictine Order. In turn, virgin land was cleared and new vineyards established. Monte Cassino was reconstructed in 717, and once more the wine-growing arts were practiced in the vineyards of St. Benedict. Monks began to grow grapes and make wine in every conceivable locale, testing even the harsh elements of Ireland and Poland.

In Italy, near Calabria, the Black Monks ran the Abbey of Vavarium. The Black Monks, a suborder of Benedictines, relaxed certain aspects of the strict code originally laid down by St. Benedict. Nearby Vavarium were several great vineyards—among them Ciro—so great that its wine had been offered as a prize to winners of the Olympic games.

The German rival to Monte Cassino was the great Abbey of Fulda, founded by St. Boniface in 744. St. Boniface was a missionary and viticulturist who planted a number of vineyards near Mainz. Fulda, however, won a special place for itself in German wine lore because it was here that the now-famous *kabinett* wines originated. Many of the abbots there were wine connoisseurs; one of them had a special cellar in which the finest wines were stored and dispensed from a secret "cabinet."

The Abbey of St. Maximin at Trier became Benedictine and established vineyards at Detzen, Leiwen, and Longuich. The best wine at Maximin was *Abtsberg*, grown at the top of the hill and drunk only by the abbot. Farther down the hill grew *Herrenberg* wine, which was reserved for the choir monks. *Bruderbar* came from still farther down the hill and was consumed by novices. The lowest vineyards produced *Biertelsberg*, a wine which was allotted to the laity.

In 613 monks planted a vineyard near Strasbourg, at Haslach, and other vineyards were established by the mid-seventh century in the lower Neckar River Valley.

The finest vineyard in Germany, however, was the eleventh-century Benedictine Schloss Johannisberg. This vineyard, located in the Rheingau, ranks even today with the world's greatest vineyards.

The monks, perennial guardians of the purity of God's grapes, eventually fell to making potions instead of wines—adding flavors and spices as they experimented with numerous recipes. Compounded by a chemist, or *pigmentarius*, such wines were known as *pigments*. Likewise, monk's wines that were exceedingly bad (for example, the wines grown at the Saint Wandrille Abbey in Normandy were notoriously loathsome) were doctored with herbs and honey in a manner recalling the ancient Greek and Roman practices.

Medieval white wines were clarified with isinglass, while red wines of the times were cleared with egg whites. Poorer-quality grapes were consumed as table grapes or used in pickling brines for cheese and ham. Inadequate wines were made into vinegar that was used much as it is today. Pomace from the presses and grape leaves were used to feed livestock, while wood pruned from the vines made very aromatic fireplace fuel.

The alliance between the monks and the peasants was a significant factor in the medieval economic structure. Many of the farmers gave up their land, including vineyards, to the monks in return for protection, recalling the sanctuary afforded the populace at Monte Cassino during St. Benedict's time. The peasants became Christians and learned the science and art of winegrowing from the monks. However, the serf-tenants of the monasteries were required to pay rent plus a *dime*, or *zehnt*, which amounted to one-tenth of their wine production. This feudal tithe gave the monks an obvious advantage over the peasants in the marketing of wine. In addition, the laity was not allowed to sell any of its wine until the monasteries had sold their production. Further, all grapes had to be pressed in the abbey's cellars, for which fees were collected from lords and serfs alike. Finally, the monasteries were usually exempt from wine taxes. This system encouraged the monks to lavish care and love on improving both their vines and their wines while peasant vineyards were forced into producing quantity rather than quality.

Most of the wines made from the peasants' grapes were quaffed shortly after they were made, certainly within a year. There was little interest in aging wines to perfection, and few winemakers among the flock cared about expert wine-mastery. The best wines were unquestionably made by the monks, whose finest efforts were dedicated, to quote André Simon, "to the greater glory of God."

Small villages began to form around the monasteries, and vineyards were planted by farmers who had mastered the new technology. As viticulture became a major form of agriculture, the great European vineyard system began to develop toward the noble structure known today.

In the Catholic Mass as performed during the Dark Ages, the laity received the wine chalice in the same manner as their priests. Following the Holy Communion, unconsecrated wine was often distributed to the peasants as well. Wine, the only known disinfectant, continued to serve as medicine and a very real relief from the pains of the times.

During the reign of Charlemagne (742-814), the Catholic church was protected and viticulture encouraged. The Saracens, who had ruined many of the Aquitaine vineyards, were driven out of France by the great emperor. New vineyards were established across Europe, some in Burgundy and the Rheinland achieving wines of particular excellence.

Both the Benedictine and Cistercian orders grew wine in Burgundy, and the monks created many of the now-famous vineyards of the Côte d'Or. Their original center of winemaking, however, was at the great Abbey of Cluny, a grand structure of huge proportions located near Mâcon, south of the modern-day center of Burgundy at Beaune. In its day Cluny was regarded as a great vineyard expanse, producing the finest wines. Today, however, the locale is known as the Mâconnais and its wine production is generally regarded as rather common.

Regulations for grape growing and winemaking were issued by Charlemagne in Germany, and it was during his era that the first records appear for the great Rheinland vineyards. Charlemagne also gave many gifts of land and vineyards to the church in Europe, properties that would later bring great wealth to the monks and clergy.

During and following Charlemagne's reign, Europe enjoyed some measure of peace and tranquility; the monasteries flourished and many grew into small cities. The citizenry of the great abbey of St. Martin at Tours, for example, exceeded twenty thousand people. Immense quantities of wine were needed for such religious communities. This period of quiescence was short-lived, however; invading Magyars, Saracens, and Vikings laid seige and terrorized the population. St. Martin's Abbey at Tours, among many others, was plundered by the raiders, but the few monasteries that survived again offered sanctuary to the meek. There can be no doubt that humanity suffered during the tenth, eleventh, and twelfth centuries. Highwaymen and other bandits roamed the countryside, and there was great conflict among the various social classes in Europe, often precipitated by famine.

This was also the period of the Crusades, wars organized by the church to regain the Holy Land for Christendom. Some historians believe that the Crusaders sampled Portuguese wines en route to the Middle East and that some soldiers found the wines so good that they remained in Lusitania. In any event, the English did settle a community at Vianna do Castekka at about that time.

The returning Crusaders brought home with them a taste for the wines of the Greek Isles, especially those of Candia (the medieval name for Crete) and Cyprus. The English called the fine wines of Candia *Malmsey.*

The Crusaders introduced a memorable vine into southern France that gained fame as the superb Muscat de Frontignan. The classic Syrah, which makes the very dark and heavy red wines of the Rhône, is said to be the same vine as the *Shiraz,* also brought back by the Crusaders from the Fertile Crescent.

During the latter part of this era new orders of monks appeared: Carthusians, Hospitallers, and Templars, bringing down the monopoly of monasticism held by the Benedictines. Much of this development in Germany is credited to noblemen, who, following Charlemagne's example, endowed the church with money, abbeys, land, and vineyards. The church became wealthy in many portions of western Europe, particularly in Germany and in Burgundy, in France.

Perhaps the finest example of a monastic vineyard was in the Côte de Nuits of northern Burgundy. In 1110, some rather poor, undeveloped land, as well as some fine vineyard property, situated near the river Vouge, was given to the Abbey of Cîteaux by Guerric of Chambolle. The Cistercian monks cultivated the Vouge land and expanded their vineyards, adding even more to their estate as they could afford it. About forty years later they built their first wine cellars. By 1336 the Cîteaux monks had composed a vineyard estate of about 125 acres around which they constructed a stone wall, thus establishing the Clos de Vougeot. Wine connoisseurs for centuries have considered the wines produced by this abbey to be among the finest of all Burgundies, both red and white. Abbot Jean de Bussière was made a cardinal after shipping thirty hogsheads of Clos de Vougeot wine to Pope Gregory XI in honor of his papal election.

Cistercian monks of Eberbach in the Rheinland cleared a portion of the dense Steinberg Forest that was given to them by the archbishop of Mainz at about the same time that the Vouge land was bequeathed to the Cistercians in Burgundy. More than 60 acres of wines were planted within a stone wall, making the Kloster Eberbach the largest and most highly esteemed vineyard in all of Germany.

The most important bestowal of vineyard property during the twelfth century, perhaps of all time, was the dowry of Eleanor of Aquitaine. By marrying her (in

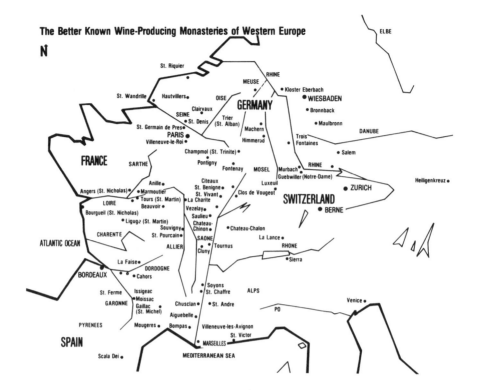

The Better Known Wine-Producing Monasteries of Western Europe

1152) Henri Plantagenet, Comte D'Anjou, Chinon, and Loire, gained a vast expanse of territory, including all the great winelands of Bordeaux. This became the possession of England and remained so for about 300 years.

Plantagenet became King Henry II of England in 1154, although he was French both by birth and parentage. During the reign of Henry II and his Bordeaux-born sons, who became King Richard and King John, a large amount of wine was shipped from Bordeaux to England. In order to maintain good trade relations, considerable quantities of wines were also shipped to England from Germany. The demand for Bordeaux wines grew steadily; a thousand casks were ordered just for the coronation of Edward II in 1307. In fact, the fine red wines of Bordeaux, especially those from the Médoc, became so popular in England that King Edward III issued regulations that forced shipping bases to be established in Bordeaux that only served English ships. A large number of ships were built as a result of this law, which was how the great English navy was born.

The thirst for "claret" (British colloquialism for Bordeaux wine) in England also led to the clearing of great expanses of vineyards in Bordeaux; the Médoc became heavily planted and more, new vineyards appeared in the region. Just as a thousand years earlier in Roman times, vines were planted in land previously used for grain, and a serious shortage of bread resulted. By the mid-fifteenth century, however, all of the English interests in French wine production had been lost; the very last Aquitaine vineyard was surrendered with the defeat of Marshal Talbot in 1453, which ended the Hundred Years War. Château Talbot remains in

Bordeaux as a fitting monument to this period of history, during which vineyards in every province of France were laid waste. With the demand for claret being much more difficult to supply, the English turned to the wines of Italy, Portugal, and Spain, among others.

King Edward III made the initial ties with Portugal for England, signing a treaty that gave Portuguese ships fishing rights off the English coast. Portuguese sailors traded their casks and skins full of green "eager" *Vinho Verde* wine for English goods. Subsequently came dry red "port" wines (not the famous sweet port dessert wines that were developed later), but they were disappointing after the superb growths of Bordeaux that the British had been enjoying for centuries. A *sack*, or dessert wine called *Osey* (*Oseye*, or *Osaye*), not to be confused with the Spanish dry sherry, was made by the Portuguese for the English. It was probably sweetened with honey since sugar was very expensive. In his *Comodytes of England*, published in the mid-1450s, Sir John Fortescue included Osey in the list of imported wines that were "out of Portugale."

The *Champagne* wines of modern times were not known in the Middle Ages—sparkling wines had not yet been invented. But there were already many vineyards surrounding Épernay and Reims in Champagne, which were producing wines similar to those of Burgundy. The great vineyards of Ay, Cumières, Damery, and Hautvillers in the Champagne Province were praised in 1398 by the poet Deschamps.

The wine-shipping center of the Loire Valley during the early 1400s was Orléans, but there were only a few growths worthy of mention in the Parisian Market. Among these were the wines of Chinon and Saint-Cyr-sur-Loire. The wines of Anjou were sold in Brittany and Normandy.

The river Yonne allowed for rather easy transportation of the wines from Chablis and Auxerre to Paris, but Burgundian vintners had difficulty trading with the provinces and countries to the north. Overland routes were physically taxing to cross with heavy loads of wine, and highwaymen were a common peril. The fine quality of Burgundy wines was enhanced, however, by the splendor and *gentillesse* with which they were presented by the dukes of Burgundy. All of this particularly impressed the Parisians, who were willing to pay the high cost of transport for these marvelous wines. As trade increased, Beaune became the center for the growing and shipping of Burgundy wines, though it did not fully establish itself in this role until the seventeenth century.

For a period of almost seventy years in the mid-fourteenth century, the popes refused to live in Rome and made their home at Avignon, on the Rhône River in the south of France. The wines of Châteauneuf-du-Pape (new home of the pope) gained instant distinction and notoriety, though it was even more difficult to transport wine to Paris from the Rhône than from Burgundy. Farther south the old Roman wine district of Narbonensis, which during the ensuing millenia after the

A tapestry showing grape harvest and pressing in medieval France. (Source: Musée de Cluny, Paris.)

fall of Rome became known as the Languedoc, continued to produce wines of high regard. French kings heavily promoted vineyard plantings there but the Languedoc wines were strong compared with the more delicate products of Bordeaux and Burgundy. Consequently, the wines of the Rhône and Languedoc were only slightly commercialized in Paris at that time.

Much of what is known about wine during the fourteenth century in England comes from the writings of Geoffrey Chaucer. The *Canterbury Tales*, in particular, has many references to wine:

> Now keep ye from the white and from the red
> And namely from the white wine of Lepe
> That is to sell in Fish Street as in Chepe.
> This wine of Spain creepith subtilly
> In other wines, growing fast by,
> Of which there rises such fumositee
> That when a man has drunken draughtes three,
> And wenith that he be at home in Chepe
> He is at home right in the town of Lepe
> Not at the Rochelle, nor at Bordeaux town.

There were then three distinct categories of wine, according to Chaucer—beverage (table) wines, dessert wines, and medicinal wines. Red beverage wines were mostly the very dark wines of Languedoc, while the whites were from Nantes or Rochelle. New wines called *must* were beverage wines that were quaffed or swilled rather than sipped and savored. Dessert wines, usually very expensive, were enjoyed for special occasions and as expressions of hospitality between friends. Some of the notable dessert types were *Grenache,* *Ribolle,* and *Romany* from Portugal and Spain, as well as *Vernage* from Italy. One favorite medieval drink in England was *Hippocras,* a medicinal wine, as the name would suggest, made of a mixture of wine and spices. Often the aristocracy would show off their wealth by also adding sugar.

In Italy there seemed to be little wine-growing progress during the Middle Ages, certainly very little was recorded. A wine called *Trubidiane,* which resembled the *Trebulan* of Caesar's time and the *Trebbiano* of modern times, was exported to London in 1373. English literature mentions the wines of Florence and *Lacrima Christi,* as well as *Leattica,* known nowadays as *Aleatico.* Some wine historians assert that no scientific viticulture existed between the fall of the Roman Empire and the Industrial Revolution. There could be little question, in any case, that Italian wines in the Middle Ages had the stamina and strength that the classical Roman wines needed to endure decades of maturation: the days of the great Falernian wines were over.

As the Middle Ages came to a close, wine had grown to encompass a very important share in trade, with activity reaching the levels of spices from the Far East and Flemish textiles. As would be expected, the heaviest demand came from the countries that could not grow wine, such as England, although monks had more than twenty monastic vineyards even there. The port of La Rochelle near Bordeaux became the most important wine-shipping point, receiving the traffic from the rivers Gironde, Dordogne, and Garonne that served the vast Aquitaine. Sea routes that had been closed down by the Arabs centuries earlier were reopened, allowing wine to be brought once more to distant markets.

By the end of the Middle Ages, the monks were, by far, the largest winegrowers in Europe. At their zenith, the Black Monks order of the Benedictines alone possessed several thousand monasteries. With well-organized and centralized labor forces the monks brought a highly professional approach to growing grapes and making wines. Many monasteries had developed extensive vineyards, often planted with a wide range of grape varieties whose performance was tested and recorded. Monastic cellars for production and aging were efficiently designed, constructed, and operated in order to maximize wine quality. The monks used calendars for planning and kept records of their data. These efforts mark the beginning of vineyard and wine classifications in Europe as they are known today.

THE RENAISSANCE

As the influence of the Renaissance began to spread from Italy, vines and wines made great advances in western Europe. France and French vineyards, in ruins at the end of the Hundred Years War in 1453, regained prosperity under Charles VII; Mathieu de Coussy, a contemporary historian, stated that "the peasants endeavored to repair their houses and to tidy up their vineyards and gardens."

New and higher standards for wines began to emerge. Louis XI, who ruled France from 1461 to 1483, prohibited the use of lesser grapes in winemaking, and the Duke of Burgundy, though a great rival of the king, nevertheless took the same action in Burgundian vineyards.

The diversity of cultures and subcultures allowed for the development of separate intellect and artistry in the Western world during the late Middle Ages. During this same era, principally the 14th and 15th centuries, a cultural trend emerged from Italy which initially pervaded much of Europe and ultimately spread to most Western nations. Doubtlessly, this new mode was motivated by the classic civilizations of Egypt, Greece, and Rome, as Europeans have continually looked back upon these ancient societies for inspiration. In particular, Italy was a nation of middle-class people who had never lost consciousness of their great Roman heritage. From this a rebirth of freethinking and scholarship was born—principally in the cities of Rome and Florence. This was the Renaissance.

The "father of humanism" was Francesco Petrarca, more well-known as Petrarch. In political exile Petrarch collected and published the forgotten works of many ancient authors, and wrote a number of treatises himself—some of which were pleas for the popes to return from the Châteauneuf-du-Pape in Avignon to Rome. Boccaccio wrote the *Decameron* in the mid-1300's and lectured in Florence on the writings of Petrarch and Dante. During the next 150 years the University of Florence became a comprehensive institution of learning and the popes, who had returned from France, became very influential in the Renaissance movement. Popes Nicholas V and Pius II were very concerned with the preservation of Roman archaeology during the mid-1400's and Pope Leo X (son of Lorenzo de'Medici, a wealthy Florentine patron of the arts) brought to Rome the idea that culture was the expression of creative artistry and gathering of knowledge—and that these things were a birthright to all people.

THE REFORMATION

Monasticism was one of the primary targets of the great religious Reformation that convulsed Europe in the sixteenth century, and it was inevitable that wine growing would also suffer heavily. Most reformers argued that monastic life was a waste of time and showed contempt for God. Martin Luther, himself an ex-friar, wrote that "monks are the fleas on God Almighty's fur coat."

There is no question that the monasteries had grown too numerous and in some cases corrupt. Some had become no more than comfortable retreats for spiritually minded ladies or gentlemen. By the 1520s, about half of the abbeys in western Europe had failed—fortunately for the history of wine, most of them were in the north where little wine was grown. Peasants did, however, sack the cellars of Kloster Eberbach, and a ransom of 18,000 gallons of wine was exacted in 1525. Protestants raided Schloss Johannisberg numerous times during the 1560s. In France the abbeys came under severe attacks during the Wars of Religion that were fought from 1562 to 1598. In one instance the Huguenots orgiastically sacked the abbey at Pontigny in Chablis while wearing monk's robes.

The monasteries remained easy prey to pillage and plunder throughout the Thirty Years War that raged in central Europe from 1618 to 1648. Some of the abbeys were to eventually recover, but never again would monastic wine growing approach the intensity and breadth it had attained during its zenith in the late Middle Ages and Renaissance.

Wine in Shakespeare's England

Water was not fit to drink in Shakespeare's time. At breakfast and midday ale and beer were drunk, while wine was taken in the evening.

Sherry, the fortified wine from Spain, was a favorite beverage in Shakespeare's time. Some wine experts insist that sherry is a "foreign wine—made and consumed by foreigners." This refers to the fact that British merchants have heavily influenced sherry's method of vinification and product standards at least as far back as 1340. Following the recapture of the wine-growing lands near Cadiz from the Moors in 1492, the British merchants gradually developed the market for sherry back in England. Sherry was known as *sacar*, a word meaning "export" in Spanish, which eventually became Anglicized into *sack*. According to the many references to sack in this period, it was probably much sweeter than the sack we know in modern times. Shakespeare was partial to Spanish sherry—the *sack* wine that is mentioned so often in his many works.

References to wines of all types abound in Shakespeare's plays. In *Much Ado About Nothing* Leonato bids farewell: "Drink some wine ere you go; fare you well." Talbot makes clear his wishes in *Henry VI:*

No other satisfaction do I crave
But only—with your patience—that we may
Taste of your wine, and see what cates you have;
For soldiers' stomachs always serve them well.

Iago, in the tragedy *Othello*, praises wine: "Come, come, good wine is a good familiar creature if it be well-used: exclaim no more against it." And there is the famous line of Brutus, in *Julius Caesar*, "Speak no more of her. —Give me a bowl of wine.— In this I bury all unkindness." Finally, from the drinking party in Act II of *Antony and Cleopatra*,

Come thou Monarch of the Vine
Plumpy Bacchus with pink eyne!
In thy fats [vats] our cares be drown'd
With thy grapes our hairs be crown'd
Cup us, till the world go round,
Cup us, till the world go round!

The peerage, vintners, and licensed tavern operators were the only people allowed to keep wine in their houses in Elizabethan England. Nearly all wines were imported from the Continent, and most of these were rather young and inexpensive, being drawn from butts, casks, hogsheads, pipes, and other wooden shipping containers. The Englishman Dr. Andrew Borde spoke of the wines he enjoyed:

I do take good Gascon wyne, but I wyl not drynke stronge wynes, as Malmesey, Romney, Romaniske wyne, wyne Qoorse, wyne Greke and Secke.

Rather,

a draught or two of Muscadell or Basterde, Osey, Caprycke, Aligant, Tyre, Raspyte, I wyl not refuse; but whyte wyne of Angeou or wyne of Orleance, or Renyshe wyne, whyte or red, is good for al men.

In 1542 Dr. Borde published a dietary, which includes the following:

moderately dronken, it doth actuate and doth quycken a man's wyttes, it doth comfort the hert, it doth scoure the lyuer; specyally yf it be whyte wyn, it doth reioyce all the powers of man and doth nowrysshe them; it doth engender good blode, it doth comforte and doth nourysshe the brayne and all the body, and it resolueth fleume; it ingendereth heate, and it is good agaynst heuyes and pencyfulness; it is full of agylyte; wherefore it is modsonable, specyally whyte wyne, for it doth mundyfye and clense wounds & sores. Furthermore, the better the wyne is, the better humours it doth engender.

Borde also advised that the Portuguese Osey wine was best taken as a dessert wine "not good to drynke with meate, but after meate."

In 1568, one of Queen Elizabeth's personal physicians, Dr. William Turner, wrote the first English-language book addressing the topic of wine. The lengthy title given to the work was "A new Boke of the natures and properties of all wines that are commonly used here in England, with a confutation of an error of some men, that holds that Rhenish and other small white wines ought not to be drunken of them that either have, or are in danger of the Stone, the reume, and divers other diseases, made by William Turner, Doctor of Phisicke."

Until the mid-seventeenth century the English called all German wines *Rhenish* whether or not they were actually from the Rhein. Perhaps the finest of the Rhenish wines were from Bacharach. Pope Pius II also felt that the wines of Bacharach were the finest from Germany. The term *Rhenish* was replaced in England by two new generic terms for German wine, *Bacharach* and *Hock*— derived from the village of Hochheim on the river Main that flows into the Rhein. These terms entered the language in the 1620s and 1630s.

The Seventeenth and Eighteenth Centuries

During the reigns of Louis XIII and XIV (1610-1715) the Anjou vineyards became one of the finest wine producers in France. This district, just west of the Touraine in the Loire Basin, was praised by Alexandre Dumas as having "le premier vin de France." Anjou eventually lost its position of popularity to other growths, among these the vineyards of neighboring Saumur, which may have given the very first fruit for sparkling wines. Most authorities, however, regard Champagne as the earliest of such wines (see below). In any case, many French wines were developing superb reputations. Perhaps Cardinal Richelieu best described the happy condition of French wine when he said, "If God forbade drinking would He have made wine so good?"

During the mid-seventeenth century war again broke out between England and France as the House of Stuart fell and the reign of Louis XIV commenced. Once more the claret wines from Bordeaux were denied the English, who had to console themselves with the dry red "ports" from Portugal, a poor substitute. One Scottish verse describes this discontent:

> Firm and erect the Highland chieftain stood
> Old was his mutton and his claret good.
> "Thou shalt drink Port" the English statesman cried.
> He drank the poison—and his spirit died.

Determined to improve the quality of these wines, British merchants went to Portugal and literally "invented" the sweet red port dessert wine-type as it is known today. The British vintners knew that the deep dark red grapes of the Douro Valley matured to a very high sugar content. When all of this sugar was fermented, the result was the strong harsh traditional port wine that had been drunk and disparaged in England. The wine masters developed a process whereby brandy was added at a precise time during fermentation, arresting further activity and preserving much of the natural sweetness in the wine. Some purists, however, quickly challenged this practice, insisting that such wines were not natural, a notion that persists in some circles to this day. Wine lodges near Oporto in Portugal still bear the names of these original port inventors and shippers: Croft, Dow, McKenzie, Offley, Sandeman, and others. Oliver Cromwell is credited by some with introducing this new port to the British Isles. Port became the wine of England, just as Madeira was adopted as the wine of the colonies in America.

Perhaps the main reason why Madeira was so widely accepted in colonial America was that King Charles II exempted wines from Madeira from the law requiring imports into America to be shipped in a British ship from a British harbor. Produce from other English possessions was prohibited from direct export. Christopher Columbus, who lived in Madeira for a time, brought his wines to the New World, perhaps blazing the trail for the eventual Madeira trade conducted by wealthy shipowners in Boston, Charleston, New York, and Philadelphia.

In France there was a keen competition between the winegrowers of Burgundy and Champagne for lower taxes and other conveniences from King Louis XIV. Both provinces produced fine red wines from the celebrated Pinot Noir vine, one of the Sun King's favorites. Louis XIV also prized Bordeaux wines, calling them the "Nectar of the Gods."

The discovery of the sparkling Champagne wine is credited to a blind monk, Dom Pérignon, cellarer at the Benedictine Abbey of Hautvillers near Épernay from 1668 until 1715. Dom Pérignon stoppered his bottles of new wine with another of his inventions, the cork, which kept the carbon dioxide gas generated during a secondary fermentation from dissipating. Upon pulling the cork and tasting the effervescent product, Dom Pérignon is said to have exclaimed, "My God, I am drinking stars!"

Fagon, personal physician to Louis XIV, was admonished for endorsing the new sparkling wine, which the Burgundians insisted was a "fast-living wine." In 1700 the Champenois met at the medical school at Reims, proclaiming afterward that Champagne was the most pleasant and wholesome wine one could drink.

Champagne was made fashionable at court by King Louis XV, whose reign brought prosperity to all the major vineyard districts in France, particularly Bordeaux. Exports were increased to Russia and the Scandinavian countries, as well as the French colonies and settlements in Africa, India, and North America. The Duc de Richelieu introduced Bordeaux to the court of Louis XV, and Madame de Pompadour had both Bordeaux and the coveted Romanée wines of northern Burgundy served at her private dinners.

The perfection of the cork as a wine-bottle closure brought a new dimension to wine-making expertise in the eighteenth century. (Spain, Portugal, and Italy all claim credit for this, though in fact it may have been mostly the work of the French monk Dom Pérignon.) It became possible to age wines in the bottle for long periods of time, dispensing with the need to drink wines young. The character of wine evolved from a healthy and hearty drink into a complex beverage that became a true art form.

A further recognition of the advances in wine was the classification of French vineyards that began in the eighteenth century. In 1723 an English wine merchant, Bruneval by name, placed four superb Bordeaux growths—Château Lafite, Château Latour, Château Margaux, and Château Haut-Brion—in a class by themselves. By the mid-1700s, most of the foremost vineyards in Bordeaux were classified, but not officially for yet another century.

THE GREAT REVOLUTIONS

In general, European wine growing suffered during the French Revolution and Napoleonic wars. Vineyards and wine cellars were damaged or destroyed, some even seized outright. The Clos de Vougeot was sold at public auction into smaller parcels. In the Rheinland Napoleon secularized all of the religious orders with the 1801 Treaty of Lunéville. As a result, many of the principal German vineyards were divided up among numerous small holders who gave their names to their parcels. Some of these vineyards are still identified by these names today.

Yet despite the ravages of war and revolution, the first half of the nineteenth century was a "Golden Age of Wine." The chemistry of Gay-Lussac introduced the first applications of scientific discipline to winemaking. Superb-quality vintages seemed to occur rather regularly, and new generations of connoisseurs emerged to appreciate them. The nobility, bankers, land barons, and the nouveau riche merchant-princes spared no expense in the development of great vineyards and wine cellars.

The English did not care much for Italian wines during the "Golden Age." Cyrus Redding observed that

> Italian wines have stood still and remained without improvement, while those of France and Spain . . . have kept pace to a certain extent with agricultural improvement and the increasing foreign demand.

Redding continued,

> There are places, however, where very good [Italian] wine is made, and something like
> care bestowed upon its fabrication; but those exceptions are the result of the care of the
> proprietor for his own individual consumption.

In 1830 German provincial officials mandated that the names of all vineyards, along with the vineyard owner's name, be recorded in a land register used as a tax roll. The register also contained such information as the vineyard soil-type, grape variety planted, and wine quality, as well as the nearest village. Although it was not originally designed as such, this eventually became a classification of vineyards in Germany. As would be expected, the first result from the register was to encourage higher demand for the better-quality wines. This brought about a desperate situation for the owners of the poorer vineyards, who were sometimes forced to sell all the wine a person could carry for just several pennies. At about the same time in France, Jean-Antoine Chaptal introduced *chaptalization*, a practice of adding sugar to deficient grapes so that fermentation would yield a higher alcohol content. Dr. Gall spread the word about this process in Germany. However, chaptalization was scorned by purists and the economic situation worsened for the poorer German wines. In despair, many of the lower-class growers sold their vineyards for a pittance and emigrated to Australia and the Americas.

A list of the best wines of Bordeaux was made for the Great International Exhibition of 1855 in Paris. French wines had been classed and divided a number of times, but this marked the first time that any official order of graded wine quality had ever been promulgated. Brokers and merchants accepted price history as the best measure of worth. There was instant criticism of the Classification of 1855—chiefly that it included only the great wines and was limited to the vineyards of the Médoc and Sauternes. Eventually adjustments were made to the Classification in order to rectify legitimate complaints, but, by and large, it has withstood the test of time very well. (See chapter 6 for a fuller discussion of the system.) Curiously, the very same noble four growths listed by the Englishman Bruneval more than a century earlier were awarded the coveted Premier Grand Cru Classe.

The advent of the 1855 Classification signaled a new era in wine growing. The practice of dividing and classifying districts, subdistricts, and specific vineyard growths was accompanied by the growing acceptance of scientific precepts. Because of the breakthroughs in microbiology made by the great nineteenth-century French chemist Louis Pasteur, people finally began to realize that fermentation was not a magical process and that spoilage was not caused by spontaneous generation; more and more vintners understood that these processes were caused by the yeasts and bacteria that Pasteur had identified. In fact, it was during his experiments with wine that he discovered microbes. In 1866 Pasteur wrote that

> when one sees beer and wine go through profound alterations because these liquids have been the host to microscopic organisms, one is obsessed by the thought that the same kind of thing can and must happen sometimes with men and with animals.

Wine masters handed down their new-found expertise to their apprentices, and succeeding generations began to leave much less to chance. Research yielded new materials and techniques by which wines could be made and preserved with consistently higher quality. The age of packaging arrived, with the widespread use of labels adorning previously naked bottles.

Private wine collections became the vogue among the aristocracy in both Europe and America. During the latter 1800s the death of Sir Walter Trevelyan brought about the probate of his London estate, which included an extensive wine cellar. Among some of the prized bottles found were some very old bottles of Hock, the oldest being from the superb vintage of 1540! Some of the 1540 vintage was opened in 1961, when it was 421 years old, and declared sound—very old, of course, but other than some browning from oxidation, the wine was pleasant.

The prospects for wine growing and wine appreciation seemed brighter than ever before, but disaster loomed just ahead.

THE PHYLLOXERA BLIGHT

The *Oidium* fungus, a powdery mildew that can devastate a grape crop, invaded France in 1847 and spread to the rest of western Europe several years later. American vines were naturally resistant to the disease, a fact that interested European winegrowers to the extent that they imported some vine stocks from the United States for experimentation. Little did anyone know that these plants carried a louse, *Phylloxera vastatrix,* which would prove to be far more destructive than the *Oidium.* It was first discovered in 1868 by Planchon in southern France. Unseen by the *vignerons,* the *Phylloxera* attacked the roots of the vines and spread throughout vineyards very quickly, killing most of the French vines in less than twenty years.

The root louse spread considerably slower in Germany than in other European countries—the first report of the scourge there came from the Palatinate (Rheinpfalz) in 1874.

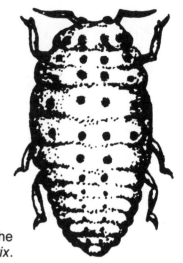

The root louse that devastated Europe's vineyards: the *Phylloxera vastatrix*.

By 1880 many vineyards on the Continent were lost, and many of the financially ruined winegrowers, thinking that the demise of the vine in Europe was upon them, emigrated to Africa, Australia, and North and South America.

One suggestion made for ridding the vineyards of the killer root louse was to flood vineyards long enough to drown the pest but not rot the vines. Unfortunately, most of the vineyards in Europe were on hillsides, which made flooding impossible.

Grafting, which had been studied since the time of the Roman naturalist Columella, proved to be the most effective technique in combating the *Phylloxera* invasion. The classic European varietal scions were grafted upon American rootstocks, which were immune to the louse. Hundreds of thousands of these rootstocks were imported from the United States each season until the massive project was completed. Never before or since have such massive resources been employed in the salvation of an agricultural industry. The project proved to be successful, and the great vineyards of Europe were preserved, thriving still today on American roots.

Appellation control by the French government required that only certain designated varieties could be replanted in each specific vineyard district (see chapter 6). This proved to be some compensation, at least, for the blight, in that many of the vague regional and subregional boundaries were more clearly defined. As well, many of the original patchwork vineyards that had existed prior to the *Phylloxera* were established anew with specific varietal selections.

Nevertheless, as mentioned before, the *Phylloxera* disaster brought ruin to many winegrowers in Europe, forcing them to emigrate in large numbers. Those that came to the United States brought new philosophies and skills to the fledgling American wine industry. This European seed found a most fertile soil in America.

THE NEW WORLD

In comparison to the 6000 years of wine-growing history in Europe, the 400-year span of American vines and wines seems miniscule. But it should be remembered that most of the major development in the Old World took place during this same 400-year span. Few modern-day European wine producers can boast of owning vineyards founded prior to the seventeenth century.

The destruction caused by Napoleon at the start of the nineteenth century and the *Phylloxera* toward its close forever altered the wine map of Europe. European wine masters had to pick up the pieces of crumbled monastic wineries and afflicted vineyards. The process of rebuilding was titanic—and so was its success. As a result, twentieth-century enophiles can now appreciate wines such as the world has never known before. The American wine industry, suffering a disaster even more devastating than the *Phylloxera*, has also undergone a massive effort of regeneration. And it has occurred, with astonishing results, in the fifty or so years since the repeal of Prohibition.

The grapevine grows abundantly in the United States. In nearly every state one type of vine or another can be grown. Of the fifty-odd species and thousands of varieties known, a greater selection of types can be grown in the United States than in any other country.

Some species of the grapevine are native to America, and, doubtless, these are what Leif Erikson found when he first visited the North American continent. the following passage comes from *The Discovery of America in the Tenth Century*, written several centuries ago by Charles C. Prasta:

Leif, son of Eric the Red, bought Byarnes' vessel, and manned it with thirty-five men, among whom was also a German, Tyrker by name. . . . And they left port at Iceland, in the year of our Lord 1000.

But when they had been at sea several days, a tremendous storm arose, whose wild fury made the waves swell mountain high, and threatened to destroy the frail vessel. And the storm continued for several days, and increased in fury, so that the stoutest heart quaked with fear; they believed that their hour had come. . . Only Leif, who had lately been converted to Christ our Lord, stood calmly at the helm and did not fear; . . . And, behold! While he spoke to them of the wonderful deeds of the Lord, the clouds cleared away, the storm lulled; and after a few hours the sea calmed down, and rocked the tired and exhausted men into a deep and calm sleep. And when they awoke, the next morning, they could hardly trust their eyes. A beautiful country lay before them . . . and they cast anchor, and thanked the Lord, who had delivered them from death.

A delightful country it seemed, full of game, and birds of beautiful plumage; and when they went ashore, they could not resist the temptation to explore it. When they returned, after several hours, Tyrker alone was missing. After waiting some time for his return, Leif, with twelve of his men, went in search of him. But they had not gone far, when they met him, laden down with grapes. Upon their enquiry, where he had stayed so long, he answered: "I did not go far, when I found the trees all covered with grapes; and as I was born in the country, whose hills are covered with vineyards, it seemed so much like home to me, that I stayed a while and gathered them." . . . And Leif gave a name to the country, and called it Vinland, or Wineland.

An enchanting story, and convincing, as wild grapevines are still prolific along the coastline of eastern America.

A ship's log kept by navigator Giovanni da Verrazano dated in 1524 made note of North Carolina vines and the possibility of making wine from them.

French Huguenots settled in Florida during the mid-1500s and made America's first wines from some of the native grapes found there. This fruit was from the species *Vitis rotundifolia*—commonly known today as the muscadine varieties. The New World grapes must have seemed strange to the Huguenot wine masters since, first of all, muscadines ripen their fruit by individual berries in small clumps, rather than in bunches, and, secondly, the flavor of the muscadines is very pronounced when compared to the more subtle taste values of the Old World *Vitis vinifera* grapes.

In 1565 Sir John Hawkins, a British admiral, reported upon winemaking from the native Florida grapes during his visits there. It seems likely that the Florida wines met with little favor among the early settlers.

Farther north, Captain John Smith wrote of his observations in Virginia during the early seventeenth century:

Of vines great abundance in many parts that climbe the toppes of highest trees in some places, but these beare but few grapes.

There is another sort of grape neere as great as a Cherry, they [probably Indian natives] call *Messamins*, they be fatte, and juyce thicke. Neither doth the taste so well please when they are made in wine.

Beauchamp Plantagenet, in a London-published text that described the colonies, made these observations of the native grapes,

Thoulouse Muscat, Sweet Scented, Great Fox and *Thick Grape*; the first two, after five months, being boiled and salted and well fined, make a strong red Xeres [Sherry]: the third, a light claret; the fourth, a white grape which creeps on the land, makes a pure, gold colored wine.

The "Great Fox" that Plantagenet mentioned was probably a variety of *Vitis labrusca*—a species that bears its heavily scented fruit in bunches, or clusters. Even in modern times *foxy* is a rather loose organoleptic term used to describe the aroma and flavor that is typical of the *labrusca* species, the variety Concord being a prime example.

Even farther north, more native vines were discovered in the early seventeenth century by the Frenchman, Samuel de Champlain, as he explored the islands of the St. Lawrence River. One of these islands was so overgrown with vines that Champlain 347 named it "Bacchus Isle." No doubt these grapes were also of the species *Vitis labrusca*.

The colonists often built their community inn or tavern near their church without much concern that the evils of wine, rum, ale, and punch drinking would contaminate their religious fervor. Between church services the worshippers would gather round the tavern's log fire, enjoying food, drink, and good fellowship. Vineyards were both public and private, but surely the wines left a lot to be desired.

Disappointment with the native American vines, and the unfamiliar wines they made, no doubt prompted the plantings of the European *Vitis vinifera* varieties in many of the colonies during the 1600s. The London Company of Virginia may have made the first attempt at growing Old World grapes in the New World. Lord Delaware brought from France some vines and viticulturists to establish the Virginia vineyards in about 1620. The project did not succeed, however, and the colonists blamed its failure on the French winegrowers' mishandling of the vines.

As the seventeenth century progressed, hope continued that the European vines could be successfully grown in the New World. Viticulture was encouraged through economic incentives and even required by law in some places. In New York wine could be made and sold without taxation. Virginia promulgated a law whereby "all workers upon corne and tobacco shall plant five vynes . . . upon penaltie to forfeit one barrell of corne."

Governor John Winthrop of Massachusetts planted vines on Governor's Island and, in Maryland, Lord Baltimore established vineyards. Near Philadelphia, William Penn had a vineyard plot where he tried to grow the classic Old World grapes. In Georgia, at Savannah, the enthusiastic Abraham de Lyon, from Portugal, planted a large-scale vineyard in 1730. Despite the encouragement of the colony, the project failed, a contemporary historian reporting that Lyon's vineyard, "which was to supply all the plantations . . . resulted in only a few gallons, and was then abandoned."

King Charles II ordered vines to be planted in Rhode Island—yet another useless attempt to grow the *Vitis vinifera*. John Mason offered to trade the British monarch all of what is now New Hampshire in return for 300 tons of French wine, but Charles II refused.

The major inspiration for the frustrated hopes of the early colonial *Vitis vinifera* pioneers was, of course, the profusion of wild vines: if the native vines grew so luxuriantly, they reasoned, then the cultivated European varieties should do all the better. The failures were, of course, not the fault of any of the *vignerons* or experimenters, but, rather, of the then-unknown *Phylloxera* root louse and several other maladies. These adverse conditions thwarted eastern American winegrowing for more than two centuries.

Widespread discouragement among the colonists over their continued failure with the *Vitis vinifera*—or with grapes of any kind, for that matter—may account for the lack of significant wine-growing advances during the early 1700s.

Thomas Jefferson maintained a very keen interest in American vineyards, but continued to import wine from Europe. As secretary of state, Jefferson chose the wines for President Washington; and when Jefferson became president, he paid for his wines out of his own pocket, keeping careful inventory records. He also assisted in stocking the presidential cellars of John Adams, James Madison, and James Monroe.

The first cultivation of native American grapes is credited to John Alexander, a Pennsylvanian whose viticultural research in the latter part of the eighteenth century brought forth the aptly named Alexander grape. The Alexander became famous for its heavy production of fruit and stalwart resistance to disease. The wine from Alexander, however, met with considerably less approbation.

Wine elevator from Thomas Jefferson's wine cellar to the dining room at Monticello. (Source: R. deTreville Lawrence, Vinifera Wine Growers Association.)

In 1809, following some of his own unsuccessful vineyard experiments, Thomas Jefferson stated that

> it will be well to push the culture of this grape [Alexander] without losing time and effort in the search of foreign vines which it will take centuries to adapt of our soil and climate.

But Jefferson was not the only early viticulturist with good foresight. William Penn also suspected that the proper course was to plant the native vines. More than a century before Alexander, William Penn advised "to fall to Fining the Fruits of the Country, especially the Grape, by the care and skill of Art . . . [rather than to send for] foreign Stems and Sets."

In Jessamine County, Kentucky, a Swiss settlement abandoned their efforts to grow the Old World *Vitis vinifera*, but they did not surrender their wine-growing talents altogether. Moving across the Ohio River to the Indiana side, the settlers founded a new colony called Vevay, namesake of the important wine-growing village of Vevey back in their native Switzerland. Native American vines were grown in the new Vevay settlement that became one of the largest grape-growing areas in America prior to the mid-nineteenth century. The whole southeastern Indiana region along the Ohio River was often referred to as "Little Rhineland." The Swiss were led by John Dufour, who insisted that some of his grapes were *Vitis vinifera*. Dufour and his grapes attracted the interest of a number of wine enthusiasts, including Thomas Jefferson and Henry Clay, but none of these experts recognized the vines as being of a European type.

Later, John Adlum, from Georgetown, D.C., introduced the *Vitis labrusca* variety Catawba, named for the Catawba River in Buncombe County, North Carolina, where the vine supposedly originated. The more delicate nature of Catawba brought it quickly to the attention of winegrowers. Without modesty, Adlum informed the world that he had given a greater service to America by introducing this new grape than if he "had paid the national debt."

Thomas Jefferson never lost his optimism that American wine growing would eventually be achieved on a commercial scale, despite his fondness for the fine wines from Europe. He foresaw in 1808 that "we could in the United States make as great a variety of wines as are made in Europe, not exactly of the same kinds, but doubtless as good." And later,

> wine being among the earliest luxuries in which we indulge ourselves, it is desirable it should be made here and we have every soil, aspect & climate of the best of wine countries . . . these South West mountains, having a S.E. aspect, and abundance of lean & meager spots of stony & red soil, without sand, resembling extremely the Cote of Burgundy from Chambertin to Montrachet, where the famous wines of Burgundy are made.

Jefferson kept a "garden book" at Monticello from 1766 to 1826 in which he kept the data of his vine plantings and experiments. Among his notes are recorded the planting of "30 plants of vines from Burgundy and Champagne with roots, 30 plants of vines of Bordeaux with roots." Several years following was another entry reporting the planting of several famous Italian vines, which included *Trebbiano, San Biovetto,* and *Aleatico,* among others. The garden book does not, however, show any significant success at the Monticello vineyard in testing the French and Italian vines.

Despite the tenacious interest that Jefferson had in wines and wine growing, he was only a moderate wine imbiber. The servants at Monticello attested to this temperance—Isaac, a member of the household staff reported that "he [Jefferson] was very fond of wine and water. . . . I never heard of his being disguised in drink."

Doubtless neither Adlum, Alexander, nor Jefferson knew that, to the West, in what is now New Mexico, the prized *Vitis vinifera* had been successfully grown more than a century before by Spanish explorers along the banks of the Rio Grande. Apparently the *Phylloxera* that destroyed the European vines in the East could not endure the hot desert sand. The variety grown was probably Mission, which had been grown in Mexico since the early sixteenth century under the direction of Cortez.

THE FRANCISCAN MONKS

Although the Papago Indians made wine from the giant Saguaro cactus in the Southwest desert since prehistoric times, winegrowing as it is now known was pioneered in western America, as in Europe, by the Roman Catholic church.

The "island" of California was first recognized by Pope Alexander VI in 1493. Spain made expeditions to explore the California coast in 1542 and 1602. The conquistadors found new frontiers to explore along the western shores of the Americas, and vineyards were established in their wake. The European vines flourished in the western New World; in fact, the new wine industry succeeded so well that, in 1595, the Spanish king decreed that new vineyard plantings be terminated in the provinces. This decree was intended, of course, to conserve sales of Spanish wine to the New World, and it remained in effect for about 150 years. It offers an interesting historical parallel to a similar decree made by Rome some 1500 years earlier to curtail vineyard plantings in its colonial provinces.

And yet, despite the order from Madrid, the Franciscan missions continued planting vines in the Americas. The first vineyard in the *Baja*, or lower California, was established at Mission Xavier by Father Juan Ugarte in the late 1690s. Development of the vines was slow since the soil was poor, thin, and rocky in that locale.

Gaspar de Portolá, explorer-captain of the Eighth Company of Dragoons, arrived in Mexico from Spain in 1767. The following year he was ordered by General José de Galvez to establish missionary settlements in *Alta* (upper) California to prohibit Russian fur trappers and British explorers from taking over the Spanish territorial claims.

De Portolá embarked upon his mission project in March of 1769 with a small force of soldiers and a devout missionary priest, Padre Junípero Serra. Serra's task was to teach the Indians the ways of Christianity in order to subdue any pagan violence that might be encountered. The procession arrived in California in July of the same year, and Serra raised the Cross that marked the first mission, which was called "San Diego." Since Padre Serra knew he would need wine, he brought the vine and planted the very first vineyard in California.

The mission chain proceeded northward, each a hard day's ride apart, along what became known as the "El Camino Real." By 1771, the vineyard at the San Gabriel Mission had become a large plot and was called the *viña madre*, or "mother vineyard," because of its superior soil and weather conditions. By the end of the eighteenth century Serra had carried his Mission vine to five outposts in southern California: San Diego, San Juan Capistrano, San Buenaventura, San Gabriel, and Santa Barbara. The vines flourished in the California climate, and the wines they produced, though perhaps not of the finest quality, were abundant. In all there were twelve missions constructed as the El Camino Real progressed northward to San Luis Obispo and beyond—the last begun by Father José Altimira at Sonoma in 1823.

The *Vitis vinifera* continued to prosper in California, under Mexican rule, until after the War of 1846. Padre Serra's Mission vine proved to be hardy and vigorous and became exceptionally well adapted to California. Some specimens eventually grew to become truly magnificent vines. The Carpinteria vine, for instance, according to the U.S. Department of Agriculture, had a trunk nearly 3 feet in diameter and once yielded 8 tons of grapes in one vintage! According to Ruth Teiser in her book *Winemaking in California* the Carpinteria vine was dug up and sent off to the 1876 Exposition in St. Louis.

BIRTH OF THE WINE INDUSTRY IN THE EASTERN, MIDWESTERN, AND SOUTHERN UNITED STATES

Perhaps the first commercial American winery was the Pennsylvania Vine Company, situated near Philadelphia, started by Pierre Legaux in 1793. Legaux was a Frenchman determined to succeed in growing French grapes, but once more such a project failed, and his only survivor was the native American variety Alexander. In the early 1820s Legaux's venture was forsaken. Another early winery was constructed near York, Pennsylvania, by Thomas Eichelberger in 1818.

Located in Orange County, New York, at Washingtonville, about 50 miles northwest of New York City, the Brotherhood Winery has a vast expanse of caves that challenge the magnificence of many in Europe. Founded in 1816 by a French immigrant shoemaker, Jean Jacques, the Brotherhood remains the oldest operating winery in the United States.

Wine master Nicholas Longworth built a majestic winery near Cincinnati, approximately 50 miles northeastward along the Ohio River from Vevay, Indiana. Longworth was so highly impressed by Adlum's Catawba grape that he planted a large acreage of the variety near his winery in the early 1820s. Longworth made the first "Champagne" in America, labeling his product with the honest name of "Sparkling Catawba." Longworth held his product in great esteem, declaring that his "Sparkling Catawba" was even superior to the sparkling wine from Champagne in France.

Henry Wadsworth Longfellow, a revered wine critic and connoisseur, was intrigued by the lofty claims of Nicholas Longworth and paid a visit to the Ohio winery in the mid-1850s in order to taste Longworth's wine. Impressed and convinced, Longfellow penned an exalted poem in 1854, entitled *Ode to Catawba Wine,* which proclaims:

> Very good in its way
> Is the Verzenay
> Or the Sillery soft and creamy;
> But Catawba wine
> Has a taste more divine,
> More dulcet, delicious, and dreamy.

Nicholas Longworth, the first
American commercial
"champagne" vintner.

The wine of Longworth must have been truly remarkable, as Longfellow's testimonial rated it superior to the French Champagne from Verzenay—a most praiseworthy comparison.

The Church, this time a Protestant denomination, also had a profound influence upon the development of the wine industry in eastern America. Elijah Fay, a Baptist deacon, is credited with having planted the first vineyard in western New York State in 1818. More notable, however, are the vineyards of central New York State nestled among the Finger Lakes. Legend has it that, when God finished making the Heavens and Earth, he laid his hand upon that particular chosen soil to bless his creation—hence, the great handlike impression that distinguishes the beautiful Finger Lakes topography. Geologists point out, however, that the gorges and hills of the Finger Lakes region resulted from the clawing effects of the Ice Age.

In either event, St. James Episcopal Church still stands today as the landmark in Hammondsport, at the southern tip of the "thumb" of the Finger Lakes, Lake Keuka, where the New York State wine industry began. Father William Bostwick propagated cuttings of Catawba and Isabella, another native *Vitis labrusca* variety, into roots and planted them behind the church in 1829 in order to make wine for the Anglican Eucharist.

The success of Bostwick's work became well known in Finger Lakes and attracted the interest of several prospective commercial winemakers. In 1860 Charles Champlin, heading several other investors, founded the Pleasant Valley Wine Company just south of Hammondsport, in Rheims, New York. The original cave was lined with stone walls more than 6-feet thick, a magnificent cellar that remains a monument to the first federally licensed winery in America.

Champlin's obsession was to make the finest "Champagne" in the New World, certainly to improve upon the already-lauded wines of Longworth in Ohio. He employed the costly and painstaking *méthode champenoise* (Champagne method of making sparkling wines). Jules Masson, a French wine master, was hired by Champlin to insure that no detail was overlooked in his determined quest for the very finest New York State "Champagne." In 1871 a tasting of some of the first wine from Pleasant Valley was held at the Parker House in Boston. Among the prestigious critics was Marshall Wilder, then president of the American Horticultural Society, who proclaimed that Champlin's sparkling wine was a "great" wine from the new "Western" world—the famous "Great Western" name was thus born and remains the trademark of the Pleasant Valley Wine Company.

The early 1860s marked the beginning of a promising era for American winegrowing. In no less than twenty states and territories significant vineyard planting and winery investments were taking place. Mary Todd Lincoln was the first to serve American wines in the White House, and French winegrowers admitted that California could grow Old World grapes well enough to be "capable of entering serious competition with the wines of Europe."

The success of Champlin and Longworth, among others, awakened new commercial wine-growing interests in the East and prompted considerable vineyard expansion, in turn bringing about a fierce competition in the marketplace for the consumer's dollar.

On the west side of Lake Keuka, several miles north of Hammondsport, the Gold Seal winery was founded in 1865 by Clark Bell and his associates. John Widmer from Switzerland founded the Widmer Winery in Naples, New York, just south of Canandaigua Lake and a few miles west of Lake Keuka. Bernard McQuaid, a Roman Catholic bishop from Rochester, founded the O-Neh-Da Vineyard near Hemlock Lake—another example of the Catholic church's influence. These were the principal ventures in entrepreneurial wine producing in the early history of the Finger Lakes Region, and they brought with them a growing need for supporting goods and services such as the manufacture of cooperage.

The new market potential for casks and vats enticed cooper Walter Taylor, descendant of a sailing ship captain, to set up a cooperage shop in the Finger Lakes Region at Bully Hill, just several miles northwest of Hammondsport. Taylor's farm was in an area known for large stands of white oak timber and, high

Walter Taylor, founder of the Taylor Wine Company, 1888. (Source: Greyton H. Taylor Wine Museum.)

on Bully Hill, overlooked miles and miles of the young but dynamic New York State wine industry. Taylor was also a winemaker, but his expertise laid in the crafting of fine cooperage, much of which was in service at the local wineries under credit agreements.

The New York State wine-producing capacity continued to grow faster than the market's propensity to consume, and the competition proved to be too much for many of the lesser wineries. Walter Taylor was ultimately forced to take action upon his delinquent accounts receivable when more and more winemakers became financially troubled. Among his collections was a significant amount of bulk wine that Taylor and his three young sons, Fred, Clarence, and Greyton, promptly placed in inventory: and so the family suddenly found itself quite deep in the wine business. During the next half-century the Taylor family parlayed this somewhat impromptu start in the wine business into one of the single largest wineries in the world.

During the mid-1800s the Catawba and Isabella grape varieties found their way to Missouri and were adapted to yield large bounties of fruit. This success attracted widespread plantings, much the same as in New York. Many of the Missouri growers were inexperienced with grapes, however, and did not recognize infestations of the dreaded Black Rot. The attack of this disease and others throughout the heartland of America caused discouragement once more, even among dedicated believers. A large number of the Old Swiss growers at Vevay, Indiana, moved to northern Ohio, where they joined German immigrants in founding the viticultural region that still exists today in the Lake Erie Islands and Sandusky area.

In Cincinnati, a Dr. Kerr introduced the variety Norton's Virginia. Some of the few grape-growing enthusiasts that remained in Missouri became interested in the new Virginia selection and planted some rather small acreages of the variety. A University of Missouri professor, George Husmann, regarded the red wine from Norton's Virginia as promising, but Nicholas Longworth proclaimed the variety worthless.

Ephraim Bull, from Concord, Massachusetts, introduced eastern viticulture to the Concord grape in 1854 after about seven years of testing. The Concord was bred from disease-resistant *Vitis labrusca* varieties primarily, and despite the astronomical cost of $5 per vine, it was of interest to the sparse wine industry remaining in Missouri.

With Norton's Virginia and Concord rekindling enthusiasm in Missouri once more, large acreages of vineyard again appeared. By the mid-1860s vineyards had expanded to very large proportions, making Missouri suddenly the leading grape-producing state in the Union. It was during this time that the first assistance came from America to help combat the *Phylloxera* root louse in Europe.

Nurserymen Bush and Meissner of St. Louis published their initial catalogue in 1869, and by 1876 a French translation was being used by European winegrowers for ordering the rootstocks necessary for the great grafting project in the Old World.

The finest years for Missouri viticulture in the nineteenth century proved to be the 1860s. Again, production exceeded demand, though, and by 1870 the Missouri growers were meeting with market resistance and had to cut back—allowing California to take the lead as the highest-ranking state in vineyard acreage, a position that the Golden State has never since relinquished. Professor Husmann also moved to California, where he proclaimed that "this [California] was the true home of the grape."

The Post and Wiederkehr families settled in the hamlet of Altus, Arkansas, during the 1880s. Descendants from these families still operate their separate wine-growing businesses nestled among the beautiful hills in the northwestern corner of the state.

As the Alexander, Catawba, Isabella, Norton's Virginia, and Concord had become champion grape producers in the North, so the muscadine variety, Scuppernong, became the pride of the South. The name was derived from the Indian word for the *sweet bay tree, Ascuponung*, which appears on early Washington County, North Carolina, maps as the name of the river there. By 1800 the name had evolved to Scuppernong, and censustaker James Blount, a decade later, reported that 1,368 gallons of wine were made in the town of Scuppernong. The following year the *Raleigh Star* termed the fruit, "The Scuppernong Grape."

North Carolina's first commercial winery was founded by Sidney Weller in 1835. He later sold the business to Dr. Francis Garrett and his brother, who were very successful with both grape juice and wine. But it was Francis Garrett's son, Captain Paul Garrett, who was to make the biggest splash with wine in the South. Paul Garrett learned the business from his uncle, and in 1900 young Garrett opened his own winery, Garrett & Co. Garrett quickly built a wine empire, with seventeen facilities in six states generating millions of dollars in revenue. His most famous and best-selling product were the wines sold under the "Virginia Dare" label.

The Montevino vineyard owned by Dr. Joseph Togno of Abbeville was a good example of wine growing in South Carolina in the 1860s, as was the Benson and Merrier Winery at Aiken.

Georgia, a top wine-producing colony and state since the mid-1700s, recorded nearly a million gallons' production per year by the 1880s. J. M. Taylor was a winegrower in Rienzi, Mississippi, during the 1870s, and, by the turn of the century, the Magnolia State could boast of no fewer than thirty-one commercial wineries in operation.

E. M. Erskine, in a British Consul report to his government in 1859 stated:

The banks of the River Ohio are studded with vineyards, between 1,500 and 2,000 acres being planted in the immediate vicinity of Cincinnati, with every prospect of a vast increase.

In Kentucky, Indiana, Tennessee, Arkansas, and generally, in at least 22 out of the 32 states now constituting the Union, vineyards of more or less promise and extent have been planted.

A special U.S. Department of Agriculture study in 1900 revealed that Alabama and Texas together had nearly 2,000 acres of vineyard, while Kansas and Missouri accounted for some 11,000 acres. New York and Ohio combined provided for more than 22,500 acres, with Pennsylvania tallying fifty-seven operating wineries.

Thomas Volney Munson generated much of the viticultural interest in the Southwest—primarily from his experimental vineyards at Denison, Texas. Munson's name is still revered by grape enthusiasts in memory of his intensive work in combating the European *Phylloxera* blight, in the breeding of grapevines, and for the book he wrote, *Foundations of American Grape Culture*. Though few of T. V. Munson's cultivars are grown commercially in modern times, his name has been immortalized by the species *Vitis munsoniana*—a name given to a native grape lineage with which he worked most of his life. It was Munson who said, "There is no more delightful and healthful employment than vine culture."

BIRTH OF THE WINE INDUSTRY IN CALIFORNIA

As merchant ships began to stop more frequently at ports along the Alta California coast, the missions of the El Camino Real came increasingly into contact with the outside world—which, in turn, brought about increased wine production during the early 1800s.

This growth was short-lived, however, as the Mexican revolt against Spain resulted in the curtailment of all agricultural endeavors by the Missions. The situation worsened, and some of the early church vineyards in California were abandoned and others destroyed by the enraged monks. Consequently, while the birth of the California wine industry must be credited to the Catholic church, its development is due primarily to the laity.

Joseph Chapman planted the first commercial vineyard in California on the Los Angeles pueblo land in 1824. Chapman was originally an Easterner who had gained experience in viticulture by working at Junípero Serra's Santa Ynez and San Gabriel Missions.

Jean-Louis Vignes, a native of Bordeaux, planted about 100 acres of vines in southern California prior to 1833. The vineyard became the property of two Sansevaine brothers, nephews of Vignes, in the 1850s. The Sansevaines reportedly brought to their vineyard cuttings of several varieties of *Vitis vinifera* from France, but no record exists of what the selections were or how they performed.

With the concentrated efforts of the monks, winegrowing had developed faster in southern than in northern California. But, with the Mexican loss of California to the United States in 1846 and the gold rush in 1849, that situation quickly reversed itself. Many European winegrowers emigrated to the San Francisco area, seeking refuge from political oppression in Europe. California welcomed this new populace and encouraged land investments for vineyards. The State Agricultural Society stated that "capital put into vineyards would bring greater returns than when outlayed in fluming rivers for golden treasures."

Much of the credit for the founding fatherhood of the north-coast California wine industry is given to Count Agoston Haraszthy, an exiled Hungarian.

Count Agoston Haraszthy. (Source: Buena Vista Winery.)

Haraszthy initially emigrated to Wisconsin in the early 1800s, building a beautiful stone winery near what is now the village of Prairie du Sac and planted grapevines. His vines died, however, presumably from either the *Phylloxera*, the harshness of Wisconsin winters, or both. In any event, Haraszthy migrated to the Sonoma Valley, north of San Francisco, about a year before the gold rush.

Haraszthy's optimism over the possibilities of quality winegrowing became very influential in northern California. He developed the Buena Vista Vinicultural Society and was determined that the wine industry should be built upon a sound foundation. Haraszthy's speeches and articles prescribed that only the finest varieties of *Vitis vinifera* should be planted in only the choicest land, and that only the latest viticultural methods be used. In 1861 Governor Downey delegated Haraszthy to make a trip to Europe so that he could select the finest varieties of grapes there and bring back cuttings of them to California. About 300 different varieties were shipped, but difficulties in handling and labeling the plant materials resulted in some of the varieties becoming either mislabeled or lost altogether. It took years to untangle the puzzle of identifying the vines—some of which, such as the now famous Zinfandel, have yet to be positively traced.

The estate and winery at Buena Vista were lavish, their cost eventually leading to Haraszthy's bankruptcy. With further financial support denied, Haraszthy rather mysteriously left America. The many classic vines of the Old World remained, however, and have since become a perpetual monument to his dedication.

A few miles to the east of Sonoma is the magnificent Napa Valley, perhaps the finest wine-growing region in all of the North American continent. The village of Yountville in the valley honors the memory of George Yount from North Carolina, who first planted Mission grapes there during the 1840s.

A number of choice European varieties were planted in the Napa Valley by the end of the 1850s, some finding their way from Haraszthy's Sonoma project and others from Samuel Brannan, who had made a selection of classic vines during a personal tour through Europe.

The reputation of the wines being grown in the little valley spread rapidly; Robert Louis Stevenson commented in the 1880s that the Napa locale was "where the soil has sublimated under sun and stars to something finer, and the wine is bottled poetry." Stevenson went on with his lauds, comparing Napa wines with those from the great growths of Bordeaux and Burgundy—namely Château Lafite and the Clos de Vougeot.

The future seemed very bright indeed, but Sonoma and Napa vines were soon attacked by the *Phylloxera* root louse in much the same manner as in Europe. California winegrowers did not notice the disease at first; unwilling to admit they had grave problems, they ignored it even after it had laid seige to entire vineyard plots.

George Yount, first viniculturist
in the Napa Valley. (Courtesy:
Bancroft Library the University
of California, Berkeley.)

Having studied wine growing in Michigan and Mississippi, Eugene Waldemar
Hilgard, of later *Hilgardia* fame, was named the first professor at the grape and
wine laboratory at the University of California. Through the work of Hilgard and
the ex-Missourian, Husmann, the *Phylloxera* was finally defeated in California as it
had been in Europe, with primarily Missouri rootstock materials used for grafting.

Paul Masson came to California from Burgundy in the late 1870s and took a job
working for Charles Lefranc. Along with his father-in-law, Étienne Thée, Lefranc
had worked vineyards a few miles from Los Gatos, south of San Francisco, since
the early 1850s. Masson married Lefranc's daughter and continued his employment in the family business. Following the death of Lefranc, Masson bought out
the interest of his brother-in-law and founded the "Paul Masson" Champagne
Company. Paul Masson was adept at making sparkling wines, and, by the close of
the 1880s, the Masson "Champagne" was winning praise in local circles. At the
turn of the century, both Great Western and Paul Masson "Champagnes" were
winning medals for excellence, even in Europe. The Paul Masson brand, dating
from the 1852 plantings of Lefranc's father-in-law, Étienne Thée, remains one of
the oldest continuous brand names in California.

With the success of such new wine masters as Masson, there was a general
feeling that the potential of the California wine industry was limitless. But as in
New York and Missouri earlier in the century, wine growing was developed far in

excess of demand. This situation was aggravated further by schemers of the "get-rich-quick" variety who manufactured poor-quality and/or immature wines. The market crashed in the late 1860s, bringing about a national depression for California wines. Some wine merchants, especially in the East, took hideous advantage of the situation by selling "strange compounds labeled in imitation of the best brands of California wines." By the celebration of the American centennial wine prices had fallen to less than 10c per gallon. Fear on the part of winegrowers led in 1879 to some of the first uprootings of American commercial vineyards. The *Phylloxera* also contributed to this decline by rampant destruction of much vineyard acreage in California.

The better-established wine producers survived the wine depression during the 1870s with minor setbacks, but the industry leaders learned that more technical and economic knowledge was required before California wines would become the American standard.

Hilgard wrote in 1879 that

> as the depression was, beyond doubt, attributable chiefly to the hasty putting upon the market of immature and indifferently made wines, so the return of prosperity has been, in great measure, the result of steady improvement in the quality of the wines marketed—such improvement being partly due to the introduction of grape varieties better adapted than the Mission grape to the production of wines suited to the taste of wine-drinking nations.

Two colossal individuals led the recovery of California wine growing in the 1880s. George Hearst made a fortune in mining, became a U.S. senator, and helped launch the career of his son, publisher extraordinaire, William Randolph Hearst. Hearst senior also purchased a 400-acre tract in Sonoma, but *Phylloxera* promptly killed his vines. Undaunted, Hearst ordered new vines grafted upon the American *Phylloxera*-resistant rootstocks, replanted, and ultimately reached a production capacity of nearly a quarter-million gallons of wine annually. Leland Stanford, railroad magnate and patron of Stanford University, built a half-million-gallon winery among the 350 acres of vineyard he owned near San Jose. By 1888 his output had reached more than a million gallons. But because of projects such as these, California vineyards were once again expanding to the point of overproduction. This depression was even worse than the one during the previous decade—grapes were sold for less than $10 per ton and wines for less than 8c per gallon.

To make matters even worse another mysterious disease was found in vineyards, principally in the Los Angeles vicinity. Vines rather suddenly became defoliated and died. This condition, which bewildered plant pathologists for decades, was finally identified as the dread Pierce's Disease, a bacterium introduced to the vines by a leafhopper insect. To date no cure has yet been found, and Pierce's Disease remains a formidable obstacle to the growth of *Vitis vinifera* and other species of vine in most southern areas of the United States.

The large wineries survived, primarily because of the seemingly limitless backing of their benefactors. But eventually they stagnated: Hearst's operation was sold by his widow to the giant California Wine Association, which in time embraced sixty-four winery properties, and Stanford's estate was purchased by Rudolf Weibel.

Some pioneers were not deterred by the economic and biological threats. In the Napa Valley near Rutherford, a Finnish sea captain, Gustave Niebaum, bought W. C. Watson's Inglenook vineyard in 1879 and built a stone winery in the Gothic style. Niebaum had an intense desire to grow the finest wine possible—an obsession that led to a strict "white-glove" policy in his winery. Inglenook in time made a name for itself as the "Schloss Johannisberg" of California. North of Inglenook, Georges de Latour, a Frenchman from Périgord, bought a grainfield and orchard property upon which he planted vines personally selected from France. Fernande de Latour, his wife, named the small estate "beautiful place"—*Beaulieu*. Like Inglenook, Beaulieu produced top-quality wines, although it wasn't until much later that Beaulieu's products were fully developed and recognized nationally.

American vintners were invited by the French to enter their wines in competition at the Paris World Exposition of 1889. The results stunned the international wine scene: the Americans were presented forty-two medals by the French wine judges! Among the winners were Beringer, Cresta Blanca, Inglenook, Krug, and Schramsberg from California, as well as Stone Hill from Missouri and Great Western (Pleasant Valley Wine Company) from New York State.

PROHIBITION

It had been building for some eighty years—a disaster worse than any disease or depression that had yet been known to American vintners. It was a reflection of profound, and perhaps too rapid, change in the fabric of American life. The dynamic advances in industrial technology, a huge influx of immigrants coupled with a population explosion that brought on increased urbanization, lingering influences from the Victorian era, Protestant sectarianism, and the Civil War: the aftermath of all of these contributed greatly to the idea that alcohol, in any form, was sinful and a detriment to the welfare of mankind.

In Kansas, prohibition of the sale of alcoholic beverages was passed in 1880. The person behind this action was the infamous Carrie Nation, who assumed, at one

Carrie Nation equipped to do battle, from a late nineteenth-century poster. (Source: The Kansas State Historical Society, Topeka, Kansas.)

time or another, the roles of judge, jury, and executioner in taking action against any facility that may have had anything to do with an alcoholic beverage. Her disregard for private property and human rights spread quickly, and, as a result, much of our early American wine history was lost as books, diaries, and journals were burned by the Prohibitionists.

The first signal of national prohibition came with the "Dry Movement," whose proponents demanded that any mention of wine be struck from textbooks and from the *U.S. Pharmacopoeia*. The "Drys" published books claiming that the word *wine* in the Bible was really grape juice, while at the same time advocating the banning of classical Greek and Roman literature that mentioned wine. By the time World War I broke out in Europe, a total of thirty-three states had voted to go dry. By 1919, the Drys had succeeded in gaining wartime prohibition. The Eighteenth Amendment to the U.S. Constitution, in conjunction with the Volstead Act, brought total prohibition in 1920.

Vintners who had foreseen Prohibition coming geared up their production and marketing forces for medicinal, sacramental, and salted cooking wines that remained legal under the Volsted Act. Some wine masters went into the grape juice business, but many were forced to close their doors altogether. Those determined to keep drinking wine did sometimes find ways around Prohibition: fake churches and synagogues were founded for the purpose of dispensing legal sacramental wines, and wine was being prescribed as "medication" for all sorts of conditions. Of all the schemes, perhaps the most blatant was the sale of a variety of grape juice products with a "pill" of dehydrated dormant yeast attached for home winemakers. The complete package was usually labeled with a printed warning not to add the "pill," "because if you do, this will commence fermenting and will turn into wine, which would be illegal." But home winemaking soon became legal, with the head of each American household allowed to make up to 200 gallons per year for personal and family consumption. Some growers converted their vineyards from wine grapes to juice and table grapes, while others uprooted their vineyards in favor of other agricultural interests. The owners of the beautiful Stone Hill Wine Cellars at Hermann, Missouri, had the novel idea of remodeling the cellars into caves for mushroom farming. The Glen Winery in Hammondsport, New York, was transformed to a storehouse for Glenn Curtiss's World War I airplane parts.

A number of vintners desperately tried to make a go of their business in secret, illegally, as bootleggers. For the most part, though, such efforts were ultimately discovered and destroyed by the "T-men" who, standing amidst the rubble, would strike triumphant poses for photographers from local newspapers— serving to warn anyone else who would dare disobey Prohibition.

Some bootleggers prospered, especially those who had access to an underground network of people, methods, and machinery that were effective against the enforcement efforts of the T-men. In fact, California vineyards grew to comprise more than 640,000 acres during the middle years of Prohibition. Most of the grapes grown were of the variety Alicante Bouschet, which shipped and kept well in storage. More important was that this variety made such a dark and heavy wine that one gallon of crushed grapes could be mixed with another gallon or more of water and sugar. The wine that resulted, often referred to as "Dago Red," gave the bootleggers a beverage they could market cheaply to the working classes.

There were many attempts made for the reversal of the Volsted Act, as well as some proposals for modification of the Prohibitionist regulations, but to no avail. Yet despite the tenacity of the federal agents, the nation was being served alcoholic beverages in countless ways, perhaps the "speakeasy" being the most colorful and memorable. The greed of the bootleggers eventually made wine expensive, however, and, even worse, Prohibition had forced the wine and liquor industry into the hands of the criminal underworld. Never before had Thomas Jefferson's pronouncement that "no nation is drunken where wine is cheap" rung truer.

Finally recognizing that Prohibition was doing the nation more harm than good, Americans began to rally around the demand for Repeal. The impetus was, of course, not from the gangsters or bootleggers, for they had built a huge lucrative illegal business. Nor did the Repeal movement originate with the legal vintners; they were, for the most part, long since out of business (unless they had been able to continue operating with the production of medicinal and/or sacramental wines). The support for Repeal came, rather, from some force resembling a national conscience. Early in December in 1933, Repeal took effect, bringing to an end fourteen years of devastation to the American wine industry.

REPEAL

Few winegrowers in 1933 believed that American vines and wines could ever be resurrected to become a viable industry again, much less ever offer serious competition to the wines of Europe, which had continued to progress during the American Prohibition. An entire generation of Americans had become accustomed to moonshine and bathtub gin. Apart from the Italian-Americans who continued to endure "Dago Red," the American people found that the table wines available had degenerated into an unfamiliar "sour" foreign-type of drink. Many users of table beverages chose to stay with beer and whiskey, which resulted in very little demand for table wines. In addition, many states voted to remain Prohibitionist, especially in the Deep South—Mississippi remaining so until 1966. Other states voted in rigorous tax laws and government control, while still others regulated alcoholic strength and heavily restricted marketing activities. Repeal came during the midst of the Great Depression, which also impeded winegrowing recovery, and, consequently, many growers and vintners remained poor.

Perhaps the only good that may have come out of Prohibition was the setting of the stage for starting all over again. The Prohibition years effectively buried many of the traditional vines, wines, and practices that had been detrimental to the advancement of the state of the wine art. With the slate swept clean, there was now an opportunity to formulate a truly American wine industry, rather than a poor imitation of the European one. In any case, American vignerons and vintners, presented with the ruins of neglected vineyards, decayed cellars, and broken lives, began their work anew.

One of the first positive steps was the formation of the Wine Institute in California by a group of experienced winegrowers led by a young newspaperman and enophile named Leon Adams. The establishment of quality standards for wines and the belief that good-quality inexpensive table wine should be made and marketed to a wine-educated American public were two of the principal ideas expressed by the founders. Despite their scarcity of funds, vintners were persuaded, under the supervision of the California State Department of Agriculture, to tax themselves as a way of funding the Wine Institute. The Institute in turn used its resources to put together the educational materials necessary in the long struggle to win Americans from whiskey to wine. Subsequently, Adams wrote *The Wine Study Course*, which over the years has proved to be one of the most significant educational tools for promoting intelligent wine consumerism.

Unfortunately, along with the Wine Institute literature, there also came an array of articles and books written by pseudo-experts disseminating wine snobbery rather than real knowledge. The notions that only certain wines went with certain foods, that only certain wines at precise temperatures should be served in certain glasses, and other nonsense, confused and frightened the potential American wine consumer.

As the wine industry was reborn, American wines were once more served in the White House during the Roosevelt Administration. Roosevelt's assistant secretary of agriculture, Rexford Tugwell, suggested a tax exemption for beer and wine in order to swing Americans away from whiskey. Dr. Tugwell also ordered two experimental wineries to be constructed: one in Meridian, Mississippi, the other at Beltsville, Maryland. Though both of the centers were fully equipped, neither was ever allowed to proceed with any research. Despite the general acceptance of Repeal, there were still many Drys in influential places. Missourian Clarence Cannon, chairman of the House Appropriations Committee and a lifelong Prohibitionist, brought an abrupt halt to the wine experiment stations, declaring "no federal money shall go to any fermentation industry!" Cannon threatened to restrict the entire appropriation for the U.S. Department of Agriculture if the wine research was not stopped immediately.

It was during the late 1930s, however, that two pioneers were to make a permanent mark on the wine industry with two very different philosophies of winegrowing.

Philip Wagner was a newspaper editor in Baltimore and an amateur winemaker who, after visiting Europe, had become greatly interested in some of the little-known French-American hybrid vines. These grape types, named for the men who hybridized them, including Maurice Baco, Louis Seibel, Kuhlmann, Seyve-Villard, and others, had been developed as an attempt to save Europe from the *Phylloxera*. The idea was to breed new cultivars of grapes from parentages of *Vitis vinifera*, *Vitis labrusca*, and a number of other species, endeavoring to combine the disease resistance and high productivity of the American selections with the flavor quality of the European lines. From thousands of crosses, many new hybrids were developed, and a few of these captured Wagner's attention. Wagner was unsatisfied with the "foxy" character of the native Concord, Delaware, Elvira, Isabella, Ives, and Niagara varieties that were used in the eastern wine industry. The hybrids held out the promise of Old World type wines, and Wagner imported a number of the most choice selections, which he then propagated in his Maryland nursery. Philip Wagner befriended many figures in the New York State wine industry—Greyton H. Taylor, one of the innovative heirs to the Taylor wine business being the most noteworthy. Taylor planted a number of Wagner's French-American hybrids; and soon cultivars such as Aurora Blanc, Seyval Blanc, Rayon d'Or, Ravat Blanc, Chelois, Baco Noir, Maréchal Foch, Léon Millot, and Chambourcin were making news on the eastern American wine scene. Other cultivars, with numbers instead of names, were also planted, and thus began many years of evaluation of the suitability of various hybrids to the rigorous conditions of the Finger Lakes region.

Fred, Greyton, and Clarence Taylor. (Source: Wine East; photo by Linda Jones McKee and Hudson Cattell.)

The hybrids were instantly rejected by the *Vitis vinifera* purists and the *Vitis labrusca* traditionalists. To this day, considerable controversy surrounds the French-American cultivars. According to some, the hybrids are a viable alternative to native grapes and a serious competitor to the blueblood *Vitis vinifera*. To others, the hybrids are bastard children not worth planting on vineyard land.

The other pioneer of the 1930s in the East was Charles Fournier, who came from Champagne in France to the Gold Seal Vineyards in Hammondsport in 1934. Fournier was warned that *Vitis vinifera* would not survive the disease and harsh winters of New York State, but Fournier experimented anyway, and, being open-minded, also planted some of Wagner's French-American hybrids. During a 1953 wine industry meeting at the Cornell Experiment Station in Geneva, New York, Fournier met Dr. Konstantin Frank, a wine grower-refugee born in Russia. Frank told Fournier that he could grow the Old World grapes in New York State by selecting the proper rootstocks in grafting. This impressed the Frenchman, and he

Dr. Konstantin Frank (center) receiving the Vinifera Wine Growers Association's first Monteith Trophy from the late Elisabeth Furness, owner of Piedmont Vineyards, and R. deTreville Lawrence, Sr., president of the association. (Source: Wine East photo by Linda Jones McKee and Hudson Cattell.)

hired Frank to work in the vineyards of Gold Seal. In a rather quiet fashion they experimented together with the growing of *Vitis vinifera*, and, during the late 1950s, succeeded in cultivating the first commercial vineyards of Old World grapes in the eastern American wine industry. Their efforts paved the way for renewed *Vitis vinifera* interest among other eastern U.S. winegrowers.

World War II took a heavy toll on American wine growing; of the 1,300-odd wineries that had been licensed following Repeal, less than 300 survived after 1945. This, however, may now be seen as the dark hour before the dawn. The American wine industry did not have long to wait for the phenomenal rediscovery of table wines that Americans were to make in the post-war years.

THE AMERICAN WINE BOOM

The interest in table wines grew quickly in the late 1940s, perhaps nurtured by returning American servicemen who brought a newly acquired taste for wine from Europe. The quest for wine technology, particularly in table wine production, was again rekindled. The American Society of Enologists was founded in 1950 at the University of California at Davis, where wine researchers followed up the pioneering work of Hilgard. Funding was subsequently made available in other states for commencing or reestablishing viticulture and enology programs of study. As both European and American wine masters conducted intensive research and testing programs, the traditions of Old World methodology started giving way to innovations based on proven procedural results and new technology.

The forward steps were by no means confined to production; there were many new ideas for the marketing of wines as well. New distribution channels opened up better access to retail-shelf space, while more and more people began to visit the wineries for touring and sampling of wines. Wine lists were no longer offered exclusively in the high-class, urban restaurants, and sales-promotion pamphlets used wine cookery recipes and down-to-earth wine-serving tips to help the common person identify with wine.

One public relations program that gained much attention was that of George Lonz, whose winery was several miles out in Lake Erie on Middle Bass Island, off the shore of Port Clinton, Ohio. Lonz, a colorful character, devised tongue-in-cheek publicity releases of his wines surrounded by cheesecake photographs of the local ladies.

In Michigan, there was innovation in new wine types, particularly wines flavored with synthetic essences and other ingredients in somewhat the same style as the ancient Greek and Roman wines. A mixture of "Champagne" and "Sparkling Burgundy," called "Cold Duck," was credited, somewhat dubiously, to Michigan invention. It became an overnight national sensation and died in much the same fashion. Michigan also enacted a protective tax to provide an economic edge to the state's winegrowers, but the anticipated growth never materialized.

These types of approaches were pursued in other states as well, but the wine boom of the post-war years was ultimately built upon the success of high-quality, low-cost table wines.

Perhaps the most important contribution of all was a simple commonsense idea employed first by James Drummond in the Sonoma Valley during the late 1870s, of *varietal* labeling. While Drummond originated the notion, it was the late Frank Schoonmaker, a devoted and highly respected American wine authority, who really earned the credit for pioneering varietal labeling. Schoonmaker's concept was that the labels of American-made wines should carry the name of the grape variety, or cultivar, rather than continuing to borrow the traditional European generic names. A wine made from Pinot Noir grapes in a style similar to that of French Burgundy would no longer be labeled "California Burgundy," but "California Pinot Noir." The great German varieties, Johannisberg Riesling and Sylvaner, were much more honest and descriptive terms on labels than, say, "California Rhine Wine."

The conversion proved to be rather easy in California, especially in the Napa, Sonoma, and other northern valley districts where many of the classic Old World varieties had been grown continuously since the Haraszthy influence a century or so earlier. In the East, however, conversion to varietal labeling proved to be more difficult for vintners. The native American grape varieties such as Concord and Niagara were not internationally known, and the French-American hybrid cultivars were not yet widely planted. Consequently, many eastern vintners retained the practice of using the European generic names such as "New York State Burgundy," "Ohio Rhine Wine," and "Michigan Chablis," among many others.

There were some dynamic easterners, though, who were bent on making a name for their wines—or for themselves. Dr. Konstantin Frank left Charles Fournier and Gold Seal in order to start his own winery, Vinifera Wine Cellars in Hammondsport, New York. The name of his establishment revealed his continued faith that European grapes could be grown commercially in the harsh Finger Lakes climate. Frank's fiery determination and Old World charm made him something of a legend among eastern enophiles.

Walter S. Taylor, son of Greyton Taylor and grandson of the founding Taylor, became the patron saint among French-American hybrid aficionados. A legend of an entirely different kind than the late Dr. Frank, Taylor has cultivated a personal style that surpasses even the antics of George Lonz.

Young Taylor was fired from the family business in the late 1960s for having made remarks to the San Francisco press, inferring that water was added excessively to the wines made by the eastern vintners, including, of course, his own family Taylor Wine Company. Banished, Taylor promptly commenced wine-production operations on Bully Hill, at the original site of his grandfather's winery and cooperage firm.

Several years later the Taylor Wine Company was sold to Coca-Cola, which insisted that Walter Taylor discontinue the use of the Taylor name on his labels. In the midst of an ensuing lawsuit, Taylor, using a felt-tip pen, drew lines through the word "Taylor" on each of his wine labels. This was followed by his drawing masks upon the portraits of his father and grandfather that were displayed upon some of the Bully Hill labels and promotional materials. Walter Taylor lost the litigation, but his brilliant manipulation of publicity endeared the Bully Hill brand to many wine imbibers.

But the greatest advances during the wine boom took place in the enormous vineyard land of California, and there were several leaders of this monumental renaissance for table wines in America.

Almadén Vineyards of Los Gatos shares its heritage and founding date with the Paul Masson winery—they both are offshoots of the Étienne Thée vineyard of

Paul Masson. (Source: Paul Masson Vineyards.)

1852. Charles Lefranc, Thée's son-in-law, took over the property and named it Almadén. Later, Masson split off and started his own winery, but Almadén continued under Lefranc's son. Charles Jones reopened the winery following Repeal and sold it to wealthy San Francisco socialite Louis Benoist in 1941. Benoist hired restaurateur Louise Savine as chef and retained wine writer Frank Schoonmaker, the champion of varietal labeling, to become the Almadén wine advisor. Another notable member of the team was Mary Lester, a public relations expert. The combination of Savine's cuisine, Schoonmaker's wine direction, and Lester's magic hospitality proved to be irresistible to wholesalers and retailers, and Almadén sales leaped up dramatically. The great entertaining style of Benoist included a yacht, seven guest houses, and two airplanes. The acceptance of Almadén premium varietal table wines in America has become a monument to marketing success. The firm was sold to the National Distillers Corporation in the early 1970s. And re-sold to Hueblein in 1987.

Another of the great names during the post-war table wine enlightenment was the Sebastiani family who were based in Sonoma at the end of the El Camino Real. Samuele Sebastiani emigrated from Tuscany in 1896 and made cobblestones until he had saved enough money to purchase the Milani winery in 1904. Surviving Prohibition by making medicinal and sacramental wines, Sebastiani gave over the

Samuele Sebastiani. (Courtesy of the Bankroft Library.)

reins of the winery in 1934 to his son August. The business had already become successful, and the name Sebastiani was well known in the bulk-blending wine trade. Gifted with foresight, August committed large sums to the planting of Barbera, Cabernet Sauvignon, Pinot Noir, and other classic Old World varieties for the consumer-goods market. August, almost always seen in bib overalls, was also a superb wine master, and built one of the largest premium wine-producing firms in America.

Christian monks, so important to the history of wine, also played a part in the post-war American table wine upsurge. In this instance it was an order of Catholic teachers founded in France by St. Jean Baptiste de la Salle in 1680. Since the early 1880s these monks had made wine at their novitiate near Martinez, California, but in 1930 they purchased a small stone cellar and vineyards located northwest of the city of Napa and renamed the property Mont La Salle. During these early years at the new facility, Brother Timothy studied chemistry and apprenticed himself to the masters of his trade. When he was made cellar master, the wine appreciators of California had found a true artist. The wines and brandy of the Christian Brothers became heavily distributed throughout the West, and ultimately growth was so rapid that Mont La Salle became too small. In 1950 The Christian Brothers bought a huge stone winery in the Napa Valley near St. Helena, and Brother Timothy expanded the output of his craft to fill the huge national demand.

In 1880 Andrea Sbarboro, a San Francisco banker, headed a foundation that helped displaced Italian and Swiss immigrant farmers settle in the Mendocino Valley. Sbarboro mortgaged plots of land to each farmer and provided food, wine, shelter, and wages in return for growing grapes—with a small portion of the wages retained for installment payments upon a twenty-five-year mortgage. The terrain was reminiscent of the hill country near Asti in the Piedmont of Italy, and so the colonists named their new homeland Asti.

Sbarboro's plan met with two initial problems: the first vintage spoiled to vinegar and the farmers refused to make any more mortgage payments. Pietro Rossi, a pharmaceutical graduate from San Francisco, agreed to take charge of the situation, and his leadership brought prosperity to the Italian-Swiss colony. Awards and medals were won for wine quality in both America and Europe. New vineyards and winery buildings were added to the colony to meet the growing pre-Prohibition demand. The El Carmelo Chapel, the famous "church shaped like a wine barrel" was built in 1907. But Rossi was killed accidentally in 1911, and the colony was taken over by the giant California Wine Association.

Rossi's twin sons, Edmund and Robert, bought back the vineyards and winery prior to the end of Prohibition, when it was supplying grapes, grape juice, and concentrate to home winemakers. In the years between Repeal and World War II, the Rossi brothers' leadership advanced Italian-Swiss Colony to become the third-

Brother Timothy, F.S.C., cellar
master, The Christian Brothers of
California.

largest winery in America. In post-war times, the production of very low-cost
table wines, along with very clever marketing programs, has made the operation
even larger.

Like the original Italian-Swiss colony immigrants, brothers Ernest and Julio
Gallo also had their roots in Asti of Piedmont, Italy. The Gallos first grew grapes at
Antioch, California, where their parents had immigrated from Italy via South
America. During Prohibition the Gallo family shipped grapes for home winemak-
ing to Chicago and New York, but instead of the common Alicante Bouschet
variety, Ernest, Julio, and their father Joseph marketed the higher-quality
Zinfandel.

Following Repeal the brothers became interested in the commercial wine business and leased a warehouse in Modesto from the Santa Fe railroad in which to
commence their initial operations. Demand for their bulk wine grew rapidly, and
by World War II the Gallo wines were also competing for consumers in the retail
marketplace. The marketing genius of Ernest and the production expertise of Julio
combined in a management team of unequaled success. In less than four decades
Gallo became the largest single winery in the world. The contemporary production facility has more than 40 acres of underground aging cellars, contains its own
glass bottle-manufacturing plant, and requires the fruit from more than 100,000
acres of vineyard each vintage.

Following the great wine boom of the 1960s and 1970s, the combined output of Almadén, Paul Masson, the Christian Brothers, Sebastiani, Italian-Swiss Colony, and Gallo accounted for more than 60 percent of the entire U.S. wine market, with Gallo alone supplying more than 25 percent.

The large wineries are not the entire story, however, especially during very recent times, when names such as Stag's Leap, Robert Mondavi, Sterling, Château St. Jean, Glenora, Haight, Meredyth, and many other small U.S. wineries are challenging the finest European competition, and in some cases, even winning against them in European-tasting comparisons.

Much of this success must be credited to the technological advances developed through academic research all across the United States. As already mentioned, the University of California at Davis has pioneered viticulture and enology research, but other institutions now also have significant programs addressed to these disciplines. Cornell University, the University of Florida, Fresno State University, Michigan State University, Mississippi State University, Ohio State University, Pennsylvania State University, the University of Missouri, and Texas A&M each have major wine-growing research and teaching efforts, and smaller programs exist at other colleges and universities. This new technology ultimately leads to the production and marketing of better-quality wines at lower cost, as well as educating American wine consumers to greater wine appreciation. This, in turn, leads to the demand for higher standards from the wine industry, plus more realistic governmental regulation. In 1980, wine consumption finally surpassed that of distilled spirits in America—the realization of a lifelong dream for Wine Institute founder Leon Adams.

The success of American winemakers and the enthusiasm of American wine consumers have not gone unnoticed in Europe: the Old World industry fully realizes that the new appreciation for wine in America represents new opportunities for them—both in marketing and investment. The European portion of the wine market in America is currently only about 22 percent, but this shows a gallonage increase from 11 million to more than 100 million since 1960. European investment in American wine-growing properties is rather commonplace nowadays—the Heidsieck-Sonoma and the Mondavi-Rothschild alliances in California being two particularly illustrious examples.

Perhaps most significant of all is the remarkable enthusiasm generated among wine appreciators for American wines of the twentieth century. With each new or enlarged chapter of the Brotherhood of the Knights of the Vine, the Les Amis du Vin, The American Wine Society, and other dynamic wine-oriented consumer groups, this enthusiastic appreciation of wine grows.

CALLAWAY

VINEYARD & WINERY

1 9 8 7

"MORNING HARVEST"

Chenin Blanc—Dry

TEMECULA, CALIFORNIA

CELLARED & BOTTLED BY CALLAWAY VINEYARD & WINERY®
TEMECULA, CALIFORNIA   ALCOHOL 12.0% BY VOL.

RESERVE

1981

Napa Valley

FUMÉ BLANC

Dry Sauvignon Blanc

ALCOHOL 13.7% BY VOLUME

PRODUCED AND BOTTLED BY

ROBERT MONDAVI WINERY

OAKVILLE, CALIFORNIA

5

THE WINES OF
AMERICA

*W*illiam Massee wrote a book about American wine that he entitled *Joyous Anarchy*, a phrase that only begins to suggest the astonishing variety of American wines. Unlike most other wine-producing countries, the United States is home to a vast number of grapevine species. Almost every state supports a variety of species and an even larger selection of hybrids. Virtually every state has a commercial wine industry of some size.

The United States encompasses a huge geographical area and climate conditions ranging from desert to rain forest and from arctic to subtropical. Compared to this country, most other major wine-producing nations, such as France or Italy, are small in size and rather uniform geographically. Because the wealth of native species made it possible to develop hybrids and rootstocks that were adapted to nearly every climate and soil condition, the grape is found nearly everywhere in this country. It is this genetic heritage that makes viticulture possible virtually nationwide.

The United States ranks sixth in worldwide production of wine, behind Italy, France, the Soviet Union, Spain, and Argentina. In consumption per capita it ranks twenty-eighth—at just over 2 gallons per person. The Italians—who not only produce a lot of wine, but also drink a great deal of it—consume about 30 gallons per person per year. American consumption of table wine has increased

The author is indebted to Elizabeth A. Schwartz for her research and writing contributions to this chapter. She has studied the American wine industry rather extensively and has written a number of articles about wine for the popular press.

TABLE 5-1   United States-Approved Viticultural Areas (1984)

	Acres of Appellation	Acres in Vineyard		Acres of Appellation	Acres in Vineyard
CALIFORNIA					
Anderson Valley	57,600	600	Willow Creek	10,000	30
Arroyo Seco	18,240	8,500	York Mountain	10,000	300
Carmel Valley	19,200	120			
Chalk Hill	17,280	1,000	**MARYLAND**		
Chalone	8,640	120	Catoctin	170,000	85
Cienega Valley	7,000	a	Linganore	57,000	52
Clarksburg	64,640	2,300			
Cole Ranch	150	61	**MICHIGAN**		
Dry Creek Valley	80,000	5,000	Lake Michigan		
Edna Valley	22,400	650	Shore	1,128,000	14,472
El Dorado	80,000	416	Fennville	75,000	a
Fiddletown	11,500	310	Leelanau		
Green Valley-Solano	1,920	400	Peninsula	211,200	150
Guenoc Valley	4,396	a	**MISSISSIPPI**		
Howell Mountain	14,080	200	Delta	a	a
Knights Valley	36,240	1,000			
Lime Kiln Valley	2,300	80	**MISSOURI**		
Livermore Valley	128,000	3,000	Augusta	a	a
Los Carneros	a	a	Hermann	51,200	102
McDowell Valley	2,230	540			
Merritt Island	5,000	425	**NEW YORK**		
Napa Valley	320,000	26,000	Finger Lakes	2,560,000	13,300
North Coast	3,008,000	68,000	Hudson River		
Paicines	20,000	4,500	Region	2,240,000	1,000
Paso Robles	614,000	4,000			
Potter Valley	27,500	1,000	**OHIO**		
Russian River Valley	96,000	8,000	Grand River Valley	46,000	2,300
San Pasqual Valley	9,000	a	Isle St. George	640	350
Santa Cruz Mountains	a	a	Loramie Creek	3,600	16
Santa Maria Valley	80,000	a	**OREGON**		
Santa Ynez Valley	182,400	1,200	Willamette Valley	3,300,000	2,000
Shenandoah Valley	10,000	1,200	**PENNSYLVANIA**		
Sonoma Valley	a	5,000	Lancaster Valley	225,000	42
Sulsun Valley	11,200	800			

	Acres of Appellation	Acres in Vineyard		Acres of Appellation	Acres in Vineyard
VIRGINIA			Ohio River		
Monticello	800,000	160	Valley (OH,		
North Fork			WV, IN,		
of Roanoke	a	49	& KY)	16,640,000	570
Rocky Knob	9,000	10	Shenandoah		
			Valley		
WASHINGTON			(VA & WV)	2,400,000	250
Yakima Valley	665,600	23,400	Walla Walla		
			(WA & OR)	175,560	60
MULTISTATE					
Lake Erie					
(NY,OH,					
& PA)	2,608,000	40,000			

a unspecified.
Adapted from *Wine Educators Chronicle* (Summer 1984).

rapidly in the last fifteen years, however, while consumption of distilled spirits in the same period declined, although, in the mid-1980s, wine consumption has leveled off.

About 76 percent of the wine consumed by Americans is made in America. Of this percentage, California is by far the largest contributor, with 68 percent. The other 8 percent is distributed among the balance of the forty-nine states. Although California is unquestionably the vinous heartland of the country, there is still a great deal of vitality in the wine industry in the rest of the nation. This is true despite a declining overall percentage of wine produced by other states. While the number of large bottling plants in the eastern states dwindles, the number of small producers who grow their own grapes and make their own wines continues to increase. State and local authorities are taking a more active role through supportive legislation in encouraging "farm wineries" to operate.

It's true that many European governments exercise far more control over vineyard boundaries, grape varietal selection, and winemaking technique than is found in America. This does not mean, in itself, that wines from America are automatically inferior. On the contrary, vastly improved technologies have been introduced into American wine growing, due to an ever-increasing commitment to research by U.S. academic institutions. Some of these technological advances, now world standards, have made possible the expansion of wine growing to new areas in America. As the number of small estate wineries grows, Americans have been showing more and more interest in wine. This in turn has sparked action by the federal government to allow American "appellations of origin," approaching the traditional European style.

Appellations of origin in America are decreed by the U.S. Congress following successful petition by organized winegrowers representing political or geographical areas. The U.S. Bureau of Alcohol, Tobacco and Firearms (BATF) administers each petition and requires that cause be shown why each individual area should be considered for such special recognition. Following approval by Congress, the appellation of origin may then be displayed upon labels of wines whose grapes have been grown within the boundaries of that particular district. The system does not yet include the restrictions and classification standards found in Europe that result in wines of many different pedigrees. Nevertheless, the federal government has, with this recognition of distinction between appellations of origin, opened the door for the initiation of an American wine classification system at some time in the future. New appellations of origin are being approved rather rapidly, and consequently the list keeps changing. The list provided in table 5-1 was in effect at the time of this writing.

Great wines are often distinguished from more ordinary ones by the grape variety used to make the wine, weather conditions during particular growing seasons, and vineyard nobility (quality). With irrigation, frost-protection devices, and other scientific breakthroughs, we have won some control over the vagaries of weather. We can do less about nobility. But perhaps it matters less: for there can be no question that it is what transpires in the winery that determines the ultimate quality of any crop, even one grown in the most prestigious vineyard under the best of weather conditions. The simple fact remains that while poor wines can be made from good grapes, good wines can never be made from poor grapes. And, in America, we can grow some very good grapes.

CALIFORNIA

California is the premier wine-producing state in the United States, producing more than 450 million gallons annually. New York, the second-largest wine-producing state, has less than one-tenth the California volume, an indication of how far California outdistances its closest state competitors in wine production. With nearly 600 wineries, the California wine industry is so large that only comparatively few of its superb members will be portrayed in detail here.

Viticultural Districts

The many vineyards and wine-growing areas of California may be geographically categorized in a variety of ways. Some of the new appellations of origin mentioned earlier help somewhat to suggest an ordering. But confusion arises even here because some appellations actually exist within others. For example, "North Coast" includes another appellation—that of "Sonoma County." In turn, "Sonoma County" includes "Dry Creek Valley." Nevertheless, we must employ some system: the outline below indicates California's major regions and districts. The cities, towns, and valleys listed within districts are subdesignations meant to serve as landmarks to help locate major vineyard areas.

NORTH COAST COUNTIES

Napa Valley

Calistoga	Oakville	Spring Mountain
Carneros	Pope Valley	Stag's Leap
Chiles Valley	Rutherford	Yountville
Mayacamas	St. Helena	
Mount Veeder	Silverado Trail	

Sonoma County

Alexander Valley	Dry Creek Valley	Kenwood
Carneros	Geyserville	Knights Valley
Chalk Hill	Guerneville	Russian River Valley
Cloverdale	Healdsburg	Sonoma Valley

Mendocino and Lake Counties

Amador	McDowell Valley	Shenandoah Valley
Anderson Valley	Potter Valley	Ukiah Valley
Eldorado	Redwood Valley	

CENTRAL COAST COUNTIES

Alameda	Carmel Valley	Contra Costa
Arroyo Seco	Cienega Valley	Edna Valley

CENTRAL COAST COUNTIES *cont'd.*

Greenfield
Hecker Pass
Livermore Valley
Monterey
Paicines

Paso Robles
Pinnacles
Salinas
San Benito
San Luis Obispo

Santa Barbara
Santa Clara
Santa Cruz
Santa Ynez
Ventura

SOUTHERN COAST COUNTIES

Cucamonga
Riverside

San Bernardino

San Diego

CENTRAL VALLEY

Clarksburg
Davis
Fresno
Kern

Lodi
Madera
Merced
Modesto

Sacramento
Stanislaus
Tulare

This is by no means an exhaustive list, but will serve to structure the discussion of California vineyards and wineries that follows.

Climate

The climate of California is dominated by two primary influences: the mountains and the Pacific Ocean. Two long ranges of mountains run from north to south through the state—the Coastal ranges on the west and the Sierra Nevadas on the east. Between the two ranges is the broad, flat Central Valley. All along the coastline small valleys and bays open channels for cool ocean air to penetrate inland, moderating temperatures and creating a broad range of climates in comparatively small areas. Fog is created where the ocean air meets the warmer inland air, and the degree to which this fog penetrates inland often determines which varieties of grapes can be grown in a given area. Terms such as *North Coast, Central Coast,* and *South Coast* in California refer to areas, some quite far inland, where the penetration of ocean air dominates, or at least moderates, the climate. The Central Valley, where this ocean influence is not felt, remains uniformly warm and dry and varies little from north to south, despite the fact that it is nearly 400 miles long.

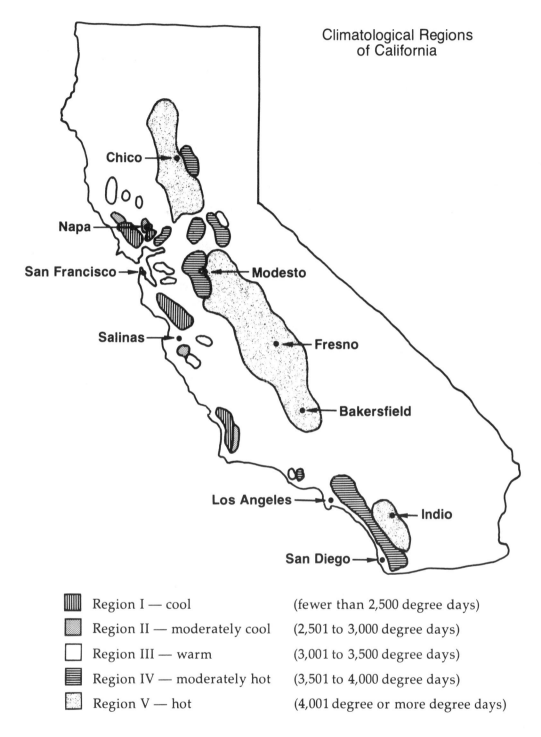

Climatological Regions
of California

	Region I — cool	(fewer than 2,500 degree days)
	Region II — moderately cool	(2,501 to 3,000 degree days)
	Region III — warm	(3,001 to 3,500 degree days)
	Region IV — moderately hot	(3,501 to 4,000 degree days)
	Region V — hot	(4,001 degree or more degree days)

Researchers at the University of California at Davis have devised a system for classifying viticultural areas according to "heat-summation" to assist growers in determining what varieties would grow best in a particular area. Heat-summation, an indication of the relative length and warmth of the growing season, is determined by calculating the total number of degree-days in a certain area. A degree-day is calculated by averaging each day's temperature, in Fahrenheit, between the last spring frost and the first autumn frost and subtracting 50 degrees, which is the temperature at which a vine becomes active. Thus, if the average temperature on a given day was 68 degrees, it would add eighteen degree-days to the total heat-summation for the area. By adding up the season-long total of degree-days you arrive at the heat-summation figure. On the basis of heat-summation, California was ultimately divided into five regions where grapes could be grown, ranging from Region 1, the coolest, to Region 5, the warmest. Region 1 is roughly equivalent to northern European vineyard regions such as the Rhein or northern Burgundy. Region 5 would be similar to a North African climate. Regions 1 through 3 are the areas best suited for growing the "noble varieties" and produce the highest-quality table wines and sparkling wines. Regions 4 and 5 are more appropriate to dessert wine and brandy production and those varieties of table wine grapes that can withstand very warm temperatures. The coastal districts generally range from Region 1 to Region 3, while the Central Valley and inland areas are Regions 4 and 5.

North Coast Counties

Napa County

North of San Francisco Bay and inland to the east of Sonoma County lies Napa County, site of the Napa Valley, California's and America's most famous wine region. (See color insert, figure 8.) Running in a northwestern arc against the eastern flank of the Mayacamas mountains, the valley is about 25 miles long and ranges from 1 to 5 miles in width. Because of the ocean influence, it is coolest in the south, where fog rolls northward from San Francisco Bay, and warms as one proceeds northward, away from the influence of the fog. At the southernmost end of the valley, where the Mayacamas mountains disappear and Napa and Sonoma Counties converge, is the Los Carneros region. This is the coolest region and is best known for table wines produced from the varieties Chardonnay and Pinot Noir. North of the city of Napa the climate begins to warm, and plantings of Cabernet Sauvignon start to dominate in the vineyards near Oakville and Rutherford. North of St. Helena to Calistoga, at the head of the valley, is the warmest region, shading into Region 3 of the University of California rating system. Most of the Napa Valley, however, falls into the Region 1 or Region 2 categories.

In addition to the ocean influence, soil and topography also play a large part in Napa viticulture. The valley floor is primarily clay while the upland soil is gravelly

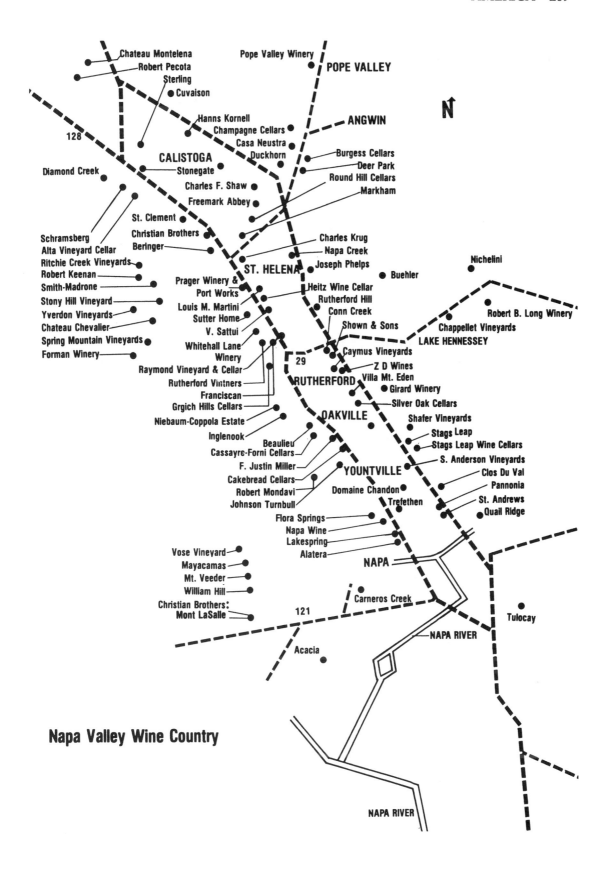

Chateau Montelena
Robert Pecota
Sterling
Cuvaison
Pope Valley Winery
POPE VALLEY

ANGWIN

N

128

Hanns Kornell
Champagne Cellars
Casa Neustra
Duckhorn
CALISTOGA
Stonegate
Diamond Creek
Charles F. Shaw
Freemark Abbey
Burgess Cellars
Deer Park
Round Hill Cellars
Markham

St. Clement
Schramsberg
Alta Vineyard Cellar
Christian Brothers
Beringer
Charles Krug
Napa Creek
Joseph Phelps
Nichelini
Ritchie Creek Vineyards
Robert Keenan
Smith-Madrone
ST. HELENA
Buehler
Prager Winery &
Port Works
Heitz Wine Cellar
Rutherford Hill
Robert B. Long Winery
Stony Hill Vineyard
Louis M. Martini
Conn Creek
Yverdon Vineyards
Sutter Home
Shown & Sons
Chappellet Vineyards
Chateau Chevalier
V. Sattui
LAKE HENNESSEY
Spring Mountain Vineyards
Whitehall Lane
Winery
Caymus Vineyards
Forman Winery
Z D Wines
Raymond Vineyard & Cellar
29
Villa Mt. Eden
Rutherford Vintners
RUTHERFORD
Girard Winery
Franciscan
Silver Oak Cellars
Grgich Hills Cellars
OAKVILLE
Shafer Vineyards
Niebaum-Coppola Estate
Stags Leap
Inglenook
Stags Leap Wine Cellars
Beaulieu
S. Anderson Vineyards
Cassayre-Forni Cellars
F. Justin Miller
Clos Du Val
Cakebread Cellars
YOUNTVILLE
Pannonia
Robert Mondavi
Domaine Chandon
St. Andrews
Johnson Turnbull
Trefethen
Quail Ridge
Flora Springs
Napa Wine
Lakespring
Alatera
Vose Vineyard
NAPA
Mayacamas
Mt. Veeder
William Hill
Christian Brothers:
Mont LaSalle
121
Carneros Creek
Tulocay
NAPA RIVER
Acacia

Napa Valley Wine Country

NAPA RIVER

loam. The upland soils drain and warm quickly—thus providing greater frost protection than the valley floor, which is much more prone to frost. Decisions about which varieties to plant in a specific vineyard area must take into account not only the heat-summation of the area, but the usual time of bud break (when buds break open and shoots commence to grow) for the grape variety and the danger of late spring frost.

Two principal roads run through the valley: Highway 29 on the west and the Silverado Trail on the east. Between them lies the valley floor. Many of Napa's wineries are nestled on the slopes and hillsides to the east and west of the valley floor in such subdesignations as Mount Veeder, Spring Mountain, Stag's Leap, Chiles Valley, and Pope Valley.

Napa Valley

Just north of the city of Napa, in the Oak Knoll district, is the historic Trefethen Vineyards, originally founded in 1886. In the late nineteenth century the wines sold under the brand name "Eshcol" were known for their outstanding quality. An "Eshcol" Cabernet Sauvignon won first prize in 1888 at the San Francisco Viticultural Fair. When the winery was sold to J. Clark Fawver at the turn of the century its fortunes waned. Fawver didn't drink wine, though he loved the vineyards. In 1940, at his death, the winery closed.

In 1968 the original Eshcol ranch and adjoining acreage was purchased by Gene and Katie Trefethen, and vineyardist Tony Baldini was hired to restore the vineyards. The Trefethen's son John became interested in reviving the winery, one of the oldest wooden-structure wineries in Napa Valley. In 1973, the first Trefethen Vineyards wines were produced. All Trefethen wines are estate bottled, though a good portion of the 500-acre wine crop goes to Domaine Chandon and other wineries. Trefethen makes varietal Chardonnay, Johannisberg Riesling, Cabernet Sauvignon, and Pinot Noir. They also produce an "Eshcol Red" and "Eshcol White," both of which are considered to be fine table wines at an excellent price. Their 1976 Chardonnay placed first in a blind tasting in Paris against some of the best white Burgundies of France.

Nestled in the bowl of an extinct volcano called Mt. Veeder in the Mayacamas mountains is the tiny Mayacamas Vineyards. These vineyards, terraced into the hillsides at well over 2,000 feet in elevation, are the highest in the Napa region. The old stone winery was built in 1889 by John Henry Fisher and was called Mt. Veeder Vineyards. Jack and Mary Taylor made their restoration of the vineyards and winery in the early 1940s a labor of love. They financed the operation by selling shares to friends at $10 per share, which entitled the owner to help out at harvest and buy the wine at reduced rates. On this very small scale the winery was successful, producing primarily Chardonnay and Cabernet Sauvignon. In 1968 the Taylors sold the winery to Robert Travers, a San Francisco stockbroker who fell in love with the wine business. Travers has maintained the high standards of the Chardonnay and Cabernet Sauvignon produced by Mayacamas. The winery is also known for occasional late-harvest Zinfandels, made when the properly matured grapes can be found. In recent years Travers has expanded the line to include Sauvignon Blanc and Pinot Noir.

The William Hill Winery, a relatively little-known winery named for its owner, has been getting rave reviews from the most knowledgeable wine critics. Hill owns approximately 700 acres of prime hillside vineyard land in Napa, one of the largest vineyard holdings in the valley. The vineyards are located primarily on Mount Veeder and Atlas Mountain. Hill believes that the highest-quality fruit is grown on hillside vineyards that produce low yields of grapes with great intensity of flavor. Working from that premise, he founded the William Hill Winery in 1976 and produced his first wines in 1978. Starting with very limited quantities, Hill produced a Cabernet Sauvignon in 1978, his first release, which was received

The ultra-modern fermentation and storage cellar at Domaine Chandon.

enthusiastically in the marketplace. His 1979 Cabernet Sauvignon and Chardonnay have also been extravagantly praised. The wines have great depth, intensity, and complexity.

About nine miles north of the city of Napa, near the town of Yountville, is Domaine Chandon, which represents the first major entry of a European wine company into California. (And it has been quickly followed by several others.) In 1973, Moët-Hennessy, the parent company of the French Champagne giant Moët & Chandon and the brandy producer Hennessy, bought 850 acres of prime land situated mostly in the cool Carneros district. The company announced plans to begin producing an American sparkling wine made in the traditional French *méthode champenoise*. A sparkling wine facility with a capacity of 3 million bottles was built near Yountville in 1977, complete with visitor facilities and a fine restaurant.

Domaine Chandon produces two sparkling wines: a Napa Valley Brut made from about two-thirds Pinot Noir, about one-third Chardonnay, plus a small amount of Pinot Blanc; and a Blanc de Noir that is 100 percent cold-pressed Pinot Noir. Cuvées are blended under the supervision of Edmond Maudière, who is also in charge of Moët & Chandon's wines in France. Domaine Chandon has been a phenomenal success story, which they attribute to the use of the highest-quality grapes coupled with nearly 250 years of experience in sparkling wine production. The winery, featuring a mini-museum containing antique vineyard and wine-making tools and equipment, is one of the premier tourist attractions of Napa Valley.

Cakebread Cellars is a small family-owned and family-operated winery in Oakville. Founded by Jack and Doris Cakebread in 1973, the winery makes Sauvignon Blanc, Chardonnay, Cabernet Sauvignon, and Zinfandel. Son Bruce Cakebread became winemaker there after graduating from the enology program at the University of California at Davis. The family owns 22 acres of vineyard in Napa Valley where their very special Sauvignon Blanc is grown. The winery, situated in the middle of the vineyards, was designed by renowned winery architect William Turnbull and won a design award from the American Institute of Architects.

When Gil Nickel bought an old stone winery in Oakville in 1979, the building had been closed since Prohibition and was in need of extensive renovation. Nickel, a member of a prominent wholesale nursery family in the Southwest, decided to replant the vineyards, restore the winery that had been built in 1885, and enter the ultrapremium wine business.

The winery is called Far Niente, from the Italian phrase *dolce far niente*, which means "it is sweet to do nothing." Nickel's first wine was a 1979 Chardonnay that was very well received. The winery now produces only Cabernet Sauvignon and

MAYACAMAS

1977
CALIFORNIA
ZINFANDEL
ALCOHOL 13½ % BY VOLUME
PRODUCED AND BOTTLED BY
Mayacamas Vineyards
NAPA, CALIFORNIA

NET CONTENTS
750 ML (25.4 FL OZ)

ALCOHOL 12%
BY VOLUME

CHANDON
Napa Valley
Brut

PRODUCED AND
BOTTLED BY
DOMAINE
CHANDON
YOUNTVILLE,CA

NAPA VALLEY
SPARKLING WINE
METHODE
CHAMPENOISE

Chardonnay, approximately 30,000 gallons of each annually when in full production. The first Cabernet Sauvignon was made in 1982 and was scheduled for release in 1985—the winery's hundredth anniversary. The old winery building, which is listed in the National Register of Historic Places, was built in the nineteenth-century style on several levels to avoid the need for pumping. Today the restored winery also has the distinction of containing the first wine cave or tunnel built in California since the late 1800s. Blasted out of hard rock, the cave extends 60 feet into the hillside.

The Robert Mondavi Winery in Oakville is an easily recognized landmark. The Spanish mission-style building with the bell tower is featured on the Mondavi varietal labels and is one of the most-photographed California wineries. Its founder, Robert Mondavi, still tireless in his 70s, is one of the most innovative and creative forces in the wine industry today. Son of Cesare and Rosa Mondavi, Robert came to California from Italy at the age of 10. When his father became a partner in the Sunnyhill winery (later Sunny St. Helena Winery), Robert came to work in the cellars. Subsequently, the family purchased the Krug winery in 1943, and Robert Mondavi got his first chance to move from bulk and jug wines to premium varietals. Convinced he could make and sell wines of the highest quality, he began his quest by replanting the Krug vineyards with better wine-grape varieties. Demand for the Charles Krug label grew, and the wine began to be sold nationally. Robert left Krug after a family disagreement and founded his own Robert Mondavi Winery in 1966.

Experimentation and education are the watchwords at Mondavi. Constantly searching for ways to improve his wines, Mondavi experiments painstakingly with fermentation techniques and methods of aging. His experiments with various types of oak and methods of coopering barrels are legendary. Mondavi's staff conducts many educational programs both at the winery and across the country. Mondavi also leads the industry in innovative marketing. In 1966 he pioneered the use of the term *Fumé Blanc* for Sauvignon Blanc produced in an aromatic, dry, wood-aged style. Since then sales have soared, increasing market potential for many other producers of the same wine type. Mondavi excels in the production of Cabernet Sauvignon and Pinot Noir, as well.

In 1980 Robert Mondavi announced a joint venture with the late Baron Philippe de Rothschild, of Bordeaux's renowned Château Mouton-Rothschild, to produce a wine combining the best of France and California. The first vintage of this wine, a 1979, was released as "Opus One."

Mondavi's commitment to remain in the vanguard of the industry has proved enormously successful. Starting in 1966 with a capacity of 100,000 gallons, the Mondavi family corporation today owns 1,100 acres of vineyard and two wineries with a combined capacity of 10 million gallons.

Trefethen
VINEYARDS

NAPA VALLEY
ESHCOL-WHITE WINE

This wine of 76% Chardonnay, 12% White Riesling, 10%
Gewürztraminer and 2% Pinot Noir "Blanc" is called "Eshcol"
to commemorate the name of our vineyard from 1886 to 1940.

GROWN, PRODUCED & BOTTLED BY
TREFETHEN VINEYARDS
NAPA, CALIFORNIA, U.S.A.
ALCOHOL 13.0% BY VOLUME

GRGICH HILLS

Napa Valley
CHARDONNAY
1981

 PRODUCED AND BOTTLED BY
GRGICH HILLS CELLAR, RUTHERFORD, CA
ALCOHOL 13.3% BY VOLUME

Moving from most modern to most traditional, Beaulieu Vineyard in Rutherford is generally considered to be the *grande dame* of the Napa Valley wineries. Founded in the early 1900s and operating continuously since that time, Beaulieu has a long and proud tradition of producing fine wines. In the lean years between the end of Prohibition and the late 1960s, Beaulieu was one of the few California wineries producing distinctive, elegant wines.

Georges de Latour, who founded the winery, had his roots in the wine industry in France. After a stint as a gold miner and some years as a purveyor of cream of tartar bought from Napa area wineries, de Latour entered the wine business on his own. Probably the most important decision he ever made was to hire a young winemaker of Russian descent named André Tchelistcheff to be his winemaker. Tchelistcheff arrived in time for the 1938 vintage and changed the face of the California wine industry. He pioneered new fermentation techniques and convinced de Latour to set aside a certain portion of the Cabernet Sauvignon for extra aging in small, oak cooperage and in the bottle. This wine, the "Georges de Latour Private Reserve" Cabernet Sauvignon of Beaulieu, has become the standard in California for Cabernet. Renowned for his discriminating palate and his ability to judge young wines, Tchelistcheff has since trained several generations of Californian winemakers.

Under the ownership of Heublein since 1969, Beaulieu has remained a leader in the production of premium table wines. Muscat de Frontignan, a distinctive dessert wine produced from a solera system dating to the 1960s, is outstanding. A new white varietal wine called "Melon," first produced in 1982, but now discontinued, was the only such varietal commercially produced in America. The grape, Melon de Bourgogne, is the variety from which the Muscadet wines of France are grown.

Just north of Beaulieu is Grgich Hills Cellars, named for its owners Miljenko (Mike) Grgich and Austin Hills. Hills, of the San Francisco coffee family, is the financial backer, and Mike Grgich is the wine-making expert of the operation. A Croatian by birth, Grgich came to this country in 1958 with a background in wine production and a degree in enology from the University of Zagreb. He worked for nearly twenty years at some of the best wineries in California, including Souverain, Christian Brothers, Beaulieu, Robert Mondavi, and Château Montelena, before getting the opportunity to start his own winery. During those years he refined his skills under the tutelage of such masters as André Tchelistcheff. Grgich became internationally celebrated overnight in 1976 when his 1973 Château Montelena Chardonnay won the gold medal in the famous comparative blind tasting by French experts of California Chardonnays and French white Burgundies. Several of the California wines did well, and the event marked the coming-of-age of California viticulture in the eyes of the world.

Grgich Hills started in 1977 and at least half of its small production each year is Chardonnay. Grgich Chardonnays consistently appear in the top ranking at competitions and tastings. They are most often described as complex with lots of varietal character. Grgich Hills also produces Sauvignon Blanc, Johannisberg Riesling, Cabernet Sauvignon, and Zinfandel.

Roy Raymond has been making wine for more than fifty years. He began working for Otto Beringer in 1933 and married Otto's daughter Mary Jane two years later. He remained at the Beringer winery for thirty-eight years, until the family sold it. At that time the Raymonds bought 90 acres on Zinfandel Lane near St. Helena and in 1974 started the Raymond Vineyard and Cellar. The winery has a capacity of 60,000 gallons, which is geared to the production of the vineyards. It's still a family operation—son Roy, Jr., manages the vineyard and another son, Walter, is the winemaker. The first estate-bottled Raymond wine, a botrytised, late harvest Johannisberg Riesling from the 1975 vintage, won a gold medal at the Los Angeles County Fair in 1977. The Raymond Cabernet Sauvignons have shown a consistently rich and powerful style.

Joe Heitz started his own winery in 1961 after years of teaching enology and working for a number of other winemakers—most notably André Tchelistcheff. The tasting room of Heitz Wine Cellars is on Route 29, just south of St. Helena. Until 1964, when Joe Heitz purchased the Spring Mountain Ranch a few miles east in the foothills, this was the winery as well. Although he produces a wide variety of wines, Heitz is without question most famous for his Cabernet Sauvignon. He has been using vineyard designations for his wines since the mid-1960s and the best known of these is "Martha's Vineyard," owned by Tom and Martha May, who sell their grapes to Heitz. Joe Heitz also produces a "Bella Oaks Vineyard" and a "Fay Vineyard" Cabernet Sauvignon, which have been attracting interest in recent years.

Heitz's winemaking style is distinctive. Although he grows some grapes himself, he prefers to purchase grapes from independent, area growers, which gives him the freedom to specialize in winemaking. He uses the word *guts* to characterize the style of wine he is striving for—a big, full-bodied character with age and depth. His Cabernets are aged for five years before release, much of that time in oak. His early Chardonnays were also outstanding, but the loss of one of his best vineyards to Pierce's Disease caused a decline in quality for a number of years. Since replanted, this vineyard should be producing again soon, and devotees of his early Chardonnays are eagerly awaiting the first release.

In 1922 Louis M. Martini, an Italian immigrant, started the L.M. Grape Products Company in Kingsburg in the southern Joaquin Valley. Believing Prohibition could not last, he survived by producing a grape concentrate for home winemakers called "Forbidden Fruit." But he wanted to produce good dry table wines, and he began building a winery on the southern edge of St. Helena in 1933 and producing wines there—while he continued to make the popular sweet wines in his first winery down south in Kingsburg. In 1940 he sold the Kingsburg winery and simultaneously released his well-made, well-aged table wines under the Louis M. Martini label—this was at a time when wines of such high grade were scarce in California. They caused an immediate sensation. His son Louis P. and his grandchildren have continued that tradition of premium-quality table wines at reasonable prices ever since.

To maintain this kind of reputation, the Martini family has kept up with the latest advances in viticulture and enology. The Martinis have been doing research in clonal selection of vines since the 1940s. They currently own vineyards in the Mayacamas Range in Sonoma County (the famous Monte Rosso Vineyards), Carneros, the Pope Valley, the Chiles Valley, the Russian River Valley, and Lake County. Each of these has been selected by the Martinis for its suitability to particular varieties. When all the sites are planted the total acreage will be approximately 1,500 acres.

All the Martini wines bear a California appellation of origin. As research has proved the superiority of certain vineyards for particular varieties, vineyard designations have been added to some of the varietal wines. Martini also sets aside some lots of wine of particular merit for their "Special Selection" designation. These wines receive additional aging before release. Martini reds such as Barbera, Cabernet Sauvignon, and Zinfandel are most often noted as their best.

Though Markham Vineyards is a relatively new winery in St. Helena, it is housed in a building dating from 1876. Formerly producers of bulk wine, Markham now makes a small amount of wine from its own vineyards in three separate locations in the Napa Valley. Each of the wines bears a vineyard designation, and owner Bruce Markham feels that the distinctive soils and microclimate of each vineyard are particularly suited to the grapes grown there. The winery currently produces Cabernet Sauvignon, Chardonnay, Johannisberg Riesling, Chenin Blanc, Sauvignon Blanc, and Muscat de Frontignan.

A short drive west of St. Helena, up the Spring Mountain Road, brings one to Spring Mountain Vineyards, probably best known today for the Victorian mansion featured in the television series, "Falcon Crest." Owner Mike Robbins began making wine in 1968 in the basement of another Victorian home in St. Helena. In 1974 he purchased the current property, famous in the nineteenth century as the Parrott estate, also a winery at that time. Robbins has built a new winery building on the site at Spring Mountain Vineyards where he makes Chardonnay, Sauvignon Blanc, Cabernet Sauvignon, and, recently, Pinot Noir. Although Robbins originally purchased many grapes from independent growers, he has

since replanted the abandoned vineyards at Spring Mountain and now makes a large share of his wines from his own grapes. Until recently, John Williams, former winemaker for Robbins at Spring Mountain, made distinguished wines both in California and New York. In addition, Williams also produced a very limited quantity of wine at Spring Mountain called "Frog's Leap," featuring a sporty frog in midair on the label.

The Christian Brothers, a Roman Catholic order of teaching brothers, decided to make wine commercially, as well as for their own sacramental use, at the same time that they moved their novitiate to Mont La Salle in the Napa Valley in 1931. The order was in severe financial straits, repeal of Prohibition was pending, and it seemed that commercial production of wine might help solve their financial problems. From that modest beginning came one of the great success stories of California wine history.

Under the guidance of the world-famous Brother Timothy, the Christian Brothers winery has developed a full line of table wines, dessert wines, and brandy. Their products are known for reliable, consistent quality and good value. Until very recently Brother Timothy eschewed vintage dating, preferring to blend his wines to consistent standards. In 1979, however, Christian Brothers began marketing vintage-dated varietals as well, in response to the changing demands of the marketplace.

Today Christian Brothers winery produces a total of about ten million gallons of wine and brandy annually. They have two facilities in the San Joaquin Valley where brandy and dessert wines are produced, as well as several other Napa facilities. The historic Greystone building in St. Helena, purchased in 1950, has been used to house their sparkling wine production, but is now reopened, following major remodeling. In 1973 an ultramodern fermenting facility was built in South St. Helena—a winery-in-the-round where all winemaking functions can be monitored from a central control area.

The Charles Krug Winery, begun in 1861, was the first commercial winery in the Napa Valley. Its founder was a Prussian immigrant who, after a few years' apprenticeship with Count Haraszthy in Sonoma, quickly developed a thriving business just north of St. Helena and established himself as the "wine king of Napa Valley" in the 1870s. In his heyday, Krug shipped wines to Europe and Mexico, as well as the East. But his fortunes declined with the onslaught of *Phylloxera,* and the winery was sold to financiers before Prohibition.

It was an ambitious Italian immigrant family that restored Charles Krug. As mentioned above, Cesare Mondavi bought the Krug property in 1943, primarily for his sons Peter and Robert, both of whom were interested in producing quality table wines. The Mondavi family quickly built a reputation for quality varietal table wines while they maintained a substantial bulk wine and jug wine business.

STONEGATE

Alexander Valley

1 9 7 9

Vail Vista Vineyard

Produced and bottled by Stonegate Winery
Calistoga, Napa Valley, California · Bonded Winery 4640
Alcohol 13.0% by volume

ALCOHOL 12% BY VOL.   750 ML. (25.4 FL.OZ.)

Hanns Kornell

BLANC DE BLANCS

CALIFORNIA
CHAMPAGNE

PRODUCED AND BOTTLED BY
HANNS KORNELL CHAMPAGNE CELLARS
ST. HELENA, NAPA VALLEY, CALIFORNIA

NATURALLY FERMENTED IN THIS BOTTLE / METHODE CHAMPENOISE

The Krug facility is often compared with the nearby Louis M. Martini winery: both are relatively large family-owned and family-operated wineries with a reputation for good and consistent quality at a reasonable price. While Martini is usually cited for its reds, the Charles Krug whites are usually the highest quality in the line. The winery also produces jug wines under the CK label.

Beringer Vineyards, at the north end of St. Helena, is one of the most popular wine attractions in the Napa Valley. Its ornate Rhine House, with 1,000 feet of limestone tunnels and caves dating from the 1870s, is one of the valley landmarks. Beringer was founded in 1876 by Frederick and Jacob Beringer, natives of the Rheinland. The winery has operated continuously since 1879 and remained in the Beringer family until 1970, when it was purchased by the Nestlé Company of Switzerland.

Beringer owns more than 2,500 acres of vineyard, primarily in Sonoma and the Carneros region. Along with a full line of premium red and white varietal wines, Beringer also produces the "Los Hermanos" line of wines, a less expensive offering of table wines in magnums and jugs. The firm recently purchased the Souverain winery in the Sonoma Valley.

Hugh Johnson, a renowned British wine writer, refers to Freemark Abbey as a "perfectionist winery." It is a partnership of seven people that includes several Napa growers and Brad Webb, the enologist who introduced California wines to French oak at Hanzell Winery in the 1950s. Located in an old stone winery building about 2 miles north of St. Helena, Freemark Abbey is distinctive because it specializes in producing a small selection of outstanding wines from the best grapes available. The winery produces about 60,000 gallons per year, primarily Chardonnay and Cabernet Sauvignon. A special Cabernet Sauvignon from the vineyard of John Bosché in Rutherford carries his name on the label and is considered to be Freemark Abbey's finest wine, but the Freemark Abbey Chardonnays are also outstanding.

Hanns Kornell Champagne Cellars is another émigré success story. Trained at Geisenheim and a third-generation winemaker, Kornell fled Germany in 1939 and arrived penniless in America. For twelve years he worked for other wineries, making sparkling wines in California, Missouri, and Kentucky. In 1952 he had saved enough money to lease a property in Sonoma, where he began making his own bottle-fermented champagnes. In 1958 Kornell bought the old Larkmead winery north of St. Helena and moved permanently to the Napa Valley. Today he produces about 250,000 gallons of méthode champenoise sparkling wines each year.

Kornell prefers Johannisberg Riesling, Chenin Blanc, and Chardonnay as the predominant wines in his *cuvée*. His "Sehr Trocken," the top of the line, is aged in tirage at least five years and is finished dry. The Hanns Kornell Brut, at .5 percent residual sugar, is still drier than most California Bruts but is distinctly Chardonnay. Kornell does not grow grapes, preferring to buy young wines from other producers in order to blend his *cuvées*.

When Robert Louis Stevenson spent his honeymoon in an abandoned mining shack on the slopes of Mt. St. Helena in 1880, he and his wife passed a pleasant afternoon visiting with Jacob Schram and his wife and tasting Schram's already famous Schramsberg wines. The visit was chronicled in Stevenson's "Silverado Squatters."

Schram's nineteenth-century success with wines was followed by a long hiatus during which the winery enterprise was revived twice, both times unsuccessfully. But, in 1965, Jack Davies, Harvard-trained business executive in search of a wine enterprise, found Schramsberg and promptly fell in love with it. He and his wife Jamie moved in and began restoring the old Victorian mansion, the long limestone caves dug by Chinese laborers, and the abandoned vineyards. Unlike Schram, Davies intended to make sparkling wine, and he has achieved outstanding success through a tenacious insistence upon top quality and the belief that it is better to do only one thing, but to do it exceedingly well.

Davies set out to make California sparkling wines that would rival the best French Champagnes. He selects primarily Chardonnay and Pinot Noir and

Remuage of *méthode champenoise* California sparkling wine in the Schramsberg Vineyards cellars. (Source: Jack Davies.)

produces all his wines by the traditional méthode champenoise. The wines are aged from two to five years in tirage before disgorging and, afterward, for several months in the bottle. Most of his production is "Blanc de Blanc" and "Blanc de Noir" but he also makes small amounts of "Cuvée de Pinot," "Crémant," and a "Réserve Blanc de Blanc" that is aged the longest of the five. The "Crémant," so-called because it has only half the normal effervescence, is a sweet wine made from the Flora grape, which was developed at the University of California at Davis and is related to Gewürztraminer. Schramsberg has grown to produce more than 100,000 gallons annually.

Schramsberg's reputation for quality attracted the attention of the French Cognac house of Rémy Martin, which was searching for a California firm to collaborate with in the production of fine California brandy, but in the French style. An agreement was made and the first brandy, R & S Vineyards California Alambic Brandy, was due to appear on the market in the late 1980s, but the alliance has since dissolved.

Sterling Vineyards, situated upon a hilltop just south of Calistoga, is unquestionably one of the most picturesque wineries in California. One ascends the crest by a tramway ride, and from atop the balconies of the beautiful Moorish-inspired winery buildings, visitors can enjoy a vista of the entire northern portion of the Napa Valley. The winery itself is a showcase of tile mosaics, fountains, elegant wall hangings, stained glass windows, and even an operating carillon.

Sterling was founded in the early 1960s by English paper magnates Peter Newton and Michael Stone, who sought to produce the highest-quality table wines principally from the varieties of Chardonnay, Gewürztraminer, Sauvignon Blanc, Cabernet Sauvignon, and Zinfandel. Fresh from the University of California at Davis, Rick Forman, now a famous California winemaker, was employed to handle the initial production responsibilities.

In July 1977, Sterling was sold to Coca-Cola of Atlanta, which marketed Sterling Vineyards wines through its newly formed Wine Spectrum. The firm continued to produce only vintage-dated, estate-bottled wines grown exclusively from Napa Valley grapes, but the varietal offerings were narrowed down to just Chardonnay, Sauvignon Blanc, Cabernet Sauvignon, and Merlot. In the latter part of 1983 the Wine Spectrum, including Sterling Vineyards, was sold to the Seagram Corporation.

Sterling has established an outstanding tradition in the mere two decades of its existence. With its own 500 acres of classic *Vitis vinifera* vineyards, it remains one of relatively few true estate wineries, that is, it grows all of its own grapes.

Château Montelena lies at the northernmost end of the Napa Valley, 2 miles north of Calistoga, nestled against the slopes of Mount St. Helena. The original winery building, an ornate French château-style stone building with castlelike

BLANC DE BLANCS

NAPA VALLEY
CHAMPAGNE

VINTAGE 1981

PRODUCED AND BOTTLED BY
SCHRAMSBERG VINEYARDS
CALISTOGA, CALIFORNIA

ALCOHOL 12.5% BY VOLUME
CONTENTS 750 MLS

STERLING VINEYARDS

ESTATE BOTTLED

1978

STERLING RESERVE

Cabernet Sauvignon

NAPA VALLEY

GROWN, PRODUCED AND BOTTLED BY
STERLING VINEYARDS
CALISTOGA, NAPA VALLEY, CALIF. ALCOHOL 13% BY VOLUME

turrets, was built in 1882 by Alfred L. Tubbs, a prominent figure in nineteenth-century Napa wine history. A Chinese couple bought the estate in 1947 and added Chinese water gardens, complete with a 5-acre lake, four islands, pagodas, and arched bridges. In 1968 Lee Pashich bought the facility and, with a partnership that he formed, renovated the winery, replanted the vineyards, and commenced producing wine under the Château Montelena label.

Far more important than the impressive building, the fantastic landscape, and the fascinating history, however, are the wines themselves. Château Montelena has been blessed since its first year (1882) with outstanding winemakers whose styles and whose wines are legendary in Napa. In 1972 came Mike Grgich (see the section on Grgich Hills above), whose first wines won instant recognition for their style and elegance. Following Grgich came Jerry Luper, trained at Fresno State University, who added an element of intensity to the wines. Château Montelena produces four wines: Chardonnay, Johannisberg Riesling, Cabernet Sauvignon, and Zinfandel. The 100 acres surrounding the winery are planted with the red varieties while the whites are purchased from other growers.

Spring Valley lies on the eastern hillsides of Napa Valley, east of St. Helena. The Joseph Phelps Winery was established on a ranch here in 1973. Phelps became involved in the California wine industry in the 1960s as the owner of a Colorado-based construction firm that had built several wineries in California. He decided to pursue his increasing interest in wine in 1973 when he hired German-born Walter Schug as his winemaker and pressed his 1973 vintage in leased quarters. By 1974 Phelps had completed his own winery, an architectural gem whose elements he had culled from his experience in building wineries. The design balances a fermenting facility on one side with an aging and bottling facility on the other. The building is united by a central bridge containing offices and the laboratory.

Phelps produces a large selection of wines, primarily from four red and four white varieties. Of the reds, Syrah, the classic variety originally from the Rhône district, is most often singled out for attention. Only a handful of wineries produce this variety in America, and Phelps was first to varietally label it. It is a personal favorite of Phelps, and one on which he lavishes a great deal of time and experimentation. Other reds are Cabernet Sauvignon, Zinfandel, and small amounts of Pinot Noir. Of the white wines, Phelps is unquestionably best known for Johannisberg Riesling done in a range of styles from dry to select late harvest. The other whites are Chardonnay, Sauvignon Blanc, and Gewurztraminer. The winery produces more than 100,000 gallons per year.

Stag's Leap Wine Cellars takes it name from the nearby rocky promontory called Stag's Leap east of the Silverado Trail. Warren Winiarski, the winemaker-operator of Stag's Leap Wine Cellars, left an academic career at the University of

1984
CABERNET SAUVIGNON
Napa Valley

Made and Bottled by
CLOS DU VAL WINE CO LTD
Napa California USA
BW-CA 4638
TABLE WINE

1977
Cabernet Sauvignon
Napa Valley
Stag's Leap Vineyards
Cask 23

STAG'S LEAP WINE CELLARS
Produced & bottled by Stag's Leap Wine Cellars, Napa, Calif. • Alcohol 13% by volume

Chicago to pursue an interest in winemaking. After an apprenticeship with several winemakers, he started producing his own wines in 1972. His 1973 Cabernet Sauvignon placed ahead of several First-Growth Bordeaux in a 1976 tasting in Paris. His 1978 Cabernet Sauvignon "Lot 2" took a double gold at the Bristol International Wine and Spirits Competition in 1982—the only American wine so honored. Stag's Leap also produces Chardonnay, Johannisberg Riesling, Merlot, Petite Sirah, and Gamay Beaujolais, but the majority of the production is still Cabernet Sauvignon.

Clos du Val, in the southern part of the Napa Valley, is located on the east side in the Stag's Leap area. Its winemaker and general manager is Bernard M. Portet who brings a strong French background to his New World enterprise. Portet was raised at Château Lafite-Rothschild where his father was *régisseur* (manager). Portet trained at a wine school in Montpelier, France, and then toured the world for John Goelet, owner of Clos du Val, in search of the best wine-growing opportunities. After two years of travel, Portet settled on the Napa Valley, and in 1972 Clos du Val was founded. Specializing in Bordeaux-style reds, the winery originally produced only Cabernet Sauvignon and Zinfandel. The Cabernet, blended with a small amount of Merlot, is more reminiscent of French Bordeaux than California Cabernet Sauvignon. Clos du Val has since expanded into Chardonnay and Pinot Noir, but Cabernet Sauvignon is still the major portion of production.

Sonoma County

Sonoma County, Napa's neighbor to the west, is a much larger county, encompassing several distinct viticultural areas. The lower Sonoma Valley is virtually a mirror image of Napa: a narrow valley hemmed in by steep hills east and west. Situated across the Mayacamas range from Napa Valley, it shares with Napa the Carneros region at the southernmost end of the valley. North of the town of Kenwood, an entire new region begins, dominated by the Russian River, which originates north of Ukiah in Mendocino County. Grapes are grown along the Russian River from Ukiah to Guerneville, near the shore of the river's terminus at the Pacific Ocean. In addition, there is the Dry Creek Valley, running northwest from Healdsburg.

The climate of Sonoma County is diverse, ranging from Region 1 at the Carneros end of the Sonoma Valley and the Guerneville end of the Russian River to Region 3 near Asti and Cloverdale to the north. Factors such as altitude, air drainage, and the direction in which vineyard slopes face also affect the choice of varieties to be planted, especially in the smaller valleys.

Buena Vista Winery

Sonoma Valley.   Facing San Pablo Bay, the Sonoma Valley is the site of the Sonoma Mission and some of the earliest sacramental and commercial wine-growing ventures in northern California. The wineries of the valley are located mostly between the towns of Sonoma and Kenwood. North of Santa Rosa, the Russian River Valley and its tributaries, the Alexander Valley and the Dry Creek Valley, dominate the viticultural scene.

First of the Sonoma wineries was Buena Vista, the property made famous by Count Agoston Haraszthy. A great deal of controversy currently exists about who first made wine and when on the Buena Vista site. Records recently unearthed seem to indicate that wine was made on that property before Haraszthy ever arrived, perhaps by General Vallejo's brother, Salvador, as early as 1849. But whatever the outcome of the historical dispute, it is certain that Haraszthy founded his own Buena Vista on this site in 1857. The vineyards surrounding the winery were planted with the numerous varieties he brought back from Europe. He constructed a series of stone tunnels and two stone barns where he made the wine. Buena Vista, subject to all the vagaries and plagues of nineteenth-century California wine history, finally succumbed in 1906 when the great earthquake devastated the property, collapsing some of the tunnels.

In 1941 Frank Bartholomew, a UPI correspondent, bought the facility in Sonoma at auction, sight unseen. Examining the property after the purchase, he

Hacienda Wine Cellars

1981 *Sonoma Valley*
PINOT NOIR

PRODUCED AND ESTATE BOTTLED BY
HACIENDA WINE CELLARS, SONOMA, CALIFORNIA
BONDED WINERY 4623 • ALCOHOL 13.4% BY VOLUME

WINES IN THE TRADITIONAL FAMILY STYLE

August Sebastiani

Country
Cabernet Sauvignon

A Dry California Table Wine

VINTED AND BOTTLED BY SEBASTIANI VINEYARDS
SONOMA, CALIFORNIA ALC. 12.2% BY VOL. BONDED WINERY 876

The Haraszthy Vineyard at Buena Vista Winery in Sonoma County.

found the ruins of the old stone barns and tunnels and discovered the history of the place. He decided to restore it and began reconstructing the buildings and replanting the historic vineyards. Bartholomew restored the Buena Vista name to prominence, especially for its Cabernets and Zinfandels. But, in 1968, planning to retire, he sold the property and retained only his home and most of the original vineyards owned by Haraszthy.

The new owners, a supermarket chain in Los Angeles, bought extensive vineyard property in Carneros—over 600 acres—and built a new facility on that property, retaining the old winery as an aging cellar and tasting room. Now owned by a West German firm, A. Racke Co., the winery has continued on a course of steady improvement in wine quality. Jill Davis, trained at the University of California at Davis and an apprentice at Beringer, has been instrumental in leading the changes during the 1980s. In 1982 a small portion of the original Buena Vista winery building was turned over to the prestigious American wine brotherhood, the Knights of the Vine, as its national headquarters. Under the direction of young Marcus Moller-Racke, Buena Vista has been renewed and is one of the premier wine producers in California.

Bartholomew, at the age of 75, started a new winery on the original Haraszthy property he had retained. Hacienda Wine Cellars, founded in 1973, is located in the old Sonoma Valley Hospital, adjacent to Bartholomew's vineyards.

The Haraszthy heritage thus lives on in Sonoma, reincarnated in two wineries, side by side. Buena Vista, on the original winery site, retains the Haraszthy Cellars name for its labels. Next door, at Hacienda Wine Cellars, the vineyards originally planted by Haraszthy still flourish, but with new plantings of vines.

Another venerable member of the Sonoma Valley wine community is Sebastiani Vineyards, dating from 1904. The history and philosophy of Sebastiani bears a similarity to that of Louis Martini in Napa Valley. Both are relatively large family-owned and family-operated wineries founded by Italian immigrants specializing in well-aged, varietal table wines. Both are best known for red wines, but continue to move with the times, improving in whites in recent years as well.

Major renovations are taking place at the original winery and new facilities are being built. A new méthode champenoise Brut was released in 1982, Sebastiani's first. An emphasis has been placed on premium, vintage-dated varietals released under the "Proprietor's Reserve" labels, including Chardonnay and Cabernet. Many of the new wines bear Sonoma Valley and Sonoma County appellations—a trend away from the old "Mountain" wines of previous years.

In also should be noted that the winery has the largest collection of hand-carved wood casks in America, making it a memorable facility to visit and tour.

Ten miles north of Sonoma in the town of Kenwood is Kenwood Vineyards. Originally the Pagani Brothers Winery, founded in 1906, it was purchased in 1970 by the Martin Lee family along with several partners. Pagani was a popular jug wine producer, but the Lees, along with the able leadership of President John Sheela, have gradually moved the winery to a line of premium, vintage-dated varietals. Kenwood is probably best known for its "Artist Series" Cabernet Sauvignon, released each October first. The original labels by prominent artists are used on the bottles of the Cabernet that Kenwood management feels will age best.

Another noteworthy label from Kenwood is the Cabernet Sauvignon made from the famous Jack London vineyards that are owned by the firm and located a few miles to the west of the winery. The "Jack London" Cabernet Sauvignon is typically softer and more delicate than the dark, heavy-bodied "Artist Series." Both are superior offerings.

At the foot of Sugarloaf Mountain just outside of Kenwood is Château St. Jean, one of the most remarkable wineries in California. In 1973 three successful table grape growers from the San Joaquin Valley purchased the Goff estate, complete with a Mediterranean villa and some precious Sonoma acreage. The partners wanted to create a fine wine "château" that would produce wines to equal those made anywhere else in the world. They appointed Allan Hemphill, a Korbel-trainee, as president. Richard Arrowood, a Sonoma County native with experience at several Sonoma wineries, became winemaker, with virtual carte

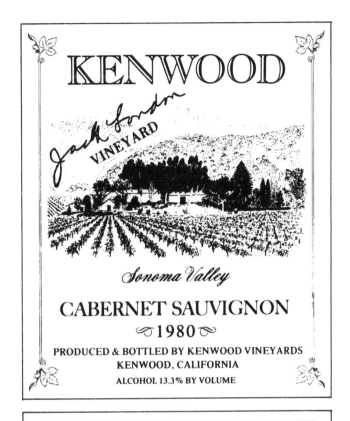

KENWOOD

Jack London
VINEYARD

Sonoma Valley

CABERNET SAUVIGNON
1980

PRODUCED & BOTTLED BY KENWOOD VINEYARDS
KENWOOD, CALIFORNIA

ALCOHOL 13.3% BY VOLUME

Jordan

ESTATE BOTTLED

1979
Cabernet Sauvignon
Alexander Valley

GROWN, PRODUCED & BOTTLED BY JORDAN VINEYARD & WINERY
ALEXANDER VALLEY, HEALDSBURG, CALIF.   ALCOHOL 12.8% BY VOLUME

blanche in equipping the new winery and making the wines. The elegant and beautifully landscaped mansion that is featured on the labels is currently used for a visitors center and offices, though there are plans to build a separate visitors facility.

The result of this ambitious and expensive undertaking has been exactly what the owners envisioned—an internationally acclaimed winery. One policy for which the winery is perhaps best known is that of individual vineyard designations on its labels. In 1980, Château St. Jean produced nine different Chardonnays, each with a distinctive vineyard designation. Some of the best known of these vineyards are "Robert Young," "Belle Terre," "Paulsen," "Wildwood," and "Crimmons Ranch." The winery owners' excellent relations with their growers and enlightened policies of shared risk have enabled them to obtain the grapes to produce extraordinary wines, especially late harvest Johannisberg Riesling. In 1984 Château St. Jean was purchased by Suntory, Ltd., a Japanese firm.

Russian River Valley.   Most of Sonoma County viticulture north of Santa Rosa is dominated by the long and meandering Russian River. Originating in Mendocino County north of Ukiah, the river wanders southward through Sonoma County to Geyserville, takes an eastward loop to define the Alexander Valley, and from Healdsburg heads south and west to the Pacific. The spectacular growth in vineyard acreage in Sonoma since the 1960s has occurred primarily in this district, especially in the Alexander Valley. Veteran vintners are finding new competition in the area from the many small wineries that continue to spring up. The newcomers are attracted by the distinctive viticultural characteristics of the locale, which ranges from a cool Region 1 around Guerneville near the Pacific to Region 3 at Asti and Cloverdale. Hillside vineyards in the southern sections of the valley are usually planted with Cabernet Sauvignon and Zinfandel while the cooler valley floor is suited to Johannisberg Riesling, Gewürztraminer, and, most recently, Chardonnay and Pinot Noir. A great deal of experimentation remains to be done before the best varieties for particular sites can be identified.

Starting from the mouth of the river and heading upstream, the first winery in the Russian River Valley is Korbel, located about 2 miles east of Guerneville, in the middle of redwood country. The Korbel brothers came to the area as loggers in the 1870s, making cigar boxes and other wood products from the lumber. When the redwood was gone, they planted grapes among the stumps. The first Korbel "champagne" was produced in 1882, making Korbel the first commercial sparkling wine producer in the state. In 1954, the Korbel family sold the winery to the Heck brothers from the same Heck family who operated Cook's Imperial Champagne Winery in St. Louis, Missouri. The Hecks introduced table wines and brandy to the line but bottle-fermented champagne is still the primary Korbel product, with annual production now in excess of 2 million gallons. Hundreds of acres of vineyards have been added, all in the coolest areas of the Russian River Valley, which the owners jokingly refer to as "Region 1/2." More of the traditional Champagne varieties have been planted recently in that area—Chardonnay and Pinot Noir, as well as Pinot Blanc—from which Korbel produces a *naturel* blend. In addition to brut, extra dry, and sec sparkling wines, the firm also produces a 100 percent Chardonnay "Blanc de Blanc" and a 100 percent Pinot Noir "Blanc de Noir." With the dramatic increase in recent years in the number of producers of méthode champenoise sparkling wines in California, Korbel no longer stands alone, but it is still very much a premium producer and currently the largest.

The tiny Dehlinger Winery is located southeast of Guerneville, not far from Château St. Jean's sparkling wine facility in Graton. Dehlinger produces only about 20,000 gallons annually. The estate's 30-acre vineyard contains Chardonnay, Pinot Noir, and Cabernet Sauvignon, plus small amounts of Merlot and Cabernet Franc. Owner Tom Dehlinger is a graduate in enology from the University of California at Davis who made wines for the Hanzell Winery before starting his own wine firm. Dehlinger is firmly recognized as a producer of distinctive wines at reasonable prices.

Mark West Vineyards, another small winery, was founded in 1976 on the south side of the Russian River, near Forestville. Named for the creek that runs alongside the property, Mark West is owned by Bob Ellis, the vineyard manager, and his wife Joan, the winemaker. In this very cool, often fogbound area, the Ellises grow Chardonnay, Johannisberg Riesling, Gewürztraminer, and Pinot Noir. The climate contributes to a refreshing, fruity acidity in the wines and small, oak cooperage adds a certain complexity to the Chardonnay and Pinot Noir.

The biggest wine attraction in the little town of Windsor, east of the Russian River and north of Santa Rosa, is Sonoma Vineyards, founded by the colorful vintner, Rodney Strong. Strong left a career in choreography for the wine business in 1959.

The first Rodney Strong wines were produced in the cellar of an old Victorian house situated in the picturesque bay village of Tiburon, just north of San Francisco. Here the premier vintage of 1959 was sold directly to local cottagers and yachtsmen. Demand for the delicious new Tiburon wines grew rapidly.

Direct-consumer wine marketing was nothing new, but the use of individual personalized labels was a fresh approach. As interest increased throughout the region, Charlotte and Rodney Strong moved their wine-making operations to Windsor in the Sonoma Valley, where their unique concept could be expanded to a custom wine mail-order service. This was another first, and burgeoning sales spawned the need for an even larger production facility.

In 1970 Strong finalized plans for the now-famous Sonoma Vineyards Winery structure. In simplest terms, the building has four wings—each radiating at equal compass points from a central core and rising to a common central peak. Specific production functions are housed in each wing, all carefully controlled from the central structure, which also provides a picturesque vantage point for thousands of visitors to see the winery and taste the award-winning wines.

Important to an improved future outlook has been a joint venture between Sonoma Vineyards and the Piper-Heidsieck Champagne-producing firm of France. The sparkling wine facility that is adjacent to Sonoma Vineyards was completed in 1982 and the first sparkling wines, called "Piper-Sonoma," were released that year. The line consists of three wines: Brut, a blend of 80 percent Pinot Noir and 20 percent Chardonnay; a 100 percent Noir called "Blanc de Noir"; and "Tête de Cuvée," 50 percent Chardonnay and 50 percent Pinot Noir. Sonoma Vineyards has also produced some creditable vineyard-designated table wines in recent years, most notably the "Alexander's River West Estate" Chardonnay and "Alexander's Crown" Cabernet Sauvignon. Recently the familiar "Sonoma Vineyards" label logo has been replaced by "Rodney Strong"—in a promotion fostered by new owners, the Renfield importing firm of New York City. Additionally, the Piper-Sonoma facility has become the sole property of Piper-Heidsieck, and Renfield has since sold Sonoma Vineyards.

A few miles north and worlds apart from the glitter of the Sonoma Vineyard complex is Foppiano Vineyards, one of the oldest family wineries left in California, founded in 1896. Foppiano has cautiously and gradually moved from a bulk wine trade to varietal wines, including Fumé Blanc, Chardonnay, and Petite Sirah, distributed under the family name. The wines from their 200-acre vineyard now bear a Russian River appellation, and the wines have evolved to be a good value for their price.

On the north side of Healdsburg is the venerable Simi winery, founded by Guiseppe and Pietro Simi in 1876. The stone building, erected in 1890, was completely remodeled several years ago, leaving only the original stone walls. Simi was a family winery from its inception until 1970, when Guiseppe's octogenarian daughter Isabelle Simi Haigh sold the enterprise to Russell Green. The winery's fortunes had waxed and waned under the Simi yoke, producing some outstanding wines in the late 1930s and declining until its sale. Green, whose vineyards in the nearby Alexander Valley supplied most of the grapes for the winery, updated some equipment and hired Mary Ann Graf as winemaker and André Tchelistcheff as consulting enologist. This outstanding wine-making team quickly turned the tide and the wines, bearing Alexander Valley appellations, once again became outstanding examples of Sonoma County's best. (Though the Simi winery is located in the Russian River region, the wines carry the Alexander Valley appellation because that is where the grapes are grown.)

The winery has changed hands several times since Russell Green acquired it and is currently owned by Moët-Hennessy, which also operates Domaine Chandon in Napa Valley. Zelma Long is the winemaker now and, inside the nearly century-old shell of the winery, the best modern equipment and small, oak cooperage have replaced the antiques inherited from the Simis.

Alexander Valley.   The Alexander Valley appellation includes the lands in the Russian River watershed from Geyserville to Healdsburg, a section in which the river makes a long loop south and then north again before heading west to Guerneville. Grapevines first were planted here in the 1840s by Cyrus Alexander, for whom the valley is named. By the late nineteenth century there were several wineries in the area—the best known of which was the Soda Rock Winery. But, in the era following Prohibition, the valley slipped into anonymity along with much of the rest of Sonoma County.

Most of the grapes grown here went to bulk producers or to wineries in other areas whose labels didn't indicate the origin of the grapes. Russell Green did much to change that, both through the Simi label and through his quest to establish a recognized Alexander Valley appellation of origin. Today there are a number of wineries within the valley, as well as vineyards owned by wineries in other areas, that use the appellation for grapes grown here. The area has been classed as Region 3, but a number of growers feel that parts of the area are Region 2.

Alexander Valley Vineyards is situated on the original Cyrus Alexander homestead. It belongs to the Wetzel family and was founded in 1975. Winemaker Harry (Hank) Wetzel III produces five estate-bottled wines from Chardonnay, Johannisberg Riesling, Chenin Blanc, Gewürztraminer, and Cabernet Sauvignon. The wines are considered to be some of the finest from the valley.

Jordan Vineyards and Winery is situated in grand style at the north end of the valley. Owner Tom Jordan first planned to buy a château in Bordeaux, but decided instead to build his own château in California and make a classic French-style claret in America. With this goal in mind he planted 275 acres of vineyard with Cabernet Sauvignon and Merlot. The opulent winery was built and equipped with state-of-the-art machinery, tankage, and French oak barrels. The first wine was made in 1976 to be released in 1980. By 1979, the decision had been made to expand to Chardonnay as well. Because of Jordan's policy of long aging before release (since 1978, the Cabernet Sauvignon is aged five years before release), only a few of the wines are available yet. Those early wines have shown promise, with the elegant style one would expect given the winery's strict philosophy.

Dry Creek, another Sonoma County appellation, covers the Dry Creek Valley from the Warm Springs Dam northwest of Geyserville to the creek's confluence with the Russian River just south of Healdsburg. Within this area, which is generally a bit warmer than the Alexander Valley, Zinfandel has been the grape most widely produced. The area had little identity in the minds of consumers prior to the arrival in 1972 of David Stare. Stare is a transplanted Bostonian who came to the Dry Creek area with plans to make wines in the style of the Médoc in Bordeaux, France. Although this has traditionally been a red wine-growing region, Stare has moved his Dry Creek Vineyards more and more heavily into white wines, primarily Sauvignon Blanc, which he markets as "Fumé Blanc." Today 80 percent of the firm's production is white wine, including Chardonnay and Chenin Blanc, which have also been very successful. The winery's small production of red wines is in Cabernet Sauvignon, Zinfandel, and Petite Sirah.

In a canyon just east of Dry Creek and not far from Geyserville is the Pedroncelli Winery, owned by the Pedroncelli family. Like Foppiano to the south, Pedroncelli is one of the old-style Sonoma County wineries that survived the Great Depression years by producing bulk wines. Within a relatively short time after the Depression, Pedroncelli began producing a few wines under is own label, and one year after John took over the winemaking from his father in 1949, the winery produced a varietal Zinfandel. During the 1950s brothers John and Jim embarked on an extensive modernization of the facility. Today they produce wines from ten varieties of grapes—white, red, and rosé—and are routinely listed in the "best buy" category in wine reviews. The quality is always consistently well above average, and the prices remain modest.

Souverain overlooks the Alexander Valley from the west side of Highway 101 near Geyserville. The history of the Souverain name is very complex: it was originally attached to a winery near Rutherford in the Napa Valley owned by Lee Stewart. A group of Napa growers acquired the property, then sold it but retained the name. The original Souverain property is now Burgess Cellars. The growers proposed to build two new wineries, one at Rutherford and the other in the Alexander Valley. These two wineries became Souverain of Rutherford and Souverain of Alexander Valley. In 1972 Pillsbury acquired both properties and less than four years later sold them again to separate buyers. Souverain of Rutherford in Napa became the Rutherford Hill Winery. The name *Souverain* and the Alexander Valley property were purchased by a limited partnership of growers from Napa, Sonoma, and Mendocino Counties, who are its current owners. Thus a name that was originally associated with Napa has now become attached to a winery in the Alexander Valley of Sonoma and is now owned by Beringer Vineyards of the Napa Valley.

The winery is a long, low building bracketed on either end by towers reminiscent of the hop kilns that once dotted the Russian River landscape. Walkways running the length of the building allow visitors to view the winemaking process, and the winery also has a superb restaurant where lunch and dinner are served. Cabernet, Chardonnay, Merlot, and Fumé Blanc are among the superior varieties. In 1982 a second label, "North Coast Cellars," joined the existing Souverain label. North Coast Cellars features a less expensive line of nonvintage wines, both varietal and generic, including Chardonnay, Gamay, and Pinot Noir.

Geyser Peak, just north of Geyserville, has appeared in a number of different incarnations since 1880, including as a bulk wine facility and a wine vinegar plant. In 1972 it was purchased by Schlitz Brewing Company of Milwaukee, later incorporated into Stroh's Brewery of Detroit. The owners undertook a massive renovation and building campaign and produced a relatively small amount of vintage-dated varietal wines under the Geyser Peak label, some with vineyard designations, while simultaneously adopting an aggressive, mass-marketing program for its less expensive "Summit" line. Innovative packaging has been the hallmark of the Summit wines, including wine in cans, six-packs, and 4-liter bag-in-box (restaurant service-type) containers. The avowed aim of the company is to strip wine of its snob image and to mass market it in areas where much larger and very savvy marketers have had little or no success.

Mendocino and Lake Counties

Heading north along the Russian River toward its source, one comes to the town of Asti, the home of the giant Italian Swiss Colony Winery mentioned in chapter 4.

About 5 miles above Asti, just north of Cloverdale, is the border of Mendocino County, the northernmost of the North Coast California wine-growing counties. Lake County borders Mendocino County to the east. Here, just north of Ukiah, is the Parducci winery. Founded in 1932, Parducci has been a champion of the Mendocino and Lake Counties growers for years. After the usual post-Prohibition period of bulk wine sales, Parducci began producing varietals and upgrading the winery acreage, largely through the impetus of the founder's two sons, John and George. Parducci has always had a local focus—using grapes primarily grown in its own vineyards and a few from neighboring growers. Following the pioneering efforts of the Parduccis, new winegrowers have come to the region, exploring previously untried microclimates and expanding acreage beyond the Russian River watershed to areas such as the Anderson Valley, McDowell Valley, Redwood Valley, and Potter Valley. Though many of the growers sell their grapes to either the Cresta Blanca winery at Ukiah or Italian Swiss Colony at Asti, a number of new wineries have appeared as well. As Napa and Sonoma become saturated with wineries, these new vineyard areas become more attractive economically and are proving to be equal in quality viticulturally.

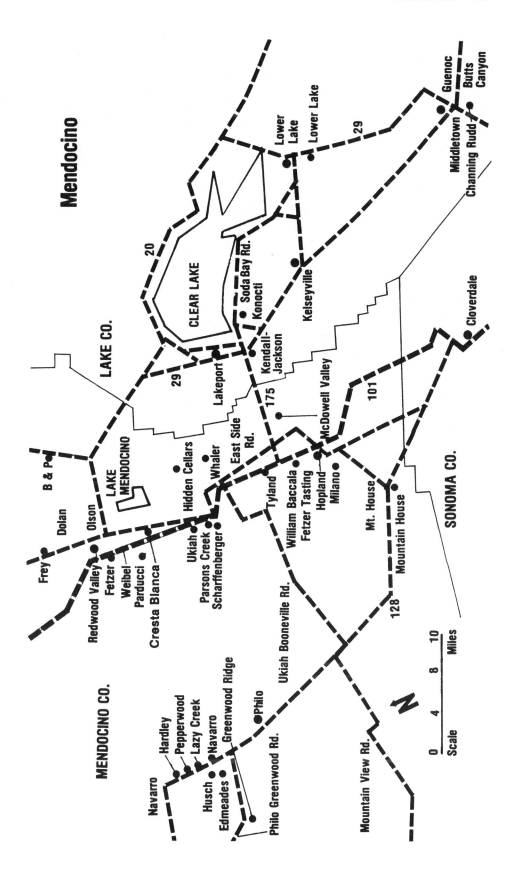

Mendocino

The Italian Swiss Colony Winery at Asti.

The Parducci brothers, who have used Lake County grapes for a number of years, have recently entered into a partnership with Lake County Vintners in a winery called Konocti Cellars. The Konocti label promises to enhance the name of Lake County grapes an an appellation of origin.

One of the newest and largest success stories in the Mendocino locale is that of the Fetzers. Originally from Nebraska, Bernard and Kathleen Fetzer moved to Ukiah from Oregon in the early 1950s. Their expertise was in lumber, but they soon became intrigued with the lush vineyards that surrounded Ukiah, the capital city of the rich and famous farmlands in the beautiful Mendocino Valley. The vines became an obsession, and the Fetzers cashed in their life insurance policies for enough capital to buy what eventually became known in the family as the "Home Ranch," a former stagecoach inn large enough to house their bounty of eleven children. The property also included a 40-acre vineyard plot and other land.

The first few crops were sold to other area vintners. Every penny they could spare after furnishing the bare necessities the Fetzers literally plowed back into their vineyards—making them bigger and better. It was only natural that such an enterprising family would sooner or later respond to the challenge of making wines equal to the quality of their superior grapes.

The Fetzer family has launched an aggressive marketing program with the same enthusiasm and relentless energy they put into production. The result has been

fetzer

1981

lake county

CABERNET SAUVIGNON

PRODUCED AND BOTTLED BY FETZER VINEYARDS
REDWOOD VALLEY, CALIFORNIA, U.S.A. ALCOHOL 12.7% BY VOLUME

McDowell Valley
Vineyards
Estate Bottled
McDowell Valley
Cabernet Sauvignon
1980
GROWN, PRODUCED AND BOTTLED BY
McDOWELL CELLARS, HOPLAND, CALIFORNIA
ALCOHOL 12.8% BY VOLUME

244   WINE APPRECIATION

success of titanic porportions. But when the iron-handed patriarch Barney Fetzer died in 1981, many thought that the days of the Fetzer wines were numbered. Little had changed, however, only some titles and responsibilities were rearranged. Eldest son John was elected to preside over the legacy, with sister Mary appointed to lead marketing and brother Jim the general manager of the winery. Ten of the eleven siblings are still directly involved with the operation of the firm, and they have made such new investments as the "Sundial" Chardonnay plot and the massive "Valley Oaks" vineyard and resort complex.

The Fetzer portfolio now embraces more than a dozen different vintage-dated varietal table wine offerings, including the "Sundial" Chardonnay and "Valley Oaks" Fumé Blanc mentioned above and Cabernet Sauvignon. The firm produces an output exceeding 700,000 cases annually—eighteenth-largest among more than 1,000 American vintners. The Fetzer winery, in just two decades, has amassed more awards and medals of quality achievements than some peers with histories spanning a century.

McDowell Valley, situated just east of Hopland, California, was named for Paxton McDowell, who settled that portion of Mendocino County during the 1850's. Existing there today is America's first solar-integrated winery—designed, constructed, and operated by Karen and Richard Keehn. Sunlight provides the energy needed for heating, cooling, hot-water, and eventually electricity, as well. McDowell Valley Vineyards wines are grown from Chardonnay, Sauvignon Blanc, Cabernet Sauvignon, Syrah, and Zinfandel, among others. Expert winemaker John Buechsenstein has no fewer than 6 gold-medal winners among his current releases—one earning "Best Of Show" honors at the 1986 National Restaurant Association competition.

Situated near Lakeport, in Lake County, is the popular Kendall-Jackson estate—headed by San Francisco attorney Jess Jackson. Winemaker Jed Steele is one of the most respected talents in all of California, and has continually won awards for superior Chardonnay, Sauvignon Blanc and Cabernet Sauvignon wines.

Mendocino and Lake Counties are becoming increasingly important quality wine districts in the vast California wine scene.

Central Coast Counties

Central Coast   refers to those counties south of Napa and Sonoma, extending down the coastline of California nearly to Los Angeles. It includes some counties that never touch the coastline, but whose topography allows coastal fogs to penetrate, making the influence of the Pacific felt. San Benito, for example, lies entirely inland, but the Monterey Bay fogs and breezes are funneled into its northern valleys, making them a cool Region 1 to Region 3. Napa and Lake

Counties are inland as well, but are included with the North Coast Counties because of their climate.

Within the Central Coast designation, the counties surrounding San Francisco Bay—Contra Costa, Alameda, Santa Clara, Santa Cruz, and San Mateo Counties—are usually separated from those to the south, primarily for historical reasons. The traditions of winemaking in these counties date from the first settlement of the San Francisco area. Many large and historic wineries are still located in this region, but, for the most part, the growing of grapes has moved elsewhere. The pressures of urbanization have driven the vineyardists south, with the notable exception of the Livermore area. In stark contrast to this historical decline, the southern counties of Monterey, San Benito, San Luis Obispo, and Santa Barbara have risen markedly in vineyard acreage during the last fifteen years. In 1982, 115,000 tons of wine grapes were grown in Monterey and San Benito Counties. In that same year, Napa produced some 98,000 and Sonoma produced approximately 99,000 tons. Although wine labels may not always indicate this, an ever-increasing proportion of premium wine grapes in California is being grown in the area south of Monterey Bay. With this growth in vineyard acreage and a parallel increase in the number of wineries in these regions, distinctive viticultural areas are beginning to emerge.

Livermore Valley.   The Livermore Valley, situated about 50 miles east of San Francisco, is an exception to the general rule about coastal California valleys where grapes are grown. It has an elevation of more than 400 feet and no coastal fogs penetrate it. The belt where grapes are grown is classified as Region 3 and parallels an old arroyo whose extremely coarse rocky soil reminded the first French settlers of southern Bordeaux. Sémillon, Sauvignon Blanc, and Chenin Blanc were some of the earliest varieties to be planted in this region, and they are still considered to be the varieties that produce some of the finest wines from the Livermore Valley.

Ernest Wente, in a brief memoir written shortly before his death in 1981, recalled twenty wineries in the Livermore Valley in his childhood and a mere 2,000 to 3,000 inhabitants during the last decade of the nineteenth century. In 1983, when both Wente Brothers and neighboring Concannon celebrated their hundredth anniversaries as vintners, only a handful of wineries remained and the population of Alameda County was well over one million. Throughout that long and tumultuous century, four generations of Wentes have survived and prospered. Today the family is doing a great deal to preserve the viticultural heritage of the Livermore Valley.

Carl Wente, founder of the winery in 1883, sold all his wine in bulk and, eventually, discouraged by Prohibition, sold the business to two of his sons,

Herman and Ernest. The Wente brothers rapidly made a name for their premium white wines in post-Prohibition California and gained national recognition when the Frank Schoonmaker firm marketed their wines across America. Herman's reputation as one of California's premier winemakers grew, and Wente became synonymous with excellent Chardonnay, Sauvignon Blanc, Sémillon, and Grey Riesling. In the early 1960s, with third-generation Karl Wente in command, the family helped pioneer the Arroyo Seco district of Monterey County as a recognized grape-growing region. Late-harvest Johannisberg Riesling grapes, some infected with noble mold, from the Arroyo Seco vineyards not only helped further the reputation of the Wente Brothers, but were instrumental in establishing the reputation of the viticultural area as well. Today, fourth-generation Wentes are affirming their viticultural heritage and continuing to pioneer in new wine-growing areas.

In 1980, the first Wente sparkling wine was produced from Chardonnay, Pinot Blanc, and Pinot Noir grown in the Arroyo Seco vineyards. The wine was released in 1983 to commemorate the winery's centennial year. In 1981, the Wente firm purchased an additional 955 acres of land in Livermore, including the original Cresta Blanca winery founded by Charles Wetmore. Management has restored the original winery building of Louis Mel, from whom Carl Wente purchased the property. On this land Sémillon and Sauvignon Blanc vines thought to have originated from Bordeaux's fabled Château d'Yquem vineyard had been grown. The building is now fully restored and remodeled into one of the most attractive sparkling wine production and hospitality facilities in America.

The commitment to wine in Monterey remains strong, and Wente is today more than ever entrenched in its original home. The appellation Livermore continues to represent some of the finest white wines available at moderate prices.

Concannon Vineyards is Wente's neighbor in Livermore and an equal in age and tradition. James Concannon emigrated from Ireland to America in the 1860s, first to New England and then west to California's Barbary Coast. It was there that he learned of Catholic Archbishop Alemany's need for additional sacramental wine. A small winery was constructed in 1883 to process the harvest of Concannon's vineyards, and the wine quickly gained favor with both clergy and laity.

James Concannon passed away just after the turn of the century, and the winery was handed down to son and then grandson—each generation dedicated to the production of premium wines. In 1986 the winery was sold to the Somerset Group, but the Concannons are still involved in the firm, with grandson Jim Concannon heading up the winery's promotional activities.

The Concannon winery now operates under the direction of Dr. Sergio Traverso, a Chilean-born enologist possessing superb talent and extensive training from the University of California at Davis. Prior to accepting the Concannon

WENTE BROS.

1985

ARROYO SECO
CHARDONNAY

Reserve

GROWN, PRODUCED & BOTTLED BY WENTE BROS.
LIVERMORE, CA • ALC. 13.6% BY VOL.

Concannon
VINEYARD

1985
CALIFORNIA
CHARDONNAY

PRODUCED AND BOTTLED BY
CONCANNON VINEYARD, LIVERMORE, CA
ALC. 13.1% BY VOL.   CONTAINS SULFITES

post, Dr. Traverso had production responsibilities at several Napa Valley wineries, including the famous Sterling Vineyards. Concannon Vineyards's Chardonnay, Sauvignon Blanc, Cabernet Sauvignon, and Petite Sirah are consistent award-winners in presitgious competitions.

Alameda County.   In the southwestern corner of Alameda County, in Mission San Jose, is the home winery of Weibel Champagne Vineyards. Situated on the historic Warm Springs property once owned by railroad magnate Leland Stanford in the nineteenth century, this vineyard area produced wines well over a century ago. The Stanford vineyards were destroyed by *Phylloxera* in the 1890s, and the property was not revived until 1945 when it was purchased by Rudolf Weibel. The winery, which is the largest private-label bottler (bottles wines under special labels for retailers and restaurateurs) of sparkling wines in the United States, makes mostly Charmat-process wines, but it also produces its own line of bottle-fermented sparkling wines by the transfer process.

In the 1960s the winery purchased over 400 acres of vineyard land in Mendocino County near Ukiah, and in 1973 built a fermenting facility there for table wine production—with an adjacent tasting room built in the shape of an inverted wineglass. This winery now produces a full line of vintage-dated, Mendocino County and Lake County varietal wines. Weibel is still best known, however, for its sparkling wines and receives most visitors at its home winery near Fremont, California.

Santa Clara County.   Santa Clara County, south of Alameda, was once home to both Almadén and Paul Masson wineries, each of which traces its history back to 1852 and French immigrant Étienne Thée (see chapter 4).

The name Almadén did not come to prominence until the 1940s when it was purchased by Louis Benoist. Benoist, like many other post-Prohibition California vintners, came under the influence of Frank Schoonmaker, who advised him to create distinctive California wines and varietal labeling for those wines. Next came "Mountain Red" and "Mountain White," to replace "Chablis" and "Burgundy." Then Almaden created a sensation with Grenache Rosé, the first phenomenally successful California rosé. As urbanization eroded the vineyards surrounding the original Santa Clara winery in Los Gatos, several thousands of acres in San Benito County were purchased—the first significant move to the south among the major Santa Clara wineries. Vineyards were planted in Paicines and La Cienega, situated about 50 miles south of San Jose. Today Almadén owns well over 6,000 acres of vineyards in San Benito and Monterey Counties.

Almadén is now an 80 million-gallon winery—third largest in the United States—and a public corporation largely owned by Heublein. It operates five separate wineries: two in San Benito, two in the Central Valley, and the home

AMERICA 249

winery in Los Gatos. The La Cienega winery, one of the world's largest wine cellars under a single roof, contains more than 37,000 small, oak barrels for aging. Almadén produces vintage-dated, estate-bottled varietals; nonvintage varietals; generics and jug wines; wines and brandy. It has recently begun a joint venture with the French firm Laurent-Perrier to produce a Chardonnay in the style of a French (nonsparkling) *Coteaux Champenoise*. First released in 1981, the wine is fermented and aged in stainless steel tankage only. The recently created "Charles LeFranc" line of premium varietals has had some notable successes, especially the "Monterey" Cabernet Sauvignon, plus a noble-mold Johannisberg Riesling and Gewürztraminer from San Benito.

Paul Masson shares far more with Almadén than the heritage of a single founder and a common home ground. After a brief ownership by Martin Ray in the 1930s, Masson was purchased by the Seagram distilling firm during World War II. Large tracts of land were acquired in the Salinas Valley of Monterey during the 1950s, and a new modern plant was constructed there to produce its table wines. In the 1970s it added acreage and a winery in the San Joaquin Valley to supplement its dessert and table wine operations. Today Paul Masson ranks just behind Almadén and the Christian Brothers in capacity and has production facilities at the Pinnacles vineyard in Monterey and in the San Joaquin Valley near Madera.

The original winery that Paul Masson built in the hills above Saratoga now is used primarily to store experimental lots of wine and for aging. The Romanesque facade is the backdrop for the famous "Music at the Vineyards" series of concerts held annually at the winery, now in its twenty-sixth year. The Pinnacles winery near Soledad is the home of the "Pinnacles Selection" wines and most of the table wines and sparkling wines from Paul Masson. The winery's famous "Rare Souzão" port comes from the San Joaquin facility.

Paul Masson, like Almadén and the Christian Brothers, produces reliable, sound wines at reasonable prices with occasional selections that are exceptional in quality. It also is the leading American exporter of wines, selling to some sixty countries around the world. It is now owned by Vintners International.

Although Mirassou ancestors have been making wine since 1854, wines bearing the Mirassou label didn't attain any significant distribution until the late 1960s. With over a century of experience in the field of bulk wine and a loyal following of customers who drove to the winery to obtain Mirassou wines, the fifth generation of the Mirassou family felt it was time to look for a market under their own label. The Mirassou family, forced to search for additional vineyard land, planted in the Salinas Valley during the early 1960s. Today the family owns about 1,500 acres, primarily in Monterey, but with a few acres still remaining in Santa Clara— enough to supply an occasional "Home Ranch" label. The current Mirassou

Mirassou Vineyards. (Source: Mirassou Vineyards.)

generation is aggressive, innovative, and anxious to assume its place as one of the first families of wine in California. The Mirassous are pioneers in mechanical harvesting and field crushing of grapes. Their latest efforts have been directed toward a greatly expanded production of méthode champenoise sparkling wines.

The San Martin Winery, located in the town of San Martin just south of San Jose, was a family-owned operation with a line of ordinary country wines catering largely to the retail, tasting-room trade. In 1973 it was purchased by a vineyard corporation called Southdown, which controlled more than 10,000 acres in Monterey County. The late Ed Friedrich, a German-born winemaker who had been employed at nearby Paul Masson, was hired, and great improvements were made in production.

The combination of better facilities, highly trained wine-making talent, and access to premium grapes initiated a complete turnaround in the wine. Four years after the Southdown purchase, the company was acquired by Somerset Importers, a division of Norton-Simon, and the greatly improved high-volume line of wines received a strong boost in national distribution. Friedrich pioneered a line of lower-alcohol "light" wines, emphasizing fruity varietal character. Today the winery purchases grapes from many Central Coast growers and has contributed greatly to increasing the popularity of such appellations as San Luis Obispo and Santa Barbara—previously little known outside of California.

Santa Cruz Mountains.   In the rugged, craggy corner where San Mateo, Santa Cruz, and Santa Clara Counties blend into the Santa Cruz mountains there exist some small, very independent wineries specializing in a style that is sometimes called "Santa Cruz Mountain Primitive." Vineyard holdings on these steep slopes are usually quite small, and many producers buy grapes from areas as far away as Mendocino, Amador, and Santa Barbara, usually designating so on the labels. Ridge Vineyards and Winery is probably the best known, and deservedly so. Here, winemaker Paul Draper makes small lots of wine, most notably of Cabernet Sauvignon and Zinfandel, from remote vineyards. These Ridge offerings are always distinctive and well made.

Just over the Santa Clara line in Santa Cruz County near Los Gatos is the David Bruce Winery. Dr. Bruce, a San Jose dermatologist, was an early proponent of the "hands off" school of winemaking. He prefers to take grapes with outstanding character and do as little as possible to them in the wine-making process. This philosophy has resulted in very distinctive wines that have been given abundant wood aging. Critical views on Dr. Bruce's wines, as one might expect, are diverse and vociferous. When well made they are generally strong and very heavy-bodied.

Salinas Valley.   The Salinas Valley of Monterey County is a long, broad valley that opens into Monterey Bay at its northern end and extends in a southeasterly direction. Ocean fogs penetrate the valley as far south as Greenfield and are so pervasive in the northern end of the valley that grapes will not adequately ripen north of Chualar. The principal grape-growing region lies between Soledad and King City, the former classed as Region 1 and the latter as Region 3. The bottomland of the valley is planted primarily with lettuce, which is why Salinas is known as the salad bowl of the country, but the grapes are planted on the benchlands on either side where the soil drainage is better. Compared to Napa and Sonoma, Monterey is relatively arid and irrigation is required for grape growing.

The Salinas Valley of Monterey County is a fascinating blend of all aspects of the California wine industry. It has a viticultural history for the most part of less than twenty-five years and so is bound by few traditions. In climate it resembles the North Coast counties, ranging from Region 1 to Region 3, and it has been planted almost exclusively with the best wine-grape varieties.

For the most part, the Salinas region has been developed by large wineries and vineyard corporations in parcels of hundreds to thousands of acres. In this way it resembles its neighbor to the east, the huge San Joaquin Valley. Monterey produces more tons of wine grapes each year than either Napa or Sonoma, but its name is little recognized beyond the borders of the state. This undoubtedly will change as more wines bearing a Monterey appellation appear across the country. Large vintners such as Mirassou, Paul Masson, Almadén, and Wente are rapidly acquainting a broad cross section of wine consumers with the name.

Almost lost within this great expanse of vineyards, however, are a handful of small firms that are proceeding in much the same way as their neighbors to the north—producing small amounts of extremely high-quality wine. The Chalone vineyard is the oldest of these, dating from 1920. Located on a windy limestone hilltop near Soledad, Chalone came to prominence in the 1970s under the direction of Richard Graff. It is currently very fashionable among Monterey winegrowers to proclaim the importance of "stressing the vines" (purposely limiting growth) in order to achieve the highest quality and intensity in their wines. One cannot help thinking that Chalone's remarkable success with its distinctive Chardonnay and Pinot Noir lends credence to the theory. At Chalone the annual rainfall averages 10 to 12 inches per year, and any irrigation water must be transported to the hilltop.

Farther south, in Greenfield, is the Jekel Vineyard—another family-owned estate winery. Brothers Bill and Gus Jekel have had spectacular success in their short history. The first Jekel Cabernet Sauvignon, a 1978 Private Reserve, placed first in a 1982 blind tasting by eleven members of the British wine trade, ahead of four 1978 First-Growth Bordeaux. The Jekel white wines—Chardonnay, Pinot Blanc, and Johannisberg Riesling—have also been enthusiastically received by consumers.

San Luis Obispo and Santa Barbara. If Monterey is considered adolescent in the history of California viticulture, San Luis Obispo and Santa Barbara, its neighbors to the south, are mere infants. With the exception of three wineries in the Templeton area, best known for Zinfandels, nearly all of the wineries in San Luis Obispo are just a few years old—the great majority of them dating from 1980 or later. Needless to say, it is difficult to attempt any evaluation of the region from such scant evidence, but there is great promise. The new wineries all cluster around either the Paso Robles area or the Edna Valley—near San Luis Obispo city.

Estrella River Winery, near Paso Robles, is an ambitious undertaking with its 1,000-acre estate and 250,000-gallon production. The distinctive winery building features a high observation tower from which one can survey the surrounding hills and vineyards. Estrella River Winery is one of the few wineries producing a true Syrah varietal. Another offering is a late-harvest Muscat Cannelli. The winery is best known, however, for truly superb and reasonably priced Chardonnay and Cabernet Sauvignon. Estrella was recently purchased by Beringer.

Below San Luis Obispo and only 6 miles from the Pacific Ocean is the Edna Valley, rated as Region 2 because of the ocean influence funneling into the valley. The Corbett Canyon Winery was the first in this area, established originally by James Lawrence in 1979. The winery has a capacity of over 750,000 gallons and produces both varietal and generic wines. Grapes for Corbett Canyon wines come from a variety of areas in both San Luis Obispo and Santa Barbara Counties.

Vineyard development in Santa Barbara County has concentrated in two areas: Santa Maria and Sisquoc to the north and the Santa Ynez Valley around the towns of Los Olivos, Solvang, and Buellton. Like San Luis Obispo, Santa Barbara's wineries are all relatively new, with great expectations but very little track record.

Firestone Vineyards, established in 1974 near the town of Los Olivos, is one of the oldest in the county. It is owned by A. Brooks Firestone, of rubber tire fame, and the Suntory Co., the Japanese distillers. The 500 acres of vineyard were planted in 1973, under the guidance of André Tchelistcheff. The 1978 Firestone Chardonnay won a double gold medal at the 1981 International Wine & Spirits

Firestone Vineyards in Santa Barbara County. (Source: Firestone Vineyards.)

Competition in Bristol, England. It was one of only five such awards given that year, and Firestone was the only American winery to receive such an honor.

Southern Coast Counties

One of the more interesting results of the wine boom of the 1960s was the discovery of a small Region 3 microclimate southeast of Los Angeles near the town of Temecula (or rather *re*discovery, since Spanish missionaries had grown wine in nearby San Diego centuries earlier). Grapes were planted in a planned agricultural/industrial development called "Rancho California." Though the region is 23 miles from the ocean at its nearest point, a gap in the coastal hills allows cool, moist breezes to penetrate the vineyards. The first to plant commercial vineyards there was Ely Callaway, a retired textile executive, who opened Callaway Vineyard & Winery in 1974, but that is now owned by the Hiram Walker distilling firm. Today there are about 2,500 acres of vines and eight operating wineries in Temecula, with several more planned. Whites have generally proved more successful than reds here, with Chenin Blanc, Sauvignon Blanc, and Johannisberg Riesling the leading white varieties. All vines are irrigated since there is scant rainfall in the area throughout the growing season.

Vineyard landscape in California's vast, flat Central Valley.

THE
FIRESTONE
VINEYARD
Santa Ynez Valley, California
Gewürztraminer
Residual Sugar 1.24° BRIX   1982   Harvest Sugar 20.4° BRIX

Grown, Produced, and Bottled by The Firestone Vineyard
Los Olivos, California, U.S.A. · Bonded Winery No.4720
Alcohol 11.1% By Volume

ESTATE BOTTLED IN OUR CELLARS BY
FICKLIN
Vineyards
MADERA
CALIFORNIA

California
PORT

ALCOHOL, 18.5% BY VOL.

Central Valley

The gigantic Central Valley lies between the Coastal range and the Sierra Nevadas in central California. It begins northeast of San Francisco and stretches southward to within 100 miles of Los Angeles, making it nearly 400 miles long. At some points it is nearly 100 miles wide. Throughout its length the entire valley is dry and warm, rating a consistent Region 4 and 5 in the University of California at Davis Classification. This incomprehensibly vast, flat valley yields more than 75 percent of the grapes grown in California.

In addition to table grape and raisin production, the Central Valley Valley has been known since Prohibition as the area that produces most of the "ports," "sherries," and other sweet dessert wines of the state. It is the home of the Flame Tokay, a beautiful seedless table grape that also produces the fine, light California brandies that have become so popular. It is also the home of the ubiquitous Thompson Seedless—the ultimate all-purpose grape used for table grapes, raisins, and good, neutral, white blending stock in wines.

What is not so generally realized is that the Central Valley now produces a vast proportion of the state's premium table wine varieties. In 1982, 81 percent of the Chenin Blanc, 70 percent of the Sémillon, 99 percent of the Barbera, and 96 percent of the Grenache grown for California wine came from the Central Valley. Improved viticultural techniques developed by Fresno State University, the University of California at Davis, as well as by local valley growers and producers have helped make this possible.

Improved winemaking practices have also contributed to the outstanding quality of America's everyday wines, which are predominantly grown in this huge valley. Temperature-controlled fermentations, stainless steel tanks, and sterile filtration are standard in the industry today—making possible the fresh, clean flavors that Americans have come to expect in their everyday wines. In fact, few Americans realize that the quality, consistency, and reliability of their inexpensive table wines are nearly unique around the world. The natural endowments of the "Big Valley" itself, the modern technology of enology and viticulture, and the determination of the state's large producers to provide good quality and good value have all combined to make the Central Valley a major center of the American wine industry.

Guild Wineries and Distilleries is one of the larger wine companies in the United States. Located in Lodi, it is a cooperative with about 1,000 member-growers. The company has seven producing wineries: six in the Central Valley and the Cresta Blanca plant in Mendocino County. Today the company produces wines under many labels, the best of which are the "Cresta Blanca" and "Winemasters" lines of varietals.

The LaMont Winery in the San Joaquin Valley. (Source: LaMont Winery.)

In the southern end of the valley, near Bakersfield, is the Bear Mountain area, named for the dominant peak on the east side of the valley. In 1966, a cooperative of grape growers bought an existing facility and started the Bear Mountain Winery. The firm produced a few varietal wines under the "M. LaMont" label, in addition to the large amount of wine sold in bulk to other wineries. The firm attracted the attention of the John Labatt Co., the Canadian brewers, who acquired the company in 1978. The winery was renamed M. LaMont and produces good, lower-priced wines. Today the firm is the property of Anheuser-Busch.

Giumarra has been in the Bear Mountain area since 1946, but has only been producing wines under their own label since the 1973 vintage. Giumarra is family owned, and many of their grapes arrive from their 4,000-acre estate surrounding the winery. Giumarra was the first winery in the southern Central Valley to produce vintage-dated varietals. In addition to the Giumarra Vineyards label, the company also produces wine under the "Breckenridge Cellars" label.

The giant of the valley is, of course, E & J Gallo. Gallo is the largest wine producer in the world, with a storage capacity in excess of 300 million gallons. The winery was founded in 1933 in Modesto by Ernest and Julio Gallo, originally operating in a rented warehouse, and is still entirely owned and operated by the brothers and their families.

It is difficult to convey either the size or the importance of Gallo in the American wine industry. Their bottling capacity of more than three million bottles per day is larger than the entire annual production of most American or European wineries. The bottling facility at Modesto has its own bottle-manufacturing plant. Their brands, in addition to Gallo, include "The Wine Cellars of Ernest and Julio Gallo," "Paisano," "Carlo Rossi," "André" Champagnes, and "E & J" Brandy. Some of their best-known generics are "Chablis Blanc" and "Hearty Burgundy," but they also produce a full line of varietal wines. The "Bartles and James" wine cooler is also a Gallo item.

In the fifty years of its existence, Gallo has single-handedly done more than any other vintner to bring wine into the American home by virtue of its national distribution network, its consistent quality standards, and its reasonable pricing. Gallo has come to mean "wine" to many Americans. The company's contributions to the American wine industry are enormous, not only in terms of consumer acceptance of wine, but also in the fields of viticultural and enological research.

It is unfortunate that the scope of this book allows room for discussion of only a few of the fine California vintners. There are hundreds more waiting to be discovered by the beginning (or experienced) wine enthusiast.

NEW YORK, PENNSYLVANIA, AND NEW ENGLAND

The early vintners of New York faced problems beyond the simple ones of climate, disease, and choice of grape variety. The region of upstate New York from Albany to Buffalo was known in the nineteenth century as the "burned-over district" because of the number of revivalists, spiritualists, utopians, and other purveyors of religious and social causes who swept through the region in waves and roused the population to a frenzy. Among these surges of moral frenzy was the temperance movement, which had it roots here as well. Twice before 1860, some sixty years before national prohibition was declared, the state passed prohibition laws that were either repealed or declared unconstitutional. The region therefore grew slowly and cautiously as a wine center, and the vintners learned to adjust quickly to adversity. That wineries like Taylor, Pleasant Valley, and Widmer have survived Prohibition, the Great Depression, and two world wars is particularly remarkable given the area's long history of distrust and persecution of the wine industry. Vintners learned early to expect the worst and prepare for it.

The New York, Pennsylvania and New England Wine Region

In eastern Pennsylvania there were early attempts to grow wine, but a significant wine industry developed only in the western end of the state. Near Pittsburgh, along the Ohio River, a utopian group called the "Harmonie Society" established vineyards and a winery in the 1920s, and wine growing in that area survived until the twentieth century. On the Lake Erie shoreline, at the town of North East, a winery was established in the 1860s, and North East remains a major wine-growing area of Pennsylvania. Most of the Lake Erie vineyards, however, are in Concord vines, planted for the fresh juice, jelly, and kosher wine industry.

Much of the finest wine growing of the northeastern American wine industry, indeed, that of the entire American East, may still be unrealized, its potential awaiting future developments. Until relatively recently, the scourge of *Phylloxera* and harsh winters have discouraged even the boldest of winegrowers from cultivating the prized *Vitis vinifera* from Europe.

The newest major stumbling block in viticulture is a disease called Crown Gall. While the disease has been observed in Europe and other parts of the world, it seems particularly prevalent in the eastern part of the United States, apparently because cold temperatures seem to aggravate the disease. No particular species of vine seems to be any more resistant to Crown Gall than another, although varieties within each species and several hybrid cultivars exhibit some degree of resistance. Nevertheless, *vinifera* plantings command much of the attention for expanded eastern U.S. viticulture.

Now that eastern growers have been having some limited success with the Old World species, and research for even better results seems promising, plantings have increased dramatically during the past decade or so. Even before these experiments with *vinifera*, eastern vintners had gradually learned how to make superior wines from some of the French-American hybrid grapes, most notably: Seyval Blanc, Vidal Blanc, Maréchal Foch, and Chambourcin. Wines beginning to flow from the better estates, made from Chardonnay, Johannisberg Riesling, Gewürztraminer, and Sauvignon Blanc, along with Cabernet Sauvignon, Syrah, and the hybrids listed above, are finding increased acceptance in the marketplace, and a few are already compared favorably (and rightly so) with the better growths of California and Europe. Obviously, the eastern wine producers are hoping to establish an international reputation for their "new" wine industry.

Finger Lakes

The Finger Lakes district of west central New York enjoys a unique combination of topography and climate. Formed by glacial erosion at the end of the last Ice Age, the Finger Lakes are a series of long and narrow parallel lakes with steep gravelly slopes. The shale soils provide good drainage and the lakes themselves, being large bodies of temporary water, lengthen the growing season in the fall and provide frost protection in the spring.

Keuka Lake, with its unique "y" shape, is the cradle of the Finger Lakes industry. Hammondsport, at the southern tip, is the home of the Pleasant Valley Wine Co., known as "Great Western" (see chapter 4). Founded in 1860 by the Champlin family, the company moved forward the wine-making skill that had been developed in Cincinnati during Nicholas Longworth's reign. Great Western sparkling wines won several major prizes internationally and became the leading champagne made in America. During Prohibition, Great Western remained open—producing wines for sacramental use under government permit. With Repeal it resumed normal operations and continued in much the same fashion until 1950, when Charles Champlin, the principal stockholder and descendant of one of the original founders, died. Ownership passed to the Taylor Wine Co. in 1961, and changes began to occur under the leadership of Greyton Taylor and his son Walter. French-American hybrids were introduced into the line and varietal table wines began to appear. In 1977 Taylor (and with it, Great Western) was purchased by Coca-Cola of Atlanta but operations remained much the same, with an emphasis on sparkling wines and development of a line of premium varietal table wines. With the 1980 vintage, Great Western introduced a line of estate-bottled premium varietal wines produced in small lots. Most notable among these new items have been a Catawba Ice Wine produced in 1981 and a Vidal Blanc in 1980.

Just south of Great Western in Hammondsport is the Taylor Wine Co. that was founded in 1880 by Walter Taylor. In 1919 Taylor bought the Columbia Winery in Hammondsport and moved there to establish a grape juice business during Prohibition. His three sons, Fred, Clarence, and Greyton, joined him, and, as the end of Prohibition neared, the Taylors prepared by updating wine production equipment and embarking upon aggressive marketing programs. They moved quickly into the marketplace and expanded rapidly to become one of the largest wineries in the United States.

In 1983 Seagram's tendered an offer to Coca-Cola to buy its "Wine Spectrum." The offer was accepted, making Taylor, and Great Western, part of the second-largest wine group (second only to Gallo) in the United States. Today the two firms are owned by Vintners International.

A few miles north of Hammondsport, on the western shore of Keuka Lake, is Gold Seal Vineyards—formerly the Urbana Wine Co. It was founded in 1865, at the end of the Civil War, by a group of local growers and merchants. Begun as a champagne house, it traditionally depended upon winemakers imported from France. Most notable of these was Charles Fournier, who came to Gold Seal in 1934 from the Champagne firm of Veuve-Cliquot in Rheims. Under Fournier's able leadership Gold Seal expanded into French-American hybrid production in the 1930s and, with the help of Dr. Konstantin Frank (see below), into growing Old World *Vitis vinifera* grapes in the 1950s. In 1950 Fournier's sparkling wine won the only gold medal at the California State Fair, the first and last year in which the competition was open to wines outside of California. In 1959 he produced Chardonnay and Johannisberg Riesling—the first commercially produced *Vitis vinifera* wines in the East. Fournier retired in 1967, but he continued to exert a positive influence upon Gold Seal until his death in 1983. In 1982 he was named "Man of the Year" by *Wines & Vines* and won the Leon D. Adams Achievement Award, the first easterner to receive either honor. Gold Seal once had the largest commercial plantings of Old World vines in the Finger Lakes region and produced outstanding Chardonnay and Johannisberg Riesling as well as sparkling wines. Seagram purchased Gold Seal in 1981 and in 1985 closed the old winery facility, moving Gold Seal wine operations to the Taylor headquarters.

The late Dr. Konstantin Frank, another notable winegrower in the Finger Lakes locale, was a Russian-born iconoclast whose personality offered a marked contrast to his quiet, soft-spoken collaborator, Charles Fournier. Dr. Frank was a fiesty, outspoken proponent of *Vitis vinifera* wine growing in the East. After surviving the vicissitudes of the Russian Revolution and two world wars in Europe, Frank, a viticulturist and enologist by training, emigrated to America in 1951. Dr. Frank had learned how to grow *Vitis vinifera* grapes in the cold climates of his native Russia and rather quickly established his expertise in the field with Charles Fournier at Gold Seal Vineyards.

Dr. Frank eventually bought his own land, planted Chardonnay and Riesling vines, and, by 1965, his own wines were on the market under the label "Vinifera Wine Cellars." He gave encouragement and firm instructions to interested growers and wine enthusiasts across the country. Many feel that the cradle of the *Vitis vinifera* wine industry in the East was Dr. Frank's porch, where he would hold forth to anyone who would listen to his views about viticulture. Dr. Frank passed away in 1985, but his work remains a source of inspiration to his many devoted followers.

High on Bully Hill, Walter Taylor, grandson of the founder of Taylor Wine, has captured the attention of the world of wine with his Bully Hill Vineyards on the old family estate. In 1970 he was fired from Great Western, where he worked with his father, Greyton Taylor, because he publicly attacked the New York industry for the practice of ameliorating wine with water. He retaliated by starting his own winery and taking for his slogan "wine without water." When he introduced the "Walter S. Taylor" brand of wines, he was promptly sued by Coca-Cola, the new owners of the Taylor brand. Walter lost the suit but won the war with a firestorm of publicity that charged Coke with trying to steal his "heritage." His colorful labels, designed by Taylor himself, are constantly changing and are collector's items themselves. Bully Hill produces a wide range of table wines, mostly from French-American hybrids, and a méthode champenoise sparkling Seyval Blanc.

Not far north of Bully Hill is Heron Hill Vineyards, founded in 1977. Winemaker Peter Johnstone and his partner John Ingle, a grape grower, have very quickly made a reputation for outstanding wines and have a collection of medals and awards from successful competition. Under the Heron Hill and the Otter Spring labels, they are producing Chardonnay and Johannisberg Riesling of consistent quality, as well as a range of wines from French-American hybrids.

West of Keuka Lake in the Naples Valley is Widmer Wine Cellars, founded in 1888. John Jacob Widmer came to the city of Naples, New York, in 1882, and, after an initial struggle to raise capital, eventually was successful in getting his winery under way. His son, Will Widmer, continued the family business, and the

SPECIAL SELECTION

VINTAGE 1982
PREMIUM FINGER LAKES REGION

ROSÉ OF DE CHAUNAC

**DRY VARIETAL TABLE WINE
FROM FRENCH-AMERICAN GRAPES**

ALCOHOL 12% BY VOLUME
PRODUCED AND BOTTLED BY
THE GREAT WESTERN WINERY
HAMMONDSPORT, NEW YORK 14840
BONDED WINERY NUMBER 1

Hermann J. Wiemer Vineyard

FINGER LAKES

Johannisberg Riesling

ESTATE **1982** BOTTLED

A wine produced from 100% Johannisberg Riesling
grapes in the finest European tradition.
PRODUCED AND BOTTLED BY
Hermann J. Wiemer Vineyard, Inc., Rte. 14, Dundee, N.Y. 14837
ALCOHOL 11.5% BY VOLUME

Widmers survived Prohibition by making supplemental grape products such as jellies and juice. Following Repeal, Widmer produced distinctive native American varietal wines, including "Moore's Diamond" and "Missouri Riesling." These caught the attention of marketer Frank Schoonmaker, who began distributing them nationally. Over the years Widmer has developed a reputation for ports and sherries made from native *labrusca* varieties, but the firm is also well known for a Niagara table wine marketed under the proprietary name "Lake Niagara." Like many of the larger family wineries, Widmer was sold in the 1960s to a financial interest, and in 1970 it passed to the R. T. French Co. of mustard fame. In 1982 the facility was purchased from French by a coalition of its operating principals and later sold again to the Canandaigua Wine Company.

North of Widmer, at the north end of Canandaigua Lake, is the Canandaigua Wine Co., home of "Wild Irish Rose." Purchased by Mack and Marvin Sands in 1945, Canandaigua began as a bulk wine distributor. A series of acquisitions and expansions followed quickly. Today Canandaigua Wine Co. is one of the largest wineries in the country. Still operated by Marvin Sands, now along with his son, Richard, the company produces "J. Roget" bulk-process sparkling wines, as well as "Virginia Dare," "Wild Irish Rose," "Manischewitz," "Widmer," "Mother, Vineyards" Scuppernong, and "Bisceglia" lines, most from native *labrusca* or *rotundifolia* grapes.

East of Canandaigua and Keuka Lake is Seneca Lake, the largest and deepest of the Finger Lakes. Forty miles long and 640 feet deep, Seneca Lake is a significant factor in the climate of the surrounding hillsides. In the 1960s and 1970s, as transportation became less of a problem and the idea of small estate wineries became a reality in New York State, a noticeable shift occurred in the concentration of vineyards from the east of Keuka Lake toward the larger and deeper Seneca and Cayuga Lakes, which afford better climatological protection. This became an important factor as cold-sensitive varieties of *Vitis vinifera* and French-American hybrids were planted. Small wineries began to appear in this region: Glenora in 1977; Wagner in 1978; Wiemer in 1979; Four Chimneys in 1980; and, in 1981, Poplar Ridge, Rolling Vineyards, Wickham, and Giasi. On Cayuga Lake's east side the same event has transpired: Plane's Cayuga Vineyard and Lucas Winery in 1980; Americana in 1981; Frontenac Point and Lakeshore in 1982. As growers also became producers of wine, the advantage of being close to a large winery diminished, and the microclimate of the vineyard became most important.

Bill Wagner, owner-operator of Wagner Vineyards, has claimed for years that the east side of Seneca Lake is the best spot in the Finger Lakes for grapes. He has been growing grapes there since the 1940s, and his father grew them before that on a site south of Lodi. In 1976 he broke ground for a winery and crushed his first grapes in 1978. His Chardonnay and Johannisberg Riesling are outstanding—displaying superior quality and garnering many coveted awards. Wagner also makes Seyval Blanc in both a semidry Teutonic style and a bone dry, wood-aged French style.

On the west side of Seneca Lake is Glenora Wine Cellars, whose managing partners own vineyards on both sides of the lake. Like Heron Hill and Wagner, Glenora is a small, new winery whose products have been distinguished by an emphasis on the highest-quality grapes and distinctive winemaking style. Since their first crush in 1977, Glenora's owners have gradually defined and clarified their goals and are now producing wines from only five grapes, all white, from *vinifera* and French-American hybrid vines. Many of the wines bear vineyard designations, among them "Spring Ledge" or "Anchor Acres." The wines are consistent medal winners in competitions entered and have received deserved attention and acclaim from wine critics nationwide.

Hermann J. Wiemer, whose winery and vineyards are situated just north of Glenora in Dundee, New York, is a native of Bernkastel, West Germany. After extensive training in all aspects of viticulture and enology, Wiemer came to the United States, where he spent a number of years as the winemaker at Bully Hill Vineyards in Hammondsport. He established a nursery business specializing in grafted vines during his years there and, in 1973, bought land to establish his own vineyard. In 1979 he produced his first wines under the Hermann J. Wiemer label. The winery produces Johannisberg Riesling in several styles: dry, late harvest, and an occasional individual bunch-selected wine. Wiemer's finely crafted, sometimes austere Chardonnay and Gewürztraminer wines are as distinctive as his accent and demeanor.

On Cayuga Lake, east of Seneca, the most notable development has been the establishment of Planes Cayuga Vineyard by Bob and Mary Plane. What began for the Plane's as an amateur interest in wine developed into a viticultural endeavor and, in 1980, culminated in a commercial winery of their own. Their farm, originally purchased as a summer retreat, showed interesting vineyard potential, and in the early 1970s they experimented with plantings of a number of varieties. By the late 1970s, the designation "Robert Plane Vineyard" began to appear on the labels of various premium wines in the Finger Lakes and rapidly became known as a trademark of superior quality. The Planes decided to commercially produce wines and crushed grapes for their own label in 1980. the 1980 Chardonnay and 1980 Chancellor Noir showed great character, and, despite a disastrous freeze in 1981, the 1982 wines appear to be of equal quality.

One of the more attention-getting entrants in the Finger Lakes wine scene during the past decade has been Casa Larga Vineyards. Located immediately southeast of Rochester in Fairport, New York, its climate is actually more affected by the Great Lakes than the Finger Lakes. Nevertheless, the Colaruotolo family has been successful in producing consistently high-quality, award-winning table wines from Old World, native, and French-American hybrid grapes.

Erie-Chautauqua-Niagara

Despite an early history of wine growing, dating from 1818 when Elijah Fay and his son Joseph planted the area's first vineyards, the Erie-Chautauqua Region in the western corner of New York State suffered the most from the long "dry" tradition of the area. Ester McNeil organized the first chapter of the Women's Christian Temperance Union in Fredonia in 1873. And Dr. Charles Welch, an ardent "dry," found a welcome home for his grape juice business in nearby Westfield in 1897. The siege of the Prohibitionists was long and stormy, and their influence remains a factor in this region.

This fact is truly unfortunate, given that the area has probably the best climate in mainland New York State for growing top-quality wine grapes. Lake Erie protects the strip of shoreline extending from Ohio through the northwest tip of Pennsylvania and across the western border of New York State from frost in spring and fall and extends the growing season significantly. This influence also extends into what is known as the Niagara Peninsula, a strip of land between Lake Erie and Lake Ontario that is the core of Canada's eastern grape industry. The majority of New York's grapes are planted in this western region, but most of the grapes are Concords, which are used primarily for juice and fresh fruit.

There are, however, two major exceptions to this rule. A great many Concord grapes grown in western New York State are shipped to two kosher wine producers, Mogen David, now owned by the Wine Group, a California corporate giant ranking in the top ten largest wine producers in this country and that produces more than 6 million gallons of wine per year. Manischewitz is the other major brand of kosher wine, produced by the Monarch Wine Co., a Canadaigua Wine Co. property located in Brooklyn, New York. However, the juice for these products is extracted at a plant in Fredonia, New York, called Fredonia Products Inc., which also produces a line of its own wines at Fredonia as well.

Another part of the western New York State wine spectrum is the handful of new small farm wineries that have emerged during the past several decades. These few have entered the premium wine field with plantings of Old World vines and French-American hybrids. First to undertake the project was Fred Johnson, a native of Westfield who opened a winery at his farm in 1961 and exclusively used his own grapes. He produces primarily French-American hybrid wines from such grapes as Seyval Blanc, Aurora Blanc, and Chancellor Noir.

In Dunkirk, just north of Fredonia, Gary Woodbury and sister-in-law Page Woodbury are operating one of the most ambitious new wineries in the region.

Frankly acknowledging his debt to Dr. Konstantin Frank for encouraging him to plant *vinifera*, Woodbury now produces Chardonnay, Johannisberg Riesling, Gewürztraminer, and a "Blanc de Blanc" champagne produced 100 percent from Chardonnay grapes.

Hudson River Region

The Hudson River Valley is one of the oldest commercial wine-growing districts in the United States. Vineyards were planted here in the 1600s in the area around New Paltz. Today most of the wines from this region are made from native *Vitis labrusca* and French-American hybrid varieties.

Hudson Valley Inset

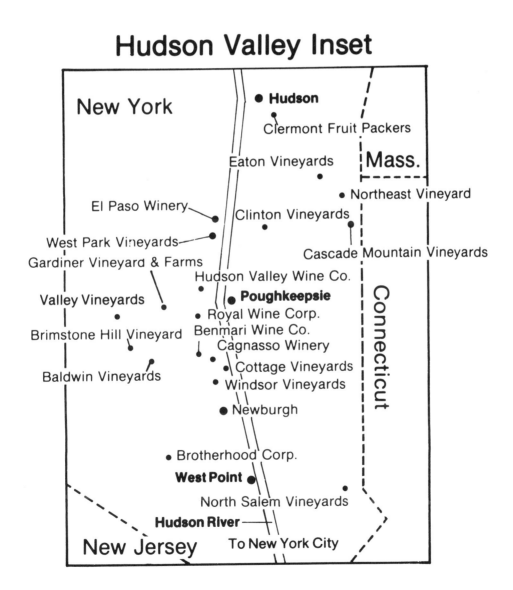

The oldest continuously operating commercial winery in America is the Brotherhood Winery: founded in 1839 near Washingtonville, New York, by Jean Jacques, it is currently operated by the Farrell family who acquired the property more than fifty years ago. Brotherhood survived Prohibition by the production and marketing of sacramental wines, and today is most famous for its dessert wines. It is the only New York winery producing a Spanish-type Flor sherry, and it also makes a variety of ports, some vintaged, which are outstanding.

Until recently the Hudson Valley Wine Company was another historic wine estate overlooking the Hudson River. It was started in 1907 near Highland, New York, by Alexander Bolognesi and occupies a magnificent 200-acre site. In 1972 it passed from the Bolognesi family to wine importer Herb Feinberg.

There are a cluster of wineries around the village of Marlboro, New York, including the old Great River Winery now owned by Windsor Vineyards of California. One of the most popular wineries in the area is the Benmarl Wine Co. owned by Mark Miller and his wife Dene Miller purchased the vineyard in 1957, when he was working as an illustrator in New York. In 1962 he moved to Burgundy for seven years and he continued working as an illustrator while developing his interest in and knowledge of wine. By 1969, when he returned to

America's oldest winery in continuous operation, the Brotherhood Winery near Washingtonville, New York. (Source: Brotherhood Winery.)

America, he was ready to undertake a winery of his own. But he chose an unusual avenue to finance it. He formed the Société des Vignerons, whose members paid a fee to support the winery and in return received the rights to the product of two vines, that is, twelve bottles of wine per year. The members also help with the crush at harvest time. Miller makes wines from Chardonnay and selected French-American hybrids and is successful in marketing the wines (that the Société members do not buy) to the New York City restaurant and retail trade. His son Eric, who served as winemaker at Benmarl in its early years of operation, started his own Chaddsford Winery in Pennsylvania.

Two small wineries on the east side of the Hudson River are producing notable wines. Ben Feder of Clinton Vineyards, a book designer by profession, produces two distinctive wines—a Seyval Blanc table wine as well as a méthode champenoise Sparkling Seyval Blanc—despite the sometimes severe weather conditions. At nearby Cascade Mountain Vineyards, novelist Bill Wetmore produces a variety of wines from French-American hybrid grapes. Wetmore is perhaps best known for his "Le Hamburger Red." He has also produced an elegant dry Ravat Blanc, though most of his wines have proprietary labels.

Long Island

Though the history of wine growing on Long Island can be traced back to the 1700s, only in the last ten years has there been significant interest in the region as a wine-producing area. Most of Long Island's wine industry is located on the North Fork of the island's East End, though some acreage has been planted on the South Fork. The waters of the Long Island Sound bordering the North Fork and the Atlantic Ocean on the South Fork give the area a growing season in excess of 200 days. The wine grapes grown on Long Island currently include such Old World varieties as Chardonnay, Johannisberg Riesling, Gewürztraminer, Cabernet Sauvignon, Pinot Noir, and Merlot. Alex and Louisa Hargrave were the first to start a winery there—producing their first wine at Hargrave Vineyard near Cutchogue in 1975. Though hundreds of additional acres have since been planted, wineries are developing more slowly, with Bridgehampton Winery (on the South Fork) producing wine in 1982 and the Lenz Vineyards of Patricia and Peter Lenz (in Peconic on the North Fork) in 1983. The superb Hargrave wines have won many accolades, and the future of wine production in the area is probably limited only by skyrocketing land values and real estate taxes that make vineyard land relatively expensive.

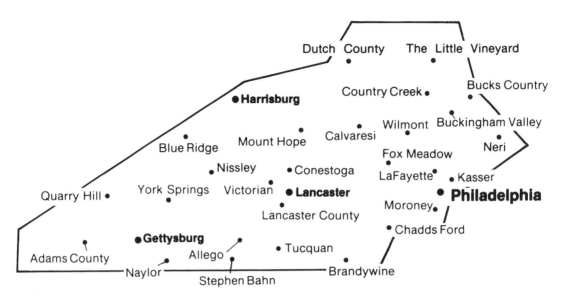

Southeastern Pennsylvania Inset

Pennsylvania

Located southwest of Westfield, New York, and just over the state line on the shore of Lake Erie is the town of North East, Pennsylvania, the gateway to midwestern wine growing. The history of this area is tied to that of western New York and, as there, the Concord vine still predominates. However, Pennsylvania positive effect on the wine industry. Today there are more than forty bonded wineries in Pennsylvania producing wines from local grapes. About half of the ing the way for a small, premium wine industry. The bill had an instantaneous positive effect on the wine industry. Today there are more than forty bonded wineries in Pennsylvania producing wines from local grapes. About half of the wineries produce 10,000 gallons or less annually. One of the foremost proponents of that legislation was Douglas Moorhead, proprietor of Presque Isle Wine Cellars. Moorhead became interested in wine while in Germany in the U.S. military service and returned to North East determined to grow Johannisberg Riesling. With the encouragement of Dr. Konstantin Frank he successfully grew a number of Old World grapes. Presque Isle opened as a home winemaker's supply business in 1964 and, with the passage of the necessary legislation in the state, began producing wine commercially in 1969.

Also quick to take advantage of the new law were a group of growers from North East headed by Blair McCord, who formed the Penn-Shore winery in 1969. Now, having grown with expanded production limits, a storage capacity of 175,000 gallons exists at Penn-Shore. The firm produces a variety of table wines and sparkling wines from *Vitis vinifera*, native *Vitis labrusca*, and French-American hybrid grapes. Five years later, in 1974, Bob and Frank Mazza opened Mazza Vineyards, a 50,000-gallon winery with distinctive Spanish-style architecture. They produce a variety of *Vitis vinifera* wines there, as well as French-American hybrid and *Vitis labrusca* wines. In 1980 the Mazzas joined forces with Charles Romito to purchase the Mt. Hope Winery in Cornwall, Pennsylvania—an attractive 32-room Victorian mansion with extensive grounds, as well as vineyards, which attracts many visitors each year.

The southeastern portion of Pennsylvania, between Harrisburg and Philadelphia, is simultaneously the state's oldest and newest viticultural region. Grape growing in this area was attempted in colonial times, and the first domesticated native grape, the Alexander, was discovered near Philadelphia before the American Revolution. But from the turn of the century until 1963, when Melvin Gordon bonded his tiny Conestoga Vineyard winery near Lancaster, Pennsylvania, there were no new wineries founded in Pennsylvania.

Located near the Delaware River, which divides Pennsylvania and New Jersey, is the town of New Hope where, in 1973, Arthur Gerold established the Bucks County Winery. Gerold, with a background in theatrical costuming, set about the wine business with an obvious flair for theater. The winery sets the stage for wine appreciation with a wine museum that includes a collection of seventeenth-century wineglasses and mannequins attired in colonial costume.

Richard Nissley retired from his bridge construction business and started a winery in Bainbridge, Pennsylvania. His wife and four children are also actively involved in the firm, which produces award-winning varietal wines and proprietary blends from *Vitis vinifera*, native, and French-American varieties.

Richard Naylor began modestly in 1978 with a cinder-block building and a small acreage of vines. His winery is located near Stewartstown, almost on the Maryland border. In addition to making fine wine, Naylor's secret of success has been in marketing the major share of his wines directly to visitors at the winery. His wines have been consistent prizewinners in competition, and, in addition to his grape wines, Naylor also produces an excellent strawberry wine called "Fragola."

New England

New England, like most of the colonial United States, has a history of Old World grape experimentation, failure, then the development of hardy native types. The area's most notable contribution was the development of the Concord grape, named for the Massachusetts town in which it was first developed by Ephraim Bull during the mid-1800s.

Chicama Vineyards on Martha's Vineyard, an island off the Massachusetts coastline, was founded by two Californians who thought the climate there was unusually mild for the Northeast. With vines from Dr. Konstantin Frank they planted 3 acres and quickly added 20 more. In 1973 they produced their first estate wines in a 4,000-gallon winery from a selection of *Vitis vinifera* varieties. Today the vineyards have expanded, neighbors are also growing grapes for the firm, and the winery has been enlarged to 20,000 gallons.

In neighboring Rhode Island, Jim and Lolly Mitchell founded Sakonnet Vineyards in 1975 on a site surrounded by water on three sides between the Sakonnet River and the Patchet Reservoir. They now have 40 acres of Old World and French-American hybrid vines with a winery production capacity of 30,000 gallons per year. They are best known for their "Rhode Island Red" and "America's Cup White," but they also produce a number of fine award-winning varietal wines including Chardonnay and Johannisberg Riesling. (The Mitchells recently sold Sakonnet to the Samson family.)

In Connecticut, Sherman Haight came to consider wine growing as an alternative to cattle and sheep for his Litchfield farm. Haight planted vineyards in 1975,

Rhode Island's Sakonnet Vineyards. (Source: Sakonnet Vineyards; photo by Steve Rosenthal.)

and in 1978 his Haight Vineyard became Connecticut's first bonded winery under a new state law that he fostered diligently. Haight's acres of vines are divided between *Vitis vinifera* and French-American hybrids. In the very first vintage Haight won awards for all three wines produced. In 1983 Haight Vineyard crushed 50 tons of Chardonnay, Johannisberg Riesling, Seyval Blanc, and Maréchal Foch.

GREAT LAKES REGION

The Great Lakes, from Lake Superior in the west to Lake Ontario in the east, provide a climatic buffer zone along their coastlines that offer protection to grapevines. The large bodies of water act as a damper on temperature extremes, softening the fluctuations. They slow down the spring and lengthen the autumn. The constant breezes caused by the difference between land and water temperatures also provide frost protection and help prevent mildew.

Southern Ohio Inset

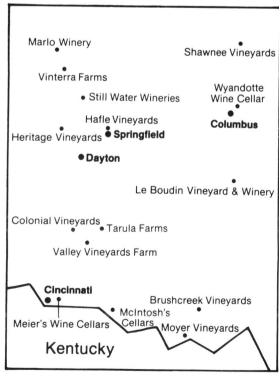

Southwestern Michigan Inset

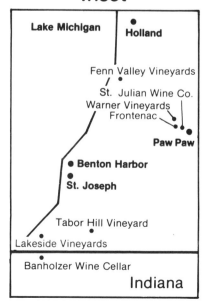

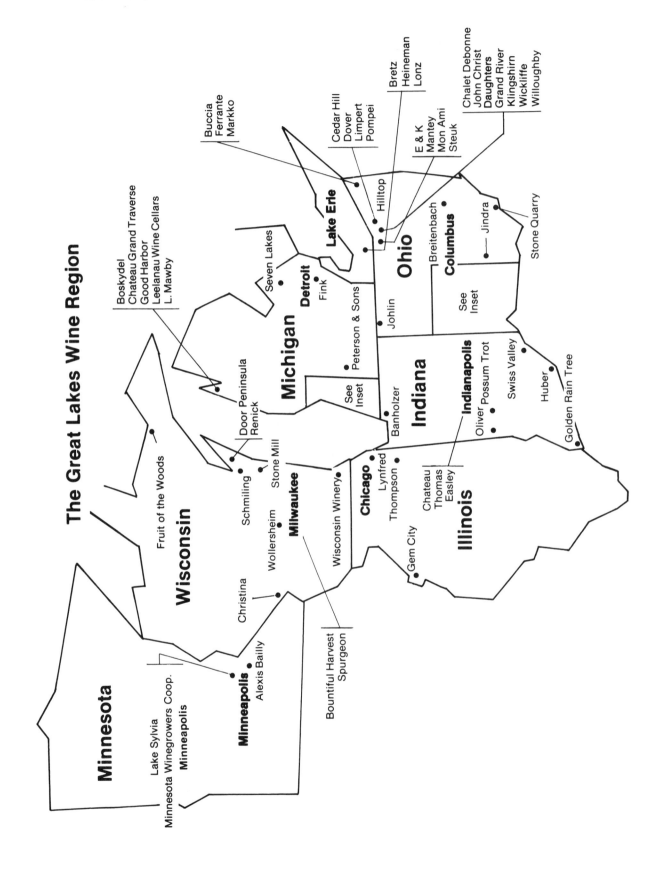

The Great Lakes Wine Region

Minnesota

Lake Sylvia
Minnesota Winegrowers Coop.
Minneapolis

Alexis Bailly

Wisconsin

Fruit of the Woods

Christina

Wollersheim

Schmiling

Milwaukee

Stone Mill

Door Peninsula
Renick

Wisconsin Winery

Bountiful Harvest
Spurgeon

Gem City

Chicago

Lynfred
Thompson

Illinois

Chateau
Thomas
Easley

Boskydel
Chateau Grand Traverse
Good Harbor
Leelanau Wine Cellars
L. Mawby

Seven Lakes

Michigan

Detroit

Fink

Peterson & Sons

See
Inset

Banholzer

Johlin

Indiana

Indianapolis

Oliver Possum Trot

Swiss Valley

Huber

Golden Rain Tree

Buccia
Ferrante
Markko

Lake Erie

Cedar Hill
Dover
Limpert
Pompei

Hilltop

E & K
Mantey
Mon Ami
Steuk

Bretz
Heineman
Lonz

Chalet Debonne
John Christ
Daughters
Grand River
Klingshirn
Wickliffe
Willoughby

Ohio

Breitenbach

Columbus

See
Inset

Jindra

Stone Quarry

Ohio

Ohio is bounded by Lake Erie on the north and the Ohio River on the south. The Ohio River Valley, the first Ohio area to be settled, was also the first to have a significant commercial wine industry. Nicholas Longworth, an ambitious young lawyer with an interest in wine, began planting vineyards in Cincinnati in the 1820s. After an initial search for the "right" varieties, he settled on the Catawba grape, which he had received from John Adlum (see chapter 4) and quickly made a fortune by producing and marketing sparkling Catawba wine. By the 1840s he had accumulated over 1,000 acres of vineyard, and numerous other growers in the area were also supplying him with grapes. But the empire fell as quickly as it had risen. By the time of Longworth's death in 1863, most of the 3,000 acres of vineyards along the Ohio River were dead, not from *Phylloxera*, but from *Oidium*, or powdery mildew, which the growers had no means of controlling at that time.

But as one star fell, another rose. In the 1830s vineyards began to appear on the Lake Erie shoreline and on the little islands in Lake Erie north of Sandusky. During the Civil War, when Longworth's empire was crumbling, the Golden Eagle Winery was opened on Middle Bass Island in Lake Erie. By 1875 it had become the largest winery in the United States, producing upwards of 500,000 gallons a year—yet it was only one of many wineries on the Lake Erie islands and the shoreline near Sandusky and Port Clinton at that time.

This second burgeoning wine industry fell to Prohibition. Of the hundreds of wineries large and small that existed at the turn of the century in Ohio, only a handful survived Prohibition and its aftermath.

Meier's Wine Cellars in the Cincinnati area is a fascinating combination of old and new and north and south in the Ohio wine industry. John Meier, the founder, dated from Longworth's era, and his winery had survived the *Oidium* plague by buying grapes from one of the Lake Erie islands. During Prohibition, when it was acquired by Henry Sonneman, Meier's Wine Cellars was a grape juice operation. Sonneman quickly popularized his "Unfermented Catawba Grape Juice." After Repeal he acquired the Isle St. George vineyards in Lake Erie and popularized the "Isle St. George" label. In 1976 Robert Gottesman acquired Meier's and quickly began to build it into a uniquely Ohio wine empire. He hired expert winemaker Ted Moulton, winner of many wine-making awards, and acquired the historic Lonz Winery, formerly the Golden Eagle Winery, on Middle Bass Island. He bought Mantey Vineyards and Mon Ami Champagne Company, both historic Lake Erie wine properties. Gottesman began removing Concord vines in 1977 and replanting his Lake Erie vineyards with *Vitis vinifera*. The main winery facility remains at its location near Cincinnati, but the unique Lake Erie wine properties, with their ambience of another era, contribute their own distinctive brands and styles.

Northwest of Cincinnati in Morrow, Ohio, is Valley Vineyards, owned by Kenneth and Jim Schucter. Ken was an executive in the automobile industry, when he tired of the corporate life and started planting French-American hybrid vines on the truck farm that he and his brother already owned. A year later, in 1970, they opened Valley Vineyards. Today Valley has 45 acres of grapes and produces more than 30,000 gallons of wine a year.

In the northeast corner of Ohio, almost on the Pennsylvania border, is Markko Vineyard, founded in 1968 by Arnulf (Arnie) Esterer. Esterer was an amateur wine buff who made the pilgrimage to Hammondsport to see Dr. Konstantin Frank and became converted to Old World grape growing. He apprenticed two vintages with Dr. Frank and then began planting Chardonnay and Johannisberg Riesling near Conneaut, Ohio. With 10 acres of vines, the Markko Winery has remained small but places a strong emphasis on quality.

Chalet Debonné Vineyards was founded in 1971 when Tony P. Debevc, recently graduated from Ohio State University in pomology, persuaded his father, Tony J. Debevc, to plant 10 acres of French-American hybrid grapes on the family farm. Together they built a winery and tasting room in the style of a chalet and commenced operations. Later they hired Mississippi State University-trained Anthony Carlucci as winemaker. Located near Madison, east of Cleveland, the winery now has 46 acres of grapes and a storage capacity of 75,000 gallons.

Michigan

Michigan's wine-growing history is not particularly long or distinguished. Although there were a few wineries in Michigan before Prohibition, they were small, located mostly on the east side of the state, and did not survive the long dry spell. Today most of Michigan's grapes are grown in the southwestern corner of the state near the Lake Michigan shore. This industry emerged circa 1900 as a result of the great demand for grape juice, and the primary variety planted was Concord. When Prohibition arrived, the demand for the Concord juice grapes increased. With Repeal, the market underwent a turnabout as demand for wine grapes increased and for Concord decreased. Michigan adopted a protectionist excise tax measure whereby wines made outside Michigan were taxed at 54c per gallon, while Michigan wines made primarily from Michigan grapes were taxed at a rate of only 4c per gallon. The Michigan wine industry survived with the help of this subsidy for several decades before the change in taste of the wine-consuming public militated toward drier, more sophisticated table wines. Traditionally, Michigan had been a producer of sweet, fruity wines.

Today the Michigan wine industry resembles that of its eastern counterparts in Ohio, New York, and Pennsylvania. The largest producers have moved toward an improved line of table wines, primarily through the introduction of French-American hybrids. They also depend heavily upon sparkling and dessert wines, in which the Northeastern wineries have always excelled. In addition, a number of small farm or estate wineries have appeared in the last decade, producing superior table wines from *Vitis vinifera* and French-American hybrid varieties. The large wineries of Michigan are clustered in a small area in southwestern Michigan, west of Kalamazoo.

New generations of owners with new ideas and an infusion of new wine-making talent brought about progressive changes in nearby Paw Paw at the St. Julian Winery and Warner Vineyards. St. Julian, under the leadership of David Braganini, grandson of the founder, opened a second winery in Frankenmuth in 1981 and a retail sales outlet in Mackinac City in 1983. At the 3 million-gallon Warner facility, Michigan's largest winery, many acres of grapes were converted from native to Old World and French-American hybrid varieties. The Warner lines of table, dessert, and sparkling wines have steadily improved and gained attention. Much of the Warner production continues to be grape juice and concentrate products.

The real revolution in Michigan winegrowing began in 1970 when Len Olson and Carl Banholzer opened Tabor Hill in Berrien County. They planted only premium *Vitis vinifera* and French-American hybrid grapes, and the wines that began to appear, most notably a late harvest Vidal Blanc, captured the attention of wine critics. Tabor Hill is now owned by David Upton, but the 1970 pioneering efforts of Olson and Banholzer continue to influence the wine industry in Michigan.

Quick to follow Olson in the southwest area was Fenn Valley Vineyards, owned by the Welsch family. Although they began initially with wines made from Washington State grapes, they produced their first estate wines in 1978. Today, Fenn Valley has a capacity of more than 100,000 gallons and frequently wins awards for product quality.

The discovery of a whole new wine-growing region in Michigan in the late 1960s is perhaps the most significant development in the state. The Leelanau Peninsula, located in the northwest section of the state, juts out into Lake Michigan. With the lake on the west and Grand Traverse Bay on the east, the vines are protected from severe winter weather. In 1965 Bernard Rink began growing French-American hybrid grapes there and in 1976 bonded a winery that he named Boskydel. In 1975 Canadian millionaire Edward O'Keefe, of the O'Keefe brewing family, planted 50 acres of *Vitis vinifera* on Old Mission Peninsula in the center of Grand Traverse Bay. Château Grand Traverse was opened shortly thereafter and now cultivates approximately 100 acres of Chardonnay and Johannisberg Riesling. Also in 1975, Charles Kalchik, a local fruit grower, began planting French-

Michigan Light
SOLERA CREAM SHERRY
Premero Añadas 1946

Cellared and Bottled by Warner Vineyards
Paw Paw, Van Buren County, Michigan
Alcohol 16% By Volume

SERVE COLD

Fenn Valley ®

FENNVILLE

Vignoles

1981
ESTATE BOTTLED

A PREMIUM WHITE TABLE WINE

PRODUCED AND BOTTLED IN OUR NATURALLY COOL CELLARS BY
FENN VALLEY VINEYARDS • FENNVILLE, MICHIGAN 49408

BWC-MI-38

American hybrids. He built a winery, Leelanau Wine Cellars, which at 85,000 gallons is currently the largest winery on the Leelanau Peninsula. The cellars are now owned by Michael Jacobson and mastered by winemaker Ed Van Dyne.

Indiana

Indiana's wine growing developed first primarily along the Ohio River Valley in the south. Arriving Swiss settlers planted vines, learned the heartbreaking lesson of *Phylloxera* and other diseases, and replanted with hardier native American grapes. Catawbas were planted to supply Longworth's wine empire in nearby Cincinnati, but succumbed to *Oidium* disease not long after the Ohio vineyards fell. Prohibition all but eradicated wine growing in the state except for home winemakers.

Indiana passed a small-winery bill in 1971, largely due to the efforts of one of those home winegrowers, a law professor from the University of Indiana named William Oliver. One year later he opened his Oliver Wine Company in Bloomington, Indiana. Today Oliver produces wine from 42 acres of grapes and makes mead from local honey. The capacity of the winery has grown to about 35,000 gallons. In nearby Unionville, Ben and Lee Sparks have undertaken winemaking on a much smaller scale. Their Possum Trot Vineyards consists of 3 acres of grapes and a winery in a remodeled barn that can accommodate about 3,000 gallons. The influence of the Sparks is felt much more widely, however, through their leadership of the Indiana Winegrower's Guild—an industry promotional association.

In the southwestern corner of the state, near Evansville, is the Golden Rain Tree Winery, the state's largest. Started in 1975 by a group of growers, the winery produces primarily French-American hybrid wines and most of the labels are proprietary. "Criterion White" as one of their best known wines and has received many prizes in state and regional competitions. It is made primarily from Vidal Blanc.

Illinois

Illinois's oldest winery is a little-known operation called Gem City Vineland on the state's western border in the town of Nauvoo. Founded in 1857 by the Icarian sect, a French utopian society that settled in Nauvoo, the winery produces a range of *Vitis labrusca* wines.

South of Chicago, in the little town of Monee, is the Thompson Winery and surrounding vineyards. The vineyard was planted in 1963 by Bern Ramey, an

LAKE ERIE
VIDAL BLANC

A Light Dry Table Wine

PRODUCED & BOTTLED BY CHALET DEBONNÉ VINEYARDS, INC
MADISON, OHIO
ALCOHOL 12% BY VOLUME

1987

Wollersheim

CHARDONNAY

Dry Wisconsin White Wine

Grown, Produced And Bottled By
Wollersheim Winery, Inc.
Prairie du Sac, Wis.

Alcohol 12.5% By Volume   Contains Sulfites

Ohio sparkling winemaker who set out to prove that fine wines could be grown there. He succeeded, but lost his vineyards to a deadly weed-killer sprayed in the vicinity. John Thompson bought the winery in 1970, restored the vineyards, and is again making wine. Most notable are his "Père Marquette" and "Père Hennepin" sparkling wines.

In Roselle, Illinois, Lynn and Fred Koehler have commenced production in their small Lynfred Winery. The initial wines have won some prestigious awards and the brand should gain deserved acclaim.

Wisconsin

Count Agoston Haraszthy, of California wine fame, first settled in Wisconsin during the 1840s, but gave up wine growing there as a bad bet. But at least one man, Bob Wollersheim, has been determined enough to try it again. In 1973 he bought the property that had once been owned by Haraszthy and still bore traces

Barrel-aging cave at Wollersheim Winery, Prairie Du Sac, Wisconsin. (Source: Robert Wollersheim.)

of his nineteenth-century vineyard and wine cellars. Wollersheim planted the vineyards with French-American hybrids. He made his first wines in 1975, and they quickly became perennial award winners. Wollersheim now has accumulated 20 acres of vineyard. The many visitors who frequent the winery are shown the wine "cave" that Agoston Haraszthy is believed to have carved in the hillside above the Wisconsin River.

Minnesota

If wine growing in Wisconsin is difficult, in Minnesota it can only be called heroic. Yet David Bailly and his daughter, Nan, are doing just that on a site south of Minneapolis on the Mississippi River. The Bailly family planted their first vineyard in 1973, but most of it was killed in the winter of 1976. They planted again and in 1977 began the practice of burying all their vines in late autumn in order to insulate them against harsh winter injury. Today they have 12 acres of vines, including Seyval Blanc, Maréchal Foch, and Léon Millot. In addition to wines made from these French-American hybrids, they also produce "Country Red," which is made from a blend of *Vitis riparia*, a native species of grape.

THE NORTHWEST

The region known as the Northwest, or Pacific Northwest, includes the wine-growing areas of Oregon, Washington, and Idaho. None of these states has a long history of commercial *Vitis vinifera* wine production, although *Vitis labrusca* grapes have been grown in Washington and Oregon for many years. Despite geographic proximity, the wine-growing locales of these three states have little in common. Oregon's winegrowers cluster along the west coast of the state between the Coast ranges and the Cascades. In Washington, grapes are grown on the east side of the Cascades in what may be described as a temperate desert. East of these two coastal states, in Idaho, the vineyards grow in river valleys at elevations of 2,000 to 2,500 feet, with moderate rainfall and fluctuating temperatures. The growth of this three-state region in the production of fine table wines has been explosive. In 1963 there was one single commercial winery in the area producing premium wines. By 1983 there were more than sixty—most of them having commenced operations in the last decade or so.

The Northwest Wine Region

Seattle   **Washington**

Famili Pucci Vin

See Inset

La Casa De Vin

Oregon

Brundage
Facelli

Ste. Chapelle
Weston

See Inset

Boise   **Idaho**

Tennyson

Washington Inset

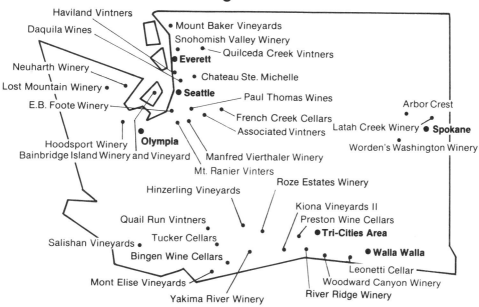

Haviland Vintners

Daquila Wines

Mount Baker Vineyards

Snohomish Valley Winery

Quilceda Creek Vintners

Neuharth Winery

Everett

Lost Mountain Winery

Chateau Ste. Michelle

E.B. Foote Winery

Seattle

Paul Thomas Wines

Arbor Crest

French Creek Cellars

Latah Creek Winery   **Spokane**

Associated Vintners

Hoodsport Winery

Olympia

Worden's Washington Winery

Bainbridge Island Winery and Vineyard

Manfred Vierthaler Winery

Mt. Ranier Vinters

Roze Estates Winery

Hinzerling Vineyards

Kiona Vineyards II

Preston Wine Cellars

Quail Run Vintners

Tri-Cities Area

Tucker Cellars

Salishan Vineyards

Walla Walla

Bingen Wine Cellars

Leonetti Cellar

Mont Elise Vineyards

Woodward Canyon Winery

Yakima River Winery

River Ridge Winery

Western Oregon Inset

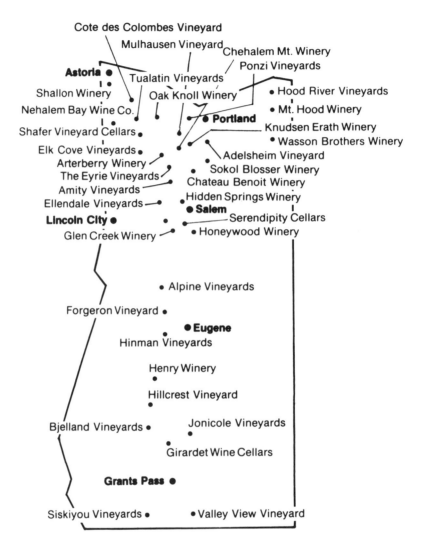

During the past decade or so some of the most coveted awards for wine-growing excellence have been won by vintners in the Northwest. The region is not simply an outgrowth of the vast California industry, but a whole new experession of quality table wine.

Traditional wine markets across America have accepted the relative newness of the Northwest wine industry much more readily than many wine-marketing experts had anticipated. Much of this is due to the state-of-the-art equipment and extremely high caliber of people employed by the new Oregon, Washington, and Idaho wineries. This is one of the nation's most interesting wine-growing regions.

Oregon

Most of the wine-growing activity in Oregon has been in the Willamette Valley just south of Portland. David Lett was one of the first to establish commercial operations there, settling in the Dundee area in 1965. Lett was in search of the best place to grow Pinot Noir, and, after deciding the Umpqua Valley to the south was too warm, he settled in Dundee, built his Eyrie Vineyards winery, and has been growing exceptional Oregon Pinot Noir ever since. He is perhaps best known for a well-publicized tasting by international experts in which his 1975 Pinot Noir placed second against the best French Burgundies personally selected for the competition by the renowned Burgundy shipper Joseph Drouhin.

Most of the excitement about Oregon wines has focused on Lett's success with Pinot Noir, a variety that can be grown in a wide variety of places but performs distinctively only in a very few. California has for years had difficulty in producing a first-class Pinot Noir. The Carneros district of Napa has shown the best promise in California, but the cool, wet, overcast climate of Oregon's west coast perhaps shows the most potential in the United States. In the 1983 American Wine Competition conducted by the Beverage Testing Institute and open to wineries throughout the United States, Oregon clearly emerged as the leading producer of Pinot Noir. Other wineries in the Willamette Valley producing distinctive Pinot Noirs are Amity and Elk Cove.

With the exception of Pinot Noir, most of the grapes grown in Oregon, especially in the cooler Willamette Valley, are white varieties such as Chardonnay, Johannisberg Riesling, and Gewürztraminer. Sokol Blosser, the most modern winery in the area, produces about 70 percent white wines. In contrast to most of the Oregon wineries that produce Chardonnay in a rich, buttery Montrachet style, Sokol Blosser's Chardonnay exhibits a fruity Chablis-type of style.

When Susan Sokol and William Blosser were first married, owning and operating a winery was little more than a dream they would entertain from time to time. Having moved to Oregon from California, then to North Carolina, and back once more to Oregon, the Blossers planted their first 18 acres of Chardonnay, Johannisberg Riesling, and Pinot Noir in the early 1970s near Dundee, Oregon. The first few crops were sold to other area vintners before the Sokol Blosser winery was completed in time for the 1977 vintage. The Blossers moved cautiously in designing, constructing, equipping, and staffing their wine-production facilities. Their dream was realized and today Sokol Blosser is one of the most respected sources of Pinot Noir wines in the United States and has grown to produce more than 20,000 cases annually from the coveted Yamhill county appellation.

One of the largest wineries in Oregon is the highly regarded Knudsen-Erath facility, a winery owned and operated by partners Cal Knudsen and Richard Erath. Their first plantings of Chardonnay, Johannisberg Riesling, and Pinot Noir were in 1969, the last is legendary for its superb quality and award-winning reputation. The Yamhill County appellation for Pinot Noir has recently become known as a giant killer in successful competitions against some of the finer red Burgundies from the Côte de Nuits in France.

The Knudsen-Erath philosophy is based on the "natural" approach of wine procesing—using knowledge and experience to help "guide" wines to become the best that they can be from each vintage of grapes. Erath explains that he does not employ ultra-high technology and equipment to "steamroller our wines." The winery is located to the west of Dundee, Oregon, and is a favorite stop for visitors traveling to and from the Pacific Coast.

Tualatin Vineyards was founded by William Fuller and William Malkmus in 1973—the name comes from an Indian word meaning "gentle flowing," in reference to a small river near their winery. Their goal was to locate a microclimate and soil upon which they could grow world-class wines principally from Chardonnay, Johannisberg Riesling, Gewürztraminer, and Pinot Noir grapes. They settled upon some lush, green foothills bordering the Willamette Valley, about 30 miles west of Portland. The site is magnificent—on clear days Mount Hood is visible 60 miles to the east.

Tualatin cultivates more than 80 acres of vineyards and harvests grapes that are closely attended throughout the winemaking processes in a winery full of quality equipment. The wines that result have more than fulfilled the aim of the founders. Tualatin Chardonnay and Pinot Noir vintages have won impressive awards in the United States and England.

Northern Oregon also seems to be most suited to sparkling wine production. Rains are often likely during the harvest, but this is not a drawback since sparkling wine production allows the wineries to harvest some of the fruit early in order to obtain higher acidity levels. Several of the wineries in the area are either already producing sparkling wines in small amounts or experimenting with formulating new cuvées. Most are made from Chardonnay and/or Pinot Noir, but some also are being produced from Johannisberg Riesling.

Another of the great pioneering forces in Oregon has been David Adelsheim, who along with his wife, Virginia, operate the innovative Adelsheim Vineyard winery in Newberg. While the many prestigeous awards for superb Adelsheim Pinot Noir portray their distinction as vintners, the Adelsheims are tireless experimenters—and most recognized for their many contributions furthering the identity and image of Oregon wines.

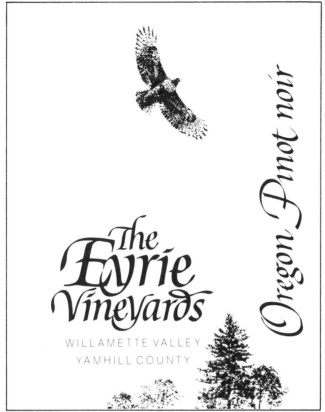

South of the Yamhill County-Dundee area, near Eugene, the Willamette Valley is pinched off by the mountains. The climate here is slightly warmer, and, in good years, the growers can produce Cabernet Sauvignon as well as the cooler varieties, such as Chardonnay and Riesling. Hinman Vineyards, Alpine Vineyards, and Forgeron Vineyard are located in this area. Each of these wineries is small, with about 20 vineyard acres each, and, with their neighbors to the north, are developing very good reputations.

Farther south near Roseburg, in the Hundred Valleys of the Umpqua, is Hillcrest Vineyards. Owner Richard Sommer planted the first commercial *Vitis vinifera* vineyard in Oregon here in 1963. Sommer is primarily interested in Johannisberg Riesling, and about 70 percent of his production is from this single variety. In 1979 he produced his first sparkling wine, a 100 percent Johannisberg Riesling, which he calls "Oregon Mist." Because the Umpqua Valley is warmer than the Willamette Valley, Sommer also grows small quantities of Sauvignon Blanc, Sémillon, Cabernet Sauvignon, and Zinfandel. The latter only ripens in exceptionally good years.

It should be noted that Oregon has several very strict producing and labeling requirements for its own wines. Oregon wines with varietal labels must contain 90 percent of the named variety, as opposed to the 75 percent mandated by U.S. law. The exception to this rule is Cabernet Sauvignon, which may contain larger percentages of Merlot or Cabernet Franc. No European generic names may be used on their *Vitis vinifera* wines, so one sees no Oregon "Chablis," "Burgundy," or "Rhine" wines. The label must also show the region in which the grapes were grown, and all grapes must come from the region shown on the label. If a label says, for example, "Yamhill County," then 100 percent of the grapes must have been grown there. These progressive laws were adopted to protect and enhance the reputation of Oregon wines and were initiated by the Oregon winegrowers.

Washington

Washington is the second-largest grape-producing state in the country, yet it lags well behind California and New York in wine production. Most of the grapes, primarily Concords, go for jams, jellies, juice, and concentrate. Some of this juice eventually ends up as wine—primarily in other states. But the core of the Washington wine industry draws on approximately 7,000 acres of *Vitis vinifera* grapes.

There were no wineries in Washington before 1933, and from that time until the mid-1960s the only commerical wines made there were from native American *Vitis labrusca* varieties, for sweet dessert wines. An attempt was made to produce wines from French-American hybrids by Boordy Vineyards of Washington (the rights to the name sold by Maryland owner Philip Wagner), but this venture did not succeed. It was the wine hobbyists of the state, who hungered for better wines and were willing to make their own, who triggered the *Vitis vinifera* wine-grape revolution in Washington viticulture. A group of amateur winemakers who were having difficulty securing reliable supplies of Old World grapes for their wine decided to plant their own vineyards and, to avoid legal complications, eventually founded their own winery in 1967. This group called itself the Associated Vintners. When André Tchelistcheff came to Washington in 1967 to assess the possibilities for a premium wine industry in the state, he sampled a wine made by one of these amateurs, and it was this that convinced Tchelistcheff of the state's potential.

The amateur group that founded Associated Vintners was a consortium formed mostly of professors from the University of Washington, each bringing expertise from a different discipline to create a successful new wine-growing entity. Although it required several moves of location to satisfy growing production needs, the firm flourished. Associated Vintners is now better known as the "Columbia Winery" and is located in Bellevue, Washington. Columbia Chardonnay is a particularly noteworthy offering.

Some of the very first Washington wines were produced by American Wine Growers, Inc. a firm created by a merger of the Pommerelle and Nawico wineries in 1954. Pommerelle was a fruit and berry wine firm in Seattle, while Nawico made dessert wines in the Yakima Valley. Their long-term project of phasing out sweet wine production was achieved, and they released their first premium dry table wines in 1967, specially labeled as the "Ste. Michelle" brand in honor of the French monastery in Normandy. Later, a group of Seattle-area investors purchased American Wine Growers and renamed the company "Ste. Michelle Vintners." In 1974 the business was sold to the U.S. Tobacco Company.

With the financial backing of U.S. Tobacco, Ste. Michelle Vintners was able to purchase historic Hollywood Farm, which had been established in the outskirts of Seattle in 1912 by wealthy lumberman Fred Stimson. A mansion designed in the Empire style was constructed upon the estate during the mid-1970s in order to house additional administrative and production facilities.

It is a grand wine manor, adorned by arboretum landscaping, serene ponds, and lush greeenery, and it is now known as Château Ste. Michelle. Visitors are cordially welcomed to tour the charming château and taste its award-winning wines in a setting that seems more akin to the aristocratic countryside of Bordeaux, France, than the northeast Seattle suburb of Woodinville, Washington.

Château Ste. Michelle produces more than 1 million gallons of wine annually, virtually all white table wines. Their varietals include Chardonnay, Chenin Blanc,

Chateau Ste Michelle

WASHINGTON
JOHANNISBERG RIESLING
1983

PRODUCED AND BOTTLED BY CHATEAU STE. MICHELLE®
B.W. #8 WOODINVILLE, WASHINGTON, ALC. 11.4% BY VOL.

Arbor Crest
WASHINGTON

JOHANNISBERG RIESLING
SELECT LATE HARVEST
1982
STEWART'S SUNNYSIDE VINEYARD

PRODUCED AND BOTTLED BY
WASHINGTON CELLARS, SPOKANE, WASHINGTON
ALCOHOL 8.5% BY VOLUME

Arbor Crest, Washington's premium wine, blends tradition with the highest standards of winemaking to produce distinctive fine wine. Only the finest premium wine will merit the Arbor Crest label.

David and Harold Mielke

On October 27, 1982, only two and a half tons of hand selected grapes were harvested for this wine. As a result of Botrytis Cinerea, these nearly dehydrated grapes produced a golden juice with 24.4° Brix. For over two months this juice was carefully observed through a cold fermentation process. Results — 140 cases of exceptional wine. Residual sugar at bottling, 8.6% by wt.

Scott Harris   WINEMAKER

Château Ste. Michelle, Woodinville, Washington. (Source: Château Ste. Michelle.)

Gewürztraminer, Muscat Cannelli, Sauvignon Blanc, Semillon, and Johannisberg Riesling—all grown in their vineyards located across the Cascade mountains in the Yakima Valley and the Columbia River Gorge. The firm also has two other production wineries in their vineyard region near Patterson, Washington.

The Preston winery was founded in 1976 just to the northeast of Pasco in Washington's southern Columbia River basin. Bill and Joann Preston planted their first classic European varietal vines in the early 1970s in fulfillment of their dream to produce top-quality table wines. Since that time they have won a very impressive list of awards for their craft: more than thirty medals just for their Chardonnay and Fumé Blanc wines alone. They also make superior Johannisberg Riesling, including some late-harvest selections, as well as Cabernet Sauvignon, Merlot, and several others. The Preston winery features an elevated tasting room situated so that visitors may enjoy wine samples while viewing a panorama of vineyards and natural countryside.

Another young winery that has gained high regard rather quickly is the Yakima River Winery, located near Prosser, Washington, and owned by Louise and John Rauner. The Rauners are innovative in their approach to the winemaking art and science. They have spent considerable time and money in devising systems of vinification and barrel aging in order to achieve their goals. The Yakima River

Winery's Johannisberg Riesling and Cabernet Sauvignon table wines have been successful in garnering awards from several prestigious wine competitions.

Yet another of Washington's fine new vintners of white table wines is the Pontin del Roza winery, also located near Prosser. In the 1860s the name "Roza" was given to a creek in the locale by General George Custer. In modern times the Roza is known as a 77,000-acre valley irrigated by water from the Cascade mountains. Wine growing has been an obsession of the Pontin family for decades, since they emigrated from Italy in the 1920s. The very first vintage, in 1984, culminated those dreams: the wines have already gained considerable attention for the awards they have won in Washington competitions.

Other Washington wineries that have received high praise for their wines, but are not in general distribution, are Hinzerling, Neuharth, and Vierthaler, located in Prosser, Sequin, and Sumner, Washington, respectively.

One of the most picturesque wineries in Washington is Arbor Crest—a renovated Romanesque mansion located on a basalt cliff known as Eagle's Nest, which is situated east of Spokane. The structure was built in 1925 by Royal Riblet, a wealthy Canadian tramway manufacturer. Today the Mielke family owns the property and has established a 100,000-gallon winery on the premises in which premium *Vitis vinifera* wines are made from predominantly Yakima Valley-grown grapes. Arbor Crest-Sauvignon Blanc is a consistent award winner.

Quail Run Vintners winery, located in Zillah, Washington, in the Yakima Valley, is managed by Stan Clarke, who specializes in the production of Morio Muskat, a white variety made famous in Germany. Clarke has recently settled out of court with management from the Quail Ridge winery in Napa, California, over a winery name dispute. As a result, Quail Run Vintners will make a name change—the new name is Covey Run.

Dr. George Stewart, a surgeon who grew up in Mississippi, had his wine thirst whetted in the late 1960s by Dr. Walter Clore, an agricultural-irrigation researcher in Prosser, Washington. Stewart tore out most of the old Catawba and Hungarian Muscat vines that existed on a farm he bought near Sunnyside in the Yakima Valley and replanted with Chardonnay, Gewürztraminer, and Cabernet Sauvignon, among other Old World varieties. The Stewart Vineyards winery was opened in 1984 and promises to become another of the increasingly highly regarded wine producers of Washington.

Most of the vineyards in Washington are in the Columbia Basin and Yakima Valley Irrigation Projects, which converted a million acres of sagebrush to productive farmland. The average annual rainfall of the region is about 8 inches because the Cascade mountains to the west block off much of the moisture from the Pacific Ocean. The soils are predominantly sandy loam, requiring only sufficient water from irrigation to make them arable. Since there is no history of *Phylloxera* in the area, many of the grapes are own-rooted rather than grafted. The greatest general difficulty for viticulture in the locale is the danger of early winter freezes. There are thousands of acres suitable for viticulture that could be developed in this area, and it seems most likely that the expansion of Washington's vineyards and its wineries will continue.

Idaho

The wine industry in Idaho is located almost exclusively in an area south of Boise along the Snake River called Sunny Slope. Vineyards are planted on southerly slopes at an elevation just under 2,000 feet. The growing season has long hours of sunlight without excessive heat, and cool nights. Grapes ripen slowly throughout the long growing season while retaining good acid levels. Growers in Idaho find abundant winter sunshine to be their greatest difficulty. Temperatures can fluctuate from below 0 at night to 50 degrees or above during the day. Reflected light from the snow cover can sunscald the vines, and the drastic fluctuations in temperature can cause vine trunk damage.

Idaho has eight wineries, the largest of which is the Ste. Chapelle Winery. It was founded in 1976 as a joint venture of Dick Symms and Bill Broich. There are 175 acres of vines planted at the winery and adjacent locales. Other grapes are purchased from eastern Washington vineyards. Chardonnay has been the most consistently successful varietal for Ste. Chapelle, but the winery is also developing exceptional Gewürztraminer, Chenin Blanc, and Johannisberg Riesling. Ste. Chapelle has also introduced a line of sparkling wines using only Idaho grapes. *Vinifera*, *labrusca*, and French-American hybrids are grown by the other Idaho vintners and growers.*

THE HEARTLAND

The European immigrants who settled the central plains of the United States transplanted their cultures to the New World. Often the sites they chose were those that most resembled their native land. French, German, and Swiss

---

*It is unfortunate that the scope of this text does not permit an individual discussion of each fine winery in the Northwest. This region is one of the most dynamic wine-growing areas in America, with many superb wines being released each year, as well as new estate wineries emerging regularly. Some of these wines are bona fide world-class products—the best of which are consistently winning the most prestigious awards in competition. The reader is encouraged to keep abreast of the developments of Northwest wine growing. One of the best publications in this regard is the *Northwest Wine Almanac*, P.O. Box 85595, Seattle, WA 98145-1595.

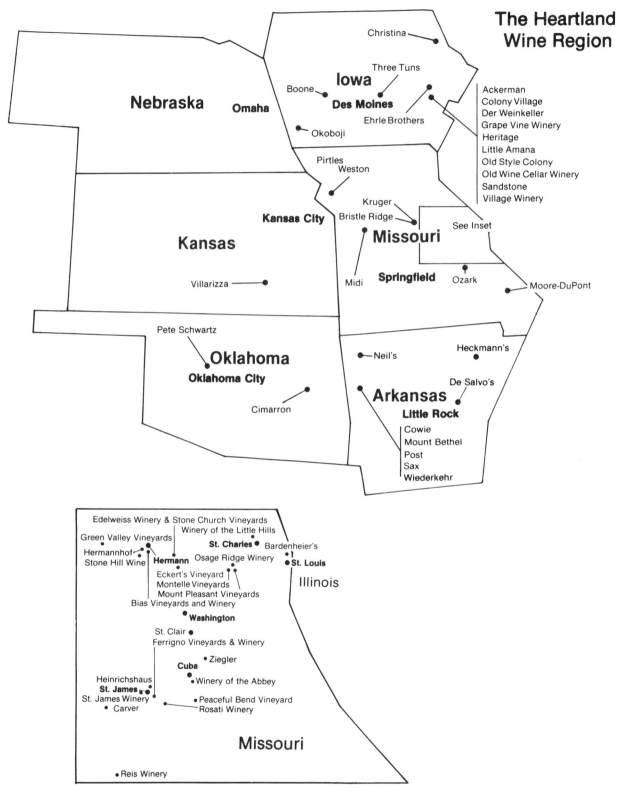

The Heartland Wine Region

Nebraska

Omaha

Christina

Iowa

Three Tuns

Boone

Des Moines

Ehrle Brothers

Ackerman
Colony Village
Der Weinkeller
Grape Vine Winery
Heritage
Little Amana
Old Style Colony
Old Wine Cellar Winery
Sandstone
Village Winery

Okoboji

Pirtles
Weston

Kruger

Kansas City

Bristle Ridge

Missouri

See Inset

Kansas

Villarizza

Midi

Springfield

Ozark

Moore-DuPont

Pete Schwartz

Oklahoma

Heckmann's

Neil's

De Salvo's

Oklahoma City

Arkansas

Cimarron

Little Rock

Cowie
Mount Bethel
Post
Sax
Wiederkehr

Edelweiss Winery & Stone Church Vineyards
Winery of the Little Hills
Green Valley Vineyards
St. Charles
Bardenheier's
Hermannhof
Stone Hill Wine
Hermann
Osage Ridge Winery
St. Louis
Eckert's Vineyard
Montelle Vineyards
Mount Pleasant Vineyards
Bias Vineyards and Winery
Illinois

Washington

St. Clair
Ferrigno Vineyards & Winery

Ziegler

Cuba

Heinrichshaus
St. James
St. James Winery
Carver

Winery of the Abbey

Peaceful Bend Vineyard
Rosati Winery

Missouri

Reis Winery

Missouri Inset

winegrowers were drawn to the valleys of the Ohio, Mississippi, and Missouri Rivers, in which they could, at least, partially replace their native Old World vineyard lands. For this reason, the history of wine growing in the heartland is often tied to small isolated pockets of European culture, separated by great distances. Although the grapevine may grow virtually anywhere in this country, the locations where it is cultivated in the interior of America have depended more on the background of its settlers than on the particular climate or soil.

Missouri

The Teutonic influence in the history of wine growing in Missouri was pivotal. Although the first wine was made in the state by French Jesuits who established a seminary near St. Louis in 1823, the cultivation of the grape was largely undertaken by German immigrants. Viticulture flowed west with the settlers, down the Ohio to the Mississippi and then up the Missouri River, arriving in Hermann, Missouri. Jacob Fugger planted the first grapes in the town of Hermann in 1843.

Built in 1847, the Stone Hill Winery in Herman once held more than 1 million gallons and was, at that time, the second-largest winery in the country. Between 1873 and 1904, a period during which the Stone Hill Winery was nationally known, the wines won eight gold medals at world's fairs. Prohibition closed the winery, the vineyards were destroyed, and an enterprising businessman turned the cellars to the cultivation of mushrooms. In 1965, James Held, sensing a renewed interest in wine in the area, moved his family into the old building and began installing wine equipment salvaged from some of the area's defunct wine operations. Vault by vault he cleared the cellars of mushroom beds and added tanks and equipment. Today the charming old winery has a capacity of 110,000 gallons and Held's German-type wines made from native American grapes are acclaimed throughout the region.

Also in Hermann is the Hermannhof Winery, whose cellars were constructed in 1852. Like the Stone Hill Winery, this is a restoration of a defunct winery. The new owner, James Dierberg, has added a wine garden and smokehouse and planted French-American hybrid vines. Located downtown near the Missouri riverbank, Hermannhof is ideally situated for the annual Mayfest held in Hermann each year on the third weekend in May.

Augusta, located on the Missouri River halfway between Hermann and St. Louis, is also a historic wine town in Missouri. Eleven wineries were operated in Augusta before Prohibition. In 1968, Lucian Dressel, a Harvard-educated accountant, decided to enter the wine business. He reopened the Mount Pleasant

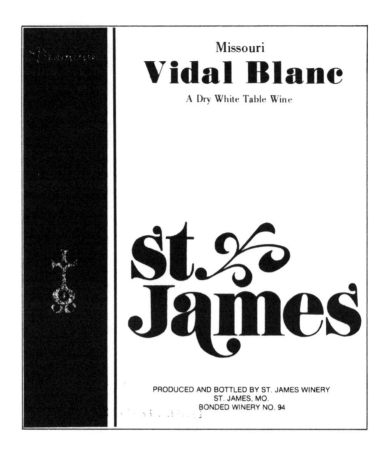

Vineyard that had been built in 1881 by Friedrich Munch. Munch was a Lutheran minister and a grape breeder who wrote a book about American viticulture. Dressel, in keeping with the history of his restored winery, makes wine from some of the old local varieties originally used by Munch, including Cynthiana (also known as Norton) and Missouri Riesling, a *Vitis labrusca* hybrid developed in Hermann during the mid-nineteenth century. His production from 45 acres of grapes includes a variety of wines produced from French-American hybrid and native *Vitis labrusca* grapes.

The area southwest of St. Louis near St. James, Missouri, is known as Big Prairie and is part of the Ozark Plateau. Most of the grapes in Missouri are grown here, primarily native *Vitis labrusca* varieties. James and Patricia Hofherr decided to build their St. James Winery here because of the proximity of vineyards to supply their initial needs. Hofherr worked at Bardenheier's Winnery in St. Louis and the Post Winery in Arkansas before starting the St. James Winery in 1970. St. James now produces table and sparkling wines from several varieties of both *Vitis labrusca* and French-American hybrid grapes primarily from their estate vineyards.

Also near St. James is Ferrigno Vineyards, which opened in 1982. Dick and Susan Ferrigno added French-American hybrids to the surrounding native *Vitis labrusca* vineyards, renovated an old dairy barn, and made eight wines from the 1981 vintage, including Vidal Blanc, Seyval Blanc, and Chancellor Noir.

On the western edge of the state, near the Kansas border, is the tiny Midi Vineyard Winery. Founded by Dutton Biggs, an architect, and George Gale, a philosophy professor, Midi is a labor of love and an avocation of wine enthusiast Gale. Not located in any particular viticultural area, with no long, proud history of winemaking to justify its existence, Midi exists because George Gale loves wine and thought he could make it there. The winery has a capacity of 7,000 gallons and 10 acres of vineyards. Wines are made from the French-American hybrid cultivars Colobel, Chancellor, Léon Millot, and Landal. Midi has doubled in size since it was founded in 1977.

Arkansas

Altus, Arkansas, is another island of wine history in the American heartland. This small area of the Ozark Plateau, settled by German-Swiss immigrants in the 1880s, still has four wineries and yet another situated only a few miles south in Paris, Arkansas. They range in size from 5,000 to nearly 2 million gallons. The best-known and most-ambitious is Wiederkehr Wine Cellars on top of St. Mary's Mountain. Johann Wiederkehr dug his cellar and made his first wine there in 1880. His grandson, Alcuin Wiederkehr, has transformed the winery into a major Arkansas tourist attraction. Today Wiederkehr Wine Cellars is an incorporated village of 100 residents, with Alcuin Wiederkehr as its mayor. It consists of the winery, almost 600 acres of vineyards, a nursery, gift shop, and superb restaurant. More important, Wiederkehr has shifted the winery production from primarily dessert wines to premium table wines made from *Vitis vinifera* and French-American hybrid grapes, as well as native American varieties. Among the best are Chardonnay, Johannisberg Riesling, and Gewürztraminer.

Farther down the hill in Altus is the Post Winery, started by Jacob Post and run by the Post family, who are cousins of the Wiederkehrs. Founded, like Wiederkehr Wine Cellars, in 1880, the winery is undergoing the same type of growth and transition but on a smaller scale. The winery produced 125,000 gallons in 1983, all of which are sold in Arkansas. Post makes wine from native muscadine, *Vitis labrusca*, and French-American hybrid grapes. Niagara and muscadine are the best-sellers at the winery, but the Posts hope to gradually wean their clientele toward drier table wines.

Iowa

There are currently fourteen bonded wineries in Iowa. Ten of these are located in the Amana area. The Amana Colonies consist of seven villages southwest of Cedar Rapids that were communally owned by a religious sect called the Community of True Inspiration. The members came in 1854 and purchased 25,000 acres of prairie for their colony. Known as the Amana Society, the colony survived in its communistic form until the Depression, when it incorporated and began paying its members wages for their work. Amana Refrigeration is the best known of the original Amana industries. Today winemaking survives there as a cottage industry, catering to tourists. Most of the wines made are fruit and berry wines, the best known of these being a rhubarb wine called *Piestengel*, which means "pie stalk."

Kansas

Dr. Robert Rizza has worked diligently to bring wine growing back to the state of the infamous Carrie Nation, and, at long last, his efforts are beginning to realize legislation that will permit winery operations in the state. He and his wife, Kitty, and their children have planted nearly 20 acres of *Vitis labrusca* and French-American hybrid grapes just south of Halstead, Kansas. *Vitis vinifera* is being studied, as are plans for the Villarizza winery.

THE ATLANTIC SEABOARD

The Atlantic Seaboard has a long and distinguished history of viticultural struggle. The Founding Fathers were men of education and taste whose determination to produce fine wines was equaled only by the problems they faced in doing so. George Washington planted vines at Mt. Vernon, but apparently little came of them since there is no record of his producing any wine. Thomas Jefferson, unquestionably the most determined of all, brought thousands of cuttings from Europe but, after thirty years of experimentation, was finally forced to admit that perhaps efforts should be concentrated on native varieties such as the Alexander.

In nearby Maryland, John Adlum, a revolutionary war veteran, experimented with European and native American varieties. His chance discovery of a vine growing in the dooryard of an inn at Clarksburg revolutionized the wine industry in a large number of states. The vine from which he took cuttings, and with which he experimented, was the Catawba—brought from North Carolina where it was said to have been growing wild near the Catawba River. Transplanted to many of the midwestern and northern states, the Catawba, with its pleasant and fruity character, became very popular among wine consumers.

In 1835, D. N. Norton of Richmond produced the variety that was ultimately to be the basis of the early Virginia wine industry. The Norton grape, as it was named, lacked the strong flavor of many native American *Vitis labrusca* and muscadine varieties. A Norton "claret," produced by the Monticello Wine Company at Charlottesville, won a gold medal at a Vienna wine competition in 1873 and a silver medal in a Paris exposition in 1878.

From this high point, though, the industry began to falter as the forces of Prohibition gathered strength and competition from other areas increased. By the time Prohibition officially arrived, the wine industry on the Atlantic Seaboard was already experiencing fiscal difficulties.

The next chapter of wine history in the area concerns a journalist from Maryland, Philip Wagner, a home winemaker with a taste for good wines. Unable to obtain grapes from California after Prohibition, he tried native American grapes and found them unacceptable. Unwilling to give up, he imported some of the French-American hybrids developed in France. He liked the wines he made from these crosses of *Vitis vinifera* and hardy American species, and he expanded his vineyard acreage. In 1945 Wagner and his wife Jocelyn bonded a winery, Boordy Vineyards, and began to sell his wine as well as nursery plants. It was the Wagner

The Atlantic Seaboard Wine Region

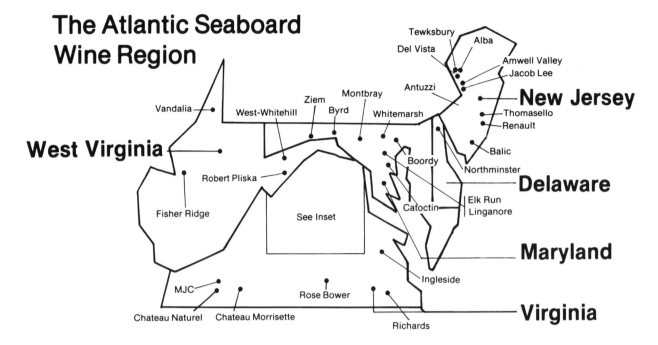

Vandalia

West-Whitehill

Ziem

Byrd

Montbray

Whitemarsh

Tewksbury

Del Vista

Alba

Amwell Valley

Jacob Lee

Antuzzi

New Jersey

Thomasello

Renault

West Virginia

Robert Pliska

Boordy

Balic

Northminster

Delaware

Fisher Ridge

See Inset

Catoctin

Elk Run

Linganore

Maryland

Ingleside

MJC

Rose Bower

Virginia

Chateau Naturel

Chateau Morrisette

Richards

Virginia Inset

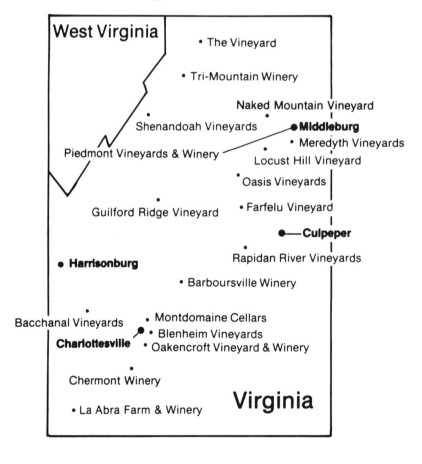

West Virginia

• The Vineyard

• Tri-Mountain Winery

Naked Mountain Vineyard

Shenandoah Vineyards

•**Middleburg**

• Meredyth Vineyards

Piedmont Vineyards & Winery

Locust Hill Vineyard

• Oasis Vineyards

• Farfelu Vineyard

Guilford Ridge Vineyard

•—**Culpeper**

Rapidan River Vineyards

• **Harrisonburg**

• Barboursville Winery

Bacchanal Vineyards

• Montdomaine Cellars

Charlottesville

• Blenheim Vineyards

• Oakencroft Vineyard & Winery

Chermont Winery

Virginia

• La Abra Farm & Winery

influence through the French-American hybrids that marked the beginning of a revolution that would rouse the eastern wine industry and take it a major step forward.

Virginia

In 1986 there were thirty-two bonded wineries in Virginia, thirty of which have opened since 1975. These small estate wineries are a direct result of the pioneering work of Philip Wagner with French-American hybrids and Dr. Konstantin Frank with *Vitis vinifera*. The climate of Virginia varies more from east to west than it does from north to south, as the coastal plain rises into the foothills of the Appalachian chain. In some portions of the state disease control is often a more decisive factor than sufficient degree-days. Accordingly, depending on vineyard site, soils, and microclimate, the wineries of Virginia grow mostly *Vitis vinifera*, French-American hybrids, or a combination of the two.

One of the first three estate wineries to open in Virginia during 1976, Meredyth Vineyards is situated in Middleburg in the foothills of the Bull Run mountains, 50 miles west of Washington, D.C. It is also one of the largest estate wineries in Virginia, producing about 20,000 gallons annually. Archie Smith, Jr., and his wife,

Gathering the grapes at Meredyth Vineyard, Middleburg, Virginia. (Source: Archie M. Smith, Jr.)

Dody, started cautiously in the early 1970s with French-American hybrid vines. Their experience proved that Old World grapes were also viable there, and the Smiths now also have 20 acres of *Vitis vinifera*, including Chardonnay, Johannisberg Riesling, and Cabernet Sauvignon. Son Archie III, Ph.D., who was a philosophy tutor at Oxford University before joining the family business in 1977, is the winemaker. His hard work and experimentation in the cellar have won Meredyth Vineyards many medals in regional and national competitions.

Also near Middleburg is Piedmont Vineyards, pioneered by the late Mrs. Thomas Furness, who chose to begin her experimental vineyards with *Vitis vinifera* vines, primarily Chardonnay and Sémillon. Planted in 1973, hers was the first commercial *Vitis vinifera* vineyard in Virginia.

West of Middleburg on the east slope of the Blue Ridge mountains near Markham is the tiny Naked Mountain Vineyard owned by Robert and Phoebe Harper. With only 5 acres of *Vitis vinifera* vines, the Harper's output is small but their wines have received good marks in the Washington area, where they are available.

Across the Blue Ridge mountains in the Shenandoah Valley is the aptly named Shenandoah Vineyards. Founded in 1977, Shenandoah now has 20 acres of vines and makes an assortment of wines from French-American hybrids, as well as Chardonnay and Johannisberg Riesling.

In eastern Virginia, on a site located between the Rappahannock and the Potomac Rivers, is the Ingleside Plantation Winery. The plantation, listed in the National Register of Historic Places, is owned by Carl Flemer and his son Doug. They compare the site to the Entre-Deux-Mer region of Bordeaux. Historically, Ingleside was a nursery operation, but Flemer became interested in wine and produced a crush of 2,800 gallons in 1980. By 1983 Ingleside was crushing 23,000 gallons and was projected to reach 50,000 gallons at full production capacity. Winemaker Jacques Recht, a French native, produces an array of superb, award-winning table wines from *Vitis vinifera* and French-American hybrid grapes, as well as a bottle-fermented sparkling wine from Chardonnay and Chenin Blanc.

Virginia has begun to attract foreign capital in recent years. Near Culpepper, southwest of Washington, D.C., Dr. Gerhard Guth, a physician from Hamburg, West Germany, purchased land and planted 25 acres of *Vitis vinifera* vines in 1978. The first wines were produced by Guth in 1981—primarily Chardonnay and Johannisberg Riesling under the Rapidan River Vineyards label. Farther southwest, near Charlottesville, is Barboursville Winery, which is owned by Zonin S.P.A., an Italian wine-marketing firm. The 850-acre farm was purchased in 1976, experimental vineyards have been planted, and wines are being produced on a small scale.

Virginia's largest winery, Richard's Wine Cellars in Petersburg, is an arm of the Canandaigua Wine Co. of New York State. Founded in 1951 by Mordecai (Mack) Sands, the winery produces native American grape and muscadine wines.

Maryland

An era in Maryland wine history ended in 1980 when Philip and Jocelyn Wagner decided to retire and sell their Boordy Vineyards winery. In the thirty-five years that the Wagners operated the winery, and indeed for ten years before that when it was a nursery operation, the names Boordy Vineyards and Philip Wagner were synonymous with progress in the eastern wine industry. Where previously dessert and sparkling wines dominated the marketplace, Wagner campaigned for dry table wines. He wrote books, propagated vines, and made wines to illustrate his point. Far more important than his wines were the converts he made to the cause of a premium table wine industry in the eastern United States. The Wagner's Riderwood, Maryland, home and adjacent Boordy Vineyards winery became the mecca of thousands of pilgrims who came to get his advice and returned home to continue his vision. The DeFord family bought Boordy Vineyards from the Wagners in 1980, and Robert DeFord III is president, general manager, and winemaker there. The winery was subsequently moved to nearby Hydes, Maryland.

Northwest of Boordy Vineyards, in the little town of Silver Run, Dr. G. Hamilton Mowbray has been operating Montbray Wine Cellars since 1966. He began with the French-American hybrid cultivars Seyval Blanc and Maréchal Foch but became convinced by Dr. Konstantin Frank that he could grow *Vitis vinifera* as well. In 1969 he produced the first commercial Old World wines in Maryland: Chardonnay and a Johannisberg Riesling. In 1974 he made history again by producing the first American "ice wine" when an October freeze caught his Johannisberg Riesling yet unharvested. In 1976 Mowbray added Cabernet Sauvignon to the list of Montbray wines, all of which are aged in oak. Montbray's production is small (7,000 gallons) and the *Vitis vinifera* wines are available only at the winery, by subscription.

Bret and Sharon Byrd opened Byrd Vineyards near Frederick in 1976. Their 1980 Cabernet Sauvignon won a gold medal at the American Wine Competition held in 1983 at the Culinary Institute of America and was the only eastern Cabernet Sauvignon so honored. Maryland's newest winery, Catoctin Vineyards, is a partnership formed between Bob Lyon, former winemaker at Byrd Vineyards, and a number of Maryland winegrowers. The first crush in 1983 was primarily of Chardonnay and Cabernet Sauvignon grapes, which have since gained a fine reputation for quality.

New Jersey

Grapes have been grown for over a century in New Jersey in the area of Egg Harbor and nearby Vineland. Egg Harbor, situated northwest of Atlantic City, is the home of the Renault Winery, which has been in continuous operation since 1868. It became well known in the nineteenth century for its sparkling wines and survived Prohibition by producing "Renault Tonic," a widely distributed over-the-counter wine tonic. Despite increased urbanization of the area, Renault still owns vineyards and produces some estate wines, one of the most interesting of which is a varietal called Noah—a native white hybrid cultivar. The firm also produces a sparkling blueberry wine that is very popular. A large collection of antique wineglasses are beautifully displayed near the entrance of the old stone winery, through which thousands of visitors pass each year.

On the opposite end of the spectrum in New Jersey is Tewksbury Wine Cellars, a small new winery that had its first crush of estate-grown grapes in 1981. Although the first wines were made exclusively from French-American hybrid and native American hybrids purchased from contracted growers, the estate plantings are Old World vines. Tewksbury, along with Catoctin, is a consistent award-winning vintner.

West Virginia

The wine industry in West Virginia is both new and comparatively small. Most of the grapes grown are French-American hybrids, although some native *labrusca* and *vinifera* are also cultivated there. The first winery in the state was Fisher Ridge, founded in 1977 at Liberty, West Virginia, by Wilson Ward. In 1981 Stephen West and Charles Whitehill founded the aptly named West-Whitehill Winery at Keyser, and a year later the Pliska family commenced operations at their Robert F. Pliska Winery at Purgitsville.

Delaware

The only winery in the state of Delaware is the tiny Northminster Winery in Wilmington, founded in 1978 by Richard Becker. It grows wines from both *labrusca* and *vinifera* vines.

THE DEEP SOUTH

Early explorers discovered a profusion of grapes growing wild in the southeast. These grapevines, now known as *Vitis rotundifolia*, or "muscadines," *Vitis aestivalis* or "summer" grapes, and *Vitis labrusca*, continue to grow abundantly along the coast. European settlers, who learned early on that imported vines succumbed to many diseases found that a pleasant fragrant wine could be made from muscadines if properly sweetened. North Carolina quickly emerged as a prime wine-growing region, with numerous small wineries commencing operation during the early 1800s. The Catawba, as mentioned earlier, was discovered in the Catawba River region of North Carolina and revolutionized the wine industry to the north and west. But it was the muscadine grape that put the South on the wine-growing map prior to Prohibition.

Captain Paul Garrett, a native North Carolinian, was raised in the southern wine business in the late nineteenth century (see chapter 4). He learned the wine trade in a winery owned jointly by his father and his uncle. When the winery changed hands and his talents were not sufficiently appreciated, young Garrett left. He started his own winery, Garrett & Co., in 1900, and by 1903 he had acquired five wineries in North Carolina plus another twelve wineries in five other states. His "Virginia Dare" label became nationally famous.

North Carolina

Muscadines have reemerged in modern North Carolina in the award-winning wines from Duplin Wine Cellar at Rose Hill. Under the leadership of David Fussell, eleven growers opened their own winery in 1975 in response to a sagging market for their grapes, most of which were going to large northern wineries. Fussell reasoned that there must be a market for Carolina grapes in North Carolina. The first crush was in 1975 and totaled approximately 3,500 gallons of Scuppernong, Carlos, and Noble—all muscadine varieties. Since then, growth has been explosive; the 1983 crush was more than 100,000 gallons. In 1980 Duplin introduced a brandy, the first to be made outside of the state of California since Prohibition. Today Duplin makes table, sparkling, and dessert wines, a traditional brandy, and a sweet Scuppernong brandy.

At the other end of the state, near Asheville, an entirely different kind of enterprise is being undertaken. There, in the mountains, lies the magnificent Biltmore Estate, a 10,000-acre private park, complete with a French château and

The Southern Wine Region

Colcord
Louisville
Kentucky
Andrew Berg

Germanton
North Carolina
Highland Manor
Tiegs
Tennessee
Nashville
Smoky Mountain
Biltmore
Charlotte
LaRocca
Duplin
Laurel Hill — Memphis
Doc's Berry Farm
Georgia Wines
Foxwood
Habersham
Tenner Brothers
Chateau Elan
Rushing
Thousand Oaks
Atlanta
B & B Rosser
Truluck
Clairborne
Monarch
South Carolina
Louisiana
Happy "B"
Alabama
Montgomery
Georgia
Jackson
Almaria
Old South
Mississippi
Perdido
Alaqua
Tallahassee
New Orleans
Lafayette
Florida Heritage
The Wines of St. Augustine
Ocala
Fruit Wines of Florida
Tampa
Florida

formal gardens. In the early 1970s William A. Vanderbilt Cecil, grandson of the original owner, became interested in growing wine grapes on the estate. Experimental vineyards were planted, French viticulturist and enologist Philippe Jourdain was hired, and an experimental winery was built. The winery was bonded in 1977, and wines were made in small lots while vineyard experimentation and expansion continued. Today there are 120 acres of vines, 109 of them *Vitis vinifera*. A large new winery and visitors center was completed in 1985. By 1994, when the winery reaches its full projected production, there will be 600 acres of Old World vines to be maintained on the estate.

South Carolina

Dr. Jim Truluck dreamed of starting his own winery in Lake City, South Carolina, after spending time in France while in the Air Force. In 1971 he began planting vines on the family farm, experimenting with muscadines, French-American hybrids, *Vitis vinifera,* and assorted other species. A winery was built in time for the 1976 vintage, and, by 1980, Truluck Vineyards had produced the first South Carolina estate-bottled *Vitis vinifera* wine, a Cabernet Sauvignon. Until recently, Dr. Truluck's son, Jay, managed the winery and vineyards. In addition to Old World vines, Truluck makes wine from selections of Carlos, Munson, Chambourcin, Cayuga, Ravat, and Seyval Blanc vines.

Georgia

Georgia is still recovering from the effects of Prohibition, as are a number of southern and heartland states. Prior to Prohibition it was the sixth-largest wine-producing state in the country. Until quite recently the only winery in Georgia was Monarch in Atlanta, established shortly after Prohibition to alleviate the Georgia peach surplus by producing fruit wine. Significant muscadine acreage still exists in the state, but most of this traditionally has been sold to wineries and other processors out of state.

One of the most remarkable new winery projects in the Deep South has been launched by pharmaceutical magnate Donald Panoz. When completed, Château Elan, an arm of Elan Pharmaceuticals, will become one of the largest estate wineries in the entire nation and will be one of the largest producers of *Vitis vinifera* wines in America outside the State of California. Plans call for over 500 acres of vineyards to be planted by the late 1980s. The premier vintage was in 1984, resulting from the first partial crops harvested from vines planted in 1982 near Braselton, Georgia, about 50 miles northeast of Atlanta. The project has received many deserved accolades from regional media, and the first wines exhibit promise. Currently, until vineyards can be brought into full production, wines are being processed in California, blended in Georgia, and sold under the "Château Elan" label.

Gay Dellinger's Split Rail Vineyards, located near Cartersville, Georgia, was the first commercial vineyard in modern Georgia history to be planted with *Vitis vinifera* and French-American hybrids. Located in the northwest corner of the state where the elevation may offer some protection from Pierce's disease, Split Rail has been growing grapes since 1978.

Stonepile Vineyards owner Tom Slick worked diligently in the lobbying effort that eventually led to the Georgia native wine legislation permitting farm wineries to operate in that state. Stonepile Vineyards is located in Baldwin, Georgia; here Mississippi State-trained winemaker Russell Jones produced wine from the first crop of estate *Vitis vinifera* and French-American hybrid grapes in 1983.

BILTMORE ESTATE

N O R T H · C A R O L I N A

CHAMPAGNE

Grown, Produced and Bottled by The Biltmore Company
Asheville, NC 28803 • BW-NC-32 • Alcohol 11.5% by Volume

1983

Château Élan

Georgia State

WHITE RIESLING

PRODUCED AND BOTTLED BY
CHATEAU ELAN LTD. BRASELTON, GEORGIA
BONDED WINERY NO. GA   ALCOHOL 12% BY VOLUME

Also in 1983 the first crush of 1,500 gallons at the B & B Rosser Winery at High Shoals, Georgia, consisted of *Vitis vinifera* from the Rosser estate vineyards and also muscadines from other in-state growers.

Florida

Except for the native muscadine, Florida has not succeeded in growing grapes for commerical purposes until very recently. *Vitis labruscas* were tried in the late nineteenth century, and, during the 1920s, thousands of acres were planted with hybrids developed by T. V. Munson in Texas. All eventually succumbed to disease and pests. Today wines are made in Florida from citrus fruits, muscadine grapes, and other disease-resistant grapes developed by research programs conducted by the University of Florida. One of the best of these new grapes is Blanc du Bois—reminiscent of Sauvignon Blanc.

Joe Midulla, who heads Fruit Wines of Florida, makes most of his wine from citrus fruits—wines that sell well to the Florida tourists. However, he is also the largest producer of Florida grapes and has a 50-acre vineyard in Pasco County north of Tampa. Red and white wines, principally from the varieties Conquistador (red) and Stover (white), from Midulla Vineyards are processed at the winery and sold in the nearby Tampa area under the "Midulla Vineyards" label. Midulla is a colorful personality and an active promoter of grape cultivation in Florida.

One of the newest, largest, and most picturesque wineries in Florida is Lafayette Vineyards founded in 1983 and situated conveniently to both locals and tourists on the eastern edge of Tallahassee. The operating partners, Gary Ketchum and Gary Cox, have enlisted the talents of award-winning winemaker Jeanne Burgess, trained at Mississippi State University. She makes high-quality proprietary products from muscadines and hybrid grapes developed at the University of Florida.

Mississippi

Despite the fact that Mississippi was the final state to vote for Repeal (not until 1966), its wine industry has undergone a dynamic rebirth—primarily due to the efforts of Dr. Louis Wise, vice president emeritus for the Colleges of Agriculture, Forestry, and Veterinary Medicine at Mississippi State University. It was Wise who pioneered the funding drive for the magnificent enology laboratory now operating at the university; this laboratory has profoundly influenced eastern U.S. wine industry development in the 1970s and 1980s.

Lafayette

BLANC Du BOIS

WHITE TABLE WINE

Produced and Bottled by Lafayette Vineyards
Tallahassee, Florida • BW-FL-31 • Alcohol Content 12% by Volume

CLAIBORNE VINEYARDS

1984

Mississippi Delta

Cabernet Sauvignon

Estate Bottled

Produced & Bottled By
Claiborne Vineyards
Indianola, Mississippi
Alcohol 11% By Volume

CLAIBORNE VINEYARDS, a small winery established in 1984, is located in the center of the Mississippi Delta Viticultural Region. We make festive wines by the traditional European methods from Vinifera and French-hybrid grapes.

The first winery to open in Mississippi since Repeal is The Winery Rushing founded by Diane and Sam Rushing, who operate what has become the state's most succesful wine-producing facility. The Rushings grow only the native muscadine vine and use its fruit in the manufacture of juice and muffin-mix products, as well as in their wines.

Dr. Scott Galbreath, successful Natchez veterinarian, has converted a pre-Prohibition beer warehouse into a quaint winery that he named the Old South Winery. The facility is used exclusively for muscadine wine production.

Clairborne Barnwell, cotton farmer, civil engineer, and vintner, opened his Clairborne Winery in 1985, near Indianola, Mississippi. Barnwell is the nephew of famous food writer Craig Claiborne, who has written food columns for the *New York Times* for many years. The chief varieties grown are Cabernet Sauvignon and Chenin Blanc, although several selections of French-American-hybrid wine varieties are also cultivated in the Delta soil at Indianola.

Tennessee

Tennessee wine production has been hampered by a long-standing controversy between wine wholesalers and vintners—a controversy that has resulted in a very restrictive native winery law. On the brighter side, Tennessee has been blessed with a large number of wine enthusiasts who have formed the very progressive Tennessee Viticultural & Oenological Society (TVOS) that has blazed the trail for continuing research and lobbying efforts for the industry in that state.

One of the most picturesque wineries in the state is located near Clarksville, about 35 miles northwest of Nashville, and is called Beachaven—named for its founder, Judge William O. Beach. Beach and his son-in-law, Edward Cooke, have constructed a Nordic-styled winery that attracts many visitors, not just because of the charm of their facilities, but also because of the superb quality of their products. Judge Beach had been well-known throughout the Deep South for years as a champion amateur winemaker prior to entering the profesional ranks in 1985. His finest products are made from *Vitis vinifera* and *Vitis labrusca* vines, but he also produces very nice wines from French-American hybrids and *rotundifolia* grapes.

The largest winery in Tennessee is the Smoky Mountain Winery in beautiful Gatlinburg, high in the mountains southeast of Knoxville. The facility produces popular wines from various grape species, fruits, and berries.

Retired Air Force officer Fay Wheeler is a principal founding partner for the highly esteemed and successful Highland Manor Winery in Jamestown, Tennessee. The production is primarily from native and French-American hybrid grapes, although a significant portion also comes from muscadine. Award-winning winemaker Irving Martin is a product of the Mississippi State University program.

After selling the family dairy business, Raymond Skinner purchased and remodeled a downtown Memphis home in 1984 into a very inviting winery facility named Laurel Hill Vineyard. *Vitis vinifera* and French-American hybrid grapes come from the Skinner vineyards, located to the east, near Lawrenceburg, Tennessee.

Kentucky

There are three operations that produce wine in Kentucky. The Kontinental Spirits Kompanie of Bardstown, Kentucky, is operated by Even Kulsveen and produces, as the name of the firm might suggest, specialty wine products. The Colcord Winery of Paris, Kentucky, was founded in 1976. Owner F. Carlton Colcord directs the production and marketing of table wines, which are the principal offerings of the firm. Glenmore Distillers also holds a BATF wine-producing permit in Kentucky.

THE SOUTHWEST

Texas

Much has been written in the last five years about the prospects of developing a wine industry in Texas. The idea of growing and producing wine in Texas does not date back very much farther. With the exception of a single winery that has been operating for 100 years, no serious interest in winegrowing emerged in the state until the 1970s. In 1974 the University of Texas, in search of a profitable industry to utilize its vast acreage in west Texas, began experimenting with grape culture. Knowing that the oil wells that swelled the university's endowment fund would one day diminish, the institution's Board of Regents hoped to find alternative uses for the land that would provide a continuing income. Experimental plots of *Vitis vinifera* vines were planted in several locations, including Van Horn and Bakersfield, and, by 1980, the university was sufficiently encouraged to proceed with commercial plantings. The Board of Regents approved the development of

320 acres and began to search for a commercial firm interested in developing the industry for the university. The interest created by the university's experiments and the glowing progress reports from the Texas Development Office generated widespread interest from the private sector. The University of Texas contracted with Gill-Richter-Cordier, a consortium combining French vineyard and winemaking expertise with U.S. marketing and management skills, to produce wine commencing with the 1984 vintage. The winery evolving from this venture is Ste. Genevieve Vineyards, which is operated out of Austin. Concurrently, in the decade during which the university was making its investigations, a dozen small, independent wineries began operations in Texas.

The overwhelming size of Texas and the vast range of climatic extremes within its borders render it difficult to generalize about suitable microclimates for viticulture. In many areas of the state, viticultural opportunities are offset by attendant

Southwest vineyard landscape.

problems, and thus any assessment becomes more a question of weighing risks than of discovering suitable sites.

The greatest successes have been in those regions of the state that combine high altitude, dry climate, and comparatively cool temperatures during the growing season. The plains of west and northwest Texas have shown the greatest promise to date. In these areas, if sufficient irrigation water is available, the only major problems growers must deal with are severe cold in the winter and dangerous hailstorms in the late spring. Aware of these conditions, the Texans have proceeded to invest and explore.

The Val Verde winery, the grandfather of the Texas wine industry, celebrated its hundredth anniversary in 1983. Located near Del Rio on the Rio Grande and the Mexican border, it is a small, family-owned winery now operated by Thomas Qualia—the third-genertion proprietor. The winery produces about 5,000 gallons of wine a year from two native American varieties, Lenoir and Herbemont. Qualia sells all of his small production to locals and tourists. He is an organic farmer who uses no pesticides or herbicides and retains a flock of geese for weed control in the vineyard.

The oldest of the new breed of wineries is located in northwest Texas near Lubbock and is called Llano Estacado, which means "staked plains." With origins similar to Associated Vintners in Washington State, Llano Estacado began with a group of professors from Texas Tech University who experimented with their own wines as amateurs. Several of these professors were chemists and agriculturists interested in developing the industry. In 1976 the firm was bonded for commercial operations, and Kim McPherson, then at Trefethen Vineyards in the Napa Valley, was hired as winemaker. The winery began cautiously with French-American hybrids but has moved steadily toward exclusively *Vitis vinifera* production. Today it makes wine from Chardonnay, Chenin Blanc, French Colombard, and Sauvignon Blanc, among others, with awarding-winning success.

On the other side of Lubbock is the prestigious Pheasant Ridge Winery, founded and operated by Jennifer and Robert Cox. Cox, once a viticultural academic at the Texas A&M Experiment Station in Lubbock, is also an expert winemaker, and his *Vitis vinifera* wines have won numerous awards—some in competition with the finest fare from California and Europe. As would be expected, Pheasant Ridge wines are in great demand and difficult to find other than at the winery itself.

There are three wineries in the Fort Worth area, the oldest of which is La Buena Vida Vineyards, founded in 1978. Owner Dr. Bobby G. Smith has 8 acres of vineyards and produces a Barbera, Carnelian, and Ruby Cabernet, in addition to a number of proprietary labels. Hindered because his winery was in dry Parker County west of Fort Worth, Smith built a retail room and production facility near Fort Worth where, by Texas law, he can sell up to 25,000 gallons directly to consumers. Smith produces a Lambrusco-style red wine called "Texas Gold" from red French-American hybrids and has recently released a cuvée of sparkling muscadine.

Sanchez Creek, in Weatherford, also in dry Parker County, was founded in 1980 by Lyndol Hart, but has since been sold to an anthropology professor named Ronald Wetherington from Southern Methodist University. Current production is about 2,500 gallons annually, and there are plans for several times that much. The 8-acre vineyard is planted primarily with red varieties of *Vitis vinifera* and French-American hybrids, and the emphasis is toward production of heavy, Rhône-style wines. First releases from the 1981 vintage were a Cabernet Sauvignon and a red blend called "Rouge."

The newest winery in the Fort Worth area is Château Montgolfier, named for the pioneer French balloonist. Owner Henry C. McDonald, in addition to his responsibilities as an orthopedic surgeon and vintner, operates a balloonport that accommodates up to twenty hot-air balloons. McDonald's own balloon is decorated with a graphic representation of an enormous bunch of grapes, the same design that is carried on the winery's label. The first release in 1983 was a Chenin Blanc of excellent quality.

Northwest of Austin, in the Highland Lakes area of Central Texas, Ed and Susan Auler are growing grapes and making wine at their cattle ranch on the shore of Lake Buchanan. The winery, called Fall Creek Vineyards, was founded in 1979, after five seasons of viticultural experimentation convinced the Aulers that grapes could be grown there successfully. The Aulers began with a mix of *Vitis vinifera* and French-American hybrid varieties, but are narrowing the number of

FALL CREEK
V I N E Y A R D S

1982

CHENIN BLANC
PECOS COUNTY

A DELICATELY FRAGRANT AND PLEASANTLY SWEET WHITE
WINE PRODUCED AT OUR WINERY IN LLANO COUNTY,
TEXAS. WE HOPE THAT THIS WINE WILL BE CONSUMED
WITH ENJOYMENT AND IN MODERATION.

ED AULER, OWNER AND PROPRIETOR
FALL CREEK VINEYARDS

ALCOHOL 11.0% BY VOLUME
PRODUCED AND BOTTLED AT TOW, TEXAS BY FALL CREEK VINEYARDS
BW-TX-23

1981

TEXAS
WHITE RIESLING
LUBBOCK COUNTY

PRODUCED AND BOTTLED BY LLANO ESTACADO VINEYARDS.
LUBBOCK, TEXAS
ALCOHOL 10.5% BY VOLUME   750 ML. (25.4 FL. OZ.)

varieties down to only the most successful Old World types. After two vintages in an interim facility, a 35,000-gallon winery was built in 1981, and additional plantings in 1984 will bring the vineyards up to 45 acres. Fall Creek wines have been well received, and Carnelian, Chenin Blanc, Emerald Riesling, and Villard Blanc all have won prizes in Texas competition.

New Mexico

Wine grapes, introduced initially by the Franciscans, have been grown in New Mexico for hundreds of years, flourishing especially in the Rio Grande and Pecos River valleys. After repeal of Prohibition many of the state's small wineries reopened, but they declined over the next several decades until, by the 1960s, the industry was virtually defunct. Now viticulture is reviving rapidly, in many cases with enormous infusions of foreign capital. Wine acreage, predominantly located in the southeast corner of the state, is increasing exponentially as foreign-based firms plant vines in hundred- and thousand-acre increments. Wineries are now being planned as acreages come into maturity.

A number of local growers are also expanding acreages, usually on smaller scales. These parcels lie principally along the Rio Grande valley from Las Cruces to north of Santa Fe. Plantings in the southern portion of the valley have been exclusively of *Vitis vinifera* varieties, but in the area surrounding Albuquerque, French-American hybrid cultivars are being grown. All the vines are at elevations ranging from 3,500 to 7,000 feet.

West Wind Winery, a new facility just built at Bernalillo, 20 miles to the north of Albuquerque, is a joint venture of Tony Claiborne and Jim Winchell. They make their wines from purchased grapes grown at Rio Valley Vineyards in nearby Belen. There are currently four other wineries along the Rio Grande in New Mexico and at least two more planned.

Viña Madre is located to the east, the only New Mexico winery on the Pecos River. The winery is owned by the Hinkle family, descendants of a New Mexico governor. Forty acres of *Vitis vinifera* were planted in 1972, and in 1978 a 40,000-gallon winery was built.

Arizona

Aside from a thriving table grape industry in southwestern Arizona, the state's wine-grape production is still embryonic. Bob Webb of Tucson, an amateur winemaker turned professional, is the man solely responsible for reviving the extinct Arizona wine industry. He began making wine in 1980 with California fruit, but by 1982 he pressed his first wines from Arizona grapes. Dr. Eugene Mielke, professor at the University of Arizona, has been working with various test sites for vineyards around the state since 1972 and feels there is great potential in the area for viticulture. For the moment the wine industry in Arizona is growing slowly, with two additional wineries opened recently.

Colorado

Colorado currently has three wineries. Jim Seewald owns the Colorado Mountain Vineyards, founded in 1978. The winery and vineyards are located on the West Slope near Grand Junction. It was the outgrowth of an interest in home winemaking, like so many of the pioneer wine establishments in other states. A vineyard was planted in 1978 to supply hobbyists and was gradually expanded into a commercial enterprise. Seewald now vinifies a small portion of his production from his own grapes, but hopes to encourage others to grow grapes in the area to supplement his vineyards. Colorado recently passed a limited winery law that grants reduced license fees and excise tax rates to wineries that produce under 100,000 gallons and utilize at least 75 percent Colorado-grown fruit for production.

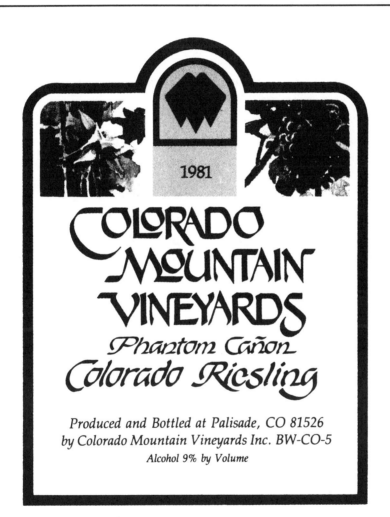

1981

COLORADO MOUNTAIN VINEYARDS

Phantom Cañon
Colorado Riesling

Produced and Bottled at Palisade, CO 81526
by Colorado Mountain Vineyards Inc. BW-CO-5
Alcohol 9% by Volume

Château d'Yquem

Lur-Saluces

1980

6

THE WINES OF FRANCE

The French mainland and Corsica total approximately 212,600 square miles—an area about 80 percent the size of Texas. Yet within this relatively small area the French cultivate more than three times the total vineyard acreage of America. (See color insert, figure 9.) About one Frenchman in every seven earns his living in some way connected with wine. Of 50 million Frenchmen, more than 1.6 million of them are winegrowers alone. One would expect the winegrowers to consume more wine than any other demographic group in France—and they do.

When one considers all the aspects of the art, there can be no question that France is the foremost country for wine growing, despite some recent dramatic advances by other nations. While Italy produces more gallons of wine than France, and Spain has more acres of vineyard, and Germany, the Soviet Union, and the United States each arguably have more advanced vine and wine technology, France has a heritage and a diversity of wine that is unmatched by any other country.

No other nation controls and regulates production of wine as strictly as France. The vineyards of France total about 3.25 million acres. While this is enormous, it pales in comparison to the 6 million acres or so that were cultivated in France in the late 1800s. The most important factor in this decline was the *Phylloxera* blight, but there have been economic pressures, too.

In 1875 France produced nearly 2 billion gallons of wine: a level never again attained. Nowadays France produces from about 700 million gallons to about 1.33 billion gallons annually. This wide disparity reflects the effects of weather on French wine yields, with drought and abundant rain following each other un-

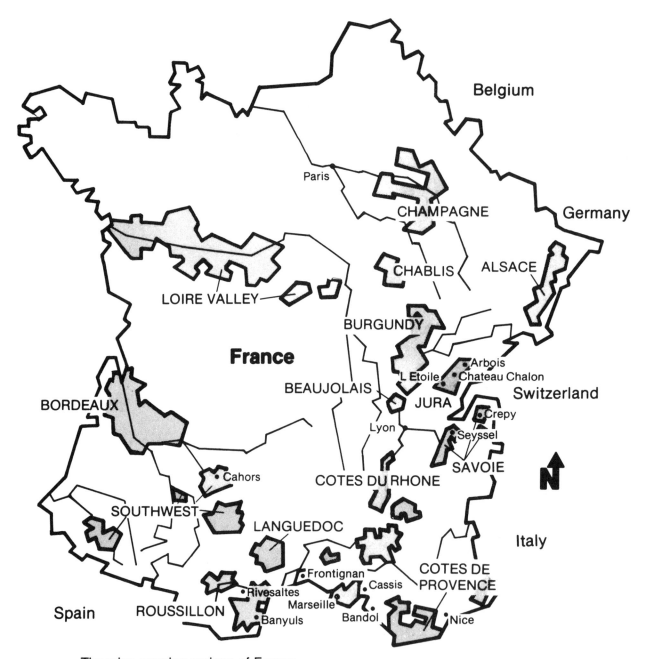

The wine-growing regions of France.

predictably. Spring and fall frosts often inflict great losses, and heavy rains and insufficient sunlight also cause losses in both quantity and quality. The median crop with a good sugar-acid ratio is often an outstanding vintage in terms of quality. The short crop with high sugar will produce small volumes of strong wine. The heavy crop with low sugar will produce large gallonages of ordinary wine. Consequently, winegrowers and wine merchants endeavor to offset the considerable yearly differences through prudent pricing in order to survive economically. There are, of course, exceptions to this, particularly in the case of the noble growths that maintain such high standards that only the finer vintages are marketed under the esteemed labels (the poorer vintages are often sold in bulk to other wineries). At the other end of this spectrum are some of the large *négociants* (shipper/merchants) that buy lower-grade wines for further processing and blending, eventually bottling finished products under their own labels. Though the label usually identifies region of origin, the individual vineyard or vintage characteristics may have been processed beyond recognition.

Prior to the nineteenth century there were few laws regulating the wines of France; the sole judge of quality was taste, and it was measured by consumer satisfaction in the marketplace. The shortage of wine following the *Phylloxera* crisis in the latter portion of the 1800s led to considerable fraud and abuse of the consumer—and the French government legislated against this in 1905 with laws that repressed "the deceits and attempted deceits of nature, quality, species, origin, and denomination of wine." Following World War I wine demand greatly increased and again dishonest merchants marketed large quantities of poor-grade wines at high prices. By 1919, exacting definitions for the appellations of origin had been determined. However, following the depression of the early 1930s, further loopholes were discovered in the viticultural regulations. Finally, the Decree of July 30, 1935, was enacted, which provided for Vins à Appellation d'Origine Contrôlée (AOC). These laws, while not perfect, have been admired by winegrowers and consumers the world over and have been used as the basis of similar legislation in other countries. Consumers desiring authentic wines from specific locales in France should learn to look for the words *Appellation Contrôlée* as a guarantee that the wine was produced from grapes grown under this French government regulation.

Since they cover the entire country, and each province has different applications and interpretations, enforcement of the AOC laws is difficult. Important as they are, the laws are obviously insufficient to guarantee a consumer any real wine quality. To this end, some districts in France are forming Commissions de Dégustation: tasting panels authorized to judge the organoleptic qualifications of wines before permitting them to be labeled.

CLASSIFICATIONS

The production of French wines is classified into four broad quality, or nobility, levels, as follows below.

AOC—Appellation d'Origine Contrôlée

Literally, the AOC translates as "wines of controlled place names." This is the most important production level and is strictly enforced in France by the INAO (Institut National des Appellations d'Origine), a private organization but empowered by the French government to "service de la répression des fraudes." Accordingly, AOC wines must be labeled with a statement that identifies the *appellation* (place name) of origin. The appellations have set boundaries, specified grape-variety requirements, and within each specific district there are also rules governing the methods of winemaking for these grape varieties. For example, even though the black grape, Pinot Noir, is grown in both the provinces of Champagne and Burgundy, the Champenois winegrowers cannot make commercial red wine from this grape as they do in Burgundy. The wine from Champagne must be white—although, prior to the invention of the sparkling champagne wine, the Champenois did compete with the Burgundians in red table wine production.

The production of most AOC wines is limited to certain maximums in most regions and subregions, although annual reassessment may permit higher levels. In total, only about 15 percent of the entire French wine production qualifies for the AOC label.

VDQS—Vins Délimités de Qualité Supérieure

This classification is translated as "wines designated as being of superior quality" that are not, however, entitled to an Appellation Contrôlée pedigree.

The VDQS wines are also controlled by the French government, but not nearly to the degree that is required for the AOC growths. This category was established in 1945 and has served to popularize many previously relatively unknown vineyards. In comparison to AOC wines, few VDQS wines are exported. Most are consumed in France. In fact, the French consume the vast majority of their own wine production; only 2 percent or so is exported to America each year.

The VDQS wines are also identified by a label that must appear on the bottle upon which either "Vins Délimités de Qualité Supérieure" is fully written out or the abbreviation "VDQS" is displayed.

Vins de Pays

Vins de Pays is translated as "wines of the area" or "country wines"—a category established in 1973 by the French government. These wines are usually rather ordinary and the designation may be applied to the wines of an entire region or to the wines of a small *commune* or village. In general, the Vins de Pays designation allows one to distinguish better from lesser wine subdistricts within an overall district of merely ordinary-quality wine growing.

Vins de Consommation Courante

As the title suggests, this is the category of the famous French *vin ordinaire,* "wine for current consumption." No origins are specified or required for these wines, which are sold and drunk about as widely and with as little discrimination as milk is in America.

Wines produced under the AOC rules are regulated by a multitude of controls, many of which vary considerably in application and enforcement. For example, not all AOC wines are subjected to organoleptic evaluation, and while vineyard boundaries are strictly maintained, a given wine may be eligible for several appellations of increasing importance depending upon the wine quality in a particular year. One of the best examples of this comes from the Montagne de Corton area of Burgundy's Côte de Beaune: where a wine may be awarded the appellation "Corton" at its best, "Aloxe-Corton" when it's of lesser quality, and merely "Burgundy" when it doesn't measure up—see below. The varieties of grapes that can be grown in specific appellations are always closely regulated, and so is minimum sugar content, which determines the alcoholic strength of the resulting wine. In some areas, such as Burgundy and Champagne, AOC regulations prescribe exact guidelines for the cultivation and trellising; while in other areas, such as Bordeaux, the vine spacings are less important. In some areas the local authorities stipulate the prices of grapes.

Each AOC has its own maximum yield limitations, termed the "Basic Yield" or the *Rendement de Base*. Generally, the finer the AOC label, the lower the limit set on the yield. Each year, local commissions can vary the Basic Yield somewhat depending on the growing conditions during the season. This variant increase is known as the "Annual Yield." Again, the amount of variance is determined by the quality echelon of each AOC. Above the Annual Yield there is a level known as the "Ceiling Yield" or *Plafond Limité de Classement* (sometimes abbreviated "PLC"), which is invariable. Production that exceeds the Annual Yield but falls within the limit of the Ceiling Yield may qualify for the AOC label by passing a taste test conducted by local authorities. When production exceeds the Ceiling Yield, then the wine lot will be tested to see if it meets the standards needed for the AOC label. If the wine lot passes, the amount up to the Ceiling Yield will carry the AOC label and the rest will go for brandy or vinegar. If a wine lot fails to pass the taste test, then it must *all* be made into brandy or vinegar, with no portion of the lot entitled to the AOC label.

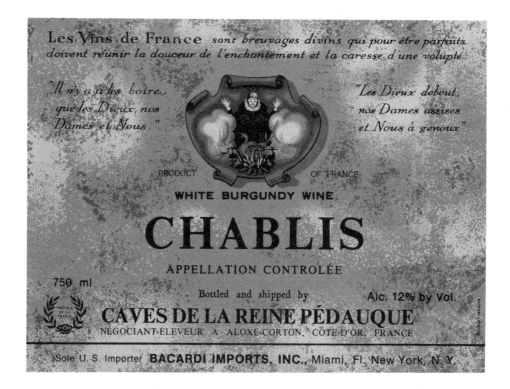

The average per capita consumption of wine in France is more than 20 gallons nowadays, ten times greater than per capita wine consumption in the United States. Thus many a Frenchman takes no more notice of his wine than Americans do of water. To him, drinking wine is natural, a custom he's grown up with.

Much of the wine imported to America from France is, of course, of a different quality from the wines that the French consume on an everyday basis. The French are frugal people, and economic pressures make it necessary to export much of their best production. Some say that as export markets become more and more competitive, these pressures may force some of the better vineyards out of business.

A Note on Classification

The French system (really, *systems*) of classifying vineyards is a common source of confusion to the wine neophyte. Not only are there a large number of terms to learn, but often the same term means something different in different regions. Discussions of the individual regions below not only considers how each separate classification system works, but it helps to clarify the subject and introduce a few general principles and definitions.

The basic idea behind the French classification systems is to establish a kind of pecking order for the various vineyards in a region. The best vineyards are ranked "First Growth" (*growth* is another term for *vineyard*), or, sometimes, "Great Growth." The second-best vineyards are "Second Growth," and so on. These rankings appear on wine labels in French, so it helps enormously to learn a few French words:

Cru—"vineyard" or "growth"

Grand—"great" or "finest"

Premier—"first" or "primary"

Deuxième—"second"

The confusion arises because individual districts use the same terms to refer to different ranking levels. For example, the Bordeaux Classification of 1855 (one of the first widely accepted systems—see chapter 4), assigned five quality levels to the best vineyards of the Médoc subregion. First-growth vineyards became known as *"Premiers Crus,"* Second-Growth vineyards as *"Deuxièmes Crus,"* and so on. For the most part this classification remains intact for wines of the Médoc. However, the St.-Émilion district, also in Bordeaux, employs its own system, in which a First Growth is known as *Premier Grand Cru* and a Second Growth as a *Grand Cru Classe.* And, in Burgundy, a *Premier Cru* takes second place to a *Grand Cru.* Further examples will only add to the confusion.

As one gains familiarity with the wines of France, however, one develops a feel for the various classification systems, sensing when it's crucial to distinguish carefully between a Grand Cru and Premier Cru and when it's not. There is no need to commit the entire apparatus to memory: with a little application one can learn one's way around the major districts and cease to worry about the minor variations.

BURGUNDY

Burgundy, or *Bourgogne* as it is known by Burgundians, is the most important wine region in eastern France. Wine growing in Burgundy preceded the Roman occupation there by several centuries. Pliny the Elder gives credit to Helvetius, a Swiss, for bringing the vine to Burgundy, while Livy insists it was Aaron, a

Tuscan. Others maintain it was the Phoenicians, who brought viticulture to the mouth of the Rhône River at Marseilles, about 600 B.C., whence it spread to Burgundy.

It was the Romans, however, who taught the Burgundii peasants, originally Scandinavians, how to cultivate the vine and make wine. Then, after some four centuries of Roman control, the Roman Catholic church began to gain dominance over the Burgundian vineyards. Monks in various religious orders planted and cultivated the many landholdings bestowed upon the monasteries by the Burgundian dukes. Wine was nearly as valuable as gold, which may be the source of the financial term "liquid assets." Consequently, the Catholic church became wealthy, and the monks began to indulge in the pleasures of cultivating wine. St. Bernard offered harsh criticism for the great wealth amassed at Cluny, the magnificent monastery in the heart of Burgundy and once the greatest church structure in France.

Many Benedictine monks moved out of luxurious Cluny in order to establish more serene abbeys. One splinter group, formed in 1098, called themselves *Cistercians*, after the bulrushes, or *cisteaux*, that grew in the swampy area where they settled, near Beaune. Their motto was "By the Cross and the Plow," an indication of their agricultural ideals. The only crop they could cultivate successfully, however, was grapes—doubtlessly from vines that were descendants of the native Allobrogian vine. The most celebrated of the Cistercian monks were those of the Clos de Vougeot, described earlier in chapter 4.

Nicholas Rolin, chancellor to the duke of Burgundy in the middle of the fifteenth century, constructed the famous Hospices de Beaune, which has held an annual auction of wines from both its own vineyards, as well as those of benefactors, ever since. This has become somewhat of a barometer of both the quality and the prices established each year for Burgundy wines.

Following the French Revolution, the large church properties were divided into small plots and sold to lay growers. Any one *vigneron* could diversify his holdings by owning a portion of any number of AOC properties—a good hedge against the unpredictable ravages of hail that shreds one vineyard or another in some years. Today, because of this division, most important Burgundy vineyards have many owners. The Clos de Vougeot, for example, is divided into more than seventy separately owned parcels. This is quite a contrast to Bordeaux, where single estates remain that are larger than some of the entire *domaines* (the Burgundian term for wine estate) of pre-Revolutionary Burgundy.

Up until the eighteenth century most of the wines grown in Burgundy were drunk from the cask. Bottling was a convenience for marketing, not aging. Desmond Seward suggests that Burgundies were lighter in color and body before the French Revolution and were characterized by clarity and a gentle fruity flavor.

In modern times Burgundy is still rather light in color, but rich in bouquet, body, and flavor.

There is a gradual change taking place in Burgundy. Traditionally, the wines of the region have been made individually by the vineyard owners. Some wines remain produced in the customary fashion, with growers holding firm to their time-honored craftsmanship. More and more grapes, however, are sold to the négociant-shippers, many of which have constructed centralized wine-producing facilities. In the view of most wine experts, this new methodology allows for the adapting of new technology and modern equipment—resulting in more consistent higher overall quality of resulting products.

The red wines of Burgundy are not generally as long lived as those from many other regions, especially the more notable Bordeaux. Some Grand Cru selections, such as Chambertin or Musigny, may take ten to twenty years to mature—but most good-quality red Burgundies are at their finest in just five to ten years.

The Region

Burgundy was defined viticulturally in 1930 by the Civil Tribunal of Dijon. It consists of four departments that have approximately 90,000 acres of vineyard:

Yonne—Chablis

Côte d'Or—the "great" growths

Saône-et-Loire—all of the Chalonnais, the Mâconnais, and the northern tip of the Beaujolais

Rhône—the balance of Beaujolais (not to be confused with the Côtes du Rhône)

Though technically Burgundy embraces the 120-mile area from Chablis down to the southern tip of Beaujolais, just north of Lyon, to many people Burgundy means simply the prestigious Côte d'Or: the "hillside of gold." This is a 37-mile strip of real estate in the heart of the larger Burgundy region. While the Côte d'Or wines are the most celebrated Burgundies, all wines grown in the area have a right to the name *Burgundy* and will be so considered in this text.

Burgundy Labels and Terms

Even the more advanced enophile can become confused with all the different Burgundian classifications, communal names, and other nomenclature. The old adage—"Respectez les crus" (learn the names of the finest growths [vineyards])—will offer some help in straightening things out. It will help even more to understand the methods by which Burgundians classify and name their wines.

In each *commune* (parish or township) surrounding a village in Burgundy, the vineyards are divided into small parcels known as *climats*. The grandest climats are known as *Grands Crus* (Great Growths) and their labels will carry *only* the climat name as the appellation—for example, Chambertin or La Romanée-Conti. One step down are the Premiers Crus (First Growth) climats. In Burgundy, the name of the Premier Cru climat may appear after the commune name on the label; for example, Beaune-Grèves, in which Beaune is the commune and Grèves the climat. The names of lesser climats may appear on the label linked to commune names so long as the lettering of the climat name is half the size of the lettering used for the commune, for example, BEAUNE-Lulanne.

Two phrases frequently found on Burgundy labels are "Mise en Bouteilles au Domaine" or "Mise en Bouteilles à la Propriété." These both translate as "bottled at the estate," or "bottled at the estate by the grower as a bottler" and are roughly equivalent to *estate bottling* as the term is used in America. (In Burgundy, the wine estates are known as *domaines*, while in Bordeaux they are usually called *châteaux*.) "Mise en Bouteilles dans Nos Caves," which translates as "bottled in our cellars," is, on the other hand, virtually meaningless. Unless the bottler is also the owner of the climat, such words say little. All wines are bottled in some kind of cellar.

Because many of the Burgundy vineyards are divided up into innumerable individual estates or parcels, it can often be difficult for the consumer to know which particular label to choose within a given appellation. One way around this is to familiarize oneself with the better *négociants,* or shippers, whose names appear on Burgundy labels. These shipping houses buy grapes and/or wine from many of the growers and may even blend wines from a particular appellation under their own label. The better négociants have a reputation to protect and are, therefore, very careful in their selecting, blending, and bottling. Consumers who look for these shippers' labels are generally providing themselves with the best chance for higher levels of quality. Among the better Burgundy shippers exporting to American consumers are Bichot, Bouchard Aîné & Fils, Bouchard Père & Fils, Joseph Drouhin, Faiveley, Louis Jadot, Louis Latour, Mommessin, Moillard, and Moreau, though this is by no means a complete list.

Chablis (The Auxerrois)

Chablis is sometimes referred to as "Lower Burgundy" because of its relatively low elevation. On a map, however, Chablis is unmistakably in the northern por-

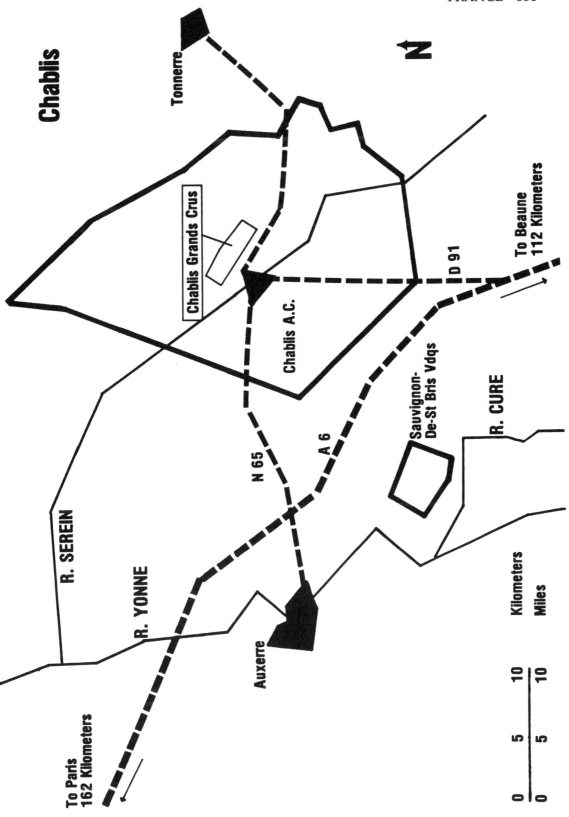

Chablis

tion of the Burgundy district, about 100 miles southeast of Paris. The entire Chablis subdistrict is properly known as the Auxerrois or Département de l'Yonne, and in addition to the renowned Chablis vineyards it also includes the vineyards of Sauvignon-de-Saint-Bris, Auxerre, and Tonnerre, among other, lesser growths. The Auxerrois is situated between the rivers Yonne and Armançon, extending southward to the villages of Avallon and Semur. It also encompasses an area about 12 miles west of the Yonne.

Chablis is a village of less than 2,000 people, situated on a stream called Le Sereine meaning, as the name may suggest, "serene," or, according to some of the locals, "evening dew." In either case, the Serein empties into the Yonne River to the north, which, in turn, eventually empties into the Seine, a system that has for centuries provided important water transportation.

There are about 4,000 acres of vineyard in Chablis, divided amongst hundreds of small growers. Only a small percentage (about 6 percent) of their production is AOC, and just one subdistrict (Sauvignon-de-St.-Bris) is designated as VDQS. To many people, the Auxerrois is synonymous with white wine, particularly the grand white AOC wines known as Chablis.

The soil strata is very calcareous, consisting of alternate beds of Kimmeridgian clay mixed with limestone. The Auxerrois has a rather severe climate for wine growing—cold, dry winters and hot, humid summers; hailstorms are common in the spring and summer. Spring frosts all too often damage or destroy the fruiting buds on the vines.

Chablis makes up about half of all the Auxerrois vineyards and produces only dry white wines from the Chardonnay variety. The wines from superior vintage years are pale golden straw in color, vinous and rather "haylike" in the nose, and possess a distinct flinty aftertaste. The Grands Crus, or "Great Growths," of Chablis are limited to a 36-hectare hillside of seven vineyards totaling 90 acres. The hillside faces southwest toward the village of Chablis. The AOC permits the names of these vineyards, Bougros, Preuses, Vaudésirs, Grenouilles, Valmur, Clos, and Blanchots, to appear on the label. La Moutonne, a small prestigious vineyard of 3 acres, was recently added as a Grand Cru. Ranking next are thirty Chablis Premier Cru wines from named vineyards. These vineyards, totaling about 500 acres, also have the natural capabilities to produce fine Chablis wines. Of these, eleven are within the village limits of Chablis and the balance in adjacent communes. In either case, the name of Premier Cru vineyards may also be included on the label.

The history of Chablis stretches back to the twelfth century. Pontigny was a Cistercian monastery founded on the Serein in 1114, and four years later the monks bought adjacent vineyards from the Benedictines of St. Martin at Tours. The Pontigny monks were undoubtedly the first to plant the great wine variety

Chardonnay in Burgundy—creating the first Chablis wine. St. Thomas à Becket was exiled to Pontigny in 1164 and spent two years there. Also during the mid-1100s a glorious church was built there that in modern times serves as a seminary and remains the oldest surviving Cistercian church in all of France.

There are other vineyards in the Chablis district aside from the Grands and Premiers Crus that can produce AOC Chablis wines. Wines from these vineyards, providing that they are within the Chablis district, can be labeled AOC Petit Chablis. No other wines can be AOC designated. The finer Chablis wines are matured in oak casks for at least eighteen months before bottling. The lesser Chablis are often bottled the very next spring after harvest or shipped in cask for on-premise draught sale. Sauvignon-de-St.-Bris is the only VDSQ-designated area in the Auxerrois and produces dry white wines from the Sauvignon Blanc variety. The St.-Bris wines are similar to Sancerre in the Loire Valley, located about 50 miles to the northwest.

The villages of Auxerre and Tonnerre produce considerable red wine from the Pinot Noir variety. Though much of the wine is of fine quality, it cannot be AOC labeled and it pales in comparison to the noble growths to the southeast in the Côte d'Or.

Côte d'Or

Burgundians are fond of proverbs, and there is one particular favorite of the people of the "slope of gold," the Côte d'Or: "If our slopes were not the richest in Burgundy, they'd be the poorest." As the Cistercian monks quickly learned nearly a thousand years ago, the red soil of the Côte d'Or is so poor that it will only grow grapes: but in combination with proper amounts of sunlight, this poor soil can produce some of the finest wines on earth. The red Pinot Noir is grown in the Côte d'Or to a richness that is rarely equaled anywhere else on earth. Tones of amber-scarlet color of soft intensity and brilliant clarity are typical of fine, aged red Burgundy, as is a distinct "coffee" nose and earthy-berry flavors.

The Côte d'Or is located about 60 miles southeast of Chablis and about 160 miles or so in the same direction from Paris. It is divided into two distinct hillsides; the highly acclaimed Côte de Nuits is located between Dijon at the north and the village of Premeaux to the south, while the Côte de Beaune reaches from Premeaux southward to include the village of Santenay. There was once a classification entitled Côte de Dijon, now defunct. Behind the two "côtes" to the west are hillside and hilltop vineyards entitled "Hautes-Côtes de Nuits" and "Hautes-Côtes de Beaune," both of which make ordinary wines.

There are about 9,000 acres of vineyard in the Côte d'Or, cultivated by hundreds of growers who produce from 3 million to 6 million gallons of precious

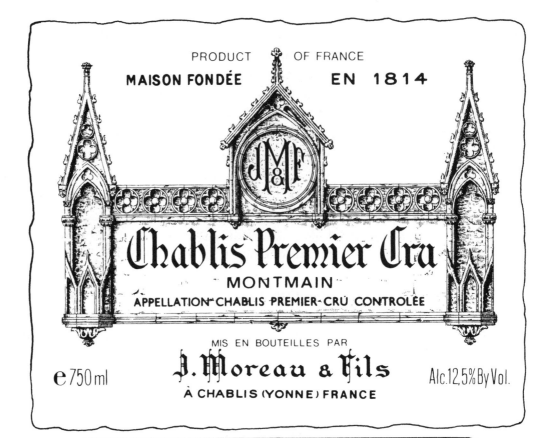

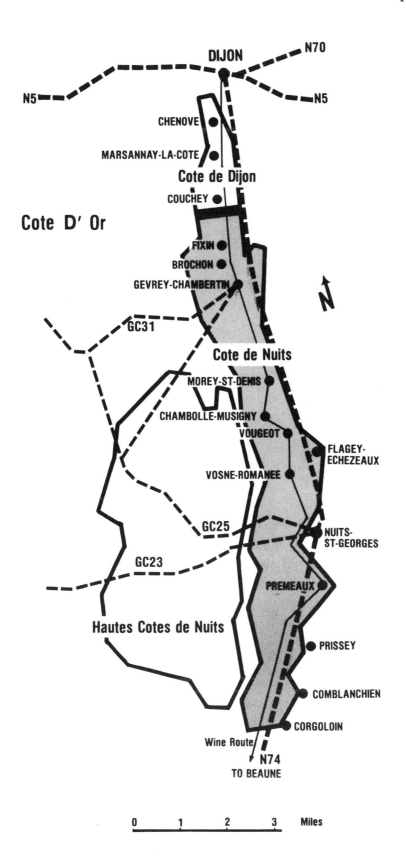

DIJON

N70

N5

N5

CHENOVE

MARSANNAY-LA-COTE

Cote de Dijon

COUCHEY

Cote D' Or

FIXIN

BROCHON

GEVREY-CHAMBERTIN

GC31

Cote de Nuits

MOREY-ST-DENIS

CHAMBOLLE-MUSIGNY

VOUGEOT

FLAGEY-
ECHEZEAUX

VOSNE-ROMANEE

GC25

NUITS-
ST-GEORGES

GC23

PREMEAUX

Hautes Cotes de Nuits

PRISSEY

COMBLANCHIEN

CORGOLOIN

Wine Route

N74
TO BEAUNE

N

0   1   2   3   Miles

wine each year. About half of the vineyards in the Côte d'Or are AOC classified, and only a few have the VDSQ designation. Red wine production dominates the regional output.

Côte de Nuits

The Côte de Nuits, which slopes gently to the east facing the Saône River, has soil of an oolitic calcareous composition mixed with intermittent iron and marl. The eastern exposure gets the early morning sun, which aids in both maximizing sunlight and also in quickly burning off the dew that can harbor disease microorganisms. Generally the land between the upper and lower levels of the slopes are the most coveted in the Côte de Nuits. The topsoil of this sector has limestone and layered fragments of crumbled rock rising from the subsoil, a mixture that is high in potassium and phosphorous compounds that are particularly well-suited to viticulture.

The northernmost village in the Côte de Nuits is Marsannay, where the great Burgundian grape Pinot Noir is grown principally for rosé table-wine production. These are generally very good rosés, but fall far short of the fine reds grown from the same grape to the south.

The great vineyards of the Côte de Nuits commence at the villages of Fixin and Brochon—situated just below Marsannay and about 6 miles south of the famous mustard-producing city of Dijon. The wines of Fixin and Brochon are complex and rich, with the best grown from nine Premier Cru vineyards. Some of the more noteworthy vintages can be quite comparable to some of the better offerings from Chambertin and Vougeot. Typically, Fixin receives less attention and is therefore sometimes overlooked by American wine consumers.

The next village to the south is Gevrey, which like many communes in Burgundy has added the name of its most famous vineyard, Chambertin, to its own—thus, Gevrey-Chambertin. There are eight Grand Cru vineyards in Gevrey-Chambertin. At the top of the list are Chambertin itself and the equally great Chambertin-Clos-de-Bèze. The other seven Great Growths all have added the name Chambertin following their own particular vineyard name, such as Charmes-Chambertin. The commune of Gevrey-Chambertin totals about 1,000 acres.

The great vineyards of Gevrey have a long and interesting history. In 630, the Burgundian Duke Algamaire bequeathed vineyards at Gevrey and Vosne to the Benedictine monks at the Abbey of Bèze. The Gevrey vineyards became known as the Clos de Bèze. Next to the Clos de Bèze was a small piece of land owned by a peasant named Bertin. He became so impressed with the quality of the wine the monks grew nearby that he planted his small property with vines and began to employ the monks' methods of wine growing. His vineyard became known as *Champ* (field) *Bertin,* eventually contracted to Chambertin. Some authorities contend that Chambertin was the favorite wine of Napoleon Bonaparte. There is no doubt that Chambertin, particularly the Clos de Bèze, remains among the finest red wine growths.

Proceeding south one approaches the commune of Morey-Saint-Denis. Among its total communal acreage of some 250 acres or so, there are five Grand Cru vineyards totaling about 80 acres. The Convent of Le Tart was founded by Cistercian nuns, sometimes called "Bernardines," in this commune in 1125. The sisters cultivated vineyards in order to demonstrate that they were true Cistercians, and their wines were thought to be as good as any in the Côte d'Or prior to the French Revolution. The old nunnery vineyard, long since called the Clos de Tart, is one of the Grand Cru growths in Morey-Saint-Denis; the Bonnes Mares, also Grand Cru, extends on into the neighboring village of Chambolle-Musigny. The other three Grand Cru vineyards of Morey-Saint-Denis are Clos de St.-Denis, Clos de la Roche, and Clos des Lambrays. In general, red wines from the commune of Morey-Saint-Denis are rich in body, bouquet, and color.

As Chambertin was added to Gevrey, so the Grand Cru vineyard of Les Musigny was added to the village name of Chambolle. It is at Musigny that the Grand Cru white wines are made in the Côte de Nuits—wines that are blessed with unforgettable bouquet and body. Law permits up to 15 percent of the white Chardonnay from Les Musigny to be blended into the reds of Pinot Noir. As a rule this is the destiny of Les Musigny Chardonnay, although rarely, the Musigny Blanc is bottled separately.

Route 74 connects all the Great Growths of the Côte de Nuits. Traveling south on this road, one reaches the next commune, the village of Vougeot. It is here that the Cistercian monks developed their legendary Clos de Vougeot as described in chapter 4. (See color insert, figure 10.) The abbey remains as a gathering center for the Chevaliers du Tastevin, a huge international wine brotherhood. Today there are only about 125 acres of AOC Grand Cru vineyard in the tiny commune of Vougeot—all planted with fine red Pinot except 5 acres of Chardonnay, which is aptly labeled "Clos de Vougeot blanc." The red wines at the Clos de Vougeot vary considerably nowadays because there are so many different parcels from which individual owners make their own wines. The best ones usually are found from the better négociant-shippers Pierre André, Joseph Drouhin, Faiveley, Jean Grivot, Leroy, and Domaine Jacques Prieur. Even when it was a single large Cistercian abbey property, though, there were different wines made by the monks. Cuvée des Papes (wine of the popes) came from the higher portion of the vineyard to the west and Cuvée des Rois (wine of the kings) came from the central portion, both about equal in quality. The third, and lowest-quality wine, was the

ALCOHOL 13% BY VOLUME

PRODUCE OF FRANCE
*Grand Vin
de Bourgogne*

RED BURGUNDY TABLE WINE
*Récolté - Élevé
et mis en bouteille
à la Propriété*

Clos-de-Vougeot

APPELLATION CONTROLÉE

GRAND CRU

1982

S. C. JEAN **GRIVOT**

VITICULTEUR A VOSNE-ROMANÉE (COTE-D'OR) FRANCE

750 ml

FILIBER NUITS – *Reprod. Interd.*

SOCIÉTÉ CIVILE DU DOMAINE DE LA ROMANÉE-CONTI
PROPRIETAIRE A VOSNE-ROMANÉE (COTE-D'OR)

ROMANÉE-CONTI

APPELLATION ROMANÉE-CONTI CONTROLÉE

9.120 Bouteilles Récoltées

Nº

ANNÉE 1976

LES ASSOCIÉS-GÉRANTS

Mise en bouteille au domaine

75 cl

PRODUCE OF FRANCE

Cuvée des Moines (wine of the monks) harvested from the lowermost division.

Still farther south on Route 74 are the fine vineyards of Flagey-Échézeaux that are 178 acres or so. Nowadays these are often included with the historic vineyards of Vosne-Romanée that border them to the south and span another 370 acres. Both are AOC Grand Cru. One poet called Vosne-Romanée the "centre pearl of the Burgundian necklace"—truly an apt description. Within Vosne-Romanée reigns what may perhaps be considered the king of all red wines: La Romanée-Conti. To Burgundy-lovers this small vineyard of 4.5 acres has no peer. Some say that nowhere else on earth are soil and sun so perfectly matched for ideal viticulture. As would be anticipated, the wines of this tiny vineyard are very expensive, often surpassing $100 per bottle for younger vintages and much more for older offerings.

La Romanée-Conti is blessed with distinguished neighbors as well—La Tâche and Richebourg, among others. All of these vineyards, along with those of Flagey-Échézeaux, were once owned by the Benedictine Abbey of Saint-Vivant at Vosne, itself bequeathed by the Duchess of Burgundy in 1232. Legend has it that the wines from La Romanée-Saint-Vivant were used to treat King Louis XIV for an illness. Exclaiming over his enjoyment of this medicine, le *Roi Soleil* (The Sun King, Louis XIV's nickname) remarked that "an illness which helps one discover such a remedy is indeed a present from heaven."

In 1720 La Romanée-Conti became the property of the Cronembourg family. Despite the efforts of Madame de Pompadour to acquire it, the tiny 4.5-acre jewel was sold again forty years later to the Prince de Conti, who added his name to make it La Romanée-Conti. In much the same fashion as at the Clos de Vougeot, the vineyards of the Abbey of Saint-Vivant became public property after the French Revolution and were subsequently auctioned off after all the buildings were destroyed so that the monks would not try to return. Curiously, the vines of La Romanée-Conti escaped the *Phylloxera* until 1945, when finally they were uprooted in favor of grafted stock. Today the estate is owned by the Domaine de la Romanée-Conti that provides for the exceptional care that must be taken to continue producing the marvelous wines of this tiny property. Together, Vosne Romanée and Flagey-Échézeaux boast of seven Grand Cru vineyards, all of which produce red wines of velvet softness and a huge coffeelike bouquet. At least part of the bouquet may be attributable to the aging of these wines in casks of precious French oak.

The principal town of the Côte de Nuits is Nuits-Saint-Georges, from which the entire grand slope gets its name. The largest village in the Côte de Nuits, it has twenty-nine Premiers Crus, which are listed at the end of this section.

The red wines of Nuits-Saint-Georges are noted for their heavy body and dark ruby color. They mature slowly, often with excessive tannin. Nowadays a multitude of wine shippers make their headquarters in Nuits-Saint-Georges primarily to centralize themselves in the Côte d'Or.

The southernmost vineyards in the Côte de Nuits are those of the commune Prémeaux, a small town that marks the border between the Côte de Nuits and the Côte de Beaune. The wines of Prémeaux are similar in style to Nuits-Saint-Georges and are entitled to use the Nuits-Saint-Georges appellation on their labels.

The high acclaim given to many vineyards in the central portion of the Côte de Nuits is not generally awarded to most of the vineyards situated at the northern and southern tips of the slope. Among the villages and parishes affected by this discrimination are Comblanchien and Prissey, near Prémeaux and, as mentioned earlier, Fixin and Brochon, which border Chambertin. Wines grown from such vineyards may be labeled "Côte de Nuits-Villages." This confers a bit of prestige and recognition on wines of generally good quality that would otherwise probably go unnoticed in the market. It also provides lower prices and typically good values to red Burgundy-enthusiasts.

Côte de Beaune

The southern half of the Côte d'Or is called the Côte de Beaune—named for the ancient city of Beaune that remains the wine center of the entire Burgundy region.

The Côte de Beaune makes both red and white table wines, but unlike the Côte de Nuits, the Côte de Beaune is famed for its whites. The hillsides of the Côte de Beaune face southeasterly and the soils have a composition similar to those of the Côte de Nuits, but perhaps with more clay and iron. Some experts say they can detect a flintiness in the white wines grown in the Montrachet and Meursault vineyards, whose soils are a light-colored marl.

To the north of the city of Beaune are the remains of the fine barrel-vaulted twelfth-century church constructed by the monks of Saulieu. Centuries before the construction of the church, in 775, Charlemagne gave the Abbey of Saulieu most of his personal Corton vineyards in nearby Aloxe (now the commune of Aloxe-Corton) hoping, no doubt, that the monks would provide him with the finest wines made from these vines. Rather ironically, Corton was also the favorite wine of Voltaire, a sworn enemy of the monastic system. Voltaire, however, is reported to have poured lesser wines for his guests and drunk the Corton himself.

The most northern vineyard locale of the Côte de Beaune is that of the Montagne de Corton, one of the most historic vineyard locales in the Côte de Beaune. This entire district was once part of the vast holdings of Charlemagne during the eighth century A.D. The eastern half of the Corton hillside is planted with the red Pinot while the southern and western portion is planted with

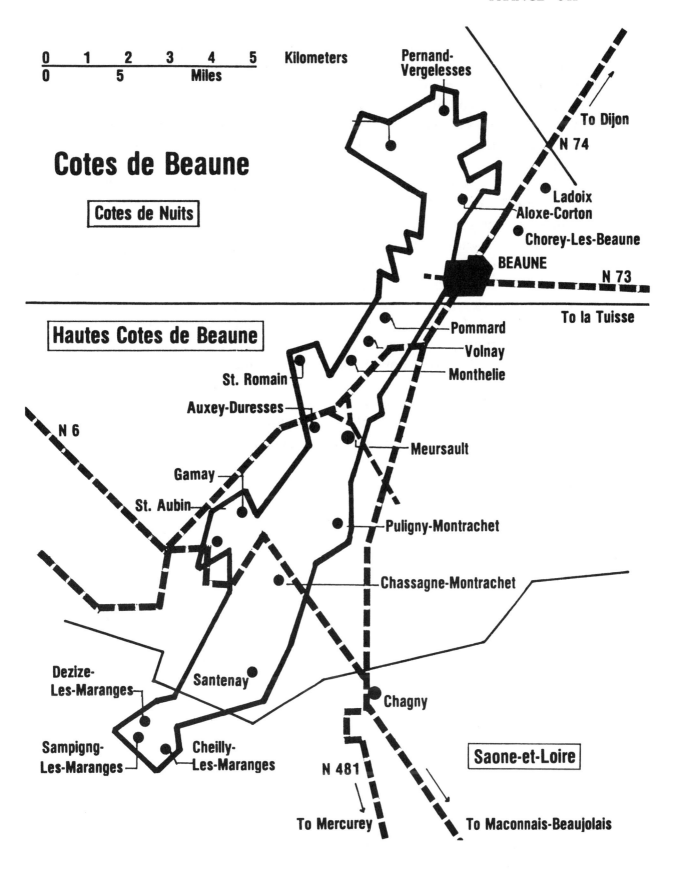

Kilometers

Miles

Cotes de Beaune

Cotes de Nuits

Pernand-
Vergelesses

To Dijon

N 74

Ladoix
Aloxe-Corton

Chorey-Les-Beaune

BEAUNE

N 73

To la Tuisse

Hautes Cotes de Beaune

Pommard

Volnay

Monthelie

St. Romain

Auxey-Duresses

N 6

Meursault

Gamay

St. Aubin

Puligny-Montrachet

Chassagne-Montrachet

Dezize-
Les-Maranges

Santenay

Chagny

Sampigng-
Les-Maranges

Cheilly-
Les-Maranges

Saone-et-Loire

N 481

To Mercurey

To Maconnais-Beaujolais

Chardonnay. Both are AOC Corton Grand Cru designated, the Pinot being the only red AOC Grand Cru in the entire Côte de Beaune. The Charlemagne and Corton Charlemagne vineyards are permitted the AOC Grand Cru for white wines only. It is often customary for the various parcels within the three Grand Cru climats to add the parcel name after the vineyard name, that is, Corton-Pougets, Corton-Grancey, etc. However, the wines are still entitled to be called Grands Crus.

Defining the exact geography for each vineyard across the "dome" of the Montagne de Corton can be an exasperating task. As can be seen in the listing of vineyards at the end of this section, this is the only place in the Côte d'Or where Grand Cru growths spill over to such an extent from one commune to another.

Legend has it that the small portion of white wine vineyards which exist upon the Corton dome were first ordered planted by Charlemagne—so that he could drink white wine in public and not stain his beard with the red.

The smallest of the three wine-growing communes in the Montagne de Corton is Ladoix-Serrigny. It is also generally regarded as the lesser in overall quality of the Corton locale. It has, nevertheless, eight Grand Cru and seven Premier Cru vineyards.

Pernand-Vergelesses is a small village around which a number of the famous Corton vineyards are situated. Wines from this village not bottled as Corton may be appropriately labeled as Pernand-Vergelesses and, as such, are generally sold for lower prices. Red Burgundy-enthusiasts can find some excellent values from both Pernand-Vergelesses and Ladoix-Serrigny labels.

Another small village, Savigny-les-Beaune, borders the commune of Pernand-Vergelesses to the west and is also a producer of superior red table wines.

The greater share of the Corton and Corton-Charlemagne vineyards of the Montagne de Corton are situated in the parish of Aloxe-Corton. Wines from both the Corton and the Corton-Charlemagne vineyards are world famous—the Corton vineyards for their superlative reds and Corton-Charlemagne for magnificent, complex whites. There are seventeen Grand Cru growths and eleven Premiers Crus in the parish.

There are thirty-four Premiers Crus among the 2,500 acres of vineyard in the commune of Beaune, which is situated to the south of Aloxe-Corton. There are, however, no Grand Cru vineyards in the commune of Beaune. It should be remembered that AOC Côte de Beaune is practically in the same area as the commune of Beaune; neither term should be confused with the appellation Côte de Beaune-Villages, which generally designates red wines grown in communes that are more famous for white wine production. All the Côte de Beaune communes *except* Aloxe-Corton, Beaune, Volnay, and Pommard are entitled to this special designation. Some of the more obscure Côte de Beaune communes, such as

Chorey-les-Beaune and St.-Romain use the Côte de Beaune-Villages designation for most of their wines. There are a variety of red and white wines produced in the commune of Beaune, some of which are identified by the vineyard name such as Beaune Clos des Mouches, whether or not it is a Premier Cru. None of them, though, are comparable to the Great Growths both to the north and south in the Côte d'Or. Beaune does have several interesting sightseeing stops, however, principally the fifteenth-century Hôtel-Dieu, now known as the famous Hospices de Beaune; the famous wine museum; and the cellars of some large négociants who vinify, blend, bottle, and ship wines from all reaches of Burgundy.

Farther south on the banks of the river Avant Dheune are the vineyards of Pommard, all of which yield exceptional red wines that are deep in color, full-bodied, and have earned the reputation of aging well. (The Dutch scholar Erasmus is rumored to have been particularly fond of Pommard.) Nearby is the smaller commune of Volnay, which lists the Premier Cru of Les Santenots among its vineyards. Pommard has approximately 820 acres of vineyard, most of which are planted with the choice red Pinot vines. Volnay, on the other hand, has only some 375 acres, although some experts proclaim Volnay as the best of the lesser red Burgundies.

In this area many of the growers make their own wine that is marketed in bulk to the négociants. Here the wine cellar, called a *chai*, is usually a small building that is at least partially buried in order to maintain stable temperatures inside. It is common to find the cellar masters of the area wielding the famous *tastevin*, a small, shallow cup in which strategically placed "dimples" are indented to facilitate the reflection of light through the wine when it is being evaluated. The tastevin, usually made of silver so that there is no other metal contamination, is about 3 or 4 inches in diameter, perhaps an inch deep at most, and often carried about by a neck strap or chain. In some of the more modern chais, however, the cellar masters have taken to using glasses in order to better examine the color and clarity of their wines.

South of Volnay and west of the AOC white wine vineyards of Meursault are the communes of Monthélie and Auxey-Duresses, which produce rather common red and white wines.

As early as the twelfth century the Cistercian monks of Cîteaux Abbey owned vineyards at Meursault, principally the superb manor vineyard of Les Perrières, now a Premier Cru. The French Huguenots destroyed the manor in the sixteenth century and the property was seized by the state after the French Revolution. Yet the huge wine cellars there have survived the tumults of history and can still be seen today. Cardinal de Bernis, beloved of Madame de Pompadour, is believed to have traditionally celebrated Mass during the mid-1700s with Meursault so that he would not grimace when confronting his Lord.

Grand Vin de Bourgogne

MEURSAULT
CLOS DE LA BARRE
Appellation Contrôlée

Mis en bouteille par MOILLARD®
Négociant-Eleveur à Nuits-Saint-Georges (Côte-d'Or) France
750 ml ℮   Product of France

FILIBER A NUITS

A FRANK SCHOONMAKER
SÉLECTION

BIENVENUE-BATARD-MONTRACHET

APPELLATION BIENVENUE-BATARD-MONTRACHET CONTROLÉE

MISE EN BOUTEILLES
AU DOMAINE

PRODUCE OF FRANCE

STILL LIGHT TABLE WINE

ANDRÉ RAMONET
Propriétaire à Chassagne-Montrachet (Côte-d'Or)

White Burgundy Wine   CONTENTS 3/4 QUART

IMP. DEVEVEY · BEAUNE

There are no Grand Cru vineyards in Meursault, but there are twenty Premier Crus—among which are Les Charmes, Les Genevrières, and Les Perrières. The reputation of Meursault rests solely on its renowned white wines, which form the bulk of its production.

In youth the wines of Meursault are crisp and fruity. The best have a delicious, lingering aftertaste. With bottle aging, Meursault wines tend to oxidize and break down, becoming dark straw in color and developing a richer bouquet. There are probably as many wine lovers who prefer younger Meursault as older. Thomas Jefferson is said to have loved the wines from Burgundy—especially those from Meursault.

Farther south are the communes of Puligny-Montrachet and the somewhat lesser Chassagne-Montrachet, which, in the opinion of many wine experts, contain the finest white wine vineyards of the Côte d'Or. Some feel that the five Grand Cru vineyards in the two Montrachets yield the finest wines that the great Chardonnay can produce anywhere on earth. There is no question that from these five vineyards—Le Montrachet, Bâtard-Montrachet, Criots-Bâtard-Montrachet, Bienvenues-Bâtard-Montrachet, and Chevalier-Montrachet—come some of the most complex and longest-lived dry white wines in the world. The finest vintages often take seven years or more to mature.

Some red wines also are produced in the southern portions of the Chassagne-Montrachet, but the great soils of Montrachet are ideal for the white Chardonnay.

At the extreme southerly tip of the Côte de Beaune are the communal vineyards of Santenay and several other small villages that produce generally rather soft but full-bodied red wines that are often marketed as Côtes de Beaune-Villages. Monks from the Abbey of Tournus once owned vineyards there. White wines of this area may be found labeled as "Bourgogne Blanc."

The fabled Montrachet vineyard.

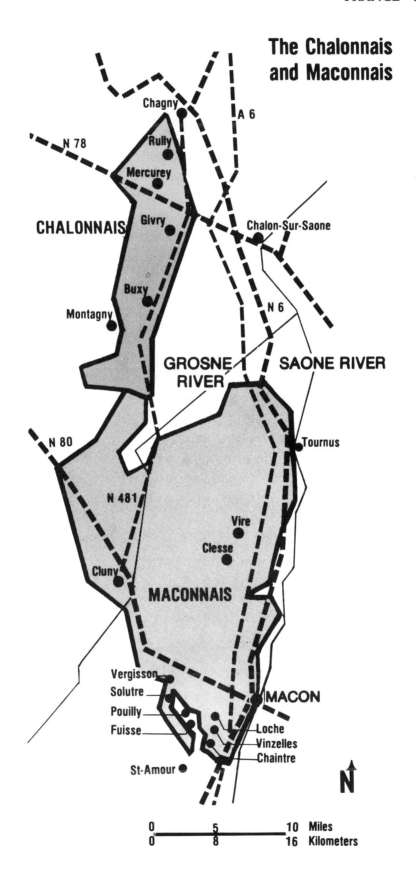

**The Chalonnais
and Maconnais**

Chagny

A 6

N 78

Rully

Mercurey

CHALONNAIS

Givry

Chalon-Sur-Saone

Buxy

N 6

Montagny

GROSNE
RIVER

SAONE RIVER

N 80

Tournus

N 481

Vire

Clesse

Cluny

MACONNAIS

Vergisson

Solutre

MACON

Pouilly

Fuisse

Loche

Vinzelles

Chaintre

St-Amour

N

| 0 | 5 | 10 | Miles |
| 0 | 8 | 16 | Kilometers |

Saône-et-Loire

Chalonnais.   The Côte Chalonnaise takes its name from Chalon-sur-Saône, a manufacturing town situated a few miles to the east of the vineyards. The Chalonnais begins near the southern tip of the Côte de Beaune and extends about 15 miles farther south to Montagny. The vineyards are planted upon the slopes of the Charollais hills which, for the most part, are exposed to the east, although a few of the sites have southeastern and southern exposures. While the lower plains have more clay and may be calcareous, soils at the upper levels have varying mixtures of limestone, clay, iron, and silica. Experts generally rank the wines from the plains and foothills as ordinary and those from the slopes as the best in the district. Pinot Noir is grown for red wines in the Chalonnais, while both Chardonnay and Aligoté are grown for white wines. Although there are no Grand Cru wines, there are twelve Premier Cru growths in the district. The district is not continuous, but rather a collection of small subdistricts that are, from north to south, known as Rully, Mercurey, Givry, and Montagny.

Rully vineyards yield both red and white wines in about equal amounts. Some of the white is made into sparkling wine. In modern times the subdistrict of Mercurey has been gaining considerable attention, some calling it by its own individual name—"La Région de Mercurey." Most of this newfound popularity stems from the improved quality of the red wines, which account for more than 80 percent of the total produced in Mercurey. Some of these approach the finesse of the Côte d'Or reds. While the red wines of Mercurey are usually less delicate and more acidic than Côte d'Or reds, they have a fine bouquet and age rather well.

Vineyards in the Chalonnais.

The wines of Givry are mostly lowland red wines and are rather harsh and have less bouquet than those from Mercurey. Montagny is entirely a white wine producer with a reputation that is gaining steadily.

Mâconnais. The Côte Mâconnais, commencing about 7 miles south of the Chalonnais, measures about 35 miles from just north of Tournus to just south of the city of Mâcon, from which the district gets its name. The Mâconnais yields a considerable amount of ordinary red and some fine white wines grown principally on steep ridges of limestone and clay valleys that range from north to south. In the western portion of this district are the remains of the huge Abbey of Cluny, the grand center of all wine growing in Burgundy before Beaune rose to prominence.

The system of AOC designation is somewhat complicated in the Mâconnais; some of its communes are shared with the Beaujolais to the south. Ordinary reds made from either Pinot Noir or Gamay may be labeled Mâcon (minimum 10 percent alcoholic strength) or Mâcon Supérieur (minimum of 11 percent alcoholic strength) if they have sufficient alcoholic strength. The best of these often add the name of their village to the label as well—"Mâcon-Viré-Villages," for example. All the white wines eligible for AOC must be made only from Chardonnay and may be labeled "Pinot" Chardonnay Mâcon or Mâcon or, with sufficient alcoholic strength, "Mâcon Supérieur." Like the reds, the whites may also take the name of the village where they were grown or, if grown from more than one village, they may be called "Mâcon-Villages."

In the southern part of the Mâconnais, below the granite cliffs, are the most famous villages in the district; here are located the fine white wine vineyards of Pouilly-Fuissé—AOC Premier Cru. Most of the fine whites from Pouilly-Fuissé and its surrounding vineyards are somewhat earthy, lacking the delicate fruity style of Chablis and the buttery richness of Montrachet. Nevertheless, these wines have a distinct character that is attractive and refreshing.

The Pouilly area is bordered by the communes of Pouilly-Loché, Pouilly-Vinzelles, and Saint-Véran that are lesser AOC-designates and produce only whites. Saint-Véran has seven small villages, some of which can also label their wines Beaujolais, which overlaps the Mâconnais at this southern tip.

Rhône

Beaujolais

The Beaujolais measures some 45 miles north to south from its juncture with the Mâconnais to just several miles north of Lyon. During the Middle Ages the Beaujolais was not part of the Duchy of Burgundy and some argue even today that there should be a separate identity for the region. The Beaujolais has its own

The vineyards of Moulin-à-Vent (the windmill) in Beaujolais. (Source: Food and Wines from France.)

governing body, as does the Mâconnais, and both of the districts have the option of classifying their wines as Bourgogne or Bourgogne Grande Ordinaire. But in the opinion of most wine experts, neither district produces a true characteristic Burgundy. The topography and soil of the Beaujolais is much like that of the Mâconnais, with a continuation of the granite hills and rather heavy soils.

The red wines of Beaujolais are almost entirely made from the Gamay that yields heavy crops compared to the more prestigious Pinot Noir. The Gamay wines of Beaujolais are fresh and cherrylike in nose and flavor. Beaujolais is sometimes purposely made in the "nouveau" style for drinking when just several weeks old—a practice only developed since World War II. American and French wine drinkers alike have taken to the Beaujolais Nouveau, and each year the hoopla grows as the first cases reach the market in the late fall. Some vintners enter competitions to see who can make the Beaujolais Nouveau the quickest— sometimes shipping the first few cases out by air freight in order to win the race. These are the exceptions, however, as the great majority of Beaujolais wines continue to be the light-bodied, ruby red, and uncomplicated standard that has made them famous and satisfying.

The Gamay is grown without aid of a trellis in many parts of the Beaujolais in a rather bushlike configuration called a *gobelet*. Beaujolais has nine Grand Cru

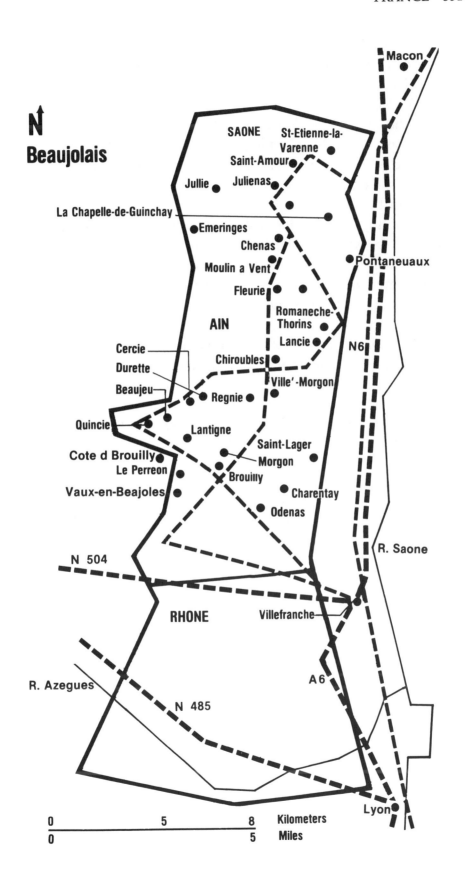

N

Beaujolais

Macon

SAONE

St-Etienne-la-Varenne

Saint-Amour

Jullie

Julienas

La Chapelle-de-Guinchay

Emeringes

Chenas

Moulin a Vent

Pontaneuaux

Fleurie

AIN

Romaneche-Thorins

Lancie

N6

Cercie

Chiroubles

Durette

'Ville'-Morgon

Beaujeu

Regnie

Quincie

Lantigne

Saint-Lager

Cote d Brouilly

Morgon

Le Perreon

Brouilly

Vaux-en-Beajoles

Charentay

Odenas

R. Saone

N 504

RHONE

Villefranche

A 6

R. Azegues

N 485

Lyon

| 0 | | 5 | | 8 | Kilometers |
| 0 | | | | 5 | Miles |

growths, all of which are located upon the rounded hills in the northern portion of the district. From north to south they are Saint-Amour, Juliénas, Chénas, Moulin-à-Vent, Fleurie, Chiroubles, Morgon, Brouilly, and Côtes de Brouilly.

The Beaujolais Grands Crus, while not on the same quality level as the Grands Crus of the Côte d'Or or Chablis, do have a richer texture and darker color than other wines in the Beaujolais. The Morgon and Moulin-à-Vent are especially heavy-bodied and may take several years of bottle aging to reach maturity. Chiroubles, Fleurie, and St.-Amour are more delicate and smooth, often ready to drink in just a year or two of aging in the bottle.

Much of the Gamay is harvested and vinified with a process called *macération carbonique*, in which the grapes are deposited into special fermentation vats without either crushing or de-stemming. Natural or added cultured yeasts commence fermentation of the grapes whose skins have been broken from handling. In a matter of two or three days, enough carbon dioxide gas is generated to begin permeating the unbroken grape skins, from which much of the flavor and a small amount of color is extracted. The must is then pressed and the resulting juice allowed to finish its fermentation in the conventional manner for red wines. The end product, after proper maturation, is a light wine in both color and body and has an unmistakeable Gamay nose.

Although most wines of the Beaujolais are red table wines, some whites are made and legally designated as Beaujolais Blanc. These are produced from Chardonnay vines near the Mâcon border in the region's northernmost extreme. Most experts consider Beaujolais Blanc something of a compromise between the regal Pouilly-Fuissé and the much more common Mâcon Blanc, both of which are produced in nearby communes.

Thirty-nine villages are designated as AOC Beaujolais-Villages or as Beaujolais followed by their village name—Beaujolais-Vaux, for instance, or Beaujolais-Beaujeu, the village from which the district gets its name. Beaujolais-Villages wines will generally have more color and body than ordinary Beaujolais.

Sparkling Burgundy.   True sparkling Burgundy wines are made under the direction of the Syndicat des Producteurs de Vins Mousseux Méthode Champenoise de Bourgogne, which guarantees that all such wines are produced in the same general manner as the sparkling wines of Champagne. The champagne method is discussed in chapter 1.

Sparkling Burgundy may be either white or red and at least 30 percent of either wine must come from noble vines, such as Chardonnay and Pinot Noir in the Côte d'Or. There are many producers of sparkling wines in Burgundy; the best are from Chablis, Nuits-Saint-Georges, Savigny-les-Beaune, Meursault, Chagny, Rully, Mercurey, and Mâcon.

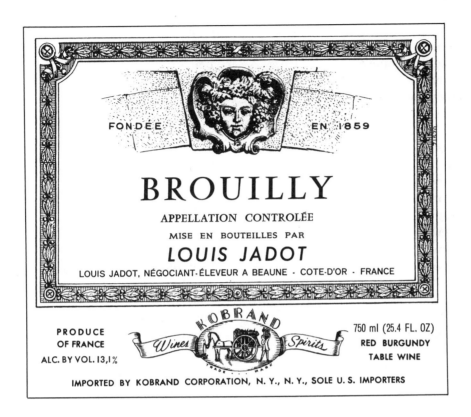

For the most part, the wines made into sparkling Burgundy are not of the same high quality as the fine table wines of the Burgundy region. In general, sparkling Burgundies are made for tourists and export—although some is consumed locally during festive events.

TABLE 6-1   Principal Communes and Climats of Burgundy

YONNE *(Auxerrois)*	Premier Cru
	Beauroy
Chablis (W)	Beugnons
	Butteaux
Grand Cru	Chapelot
	Châtains
Blanchots	Côte de Fontenay
Bougros	Côte de Lechet
Clos	Côte des Près Girots
Grenouilles	Epinottes
Moutonne	Forêts
Preuses	Fourchaume
Valmur	Fourneaux
Vaudésir	L'Homme Mort

Lys
Mélinots
Montée de Tonnerre
Montmains
Monts de Milieu
Morein
Pied d'Aloup
Roncières
Séché
Troesmes
Vaillons
Vaucoupin
Vaudevey
Vaugiraud
Vaulorent
Vaupulent
Vosgros

CÔTE DE NUITS

Marsannay-la-Côte (R)

Fixin (R)

Premier Cru

Arvelets
Cheusots
Clos du Chapître
Hervelets
Meix-Bas
Perrière
Queue de Hareng
En Suchot
Le Village

Gevrey-Chambertin (R)

Grand Cru

Chambertin
Chambertin-Clos de Bèze
Chapelle-Chambertin
Charmes-Chambertin
Griotte-Chambertin
Laticières-Chambertin
Mazis-Chambertin
Ruchottes-Chambertin

Premier Cru

Bel Air
La Boissière
Cazetiers
Champeaux
Champitonnois
Champonnets
Clos du Chapître
Cherbaudes
Closeau
Combe-aux-Moines
Combottes
Corbeaux
Craipillot
Ergots
Estournelles
Fontenay
Gémeaux
Goulots
Issarts
Lavaut
Perrière
Poissenot
Clos Prieur
La Romanée
Clos St.-Jacques
Véroilles

Morey-St.-Denis (R)

Grand Cru

Bonnes Mares
Clos des Lambrays
Clos de la Roche
Clos St.-Denis
Clos de Tart

Premier Cru

Clos Baulet
Blanchards
Brûlées
Clos Bussière
Chaffots
Charmes

Charrières
Chénevery
Aux Cheseaux
Façonnières
Genevrières
Gruenchers
Millandes
Monts Luisants
Clos des Ormes
Riotte
Côte Rôtie
Ruchots
Sorbés
Clos Sorbés

Chambolle-Musigny (R)

Grand Cru

Bonnes Mares
Musigny (W)

Premier Cru

Amoureuses
Baudes
Beaux-Bruns
Borniques
Charmes
Châtelots
Combottes
Aux Combottes
Cras
Derrière-la-Grange
Fousselottes
Fuées
Grosseilles
Gruenchers
Hauts-Doix
Lavrottes
Noirots
Plantes
Sentiers

Vougeot (R)

Grand Cru

Clos de Vougeot

Premier Cru

Clos de la Perrière (R)
Petits-Vougeots (R)
Vigne Blanche (W)

Vosne-Romanée (R)

Grand Cru

Échézeaux
Grands Échézeaux
Richebourg
La Romanée
Romanée-Conti
Romanée-St.-Vivant
La Tâche

Premier Cru

Beaux-Monts
Brûlées
Chaumes
Gaudichots
Grande Rue
Malconsorts
Petits-Monts
Clos des Reas
Reignots

Nuits-St.-Georges (R)

Premier Cru

Aux Argillats
Les Argillats
Boudots
Bousselots
Cailles
Chaboeufs
Chaignots
Chaîne-Carteau

Champs-Perdrix
Cras
Crots
Damodes
Didiers
Hauts-Pruliers
Murgers
Perrière
Perrière-Noblet
Porets
Poulettes
Procès
Pruliers
Richemone
Roncière
Rousselots
Rue-de-Chaux
St-Georges
Thorey
Vallerots
Vaucrains
Vignes Rondes

Prémeaux (R)

Premier Cru

Clos des Argillières
Clos-Arlots
Clos des Corvées
Clos des Grandes Vignes
Corvées-Paget
Clos des Forêts
Clos de la Maréchale
Cerdrix
Clos St-Marc

CÔTE DE BEAUNE

Ladoix-Serrigny

Grand Cru

Carrières (RW)
Grandes Lolières (RW)
Basses Mourettes (W)

Hautes Mourettes (W)
Moutottes (W)
Le Rognet et Corton (W)
La Toppe-au-Vert (RW)
Vergennes (RW)

Premier Cru

Basses Mourettes
Bois Roussot
Le Clou d'Orge
La Corvée
Hautes Mourettes
Joyeuses
Micaude

Pernand-Vergelesses

Grand Cru

Charlemagne (W)
Corton (R)

Premier Cru

Basses-Vergelesses
Caradeux
Creux de la Net
Fichots
Île de Vergelesses

Savigny-les-Beaune (R)

Premier Cru

Basses-Vergelesses
Bataillère
Charnières
Clous
Dominode
Fourneaux
Grands-Liards
Gravains
Guettes
Haut-Jarrons
Haut-Marconnets

Lavières
Marconnets
Narbantons
Petits-Godeaus
Petits-Liards
Peuillets
Redrescuts
Rouverettes
Serpentières
Talmettes
Vergelesses

Aloxe-Corton

Grand Cru

Bressandes
Charlemagne
Chaumes
Combes
Corton
Fiètres
Grèves
Languettes
Maréchaudes
Meix
Meix-Lallemand
Paulands
Perrières
Pougets
Renardes
Clos du Roi
La Vigne au Saint
Village
Voirosses

Premier Cru

Chaillots
Coutière
Fournières
Guérets
Maréchaudes
Meix
Moutottes
Pauland
La Toppe-au-Vert

Valozières
Vercots

Beaune (R)

Premier Cru

Aigrots
Avaux
Bas des Teurons
Blanches Fleurs
Boucherottes
Bressandes
Cent Vignes
Champs Pimonts
Chouacheux
Coucherias
Cras
Écu
Epenottes
Fèves
En Genêt
Grèves
Sur-les-Grèves
Marconnets
Mignotte
Montée Rouge
Montrevenots
Clos des Mouches
Clos de la Mousse
En l'Orme
Perrières
Pertuisots
Reversées
Clos du Roi
Seurey
Sizies
Teurons
Tiélandry
Toussaints
Vignes Franches

Chorey-les-Beaune (R)

Côte de Beaune (R)

Pommard (R)

Premier Cru

Argillières
Arvelets
Bertins
Clos Blanc
Boucherottes
Chanière
Chanlins-Bas
Chaponnières
Charmots
Combes-Dessus
Clos de la Commaraine
Croix-Noires
Derrière St.-Jean
Épenots
Fremiers
Jarollères
Clos Micot
Petits-Épenots
Pézerolles
Platière
Poutures
Refène
Rugiens
Saussilles
Clos du Verger

Auxey-Duresses (R)

Premier Cru

Bas des Duresses
Bretterins
Duresses
Ecusseaux
Grands Champs
Reugné
Clos du Val

St.-Romain (RW)

Volnay (R)

Premier Cru

Angles

Aussy
Barre
Bousse d'Or
Brouillards
Caillerets
Caillerets-dessus
Carelle sous la Chapelle
Carelle-dessous
Champans
Chanlin
Clos des Chênes
Chevrets
Clos des Ducs
Durets
Fremiets
Lurets
Mitans
Ormeau
Petures
Pitures-dessus
Pointes d'Angles
Pousse d'Or
Robardelle
Ronceret
Santenots
Taille Pieds
En Verseuil
Volnay

Monthélie (R)

Premier Cru

Cas Rougeot
Champs-Fulliot
Duresses
Gaillard
Gauthey
Lavelle
Meix-Bataille
Riottes
Taupine
Vignes Rondes

Meursault

Premier Cru

Bouchères (RW)
Caillerets (RW)
Charmes-dessous (RW)
Charmes-dessus (RW)
Cras (RW)
Genevrières-dessous (RW)
Genevrières-dessus (RW)
Goutte d'Or (RW)
Jennelotte (RW)
Perrières-dessous (RW)
Perrières-dessus (RW)
Petures (RW)
Pièce-sous-le-Bois (RW)
Plures (R)
Porusot (RW)
Santenots-Blancs (R)
Santenots-dessous (R)
Santenots du Milieu (R)
Sous le Dos d'Âne (RW)

Puligny-Montrachet (W)

Grand Cru

Bâtard-Montrachet
Bienvenue-Bâtard-Montrachet
Chevalier-Montrachet
Montrachet

Premier Cru

Caillerets
Chalumeaux
Champs-Canet
Clavoillons
Combettes
Folatières
Garenne
Hameau de Blagny
Pucelles
Referts
Sous le Puits

Chassagne-Montrachet

Grand Cru

Bâtard-Montrachet (W)

Criots-Bâtard-Montrachet (W)
Montrachet (W)

Premier Cru

Abbaye de Morgeot (RW)
Boudriotte (RW)
Brussolles (RW)
Caillerets (W)
En Cailleret (R)
Champs Gain (RW)
Chenevottes (RW)
Grandes Ruchottes (RW)
Macherelles (RW)
Maltroie (RW)
Morgeot (RW)
Romanée (RW)
St.-Jean (RW)
Vergers (RW)

Le Montrachet (W)

St.-Aubin (R)

Santenay (RW)

Premier Cru

Beauregard
Beaurepaire
Comme
Gravières
Maladière
Passe Temps
Clos des Tavannes

SAONE-ET-LOIRE
(Communes)

CHALONNAIS

Rully (RW)
Mercurey (R)
Givry (R)
Montagny (W)

MÂCONNAIS

Pouilly-Fuissé (W)
Pouilly-Loché (W)
Pouilly-Vinzelles (W)
St.-Véran (W)
Mâcon Superieur (RW)
Mâcon (W)
Mâcon-Villages (RW)

Chénas
Moulin-à-Vent
Fleurie
Chiroubles
Morgon
Brouilly
Côtes de Brouilly

BEAUJOLAIS GRANDS CRUS (R)

St.-Amour
Juliénas

W = principally or exclusively white wine production
R = principally or exclusively red wine production
RW = both white and red wine production

Red wines grown in specific communes located in the Côte de Nuits may be labeled "Côte de Nuits-Villages."

Red wines grown in predominantly white wine communes in the Côte de Beaune may be labeled "Côte de Beaune-Villages."

Grand Cru vineyards (climats) are labeled with simply the vineyard name. Premier Cru vineyards are labeled with the name of the commune attached to the name of the vineyard.

Mâcon or Mâcon-Villages white wines made from Chardonnay may be labeled as "Pinot Chardonnay Macon."

There are thirty-nine villages entitled to the label "Beaujolais-Villages" or to the label "Beaujolais" followed by the name of the village in which the wine was grown.

BORDEAUX

The seaport city of Bordeaux is built alongside the Garonne River, some 60 miles from the coast. Downstream from Bordeaux the Garonne River merges with the Dordogne to form the Gironde River, which empties into the Atlantic Ocean. Bordeaux was the capital city of the ancient province of Gascony, the setting for many chivalrous tales. Today it is the fifth-largest city in France. Wine is, by far, its most famous and important export.

The flavor of San Francisco is reminiscent in Bordeaux—the ships at portside, the hurried cosmopolitan flair amongst a concentration of humanity, and the distinct wine and food ambience which pervades the community. Bordeaux even has a smaller version of the Golden Gate bridge which spans the Gironde from

Bordeaux

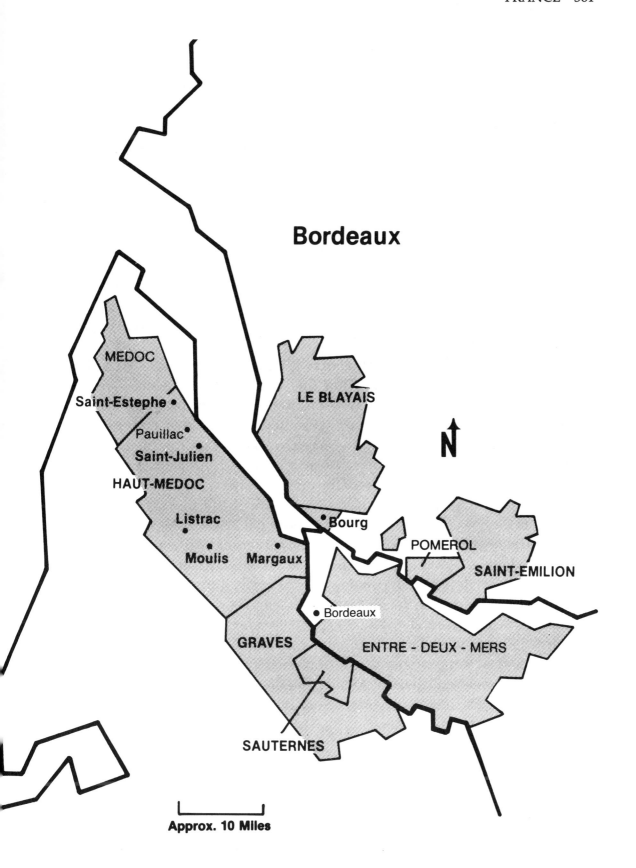

MEDOC

Saint-Estephe •

Pauillac •
Saint-Julien •

HAUT-MEDOC

Listrac •

Moulis • Margaux •

LE BLAYAIS

N

• Bourg

POMEROL

SAINT-EMILION

• Bordeaux

GRAVES

ENTRE - DEUX - MERS

SAUTERNES

Approx. 10 Miles

"Centre Ville" to the north towards Libourne. Most importantly, both cities have great vineyards flourishing at their perimeters.

Bordeaux vineyards total approximately 190,000 acres and yield about 50 million gallons of wine annually. Of this production, about 60 percent is white, and the balance is red table wines; sparkling wines represent a miniscule proportion of the production. While such Bordeaux reds as Château Lafite-Rothschild, Château Haut-Brion, Château Margaux, and Chateau Latour are among the most celebrated and coveted wines in the world, Bordeaux whites, especially those produced in the Sauternes district, can also attain magnificent heights.

Bordeaux not only produces some superlative wines, it also produces great quantities of wine: its wines account for about half of all the AOC wines grown in France, making it the largest-producing region in quantity. There are approximately 24,000 winegrowers in Bordeaux, only a few of whom grow wine of any noteworthy nobility. Whereas Burgundy has small *climats* divided among different owners, in Bordeaux the large wine estates (called *châteaux*) usually belong to just one owner.

The term *claret*, which today refers to red Bordeaux wines, dates back to the Middle Ages. Opinions differ as to how this term was coined: some conjecture that all light-colored red wines (some of which were made by blending white and red wines together, a practice no longer permitted) were known as *clairet*, meaning "light" or "clear." Gradually, the term began to be used by the English only for red wines. Later on, it gained its present-day sense of red Bordeaux. It may well be that the term *claret* was another case of the British adopting a foreign word into the English language in slightly altered form—just as they anglicized *sherry* from *Jerez*, the name of the Spanish town that was stamped on the casks of its famous wines.

Louis XIV is credited with spreading an appreciation for Bordeaux wines throughout France. The Sun King called the wines of Bordeaux the "Nectar of the Gods," and many less august persons are still inclined to agree with him.

Nobles in poor favor were sometimes banished to Bordeaux. This was the fate of the Duc de Richelieu in the mid-eighteenth century. There is a story that Richelieu's friends played a trick on him and switched the labels on a bottle of Bordeaux and a bottle of Burgundy. Richelieu proclaimed the wine labeled Burgundy superior, but when his friends revealed it was actually a Bordeaux, he adopted these wines as his favorites from then on. Richelieu's support gave Bordeaux a big boost in popularity. Soon after, even Madame de Pompadour, mistress of Louis XV, began to serve Bordeaux at her famous private dinner parties. In 1723 a glass factory was founded in Bordeaux and "château bottling" was begun. It was not until 1797, however, that the entire vintage of the prestigious Château Lafite was bottled in glass. The practice of château bottling fine Bordeaux estate wines arose in response to demands from merchants who wanted some guarantee that the wines they sold were not being blended with lesser growths. It was not until the late nineteenth century, however, that château bottling was a common practice throughout Bordeaux.

Thomas Jefferson loved many different types of wines, not the least of which were the fine wines of Bordeaux. Among the châteaux that he particularly favored were Châteaux Latour, Margaux, Haut-Brion, and d'Yquem (truly superb choices, as these were eventually selected from the thousands of Bordeaux châteaux to become four of only five First Growths classified in 1855).

As the popularity of Bordeaux wines grew rapidly during the late eighteenth and early nineteenth centuries, it became clear to enthusiasts that some growths were consistently superior to others, and some were indeed superlative. The great Paris Exposition of 1855 provided the occasion for the first official classification of Bordeaux wines. From thousands of Bordeaux vineyards, sixty-two were chosen "Great Growths" (Grands Crus), and this category was further broken down into five classes of First Growth, Second Growth, and so on. There were only five châteaux awarded the coveted First Growth status, three reds from the Haut-Médoc, one from Graves, and one white from Sauternes. Respectively, these were Château Lafite, Château Latour, Château Margaux, Chateau Haut-Brion, and Château d'Yquem.

One step below the Great Growth category of the 1855 Classification was the "Exceptional Growth" (Cru Exceptionel) category; below this were the "Bourgeois" and "Artisan" categories (Cru Bourgeois and Cru Artisan). *Cru Bourgeois* is currently a term recognized under the European Economic Community (EEC) rules.

As might have been expected, this classification aroused considerable furor in the Bordeaux wine-growing and wine-shipping communities, some of which continues even today. In fact, it was only relatively recently that Château Mouton-Rothschild was elevated from Second Growth to First Growth in the Haut-Médoc. Other Bordeaux districts employ different classification systems. The wines of the Saint-Émilion district (see below) were officially classified in 1955 under a system that dispensed with numbered rankings. Instead, the highest ranking is Premier Grand Cru; next is Grand Cru; and the bulk of the lesser châteaux are simply categorized as "other principal growths."

The golden period of the mid-nineteenth century was followed by the devastations of *Oidium* and *Phylloxera* and in the twentieth century by two world wars. Happily, Bordeaux escaped the large-scale destruction that many of France's less fortunate wine-growing regions suffered.

England continues to thirst after claret, as it did in the Middle Ages, and the example set by Thomas Jefferson has spread throughout America. These two countries, along with Belgium, make up Bordeaux's three largest export markets.

Japan and the Soviet Union have been importing more and more Bordeaux in recent years.

The fine reds of Bordeaux are made principally from the variety Cabernet Sauvignon—thought by some to be the ancient *Vitis biturica*—originally a grape from northern Spain. In addition, most of the château vineyards are also planted with Merlot and/or Malbec in combinations that satisfy the critical demands of each owner and *maître de chai* (cellar master in charge of winemaking). The *régisseur*, the "manager," may also have a say in varietal-choice blending. Other red varieties found in Bordeaux are Cabernet Franc, Bouchet, and Verdot. The whites of Bordeaux are made from Sémillon, Sauvignon Blanc, and Muscadelle.

A country home situated on a vineyard estate in Bordeaux is called a *château*. These are often grand structures, although they need not be. French law prohibits the word *château* upon a Bordeaux wine label unless there is a bona fide vineyard existing on the property. There are also the following legal conditions:

- The château must be entitled to the appropriate AOC.
- The château name must be authentic, constant, and in conformity with local requirements.
- Winemaking from the grapes grown on the estate must take place at the château.

One rather common misleading statement found on Bordeaux labels is "Mise en Bouteilles au Château Mystère" (or some other château name). If the château has no relationship to a vineyard, then such a statement is virtually meaningless. Shippers, for example, may do business in offices within some château (or other building), bottling wines purchased from other vineyards. Such wines may be all right, but they are not château bottled in the commonly accepted sense of being grown on the château estate and bottled in the same château's cellar.

Château-bottled wines are sealed with corks upon which the château's name and the vintage year is branded. This is designed to provide a guarantee that the wine really was Mise en Bouteilles au Château, meaning "placed in the bottle at the château."

As French wine labels go, a Bordeaux wine label can be comparatively simple to read and understand. Bordeaux labeling follows these general rules:

- Appellation d'Origine Contrôlée is required to be displayed.
- The name of the château is not required but is almost always displayed.
- The classification of the growth is not required to be displayed, and usually the Premier Grand Cru and Grand Cru (First and Second Growths, respectively) châteaux do not add their *classe* to the label; their names are well

known and can stand alone as indications of quality. This does cause some confusion at times, though, as the growths graded lower than Grand Cru *never* display their class, but will instead carry such statements as "Grand Cru de St.-Julien" or "Grand Cru Classe," which does not refer to a particular class, but is rather a general statement that the vineyard is "great."

- The vintage need not be displayed, although the best growths almost always indicate the vintage year on their labels.
- The statement of château bottling "Mise en Bouteilles au Château" or the like is not required, but, again, the best châteaux always make the quality-guarantee statement of château bottling.
- The name and address of the proprietor is required on the label.

Bordeaux has four general appellations: Bordeaux, Bordeaux Supérieur, Bordeaux Rosé (Bordeaux Clairet), Bordeaux Mousseux (sparkling) and forty-two communal or regional appellations.

The Bordeaux region is divided into five major districts, each with its distinctive wines and outstanding châteaux. The Médoc district contains some of the very greatest wine estates in the world, among them Château Lafite-Rothschild, Château Latour, and Château Margaux (all ranked as First Growths in the 1855 Classification) and Château Mouton-Rothschild (awarded First-Growth status in 1973, the only change ever made in the original classification). Graves, named for its gravelly soil, produces reds and whites of equal note and contains Château Haut-Brion, another First Growth of the 1855 Classification. The Sauternes district is known primarily for its luscious, sweet white wines—the most splendid of which comes from the fabled Château d'Yquem, the only 1855 classified First Growth to produce white wine. Both Pomerol and Saint-Émilion are primarily red wine districts; their wines, especially those of Saint-Émilion are a bit fuller and heartier than those of the Médoc. The two most celebrated châteaux of Saint-Émilion are Château Ausone, whose ancestry and name date back to ancient Rome, and Château Cheval-Blanc. In Pomerol, Château Pétrus has achieved the greatest renown, and its wines command worldwide respect and extremely high prices. The wines from these three châteaux are every bit the equal of the finest Médocs.

There exists a number of small marketing organizations that operate in Bordeaux to satisfy the distribution of many of the château-produced wines. Some châteaux market independently and still others contract with large shipper-négociants. Kobrand, Heublein, and Schieffelin are among the most well-known importers of Bordeaux wines into America, but the giant Château & Estate Wine Company (a division of Seagram) perhaps imports more than all of the others combined.

One last point to raise before the district-by-district discussion, however, concerns the question of how class reflects quality. One should always expect First-Growth wines to be superb, but this does not mean that Second-Growth, or even Fifth-Growth, wines should be grossly inferior. It is important to remember that the Bordeaux classification system is designed only for the top several hundred chateaux among several thousand existing there. Consequently, a fourth or fifth growth in the Médoc remains a pedigree of superb nobility—certainly far from any notion that such wines are fourth or fifth class.

Médoc

The Médoc, particularly the higher portion, the Haut-Médoc, is the single most-important subdistrict of the entire Bordeaux region. About 7 miles wide and 35 miles long, it is situated between Jalle de Blanquefort just north of the city of Bordeaux and extends northwestward to Pointe de Grave along the left bank of the Gironde. The lower Médoc—some 40 percent or so of the Médoc—is the northwest portion, and it has quite sandy soil that produces rather common red wines. The Haut-Médoc soil is a quartz-gravel rich in iron oxide upon a clay subsoil. The gravel stones, called *cailloux*, retain heat from the daytime sun and thus aid in ripening the grapes. The cailloux also allow drainage from excess

Pruning the vines during the spring in the Médoc (Source: Bordeaux Wine Information Bureau.)

rainfall. When young, fine red Bordeaux wines are nearly undrinkable—densely purple in color, astringent from unmellowed tannins, and, in general, rather awkward. But when patiently matured in French oak puncheons and aged in bottles, Bordeaux is typically heavy-bodied, of a rich, dark garnet-ruby color, and exemplifies many different delicious orchestrations of black currant, bell pepper, wood, and creosote flavors. Along with the Côte de Nuits of Burgundy, the Médoc yields some of the very finest and most expensive red wines on the face of the earth.

The 1855 Classification still rules in the Haut-Médoc, where the Great Growths yield only red wines. A few whites are grown, but these are only entitled to the AOC Bordeaux label. There are twenty-seven communes in the Haut-Médoc, of which seven, St.-Estèphe, Pauillac, St.-Julien, Margaux, Haut-Médoc, Listrac, and Moulis are entitled to their own appellations on their labels. Along with the many internationally known châteaux of the Médoc are several wine-producing cooperatives and, of course, many lesser châteaux.

Perhaps the single most-famous wine producer in the world is Château Lafite-Rothschild, beautifully situated on a ridge in the commune of Pauillac. It was christened the "Prince of Vineyards" during the Middle Ages by a magistrate who felt it was a superior growth. Louis XV preferred Lafite, and, in keeping with the mode of the court, Madame de Pompadour also began serving the wines from Château Lafite. Prior to the French Revolution, Château Lafite was owned by Nicholas Pierre de Pichard, then high court president of the Parlement de Bordeaux. The property was sold by the state in 1797 to the Dutch family Vandenbergh, who in turn sold the property to young Rosalie Lamaire in 1821. Lamaire sold Lafite to Sir Samuel Scott, an English banker, who sold the estate back to the Vandenberghs. In 1867 it was purchased by Baron James de Rothschild. It then became Château Lafite-Rothschild and still remains in the hands of the Rothschild descendants. Château Lafite-Rothschild has 312 acres, of which a little more than half are planted with vineyards. About 60 percent of the vines are Cabernet Sauvignon; the balance are the Merlot and Cabernet Franc varieties. Annual production is about 45,000 gallons (or 20,000 cases). Lafite is very dark and full-bodied, yet it is also delicate and thus easily overpowered by spicy food. It exhibits the typical black currant and "cigar box" "nose" that is found in the finest Bordeaux growths. Since 1797 a number of bottles from each vintage have been placed in a cellar vault, which now holds more than 80,000 bottles. This was a treasure that was reserved for Nazi Air Marshal Hermann Goering during the German occupation of France in World War II. Ironically, the wine cellar remained in the hands of the Jewish Rothschilds. Today a rare bottle will be removed for a special purpose: one was an 1832 vintage magnum (double bottle), which sold for a then-world record price of $31,000 to Memphis,

The fabled Château Lafite-Rothschild. (Source: French Wine Board.)

Tennessee, restaurateur, John Grisanti, in 1982. However, the current record price for a wine purchase is $156,450, paid by Christopher Forbes (son of *Forbes* magazine magnate, Malcolm Forbes) for a bottle of Château Lafite 1787 thought to have once belonged to Thomas Jefferson.

Compared to Lafite, Château Latour, also classified "First Growth," is small, only about 100 acres in all. The owners of this ancient Pauillac estate took sides with the English Plantagenets during the Hundred Years War and lost their castle in the destruction that accompanied the final battle, when the English General John Talbot was killed and the Aquitaine reverted to French rule. Only the tower remains, whence the name Latour (the tower) and the logo prominent on the labels of Château Latour. The property was purchased in 1670 by de Chavanaz, councillor to Louis XIV, and seven years later was passed on to the Clauzel family. Through marriage it became the property of the de Ségur family and has remained among descendants of that family ever since—although in 1842 a corporate Sociéte Civile de Château Latour was established to manage the estate. The Latour vineyards are planted with about two-thirds Cabernet Sauvignon, and the balance is Malbec and Cabernet Franc. The annual production is about half that of Château Lafite. Château Latour may be the most robust of the Médoc First Growths.

Château Mouton-Rothschild, also located in the commune of Pauillac, was classified a Second Growth in the 1855 Classification. Due to owner Baron Philippe de Rothschild's monumental diligence in improving wine quality,

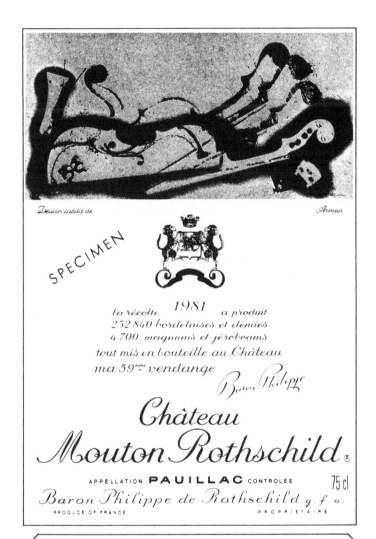

The immaculate cellars of Château Mouton-Rothschild.

however, the wines of Mouton gradually became accepted on a par with those of the other First Growths of the Médoc and were officially recognized as such in the late 1970s.

The Duke of Gloucester owned the property in 1430, and, after passing through several other proprietors, Château Mouton became the property of the Duc d'Épernon in 1587. It remained in the hands of that family until 1741, when Baron Brane became the owner. Baron Nathaniel de Rothschild purchased the estate in 1853 and added his name to form the now-familiar Château Mouton-Rothschild. It has remained a Rothschild property ever since.

The vineyards of the estate total about 150 acres and are planted almost exclusively with Cabernet Sauvignon that, treated with extraordinary care in the winemaking processes, yields great red wines with powerful bouquet and superb flavor. Texas wine wholesaler Tony LaBarba recently paid $38,000 for an 1870 Château Mouton-Rothschild.

Originally, the estate of Château Margaux in the commune of Margaux was known as Château Lamothe and belonged to the king of England. After passing through the hands of several owners, Margaux became the property of Count Fumel, Lord of Haut-Brion, who planted vineyards on the property for the first time in 1750. After the French Revolution the state sold Château Margaux to the Marquis de la Colonilla, who tore down the old building and built the present Grecian-style château. After several more owners the property came to rest in the hands of the Société Viticole de Château Margaux that managed wine operations

PRODUCE OF FRANCE

Château Giscours

GRAND CRU CLASSÉ EN 1855

MARGAUX

1979

APPELLATION MARGAUX CONTROLÉE

S.A. D'EXPLOITATION DU CHATEAU GISCOURS FERMIÈRE DU GROUPEMENT AGRICOLE FONCIER

NICOLAS TARI, GÉRANT

75cl MIS EN BOUTEILLES AU CHATEAU

BORDEAUX WINE   PEARTREE   ALCOHOL 12.5 % BY VOL.

PEARTREE IMPORTS INC., NEW YORK, N.Y.

750 ML   SOLE U.S. IMPORTER

CRU CLASSE EN 1855

CHATEAU DU TERTRE

ARSAC

— 1981 —

APPELLATION MARGAUX CONTROLÉE

MIS EN BOUTEILLES AU CHATEAU

S.C.A. Château du Tertre, propriétaire à Arsac

75cl

G. CHARIOL BORDEAUX   Product of France

amidst financial difficulty. It once belonged to Pierre Ginestet of the great wine-shipping family. The Margaux vineyards are spread over approximately 150 acres of the total 625-acre estate. Some 90 percent of the vines are Cabernet Sauvignon, which produces in the best years wines that may well be the finest of Bordeaux. One section of the property is planted with vines that yield white wines. These are permitted only an AOC Bordeaux classification and are labeled "Pavillon Blanc de Château Margaux."

There are another fourteen Second Growths in the Médoc that, in the better vintages, often produce wines of such high quality that even the experts cannot tell the difference between them and First Growths. Consequently, the prices remain very high. The real values may come from the Third-, Fourth- and Fifth-Growth vineyards of the Médoc, bringing prices that are often reasonably affordable. One must remember that while vineyard soils have only rather slight differences from one section of the Haut-Médoc to another, there is a wider disparity between winemaking skills and vintage years among the lesser growths. These make up a very large number of choices with which the enophile must experiment in the quest for value. The major growths of the entire Bordeaux region are listed at the end of this section.

Graves

Graves is named for the gravel plain upon which its best vineyards are established. The district, about 38 miles long, borders the Médoc to the south and includes the city of Bordeaux. It extends southeastward just past the village of Langon.

The gravel topsoil is supported by a subsoil of chalk, clay, and ironstone, all of which are thought by connoisseurs to infuse the wines of the Graves with an earthy taste termed the *goût de terroir*. The wines from the vineyards bordering the Médoc are mostly red and are the finest of the district. At the center of the Graves, dry white wines are grown to good quality and, at the southeasternmost tip, mostly ordinary wines are to be found. Generally the red wines of Graves are as good as those of the same class in the Médoc, perhaps somewhat less full-bodied and with a bit less bouquet and flavor. Some experts call them more velvety.

Graves has only one 1855-classified First Growth—that of the famous Château Haut-Brion in the commune of Pessac. It belonged to the Lord d'Aubrion during the Middle Ages and in October of 1529 was given over to Jean de Pontac as part of the dowry of Jeanne de Bellon, a daughter of Pierre de Bellon, Lord of the Haut-Brion manor and Mayor of Libourne. It remained in the Pontac and Fumel families until the French Revolution. In 1801 Charles de Talleyrand-Périgord, minister of

CHATEAU HAUT BRION
1981
GRAVES
Premier Grand Cru Classé
Appellation Graves Contrôlée
75 cl
Mis en bouteilles au Château   *Domaine Clarence Dillon s.a. Pessac, Gironde*
G. CHARIOL - BORDEAUX   PRODUCE OF FRANCE   MARQUE ET BOUTEILLE DÉPOSÉES

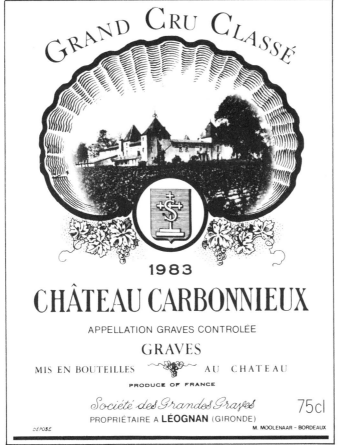

GRAND CRU CLASSÉ
1983
CHÂTEAU CARBONNIEUX
APPELLATION GRAVES CONTROLÉE
GRAVES
MIS EN BOUTEILLES   AU   CHATEAU
PRODUCE OF FRANCE
Société des Grandes Graves   75cl
PROPRIÉTAIRE A **LÉOGNAN** (GIRONDE)
DÉPOSÉ   M. MOOLENAAR - BORDEAUX

foreign affairs for France, acquired Château Haut-Brion and sold it three years later to a Parisian banker. After several more owners the estate was purchased by Joseph-Eugène Larrieu in 1836 and remained in his family until 1923, when a small company was formed to manage the château. A dozen years later Château Haut-Brion was bought by the American banker Clarence Dillon, father of the former American ambassador to France, C. Douglas Dillon.

Château Haut-Brion produces about 25,000 gallons of wine annually from about 105 acres of undulating vineyards. Experts say that the wines from this château are as tasty as the three Médoc First Growths, but with more finesse and less body and richness, creating an almost-silken taste.

There are another fifteen châteaux in the Graves that have Second-Growth credentials. Most of these have this classification for both red and white wine production and are distributed in the communes of Pessac, Talence, Villenave-d'Ornon, Cadaujac, Léognan, and Martillac. Other lesser growths, some of superb value, can also be found in these communes as well as in Mérignac, Gradignan, Beautiran, Castres-Gironde, and Portets.

Sauternes

In comparison with the giant districts of Médoc and Graves, Sauternes is tiny. Basically triangular in shape, the Sauternes district is 7 miles on each side and nearly surrounded by the Graves. Sauternes nowadays encompasses five communes: Sauternes, the even smaller Barsac, Preignac, Bommes, and Fargues. Sometimes neighboring Cérons is included in the district as well. The area of all of these districts combined is still less than 10 percent the size of the Graves.

There is a fascinating microclimate effect that takes place in the Sauternes—both the morning mist and the midday autumn sun are more intense than the norm of the Graves. The best topsoils are on rolling upland gravel with a subsoil of clay and sandstone, with somewhat more limestone in the Barsac. Only white wines are grown in this district and nearly all of these from the varieties Sémillon and Sauvignon Blanc. The variety Muscadelle is disappearing because its wine becomes dark and woody (maderizes) too quickly in the cellars.

The grapes are picked overripe: they are left on the vines until they become infected with the famous noble mold called *pourriture noble* by the French and *Botrytis cinerea* by microbiologists. This mold permeates the skins of the fruit and allows water to evaporate from the interior of each grape berry. If the weather conditions cooperate and no rain falls during this critical period, thus preventing such molds as *Penicillium* from developing, then the *botrytis*-infected grapes yield an exceedingly luscious, sweet nectar, which is reminiscent of fig and raisin flavors. In order to qualify for the AOC Sauternes label the resulting wine must reach at least 13 percent alcohol and still retain a high level of sweetness from the remaining unfermented sugars. This level cannot be specified due to the differences in concentration of natural grape sugars from one vintage year to another. Generally, however, Sauternes sweetness is from 3 to 7 degrees extract—an analytical figure roughly equivalent to percentage of sweetness by weight. If it does not meet these requirements, then the wine may only be classified as AOC Bordeaux. Some connoisseurs rate the fine vintages of Sauternes as the finest sweet white wines that exist. There are others who argue that the late-harvest wines from Germany are equal or even superior.

There is only one First Growth in the Sauternes district, and it is also the only white wine First Growth in Bordeaux: this is the fabled Château d'Yquem. It is named for Michel Eyquem Seigneur de Montaigne, an extravagant patron of the arts who was an owner of the estate during the Middle Ages. Montaigne, who had himself awakened each day by gentle tunes from the flute, offered these profound thoughts concerning the good life: "Drinking wine at two meals a day, in moderation—surely the good Lord did not intend us to be restricted to so little. The Ancients spent all their days and night drinking."

Château d'Yquem, for centuries the reigning queen of Sauternes' vineyards.

In 1782, when Ambassador Thomas Jefferson first arrived in Bordeaux, having walked most of the several hundred miles from Paris, he entered in his journal that the best white wine of France was the Sauternes of "Monsieur d'Yquem." That wine was not, however, the same lusciously sweet product from the noble mold that we know in modern times, but rather a fine table wine made by more traditional methods.

Passed through a number of owners by sales and marriage dowrys, Château d'Yquem eventually became the property of the Lur-Saluces family who still own the estate. The vineyards total about 230 acres across the entire 370-acre domain. Sémillon is planted in 75 percent of the vineyards, while the other 25 percent is Sauvignon Blanc. The annual average production is about 30,000 gallons of the precious (expensive) sweet golden wine.

There are another eleven Premier Cru vineyards in Sauternes; this classification, however, is roughly equivalent to Second-Growth status in the Graves or Médoc.

St.-Émilion

Some 20 miles or so northeast from Sauternes and Graves across the vast Entre-Deux-Mers is the ancient village of St.-Émilion, capital of the wine-growing district of the same name. The finest estates are situated on slopes or *côtes* of limestone hills that border the old city and plateau vineyards, confusingly called *graves* because of the gravel-type soil found there.

The côtes are divided into three separate locales known as Paire, La Madeleine, and Canon, a total area some 2 miles wide and 5 miles long. It is this area where the ancient Roman poet Ausonius built his villa and planted his vineyards; this is the property now known as Château Ausone. Many relics of the estate's antiquity may still be seen, among them a chapel in which there are the remains of a mural depicting the Last Judgment. The Dubois-Challon family now owns and manages the property. The wines are of very high quality and on a par with any fine red wine growth in Bordeaux. The average vintage yields about 6,000 gallons of wine.

There are fine vineyards in the lowlands, as well, but these are more prone to frost damage. On the other hand, the sand and gravel soil is thought to give these wines more body and distinction than those of the côtes—making the lowland wines perhaps more reminiscent of rich Burgundy than the standard Médoc. Among the best estates of the St.-Émilion plain is that of Château Cheval-Blanc, which gets its name from the ancient "White Horse Inn." Travelers on their way to and from the nearby town of Libourne would stop there for food and drink. It was built in 1269 by the Englishman Roger Leyburn. Neighboring sharecroppers

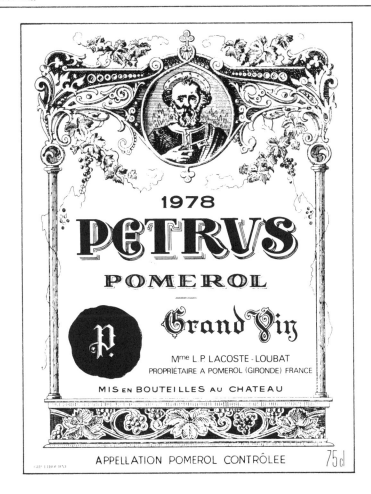

planted the first vines there. Gradually, as they left, the estate was formed from their remaining vineyards. Château Cheval-Blanc is today owned by the Fourcaud-Laussac family, who have handed the property down from generation to generation for many years. The wines from this estate, noted for their delicacy and softness, have an exceptionally fine bouquet in some years.

In 1955 the vineyards of St.-Émilion were classified as twelve "Premiers Grands Crus" that roughly equal in quality to the Second Growths of the Médoc and Graves—although Château Ausone and Château Cheval-Blanc head the list and may be considered superior, perhaps as "Class A," while the remaining ten growths are "Class B." There are another sixty-six "Grands Crus" that include some fine growths. Though these are intermingled in an alphabetical listing and not divided into ranked classes, they may be considered equivalent to the Third, Fourth, and Fifth Growths of the Médoc and Graves.

Pomerol

The district of Pomerol lies to the northwest of St.-Émilion—between the St.-Émilion lowland and the river Barbanne. The two districts are quite close: in fact there is less than a half-mile between Château Cheval-Blanc and Château Pétrus, which is generally considered the best growth in Pomerol.

The soil profile is much the same as the St.-Émilion plateau, with an ironstone subsoil beneath the finest Pomerol vineyards. The AOC Pomerol is authorized only for red wines, and there are no distinct classifications of growths. To the north and northeast of Pomerol lay, respectively, the subdistricts of Lalande-de-Pomerol and Néac. Lalande is situated upon higher and somewhat more fertile ground than Pomerol, but the wines are generally considered a bit inferior.

The best Pomerols are typically described as being the most slowly developing reds grown in Bordeaux, with much less softness and finesse than reds from the other major districts. Nevertheless, low prices and improving quality have begun to bring more and more Pomerols to the attention of the wine world.

TABLE 6-2   Principal Château Estates of Bordeaux

HAUT-MEDOC	Second Growth
Margaux (R)	Château Brane-Cantenac
	Château Durfort-Vivens
First Growth	Château Lascombes
	Château Rausan-Sègla
Château Margaux	Château Rauzan-Gassies

Third Growth

Château Boyd-Cantenac
Château Cantenac-Brown
Château Desmirail
Château Ferrière
Château Giscours
Château d'Issan
Château Kirwan
Château Malescot-St.-Exupéry
Château Marquis d'Alesme-Becker
Château Palmer

Fourth Growth

Château Marquis-de-Terme
Château Pouget
Château Prieuré-Lichine

Fifth Growth

Château Dauzac
Château du Tertre

St-Julien (R)

Second Growth

Château Ducru-Beaucaillou
Château Gruaud-Larose
Château Léoville-Barton
Château Léoville-Las-Cases
Château Léoville-Poyferré

Third Growth

Château Lagrange
Château Langoa-Barton

Fourth Growth

Château Beychevelle
Château Branaire-Ducru
Château St.-Pierre
Château Talbot

Pauillac (R)

First Growth

Château Lafite-Rothschild
Château Latour
Château Mouton-Rothschild

Second Growth

Château Pichon-Longueville
Château Pichon-Longueville (Lalande)

Fourth Growth

Château Duhart-Milon-Rothschild

Fifth Growth

Château Batailley
Château Clerc-Milon
Château Croizet-Bages
Château Grand-Puy-Ducasse
Château Grand-Puy-Lacoste
Château Haut-Bages-Libéral
Château Haut-Batailley
Château Lynch-Bages
Château Lynch-Moussas
Château Mouton-Baronne-Philippe
Château Pédesclaux
Château Pontet-Canet

St.-Estèphe (R)

Second Growth

Cos d'Estournel
Château Montrose

Third Growth

Château Calon-Ségur

Fourth Growth

Château Lafon-Rochet

Fifth Growth

Cos Labory

Haut-Médoc (R)

Third Growth

Château La Lagune

Fourth Growth

Château La Tour-Carnet

Fifth Growth

Château Belgrave
Château de Camensac
Château Cantemerle

Listrac (R)

Moulis (R)

GRAVES

First Growth

Château Haut-Brion (R)

Cru Classe

Château Bouscaut (RW)
Château Carbonnieux (RW)
Domaine de Chevalier (RW)
Château Couhins (W)
Château Couhins-Lurton (W)
Château de Fieuzal (R)
Château Haut-Bailly (R)
Château Laville-Haut-Brion (W)
Château La Mission-Haut-Brion (R)
Château Malartic-Lagravière (RW)
Château Olivier (RW)
Château Pape-Clément (R)
Château Smith-Haut-Lafitte (R)

Château La Tour-Haut-Brion (R)
Château La Tour-Martillac (RW)

SAUTERNES (W)

Premier Grand Cru

Château d'Yquem

First Growth (Premier Cru)

Château Climens
Château Coutet
Château Guiraud
Clos Haut-Peyraguey
Château Lafaurie-Peyraguey
Château Rabaud-Promis
Château Rayne-Vigneau
Château Rieussec
Château Sigalas-Rabaud
Château Suduiraut
Château La Tour-Blanche

Second Growth

Château d'Arche
Château d'Arche-Lafaurie
Château Broustet
Château Caillou
Château Doisy-Daëne
Château Doisy Dubroca
Château Doisy-Védrines
Château Filhot
Château Lamothe
Château de Malle
Château Nairac
Château Romer-du-Hayot
Château Suau

ST.-ÉMILION (R)

First Growth (Premier Grand Cru)

Château Ausone

Château Beau-Séjour
Château Beauséjour
Château Belair
Château Canon
Château Cheval-Blanc
Château Figeac
Clos Fourtet
Château La Gaffelière
Château Magdelaine
Château Pavie
Château Trottevieille

Grand Cru Classe

Château L'Angélus
Château L'Arrosée
Château Balestard-la-Tonnelle
Château Bellevue
Château Bergat
Château Cadet-Bon
Château Cadet-Piola
Château Canon-la-Gaffelière
Château Cap-de-Mourlin
Château La Carte et Le Châtelet
Château Chapelle-Madeleine
Château Chauvin
Château La Clotte
Château La Clusière
Château Corbin
Château Corbin-Michotte
Château La Couspaude
Château Coutet
Château Le Couvent
Château Couvent-des-Jacobins
Château Croque-Michotte
Château Curé-Bon-la-Madeleine
Château Dassault
Château Faurie-de-Souchard
Château Fonplégade
Château Fonroque
Château Franc-Mayne
Château Grand-Barrail-Lamarzelle-Figeac
Château Grand-Corbin
Château Grand-Corbin-Despagne
Château Grand-Mayne
Château Grand-Pontet
Château Grandes-Murailles

Château Guadet-St.-Julien
Château Haut-Corbin
Château Haut-Sarpe
Clos des Jacobins
Château Jean-Faure
Château La Dominique
Château Laniotte
Château Larcis-Ducasse
Château Larmande
Château Laroze
Clos La Madeleine
Château Matras
Château Mauvezin
Château Moulin-du-Cadet
Château L'Oratoire
Château Pavie-Décesse
Château Pavie-Macquin
Château Pavillon-Cadet
Château Petit-Fourie-de-Souchard
Château Le Prieuré
Château Ripeau
Château St.-Georges-Côte-Pavie
Château Sansonnet
Château La Serre
Château Soutard
Château Tertre-Daugay
Château La Tour-Figeac
Château La Tour-du-Pin-Figeac
Château La Tour-du-Pin-Figeac (Moueix)
Château Trimoulet
Château Troplong-Mondot
Château Villemaurine
Château Yon-Figeac

POMEROL (R)

First Growth

Château Pétrus

Important Châteaux

Château Beauregard
Château La Cabanne
Château Certan de May
Château La Conseillante

Château La Croix	Château Lafleur
Château La Croix-de-Gay	Château Latour à Pomerol
Clos L'Église	Château Nénin
Château L'Enclos	Château Petit-Village
Château L'Évangile	Château La Pointe
Château Feytit-Clinet	Château Rouget
Château La Fleur Gazin	Château de Sales
Château La Fleur-Pétrus	Château Trotanoy
Château Gombaude-Guillot	Vieux Château Certan

W = *principally or exclusively white wine production*
R = *principally or exclusively red wine production*
RW = *both white and red wine production*

CHAMPAGNE

Champagne is first a place—an ancient French province that today falls mostly within the Département of the Marne. It is located about 100 miles east and slightly north of Paris, a mere hour or so on the express train. Champagne is also a wine that many consider to be the most luxurious of wines, perhaps even the most enthusiastically celebrated, and certainly the festive wine par excellence. Champagne—true Champagne—is a sparkling wine made in a strictly regulated fashion from certain grapes grown only within a specifically delimited Champagne district. This district has two capital cities, Reims and Épernay, and, as one might expect, they are great rivals.

True Champagne is known the world over as a delightfully sparkling, or effervescent, wine, a wine that is a symbol of affluence, class, high living, and good times. It was not always so. For centuries the wines from the province of Champagne were mostly red table wines in much the same general style as those of Burgundy.

The Champagne city of Reims has a history dating back to Roman times. In 496 A.D. Saint Remi, then Bishop of Reims, laid the crown upon the head of Clovis, the first Christian king of France. Each succeeding French monarch was crowned in Reims thereafter. There are many references to the Champagne wines in Saint Remi's *Testament*, including mention of specific vineyards. Pope Urban II praised the wines from the area of Reims in the eleventh century, as did Pope Leo X in the early 1500s. In fact, the nonsparkling red wines of Champagne had no competition in Paris until the seventeenth century when the wines of Burgundy first became fashionable and then, some time later, the wines of Bordeaux caught on.

Champagne

The competition that ensued delighted Louis XIV who, apart from thoroughly enjoying these good wines, began to gain a great deal of revenue from their taxation.

The wines of Burgundy were probably superior to those of Champagne, a condition that may have prompted the eventual acceptance of Dom Pérignon's sparkling Champagne wine in the late 1600s. Pérignon was born in January 1638 at Saint-Menehoulde and became a Benedictine monk at the age of nineteen. He was appointed wine master of the Abbey of Hautvillers, near Épernay, in 1668. Despite the popular belief that Dom Pérignon invented Champagne, he probably did not. He made better wines in Champagne than had been made before his time, and he did in fact make sparkling Champagne wines, but his fame should be put in the proper perspective. He was an expert blender, and he mastered the effects of interrupted fermentations caused by cold winter temperatures. Almost certainly there were sparkling wines made decades earlier in the Loire at Saumur by winemakers who had found that wines bottled during the winter "rest" would continue to ferment after the spring warming. Because the carbon dioxide gas generated during the second fermentation could not escape, it became dissolved in the bottled wine, causing an effervescence or sparkling effect when the wine was uncorked and poured. The "magic" of this process was, like all fermentations, believed to be a mystical reaction, and winemakers had little control over it until Joseph-Louis Gay-Lussac formulated in 1810 the relationship of sugars in fermentation and created the densimeter. This device allowed the precise measurement of sugar in the wine before bottling and the secondary fermentation. This, in turn, permitted the winemakers to control the amount of carbon dioxide gas generated, resulting in far fewer exploded bottles from excessive fermentation or flat wines from insufficient fermentation. The technology today is, of course, far more advanced, but the basic principle remains the same. The modern-day method of making sparkling wines is discussed below.

Though he may not have been the inventor of Champagne, Dom Pérignon was, however, the first to demonstrate the fine effects of corks used as bottle seals. For that alone credit is due him—not just in Champagne but throughout the entire world of wine.

There are approximately 55,000 acres of vineyards in the province of Champagne and about 16,000 growers. Production ranges from 3.5 to 11 million gallons, of which about 80 percent is AOC designated and only a trace is VDQS. More than 90 percent is white wine production, much of the balance being sparkling rosé wines that have become somewhat more popular recently.

One of the modern-day heroes of Champagne is the late Comte Robert-Jean de Vogue of Moët & Chandon who, at the beginning of World War II, resisted the efforts of the Nazis to loot the cellars, an effort that led to his imprisonment in a German concentration camp. Perhaps even more creditable was Vogue's founding of the Comité Interprofessionelle du Vin de Champagne (CIVC) in 1942, an organization that regulates vineyard practices and wine production in the province. This organization continues to function as the authority over Champagne, and today is governed by a board that has an equal number of grower and winery representatives. It is funded through a marketing order on each kilogram of grapes and each bottle of wine sold.

The climate of Champagne brings cold winters but also long summers. Frost can damage buds in the spring, and the finest vineyards employ heating units and other such frost-abatement devices. The CIVC determines when harvest should begin each year and how many grapes may be harvested per acre—both determined by the effects of the growing season on the grapes.

The soil of Champagne is one of the most famous in viticulture: the best vineyards are planted upon a base of belemnitic and oolitic chalk, a layer raised up from earthquakes that occurred millennia ago. The chalk rests under a shifting topsoil layer and absorbs heat in the fall to assist ripening. Sometimes topsoil must be replaced with organic deposits from the nearby hilltops. The chalk, which is easily worked by the vignerons today, provided the ancient Romans with a material that could be readily extracted to form vast storage caves underground. Many of these caves remain, and they have long since been used as wine cellars. In fact, the cellar master in Champagne is called the *chef des caves*.

However, Champagne's famous chalky soil varies in composition and quality across the region. The soil constituency is the crucial determinant of vineyard quality in Champagne—quality being a figure precisely calibrated by the CIVC authority from 75 percent in grade up to the maximum grade of 100 percent. As one might expect, vineyards with the highest percentage ratings are quick to

Chalk subsoil in the vineyards of Champagne. (Source: Food and Wines from France.)

make such numbers available to the public while those of lower stature tend to keep quiet about their ratings.

Some experts insist that the 100 percent classification is the same as a "First-Growth" classification—or equal to a "Grand Cru" as designated in Burgundy. Similarly, the growths that are stipulated as more than 90 percent but less than 100 percent may be considered as "Premier Cru." Any vineyard with a classification less than 90 percent may be regarded as without any type of "Cru" pedigree.

Champagne is divided into two main regions: Region I, which contains the classic vineyards surrounding Reims and Épernay; and Region II, the Aube and Haute-Marne, which are located farther south.

There are three main districts in Champagne I: the Montagne de Reims, the Vallée de la Marne, and the Côte des Blancs, from north to south, respectively. A listing of principal Champagne I vineyards is provided at the end of this section.

The Montagne has a subdistrict that is called the Basse-Montagne, a producer of lesser-quality sparkling wines. The Haute-Montagne encompasses the eastern and northern portions of the Montagne de Reims and extends for 15 miles from Tauxièrres to Verzenay. It boasts no fewer than eight 100 percent communes and five more that meet or exceed 90 percent in the quality scale. The Montagne is known for yielding heavy-bodied, vinous wines.

The Vallée de la Marne surrounds the other capital of Champagne I, Épernay, and, as its name suggests, borders the Marne River on both sides. The Vallée has eight growths of 90 percent quality or more, but only two 100 percent growths, one being the most famous vineyard of all Champagne, the Ay. The wines from this district are typically more fruity than those from Montagne.

The Côte des Blancs is noted for wines of finesse—perhaps due to the large portion of white grapes grown there, as the district's name suggests. There are two 100 percent growths in the Côte des Blancs, those of Cramant and Avize, and another six growths of 90 percent quality or more—some of which qualify with both white and red grape production.

There are only three varieties of grapes that the AOC allows to grow in the Département of Champagne I: Pinot Noir and Pinot Meunier, both red-skinned varieties, which are predominantly grown in the northern subdistricts of Montagne and Marne, as well as the white Chardonnay that pervades the Côte des Blancs and is labeled as "Blanc de Blanc" (white from white).

Few nonsparkling wines remain in the Champagne I region: the whites of Sillery and the reds of Bouzy being the most notable. All of these wines, now under EEC regulation, must be labeled with the designation AOC *Côteaux Champenois*; only sparkling wines from Champagne are allowed the distinction of AOC *Champagne*. The red wines from Bouzy are blended with whites in order to make pink, or rosé, Champagne—the only AOC Champagne rosé wine allowed by the EEC to be blended from red and white wines.

The soils of the Aube and Haute-Marne in Champagne II are diverse, being chalky in the vineyards that flank the upper region, and of Kimmeridgian limestone, similar to the soil composition of Chablis, in the lower portion. A few red table wine producers still remain in Champagne II, along with some still and sparkling white and rosé vintners. While a few of the vineyards are classified over 80 percent, most are not. The Riceys vineyard is the region's most noteworthy. In addition, a wide range of grape varieties are cultivated in the Aube and Haute-Marne.

The CIVC allows only 159.8 gallons of juice to be extracted per ton of grapes in the making of Champagne wine. Of this, 75 percent, or 120 gallons, is the free-run juice that flows from the grapes prior to pressure applied from the press. The *vin de cuvée* is the combined juice of the free-run and the first, second, and third pressing. The fourth and fifth pressings are called the *premieres tailles* and the sixth pressing the *deuxièmes tailles*—both of which are of lesser quality and are usually fermented separately, but may also be blended into the final cuvée for secondary fermentation in the bottle. Oftentimes additional pressings are made to extract a low-quality juice called *rebeche* that, along with the pomace, is fermented into

The grape harvest in Champagne: workers carrying the grapes to the presses.

brandy called *eau-de-vie de marc de Champagne*. Sometimes the premieres and deuxiemes tailles are also made into brandy called *eau-de-vie de vin de Champagne*.

As would be expected, the pressing of the black Pinot Noir and Pinot Meunier varieties often yields juice that has varying amounts of pink color—all of which is oxidized into the golden hue familiar to connoisseurs of the *blanc de noir* (white from black).

Some of the finest Champagnes result from grapes that have been given the benefit of *épluchage*. This is an expensive task in which experienced sorters inspect each bunch of grapes closely and cull by hand defective berries or bunches prior to pressing. Cuvée wines are made in the traditional dry white-wine manner.

A precise amount of sugar, nutrients, and yeast starter are added to the young wine, which is then poured into specially constructed bottles that can withstand the ensuing pressure. The wines ferment in *tirage*—which refers to the laying of the bottles horizontally in tiers—and the process may take several weeks to several years. After all the available sugars are fermented, the yeasts disintegrate and impart their flavor to the wine if it is left in contact with the sediment long enough. In the *remuage*, or "riddling," the bottles are placed neck down so that the yeast sediment can gather at the temporary crown cap used to seal the bottle. Each day, the riddler will lift each bottle slightly several times, give it a quarter turn, and firmly replace it so as to jar the sediment downward. After clearing, the wine is refrigerated and a small ice plug is frozen about 1 inch or so above the cap. The *désgorgeur*, or "disgorger," will then remove the cap, and the head pressure inside the bottle will expel the plug—taking it with the sediment. The wine is quickly given a *dosage*—a sweetener and preservative—then corked and wire hooded to provide the final seal. This entire process, known as the *méthode champenoise*, is discussed in detail in chapter 1.

Champagne production and marketing is dominated by a group of wineries known as Champagne houses, located in the major towns of the Champagne region. Each house has its own "house style"—a blend recipe that insures a consistent and uniform product from year to year. Though Champagnes are considered luxury wines and command fairly high prices, there are gradations of Champagnes offered by the various houses. The lowest in price are usually the nonvintage Champagnes, which are blends of wines made from different years of growth. The Champagne houses will declare a vintage only in years when the wines are superior; some connoisseurs consider vintage-dated Champagne a more complex and longer-living wine than nonvintage. They usually cost more money. Many Champagne houses have a still higher grade of wine that may be labeled *tête de cuvée* or *cuvée speciale*. These are the finest wines from vintage years, usually from the first pressings of the top-quality grapes. The houses usually offer them under special, super-premium labels, the best-known example being Moët

The *méthode champenoise:*
(1) *Remuage* (riddling), (2)
Le dégorgement
(disgorging), (3) *Le dosage*
(addition of sweetener).

& Chandon's "Dom Pérignon." While these special labels and quality statements carry no official meaning, many consumers rely on them as indications of the finest product a particular house has to offer. Needless to say, the wines are very expensive.

Among the finest Champagne houses that sell to the American market are Bollinger, Charles Heidsieck, Piper-Heidsieck, Krug, Laurent-Perrier, Moët & Chandon, Mumm, Perrier-Jouet, Pol Roger, Pommery, Roederer, Ruinart, Taittinger, and Veuve Clicquot-Ponsardin.

Other categories of Champagne depend on the grape types used and the sweetness level achieved. Blanc de Blanc Champagnes are made from the white Chardonnay exclusively, and many experts consider them the finest wines made in the province. The sweetness level of a particular Champagne is specified on the label. The sweetest products are labeled *doux* (sweet); slightly drier but still on the sweet side is *demi-sec* or *demi-doux* (semidry). *Sec* (which is French for dry) is the next level up in dryness, but even these wines are not entirely dry. The very driest Champagnes are called *brut*, and these are usually the highest in quality because there is less sweetness to mask imperfections.

TABLE 6-3   Champagne—Principal Growths

CHAMPAGNE I

Montagne de Reims (WSp)	Premier Cru (90 to 99% WG)
Haute-Montagne	Montbré Trépail Villers-Marmery Villers-Allerand
Grand Cru (100% BG)	
Ambonnay Beamond-sur-Vesle Bouzy Louvois Mailly Puisieulx Sillery Tauxières-Mutry Verzenay	*Basse-Montagne (WSp)* Premier Cru Écueil Les Mesneux Sacy Trois-Puits Ville-Dommange
Premier Cru (90 to 99% BG)	Vallée de la Marne (WSp)
Chigny-Les-Roses Ludes Rilly-La-Montagne Verzy	Grand Cru (100% BG) Ay Tours-sur-Marne

Premier Cru (90 to 99% BG)	Grand Cru (100% WG)
Avenay	Avize
Bisseuil	Cramant
Champillon	
Choilly	Premier Cru (90 to 99% WG)
Cumières	
Dizy-Magenta	Bergères-Les-Vertus
Hautvillers	Cuis
Mareuil-sur-Ay	Grauves
Mutigny	Le Mesnil-sur-Oger
Pierry	Oger
	Oisy
Premier Cru (90 to 99% WG)	Premier Cru (90 to 99% BG)
Choilly	Bergères-Les-Vertus
Tours-sur-Marne	Cuis
	Grauves
Côte des Blancs (WSp)	Vertus

BG = black grapes only qualify for classification
WG = white grapes only qualify for classification
WSp = white sparkling wines made exclusively
R = red table wines made principally or exclusively

ALSACE

The Alsace may be aptly described as a "bit of Germany transplanted in northern France." It is the only major French wine-growing region not to have, at least in part, a Roman origin.

There is evidence that supports the idea that grapes were grown in the Alsace during the reign of Emperor of the West Charlemagne. The Treaty of Verdun, drafted in 870 A.D., allotted Louis the German the Province of the Alsace "in order that he might have wine in his new kingdom." As the Alsatian wines' reputation for quality grew, a dynamic trade evolved with the Northern European states.

In fact, up to the late 1600s, the Alsace was a Germanic state. After the Thirty Years War it became part of France. But following the Franco-Prussian War, Alsace again became German. World War I brought the district under French rule once again, and it has remained French ever since. Nevertheless, its language, customs, architecture, and wine-growing style remain Teutonic in flavor.

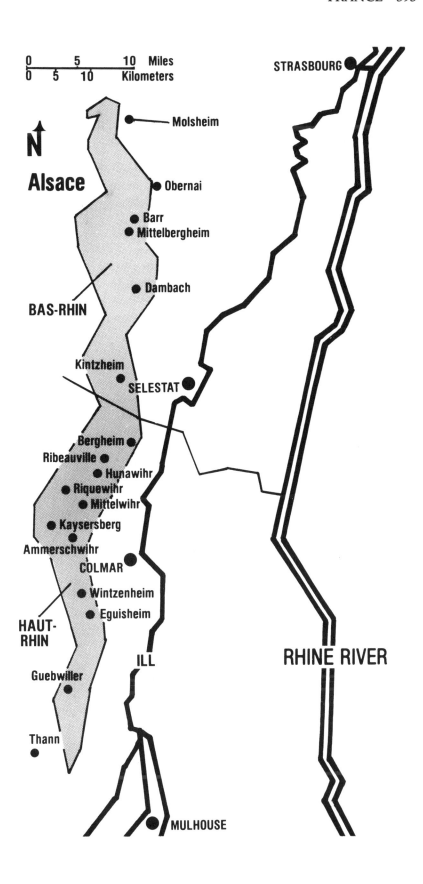

0   5   10   Miles
0   5   10   Kilometers

N

Alsace

Molsheim

Obernai

Barr
Mittelbergheim

Dambach

BAS-RHIN

Kintzheim

SELESTAT

Bergheim
Ribeauville
Hunawihr
Riquewihr
Mittelwihr
Kaysersberg
Ammerschwihr
COLMAR
Wintzenheim
Eguisheim

**HAUT-
RHIN**

ILL

RHINE RIVER

Guebwiller

Thann

MULHOUSE

STRASBOURG

The Alsace is a rather narrow strip of land some 60 miles long parallel to the west bank of the Rhein (Rhine) River. The capital city is Colmar, which divides the northern Bas-Rhin subdistrict from the southern Haut-Rhin. In total, the Alsace has approximately 30,000 acres of vineyards operated by about 9,000 growers. Production ranges from about 11 to 20 million gallons of wine per year. The finest growths are located in the Haut-Rhin: there 95 percent of the production is white table wines, of which 90 percent are AOC designated. The Bas-Rhin produces about 90 percent white table wines, but only 55 percent are AOC labeled. The VDQS growths are negligible.

The hillside soils of the Alsace are varied; gneiss, gravel, granite, irrigated marl, and limestone can be found in different locales. In the superior Haut-Rhin the better vineyards are planted upon calcareous slopes exposed to the south and southeast. In both subdistricts the lesser wines are grown upon the lower valley plains.

The Alsace is located more than 500 miles inland and, consequently, is not significantly affected by the tempering effects of ocean currents. Summers are hotter and winters are colder than in any other major French wine-growing

The hilly vineyards of Alsace.

region. The Vosges mountains to the west offer both protection from the inclement weather that usually approaches from that direction and water for the vineyards from tributary streams that run down from the slopes to feed the Rhein River.

Alsatian wines are distinguished primarily by the names of grape varieties grown in the vineyards, rarely by designations of geographic area or growth limitations.

There are six noble vines that are grown in the Alsace. The most famous is the Johannisberg Riesling, producer of superb white wines—some the equal of the finer growths of Germany, whence the variety originates. But the pearl of Alsace is Gewürztraminer. In years gone by the variety was simply called Traminer, but a sport (a genetic mutation) was discovered that was thought to produce superior wines of spicy, or *Gewürz*, character. The Gewürz was propagated and widely planted in modern times. The other four varieties found in Alsatian vineyards are Muscat, Pinot Gris (sometimes called Tokay d'Alsace), Pinot Blanc, and Sylvaner—the latter remaining the variety cultivated most widely.

Both Alsace and Vin d'Alsace are permitted AOC designations. If a variety name is used in conjunction with these designations on the label, then all the wine must be made from that grape. Alsatian AOC wines must have a minimum alcohol strength of 8.5 percent, and grapes must be harvested within the regulations set forth by the Comité Régionale d'Experts. The Alsatians usually bottle their wines in the tall slender green bottle known as the *flûte d'Alsace,* and all bottling of Alsatian wines must take place in Alsace.

When ordinary wines are blended with those from noble grapes, the AOC designation Alsace Edelzwicker is permitted, although the name, or names, of the noble grapes cannot be displayed on the label. A few AOC sparkling wines called Alsace Crémant are made. Alsatian vintners sometimes add the name of a commune to their labels, such as Riquewihr or Éguisheim. The addition of a vineyard name is also rather common—Sporen or Kanzlerberg, for example. Labels that indicate grape name *and* shipper, grower, or vineyard are likely to be found on the best wines.

Alsatian Grand Cru wines are a new entity. The AOC currently established delineated boundaries for some vineyards. AOC Alsace Grand Cru requires a minimum of 10 percent alcohol for wines made from Johannisberg Riesling and Muscat. Eleven percent is minimal for Gewürztraminer and Pinot Gris.

The wines of the Alsace are diverse, ranging from the finer crisp dry whites from the Pinot Blanc to the superb dry and medium-dry whites from Johannisberg Riesling and Gewürztraminer. The wines from Muscat are sometimes made sweet and are generally thought of as lesser in quality than the wines made from the other five noble varieties. The heavily planted Sylvaner makes both ordinary and superior wines in the Alsace. The wines from the Alsatian growths are appearing more often on the shelves of American wine stores.

Some of the more reliable vintners are Dopff & Irion, Hugel & Fils, Preiss Henny, Schlumberger, Trimbach, and Alsace Willm.

TABLE 6-4   Alsace—Principal Growths

HAUT-RHIN

Ammerschwihr
  Erlenbrunn
  Froehn
  Griess
  Hahnen
  Hasengrab
  Kaefferkopf
  Probstgart
  Schloss Meywihr
  Sommerberg

Béblenheim
  Altkirch
  Haring
  Schiff
  Sonneglanz

Bergheim
  Altenberg
  Blosenberg
  Kanzleberg
  Rotenberg

Colmar
  Harth

Éguisheim
  Eichberg
  Pfersigberg

Guebwiller
  Kitterlé
  Wanne

Hunawihr
  Muhlforst

Ingersheim
  Florimont

Kaysersberg
  Schlossberg

Kientzheim
  Clos des Capucins
  Fürstentum

Mittelwihr
  Mandelberg

Ribeauvillé
  Geisberg
  Hagel
  Kirchberg
  Osterberg
  Zahnaeker

Riquewihr
  Dambaechal
  Gehei
  Hoppler
  Oberberg
  Schoenenberg
  Sporen
  Weissengrund

Rouffach
  Langenzug
  Bollenberg

Sigolsheim
  Mambourg

Soultzmatt
  Weingarten
  Zinnkoepflé

Thann
  Le Rangen

Turckheim
  Brand

Voegtlinshoffen
  Hatschbourg
  Grosskohlausen

Westhalten
  Clos St.-Landelin
  Steinstück
  Strangenberg

Wettolsheim
  Kalkgruber
  Steingrubler

Wintzenheim
  Hengst
  Wartsein

Wuenheim
  Côte d'Ollwiller
  Schweighof

Zellenberg
  Buergen

BAS-RHIN

Andlau
  Kastelberg
  Mönchberg
  Wibelsberg

Barr
  Freiburg
  Gansbrönnel
  Kirchberg
  Krug
  Pfloeck
  Ritteney
  Zisser

Bernardville
  Hüelland

Bernardswiller
  Buhl
  Dorenberg
  Mittelgewand
  Offenberg
  Stritt

Blienschwiller
  Broch
  Kley
  Mittelberg
  Oberberg
  Rott
  Winzenberg

Châtenois
  Hahnenberg

Dieffenthal
  Gabelsfach
  Hagelbukel
  Victoriaberg

Dorlisheim
  Alberberg
  Bromberg
  Weilerthal

Eichhoffen
  Duttenberg
  Lerchenberg

Fundenheim
  Alter Rebberg

Goxwiller
  Bannscheid
  Ziegerlgässel

Heiligenstein
  Frauelsberg
  Gesetz
  Hinderkirch

Irmstett
  Kirchstück
  Schildstück

Itterswiller
  Kirchberg
  Süssenhart

Mittelbergheim
  Berg

Brandluft
Brückel
Hagel
Rotland
Trotzenberg
Zotzenberg

This is a list of communes and specific vineyards that are generally recognized as superior growths.

Noble varieties: Johannisberg Riesling, Gewürztraminer, Pinot Gris (Tokay d'Alsace), Muskat, Pinot Blanc, Sylvaner

LOIRE

The Loire Valley vineyards were most likely established by the Romans during the first and second centuries A.D. In the fourth century St. Martin of Tours became the first monk to grow grapes in all of western Europe, and his memory, still vivid amongst the Touraine, is honored each year. The red cloak of St. Martin remains one of the most sacred relics in France.

About 1,000 years after the death of St. Martin, Rabelais wrote in his stories of Pantagruel and Gargantua about the power of the Loire wines to enhance virility.

During the Renaissance the many red, white, and rosé wines of the Loire began to improve in quality, and, as they did, producers turned from exporting their wines to England and the Netherlands to supplying the thirst of Paris and other internal markets. In modern times the inexpensive wines of the Loire Valley find their way to many export markets, not the least of which is America.

The Loire River is about 625 miles long, France's longest, and its many tributaries include the Cher, Indre, Layon, Loir, Sèvre, Vienne, among others. Along the banks of these rivers lay the four important wine districts of the region: from east to west these are the Upper Loire, the Touraine, Anjou, and the Nantais. The vineyard area is massive—about 360,000 acres spread among approximately 230,000 growers, if one includes all the ordinary growths.

Upper Loire

The Upper Loire, sometimes called the Nivernais, contains only about 5,000 acres and are located mostly upon the right bank of the Loire between the villages of Gien at the north and La Charité at the south. The white wines are the most famous here, particularly those made from Sauvignon Blanc, sometimes called Blanc Fumé by the locals, grown on calcareous soils. They are called *fumé* because of their heavy, smoky bouquet. The Nivernais is divided between two main subdistricts, AOC Sancerre and AOC Pouilly-sur-Loire, the latter not to be confused with Pouilly-Fuissé of the Mâconnais, to which it has no relationship. The Pouilly-sur-Loire is further subdivided to distinguish AOC Blanc-Fumé-de-Pouilly—the most distinctive growth in the Nivernais. Like most of the Loire wines, they are best drunk young while the flavors are fresh and fruity. Wines from the Pouilly-sur-Loire are marketed as "Pouilly Fumé" by some shippers in France. The epitome of Pouilly and Sancerre is beautifully exemplified by the grand Château du Nozet—owned by Baron Patrick de Ladoucette. The estate produces some of the finest dry white wines in France.

Also in the Upper Loire district are the AOC vineyards of Quincy near the Cher River and Reuilly further to the west. Quincy vineyards are planted with Sauvignon Blanc on poor gravel soil, while Reuilly cultivates the same variety upon Kimmeridgian marl—both yielding white wines that are most pleasant when consumed before any significant aging takes place.

To the northwest are the two final subdistricts in the Upper Loire: the Coteaux de Gien that cultivates the red varieties Gamay and Pinot Noir, but is better known for its whites from both noble and ordinary varieties; and the Coteaux de l'Orléanais, which surrounds the city of Orléans and produces mostly ordinary red and white wines, along with a small amount of fine Chardonnay.

Touraine

The vast AOC Touraine vineyards, covering about 120,000 acres, yield mostly ordinary wines, although a few exceptional growths are beginning to gain prominence. The soil in the better subdistricts of the Touraine is primarily clay and limestone over a subsoil of tufa chalk, a porous pumicelike chalk produced by volcanic activity, which retains both heat and moisture well. The most famous wine from the Touraine is the AOC Vouvray, made both dry and sweet, still and sparkling—all from the Chenin Blanc variety (sometimes called "Pineau de la Loire" in the Loire wine trade) first introduced by St. Martin 1,600 years ago. On the other side of the river, to the south, the vineyards of Montlouis grow similar wines. In the western Touraine are the vineyards of AOC Bourgueil that grow wines with a distinct raspberry-like taste from the Cabernet Franc (called *Breton* by the locals). The most notable communes are AOC St.-Nicholas-de-Bourgueil and the famous AOC Chinon, where the fabled King Henry II of England lived.

Alexandre Dumas spent much of his younger life in Orléans and the Touraine, which no doubt influenced his bon vivant lifestyle. He once remarked that history would remember him for his *Grand Dictionnaire de la Cuisine*—not for *The Three Musketeers*. The Dumas food dictionary is a rare book that runs to 818 pages in the unabridged edition and includes suggestions for serving wines with such exotic dishes as elephant's feet and kangaroo.

Anjou

Some connoisseurs insist that the finest wines of the Loire are grown in Anjou, although its vineyard acreage is dwarfed by the Touraine. In the east there is limestone out of which many notable caves have been carved, and to the west the soil is shallow and schistous. The white wines of AOC Anjou are made from Chardonnay, Chenin Blanc, and Sauvignon Blanc, and some are made *pétillant*—only slightly sparkling, or "crackling." The AOC also permits red wines made from Cabernet Sauvignon, Cabernet Franc, and Pineau d'Aunis, as well as a separate AOC red wine called Anjou-Gamay.

Undoubtedly the most internationally famous wines of the Anjou are the AOC Rosé d'Anjou wines made to a medium-dry sweetness from blends of Gamay and Gros Lot. AOC Cabernet d'Anjou-Rosé and AOC Cabernet de Saumur Rosé are made exclusively from the red Cabernet varieties. Both red and white wines from the Saumur, a subdistrict of Anjou, are permitted the AOC-Saumur designation. The best-known Saumurs are sparkling wines made by the méthode champenoise. AOC Saumur-Champigny produces red wines from Cabernet grapes. On the north side of the Loire River lies the AOC subdistrict of Anjou Coteaux de la Loire from which delicate dry and medium-dry white wines are made from Chenin Blanc. The small commune of Savennières is situated near a volcanic deposit, upon which are four slopes that yield the highest quality wines of the area: Coulée de Serrant, Château d'Epiré, Roches-aux-Moines, and Clos-du-Papillon. At the most western reaches of the Anjou district are two more subdistricts—AOC Coteaux du Layon and AOC Coteaux de l'Aubance—named for the rivers that run through each subdistrict. Both of these subdistricts produce fine white wines from Chenin Blanc, but they are considerably sweeter than the wines of Savennières. At the vineyards of AOC Quarts de Chaume and AOC Bonnezeau, the noble mold grows and, as may be expected, the wines here are quite similar to those of Sauternes in Bordeaux.

Nantais

Nearest the ocean is the Nantais district—noted for a mild climate that the ocean moderates. The finest vineyards are located upon the slopes that border the Loire

River, with soil made of clay upon a mineral-rich granite subsoil. The wine of the Nantais is AOC Muscadet from the grape of the same name. When young, dry white Muscadet is tart and crisp with a rich fruity nose, but it ages quickly, losing its elusive character. The district has two subdistricts, the AOC Muscadet de Sèvre-et-Maine and Muscadet des Coteaux de la Loire, both of which are recognized as superior growths—the former the very finest.

TABLE 6-5 Loire—Principal Growths

ANJOU

Anjou-Gamay (R)

Rosé d'Anjou (Ro)

Cabernet d'Anjou-Rosé (Ro)

Saumur (W & SW)

Saumur-Champigny (R)

Cabernet de Saumur Rosé (Ro)

Anjou Coteaux de la Loire (W)
   Savennières
   Coulée-de-Serrant (WSup)
   Château d'Epiré (WSup)
   Roches-aux-Moines (WSup)
   Clos-du-Papillon (WSup)

Coteaux de L'Aubance

Coteaux du Layon
   Quarts de Chaume (WSup)
   Bonnezeaux (WSup)

NANTAIS

Muscadet (W)

Muscadet de Sèvre-et-Maine (WSup)

Muscadet des Coteaux de la Loire (WSup)

TOURAINE

Vouvray (RW, SR, & SW)

Bourgueil
   St.-Nicholas-de-Bourgueil (R)
   Chinon (R)

Coteaux du Loir
   Jasnières (W)

UPPER LOIRE REGION

Quincy (W)

Reuilly (W)

Sancerre (WSup)

Pouilly-sur-Loire (WSup)
   Blanc-Fumé-de-Pouilly (WSup)

Menetou Salon (RW & Ro)

R = red
W = white
Ro = rosé
Sup = superior
SW = sparkling white

The Nantais has two VDQS subdistricts as well. The first is the Gros Plant du Pays Nantais, which makes a white wine from the Folle Blanche variety. The other is the Coteaux d'Ancenis, bordering Anjou, which produces rosé and red wines from Cabernet Sauvignon and Gamay, as well as whites from Chenin Blanc.

Obviously the Loire Valley produces a wide range of wines, many of which are steadily improving and gaining more attention in the world marketplace. For the most part they remain light-bodied wines, and the majority of them are best drunk when in their youth.

CÔTES DU RHÔNE

The Rhône Valley stretches about 120 miles from Lyon southward to Avignon and has approximately 220,000 acres cultivated by more than 120,000 growers. It is divided into two main parts—the northern Rhône and the southern Rhône.

The soils in the north are granitic and schistose on steep slopes bordering both sides of the river. To the south the vineyard land is clay-limestone, sometimes strewn with red stones left by glacier activity.

The Rhône Valley is one of the most picturesque wine-growing regions in France. In the north the steep slopes and cliffs are reminiscent of some areas in the Rheinland, with terraced vineyards leading down to the river where house-barges and other traffic slowly pass by. The southern Rhône has many fruit orchards, as well as vineyards, which help to compose a natural and agricultural landscape of breathtaking beauty. A tour of the region will bring one close to many ancient Roman relics, along with other historic points of interest. Including the many fine restaurants to be found in the cities and villages along the river, the Rhône Valley is a vacationland *par excellence* for the enophile seeking to "get away from it all."

The weather of the Rhône Valley can often be quite harsh. There are four seasons in the north, but the south has a more Mediterranean climate with just two seasons, summer and winter. The entire region is vulnerable to the *mistral*—a cold glacier katabatic (flowing downward) wind that sweeps down from the Alps. The mistral often damages vineyards through both bitter cold and high wind. Rhône wines, as one might imagine, are characteristically robust and hearty.

Northern Rhône

The northernmost growth of the Rhône is AOC Cote Rôtie that clings to the west bank of the river. The Syrah variety is grown for reds and the Viognier for

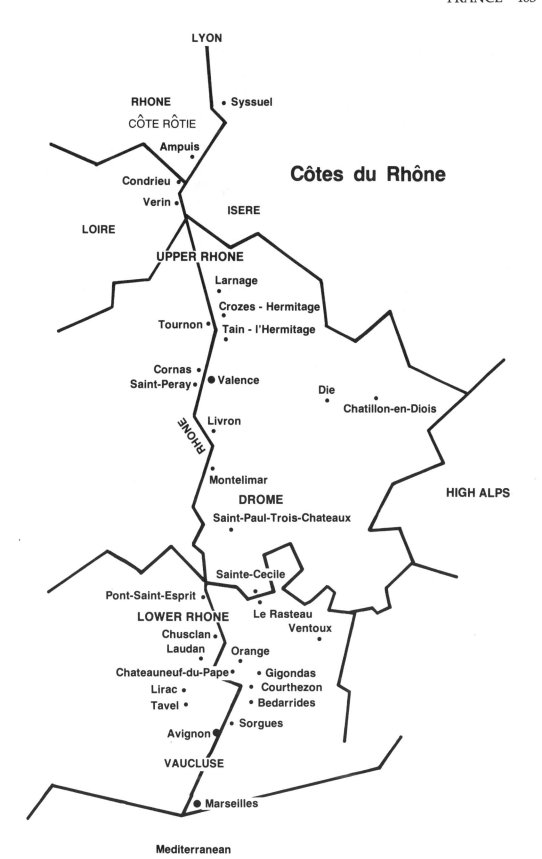

whites. Côte Rôtie is subdivided into two portions, the Côte Brune and the Côte Blonde—according to legend, named for the two daughters of a medieval owner, one a brunette and one a blonde. If one looks closely at the soils in the two subdistricts, one notices that the one is dark with iron oxide and the other pale with limestone. Côte Rôtie, in any event, is best known for its red wines, which are heavy and dark, typically rich in berrylike flavor.

The vineyards of AOC Condrieu border Côte Rôtie to the south and are entirely planted to the Viognier, which yields long-living white wines that are full-bodied. Within the Condrieu is the tiny vineyard of AOC Chateau Grillet—only about 2 acres.

South of Condrieu is AOC St.-Joseph, where the Rhône Valley begins to broaden somewhat, nearly all the wines produced are red from the Syrah—although the AOC permits white wines to be produced there as well. AOC Cornas borders St.-Joseph to the south and produces similar wines, although they have a tendency to be very tannic and heavy-bodied.

On the east side of the river, opposite the town of Tournon, is the village of Tain-l'Hermitage. Bordering the village to the east and northeast lay the famous vineyards of AOC Hermitage. Here, reds that are dark and pleasantly astringent are produced only from the Syrah, while whites are grown from the Marsanne and Roussane varieties. There are three vineyards that are recognized as First Growths—les Bessards, le Meal, and les Greffieux—and there are ten Second Growths. Bordering the Hermitage vineyards are AOC Crozes-Hermitages: vineyards that yield lighter wines, but many of them are superb, nevertheless.

Back across the river to the west side and south past Cornas is the commune of St.-Péray. Only white wines are produced there, from both Roussane and Marsanne vines. When the wines are made sparkling by the methode champenoise, as they frequently are, they may carry the AOC St.-Péray *mousseux* designation.

Two more districts lay in the northern Rhône, those of AOC Clairette de Die, producer of sparkling wines made from the Clairette grape, and AOC Châtillon-en-Diois—primarily known for red wines from Pinot Noir, but a producer of whites and rosés, as well. Both of these subdistricts are located about 30 miles east up the Drôme tributary near Savoie.

Southern Rhône

Proceeding south from Valence one enters into the southern half of the Rhône. Côtes du Vivarais lies to the west of the river and has twenty-two wine-growing villages nestled in the hills west of Montélimar. Eleven of these are permitted

VDQS for red, white, and rosé wines from a dozen or so varieties of grape. On the east side of the river is the AOC Coteaux du Tricastin, recently elevated from VDQS, where twelve villages grow the varieties Carignan, Grenache, and others to produce mostly red wines.

Southeast of Tricastin, scattered in the hills near the town of Nyons, are located another eleven villages, known collectively as Les Baronnies. Five of the villages can add their name to AOC Côtes du Rhône, while the other six are permitted VDQS Haut-Comtat. The wines from yet another eleven villages, when blended together under strict rules governing alcohol strength and taste, are entitled to the name AOC Côtes du Rhône-Villages. One of these villages, Gigondas, now has its own AOC for rosé and red wines produced from up to 65 percent of the Grenache variety. The general term *Côtes du Rhône* without any village name can be used for wines from over 100 communes in the area.

Upon the slopes of Mont Ventoux are the AOC Vins Doux Naturels, Rasteau, and Muscat de Beaumes-de-Venise. These are wines made in a fashion similar to other dessert wines in which the primary fermentation is arrested by the addition of brandy in order to preserve some of the natural grape sugar and fruit flavor. Rasteau, made primarily from Grenache, often takes on a flavor called *rancio*—best described not as rancid, as the name might suggest, but as rather caramel and nutlike in flavor. Muscat de Beaumes-de-Venise is made from Muscat and, despite the preservative effects of the brandy fortification, is best drunk when young before the Muscat fruitiness is lost.

Châteauneuf-du-Pape

The Côtes du Rhône region ends at the junction of the Durance and the Rhône Rivers, south of the city of Avignon. Clement V, previously bishop of Bordeaux, was coronated pope here in 1305, becoming the first of seven popes to reside in Avignon during the fourteenth century. He was also the first occupant of Châteauneuf-du-Pape—"the new home of the pope"—a large castle situated upon a bend of the Rhône River about 7 miles north of Avignon. Today only a fragment of the original castle remains. The vineyards are said to have been established before the arrival of the Romans. Today the wine of AOC Châteauneuf-du-Pape is unquestionably the most famous in all the Rhône, continuing to command the same high regard it has enjoyed for nearly twenty centuries. There are eight grape varieties grown in the Châteauneuf-du-Pape vineyards, principally Grenache, which may constitute 40 to 50 percent of the final blend each vintage. Syrah is permitted in amounts from 10 to 30 percent, with Cinsault, Mourvèdre, Vaccarese, Clairette, Terret Noir, and Picpoul making

The stony vineyards of the Châteauneuf-du-Pape district. (Source: Comité Interprofessionnel des Vins des Côtes du Rhône.)

up the balance. The rather varied soils at Châteauneuf-du-Pape are particularly noteworthy for the large stones commonly found on the vineyard floor.

Across the river from the Châteauneuf-du-Pape to the west side is the district of AOC Tavel—world-famous for its superb dry rosé wines. These are made from Grenache, Clairette, and Bourboulenc grown on soils as stony as those of the Pape vineyards, but also containing limestone chips. Curiously, Tavel makers eschew the bottles traditional for Burgundy and Rhône wines, preferring to bottle their wines in the tall flûte d'Alsace instead. To the north of Tavel is AOC Lirac, also possessed of stony soils and best known for its red wine.

TABLE 6-6 Côtes de Rhône—Principal Growths

NORTHERN RHONE	
Côte Rotie	St.-Joseph
Côte Brune (R)	AOC (R&W)
Côte Blonde (R)	Condrieu
	Château Grillet (W)

Cornas
  AOC (R)

Hermitage
  Les Bressards (R1)
  Le Meal (R1)
  Les Greffieux (R1)
  Crozes-Hermitages

St.-Péray
  Clairette de Die (SR & SW)

SOUTHERN RHONE

Les Baronnies
  Côtes du Rhône-Villages (R)

Mont Ventoux
  Rasteau (SR)

Muscat de Beaumes-de-Venise (SW)

Côtes du Vivarais
  VDQS (RW & Ro)

Châteauneuf-du-Pape
  AOC (R1)

Côteaux du Tricastin
  AOC (R)

Tavel
  AOC (Ro)

Lirac
  AOC (RW & Ro)

R = red
W = white
Ro = rosé
S = sparkling
1 = Rhône First Growth

THE MIDI

The Midi is the largest wine-growing region of France and one of the oldest, as well. The Midi wines have been, at best, ordinary until recent years, when new plantings of better grape varieties and modernized wine-making processes have improved the quality.

The region is bordered by the Rhône River to the east and Spain to the southwest. Principal vineyard districts in the Midi are Corbières, Languedoc, Minervois, and Roussillon.

Many people are reminded of the Monterey region of California when visiting the Midi in the southernmost reaches of France. It is a charming countryside consisting of a rolling terrain sloping down from the Alaric Mountains to a romantic seaside resort area. The Midi vineyards, cultivated upon all sorts of trellises and some upon no trellis at all, comprise a massive expanse of wine growing.

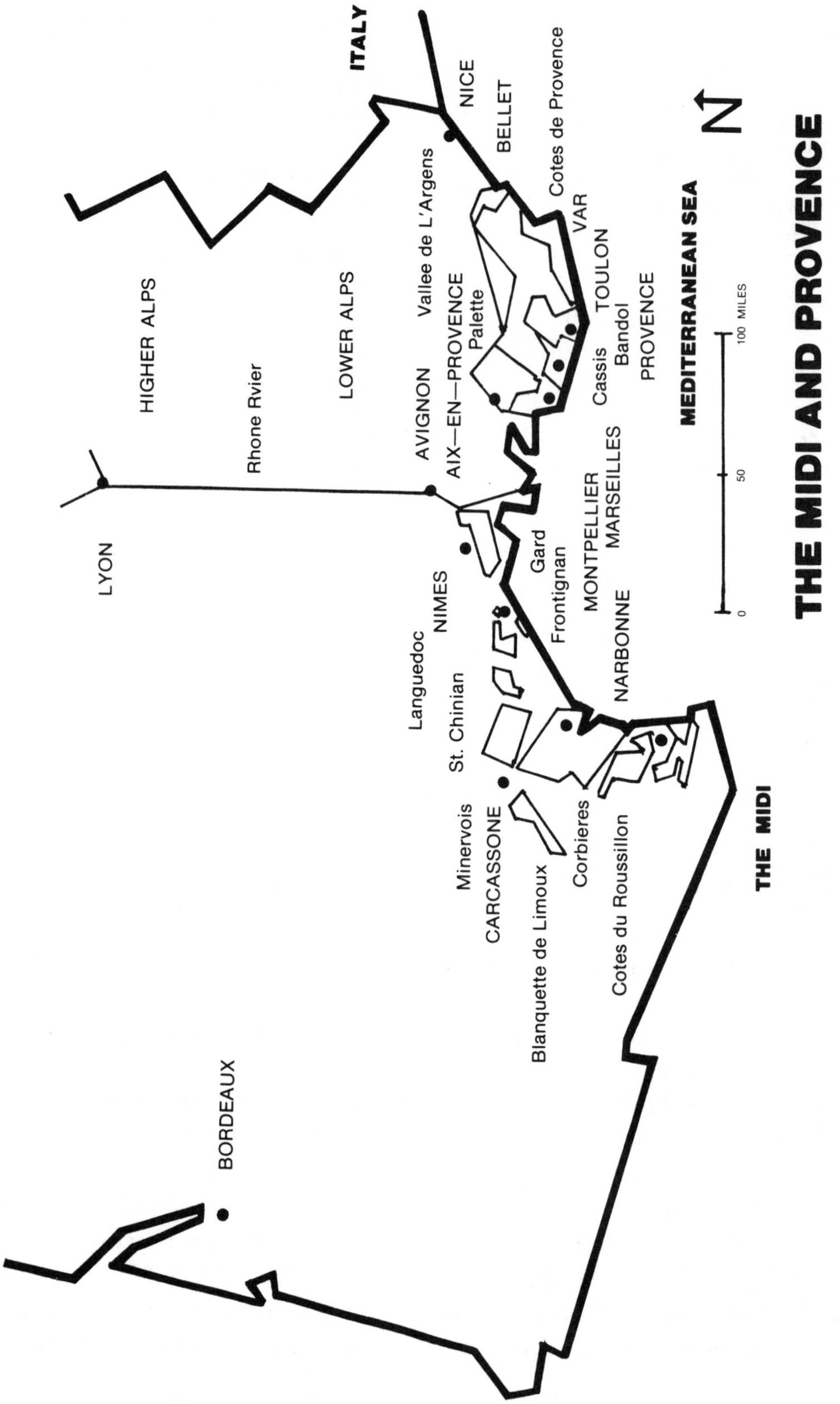

THE MIDI AND PROVENCE

ITALY

NICE

BELLET

Cotes de Provence

VAR

TOULON

Bandol

PROVENCE

Cassis

Palette

Vallee de L'Argens

AIX—EN—PROVENCE

AVIGNON

MEDITERRANEAN SEA

MARSEILLES

MONTPELLIER

Frontignan

Gard

NARBONNE

NIMES

Languedoc

St. Chinian

Minervois

CARCASSONE

Corbieres

Blanquette de Limoux

Cotes du Roussillon

THE MIDI

HIGHER ALPS

Rhone Rvier

LOWER ALPS

LYON

BORDEAUX

N

0   50   100 MILES

Corbières

The rolling hillside vineyards of the Corbières reach southeast from Carcassonne, a city centered by a magnificent eleventh-century abbey, to the ancient Roman wine-growing capital city of Narbonne. White, rosé, and red wines are grown in the Corbières, but the reds—primarily from the Carignan and Grenache grape varieties—are the most notable.

The Corbières, accorded the VDQS seal, is characterized by thousands of growers supplying large cooperative wineries. Macération carbonique, a relatively new method by which crushed red grapes are stored prior to pressing in chambers filled with carbon dioxide gas, has resulted in more distinctive wines with broader consumer appeal.

Languedoc

The modern-day Côteaux de Languedoc coincides with the site of ancient Narbonensis, the area occupied some 2000 years ago by Roman soldiers and the earliest wine-growing center in France that is recorded in history.

Most of the vin ordinaire grown in France comes from the Languedoc, although some of the hillsides are rated VDQS. The major portion of the vast vineyard acreage of the Languedoc is located in the Departement of Hérault, with other huge establishments also in Aude and Gard. The finest wines of the region are reds, principally those produced from macération carbonique processing and grown in the Berlou Valley, Faugères and St.-Chinian. In addition to the predominantly red wine production of the Languedoc, there are some noteworthy sweet white wines grown from Muscat vines at Frontignan. A highly regarded semidry white sparkling wine, Blanquette de Limoux, is produced at Limoux, thought by some to have preceded the first of such wines from Champagne.

Minervois

Though Minervois is the smallest of the giant wine-growing districts of the Midi, it often receives the highest praise from wine experts. It is authorized the VDQS seal for a 40-mile long portion of the north bank of the river Aude, northwest of Narbonne. The district is characterized by gravel flatlands nearest the river and a higher plateau farther back.

As with the other Midi districts, the Minervois produces mostly red table wines, although whites and rosés are also made. The reds, however, are the best, particularly those from Carignan and Grenache vines.

Roussillon

The Midi district of Roussillon is centered on the seashore village of Perpignan—progressing inland along valley hillsides. Carignan, Grenache, and Mourvèdre grapes yield very dark and heavy red table wines. The Côtes du Roussillon recently have been elevated to AOC, due primarily to improvements in red table wine production. Principal wine-growing villages in the appellation are Caramany, Collioure, and Latour-de-France.

Roussillon has greatest fame as the district that produces most of France's sweet dessert wine. The methods for making brandy were first described in detail by a Montpellier physician, Arnaldo da Villanova, who introduced the still from Moorish Spain during the thirteenth century. The resulting brandy is used in making sweet red wine, *vin doux naturel*—similar in production and style to the classic ports of Portugal. With aging, the sweet red fortified wines of Roussillon become maderized, taking on a flavor called *rancio* (caramel and nutlike flavor) by the neighboring Spanish.

PROVENCE

Despite the glorious early history of Provence, it has only recently made wines that can compete with those from the neighboring Rhône and Midi districts.

Rather strong, but neutral-flavored rosé wines have traditionally been made from Carignan, Cinsault, Grenache, Mourvèdre, and Syrah grapes. New varieties have been planted which, along with better enological methods and controls, led, perhaps prematurely, to the upgrading of the Côtes de Provence from VDQS to AOC in 1977.

There are four subdistricts in the huge appellation of Provence—which stretches from just east of Marseilles along the Mediterranean coast to Italy and inland to the Alps. Bandol, the largest of the subdistricts, is located just west of Toulon and produces distinctive red table wines, as well as more common white and rosé table wines. The Cassis district, which surrounds a fishing-port city of the same name, is perhaps best known for good white table wines. Northeast of Marseilles is the tiny subdistrict of Palette, best known for red wines from Château Simone. At the extreme eastern border of Provence is Bellet—situated between Nice and the mountains to the north. Bellet produces good table wines, but none are outstanding.

The Côteaux d'Aix-en-Provence is situated around the university city of Aix-en-Provence; it is known only for some pleasant, ordinary white, rosé, and red table wines, the best of which are VDQS.

MINOR DISTRICTS

There are three separate districts—the Jura and Savoie, the Southwest, and the island of Corsica—that may be considered together as the minor wine-growing regions of France. While these districts are minor as regards geographical size, they are not necessarily minor in wine quality. In particular, Savoie and Bergerac in the Southwest produce consistently high-quality wines. Unfortunately, the wines of France's minor districts are a rarity in most of America's wine markets.

Jura and Savoie

The Jura and Savoie are located due east of Burgundy, situated on the eastern border between France and Switzerland. The principal wines of the Jura are light reds from Poulsard, Trousseau, and Pinot Noir grapes—and a white, *Vin Jaune*, which with aging develops a distinctive bouquet and golden color tones. The three principal AOC are the Côtes du Jura, Arbois, and Château-Chalon—the latter being a commune, not an estate.

The Savoie, the most mountainous wine-growing region in France, is located upon the Rhône River, just southwest of Lake Geneva. Most Savoie is white table wine, the best of which is grown at Crépy. Fine sparkling wines from Seyssel are building a good reputation.

The Southwest

There are five subdistricts in the region situated south of Bordeaux, known as the Southwest.

Bergerac

The wines of Bergerac are rather evenly divided between red and white table wines—the best being predominately sweet white wines. Many are reminiscent of Sauternes, but without the great acidity, heavy richness, and fruitiness. The principal grape for the whites is Sémillon; the principal grape is Merlot for the reds. Monbazillac, a cooperatively operated château, is the most noteworthy growth in the area. Also located in Bergerac are the Côtes de Saussignac and Montravel.

Cahors

The Cahors district is located on the Lot River and is best known for superior red table wines made primarily from Merlot, Syrah, and Tannat grapes.

Gaillac

Some experts believe that the Gaillac may have existed as a wine-growing area even before Bordeaux—prior even to the Roman occupation of the Midi. In modern times wine production in Gaillac is dominated by large cooperative wineries, which make rather neutral white, rosé, and red table wines.

Madiran

Wines from Madiran are considered by some to be the best red table wines of the Southwest. They are made principally from Cabernet Sauvignon and Tannat grapes, although other varieties are grown for reds in the Madiran as well. A white wine, Pacherenc du Vic Bilh, is grown from blends of Sauvignon Blanc, Sémillon, and other white grape varieties.

Jurançon

The vineyards of the Jurançon are situated south of the town of Pau on the lower slopes of the Pyrénées in a very picturesque setting. The two predominant grapes grown in the subdistrict are Gros and Petit Manseng—which yield exceptionally rich, strong, and aromatic white table wines.

Corsica

The sunny island of Corsica, located north of Sardinia and due west of Italy, is heavily influenced by Italian culture. Corsica's most famous historical figure is, of course, Napoleon Bonaparte. The island is replete with beautiful mountain vineyards that yield ordinary, but dry and strong, wines made principally from the white grapes Malvoisie, Trebbiano, and Vermentino—along with the red grapes Nielluccio and Sciaccarello.

The principal appellations of note in Corsica are Côteaux d'Ajaccio, Patrimonio, Figari, Porto-Vecchio, Sartène, and Ghisonaccia-Aleria.

Erzeuger-Abfüllung
Fürst von Metternich - Winneburg'sche Domäne
Schloss Johannisberg im Rheingau

Fürst von Metternich

Qualitätswein mit Prädikat · Alc. 10% by Vol.
Contains sulfites · Net Contents: **750mle**
A.P.Nr. 26026011 86 · Product of W.-Germany

Schloss Johannisberger

Kabinett
1985er Rheingau · Riesling

7

THE WINES OF
GERMANY

The square mileage of West Germany totals only about two-thirds that of California, and German vineyards are just over 225,000 acres—less than one-third of the vineyard area of California. The Germans are not the world's greatest wine consumers either, owing, in part, at least, to their thirst for beer. By most counts the per capita wine consumption is just less than 10 gallons annually. By far, the largest export markets are in the United Kingdom and the United States. The importance of Germany as a wine-producing nation arises from a narrow range of unique wine products that have been created through magnificent dedication and struggle against the elements of nature.

The vineyards of Germany lay at the very northern limits of the zone where grapes may be commercially grown for fine wines. Farther north the summers are too short to provide enough heat-summation for adequate ripening of grapes. With marginal weather conditions the rule rather than the exception, the German wine-growing situation is precarious even within the chosen boundaries. And while the steep mountainside vineyards along the famous German rivers are breathtakingly beautiful, the soil is generally poor, and what little of it exists is often lost to violent rainstorms—arduously carried by hand back up again. Consequently, Germany challenges its winegrowers merely to gather any yield at all, let alone one of superior stature.

The reward for conquering these handicaps is some of the most delicious white wines in the world. While many other countries have planted German wine grapes, no other nation has yet succeeded in matching the many complex nuances of flavor in Germany's white wines, which range from subtly charming to bold in floral bouquet and heavy in body. This uniqueness is due, in part, at least, to the

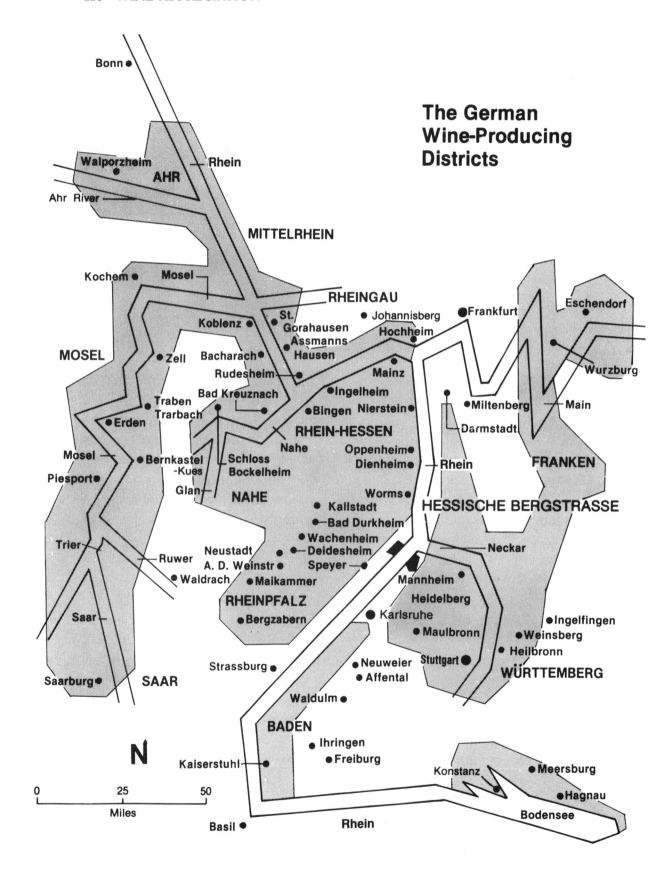

The German Wine-Producing Districts

Bonn

Walporzheim
AHR
Rhein
Ahr River

MITTELRHEIN

Kochem
Mosel
RHEINGAU
St.
Johannisberg
Frankfurt
Eschendorf
Koblenz
Gorahausen
Hochheim
Assmanns
MOSEL
Zell
Bacharach
Hausen
Wurzburg
Rudesheim
Mainz
Main
Traben
Bad Kreuznach
Ingelheim
Miltenberg
Trarbach
Bingen
Niersteln
Darmstadt
Erden
RHEIN-HESSEN
Mosel
Nahe
Oppenheim
Rhein
FRANKEN
Bernkastel
Schloss
Dienheim
-Kues
Bockelheim
Piesport
Glan
NAHE
Worms
HESSISCHE BERGSTRASSE
Kallstadt
Bad Durkheim
Trier
Wachenheim
Neckar
Ruwer
Neustadt
Deidesheim
A. D. Weinstr
Speyer
Mannheim
Waldrach
Maikammer
Heidelberg
Ingelfingen
RHEINPFALZ
Karlsruhe
Weinsberg
Saar
Bergzabern
Maulbronn
Heilbronn
Stuttgart
Neuweier
WÜRTTEMBERG
Strassburg
Affental
Saarburg
SAAR
Waldulm

N

BADEN
Ihringen
Freiburg
Konstanz
Meersburg
Kaiserstuhl
Hagnau

0   25   50
Miles

Basil
Rhein
Bodensee

great diversity of soils in each of the principal wine-growing regions: some calcareous, others of loess, slate, and volcanic stone, among other types. German wines show their origins and have never been reproduced elsewhere.

The wine land of Germany is situated in the southwestern portion of the nation, cut through by the fiftieth parallel of north latitude. Though the northern location and steep slopes of the vineyards present hazards, there is some compensation in planting vineyards near rivers, whose waters help in tempering the climate by bringing a more constant day-night temperature. In addition, mist and fog rise from the rivers during the vintage season and offer some protection from early frosts.

THE WINE-GROWING DISTRICTS OF GERMANY

The major wine river is the Rhein, which flows northward and teems with both commercial and pleasure craft. Progressing along from the Rhein south to north, one comes to the wine-growing districts of Baden, Rheinpfalz, Rheinhessen, Hessische Bergstrasse, Rheingau, and Mittelrhein. Württemberg is a region in the vicinity of the Neckar River, while the Franken district follows the meanderings of the Main River. Both the Neckar and the Main are tributaries of the Rhein. The balance of Germany's wine regions are named for three more tributaries of the Rhein: the Nahe, the Ahr, and the Mosel-Saar-Ruwer—the last being, in itself, a system of rivers.

Despite the fact that the Rheingau is one of the smallest wine-growing regions in Germany, it is considered by most wine experts to be the most prestigious. The much larger Mosel-Saar-Ruwer, however, rivals the Rheingau in prestige and nobility of its vineyards. Both regions contain many vineyards that have yielded superb wines for decades and, in some cases, centuries. In recent years, some wines from the Rheinpfalz, the Rheinhessen, and, especially, the Nahe, have also become popular in American markets.

Nearly 90 percent of all German wines are white and come from a range of different varieties, some of which are restricted to only certain vineyard locales and others of which may be cultivated in any region. With this wide choice available, one would expect a diversity of wine types and styles, especially considering that the average vineyard estate embraces less than 2.5 acres. Nevertheless, most vintners orchestrate only a few varieties, at most, into blends that are subtle variations upon a typical regional theme. In general, the northern regions, principally the Mosel-Saar-Ruwer, the Ahr, and the Mittelrhein, yield wines with a distinctive flowery bouquet with tart, fruity flavors. In the central districts of the Rheingau, the Nahe, and the Rheinhessen, the wines are a bit richer and more complex, with lingering aftertastes. To the south, in the Rheinpfalz and the Baden particularly, the style is more mild, yet these districts also produce heavier-bodied wines with more boldly pronounced and powerful fragrances and flavors.

Without question the great *Johannisberg Riesling*, often called "White Riesling" in California, or just "Riesling," is the most noble grape in Germany. It accounts for about one-fifth of all vineyard plantings in the nation and responds to deficiencies of soil fertility and rainfall with profoundly rich, speckled golden grapes. It is the wines grown from Riesling that garner most of the world's accolades for elegant German wines. The grape, however, is difficult to ripen since it needs lots of sunshine to reach maturity, often more sun than nature provides in West Germany.

At one time *Silvaner* was the most widely cultivated variety in Germany, but today it accounts for less than 10 percent of total vineyard acreage there. Although it ripens considerably earlier than Riesling and produces consistently larger crops, the wine quality of Silvaner has never been rated as high. In 1882, Professor Müller of Thurgau, Switzerland, succeeded in crossing the two varieties in order to achieve a grape with Riesling-like wine richness and Silvaner-like vineyard characteristics. The now-famous *Müller-Thurgau* cultivar has become the most widely cultivated vine in Germany, with more than 25 percent of the German vineyards now planted with it. Other principal grape varieties in the country are *Gewürztraminer*, renowned in the French Alsace, *Ruländer*, known as Pinot Gris in France, and *Spätburgunder*, the very same as Burgundy's Pinot Noir.

THE HISTORY OF WINE GROWING IN GERMANY

The first vine to grow in Germany was probably the *Vitis silvestris*—a native vine dating back much earlier than the Roman introduction of *Vitis vinifera* at the beginning of the Christian Era. Wine was considered a staple by the Romans. Each soldier was allotted, and required to drink, one liter per day. Consequently, great quantities of wine were needed, and the fresh wine from the local environs was much preferred to that which was shipped from the Roman cellars. The Roman settlers were not initially encouraged, and for some time were even prohibited, to plant vines. Because there was a serious grain shortage in Italy and the emperors hoped the new provinces in western Europe would fill that need, the planting of vines was, in many Roman provinces, therefore forbidden. However, the steep hillsides and cliffsides of the Rheinland could obviously never serve as grainfields, and thus it was on these precipitous slopes that the Teutonic natives were first called upon to establish the great vine growths of Germany.

The influence of the Roman occupation lives on in such winemaking terms still used in Germany today as *flasche* (bottle) from the Latin *flasca*, *keller* (cellar) from *cellarium*, and *winzer* (vintner) from *vinitor*, among many others.

From the early 400s to the middle 700s, Goths, Huns, Vandals, and Visigoths laid siege to the German provinces time and time again. As the Roman empire and its once-mighty legions were destroyed, so were cellars, as well as the books, journals, and records of vineyards, wineries, and wines that might have provided a major historical link with the earliest German wine growing.

During the first half of the seventh century, there were many vineyards cultivated in the Rheinland. Among these were the Haslach monastic vineyards situated near Strasbourg, and the Ladenburg vineyards located in the lower Neckar River Valley. The Wissemburg Abbey owned more than a dozen vineyards in Grünnesbrunnen, Lautenbach, and other sites in 644.

In the eighth century, Charlemagne became the driving force for renewing many vineyards in Germany, and he is credited with planting the original "Schloss Johannisberger" vineyard in what is now the Rheingau. Charlemagne brought monks who were educated in the arts of viniculture in other parts of Europe into Germany and charged them with regenerating the once-great wine industry there.

In 843 the Rheinland fell to King Louis the German, and a great cache of wine also fell to the victors. Indeed, the region had come to be known as the "wine cellar of the German empire." During the next several centuries wine growing expanded beyond even the northern limits established today. As might be expected, grapes rarely ripened, and the highly acidic wines that resulted were sweetened with honey and sometimes spiced as well.

The beginnings of such famous present-day vineyards at Geisenheim and Rüdesheim on the north bank of the Rhein River, in what is now known as the Rheingau district, date back to the ninth century. They owe their existence largely to Charlemagne's influence in promoting the use of wine in households at that time. Charlemagne gave land to the German Roman Catholic church (as well as the French Roman Catholic church in Burgundy), and his successors maintained this tradition of benevolence for several centuries. During the Middle Ages, the Catholic church became, by far, the largest single owner of vineyards in Germany, some of these vineyards being then the finest in the land. As a consequence, the Catholic church emerged as a very wealthy entity as well as a very powerful spiritual force.

During the eleventh century a medieval archbishop bequeathed to the Benedictine monks of St. Alban's Priory the *Mons Episcopi*, or "Bishop's Hill," overlooking the Rhein River at the village of Winkel. It was renamed *Johannisberg*, or "St. John's Hill," and eventually became "Schloss Johannisberg"—today the most famous winery in Germany.

The supreme work by the Catholic church in Germany was carried out during the twelfth century at the large vineyard of Steinberg located near Hattenheim and Schloss Johannisberg in the Rheingau. Here, the Cistercian monks created the *Kloster Eberbach*, the most magnificent vineyard in the entire nation. The monks devoted themselves to attaining the highest possible wine quality, but they achieved quantity, too: the abbey warehouse in Cologne grew to hold more than 100,000 gallons and had its own flotilla of barges to carry wines in trade to the British Isles and other markets in Europe.

Another monumental abbey, the *Mühlen Brunnen*, or "Mill Well," was constructed near Speyer by the Knight Walter von Lomersheim in the mid-1100s. It is thought that St. Bernard inspired the project when he visited to preach for the Second Crusade. The great monastery prospered magnificently, eventually acquiring more than 100 vineyard parcels on both sides of the Rhein River. Some experts believe that it was also St. Bernard who brought the classic red Burgundian Pinot Noir vine from France and introduced it to the Kloster Eberbach. It was renamed *Blauburgunder*, and, later, *Spätburgunder*, but, in any event, it did not make good wine in the abbey vineyards. It was taken farther west downriver to Assmannshausen, where it yielded much better quality, and remains today the principal red wine variety in Germany's predominantly white Rheingau wine region.

The medieval wine markets played a very important role in the economic development of the many towns and villages in which they operated, particularly because of the revenue that was generated by different types of vine and wine taxes. During the German Renaissance there was a trend toward developing higher quality wines, which led to many new plantings of Riesling. Unfortunately, the Thirty Years War, fought on Rhenish soil, brought massive destruction once again to vineyards and cellars, as it did to all aspects of life in the Rheinland.

Recovery was slow, and the selection of wine varieties remained for the most part an arbitrary decision. It wasn't until the eighteenth century that the government began to prohibit indiscriminate vine choices.

In 1716 Schloss Johannisberg and all the monastic vineyards of the Rheingau came under the control of the Prince-Abbot of Fulda. The dual title had evolved from the merger of two formerly separate offices—that of the Primate of the Imperial Abbots and the Hereditary Chancellor of the Empire. By 1752 the office had been elevated even further to the level of a Prince-Bishop, and successive monarchs ruled the tiny principality with regal splendor. One of the many duties of the Prince-Bishop was to announce the starting date for the vintage season. A notoriously absent-minded Prince-Bishop forgot the proclamation in 1775, and the fruit on the vines began to shrivel and mold from overripeness. Frantic with worry, the monks of Johannisberg dispatched a courier to Fulda in order to secure permission to commence the harvest. The horseman was held up either by a highwayman or an attractive young lady—the tellers of the story divide nearly equally at this point. In any event, by the time the youth returned, the Schloss's grapes had already rotted with *Edelfäule,* or "noble rot" the very same *Pourriture Noble* of French Sauternes. The monks gathered the moldy fruit and made wine from it, nevertheless; the result, to their surprise, being a magnificent dessert wine. This tradition has lived on. Today such wines are known and revered as the famous *Beerenauslese* and *Trockenbeerenauslese* wines, described in detail later in this chapter.

The ecclesiastical ownership of German vineyards ended with Napoleon's invasion from France. The monastic vineyards were parceled out to private owners. Most of the secular estates became property of the provincial governments, and trade barriers rather quickly arose between the states. By 1834 the German Customs Union did away with all such commercial restrictions in the country, and this created an immediate demand for the better wines, especially those grown from the well-known vineyards of Riesling. Demand for the superior Rheinland and Mosel wines also grew steadily, spurred considerably by a number of exceptionally favorable growing seasons, until the mid-1800s, when demand began to surpass supply. In 1871 Bismarck reclaimed the Alsace from France, and German wine shippers happily added the quality Alsatian wines to their inventories of fine selections, which had greatly diminished.

Germany was, of course, infected along with France by the *Phylloxera* root louse—the first report of the pest's arrival coming from the Rheinpfalz in 1874. Noble and common vineyards alike were completely obliterated. But in the long run not all of the effects were negative. The clearing of old, lower-class vineyard sites provided an opportunity for upgrading vineyards by replanting with American rootstocks, impervious to the *Phylloxera,* and grafting atop fruiting scion wood from improved plant materials.

The nobility of German wine is due, at least in part, to nearly 2,000 years of struggle on the part of German winegrowers. The hard-won fame of German wine continues in modern times, although today dynamic improvements are fostered largely by research—making Germany perhaps second only to the United States in contributing to the improvement of the wine industry through science and innovation.

GERMAN WINE LAW AND NOMENCLATURE

The wine-growing lands of Western Germany are classified into eleven *Gebiete,* or regions. Each region is further divided into *Bereiche* (districts) there being a total of thirty-two Bereiche within the eleven German Gebiete. Within each Bereich there are specific vineyard locales, or parcels, called *Einzellagen,* which may be roughly compared to the *climats* of the Burgundy region in France (see previous chapter). There are more than 2,500 Einzellagen in Germany, and, in some instances, Einzellagen that have similar geographical characteristics are grouped together into what are known as *Grosslagen,* or collective vineyards. Some individual vineyards may be referred to as *Lagen.* Wine-growing villages are known in Germany as *Gemeinden,* and an individual wine-producing estate is called a *Weingut.* Here is an example of how such terms are used to describe a specific wine:

Weingut:	Dr. H Thanisch
Lagen:	Doktor
Einzellagen:	Bernkastel
Bereich:	Bernkastel
Gebeit:	Mosel-Saar-Ruwer

See the end of this chapter for listings of the Gebiete, Bereiche, and Gemeinden.

The West German Wine Law is not addressed to geographical classifications of vineyards as in France, but is designed instead to assure consumers that each stage of the wine-making process has been performed in accord with precise government regulations.

Grapes must contain strictly stipulated degrees of sugar content at harvest in order to legally carry labels designating specific type and quality. Poor weather often leaves grapes unripe, or deficient in the required sugar content, a condition rectified in either case by *chaptalization*—the addition of sugar to the fermenting wine must. This is a practice performed in many of the wine-growing regions of Europe, including the Alsace, Bordeaux, and Burgundy in France. The European authorities, however, strictly regulate the amount of sugar added, permitting only the amount sufficient to achieve minimum alcohol levels from fermentation. Most of the superior growths are not allowed any added sugar.

German winegrowers report grape harvest data to government inspectors who are authorized to inspect vineyards and cellars, as well as the wines themselves.

These inspectors use the results of wine analyses performed at designated testing stations to authenticate specific requirements regarding grades of quality. Under the 1982 West Germany Wine Law there are two categories of wine quality: *Tafelwein*, or ordinary table wine, and quality wine, called *Qualitätswein*.

Tafelwein is the lowest grade of wine produced commercially in Germany. It is legally made in just five regions (Main, Mosel, Neckar, Oberrhein and Rhein) and only from specified grape varieties. Tafelwein never carries a vineyard name on the label and is generally drunk as the everyday wine of Germany. *Deutscher Tafelwein* must be made entirely of German-grown wine, while wine designated merely *Tafelwein* may be a blend of German and European Economic Community (EEC) wines. Wine labeled just plain *wein* may be wine grown and vinified outside the EEC. *Deutscher Landwein*, a new category of Tafelwein, is wine with a bit more character than the ordinary grade, and the label may carry the name of one of the fifteen regions in which it is permitted to grow Landwein. Both Tafelwein and Landwein may be chaptalized.

Qualitätswein is divided into two subcategories: *Qualitätswein bestimmter Anbaugebiete*, or QbA (quality wine of designated regions), and *Qualitätswein mit Pradikat*, or QmP (quality wine with special qualifications). The QbA wines must originate from one of the eleven Qualitätswein regions of Germany and be made from government-approved grape varieties. Further, grapes grown for the QbA wines must have achieved sufficient ripeness each vintage to result in wine that has the typical style of bouquet and flavor that is traditional to the region—although chaptalization is also permitted. It is in the QbA category that the largest quantity of German Qualitätswein wine is made and marketed. The QmP wines, which may not be chaptalized, are wines that exhibit special attributes and distinction. As one would expect, the QmP category is the classification awarded to the very finest wines of Germany.

All Qualitätswein must be tested by the government at a regional analysis laboratory. Following testing, and with final approval, a *Prüfungsnummer*, or national certificate number, is issued to each wine. This number consists of up to eleven digits, for example, 43417141579. The last two digits indicate the application year (79). The preceding three digits (415) denote the serial number given to the vintner's application, and the next three digits (171) reveal the vintner's own code identification. The next two digits (34) disclose the vintner's village code, and the first digit (4) gives the particular inspection station that did the testing.

Each QmP wine *must* also display one of six special distinctions upon the label. These special attributes are addressed primarily to the relative time and ripeness condition of the grapes at harvest. In the following list, these designations are ranked in ascending order of quality:

Kabinett—wines made from grapes harvested at peak ripeness. They must have at least 17.8 degrees Brix (percentage of sugar and other dissolved solids by weight). Finished wines usually contain little, if any, residual sweetness (the name is derived from special wines once reserved in "cabinets" at the Kloster Eberbach).

Spätlese—"late harvest" wines made from grapes harvested at least seven days after peak ripeness and after having reached at least 20.4 degrees Brix naturally in order to enhance organoleptic constituency. They may have some residual sweetness, but they are usually relatively dry.

Auslese—"select harvest" wines made from late harvest grapes of specific variety and origin, each bunch specially selected for superiority. The natural Brix level must be between 21.6 degrees and 30.2 degrees. In exceptional vintages these wines may be infected with Edelfäule (noble mold). They are generally somewhat sweet.

Beerenauslese—means "berry selection." These are wines made from auslese grapes that have reached at least 28.0 degrees Brix. From each bunch, vintners select out by hand individual berries that have been infected with Edelfäule, generally a phenomenon that occurs only several vintages per decade. The finished wines are sweet and expensive.

Trockenbeerenauslese—means "dried berry selection." These wines are made from auslese grapes that have reached at least 36.0 degrees Brix. The individual berries that have been infected with Edelfäule and dried to a raisinlike form are selected by hand from each bunch. These wines are very rare, very sweet, and very, very expensive.

Eiswein—means "ice wine." These wines are made from either fully ripened or overripened grapes that are harvested while naturally frozen and prior to thawing. The finished wines are very concentrated in bouquet, flavor, and sweetness. They are a rarity and very expensive.

There are other designations as well, which may be employed on German wine labels, if the wine qualifies:

Anbaugebiete—Qualitätswein regions: Ahr, Hessische Bergstrasse, Mittelrhein, Mosel-Saar-Ruwer, Nahe, Rheingau, Rheinhessen, Rheinpfalz, Franken, Württemberg, and Baden.

Bereich—district within an Anbaugebiet.

Einzellage—a specific vineyard (estate, family, cloister, etc.).

Erzeugerabfüllung—"estate bottled." The grapes were grown by the same proprietor who vinified and bottled the wine.

Gemeinde—communal or parish vineyard (often cooperatives).

Eiswein (ice wine) grapes ready for harvest. (Source: German Wine Information Bureau.)

Grosslage—a collective site or group of vineyards having similar soil and climatic
  conditions.

Halbtrocken—"half dry." This term may be used on the label providing that the
  wine does not have in excess of 1.8 percent by weight of residual sugar.

Jungferwein—"virgin vintage." The very first wine made from a newly planted
  vineyard; the same as *première vendange* in France.

Liebfraumilch—this term was originally *Liebfrauminch* (*minch* is an old German
  word for "monk"), and, thus, Liebfrauminch was wine belonging to the monks
  of the *Liebfrauenkirche*, or the "church of the loving wife" (St. Mary, mother of
  Jesus Christ). As the language evolved the *n* in *minch* became an *l*, and, hence,
  Liebfraumilch. Some contend that this word originated as *Liebfraumilch* and is
  thus translated as the "milk from the loving mother," but this is not the case.
  The Liebfrauenkirche vineyards surround the Worms church, now known as
  the *Liebfrauenstift*, and yield about 4,000 gallons of wine annually, far less than
  the vast amount of Liebfraumilch marketed each year. Consequently, nowadays any Qualitätswein Rhein wine grown in any Rhein district (Rheingau,
  Rheinhessen, Rheinpfalz, and Nahe) may be labeled Liebfraumilch as long as
  the label displays no other names to indicate a more specific origin. If the wine
  qualifies, Liebfraumilch may also display the special designations *Kabinett* or

Spatlese. The grapes for Liebfraumilch must have at least 14.8 degrees Brix natural sugar content. The names of the grape varieties used in making Liebfraumilch may not be displayed on the label, but the wines must exhibit the character of superior German wine grapes.

May Wine—this is derived from an old German custom called the "mixing of cups," in which a *Bowle*, or "cup", is used to mix convivial drinks. One of these drinks is "May Wine," in which the Bowle is used to blend ordinary light wine and strawberries along with *Waldmeister*, the fragrant woodruff—an herbal plant found growing wild in German forests. The mixture is then sweetened with sugar. (The strawberries may be replaced with peaches or pineapple, or some portion of these and/or other fruits may be mixed together.) Some May Wines are bottled (generally using fruit and woodruff essences), but genuine May Wine is made and consumed fresh from the Bowle during the late spring.

Moselblümchen—translated as "little blooms from the Mosel," this is generally a very inexpensive wine produced anywhere in the Mosel. It is considered only as Tafelwein by the German government.

Sekt—sparkling wine, usually made by the *Charmat* bulk method.

Strohwein—"straw wine." These wines are made from late harvest grapes allowed to dry on straw into a raisinlike form. The finished wines are very sweet.

Trocken—"dry." This term may be used on the label providing that the wine does not have in excess of .9 percent by weight of residual sugar, and residual sugar may not exceed total acidity by more than .2 percent by weight.

Weinbaugebiet—Tafelwein regions: Main, Mosel, Neckar, Oberrhein, and Rhein.

Weinlese—"vintage." If displayed on the label, guarantees that at least 95 percent of that wine was vinified from grapes harvested in the specified year (5 percent is allowed from other years to make up for losses due to evaporation and seepage from casks). Unless a bottle is designated *Erzeugerabfüllung*, the year stated alone without the suffix "-er" (such as "1979-er") only verifies that the wine was *bottled* in that year: it does not necessarily mean that at least 95 percent of the wine was vinified from grapes harvested in the specified year.

The labels of the better German wines will carry the name of the village (usually with "-er" added to the end) and the vineyard name; for example, Bernkasteler Doktor, indicating that the wine comes from the Doktor vineyard of the village of Bernkastel. A wine labeled with a village and vineyard name is likely to be superior to a wine with only a Bereich (district) name. For example, Niersteiner Brudersberg will be finer wine than one labeled simply Bereich Nierstein. It works much like the French system, whereby an appellation St.-Julien (commune name) is superior to an appellation Médoc (district), which in turn is better than an appellation Bordeaux (region).

Some shippers of German wines choose to add still other designations to labels for export wines—often expressed in English due to the large trade with the United States and other English-speaking nations:

Produced & Bottled by—indicates only that the bottler actually produced at least 75 percent of the wine.
Made & Bottled by—indicates only that the bottler actually produced at least 10 percent of the wine.
Bottled at Winery—indicates that the wine was bottled at the same location where it was produced and/or blended.
Blended or Cellared or Prepared or Selected—vague terms, may be essentially meaningless.

German-grown wines that are varietal labeled, that is, indicating upon the label the variety of grape from which the wine was made, must have at least 85 percent of that specific variety as the source of that particular wine.

Typically, German wines are bottled in the tall slender *Schlegelflaschen*, with bottles of amber-colored glass generally used for wines grown in the Rhein regions and green for wines from the Mosel-Saar-Ruwer. The short flagon, or *Bocksbeutel*, is commonly employed for wines grown in the Franken region and occasionally used for Baden wines.

Control and regulation of one sort or another over German wine growing dates back even before the days of Charlemagne. But most of the modern-day regulations have arisen as a result of recent technological advances in quality control and increased sophistication in identifying wine characteristics. Certainly the greatest achievements in accuracy in labeling have taken place since the end of World War II.

To the beginning appreciator of wines, German vineyard names can be rather imposing as regards both pronunciation and meaning. The late Frank Schoonmaker, in his book *The Wines of Germany,* had an excellent suggestion for overcoming this obstacle. He pointed out that if the neophyte would memorize just a few German words and their English translation, he or she could make sense of the vineyard titles. The following list is a start:

Berg	hill
Burg	castle
Dom	cathedral
Garten	garden
Herren	men, lords
Hof	court, manor house

| Kloster | monastery, convent |
| Stück | tract of land |

German vineyard names are quite colorful. They range from the dove (Taubenberg) to the dragon (Drachenstein) and from heaven (Graacher Himmelreich) to hell (Johannisberger Hölle). With a little time and effort devoted to building up this list, one can soon become adept at unraveling the meanings of even the most complicated German vineyard names.

Some of the largest and most well known shippers of fine German wines to the United States are Deinhard, Guntrum, Kendermann, Müller, and Sichel.

BADEN

Baden is the southernmost Qualitätswein region of West Germany. Beginning with the Bodensee at its extreme southeast end, the district proceeds along the north bank of the Rhein westward to the city of Basel, in Switzerland, where the river turns northward. The Baden extends north a total of approximately 250 miles, ending at the borders of the Franken Anbaugebiet. Seven Bereiche and seventeen Grosslagen are to be found in the region.

With a sum of more than 35,000 acres of vineyards, Baden is the third-largest wine region in Germany—and the most varied. Soils cover a range of different consistencies including clay, gravel, limestone, loess, shell-lime, and volcanic stone. Approximately 38 percent of the vines cultivated are Müller-Thurgau; another 13 percent is Rülander; 9 percent are Gutedel; and about 7 percent or so are devoted to Riesling. Red wines from Spätburgunder account for approximately 20 percent of the wine production in Baden. Most Baden vineyards have been replanted during the past several decades in a massive project undertaken with the latest viticultural technology.

Bereiche Bodensee, isolated from the main portion of the Baden, encompasses less than 1,000 acres of vineyards. The specialty of the district is a rosé wine made from Spätburgunder called Weissherbst.

The major share of the Baden vineyards are along the east bank of the Rhein, between Basel and Heidelberg, with the heart of the region between the cities of Freiburg and Karlsruhe. Kaiserstuhl-Tuniberg, situated around an extinct volcano, is the largest Bereiche in this area. The volcanic ash soil has a pronounced effect upon the wine, imparting a distinctively smoky element to the bouquet and a metallic component to the flavor. Other important Bereiche in the Baden heartland are Markgräflerland, Breisgau, and Ortenau.

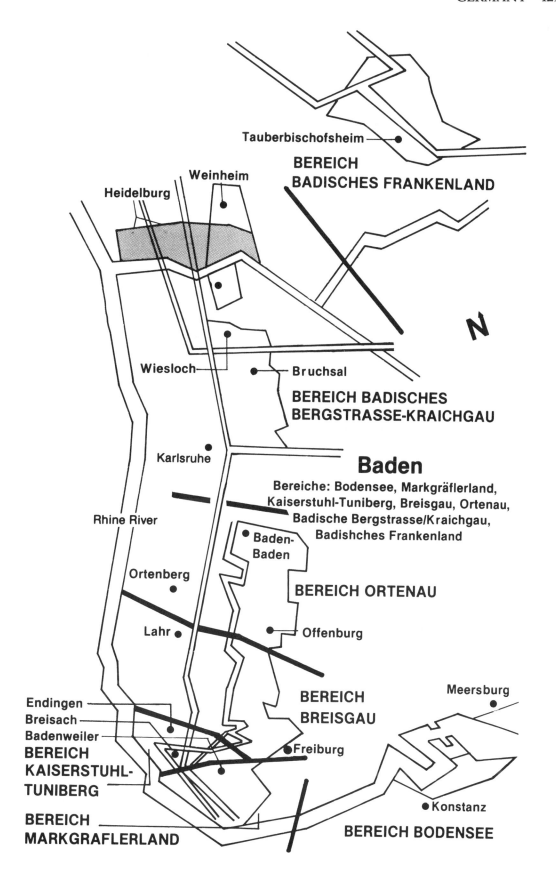

Tauberbischofsheim

BEREICH
BADISCHES FRANKENLAND

Weinheim

Heidelburg

N

Wiesloch — Bruchsal

BEREICH BADISCHES
BERGSTRASSE-KRAICHGAU

Baden

Bereiche: Bodensee, Markgräflerland,
Kaiserstuhl-Tuniberg, Breisgau, Ortenau,
Badische Bergstrasse/Kraichgau,
Badishches Frankenland

Karlsruhe

Baden-
Baden

BEREICH ORTENAU

Rhine River

Ortenberg

Offenburg
Lahr

Meersburg

BEREICH
BREISGAU

Endingen
Breisach
Badenweiler
Freiburg
BEREICH
KAISERSTUHL-
TUNIBERG

Konstanz

BEREICH
MARKGRAFLERLAND

BEREICH BODENSEE

Farther north, bordering the romantic city of Heidelberg, is Bereiche Badische Bergstrasse/Kraichgau, which produces heavy-bodied wines replete with flowery fragrance and good acidity balance.

Situated at the far reaches of the Baden Anbaugebiet is Bereiche Badisches Frankenland, which, as the name suggests, borders the Franken region. The wines of this district are often similar to those of Franken, to the extent that some are bottled in the squat Bocksbeutel bottle.

WÜRTTEMBERG

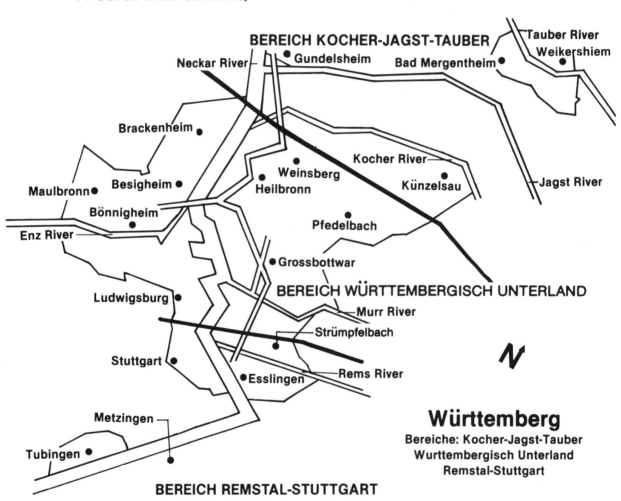

The Württemberg Anbaugebiet is the fifth-largest wine-growing region of Germany, with more than 21,000 acres of vineyards under cultivation. It is located east of Baden on both banks of the Neckar River, which flows into the Rhein at the city of Mannheim. The capital city of the region is Stuttgart, one of the most dynamic industrial centers of the nation.

As in Baden, much of the wine produced in Württemberg is also consumed there—comparatively little is exported. The finest wines of the region, as may be expected, are grown from the classic Riesling, but the *Trollinger* vine is cultivated widely throughout Württemberg and yields distinctive red and rosé table wines. The "Black Riesling," or *Schwarzriesling*, is another important red wine variety of the region; this is the very same vine as the Pinot Meunier of the French Champagne district. Spätburgunder and *Portugieser* are also cultivated in significant acreages.

There are three Bereiche in Württemberg, commencing with Remstal-Stuttgart at the south and proceeding northward downriver to Württembergisch Unterland and finally Kocher-Jagst-Tauber. Cooperatives dominate the great majority of winegrowing throughout the region.

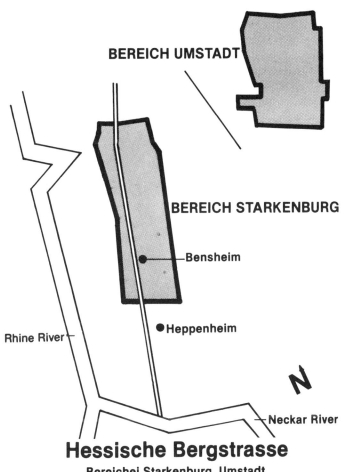

Hessische Bergstrasse
Bereichei Starkenburg, Umstadt

HESSISCHE BERGSTRASSE

With just less than 1,000 acres of vines the Hessische Bergstrasse is the smallest Anbaugebiet in West Germany. The region, which borders the Baden to the north, is nearly surrounded by rivers—the Neckar to the south, the Main to the north, and the Rhein to the west.

The principal grape varieties of the Hessische Bergstrasse are the Riesling and Müller-Thurgau. The former is predominant in the southern Bereich Starkenburg, while the latter is most commonly found in the northern Bereich Umstadt. Within these two Bereiche the tiny region is made up of three Grosslagen—all of which typically produce wines that are full-bodied, fragrant, and somewhat low in acidity. As in Württemberg, most of the wine production in Hessische Bergstrasse is generated by cooperatives, and the greatest share of the yield is also consumed locally.

FRANKEN

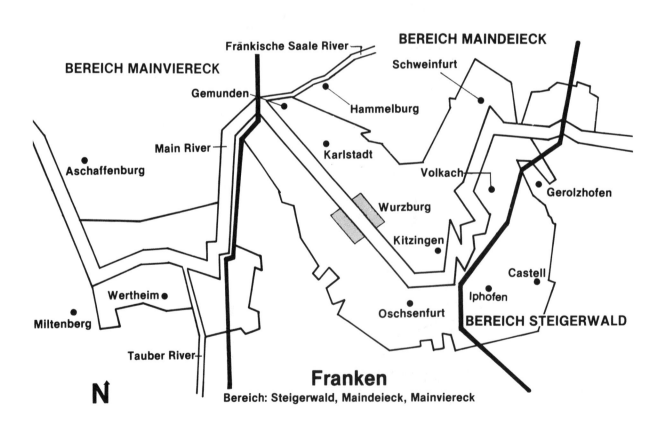

Franken
Bereich: Steigerwald, Maindeieck, Mainviereck

The Franken, about 40 miles east of Frankfurt, is in the northwest corner of Bavaria, where the Main River joins the Rhein. It is the seventh-largest wine-growing region in Germany, and, without question, the most distinctive. Much of the character of Franken wines is due to a climate that typically brings heavy rainfall and bitter cold winters along with early autumn frosts. Consequently, the early-ripening Müller-Thurgau has found great acceptance in the region, now accounting for about half of all vines cultivated there. Silvaner represents approximately 23 percent of all plantings, and the late-ripening Riesling only 2 percent. Another token of Franken's individuality is its traditional Bocksbeutel, the round-bodied flagon in which Franken wines are bottled. Legend says it evolved because it was more easily concealed under the monk's habit than the long Schlegelflaschen employed in the other German Anbaugebiete.

The most western of Franken's three Bereiche is Steigerwald. This is a comparatively small district and grows its vines on predominantly clay soil that some experts say imparts a rather honeylike bouquet and flavor.

There are nine Grosslagen in Bereich Mandreieck, and vineyards are cultivated upon predominantly limestone soils, yielding, in general, the best wines of the entire region. At the center of Bereich Mandreieck is the old Gothic city of Würzburg, the capital city of Franken. The most famous vineyard in this district is the Stein, from which is derived the generic term, *Steinwein*, used by many wine enthusiasts to refer to all Franken wines. Legally, however, only wines grown specifically in the Stein vineyard can be labeled "Stein."

To the far west is Bereich Mainviereck, where sandstone and loam soils yield wines that, in the best vintages, can be powerfully rich and fruity.

RHEINPFALZ

The Rheinpfalz produces more wine annually than any other Anbaugebiet in Western Germany—although its 54,000 acres of vineyards ranks second to the 58,000 acres of neighboring Rheinhessen. It is bordered by approximately 50 miles of the Rhein River to the east and by France to the southwest.

Its name derives from the Roman *palatium* for "palace." This is also the origin of the English name for the region: the Palatinate. During the Middle Ages, the Rheinpfalz was the "Wine Cellar of the Holy Roman Empire." Whatever building an emperor chose for his headquarters during a visit to the region would become a palace, or *palast*, in German. It eventually became modified to *pfalz* and, hence, the "Rheinpfalz."

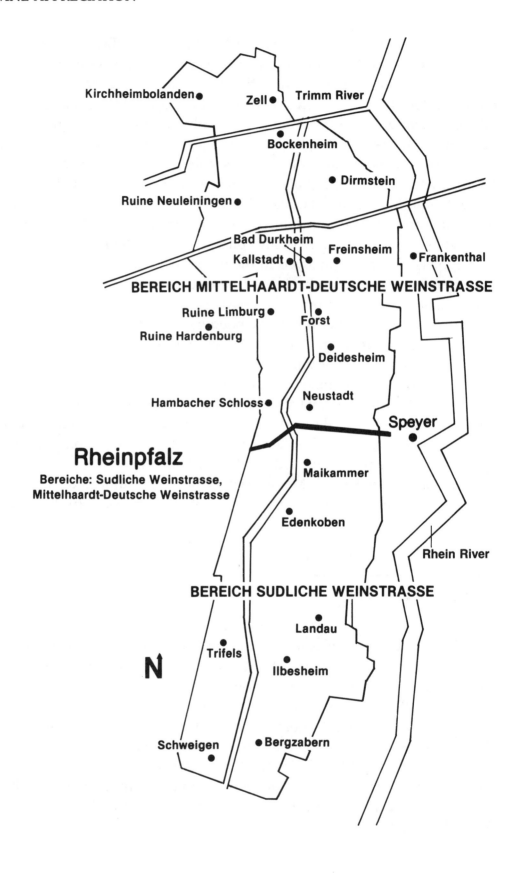

Kirchheimbolanden ●

Zell ●

Trimm River

Bockenheim ●

● Dirmstein

Ruine Neuleiningen ●

Bad Durkheim

Kallstadt ● ● Freinsheim ● ● Frankenthal

BEREICH MITTELHAARDT-DEUTSCHE WEINSTRASSE

Ruine Limburg ●

Forst ●

Ruine Hardenburg ●

● Deidesheim

Hambacher Schloss ● Neustadt ●

Speyer ●

Rheinpfalz

**Bereiche: Sudliche Weinstrasse,
Mittelhaardt-Deutsche Weinstrasse**

● Maikammer

● Edenkoben

Rhein River

BEREICH SUDLICHE WEINSTRASSE

● Landau

N

Trifels ●

Ilbesheim ●

Schweigen ● ● Bergzabern

About one-quarter of all vineyards in the region are devoted to Müller-Thurgau vines, with 14 percent Riesling and 10 percent or less for each of the Silvaner, Kerner, Morio-Muskat, Portugieser, and Scheurebe varieties.

Despite its size, the Rheinpfalz has only two Bereiche. On the southern side is Bereich Südliche Weinstrasse. Wine growing in this historic district has made great strides in modernization due to new plantings and updated wine-making techniques. Much of this progress has resulted from government support and the emergence of cooperative vintners. The Südliche Weinstrasse, once known chiefly for ordinary wines, is achieving growing renown for its fine varietal wines.

The *Deutsche Weinstrasse,* or "German Wine Route," which predates even the Roman occupation, remains a very picturesque landscape guarded by the Haardt Mountain Range. Bereich Mittelhaardt-Deutsche Weinstrasse is the heart of the great Rheinpfalz vineyards, particularly the countryside between Neustadt and Kallstadt. This is where many of the Riesling vineyards are cultivated, and they yield wines that are typically delicate and unassertive with a finesse that attractively matches with many dinner entrées. The town of Wachenheim is the center of this small subdistrict. The village of Forst is located upon a soil of black basalt that exists nowhere else in the country. This soil imparts a coarseness to the Riesling grapes that is perhaps best exemplified by the wines of the most famous vineyard in the area, the Jesuitengarten. Deidesheimer is a name rather commonly found in American wine markets, and with good reason—the village of Deidesheim is one of the largest producers of quality wine in the entire Rheinpfalz. Another notable wine-producing village in the Bereich is Ruppertsberg.

RHEINHESSEN

As mentioned in the previous section, the Rheinhessen has the largest acreage of vineyards in Germany and is the nation's second-largest producer of wines. It is bordered by the Rhein River both to the east and the north and to the west by the Nahe River. The Rheinhessen is a region of rolling hills and valleys in which there is a wide array of soil types, microclimates, and, therefore, of vine varieties cultivated. Approximately 23 percent of Rheinhessen vineyards are planted with Müller-Thurgau; Silvaner makes up about 15 percent. Other significant varieties are Bacchus, Faber, Kerner, Portugieser, Riesling, and Scheurebe.

There are three Bereiche in the Rheinhessen: the southernmost being Bereich Wonnegau. Its name derives from the German word *Wonne,* meaning "bliss." At the ancient city of Worms one finds the famous vineyards of the

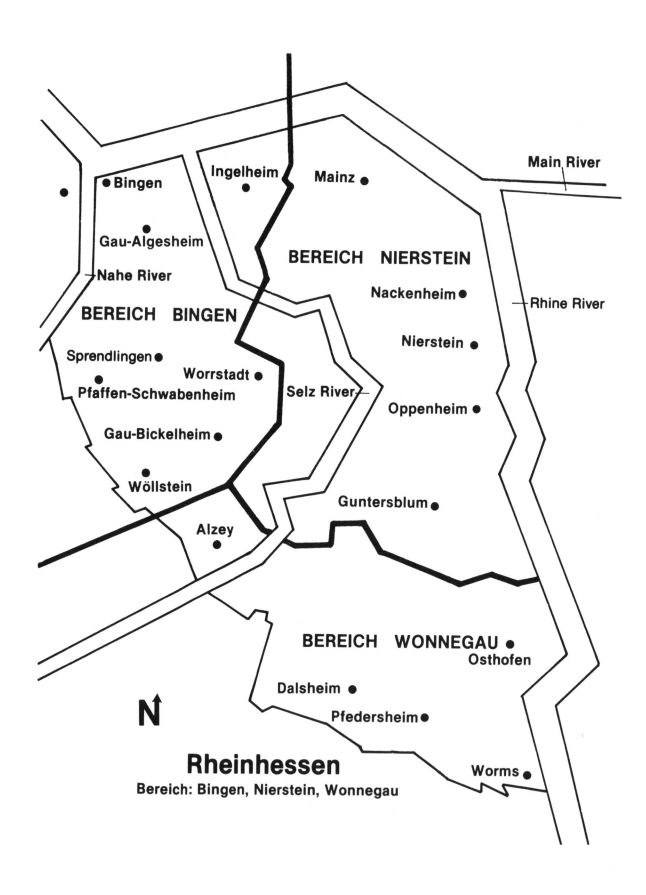

Rheinhessen

Bereich: Bingen, Nierstein, Wonnegau

Liebfrauenkirche—the birthplace of Liebfraumilch. This landmark city also divides the Rheinhessen from the Rheinpfalz. Chalk, loam, marl, sandstone, slate, and other soil types can be readily identified in the area and yield wines that become lighter and fresher as the altitude ascends. The village of Alzey is the center of wine growing in the Wonnegau district.

The finest of Rheinhessen wines are generally considered to originate from Bereich Nierstein. The district, characterized by its red slate soils, extends from Guntersblum north to the ancient city of Mainz.

Mainz has a wine history dating as early as 38 B.C., when Roman soldiers established a camp next to a Celtic community and were rationed wines from Italy. Some twenty-five years later Emperor Augustus's stepson, Drusus, launched his campaign against the Teutons from that headquarters. Mainz eventually became the seat of the Commander in Chief of Germania Superior (upper Germania) and the site of new vineyard plantings.

Up from the riverbanks the hillsides of the Mainz area are fashioned into terraces upon which grapes often ripen to yield very high quality wines—not overpowering, but with both substance and elegant, floral bouquet. One note-worthy village is Oppenheim, known for soft wines from gentle slopes. As the name Bereich Nierstein would suggest, the most important town in the district is Nierstein. Exceptionally fine vineyards in the area are Brückchen, Brudersberg, Hipping, Klostergarten, Kranzberg, and Pettenthal. Niersteiners and Oppenheimers are commonly found in American wine markets.

The wines of Bereich Bingen, not surprisingly, have many qualities in common with the wines grown in neighboring Nahe to the immediate west across the Nahe River. The Bingen slopes impart a full-bodiedness and rich flavor to their wines, which are generally more intense than the products typical of the other Bereiche in the Rheinhessen Anbaugebiet. Of particular note are wines grown at the towns of Scharlachberg and Ingleheim. The latter was once the site of Charlemagne's personal vineyard estate.

NAHE

The 11,000 acres of vineyards in the Nahe rank it sixth among German Anbaugebiete. It borders the Rheinhessen to the east and the Rhein to the north. Most of its vineyards are carved into steep slopes that form the banks of its namesake, the Nahe River. The topography has an austerity that is very picturesque: cliffs, terraces, and small sleepy villages centered on the city of Bad Kreuznach.

The Nahe has two Bereiche—the southernmost is Bereich Schlossböckelheim, surrounding a village of the same name. The slate soils of this district produce wines that recall the green-apple freshness and flowery bouquet of the wines of the Mosel region over the mountains to the west. The most famous vineyard of Schlossböckelheim is the Kupfergrube, which, as the name indicates, was once the site of a copper mine.

Bereich Kreuznach also surrounds its namesake, Bad Kreuznach, an industrial city perhaps better known as the home of Seitz-Werke, the manufacturer of some of the world's finest-quality winemaking equipment and machinery. A spa is also located there that dates back to the Middle Ages. The best vineyards of Bereich Kreuznach yield truly fine wines, which lead some to argue that the Nahe, in this area, serves as the transition between the great wines of the Mosel and the revered Rheingau. The best vineyards are Brückes, the four Kausenbergs, Kahlenberg, Krötenpfuhl and Steinweg.

Hillside vineyards of the Nahe. (Source: German Wine Information Bureau.)

In America consumers can often find wines from the large Anheuser wine estates, which include vineyards in both of the Nahe Bereiche.

RHEINGAU

While only about 3 percent of the total German vineyard acreage falls within the boundaries of the Rheingau, it is nevertheless one of the most important wine-growing districts in the nation. Steeped in a history of vinous excellence, the Rheingau continues to produce some of the world's most aristrocratic wines.

All of the vineyards of the Rheingau lay on the northern side of the Rhein River and are protected from the harsh north winds by the Taunus hills. There are approximately 7,200 acres of vineyards cultivated in the Rheingau—of which 78 percent are planted with the classic Riesling, about 11 percent with the hybrid Müller-Thurgau, and 6 percent with Silvaner. Some red varieties are also grown in the region. The river provides a temperature buffer that aids in protection against frost and also increases the humidity level during the ripening season in autumn, which is necessary for the proper development of the Edelfäule. Soils at the western end of the Rheingau Anbaugebiet are slate rock on steep slopes and evolve farther east to a red schistous consistency near the village of Rüdesheim.

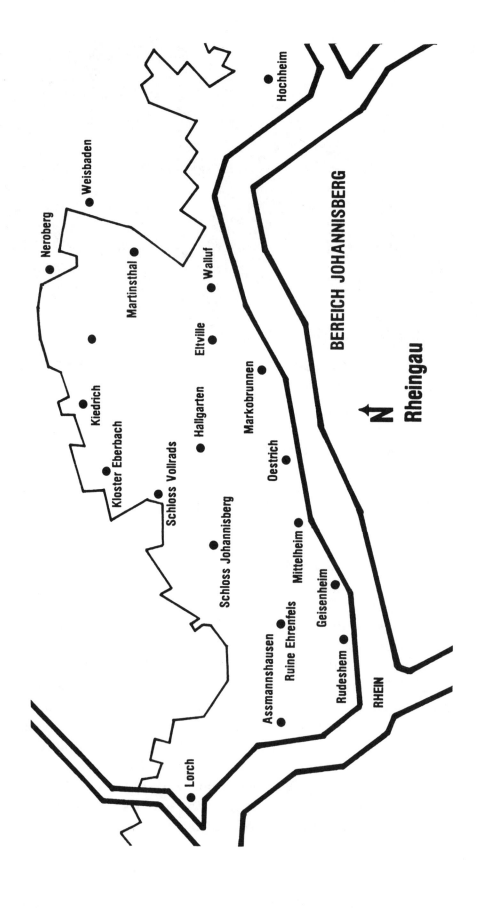

Verband deutscher Prädikats-Weingüter e.V.

Unsere Mitglieder besitzen Lagen von Weltruf!

Vereinigung Rheingauer Weingüter e.V.

SCHLOSS VOLLRADS

Rheingau Riesling
1983er KABINETT
blaugold
Qualitätswein mit Prädikat

Alc. 8,5% by Vol.

Erzeugerabfüllung
Graf Matuschka-
Greiffenclau
Oestrich-Winkel
Rheingau
Produce of Germany
A.P.Nr.
2707401685

e 750 ml

39

BOTTLED AND SHIPPED BY: ABGEFÜLLT DURCH: MIS EN BOUTEILLE PAR:

Gustav Adolf Schmitt

NIERSTEIN · GERMANY · ALLEMAGNE

White wine
Vin blanc

Registered
Trade Mark

WEINBAU
SEIT
1618

Produce of Germany
Produit d'Allemagne
de l'Ouest

1980 Oppenheimer Krötenbrunnen Beerenauslese
Qualitätswein mit Prädikat - A. P. Nr. 4 907 265 138 81
RHEINHESSEN
Light White Rhine Wine - Alcohol 12% by volume
Imported by: G. A. Schmitt & Co., USA, Wakefield, Ma.

750 ml

136 E

Continuing east the earth becomes loess and quartzite, best exemplified by the famous Schloss Johannisberg vineyards.

There are twenty-eight wine villages in the Rheingau, most of which are classic names, well known to connoisseurs of German wines. The region has only one Bereich, that of Johannisberg. It has ten Grosslagen and more than a hundred Einzellagen.

On the upper slopes of Rheingau the village of Rauenthal, about 2 miles north of Eltville, is recognized as an exceptional source of rich aromatic white wines. Superior vineyards are Baiken, Langenstück, and Wülfen. The villages of Kiedrich and Hallgarten also have vineyards that produce fine white Rheingau wines.

Along the riverbank is the village of Erbach, near the village of Hattenheim. Between these two communities is the legendary vineyard of Marcobrunn, named after the *Marcobrunnen* (boundary fountain). For decades a dispute raged over whether the long-lived wines from that vineyard were officially "Erbachers" or "Hattenheimers." In 1971 German authorities pronounced the growth an Erbach. But Hattenheim can console itself with the classic Steinberg vineyards created by Cistercian monks in the twelfth century: these vineyards retain their Hattenheim origin and yield white wines considered by some experts to be among the finest of the country. Two miles to the north is the great Abbey of the Kloster Eberbach, which is 850 years old, immaculate, and a proud monument to its glorious heritage. Both the Steinberg and Kloster Eberbach are properties of the West German State.

One of the most highly revered wine estates in Germany is Schloss Vollrads, which is located near the village of Winkel. The wines are elegant Rheingaus with a fruity tartness that has become the distinctive style of the manor.

To the west is the most glorious of German vineyards, the famed Schloss Johannisberg. Vines extend from in front of the old palace down toward the Rhein River and yield vintages of luscious white wines that are often the most expensive in the nation. Schloss Johannisberg identifies different grades of wine by different colors of capsules used to seal and dress the top of the bottle over the cork. Since Napoleonic times the estate has been owned by the von Metternich family. Both Schloss Vollrads and Schloss Johannisberg are permitted to label their wines with only the name of the estate—a vineyard site is not needed.

Also located in the Rheingau is the little village of Geisenheim, home of Dr. Helmut Becker and his well-known center for research and teaching in viticulture and enology.

Farther west in the region is the village of Rüdesheim, where vineyards are terraced into steep slopes known as the "Rüdesheimer Berg." As would be expected, this very poor soil yields wines of rich color, body, and flavors, the most notable of which are the Einzellogen Bischofsberg, Berg Roseneck, Berg Rottland, and Berg Schlossberg.

Schloss Johannisberg, one of the crowning glories of Germany's vineyards. (Source: Schloss Johannisberg.)

Proceeding toward the western extreme of the Rheingau is Assmannshausen, where the black Burgundian grape, Spätburgunder (Pinot Noir), makes up more than half of the vines cultivated in the village. These red wines are generally considered to be some of the most important grown in the nation.

MOSEL-SAAR-RUWER

The Mosel River runs about half of its entire length in France before becoming the border between Germany and Luxembourg. It then proceeds northward and finally runs as a tributary into the Rhein. It flows in so serpentine a course that it takes about 150 miles to progress less than half that distance as the crow flies. There are four Bereiche in the Mosel-Saar-Ruwer Anbaugebiet: Zell/Mosel, Bernkastel, Obermosel, and Saar Ruwer.

The Mosel-Saar-Ruwer is the fourth-largest wine-growing region in Germany, with just a little over 30,000 acres in cultivation. It produces virtually all white wine, principally from Johannisberg Riesling, which constitutes 56 percent of the vineyards, and Müller-Thurgau, at about 23 percent, along with a significant share of Elbling.

SHIPPED BY DEINHARD & CO. KOBLENZ/RHEIN · GERMANY

MOSEL · SAAR · RUWER

19  83

Bernkasteler Doctor
Riesling Auslese

Qualitätswein mit Prädikat · A. P. Nr. 157628102484

Erzeugerabfüllung · Estate bottled · Gutsverwaltung

Bernkastel-Kues/Koblenz

PRODUCT OF GERMANY   750 ml   MOSELLE WINE
ALCOHOL 9 % BY VOL.

SHIPPED BY DEINHARD & CO. KOBLENZ/RHEIN · GERMANY

MOSEL · SAAR · RUWER

19  83

Wehlener Sonnenuhr
Riesling Kabinett

Qualitätswein mit Prädikat · A. P. Nr. 157628101884

Erzeugerabfüllung · Estate bottled · Gutsverwaltung

Bernkastel-Kues/Koblenz

PRODUCT OF GERMANY   750 ml   MOSELLE WINE
ALCOHOL 9 % BY VOL.

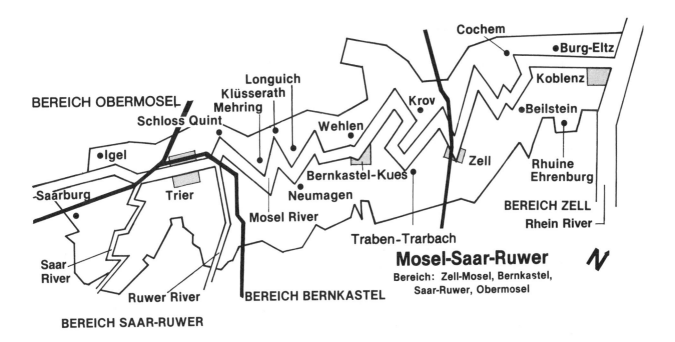

The southwestern portion of the Mosel Anbaugebiet is called the Obermosel, and it is here that the Saar and Ruwer tributaries join the Mosel River. In this region, at Trier, one can see the ruins of the ancient Roman city, a monument to a wine-growing heritage reaching back more than 2,000 years. A combination of calcareous soils with sandstone and slate outcroppings commonly found in the Saar and Ruwer, along with the typically coarse fruit from the predominant Elbling vines, result in good, but somewhat harsh, wines from this district in most years. When the wines are extremely harsh, the winegrowers of the area make what they call, with tongue-in-cheek, *Dreimannerwein,* or "three-man wine": "It takes two men to force a third to drink it!"

Wiltingen produces the finest wines in the Bereich Saar-Ruwer, and Scharzhofberg is another famous wine-growing village in the district.

The Bereich Bernkastel has a breathtakingly beautiful countryside and wines to match; indeed, some of the the finest wines grown in all Germany. The capital city of the district is generally recognized to be Bernkastel, a village with a Brothers Grimm storybook charm and home of the legendary "Bernkasteler Doktor" vineyard. In 1360, the "Doktor" wine was, according to the most widely accepted version of the legend, offered to the seriously ill Archbishop of Trier by winegrower Ritter von Hunolstein. Von Hunolstein was a personal friend of Archbishop Boemund II, and, feeling desperate to help in some way, prepared a bottle of the best wine from his Bernkastel vineyards and managed to get it into the hands of the ailing prelate. The Archbishop skeptically accepted the wine—doubtlessly feeling that all it could do was ease the discomfort of fever and pain. After consuming several glasses, Boemund fell asleep, and, when awakened the next day, proclaimed a full recovery from his illness. He delightedly decreed to all about Von Hunolstein's wine, "this splendid doctor cured me!" Since then, the vineyard has received countless accolades regarding its healing powers. Eventually the property became part of the estate of Dr. H. Thanisch, who is often mistakenly thought to have been the original "Bernkasteler Doktor." Across the river to the southwest is Piesport, home of the famous "Piesporter Goldtröpfchen" wine—the "little drops of gold." The Mosel River at this point has numerous sharp bends in its course, and the very steep mountainside and cliffside vineyards, planted mainly with Riesling on both sides, make an unforgettably austere sight.

Other important vineyard towns of the Bereich Bernkastel are Brauneberg, Erden, Graach, Wehlen, and Zeltingen. Wehlen is well known for its "sun dial" vineyard, the *Sonnenuhr*, named after a sun dial carved in one of its cliffs. The steepest vineyards of the entire Mosel are found at Erden, the most remarkable being the *Treppchen*, or "little stairway." Erdener wines are typically fresh and somewhat spicy and exhibit a certain stoniness. Graacher wines—often very fragrant but light and of good acid-sugar balance—are thought by some to be among the best of the Mosel. Braunebergers and Zeltingens are rich and full-bodied with distinctive bouquet and flavor.

In Zell/Mosel, to the north, the hybrid cultivar Müller-Thurgau is gaining popularity with increased plantings. The riverbanks are not as steep there, and soils gradually become richer as the river nears its confluence with the Rhein at the city of Koblenz. The central town of Zell is the home of the renowned *Kellar Schwarze Katze*. Legend has it that, many years ago, a very superstitious innkeeper from Zell, having farmed all his life with small success, as a last resort turned to growing grapes. During the spring of his new vineyard's first crop year, on a cold and rainy day, a black cat happened through the vines, saw the man, hissed and spat at him, and backpedaled away. The man fell into despair, but his depression slowly lifted as his grapes ripened to perfection and the wine from them was superb. In gratitude, the man promptly named his new enterprise *Kellar Schwarze Katz*, or "Black Cat Cellar." To this day, it is said that no dogs are allowed in the old Electoral Castle Inn in Zell.

MITTELRHEIN

The Mittelrhein begins where the Rheingau ends and proceeds northwesterly some 60 miles to the city of Bonn. It is in the Mittelrhein that the steepest cliffside vineyards in Germany are cultivated, many of which in their precarious situation offer the utmost challenge to the desire to grow wine. A visit to the vineyards of

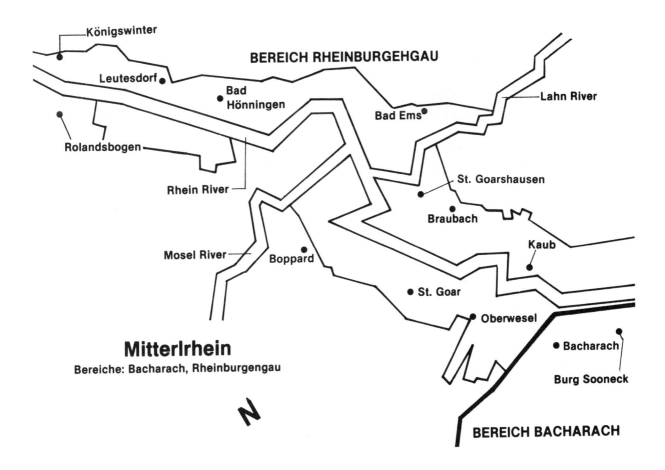

Königswinter

BEREICH RHEINBURGEHGAU

Leutesdorf

Bad Hönningen

Lahn River

Bad Ems

Rolandsbogen

St. Goarshausen

Rhein River

Braubach

Kaub

Mosel River

Boppard

Mitterlrhein
Bereiche: Bacharach, Rheinburgengau

St. Goar

Oberwesel

Bacharach

Burg Sooneck

N

BEREICH BACHARACH

the Mittelrhein is not for the fainthearted, but the region has the attractions of legendary castles and ancient ruins perched upon rocky peaks along with natural scenery of unmatched beauty.

Nearly three-quarters of the vines tendered in the Mittelrhein are Riesling, with 11 percent planted with Müller-Thurgau. The wines of the region are almost always very tart and, when excessively so, are generally marketed in bulk for the production of sparkling wines, which the Germans term *Sekt*.

The most important village in the region is that of Bacharach, although the villages of Boppard, Oberwesel, and St. Goarshausen also have vineyards with either historic value, good quality wine production, or both.

AHR

The most northern of Germany's wine Anbaugebiete is the Ahr, the only region where more red wine is grown than white. Only the Hessische Bergstrasse is

Mittelrhein vineyards at St. Goarshausen. (Source: German Wine Information Bureau.)

smaller than the Ahr, which totals just a bit more than 1,000 acres of vineyards. The vineyards of the region line steep hillsides along both banks of the Ahr River for about 15 miles until it joins the Rhein at Bonn.

Approximately 32 percent of the vines cultivated in the Ahr are Spätburgunder, with another 28 percent devoted to Portugieser. The resulting red wines are light and fruity, and most of them are consumed locally.

TABLE 7-1   The Anbaugebiete, Bereiche, and Principal Wine-Growing Villages of Germany

AHR	Markgräflerland
	Auggen
Walporzheim	Ehringen
Bad Neuenahr	Efringen-Kirchen
Remagen	
	Kaiserstuhl-Tuniberg
BADEN	Achkarren
	Ihringen
Bodensee	
Meersburg	Breisgau

Glottertal
Lahr

Ortenau
 Baden-Baden
 Durbach
 Neuweier
 Ortenberg

Badische Bergstrasse/Kraichgau
 Karlsruhe
 Weingarten
 Weinheim
 Weisloch

Badisches Frankenland
 Tauberbischofsheim

FRANKEN

Mandreieck
 Dettelbach
 Gemünden
 Hammelburg
 Karlstadt
 Kitzingen
 Ochsefurt
 Sommerhausen
 Volkach
 Würzburg

Mainviereck
 Grossostheim
 Hörstein
 Wertheim

Steigerwald
 Abtswind
 Castell
 Frankenberg
 Iphofen
 Rödelsee
 Zeil

HESSICHE BERGSTRASSE

Starkenburg

Bensheim
Heppenheim

Umstadt
 Zwingenburg

MITTELRHEIN

 ·
Bacharach
 Bacharach
 Niederheimbach

Rheinburgengau
 Bad Ems
 Boppard
 Braubach
 Kaub
 Königswinter
 Hammerstein
 Oberwesel
 St. Goarshausen
 St. Goar

MOSEL-SAAR-RUWER

Bernkastel
 Bernkastel-kues
 Detzem
 Graach
 Kröv
 Longuicher
 Neumagen
 Piesport
 Reil
 Traben-Trarbach
 Wehlen

Obermosel
 Igel
 Mesenich

Saar-Ruwer
 Trier
 Wiltingen

Zell/Mosel
 Cochem

Koblenz
Winningen
Zell

NAHE

Kreuznach
  Bad Kreuznach
  Langenlonsheim
  Wallhausen

Schlossböckelheim
  Meddersheim
  Niederhausen
  Schlossböckelheim

RHEINGAU

Johannisberg
  Assmannshausen
  Eltville
  Geisenheim
  Hallgarten
  Hattenheim
  Hochheim
  Kiedrich
  Oestrich
  Marcobrunn
  Rauenthal
  Rüdesheim
  Winkel

RHEINHESSEN

Bingen
  Bingen
  Gau-Bickelheim
  Ingelheim
  St. Johann
  Worrstadt

Nierstein
  Albig
  Alsheim
  Bodenheim (Mainz)
  Guntersblum

Nierstein
Oppenheim

Wonnegau
  Alzey
  Bechtheim
  Hohen-Sülzen
  Osthofen
  Westhofen
  Worms

RHEINPFALZ

Südliche Weinstrasse
  Bad Bergzabern
  Eschbach
  Godramstein
  Maikammer
  Schweigen
  St. Martin
  Walsheim

Mittelhaardt-Deutsche Weinstrasse
  Bad Dürkheim
  Bockenheim
  Deidesheim
  Forst
  Freinsheim
  Kallstadt
  Kirchheim
  Neustadt
  Ungstein
  Zell

WÜRTTEMBERG

Kocher-Jagst-Tauber
  Criesbach
  Gundelsheim
  Weikersheim

Remstal-Stuttgart
  Grossheppach
  Metzingen
  Schnait
  Stetten

Württembergisch Unterland
  Abstatt
  Besigheim
  Grossbottwar
  Harsberg

Heilbronn
Lauffen
Vaihingen/Enz
Weinsberg

FATTORIA DELLA
AIOLA
CHIANTI CLASSICO

DENOMINAZIONE DI ORIGINE CONTROLLATA

1978

IMBOTTIGLIATO ALL'ORIGINE DAL DOTT. G. MALAGODI
NELLA FATTORIA DELL'AIOLA-VAGLIAGLI-ITALIA

NET. CONTENTS 750ml.   R.I. 73/SI   ALCOHOL 12.5% BY VOL.
PRODUCT OF ITALY   RED WINE

SOLE AGENT: PATERNO IMPORTS CHICAGO, IL

8

THE WINES OF
ITALY

The Italian mainland totals about 116,000 square miles—an area just slightly larger than the State of Arizona. Within this comparatively small geographical region, the Italians often produce more than two billion gallons of wine annually, more than four times the total volume of wine produced in the United States each year. Italian vineyard acreage is approximately four million acres. About three-quarters of the Italian wine produced is also drunk in Italy, which leads the world in per capita wine consumption, the current figure being approximately 30 gallons per person per annum.

The Italian peninsula reaches from the thirty-seventh to the forty-seventh parallels of north latitude, stretching from the Alps to within a few miles of Africa. Much of the terrain is austere and mountainous—the Alps, along with the Dolomites form the northern border, while the Apennines divide almost the entire length of the country. In the northern provinces that border France, Switzerland, Austria, and Yugoslavia, the winters are cold and summers hot, though the climate is somewhat tempered by the Alpine barriers to the north winds and the waters of glacier-formed lakes. South of the Po River the climate takes on a more temperate character, with warmer winters and cooler summers; the wines seem to exhibit the same character: they tend to be subtle, without the distinctiveness of the wines grown in the upper Italian vineyards. In southern Italy the climate is typically Mediterranean, with warm winters and very hot and humid summers, resulting in many wines that are strong and rather common. There are few places in Italy where vineyards do not constitute the major share of the agricultural enterprises. In Italy the vine is cultivated virtually everywhere,

453

whether it be the coastal plains, the plateaus, or upon the mountainsides. About 30 percent of the national work force in Italy is employed exclusively in vineyards, most of which are owned by farmers in parcels that average less than 3 acres each.

Italy's diversity of climates is matched by a diversity of soils from one region to another. The result is a wider range of wine types than most other countries offer, with variation even within individual regions. There are also many different varieties of the vine grown in Italy. Some are grown just regionally; for example, Barbera, Cabernet Sauvignon, Dolcetto, Freisa, Merlot, Nebbiolo, and Pinot Noir are each limited to a single region. Others, such as Malvasia, Moscato, Sangiovese, Trebbiano, and Verdiccio are planted in two or more regions.

There are nearly 200 different types of Italian wine recognized officially by controlled denominations (see explanation of DOC below). Such wines make up less than 10 percent of the 2 billion-gallon annual production. It is, however, from this small portion that most of the wines reaching American retailers and restaurants are grown.

The largest export markets for Italy's wines are Germany, Switzerland, the United States, the United Kingdom, and France. The major share of these exports are shipped to wine-blending houses in Germany and France for the production of low-cost, high-volume products. More Italian wine is imported into the United States than French, German, Portuguese, and Spanish wine imports combined.

THE HISTORY OF WINE GROWING IN ITALY

There are records of Italian wine growing that predate Rome, although, of course, the most fully documented history of Italian wines begins with the Roman Empire. Rome spread the science and art of viticulture throughout what is now Western Europe.

The many writings of Cato the Elder, Columella, and Pliny the Elder, among others that have come down through history, portray an Italian wine-growing art that was remarkably advanced even before the emergence of Christianity. There is considerable evidence to suggest that the Roman vineyards of 2,000 years ago were quite similar to some of those in modern Italy. University of Maryland archaeologists have excavated an ancient vineyard from beneath the volcanic debris at Pompeii, the ancient Roman city destroyed by eruption of Mount Vesuvius in 79 A.D. They discovered that vines were planted about 4 feet apart and trained onto chestnut, poplar, and willow trellis stakes, with several hollows at the base of each vine to collect and hold rainwater. Such cultivation practices are still employed in many Italian vineyards today. The citizens of ancient Pompeii enjoyed outdoor restaurants and wine retail shops. A typical wine merchant would provide tables and seats for customers and display his wines on shelves where cups and glasses also were stored. The wine "bartender" would pour and serve wines from a countertop that faced the street.

The Dark Ages, which followed the fall of the Roman Empire, were an era in Italy when very little was chronicled; some feel that perhaps wine growing ceased to exist there for several centuries, since it is not until the ninth century that there are indications that the Italians resumed the culture of the grape. It was during this period that Greek-speaking refugees from the Byzantine conquest of Greece founded the Greco di Gerace—a beautiful cathedral and the largest in Calabria. These refugees grew the fabled *Greco di Gerace* white wine on soils so poor that often two vines had to struggle to yield just one bottle.

Greco di Tufo, also white, and one of the lightest of Italian wines, has early origins similar to the headier Greco di Gerace. Both wines have their roots in the

Roman statue of goddess of Ebe at Trento. (Source: Flavio Fuganello, Italian Wine Promotion Center.)

Catholic church: Greco di Tufo comes from the hermitage of St. William, built high upon Monte Vergine in Campania during the eleventh century, which to this day is still under Benedictine rule.

In 1282, a Florentine wine merchants' guild was formed—perhaps the first such regulatory body for marketing wines, and unquestionably the ancestor of the modern-day *consorzi* (see below) that operate throughout Italy.

Most of the wine produced in Italy during the Middle Ages was consumed there, although there are some fourteenth- and fifteenth-century records of northern Italian wines being shipped to England. Even so, there is little evidence that the Italian wine-growing industry was being rebuilt with any enthusiasm or even much effort during the Middle Ages or through the Renaissance; although, curiously, very elaborate glassware for wine service developed in Italy in the sixteenth and seventeenth centuries. It was not until the mid-1700s that Italian wine growing began to attract agricultural scholars. Even then, another century or more passed before any improvement in wine products became noticeable. Cyrus Redding, a British wine enthusiast, wrote of his experiences during an 1850 trek

Medieval Italian fresco of the grape harvest and pressing, from the Castello Buon Consiglio in Trento. (Source: Flavio Faganello, Italian Wine Promotion Center.)

through Italian wine country that "Italian wines have stood still and remain without improvement."

In the early 1930s the consorzio system was introduced in Italy. An Italian governmental decree authorized the creation of local winegrowers associations or leagues called *consorzi* (consortiums), each with its own constitution designed to regulate wine production and marketing in that particular locale. The consorzi created geographical limits and production standards and authorized district names of origin that had real meaning. The consorzi also enforced national regulations and promoted Italian wine exports. This was the first national effort to regulate Italian wines and to formulate definitions and standards.

The consorzio system had several early problems, including the differences in the individual constitutions from region to region, and renegade vintners who refused to acknowledge parts or all of the authority. Yet in spite of the difficulties, the consorzi were the first step toward organizing the then-vast and chaotic vineyards of the nation.

DENOMINAZIONE DI ORIGINE CONTROLLATA (DOC)

In 1963, the Italian government issued the Italian Wine Law that set up the basis for wine industry control according to the principles endorsed by the European Economic Community (EEC). This comprehensive wine statute, modeled closely on the French Appellation Contrôlée laws, specifically defines areas of production, designates the grape varieties that may be grown in the various regions, and regulates wine quality. The Italian wine decree is known as the DOC statute—DOC stands for Denominazione di Origine Controllata, which means "controlled appellation of origin."

The original law established three different grades of wines: wines of the lowest grade were designated *Denominazione di Origine Semplice*. Wines in this category originated within specified areas, but the production methods were not defined. This grade was subsequently replaced by the EEC grade *Vino da Tavola* (table wine).

The next grade up, and the most well-known, is the *Denominazione di Origine Controllata*, usually abbreviated DOC on wine labels. In order to qualify for this category, the wines must conform to production rules laid down for each particular region of origin. The regulations for DOC wines also govern bottling, alcohol levels, and aging requirements. A DOC wine will carry the initials DOC on a red label affixed to the bottle. A national twenty-eight-member committee of both industry and government officials considers applications from vintners for DOC recommendation. Upon the committee's advice, the applications are processed by the Ministries of Agriculture, Commerce, and Industry and eventually DOC status is conferred by presidential appointment. In order for a table wine to receive the DOC seal, at least 20 percent of the vineyards in the region must meet the standards and be endorsed. For dessert and sparkling wines, 30 percent is required.

The highest category is *Denominazione di Origine Controllata e Garantita*, or DOCG, which means that the appellation of origin is controlled and guaranteed. This designation is reserved for wines of the highest distinction. At present there are only four such wines: *Barolo* and *Barbaresco* from the Piedmont and *Brunello di Montalcino* and *Vino Nobile di Montepulciano* from Tuscany.

Depending upon the region involved and the assigned category, Italian wines may be geographically designated with the name of a large region such as *Chianti*, or a district such as *Asti,* or a village such as *Montalcino*. Wines may also be named for the sole or primary grape variety used in their production, but, if they are DOC designated, then they must also carry the name of the place where the grapes were grown, such as *Nebbiolo d'Alba*, where Nebbiolo is the grape and Alba the place-name.

The term *Classico* on a label signifies that the wine was grown from an inner, and superior, portion of a larger region: for example, *Chianti Classico* is the choice inner district of the Chianti region of Tuscany. When the DOC seal is approved, other terms of identification may also appear on the Italian wine label, terms such as *imbottigliato* (bottled) in *zona d'origine* (in the growing area), *nello stabilimento* (on the producer's property) or *tenuta* (estate). A number of other terms also commonly appear on labels. The *vendemmia* (vintage) is usually revealed by the *annata* (year). Wine descriptive terms are also allowed, such as *riserva* (reserve), *vecchio* (old), and *superiore* (superior in age and alcohol strength), but these have different levels of meaning depending on the region and vintner. White wines are *bianco*, reds are *rosso*, rosés are *rosato*, dry is *secco*, and *dolce* means sweet. *Abboccato* means "slightly sweet." Sparkling wines are called *spumante* in Italian, and wines made from dehydrated grapes are known as *passito*.

Finally, if the vintner is a consorzi member, a paper seal is placed over the closure or capsule of the bottle, which indicates membership in a particular consorzio.

Wines are grown all over the Italian peninsula, with each region producing its distinctive varieties and styles. Though the northern Italian provinces of the Piedmont, Veneto, and Tuscany are generally regarded as the leaders in quality wine production, fine wines may be found in almost every part of Italy. Some of the most popular names of importers and shippers of Italian wines in U.S. markets are Bolla, Buckingham Wile, Garneau, International Vintners (Heublein), Paterno, Renfield, and Villa Banfi.

The following is a discussion of the primary wine regions of Italy.

PIEDMONT

Piemonte means, literally, the "foot of the mountain." Many wine experts consider the region one of the finest wine districts in all of Italy. The province, which is located in the far northwestern corner of the country at the foot of the Alps, surrounds its principal wine city of Asti, southeast of Turin (Torino).

The Piedmont is most famous for red table wines from Barbera and Nebbiolo grapes and for white wines, both of the table and sparkling types, made from several Moscato varieties. Annual production is about 115 million gallons, which ranks it seventh-largest of Italy's provinces. The Piedmont is also the home of the first commercially produced aperitif wines, sold out of Torino during the late eighteenth century. Today the well-known Italian sweet vermouth is made by infusing a base wine with different barks, herbs, and spices—the secret recipe of Cinzano is said to be made of no less than ninety-two such ingredients.

Two of the most important wines in Italy—Barolo and Barbaresco—are made in the Piedmont from the Nebbiolo grape. Barolo, the best known of the two, from the district of the same name, usually needs rather extensive aging in both cask and bottle;some vintages can last for decades. Barbaresco, grown in a neighboring area, is softer than Barolo and usually has less body and slightly less color. Both Barolo and Barbaresco are in the DOCG category. No fewer than thirty-six DOC-classified wines are grown in the Piedmont region; they are listed in a table at the end of this chapter. *Gattinara* and *Ghemme* are made from Nebbiolo wines blended with wines from other varieties grown in the region. These are generally considered somewhat inferior to Barolo and Barbaresco, but still better than the simple varietal Nebbiolo wines, the best known of which is *Nebbiolo d'Alba.*

Though the Nebbiolo grape is the more highly regarded, the famous Barbera grape is far more widely planted in the Piedmont. Wines made from Barbera are normally dry, fruity red table wines—dark and somewhat astringent. *Barbera d'Asti* is one of the wines of the type most frequently found in the marketplace. The variety is also made into somewhat sweet wines, as well as *frizzante* (semi-sparkling) wines.

Grignolino, Freisa, and Dolcetto are other varieties of grapes that yield notable red wines in the Piedmont. Grignolino typically produces light, dry red wines,

On the hillsides of the Piedmont, trellises supported on stone pillars provide maximum sun and warmth to the prized Nebbiolo grapes. (Source: Italian Wine Promotion Center.)

while the more widely cultivated Dolcetto is a bit more flavorful and full-bodied. Some authorities say they detect a nose of violets in superior wines from the Freisa. Three good examples of these are *Grignolino d'Asti, Dolcetto d'Alba,* and *Freisa di Chieri.*

Asti Spumante, one of the best-known Italian sparkling wines in American markets, is made from the Moscato grape—thought by most viticultural experts actually to be several slightly different Muscat varieties. Virtually all Asti Spumante is made by the *Charmat,* or bulk process. Asti vintners also employ the Moscato in making semisweet white table wines.

VAL D'AOSTA

Located north of the Piedmont, and in the extreme northwestern corner of Italy, the Val d'Aosta is the smallest viticultural region in Italy, perhaps more famous for ski resorts than wine growing. The snow-capped Alps rise high above the hillside vineyards along the Aosta Valley. The comparatively small yield of richly concentrated Nebbiolo grapes is made into a wine called *Donnaz*, a rather harsh almond-flavored wine that is the best known in the region. Petit Rouge grapes are grown at higher elevations and produce *Enfer d' Arvier*. Both Donnaz and Enfer d'Arvier are DOC-classified wines.

LIGURIA

To the south of the Piedmont in the Italian Riviera is the Ligurian wine-growing region. While it may not be the most important wine producer in Italy, Liguria is surely one of the country's most picturesque. At its center is the historic port of Genoa, and in the southern portion of La Spezia, growers have carved vineyards into the cliffs, many of which can only be reached by boat. Between the cliffs and the sea a delicate dry white wine called *Cinqueterre* is made—the name refers to the five villages that are located there. Cinqueterre is made from blends of Albarolo, Bosco, and Vermentino grapes and is DOC classified.

Dolceacqua, a soft, dry red wine, sometimes called *Rossese di Dolceacqua*, is another DOC wine grown in the Liguria region.

LOMBARDY

The Lombardy region, located northeast of the Piedmont, is one of the largest districts in Italy. The region surrounds its capital city of Milan. In the northern portion of the province is the Adda River, which flows through the Valtellina: a basin of principally Nebbiolo vineyards that produces some of the most famous red wines of the region. Most of the wines of the Valtellina are named after subdistricts, and the vineyards, many of them part of beautiful landscapes, rise up the hillsides into the Alps to an altitude over 2,500 feet above sea level. Of highest regard are the subdistricts of Grumello, Inferno, and Sassella. *Sfursat* is a very heavy-bodied red wine made from partially dried grapes grown in the Valtellina.

In the Pavia area within the southern heart of the Lombardian wine-growing region is situated the Oltrepò Pavese district. The red wines of Oltrepò Pavese have been internationally famous for centuries.

A rather dark rosé called *Chiaretto del Garda* (*Chiaretto* means *claret*) is made from Gropello grapes grown on the southwestern shores of Lake Garda, which borders the region of Veneto.

The DOC list (see the table at the conclusion of this chapter) includes thirteen Superior Growths.

VENETO

The Veneto, with annual output of some 250 million gallons, ranks third in the volume of wine produced by an Italian province. Veneto is situated between the Piave and Po rivers and Lake Garda. Lake Garda is a very popular resort area in northern Italy. To the north it is a mountainous region, but it flattens to the southeast as it approaches its capital, Venice.

The region has been awarded fifteen DOC wines, of which several are world famous. One of the most well-known Veneto wines is *Bardolino,* a red table wine grown from Corvina and Molinara vines, often blended with Rondinella and other grapes. Minimum alcohol allowed by regulation is 11.5 percent. Bardolino is grown within a group of sixteen communes in the province of Verona on the southeastern shores of Lake Garda. Six of these communes form the inner Bardolino Classico district. Bardolino must be aged in provincial cellars for at least one whole calendar year before being labeled as Bardolino Superiore. Some vintners also make frizzante Bardolinos.

Another of the fine Veneto wines is *Valpolicella,* which hails from vineyards grown on the hillside facing the Adige River to the east of Bardolino. Valpolicella is blended from essentially the same varieties as Bardolino and is grown in nineteen communes, five of which have been awarded the Valpolicella Classico title. Wines grown exclusively in the Valpantena Valley may also add the Valpantena name to their labels, for example, *Valpolicella Valpantena. Recioto della Valpolicella* is made from grape berries that ripen only on the outside of the bunch—those choice berries that receive the most exposure to the sun. Such production is much more controlled than the standard Valpolicella. The minimum alcohol strength required for Valpolicella is 12 percent and, if aged for at least one year like Bardolino, it may be labeled *Valpolicella Superiore.*

A very fragrant white table wine is made from the Prosecco grape, grown in the hills around the village of Conegliano, north of Venice. The Veneto also produces many fine reds from Cabernet Sauvignon and Merlot; vintners characteristically add a local name to the grape varietal such as *Cabernet di Pramaggiore* and *Merlot di Montello.*

RICASOLI™

SOAVE

DENOMINAZIONE DI ORIGINE CONTROLLATA

ITALIAN LIGHT DRY WHITE WINE

IMBOTTIGLIATO NELLE CANTINE DI GAIOLE IN CHIANTI DALLA

CASA VINICOLA BARONE RICASOLI

FIRENZE - ITALIA

750 ML   ALCOHOL 11.5% BY VOL.

PRODUCT OF ITALY

IMPORTED BY BROWNE VINTNERS CO.
NEW YORK, N.Y.
SOLE DISTRIBUTORS IN THE U.S.A.

VALPOLICELLA

CLASSICO

SUPERIORE

RUFFINO

750 ml - e   SCHIEFFELIN & CO. · NEW YORK   Alc. 12%
(25.4 fl oz)   IMPORTERS   SOLE U.S.   by vol.
                  SINCE 1794   DISTRIBUTORS

Located about 12 miles east of Verona is the small town of Soave, which gives its name to the fine white wine that is made there. The grape varieties Trebbiano (Ugni Blanc) and Garganego are grown upon soils that are primarily of clay. *Recioto di Soave,* like the Recioto della Valpolicella, is made from the outer berries of each bunch of grapes and is also restricted in production in much the same manner. *Soave Classico* and *Soave Superiore* wines are controlled in similar fashion to Bardolino and Valpolicella.

In the Euganean hills of the Padua province there are vineyards that are more than 1,000 years old. Seventeen communes there produce white and red wines called *Colli Euganei.*

TRENTINO-ALTO ADIGE

The Trentino-Alto Adige is the most northern of the Italian regions and is better known to some as the Italian Tyrol. As the Alsace is a bit of Germany in France, so

Terraced vineyards in the Trentino region (Dolomite mountains in background). (Source: Italian Wine Promotion Center.)

the Trentino-Alto Adige is an Alpine region of Italy reminiscent of Austria and Switzerland. Viticulture in the region dates back to ancient times, to the very formation of the Roman Empire; then, as now, parts of the Adige Valley from below Trento to Bolzano and Merano were literally covered with vineyards. The Alps provide a barrier for the Adige vineyards—protecting them from harsh temperatures and winds from the north.

The wines, like the region itself, recall Austria and Germany. One notable area of white wine production from Pinot Bianco (Pinot Blanc), Gewürztraminer, and Johannisberg Riesling vines is the village of Terlano.

Red wines from the upper part of the region, approaching Bolzano, are a bit astringent, but usually well balanced. Lago di Caldaro is one highly regarded red wine area, as is Santa Maddalena.

The lower valley, the Trentino, cultivates vineyards of the Teroldego grape, which yields heavy red table wines of the same name—usually with a bitter, rather nutty aftertaste. Cabernet Sauvignon, Moscato, Pinot Noir, and Johannisberg Riesling are also grown in the Trento vicinity. *Casteller* is a noted, rather dense rosé that is grown in the lower valley and is DOC classified—one of the eleven DOC wines assigned to the entire region.

FRIULI-VENEZIA GIULIA

In this comparatively small district on the Adriatic Sea in northeastern Italy bordering Yugoslavia and Austria, wine has been grown for so long that no one can be really sure when wine growing commenced—certainly long before the birth of Christ.

Collio, a small locale west of Gorizia, produces mostly white table wines, but some sparkling whites are also entitled to the DOC *Collio Goriziano* distinction. The principal grape varieties grown are Ribolla, Malvasia, and Tocai. These and other varietal names, such as Pinot Bianco, Pinot Nero (Pinot Noir), and Traminer, can be added to the DOC Collio Goriziano entitlement provided the wine bearing that designation has been made exclusively from the variety named on the label.

EMILIA-ROMAGNA

The Emilia-Romagna, which borders Lombardy and Veneto to the south, has the second-largest volume of wine production of any region in Italy, with nearly

280 million gallons made each year. Most of the wine from this region is also consumed there, although there is one remarkable exception—that of *Lambrusco*. *Lambrusco di Sorbara* is a rather frizzante, semi-dry red wine with a bouquet that some say is reminiscent of violets, like the Friesa wines from Piedmont. It must have an alcohol content of at least 11 percent to be so labeled and is grown in ten communes in the province of Modena. Other wines, made chiefly from Sangiovese and Trebbiano grapes, are also grown and shipped from the Emilia-Romagna. Principal among these are *Trebbiano di Romagna*, grown near Forli, Ravenna, and Bologna. Albana grapes yield white table wines of the same name grown from northern vineyards upon the slopes of the Apennines. There are twelve DOC-classified wines in the Emilia-Romagna.

TUSCANY

Tuscany, located directly south of Emilia-Romagna, is considered by many wine authorities to be the single most important region in Italy, and, perhaps even more significant, the most characteristically Italian.

The Etruscans cultivated vineyards in Tuscany during the ninth century B.C. The Romans who followed them advanced the wine-growing arts, and, during and after the fall of the Roman Empire, the Christians advanced them even further. During the Middle Ages various factions in Florence and Siena fought bitterly for control of the Tuscan wine-growing regions. Florence, the beautiful capital of Tuscany, was also the city where the Renaissance first flowered.

Tuscany was home to Catherine de' Medici; it was she who carried haute cuisine to France following her marriage to Henry II and taught the French how to use a fork at the table. Tuscany was also the birthplace of Amerigo Vespucci, Leonardo da Vinci, Machiavelli, and Giovanni da Verazano. It was in Tuscany where Michelangelo worked, as did Galileo, and many other noted geniuses in the arts, crafts, and sciences. Wine, along with olive oil, was, and still is, the most important agricultural product of the region.

Tuscany, which borders the Emilia-Romagna to the south, cultivates some very famous and noble growths, as well as some that are only ordinary. The wines of the province have been grown for centuries upon the hills and open countryside vineyards that surround the Tuscan villages and cities—some vines are grown even within city walls. There are thirteen DOC wines classified in Tuscany, of which two have been elevated to DOCG status (see below).

Perhaps the best known of all Italian wines is *Chianti*, a dry everyday red wine grown primarily from Sangiovese vines. In recent years the Tuscans have had difficulties establishing precise boundaries for the Chianti region as well as for *Chianti Classico,* the central district. Chianti Classico wines must have an alcohol content of at least 11.5 percent, and yields from the best vineyards are limited.

Some of the Chianti wines are made by the traditional system called the *Governo* process in which up to 10 percent of the grapes are left to dry while the rest ferment. After the fermentation is completed, the dehydrated *passiti* grapes are added to the new wine, which restarts fermentation; some of the sweetness and most of the fruitiness remain, however, and the result is a fresh red wine that can be drunk young. Chianti is typically full-bodied with a flowery bouquet and a somewhat tannic, or astringent, sensation to the palate. If a Chianti wine contains a minimum of 12 percent alcohol and is allowed to age for two years or more, vintners may add the term *vecchio* (aged) to their labels. Chianti Classico may also be labeled vecchio under the same conditions except the alcohol content must be at least 12.5 percent. After three years of aging, both Chianti and Chianti Classico may be entitled to the distinction of *riserva.* Surrounding the central Chianti Classico region are six consorzi districts that may use the term "Chianti" in labeling as long as it is followed by the name of the particular district in which the grapes were grown. These are: *Chianti Colli Arentini, Chianti Colli Fiorentini, Chianti Colli Pisane, Chianti Colli Senesi, Chianti Montalbano,* and *Chianti Rufina.*

In total, about 125 million gallons of wine are produced each vintage in the entire region of Tuscany.

Since the 1200s the *Vin Nobile di Montepulciano* has been grown as a religious wine by the local aristocracy. By the 1300s it was already being exported and is reputed to have been a favorite of Pope Paul II. Deep red in color, it is made principally from the Prugnolo Gentile vine, which some believe to be a superior type of Sangiovese. It must have at least 11 percent alcohol and two years' aging in cask and may become riserva after three years' aging or riserva speciale after four years.' Vin Nobile di Montepulciano may age well in the bottle for another several decades.

Perhaps the most noble red wine of all Italy is that of *Brunello di Montalcino.* The Brunello vine is a cousin of the Prugnolo Gentile variety, another of the so-called superior Sangiovese cultivars. The village of Montalcino is located south of Siena and the soils of the area yield dark, heavy-bodied fruit that makes wines that must be aged for a minimum of six years just to become riserva. Brunello wine must be vinified in the commune of Montalcino. It is often aged for decades before bottling and may be aged for decades more before being released for sale. Some vintages become among the most expensive table wines in the world.

White Chianti wines are unknown, but some white wines are made in Tuscany from Malvasia and Trebbiano vines.

MARCHES

The Marches, located east of Tuscany on the Adriatic coast, is another of Italy's ancient wine-growing districts. It principally produces white wines made from the Verdicchio grape. These are best when drunk young since they are strong in alcohol, often astringent, and have a fruitiness that does not endure long periods of aging.

The same Verdicchio grape is also made into a crisp dry white wine that is sold in an amphora-shaped bottle; this Verdicchio is the best-known wine grown in the coastal vineyards of the Adriatic Sea. Verdicchios from Castelli di Jesi and Matelica, both somewhat inland, are also highly noteworthy.

In all, there are nine DOC-classified wines in the Marches.

UMBRIA

This region, in the heart of Italy, has many vineyards planted upon the Apennine mountain slopes that face westward and in the valley of the Tiber. In ancient times boats carried large volumes of wine from Umbria down the Tiber to Rome.

In the higher portion of the Tiber Valley is Torgiano, a small district that embraces Assisi, famous as the home of St. Francis. Today the area produces red and white DOC-*Torgiano* wines from Canaiolo, Sangiovese, and Trebbiano grapes.

Downriver, just north of Lake Bolsena, is Orvieto, an ancient Etruscan town that makes the well-known wines of the same name, grown principally from the Trebbiano variety, but also from Malvasia Greco and Verdello grapes. The DOC-qualified wine labeled *Orvieto* must have at least 12 percent alcohol; it may be either dry or sweet and is sometimes frizzante. In Roman times, Orvieto was a holy shrine, and misuse of vineyards was severely punished.

The traditional pride of Orvieto has been the *abboccato*, or semisweet white wine, although in recent years the dry *secco* has become popular as well. During some vintages the noble mold, called the *muffa nobile* in Italy, grows in the humid river valley, bringing more richness to the wines grown there.

The third DOC wine of Umbria is *Colli del Trasimeno*. This wine comes from the district that is located along the border with Tuscany and produces red wines from Gamay, Ciliegiolo, and Sangiovese grapes; the wines often bear a similarity to those of its famous Tuscan neighbor. White wines are also made in Colli del Trasimeno—chiefly from Trebbiano, Malvasia, and Grechetto vines.

LATIUM

The province of Latium embraces Rome and the lower Tiber River basin. Situated in the upper portion of this district, near Lake Bolsena, is the village of Montefiascone, from which the fabled sweet white wine called *EST! EST!! EST!!!* originates. While there are a number of different stories explaining how this name originated, the most widely recognized version has to do with the German Bishop Fugger of the diocese of Fulda in Franconia during the twelfth century. While traveling through Italy, Bishop Fugger quite naturally wanted to make his trip as enjoyable as possible, so he sent a forerunner to seek out good inns with superior wines. The forerunner was to mark the chosen inns by writing the word *est* upon the door, apparently an abbreviation for *vinum bonum est,* or "the wine is good." The wine at Montefiascone must have been truly superior since the door of the inn in that village was marked with EST! EST!! EST!!!. The bishop obviously agreed wholeheartedly as he abandoned his journey and dwelled in Montefiascone for the rest of his life. The bishop's wine was a sweet dessert wine made from Moscato grapes, but today EST! EST!! EST!!! is made both dry and sweet from Trebbiano blended with Malvasia.

The volcanic Alban hills that rise up south of Rome are known as *castelli* and have produced wines since the first Greek settlers arrived there millennia ago. In modern times, the vineyards, planted amidst ancient castles, yield *Frascati,* the most famous of the wines of the *Castelli Romani.* Most typically, Frascati is made dry and very fragrant, with a strong flavor of the grape—known locally as the *abboccato* style. It is also made semisweet, sweet, and sparkling. The grapes grown for Frascati are Malvasia and Trebbiano. *Marino, Colli Albani,* and *Colli Lanuvini* are other white table wines grown in the area. Some red wines are also made in Latium from Cesanese and Sangiovese grapes, but they are not well known outside of the area.

Latium lists eighteen DOC-classified growths.

ABRUZZI

Abruzzi is one of the newer wine districts in Italy, having been largely developed since World War II. It is located east of Latium and produces a red wine called *Montepulciano d'Abruzzo,* which should not be confused with the Vin Nobile di Montepulciano of Tuscany although they are similar in rich color and flavor. The Montepulciano d'Abruzzo is typically slightly lighter in body and less tannic than Vin Nobile di Montepulciano. Perhaps the most important wine of the district is *Trebbiano d'Abruzzo,* a white wine that is often of good quality despite a typically low acidity. Most of the grapes of the region are grown in the narrow plain on the eastern coast of central Italy.

CAMPANIA

The beautiful Campania region, surrounding Naples on the west coast of Italy, is a region steeped in history. This region includes the renowned vineyards of *Lacrima Christi* that grow on the famous volcanic soil of Mount Vesuvius. Several legends have arisen to explain the origin of this name. In one of the most popular, Lucifer, as he was cast out of Paradise, stole a portion of the revered soil and cast it iniquitously into the Gulf of Naples—to this day called "the bit of Paradise dropped by the Devil." It also is said that Christ once visited the area and, looking upon how the Devil's work could lure people into sin, was moved to tears. Where His tears fell upon the Campanian slopes, vines of sacred origin sprang forth and produced the white wine of the Lachrima Christi: the "tears of Christ." Some red Lachrima Christi is also made, but it is not generally as highly regarded as the white.

One white wine of merit mentioned earlier in this chapter is called *Greco di Tufo,* or the "Greek wine grown on boiled stone." The Tufo is similar to the soils in the Touraine in France and so are the wines these two districts produce.

Fiano di Avellino, a white, and *Taurasi,* a red, are also popular wines grown in the mountainous vineyards of Campania. *Solopaca* is medium-range red produced in the northeastern sector of the Campania.

The island of Ischia, not far from Naples, produces both whites and reds.

The Campania has a total of eight DOC-classified growths.

APULIA

The Apulia, the "heel" of the Italian "boot," is the fourth-largest wine-producing region in Italy. The wines grown there are mostly very common but strong, and many of them are used as vermouth-base wines or exported to France and Germany for use as blending wines in the production of European Economic

Community (EEC) table wines. Inexpensive Apulian wines became so popular in France during the early 1970s that many French winegrowers, especially in the Midi, became concerned about the heavy volume of the Italian imports. In 1976 the first of several riots erupted on the docks of Marseilles over the unloading of wines from Apulia. The situation continues to be a source of tension in both France and Italy.

A heavy-bodied, sweet red varietal dessert wine made from Aleatico is perhaps the most noteworthy bottled wine grown in the Apulia.

Inland, between Bari and Foggia, good white, rosé, and red table wines can be found at the Castel del Monte; the rosé, which receives the most acclaim, is thought by some to be one of the best rosé wines in the country. San Severo, in the north of the region, produces a strong red wine from the Montepulciano grape and also a heady generic white wine. To the south a good white table wine called *Locorotondo* is grown.

While Apulia has fifteen DOC-listed wines, few are well known or widely distributed in the United States.

BASILICATA

The soils of the Basilicata are probably the worst in all of Italy, and wine growing is the only agriculture that is attempted upon the slopes of the dormant volcano Mount Vulture. The best wine in the province is *Aglianico del Vulture,* a dark red table wine, usually astringent. With three years of aging, Aglianico may be labeled vecchio, and with five years of aging the mellowed red can be sold as riserva. White table wines grown from Malvasia and/or Moscato grapes are also popular in local consumption.

CALABRIA

The terrain of Calabria—rugged and austere—is breathtakingly beautiful, and the region is perhaps more famous for its scenery and for being the "toe" of the Italian "boot" than for any of its wines. One possible exception is that of *Greco di Gerace,* famous since Roman times, a dark golden dessert wine that some say has a bouquet reminiscent of orange blossoms. What little is offered for export brings high prices. The table wines grown at Cirò date back to Grecian times and are popular for the most part only in Italy. *Donnici, Pollino,* and *Savuto* are DOC-Calabria red wines made from blends of mostly red, but also white, grapes.

SICILY

Sicily is Italy's largest producer of wine—some 285 million gallons annually. Sicily also ships considerable amounts of wine in bottle and bulk to other provinces and countries.

The wines from Sicily have been famous for centuries, and evidence of wine growing on the island goes back to Grecian times. In the Sicilian city of Syracuse, originally a Greek colony, archaeologists have found many ancient coins bearing the head of Bacchus on one side and a bunch of grapes on the other. However, the best Sicilian winegrowers have never competed aggressively in the world's wine markets and, consequently, many of the truly fine wines from the region are relatively unknown outside its confines.

The finest of Sicily's bottled wines is *Marsala,* a dessert wine first made there by Englishman John Woodhouse in 1773. Marsala production begins with blends of table wines made from the varieties Catarratto, Grillo, and Inzolia. *Vino cotto,* or "cooked wine," which is really just juice boiled down into a sweet concentrate, is added to the blends, along with brandy, in order to create the strong sweet Marsala. The cooking and aging oxidize color pigments and caramelize the sugars of the wine in the process called *Maderization,* named after the process used to make Madeira wine. Marsala, after four months of aging, can be called *fine* and may be either dry (and light) or sweet (and dark). *Marsala superiore* must be aged in casks for at least two years. If no vino cotto is added and if the wine is kept in a solera fractional blending and aging system for at least five years, the resulting wine may be called *Vergine,* a drier and lighter Marsala. (The solera blending and aging system is fully described in the Spanish sherry portion of chapter 9.) Marsala Speciale wines are also made with the addition of fruit, nut, or other flavors.

Another Sicilian dessert wine is made from late-harvested Zibibbo grapes, which result in a strong amber product known as *Moscato Passito di Pantelleria.*

The best table wines, both white and red, are grown west of Palermo and are bottled under the brand labels "Corvo" and "Regaleali." The white wines of Etna, produced mostly from the Carricante grape in the Province of Catania, are also worth mention. When grown in the commune of Milo and produced from at least

80 percent Carricanto grapes to an alcoholic strength of at least 12 percent, the wines may be labeled *Etna superiore.*

Ten DOC wines are listed for Sicily.

SARDINIA

Despite the fact that fourteen DOC-classified growths are established in Sardinia, Sardinian wines are for the most part not commercially important as exports and they are rarely found off the island. One white varietal wine made from Nuragus and a red from Cannonau are considered by experts to be the finest table wines in the district. Perhaps the most typical of Sardinian wines is the dessert wines called *Vernaccia di Oristano*—very similar in nature to sherry.

TABLE 8-1 The DOCG (Denominazione di Origine Controllata e Garantita) Wines of Italy

PIEDMONT	*TUSCANY*
Barbaresco	Brunello di Montalcino
Barolo	Vino Nobile di Montepulciano

TABLE 8-2 The DOC (Denominazione di Origine Controllata) Wines of Italy

ABRUZZO	Ostuni Bianco
	Ottavianello di Ostuni
Montepulciano d'Abruzzo	Primitivo di Manduria
Trebbiano d'Abbruzo	Rosso di Cerignola
	Salice Salentino
	S. Severo
APULIA	
	BASILICATA
Aleatico di Puglia	
Cacc'e mmitte di Lucera	Aglianico del Vulture
Castel del Monte	
Copertino	*CALABRIA*
Locorotondo	
Martina or Martina Franca	Cirò
Matino	Donnici
Moscato di Trani	Pollino
Ostuni	Savuto

CAMPANIA

Fiano di Avellino
Greco di Tufo
Ischia Bianco
Ischia Rosso
Ischia Bianco Superiore
Lacryma Christi del Vesuvio
Solopaca
Taurasi

EMILIA-ROMAGNA

Albana di Romagna
Bianco di Scandiano
Colli Bolognesi-Monte S. Pietro
Gutturnio dei Colli Piacentini
Lambrusco Grasparossa di Castelvetro
Lambrusco Reggiano
Lambrusco Salamino di S. Croce
Lambrusco di Sorbara
Monterosso Val d'Arda
Sangiovese di Romagna
Trebbiano di Val Trebbia
Trebbiano di Romagna

FRIULI-VENEZIA GIULIA

Aquileia
Collio Goriziano or Collio
Colli Orientali del Friuli
Grave del Friuli
Isonzo
Latisana

LATIUM

Aleatico di Gradoli
Bianco Capena
Cervetri
Cesanese del Piglio or Piglio
Cesanese di Affile or Affile
Cesanese di Olevano Romano or
   Olevano Romano
Colli Albani
Colli Lanuvini
Cori

Est! Est!! Est!!! di Montefiascone
Frascati
Marino
Merlot di Aprilia
Montecompatri-Colonna
Sangiovese di Aprilia
Trebbiano di Aprilia
Velletri
Zagarolo

LIGURIA

Cinque Terre
Cinque Terre Sciaccatrà
Rossese di Dolceacqua or Dolceacqua

LOMBARDY

Botticino
Cellatica
Colli Morenici Mantovani del Garda
Franciacorta Pinot
Franciacorta Rosso
Lugana
Oltrepò Pavese
Riviera del Garda
Riviera del Garda Bresciano
Tocai di S. Martino della Battaglia
Valcalepio
Valtellina
Valtellina Superiore

MARCHES

Bianchello di Metauro
Bianco dei Colli Maceratesi
Falerio dei Colli Ascolani
Rosso Conero
Rosso Piceno
Sangiovese dei Colli Pesaresi
Verdicchio dei Castelli di Jesi
Verdicchio di Matelica
Vernaccia di Serrapetrona

PIEDMONT

Asti Spumante

Barbera d'Alba
Barbera d'Asti
Barbera del Monferrato
Boca
Brachetto d'Acqui
Caluso Passito
Caluso Liquoroso
Carema
Colli Tortonesi
Dolcetto d'Acqui
Dolcetto d'Alba
Dolcetto d'Asti
Dolcetto delle Langhe Monregalesi
Dolcetto di Diano d'Alba
Dolcetto di Dogliani
Dolcetto d'Ovada
Erbaluce di Caluso
Fara
Freisa d'Asti
Freisa di Chieri
Gattinara
Gavi or Cortese di Gavi
Ghemme
Grignolino d'Asti
Grignolino del Monferrato Casalese
Lessona
Malvasia di Casorzo d'Asti
Malvasia di Castelnuovo Don Bosco
Moscato d'Asti
Moscato Naturale d'Asti
Nebbiolo d'Alba
Rubino di Cantavenna
Sizzano

SARDINIA

Campidano di Terralba or Terralba
Cannonau di Sardegna
Carignano del Sulcis
Girò di Cagliari
Malvasia di Bosa
Malvasia di Cagliari
Monica di Cagliari
Monica di Sardegna
Moscato di Cagliari
Moscato di Sorso-Sennori
Nasco di Cagliari

Nuragus di Cagliari
Vermentino di Gallura
Vernaccia di Oristano

SICILY

Bianco Alcamo or Alcamo
Cerasuolo di Vittoria
Etna
Faro
Malvasia delle Lipari
Marsala
Moscato di Noto
Moscato di Pantelleria
Moscato Passito di Pantelleria
Moscato di Siracusa

TRENTINO-ALTO ADIGE

Alto Adige
Caldaro or Lago di Caldaro
Casteller
Colli di Bolzano
Meranese di Collina
Santa Maddalena
Terlano
Teroldego Rotaliano
Valdadige
Valle Isarco
Vini del Trentino

TUSCANY

Bianco della Val-di-Nievole
Bianco di Pitigliano
Bianco Vergine Val di Chiana
Carmignano
Chianti
Elba Bianco and Rosso
Montecarlo Bianco
Montescudaio
Parrina
Rosso delle Colline Lucchesi
Vernaccia di S. Gimignano

UMBRIA

Colli del Trasimeno

Orvieto
Torgiano

VAL D'AOSTA

Donnaz
Enfer D'Arvier

VENETO

Bardolino
Bianco di Custoza
Breganze

Cabernet di Pramaggiore
Colli Berici
Colli Euganei
Gambellara
Merlot di Pramaggiore
Prosecco di Conegliano-Valdobbiadene
Soave
Recioto della Valpolicella-Amarone
Recioto di Soave
Tocai di Lison
Valpolicella
Vini del Piave

LA CONCHA®

GONZALEZ BYASS
JEREZ

JEREZ - XÉRÈS - SHERRY

PRODUCED AND BOTTLED IN JEREZ. SPAIN

750 ML.   IMPORTED   ALC. 20°/₀ VOL.   EMB. 222

LIT HURTADO JEREZ

SOLERA MEDIUM AMONTILLADO
SHERRY

9

THE WINES OF
SPAIN AND
PORTUGAL

SPAIN

The Carthaginians and the Greeks followed the Phoenicians, and the Greeks brought even more and newer technology to the viticulture of the Iberian natives.

Hannibal used Spain as a base for the conquest of Rome in the third century B.C. During the Second Punic War, he crossed the Pyrenees and the Alps to attack Italy, but was cut off from Spain by Roman forces. This marked the first occupation of Hispania by the Romans, but it was several hundred years more before the Iberian provinces were totally secured for the Roman Empire.

The Romans spread wine growing to the northern provinces of Spain during the first two centuries after the birth of Christ. The eastern coastal areas of Tarragona, Andalusia, and Alicante were already relatively heavily developed during these early times.

In the fifth century the Iberian peninsula was pillaged by Germanic invaders. Though wine growing suffered enormously, it nonetheless survived.

The Moors occupied southern Spain from the early eighth century until the fifteenth century. Despite the Islamic prohibition of alcohol, there is plenty of

"Wine Drinkers or the Triumph of Bacchus" by Velasquez. (Source: Museo del Prado, Madrid.)

Medieval view of "Xeres de la Frontera," the modern-day sherry region. (Source: Sherry Institute of Spain.)

evidence to suggest that the Moors enjoyed the Hispanic wines to the fullest. The poet Al-Motamid wrote in the eleventh century:

I certainly intend
Complaining to my friend
About this glass, alack
Garmented all in black.

I set therein to shine
The sunlight of the wine
The sun is sinking thence
To darkness most intense.

During the Middle Ages, wine was one of Spain's most important products, but it was not until the tenth century that the Spanish wine export trade began to flourish. This continued until the twelfth century, when economic conditions pushed Spain outside of the mainstream of European trade. Consequently, more and more of the Hispanic wines were consumed domestically.

Alfonso X led his forces into Jerez, near Cádiz, in southernmost Spain, in 1262. His victory confined the Moors and their antiwine influence to Granada and several ports along the Mediterranean coast near Cádiz. During the next 150 years or so, the Christians gradually gained control over Spain, although both Moorish and Jewish influence lingered on in the language and politics. With the marriage of Isabella I, queen of Castile, and Ferdinand II, king of Aragón, in 1469, Spain made a great advance toward uniting as a single nation. Laws were recodified, the judicial system was reorganized, and the absolute monarchy that emerged centralized the powers of government. Isabella and Ferdinand were dynamic as well as powerful: it was during the same year (1492) that Christopher Columbus made his voyage of discovery to the New World under their sponsorship and the last Moors were driven out of Granada. Part of the development in this "new" Spain included a rejuvenation of vineyards—especially in the Cádiz and Granada frontiers. Spain's Catholic monarchs had many political and economic differences with other European nations, particularly England, and this served to soften trade even though some of the Spanish wines had gained superb reputations abroad. A raid by Sir Francis Drake on Cádiz in 1587 resulted in the seizure of more than 350,000 gallons of sherry wine, but the booty only created more demand for the product back in England.

One of the most famous of the Iberian wines during and following the Renaissance was "sack," the English name for sherry, which probably evolved from the word *sacar*, Spanish for "export." Shakespeare delighted in Spanish sherry, and it is mentioned in many of his works; for example, in *Henry IV* Falstaff explains,

> If I had a thousand sons, the first human principle I would teach them should be,—forswear thin potations and to addict themselves to sack.

and

> A good Sherris-sack hath a two-fold operation in it. It ascends me into the brain; dries me there all the foolish and dull and crudy vapours which environ it; makes it apprehensive, quick, forgetive, full of nimble, fiery, and delectable shapes; which delivered o'er to the voice,—the tongue,—which is the birth, becomes excellent wit.

In the early 1700s Spanish wines again lost popularity, to some extent due to the Methuen Treaty in 1703 that favored the Portuguese wine imports into England. But the demand for sherry expanded greatly again during the latter part of the eighteenth century and the beginning of the nineteenth. During this era many of the present-day, large sherry houses in Jerez were founded.

Spanish table wines for the most part, however, had been a dead issue since Moorish occupation, and they remained so until the *Phylloxera* invaded the vineyards of France, Germany, and other northern European wine-growing nations in the 1860s. The demand that could not be supplied by the customary growths opened the door to the Spanish winegrowers. But the new markets were not handled properly, and disorganization created confusion and discord. Eventually, the *Phylloxera* invaded Spain as well, and by the end of the nineteenth century, the Spanish wine industry was in shambles.

The twentieth-century resurrection of Spanish wine growing has been nothing short of magnificent. Resurging from its post-*Phylloxera* low ebb, Spain now has approximately 4.5 million acres—more acres of vineyard than any other country in the world. From this expanse, about 750 million gallons of wine are produced annually, which does not, as yet, approach the per-acre efficiency of U.S., Italian, or French yields.

The entrance of Spanish wines into the international marketplace has had an important influence upon the winegrowers of Spain; for the most part this has improved the quality and raised the reputation of Spanish wines. It was only in 1970, however, that the Ministerio de Agricultura promulgated the Statute of Vines, Wines, and Spirits. This set of regulations empowered twenty-odd regional committees called *consejos* to enforce the new system of Denominacións de Origen (DO)—similar in nature to the Italian DOC and the Portuguese Denominaçãos de Origem.

There is an oceanic coastal climate in northwestern Spain similar to that of neighboring Portugal to the south. Winds from the southwest touch upon the cool mountains and humidity becomes rain, often quite abundant rain. To the east and south the levels of rainfall taper off dramatically until, particularly in some of the plateau regions, there is only scant precipitation.

Switzerland is the only European country more mountainous than Spain, and from the beautiful peaks of central Spain five major rivers arise. These drain the upper wetlands and provide moisture to the parched plateaus and lowlands, thus permitting the many different vineyard regions of Spain to exist. The Douro flows westerly through the great Portuguese vineyards that bear port wine and on to the Atlantic at the cities of Vila Nova de Gaia and Oporto. The Tagus also flows westerly to the Portuguese Atlantic, first passing through the Extremadura and Lisbon. The Guadiana River crosses through the heart of the famed La Mancha region before it travels down southeastern Portugal and joins the Atlantic. The Guadalquivir runs southerly through the renowned sherry vineyards past the sherry capital city of Jerez de la Frontera. The fifth river, the Ebro, flows through the entire length of the Rioja and southeastward through the Catalonia wine district before eventually feeding the Mediterranean.

The wines of northern Spain, perhaps best exemplified by those from the Rioja region, are considered by many to have the most character and highest quality of all Spanish wines. The central regions of Spain grow most of the nation's common and inexpensive *vino de mesa*, or "table wine." The south is best known for dessert wines, with two products—sherry and Málaga—enjoying worldwide fame. Exceptions do exist in each region, however, and these general statements are meant only as an overview.

Rioja

This region is the most northern of the Spanish wine-growing districts, located less than 75 miles from the southwestern border of France. Its name comes from the *Rio Oja*, or the "Oja River," a tributary that joins the Ebro at the town of Haro.

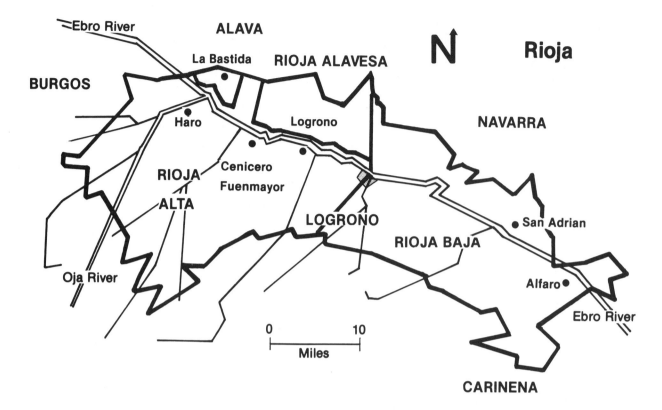

When the *Phylloxera* invaded Bordeaux, many of the winegrowers there crossed over into Spain, and particularly the Rioja, bringing with them French wine-growing expertise and high hopes to fill the world demand for wine with Spanish wine products. The French heritage lingers, and in modern times the wines of Rioja are made in the French manner; in fact, some critics say that these Spanish wines could be much better if they were not aged so long in the *barricas* (the equivalent of the 225-liter oaken *barriques* of Bordeaux), which impart a vanilla character to the reds in particular. Indeed, such changes are currently taking place in Rioja, with its "new" reds becoming some of the best buys available.

Both white and red table wines are grown in the Rioja, reds principally from the Tempranillo and the Garnacho grapes, the latter of which is the same grape variety as the Grenache of the Rhône in France. White Rioja wines are grown from the Viura grape, also known as the Macabeo in Catalonia, and the classic Malvasia. Riojas are typically made in very large *bodegas* (wine cellars), as opposed to the many small *chai* of Burgundy or *Weinkellerei* of Germany. There are only fifty Rioja bodegas that are permitted by DO regulations to export their wines.

The western portions of the Rioja, the Alta and Alavesa, have a moderate climate—without excessive rainfall or hot summer temperatures. The environment changes drastically, however, as one proceeds down into the Rioja Baja. There the climate becomes nearly arid and very hot. As would be expected, the

PRODUCT OF SPAIN

Privilegio
del Rey Sancho
RIOJA
RED TABLE WINE

PRODUCED & BOTTLED BY BODEGAS DOMECQ, ELCIEGO (ALAVA) SPAIN

1980

Pedro Domecq

ALC. BY VOL. 12%   750 ml.

ALCOHOL 12%
BY VOLUME   750 ML.

Codorníu

BLANC DE BLANCS
MÉTHODE TRADITIONNELLE CHAMPENOISE
VINTAGE 1985
SPARKLING WHITE WINE
CODORNIU, S.A.-SANT SADURNI D'ANOIA-ESPAÑA

EMB. 375-B   CAVA   R.S.I. 30. 279/B

wines grown at the Alta are more acidic and full-bodied, while the Baja wines are strong and bland. It is common to find wines blended together from all three districts in the region. This ensures a consistency of production, without the yearly variation of vintages that is customary in other European vineyard locales.

The post of Consejo Regulador—the "wine Governor" of Rioja—was established in the 1920s to administer wine production and wine-marketing activities in the region. Appointments for the position are made by the Spanish Minister of Agriculture. A station is maintained in the city of Haro for the analysis and inspection of Rioja wines assigned for export. There are also inspectors who make checks in the vineyards and bodegas to see that regional regulations are complied with. The principal types of Rioja are as follows:

Clarete—light reds with a fruity bouquet
Tinto—dark reds, full-bodied and strong in alcohol
Rosado—rosé wines, either light and dry or heavier and sweeter
Blanco—white wines, both dry and green or sweet and golden from maturity
Reservas—red wines chosen from the better vintages and aged for at least six
          years before bottling

In recent years the wines from Rioja have become popular in the United States, primarily because their reasonable prices and increasing quality are becoming recognized as good values.

Navarra

The Navarra, which borders the Rioja to the north and east, produces both red and white wines that are similar in nearly every way to those of the Rioja Baja—the best grown at Puente de la Reina and the Señorio de Sarria.

Catalonia

The Catalonian wine-growing region of Spain is located approximately 100 miles east of the Rioja and Navarra. The Ampurdán-Costa Brava sits somewhat apart from the main body of the Catalonia region, whose centers are the cities of Barcelona, Sitges, and Tarragona. Good-quality dry red and white table wines, as well as sweet dessert wines, are grown in the Ampurdán-Costa Brava district. None, however, is classified by the DO.

Just north of Barcelona are the vineyards of the Alella district, which are classified by the DO. Alella white table wines are grown principally from the grape varieties Macabeo and Malvasia; while reds are made from Garnacho and Tempranillo. The general practice is to blend wines grown from the north and south slopes in order to balance acidity and then to age the resulting blended wines in oak cooperage from one to three years before bottling.

Embracing the port of Sitges is the sandy lower sector of the Panadès district, known principally for "Malvasia de Sitges," a sweet, light amber dessert wine made, as the name suggests, from Malvasia grapes, but with some Sumoll blended in. In the higher limestone soils of the Panadès uplands are vineyards planted with the varieties Macabeo and Parellada, which yield fine dry white table wines. Sparkling wines (*espumosos*) are also made in the Panadès by the bulk system, and by the French *méthode champenoise*. The best are those made from white grapes that are selected for superior quality, in much the same fashion as the *épluchage* selection process is performed in France's Champagne region. Extra-dry Spanish espumoso is called *bruto*; near-dry is *seco*; sweet is *dulce*. Again borrowing from the French, *semiseco* and *semidulce* are "semi-dry" and "semi-sweet," respectively.

Tarragona has endured a reputation for producing very strong red dessert wines of poor quality, known as "Red Biddy" in England. In recent years, though, as Tarragona has made a name for itself in quality aperitif wine production, this earlier reputation has waned. There are two other noteworthy products from the expansive district: an altar wine made for the Vatican and *sangria*, the latter a light red wine mixed with citrus fruit slices, sparkling soda, and a dash of brandy—all the rage in the United States during the late 1960s and early 1970s.

Within the Tarragona district there is an inner region, somewhat equivalent to Italy's "classico" designation, called the *Priorato*. The Priorato gets its name from the priory of a Carthusian monastery called Scala Dei—now only ruins upon the volcanic slopes of the Sierra de Montsant. Dry red wines, grown from Cariñena and Garnacho Negro vines, are often vinified to more than 16 percent alcohol content by volume. Sweet dessert wines are also classified as DO Priorato and grown principally from Garnacho Blanco, Macabeo, and the great Pedro Ximénez vines. Also made in Priorato is a wine-related beverage called *mistela*. Mistela is nothing more than brandy added to grape juice before any fermentation takes place. While some mistela is consumed straight, most of it is used for blending in making other dessert and aperitif wines.

In recent years some of the larger, better-known vintners of Catalonia have found great success in American markets. Among these firms are Vinedos Torres, Cordorniu, and Freixenet—the latter two producers of highly regarded sparkling wines. Freixenet has just completed construction of a large winery in the Sonoma Valley in California.

Cariñena

As regions go in Spain, the Cariñena is rather small, even when neighboring Aragón is included. It is located between the Rioja and Catalonia in the northeastern part of Spain.

Very strong table wines, both red and white, are grown in Cariñena, primarily from the grape varieties Garnacho Negro, Garnacho Blanco, and the region's own Cariñena (the same as Carignan). There are also various types of dessert wines produced in the region. The lower portion of the Cariñena is important primarily for the production of blending wines while the upper reaches yield more well-balanced table wines with a comparatively delicate flavor.

The Aragón claretes, particularly well thought of by some experts, resemble the light-colored red table wines from the upper Rioja.

La Mancha

Situated about 150 miles south of the Rioja, La Mancha is renowned as homeland of the literary character Don Quixote. The region is a high plateau upon which about a third of all the table wine grown in Spain is produced.

The soils of La Mancha are a poor chalky base with an arid topsoil; even the best section is called the *Valdepeñas,* or the "valley of stones." Red wines grown in the DO Valdepeñas from Cencibel and Garnacho Negro grapes have a good reputation, as do the whites made from Airén, Cirial, and Pardillo. The La Mancha landscapes are green in spring, but become gold in the arid summer when the only moisture available is that which the chalky subsoil has retained from the previous winter rains.

Most of the wines of La Mancha are dry, bland, and thin-bodied and are grown primarily for blending with wines in other regions and for export in bulk. Some La Mancha wines are distilled at the brandy center of Tomelloso.

Levante

The Levante is another huge Spanish vineyard region. It is bordered by more than 100 miles of the Mediterranean along the southeast coastline of Spain and to the west by the vast La Mancha plateau.

The best of the Levante wines are grown in the Utiel-Requena; almost all of the dry red, white, and rosé table wines in this region are of a strong and earthy character, typical of wines from rich soils.

The northern portion of the region is centered on Valencia, the third-largest city in Spain. Here, along with the Utiel-Requena, is the district of Valencia, named for the port city. The southern reaches of the Levante include the districts of Almansa, Jumilla, Yecla, and Alicante that surround the capital port of Alicante on the Costa Blanca.

Galicia

Both white and red wines are grown in Galicia—although most are red. While the major share of Galician wines have no effervescence, some are slightly *pétillant*, and others are noticeably bubbly. It is in Galicia that the "green wines" of Spain are produced, wines similar to Portugal's *vinho verde* that are discussed later in this chapter. Green wines are made from green, unripened white or red grapes and are generally quite acidic on the palate. These types of wines are often described as "eager" wines, perhaps due to the eagerness of the wine masters to gather the fruit before it reaches maturity in the vineyards. Not all of the Galician wines are green, however; some, in fact, when aged six years or more, become *reserva*.

The Galician Province of Orense is located along the northern border of Portugal and is made up of three districts: the Ribeiro, Valdeorras, and the Valle de Monterrey.

The largest of these districts is the Ribeiro where red table wines of good balance are grown from Garnacho Negro, Caino, and Brancellao vines. Whites are made from Treixadura and Albariño.

Valdeorras vineyards are planted upon gently sloping hills that rise to elevations over 2,500 feet. The varieties Garnacho Negro, Alicante, and Mencia yield good red wines—and Godello Blanco yields good whites.

The vineyards and wines of the Valle de Monterrey are similar to those of Valdeorras, although some experts insist that the Monterrey reds are more full-bodied.

Extremadura and León

The Douro River flows through the rural reaches of the Provinces of Badajoz and Cáceres, which together make up the Extremadura. The clay, granite, and slate soils yield good wines in some locales, but few are exported. The best red table wines are grown from Almendralejo, Garnacho Negro, and Morisca grapes. Cayetana, the most prominent white variety of the Extremadura, is blended with wines from Lairén, Moscatel, and Macabeo grapes, along with the classic sherry varieties of Palomino and Pedro Ximénez.

The Provinces of Léon and Zamora produce a large amount of ordinary wines (called *corrientes*) although some superior growths are noted from La Bañeza and Toro.

Montilla and Moriles

The Montilla and Moriles region is located about 75 miles south of Valdepeñas and about 20 miles to the southeast of Córdoba. Soils vary in the region, but are predominantly calcareous in nature. The principal vine variety grown in the vineyards there is the Pedro Ximénez, which is vinified into a very strong wine that is similar to sherry and Madeira. Although Montilla is not fortified with brandy, it reaches an alcohol content nearly as high as sherry's naturally.

The light, medium, and dark wines of Montilla were once even more popular than those of the sherry region to the south. The famous *Amontillado* wines of sherry translate as "like the wine of Montilla"—an indication of how highly esteemed these wines were and how similar sherry wines are to those of Montilla.

The bodegas of Montilla recall ancient Roman times as they still use huge earthenware amphorae, called *tinajas,* to store and ferment the wines. These containers are often more than 7 feet in height and contain more than 700 gallons. Lined up in rows, they make a most impressive sight.

Málaga

Málaga is another Spanish wine-growing region that is rich in history, with many signs of the Roman occupation still remaining. At the center of the region is its capital city of Málaga, which is beautifully situated upon the famous Costa del Sol.

The mild climate yields lush grapes from the varieties Pedro Ximénez and Moscatel, the latter dried into raisins before the juice is extracted and the dark brown sweet and semisweet Málaga wines are fermented. Like the wines of Montilla, the wines of Málaga were well known long before the sherries of neighboring Jerez de la Frontera.

Lagrima is considered by many to be the best type of Málaga and is made entirely from raisins. *Mountain* Málaga is, as the name indicates, grown from mountain grapes and makes a wine that is drier and lighter than lagrima. *Virgin* is the driest of the Málaga wines.

Huelva

While Málaga is located at the eastern end of the Spanish Andalusia, Huelva is at the western end, with the Jerez region nestled in between.

The climate, soils, and grape varieties cultivated in the Huelva are very similar to those of neighboring Jerez, although experts agree that the Huelva wines lack the delicate character of many sherries.

The best-known districts are the Almonte, Bollullos del Condado, Bonares, Paterna, and Moguer—the latter producing the sweetest wines of the region.

Jerez de la Frontera (Sherry)

The Greek historian Theopompos thus referred to the ancient capital of the Spanish sherry region in the fourth century B.C.: "Xera, city situated in the proximity of the Columns of Hercules."

But *Xera*, on Spain's south coast near modern-day Gibraltar, was already an old city by the time of Theopompos—for the Phoenicians had founded a settlement called *Shera* there in the eleventh century B.C.

The Roman agriculturist Columella lived in Cádiz, located on the Mediterranean coast about 5 miles south of Xera, then called *Ceritium*, and wrote that Ceritium was already an important wine-growing center in Roman times. The conquering Moors were to rename it again—this time *Xerez*, which they pronounced "Scheris." The medieval wine of the Moslem occupation was simple and sweet, made so by boiling down freshly pressed juice into syrup that was added to wines after fermentation.

The history of sherry wine commenced with the invasion of Xerez in the mid-thirteenth century by Alfonso X, who encouraged the expansion of wine growing in his new "frontier," hence the name *Jerez de la Frontera*.

The citizenry of Jerez de la Frontera were instrumental in preparing Christopher Columbus for his voyages to the New World. In 1493, they contributed more than 1,200 bushels of wheat to the stores for his second journey to the west.

It was in the large monastery called "Of the Defense of the Blessed Virgin Mary" that many faithful believe the first sherry-base wine was fortified with brandy during the year 1475. Some credit the Moors with inventing the brandy-distillation process during their occupation of Xerez—although other historians suggest that if this were the case, then Spanish brandy would have been exported long before sherry.

In any event, sherry today is a wine fortified with added brandy and made largely from Palomino grapes grown in an officially designated sherry region around the city of Jerez. After the grapes achieve a state of overripeness, all of their sugar is fermented to make a strong wine. After fermentation, the wines are lightly fortified with grape brandy, and it is at this point that the distinction is made between the *fino* sherry and the *oloroso*: the finos will devolop a thick layer of surface-growing yeasts known as *Flor*, and it is this that imparts the distinctive nutlike flavor and amber color. The darkest and sweetest sherries, sometimes known as "cream" sherries, are *olorosos*. *Amontillado* sherries are often described as "medium" sherries—and, in fact, they are more fully developed finos, darker and heavier-bodied than the amber finos but not as sweet or rich as an oloroso. Sherries termed *raya* are lesser-grade olorosos, generally used for lower-priced sherry blends.

The climate of the sherry region is, except for hot summers, rather mild. Prevailing southwesterly winds bring only a bit more than 20 inches of rain during most years, most of which falls in late autumn.

This precious rain is absorbed by the all-important soil of the region, which has high consistencies of chalk. Albariza soil, for example, has approximately 40

Vineyard scene in the sherry region. (Source: Sherry Institute of Spain.)

percent chalk content. Other principal districts that have this valued soil are Añina, Balbaina, Carrascal, and Macharnudo. The principal variety grown in the Albariza is the Palomino, which yields the finest of the fino sherries.

Albarizona soils, which have only about 25 percent chalk, produce good-quality wines but they do not rank with those of Albariza. *Arena* soils are sandy, with only about 10 percent chalk; while *Barro* soils have about the same amount of chalk, but are generally of a clay consistency. The sherries produced from both Arena and Barro vineyards are for the most part coarser and sweeter than the finest-quality sherries.

The arid conditions in the Jerez de la Frontera vineyards make labor there arduous, although mechanization has alleviated much of the hardship during the past several decades. The chalky soils dry into a crust, which must be broken up each year, and shallow ditches are dug along the rows in which to conserve the autumn rains. As in the French Beaujolais, some vineyards are managed without benefit of trellising, but this is changing since better fruit quality and greater economic efficiencies have been attained through the use of modern training systems.

Nowadays the golden ripe Palomino grapes of the Jerez de la Frontera are harvested and immediately taken to wineries for crushing and pressing. The

Sherry grapes drying in the vineyards prior to crushing and pressing. (Source: Sherry Institute of Spain.)

Pedro Ximénez and Moscatel grapes continue to be dried in more traditional style on woven grass mats before being shipped to the sherry house wineries. The fruit from each vineyard locale is kept separate so that wine masters can judge the elements to take from each growth to make a final product that will be consistent from year to year.

The juice from raisinized Pedro Ximénez and Moscatel grapes are made into a very sweet *mistela* by the addition of brandy—a more delicate *dulce mistela* is sometimes made from the Palomino. A "color" wine is also made by concentrating even further the juice from Pedro Ximénez and Moscatel grapes and blending the resulting syrup with unconcentrated juice prior to fermentation.

Using the new wines, along with mistelas, brandy, and color wines, the sherry wine masters then compose blends that are married and stabilized into light and dry finos, the medium-dark and medium-sweet amontillados, and the very dark and sweet olorosos.

One malady that is characteristic of the grapes from the Jerez de la Frontera vineyards is a deficiency in acid strength. Wines made from low-acid grapes are more subject to microbial degradation and are generally more difficult to stabilize than balanced wines. This deficiency is overcome in the sherry region with a

IMPORTED

HARVEYS ®

BY APPOINTMENT TO
HER MAJESTY QUEEN ELIZABETH II
WINE MERCHANTS
JOHN HARVEY & SONS LIMITED BRISTOL

BRISTOL CREAM ®

CHOICEST FULL PALE SHERRY

SHIPPED & BOTTLED BY
JOHN HARVEY & SONS LIMITED, 12 DENMARK STREET, BRISTOL, ENGLAND.
FOUNDED 1796

CONTENTS 750ml.   ALCOHOL 20% BY VOLUME
PRODUCE OF SPAIN

BY APPOINTMENT
TO HER MAJESTY
QUEEN ELIZABETH II

WINE MERCHANTS
GEO. G. SANDEMAN
SONS & CO. LIMITED

Imperial Corregidor

RAREST VVO. OLOROSO

Sherry

made and bottled by
Sandeman Hnos. y Cia.
Jerez Spain

SANDEMAN ®

ESTABLISHED IN THE YEAR 1790

'E2374-CA'

ALC. 21% BY VOL.

PRODUCE OF SPAIN

CONTENTS 750ML

process called "plastering," in which gypsum (called *yeso* in Spain) is dusted upon the grapes.

There is modernization in the sherry wineries, too. The pressing of the crushed (but not destemmed) grapes is principally performed with large mechanical presses, rather than the traditional barefoot "treading" in the *lagares* (shallow, wooden vats).

The primary fermentation takes place tumultuously in the Jerez bodegas for about three or four days in the hot autumn temperatures, resulting in an alcohol content of about 12 percent by volume. In the traditional process the new wines were allowed to rest for three months in the sherry *butts* (oaken casks of about 132 gallons capacity) filled to only about 110 gallons, leaving *ullage,* or "air space," of about 22 gallons. Traditionally, this air exposure has had several different effects:

> If a surface-growing yeast called a Flor, the wine "flower," appears and the famous nutlike flavor develops, brandy is added up to about 8 percent—these wines are temporarily classified as *finos,* but some will eventually become *amontillados* and *olorosos.*

> If a caramel-like bouquet and dark color develops, brandy is added up to about 18 percent to arrest further oxidation, these wines are preliminarily designated as *rayas.*

> If an infection of vinegar bacteria, *Acetobacter,* develops, the wines are distilled into brandy.

Today, however, most of the large sherry houses employ much more advanced technology to control the course of microbial transformation. This, of course, balances the amount of each type of wine result desired and maximizes product quality, inventory, and operating efficiency.

After the initial "rest" of the new *añada* (vintage) wines, they are reevaluated and reclassified approximately every six months. Each vineyard's wine is eventually decreed a quality level, after which it is introduced to one of the appropriate *soleras* in the bodega. A solera is a fractional blending system made of rows of stacked sherry butts called *criaderas.* Once each year a prescribed amount of wine (up to 50 percent of the total volume) is taken from each of the butts in the last criadera in the solera for final blending. The void left in the final criadera is replaced with wine taken in the same manner from each butt in the next criadera, which, in turn, is refilled with wine from the next, and so forth, through perhaps as many as fifteen or more criaderas in the entire solera. The new *añada* replaces the void left in the first criadera.

José Domecq, the famous "nose" examines some new sherry from the solera in his bodegas. (Source: David Alan Harvey, © National Geographic Society.)

This process brings a superb consistency to the sherries from each solera and, because such wines depend upon long periods of aging, the solera also continuously effects an older and older cumulative age for the entire lot of wines in the system.

Finos are younger sherries and, therefore, fewer criaderas are employed in a fino solera than for the older, darker amontillados or the very dark olorosos. Of these three types, finos have the lowest alcohol content and olorosos the highest (18 to 24 percent) with amontillado in between. Because the storage butts in the criaderas are wooden and therefore somewhat porous, the water in the sherry wines can slowly evaporate since water is a very small molecule. The much-larger alcohol molecule is retained inside the butts, causing, in time, the alcohol percentage to increase. The longer the period of storage, the higher the alcohol percentage increase.

One special type of sherry is grown and matured in Manzanilla, located near the port of Sanlúcar de Barrameda. This is the region of the high-chalk Albariza soils adjoining the sea a dozen miles northwest of Jerez de la Frontera. The true Manzanilla is made and matured by the sea, which imparts a profound salty bouquet and flavor to the wine. Manzanilla is one of the most popular wines in the current Spanish wine marketplace.

Diagram of a solera fractional blending system

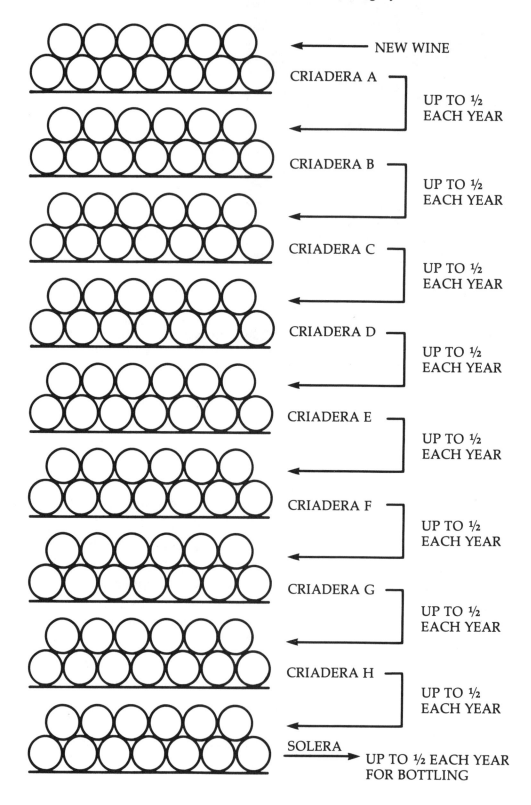

Cellar workers blending sherry from *criadera* to *criadera* in the solera. (Source: Sherry Institute of Spain.)

Some of the most respected names in sherry are Duff Gordon, Gonzalez Byass, Harvey's, Pedro Domecq, Sandeman, and Williams and Humbert.

TABLE 9-1   Spain—Principal Growths

CARIÑENA AND ARAGON	Panadès
R, W TW,	W TW, W DW & W SpW
W DW	Tarragona
	W
Cariñena	Priorato
Aragón	R TW
	W DW
CATALONIA	
	EXTREMADURA AND LEON
Alella	R, W TW
R, W TW	
Ampurdán-Costa Brava	Extremadura
R, W TW	León
R, W DW	

GALICIA
R, W TW

Ribiero
Valdeorras
Valle de Monterrey

HUELVA
W DW

Almonte
Bollullos del Condado
Bonares
Moguer
Paterna

JEREZ DE LA FRONTERA
W DW

Fino
Amontillado
Oloroso
Manzanilla

LA MANCHA
R, W TW

Valdepeñas

LEVANTE
R, W, & Ro TW

Utiel-Requena
Valencia

Alicante
Almansa
Jumilla
Yecla

MÁLAGA
W TW

Lagrima
Mountain
Virgin

MONTILLA AND MORILES
W DW

Montilla
Moriles

NAVARRA
R, W, & Ro TW

Navarra

RIOJA
R, W & Ro TW

Alavesa
Alta
Baja
    Clarete
    Tinto
    Rosade
    Blanco
    Reserva

R = red
W = white
Ro = rosé
TW = table wine
DW = dessert wine
SpW = sparkling wine

PORTUGAL

Wine growing in Portugal began, as perhaps in Spain, with the Phoenicians—although Portugal did not then exist as an autonomous political entity.

Following the establishment of the initial wine-growing industry by the eastern traders, the Greeks arrived and contributed their expertise, and after the Greeks came the Romans, with even more advanced technology. In the south of the Iberian peninsula, Roman *dolia* (large amphorae) have been found that closely resemble the *tinajas* that are still employed in the area. The Greek geographer Strabo (c. 63 B.C.-21 A.D.) told of how vineyards were being planted along the western coast of what is now Portugal and Spain.

While the conquering Moors made winegrowers throughout Iberia suffer, they did not discourage viniculture. Following the Christian reconquest, the lands of the region, including neighboring Lusitania to the south, were divided up into large estates, and most vineyards disappeared. The few wines that remained were chiefly thin and of poor quality.

The first date of importance in the more recent history of Portuguese wine growing is 1093, the year King Alfonso VI of Castile arranged the marriage of his illegitimate daughter Teresa to Count Henry of Burgundy. The dowry included large Portuguese estates, and Count Henry brought many vines, no doubt Pinot Noir, with him to his new lands. This region would later be named *Guimarães*. The native Portuguese immediately adopted the new vines and renamed them *Tinta Francisca*, or *Tinta da Franca* and *Francesa*, all of which translate as "French Red." The wines were also restyled, and the resulting products were much heavier and richer than the wines that had been previously grown in the region.

Count Henry's domain, stretching from the Minho to the Douro in what is now northern Portugal, became known then as the *Terra Portugalensis*—and Henry extended the borders even farther through his successes in intervening in civil wars. Henry's son Alfonso, upon succeeding to rule of these lands, promoted himself to Duke, then Prince, and, finally, King of the Terra Portugalensis. However, his cousin, Alfonso VII, himself successor to King Alfonso VI of Castile, did not take kindly to the usurpation of these titles and declared war on the ascender in 1130. An ensuing peace brought little respect for the position of the Portuguese leader. Eventually, King Alfonso VII, within the structures of the Treaty of Zamora, acknowledged the royal status of his cousin and granted him the title of King of Portugal. The Pope did not concur, however, and would recognize only a dukedom for Alfonso I of Portugal.

Throughout the next two generations of monarchs, the Portuguese wine industry became well-established, and trade with England started up again. During this time, the Portuguese borders were expanded through the conquest of such strongholds as Cintra and Lisbon, and later the Crusaders, Templar Monks, and the Knights Hospitalers of Santiago helped to add even more land.

King Alfonso II encouraged his nation's growth and industry, particularly that of wine growing. However, he was excommunicated from the church for various infractions and replaced by his brother, Dom Dinis. Dinis was also progressive and organized the first vineyards in the Douro district of Portugal.

In 1353 Dinis's son, Alfonso IV, and England's Edward III negotiated a treaty that exchanged Portuguese wine for fishing rights off the coast of England. This wine, called "port," was dry red wine of poor quality, especially compared with the fine red wines of Bordeaux that had already been shipped to Britain for two centuries. Another wine, probably from the Oporto area, called *Osey*, was also exported to England, but the British admired this rich golden dessert product that was most likely sweetened with honey. A poem of the times relates that:

Portyngalers . . . ,
Whose merchandise cometh much into England.
Their land hath oil, wine, osey, wax and grain.

Lisbon, a large port and trade center during the fifteenth century, may have introduced the West to spices, tea, and other treasures from the East. Portuguese sailors of the day were renowned for their adventuresome spirits and fearless dispositions. Among these was João Gançalves, also known as Zarco the blue-eyed. Zarco boldly sailed into the forbidding Atlantic and discovered the rocky isle of Madeira, located about 400 miles west of the northwestern African coast. In colonizing the island, Zarco set fire to the forests—fires that were reported to have lasted almost seven years. The ashes may have given fertility to the sparse volcanic soil as the *Madeira* vineyards flourished, but wood for building the casks needed for wine storage was, of course, lost to the great fire. Visiting the island in 1455, a Venetian traveler, Alvise da Mosta, praised the Madeira wines, especially those made from the Malvasia vine, which produced huge bunches of grapes. This reputation spread quickly, and by the end of the fifteenth century the popular Cretian *Malmsey* wines exported to England had to compete with Madeira.

Following the defeat of King Sebastian in 1580, Philip II of Spain marched into Portugal and brought an end to the wine trade with England. Sixty years later the House of Bragança was restored in Portugal, and some trade was resumed; relations, however, were strained, perhaps partly because of the poor-quality dry red wines being shipped from Oporto.

A poem reveals the discontent with port wine:

Mark how it smells. Methinks, a real pain
Is by its colour thrown upon my brain.

I've tasted it—'tis spiritless and flat
And it has as many different tastes,
As can be found in compound pastes . . .

Determined to improve the quality of these wines, British merchants went to Portugal themselves during the latter 1600s and literally "invented" the sweet red *port* dessert wine-type as it is known today. The English vintners knew that the deep, dark red grapes of the Douro Valley matured to a very high sugar content. When all of this sugar was fermented, the result was the dry, strong, harsh traditional port wine that had become notorious in England for its unpleasantness. The wine masters developed a process whereby brandy was added at a precise time during fermentation—arresting further activity and preserving much of the natural sweetness in the wine.

This practice, however, was quickly challenged, as purists insisted that such wines were not natural, a complaint that continues to be made in some circles even in modern times. The British wineries, or "wine lodges" that still operate near Oporto in Portugal bear the names of some of the original inventors and shippers—Croft, Dow, McKenzie, Offley, Sandeman, and others. (For a discussion of port in modern times, see the section on the Douro region below.)

Oliver Cromwell is credited by historians with introducing the new sweet port dessert wine to England, and it soon became the favorite wine of the nation, just as Madeira became the preferred wine in the British colonies.

Perhaps the reason why Madeira was so popular in colonial America was that King Charles II excepted wines from Madeira from the requirement of being shipped in a British ship from a British harbor. Produce from other English possessions and territories was prohibited from direct export. Christopher Columbus lived in Madeira for a time, and, in bringing his wines to the New World, he perhaps blazed the trail for the eventual shipping of Madeira by wealthy shipowners in Boston, Charleston, New York, and Philadelphia.

It was at Oporto that the first cylindrical bottles were employed for wine aging—at about 1770. Prior to this, bottles were rather short flasks: they could not be laid down, and thus the corks would not stay wet. Instead they had been stored upright, and when the corks dried out, air entered the bottles, allowing for deterioration from oxidation.

Tiny Portugal ranks eighth in world wine production, but is first in the density of vineyards compared to total land area. It produces about 350 million gallons of wine per year from some 900,000 acres of exquisitely beautiful vineyard locales. The average annual per capita consumption is about 20 gallons of wine per person.

The wine-growing regions of Portugal rise steeply from the narrow coastal Atlantic plain to the high mountains that dominate most of the stark countryside.

In many areas the mountainsides must be terraced in order for the vineyards to exist. The many hardy laborers who dedicate their lives to wine growing in Portugal tend the vineyards almost like gardens, doing a good deal of the work by hand. Much of the soil, in the northern part of the country especially, is granitic and must be broken up manually. The magnificent terraces and walled vineyards of the Douro are built upon schistous soils while in the expansive lower regions the vines exist upon blazing hot sand.

The climate is determined by the cool Atlantic southwesterly winds that bring a good deal of rain inland, resulting in a rather wet growing season in the Serra mountain ranges.

The ordinary white, rosé, and red wines of Portugal are called *vinho de consumo* and are made without demarcation. Much of the popular rosé wine imported into America originates from blends of *consumo*.

The responsibility for control over Portuguese wines is held by the Junta Nacional do Vinho (JNV), which is headquartered in Lisbon. (Port wine control is excepted from this jurisdiction as it has its own institute in Oporto.) This organization coordinates the work of local, regional, and federal authorities in somewhat the same manner as the federal DOC cooperates with the regional *consorzi* in Italy. The JNV monitors standards of production quality and controls both vinifying and marketing practices, as well as directing the issuance of Denominaçãos de Origem. Most of the enforcement operations are delegated to regional authorities.

Demarcated wines undergo laboratory testing to ensure that they meet the particular specifications set by the authorities with jurisdiction in each region. In bulk wine shipments, containers are sealed with metal devices attached to prevent tampering. Bottled wines from Portuguese-demarcated areas have a printed seal, which varies according to region, drawn across the bottle neck and cork before capsuling.

At this time there are just seven regions that have been authorized by the JNV, but others are sure to follow as soon as wine qualities can be improved sufficiently to warrant demarcation.

Minho

The Minho, located in the northwestern corner of Portugal, is the region of the *vinhos verdes*, or "green wines," sometimes called "eager wines" because they are produced from grapes that have not fully ripened in the vineyards. The notion that vinhos verdes are made from green-skinned grape varieties is a fallacy—in fact, more than 75 percent of vinho verde results from red grapes. The immature fruit is high in malic acid, and malolactic fermentations that break down this acid result in a cheesy taste as well as some effervescence that is common in vinho verde. Also, vinho verde is often found to be astringent or tannic, which results from the grapes being vinified without removing the stems.

The vines in the Minho are often cultivated to heights of 8 feet above the vineyard floor in an overhead system that provides shade for other crops beneath the trellises. The black Vinhao variety is the most heavily planted, and Azal Tinto, Borracal, and Espadeiro are also popular. White varieties are Alvarinho, Azal Branco, and Dourado.

There are approximately 90,000 winegrowers in the Minho region producing more than 60 million gallons per year. The districts that comprise the Minho are: Amarante, Basto, Braga, Lima, Monçao, and Peñafiel.

The Dão, Bairrada, and Tràs-os-Montes

The Dão is a high plateau region of granite soils divided by steep canyons and bordered by mountains. It is situated in the north-central section of Portugal, about 40 miles south of the Minho. The region takes its name from the Dao River, which cuts through it in a southwesterly direction and flows as a tributary into the Mondego River. Since very early times, the wines of this locale have been rather common; it is known, for example, that in the thirteenth century the citizenry voted to prohibit sale of any wines made outside the region so long as stocks of the native Dão wines were still unsold in inventory. Since the establishment in 1942 of the regional authority, the Federaçao dos Vinicultores do Dão, wine quality has improved along with labeling standards.

There are about 50,000 acres of vineyards in the neighboring districts of the Dao, Bairrada and Tràs-os-Montes (across the mountains), some planted at more than 5,000 feet in elevation. In contrast to the Minho, the vineyards of the Dao are maintained on a low-trellis system. Mostly bland red wines are made from the varieties Tourigo, Preto Mortagua, and Tinta Pinheira, the last thought to be a descendant of the great French Pinot Noir brought centuries ago by Count Henry of Burgundy. Whites are made from Doura Branca and Arinto, the Arinto thought to be a descendant of the German Riesling.

At the center of these three regions is the ancient Roman crossroads town of Viseu. All of these locales grow *vinhos maduros,* or "mature wines," from ripened grapes. Two of the landmark towns are Pinhel, noted for its rosé table wines, and Agueda, an area that makes wines that may be described as somewhere between vinho verde and vinho maduro.

Carcavelos

In the tiny Carcavelos region, which measures less than 80 acres, vines are grown upon alluvial solid deposits that border the Tagus estuary. A red dessert wine grown from the Galego Dourado vine is made to varying sweetness levels. Rare nowadays, the wines of Carcavelos are treasured in the Scandinavian countries, where the drier versions are taken as aperitifs.

Estremadura

The Estremadura region is located north of Lisbon and is usually divided into two main districts: the "plain" and the "ocean."

The wines from the plain, the valley of the Tagus River, are reds from Cartaxo and reds and whites from Almeirim, Bucelas, and Torres Vedras. Most of these wines are consumo.

The soils of the ocean district, subdivided into the northern Alcobaça and the Colares in the south, are typically of heavy clay in consistency. Some of the very oldest vineyards in the world exist in the Colares. The sand is so deep and hot in this locale that the *Phylloxera* could not wreak its damage here during its late nineteenth-century rampage. Consequently, the vines of Colares survived the scourge. To keep the grapes from burning, the vines must be propped up from the sand in the summer and early fall.

Setúbal

South of Lisbon in the upper portion of the Setúbal are the vineyards of Azeitão and Palmela. These, like the vineyards of Colares, continue to flourish with un-grafted vines that resisted the *Phylloxera*. The vineyards are bordered by the sea and the towering limestone Arrábida hills. The white Moscatel do Setúbal grape and the red Moscatel Roxo are both vinified into a golden dessert wine aptly named Sebutal Muscatel, thought by many wine experts to be the finest muscatel in the world and by others to be the best dessert wine of all.

It is in the Setúbal where many of the exported rosé wines are grown, but these have not been given, as yet, any demarcation. These wines are made primarily from the varieties Alvarelhão, Bastardo, Mourisco, and Touriga and some are made *pétillant* from artificial carbonation.

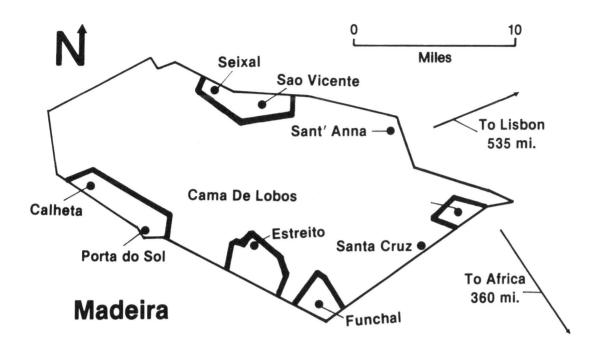

Madeira

The isle of Madeira is only 30 miles long and scarcely 16 miles wide—and only about one-third of the land surface is suitable for viticulture. The entire island is a dormant volcano dotted with high cliffs and caves, and most of the arable land must be created by breaking up the lava with pick and shovel.

The vines grown include *Malvasia*, which the British often referred to as Malmsey, a variety originally brought to Madeira from Crete; Bastardo, often mentioned by poets of the eighteenth and nineteenth centuries; and Terrantez. Perhaps the most important variety is the Sercial vine, thought to be a relative of the German Riesling.

In modern times, Madeira is made in classic dessert-wine style. Grapes are crushed by bare-footed men in *lagares* (shallow open-top vats) and the resulting must is carried in goatskins to the winery lodges—most of which are in the capital city of Funchal. Following fermentation, the wine is aged for six months or so in the heated cellars called *estufa*, where temperatures of about 110 to 115 degrees Fahrenheit "bake" the wine. For the sweeter *Malmsey* and *Bual Madeiras*, the *estufado* baking process is performed after brandy is added to fortify the wine. The drier *Sercial* and *Verdelho Madeiras* are baked in estufa before the fortification brandy is blended in.

Legend has it that some casks consigned to a colonial American buyer were once accidentally topped-up from a barrel of rainwater. The Madeira shippers

A *Frank Schoonmaker*
S E L E C T I O N

PURVEYOR TO HER MAJESTY   THE QUEEN OF DENMARK'S HOUSEHOLD

WARRE'S

750 ML   ALC. BY VOL. 20%

1975
VINTAGE
PORTO

PRODUCE OF PORTUGAL
Shipped by
WARRE & CA. LDA. OPORTO
Established 1670
IMPORTED BY: FRANK SCHOONMAKER SELECTIONS
NEW YORK, N. Y.

BY APPOINTMENT TO   HER MAJESTY THE QUEEN

WINE MERCHANTS
GEO. G. SANDEMAN SONS & CO LIMITED

FINE RICH
MADEIRA

SANDEMAN.®
Established in the year 1790

PRODUCE OF MADEIRA (PORTUGAL)
BOTTLED BY THE MADEIRA WINE CO. LDA., FUNCHAL
FOR GEO. G. SANDEMAN SONS & CO. LTD.,
Contents 750 ML   Alc. 17.8% by vol.
IMPORTED BY CHATEAU & ESTATE WINES CO., NEW YORK, N.Y.

discovered this mistake only after shipment and expected a wrathful response. However, the lighter Madeira wines were received even more warmly than the traditional product—and reorders were placed for larger shipments. This legend continues, with "Rainwater" Madeira still commercially produced.

There remain a few bottles of *Madere de Napoleon*, which was produced in 1772. This was offered to Napoleon in 1815 on his way to exile at St. Helena, but he was too ill to take any.

In our times Malvasia, or Malmsey, is obtained from the pressing of the ripest of the grapes grown in the hottest region of the island. Sercial is produced from the Teutonic varieties grown upon the peaks and cliffs, some from sites suspended in truly precarious positions. Sercial Madeira is not usually drunk until it is at least eight years old, and it may be aged much longer before consumption.

Douro (Port)

Aside from more modernized equipment, the making of contemporary sweet *port* wine has not essentially changed since it was first produced by the English in the lodges several centuries ago.

Port is a fortified wine made from sweet red grapes that are crushed and fermented so as to use about half of the natural grape sugar, at which point brandy is added to raise the alcohol content sufficiently to stop fermentation (by inhibiting any further yeast action). Because port contains unfermented grape sugars, it is by definition sweet. The British, who have long since dominated port production and trade, consider it the supreme after-dinner drink.

Vineyard conditions in the Douro are extreme in both climate and soil. The climate is biting cold in winter and reaches more than 100 degrees Fahrenheit during most summers. Rainfall often measures more than 50 inches per year. The rocky shale in the mountainsides and cliffs is composed of a compressed clay that commonly protrudes from a dense granite overlayment. The labor required to plant just a small vineyard upon a terrace supported by a high wall is monumental. The earth is often so unmanageable that explosives are needed to make the holes for planting the vines. There are few nutrients, save potassium, in the soil. Few other plants, and no other crop, could be grown economically in such a locale. Yet it remains one of the most beautiful vineyard regions on earth.

The finest growths are situated near Pinhão, located in the center of the Douro approximately 60 miles east along the Douro River from the great English wine lodges in the city of Vila Nova de Gaia.

More than thirty grape varieties are grown in the Douro for port, among the best being Alvarelhão, Mourisco, Tinta Cao, Tinta Francisca, Souzão, and

Terraced port wine vineyards of the Duoro River Valley in Portugal. (Source: Forrester & ca., Limitada, Vila de Gaia, Portugal.)

Touriga. While many of the lodges now employ modern machinery in the vinifying processes, at some of the more traditionally operated firms barefooted men still crush the grapes in lagares. Most experts agree that the differences in resulting product quality are not distinguishable.

The vintage begins in September with the gathering of grapes, crushing, and fermentation. As the fermenting process converts sugar to alcohol, wine masters monitor progress until just the right amount of sweetness remains in the fermenting must—then brandy at a strength of 155 degrees proof (about 77.5 percent alcohol), which must be purchased from the grower's cooperative, is added to arrest the fermentation and raise the alcohol content up to about 19 percent by volume. Each vintner individually sets his own precise sweetness standards, most ranging from between 10 and 13 percent sugar by weight.

Of the 30 million gallons or more of wine that is made annually in the Douro, only about one-third is *approveitado* (government-approved) for port. This is determined by a "points" system that is governed by the Instituto do Vinho do Porto and outlined in table 9-2.

Once a new wine is judged suitable to be processed into precious port, it is taken from its *quinta*, or estate lodge, in oaken *pipes* of about 145 gallons capacity and shipped to one of the port lodges in Vila Nova de Gaia. These days,

Crushing port wine grapes in the traditional lagares.

semitractor and trailer units and railroad cars haul much of the new port to the city. But up until recent times, when hydroelectric-generating dams made the trek impossible, single-sailed boats called *barcos rabelos* hauled the pipes down the river across the rapids. At the port lodges, the wines age in wooden barrels until they have reached maturity. Most ports are blends of various wines and vintages, with each lodge blending to maintain its own consistent style. The new wine is stored in large wooden casks called *toneis* that can hold about 3,000 gallons each. When these wines receive long periods of aging in wood casks, they are known as "wood ports." There are five distinct types of "wood ports": *Ruby port* ages for about four years in pipes before bottling. *Old ruby port* matures for seven years prior to bottling. *White port* (popular in France as an aperitif) is made from white grapes and vinified in a fashion similar to ruby port. *Tawny ports* are rather amber in color, the result of aging periods of more than eight years in wooden pipes.

When the port producers or shippers feel that the year has been truly exceptional for the production of fine port, they "declare" a vintage—something that only happens about one year out of every five. Of all ports, vintage port is deepest ruby in color and fullest in flavor. The wines are aged in pipes for only about two years before bottling, but they are given the benefit of long periods of aging in the bottle before being shipped. Despite the claims of some authorities, vintage ports will not live forever, they are generally at their best with from ten to thirty-five years of aging. Vintage ports are more expensive than most wood ports, but, in the opinion of many connoisseurs, they are well worth it. Few wines have received the accolades bestowed on well-aged vintage port.

There are also *Late-Bottled Vintage ports* made—sometimes simply labeled as *LBV port*. These are aged about twice as long as vintage ports, have a lesser degree of color and flavor generally, and cost less than fine vintage ports, but can be a good value when produced by one of the better lodges.

The famous "crusted ports" are made in much the same manner as the vintage ports, except that they are blended from at least two separate vintages and are aged for much longer periods of time in the bottle. During this aging, the sediment that develops hardens into the familiar crust.

TABLE 9-2 Elements Governing Authorization of Vineyards

(a) Elements	Minima	Fixed	Maxima
		Points Awarded	
Productivity	+900	—	−120 (for lowest production)
Altitude	+900	—	−150 (for lowest altitude)
Geographical position	+50	—	−600
Upkeep	+500	—	−100
Soil-Granite		−100	—
Mixture	—	+150	—
Schist	—	−100	—
Grape qualities	+300	—	−150
Gradient	+100	—	−100 (for steepest gradient)
Position in relation to climate conditions	0	—	−60 (for best shelter)
Age of vines	0	—	−50 (for oldest)
Distance between roots	+50	—	−50 (for greatest distance)

(b) Classes of Vineyards	Total Points Awarded	Permissible Usage for Port in Litres per 1000 Vines
Class A:	1200 or more	600
Class B:	1001-1200	570
Class C:	901-1000	520
	801-900	490
Class D:	701-800	330
Class E:	501-600	220
	401-500	190
Class F:	below 400	0

Points per class are subject to annual review.

The port lodge may not ship more than one-third of its inventory in any single year. The port vineyard region is entitled to the "Alto Douro" name for labeling and is divided into the *Baixo Corgo*, where from one to one and one-half bottles of wine can be produced from each vine, and the *Cima Corgo*, where only one-half bottle is permitted. Of all the port wine made, only about 10 percent is consumed in Portugal.

Apart from the controls exercised on port production by the Instituto do Vinho do Porto, there is also a winegrower's union called the Casa do Douro, which was formed in 1933. This cooperative regulates trade and manufactures the brandy that is used in arresting fermentations. There is also the Gremio dos Exportadores do Vinho do Porto, a shippers' association.

Dwarfed by the immense international popularity of port, the table wines made in the Douro are often forgotten. Undemarcated red table wines are the most highly thought of—particularly those of Ferreirinha. The giant SOGRAPE—Vinhos de Portugal SARL uses grapes from the Douro and Dão in the blending of its famous "Mateus" rosé table wine, which is blended, processed, and shipped from Oporto.

The great port-wine names are Burmeister, Cockburn, Croft, DaSilva, Dow, Ferreira, Fonseca, Graham, Mackenzie, Noval, Offley Forrester, Sandeman, Taylor, and Warre.

TABLE 9-3   Portugal—Principal Growths

CARCAVELOS	White Port
	Tawny Port
Carcavelos R DW	Oporto-Bottled Port
DAO AND TRAS-OS-MONTES	Ferreirinha R TW
Vinhos Maduros R, Ro, W TW & SpW	*ESTREMADURA*
Agueda	
Bairrada	plain
Pinhel	Almeirim R&W TW
	Bucelas R&W TW
Vila Real Ro TW	Cartaxo R TW
	Torres Vedras R&W TW
DOURO	ocean
	Alcobaca W TW
Port R&W DW	Colares R TW
Vintage Port	
Crusted Port	*MADEIRA*
Wood Port	
Ruby Port	Bual W DW
Old Ruby Port	Malvasia W DW

Sercial W DW
Verdelho W TW

MINHO

Vinho Verde R & W TW
  Amarante
  Basto
  Braga
  Lima

Moncao
Peñafiel

SETÚBAL

Azeitao W DW
Palmela W DW

Ro TW

R + red
Ro + rose
W + white
TW + table wine
DW + dessert wine
SpW + sparkling wine

PRODUCT OF SPAIN

LIGHT FINO
Solera Reserva "JARANA"
SHERRY

PRODUCED AND BOTTLED BY

JEREZ SHERRY

ELO

ANTIGUOS VIÑEDOS Y BODEGAS DE LA
FAMILIA LUSTAU RUIZ–BERDEJO
FUNDADOS 1896

EMILIO LUSTAU
JEREZ
ESPAÑA

ALC 15,5 % BY VOL.

750 ML

Selected by EUROPVIN - CANNAN & WASSERMAN

IMPORTED BY
PRESTIGE WINE CORP.
NEW YORK, N.Y.

Emb 2083-CA

RIS 302379/CA

GRAND VIN
DU PAYS DE VAUD

CLOS DE BARIN

LA CÔTE
DORIN PREMIER CRU DE
LA CÔTE VAUDOISE

CERTIFIE D'ORIGINE

Récolte exclusive de la propriété
élevée et mise en bouteilles dans la tradition vigneronne
par Uvavins-Vaud   Morges-Tolochenaz

233.7

10

THE WINES OF AUSTRIA, SWITZERLAND BELGIUM, LIECHTENSTEIN, AND LUXEMBOURG

T he five countries considered in this chapter, particularly Switzerland, have been making strides in recent years in wine production and quality. While it's true that none of the five ships much wine to the United States, it's also true that each is shipping more than it used to. Not surprisingly, the wines of these Western European countries have a good deal in common with the wines of their larger wine-producing neighbors: Viticulture in Austria, Liechtenstein, and Luxembourg is quite similar to viticulture as it is practiced in Germany. The wines of Belgium have a kindred relationship to those of France; and Swiss winegrowing, while its principal character is French, also exhibits marked German and Italian traits.

During the past decade or so, Austria has emerged from relative obscurity to become the fifteenth-largest producer among wine-growing nations—much of this progress is the result of an aggressive export program. This recent success, however, may soon collapse in the face of the much publicized antifreeze scandal in Rust, Austria, a situation that is explained in detail later in this chapter.

Switzerland has broadened its vineyard perspective. Most texts devoted to wine geography divide Switzerland into three major viticultural regions, but one can now identify six distinct regions of very diverse character.

AUSTRIA

The wine-growing regions of Austria are all located in the eastern part of the nation, distributed in the 150-mile sector that is bordered by Czechoslovakia to the north and Yugoslavia to the south. The Austrian wine land is replete with rivers—the main artery in the north being the Danube.

The climate of the principal Austrian wine-growing regions is drier and warmer than most vineyard regions in West Germany. This is due primarily to the Alps east of Austria that create a barrier to cold westerly winds and rain-filled clouds. As a result, grapes grown in the dry Continental Basin often reach the overripe state necessary to produce the prized late-harvest *Beerenauslese* and *Trockenbeerenauslese* wines.

Grape seeds have been found in Austria that are estimated to be more than 2,500 years old, indicating that vines were harvested—and perhaps wine made—there at that time.

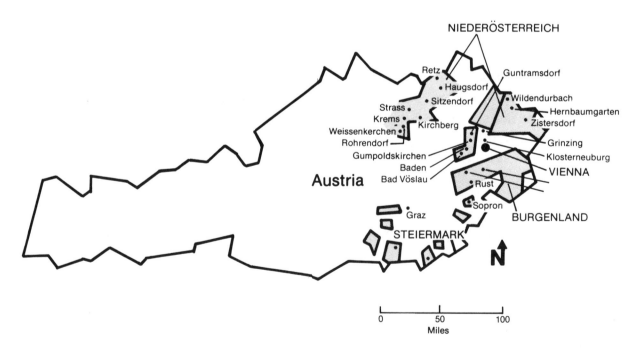

The Austrians, like most Western European peoples, first learned the art of viniculture from the Romans during their occupation. When Germanic tribes overran the Roman Empire, winegrowing, for all intents and purposes, ceased to exist. Charlemagne, through his decrees for the planting of vines, began the resurrection of the wine arts in Austria during the Middle Ages.

Among the most active forces in the reestablishment of Austrian winegrowing were the monasteries. One of the finest of these is Heiligenkreuz, built by St. Leopold in 1141, near Mayerling, in the Vöslau region. It remains one of the most splendid examples of Cistercian monastic architecture in the country, and its still-flourishing vineyards bring to mind the memory of many vintages of flowery white wines enjoyed in the nearby Vienna Woods.

During the early 1100s Viennese winegrowers maintained a powerful association, one that rigidly restricted wine imports allowed into their region. These restrictions were no doubt at least one reason why Austrian wine quality generally suffered during the next few centuries. In 1582 Johannes Rasch wrote an impressive book about the need for upgrading Austrian viticulture. This work unquestionably influenced the Austrian Imperial Court to ratify a wine-quality classification system although this did not come about until 1673.

It is in Austria that one finds *Heurigen*, a word literally translated as "young wine," but which refers to the fresh jug wines available at low prices in the many Vienna wine pubs. The first Heurigen became available in 1780 when Empress Maria Theresa proclaimed that each winegrower was to be allowed to sell wine made from his or her own vines without having to pay taxes. As new wines became marketable in November, the vintner would display a crown or wreath of straw or fir above the entrance door of the establishment, advertising to passersby that the Heurigen was ready. With the new vintage, the vintner would welcome new friends and renew ties with old ones. By the following November, when a new Heurigen was ready, the old wines became *alte wein*, or "old wine." The popularity of this tradition has made Heurigen one of the most famous wines in Austria.

Austria embarked upon an ambitious program of change for its wine industry during the early 1970s. Previously, Austria had only a rather loose set of national wine regulations that did little to define origins or set production controls. When neighboring Germany adopted its new wine law in 1971, the Austrian government took steps to enact a very similar set of regulations, the major categories of which are:

Tafelwein	natural grape sugar must have reached a minimum of 13 degrees Brix

Qualitätswein | natural grape sugar must have reached a minimum of 15 degrees Brix, alcohol level must be at least 9.5% and the label must display the wine's geographical origin

Kabinett Wein | natural grape sugar must have reached a minimum of 17 degrees Brix and no sugar or juice concentrate may be added, and the label must display the wine's geographical origin

Besonderer Reife (Lesearten) | Kabinett Wein that has higher natural grape-sugar levels and also exhibits organoleptic characteristics that are typical of overripe grapes, and the label must display the wine's geographical origin

Spätlese | natural grape sugar must have reached a minimum of 19 degrees Brix, and the label must display the wine's geographical origin

Auslese | natural grape sugar must have reached a minimum of 21 degrees Brix, and the label must display the wine's geographical origin

Beerenauslese | natural grape sugar must have reached a minimum of 25 degrees Brix, and the label must display the wine's geographical origin

Ausbruch | natural grape sugar must have reached a minimum of 27 degrees Brix, and the label must display the wine's geographical origin

Trockenbeerenauslese | natural grape sugar must have reached a minimum of 30 degrees Brix, and the label must display the wine's geographical origin

Eiswein | natural grape sugar must have reached a minimum of 22 degrees Brix, the grapes must have been naturally frozen, and the label must display the wine's geographical origin

The addition of sugar is permitted under much the same circumstances as in Germany. Should natural grape sugar fall below the minimum of 13 KMW (an acronym for *Klosterneuburger Mostwaage*—a measure of sugar density by percentage of total weight that is virtually identical to the more familiar Brix measurement used throughout the United States) for a particular vintage, then the wine may be chaptalized provided the sugar addition brings the resulting juice only up to the 13 KMW minimum. A maximum addition of 5KMW is allowed under any condition.

One of the chief differences in the Austrian quality levels and those of Germany is the higher sugar requirement in Austria. This results from the warmer and drier climate that generally yields fruit of higher natural-sugar content in Austria. Another difference in the Austrian system has to do with testing. No *Prüfungsnummer* is awarded in Austria, but, instead, wines that successfully pass the taste testing of government Cellar Inspectors may be awarded the *Weingütesiegel*, or "Austrian Wine Seal." This seal is circular and colored red, white, and gold and should not be confused with the triangular Austrian Trade Mark (Österreichermarke) that is placed upon some wines that have not earned the quality-wine seal.

Austrian wine-labeling laws allow the bottle label to carry the name of a region (for example, Niederösterreich), a district (for example, Wachau), and a village (for example, Weissenkirchen). The name of the grape variety, for instance, the pervasive Grüner Veltliner, is also permitted, either alone or in combination with the geographical origin. It is also common on Austrian wine labels to find brand names of vintners combined with the appellation of origin. When a geographic claim is made for a white wine, that wine must have originated *entirely* from that designated locale. Austrian red wines are allowed to be blended with up to 15 percent of wines from outside the specified area.

In Austrian usage, the word *Reid* (that literally translates as vineyard) is closely related to the German term *Einzellage*, or "distinctive individual vineyard parcel." Some wines produced in Austria carry individual reid names upon their labels, but such wines are rarely shipped to America and can be found only at the largest and most fully stocked metropolitan wine retailers.

Niederösterreich

The Niederösterreich, located in the northeastern corner of Austria, is the largest wine-growing region of the country. It is often referred to as "lower Austria" due to the lower elevations of the land that borders both banks of the Danube that flows through the central part of this beautiful countryside.

Vineyards in the Niederösterreich embrace the romantic old city of Vienna both to the north and the south. Soils in the region are varied—lowland soil is composed of chalk, gravel, sandy loess, and schist.

There are eight districts in the Niederösterreich: Baden, Falkenstein, Krems, Langenlois, Retz, Traismaur, Vöslau, and Wachau. The wines of the Niederösterreich are typically white, light, and dry although, because of the relatively higher grape-sugar levels attained, some are also strong. The Grüner Veltliner is very heavily planted in this region.

Forty miles to the west of Vienna is the town of Krems, with its lovely display of vineyard slopes directly facing the Danube. To the northeast of Krems is the Langenlois district, with several miles of the Kamp River Valley connecting the two districts. While both white and red table wines are produced in the Langenlois, the strong, aromatic Rieslings are the most particularly noteworthy products of the district. To the southwest of Krems is the famed Wachau district. One could almost mistake the Danube for the Rhein as it flows past the storybook villages of Weissenkirchen and Dürnstein. The white wines grown there are also reminiscent of Rhein wines, but perhaps more tart and less complex. It was in Dürnstein that Richard Lion-Heart was imprisoned and held for ransom during the twelfth century. Though arguments on the subject persist, it is generally conceded that the Wachau is the nation's finest-quality wine-growing district.

Just east of Krems is the small village of Rohendorf, of importance primarily as the home of Lenz Moser. Moser has been a dynamic advocate of twentieth-century high-tech vineyard cultural and training methods, and his teachings have helped revolutionize viticulture not only in Austria but in many other nations as well. Moser's sons continue his fine work and manage the family wine-growing estate.

Ringing Krems and the Langenlois are the Niederösterreich districts of Retz at the extreme northwest, Wildendurnbach and Falkenstein at the far northeast, and Vöslau at the farthest point south—the last being about 25 miles south of the capital city of Vienna.

Perhaps the best-known wine of Austria is the legendary *Gumpoldskirchner*, grown in the Baden district from Rotgipfler vines. These rich golden wines are the product of grapes grown upon the slopes situated below the exquisite resort town of Gumpoldskirchen. Eventually these slopes lead down to the Danube, 15 miles to the north in Vienna.

Vienna

Vienna, Austria's smallest viticultural region, is bordered both to the south and the north by the Niederösterreich. The Vienna region contains about 1,000

Heurigen—many of which, in addition to the new wine, also offer *sturm*, a partially fermented wine akin to the *spritzen* of German Oktoberfest fame. The importance of Vienna wine growing lies not in its size, which is diminutive, but in the social activity and tourist traffic it engenders; principally in the many Heurigen. The most noteworthy Vienna vineyard districts are Grinzing, Nüssdorf, and Sievering.

Burgenland

The Burgenland, located about 25 miles to the southeast of Vienna, is the source of some of the most impressive wines grown in Austria. In the center of the region is the large lake Neusiedler See that tempers the climate of the area and provides humidity to nurture the precious *Edelfäule,* or "noble rot." Because of these conditions it is common for up to half of the Burgenland's white wine production to reach the upper KMW sugar levels. A few of the finer estates may produce, in some years, a preponderance of Beerenauslese and Trockenbeerenauslese wines. Typically, these are rich and strong.

The most widely cultivated grape varieties of the Burgenland are the Müller-Thurgau, Neuburger, and Weissburgunder. Gewürztraminer, Muskat-Ottonel, Riesling, and Welschreisling vines are planted to a lesser extent in the region.

There are two subdistricts in the Burgenland: Neusiedler See and Rust. Neusiedler See white wines are generally superior Austrian growths, but this district is probably best known locally for some of its red wine production from *Blaufränkischer* (Pinot Noir) and *Blauer Portugieser* (Merlot). Rust is the best known of the two subdistricts, primarily due to the antifreeze scandal that was worldwide news during the summer of 1985. A number of wines from Rust were found to contain diethylene glycol, commonly used as a refrigerant, added in an apparent attempt to increase sweetness levels without the addition of sugar. Ingestion of this chemical in sufficient amounts can cause brain and kidney damage. This scandal has had a devastating impact on the entire Austrian wine industry.

Rust is also where *Ruster Ausbruch* originates—a Trockenbeerenauslese that often achieves the high quality of German wines of the same type.

Steiermark (Styria)

The Steiermark region is composed of five comparatively small districts stretching from the southwest to the southeast of Graz and on both sides of the Mur River. The terrain is stark, with many vineyards established upon the poor rocky soils of the Alpine foothills. Much of the abundant rainfall either quickly runs down the steep slopes or arrives during the dormant season, without adding much to the moisture levels in the vineyards.

Southern Styria and Klöch-Oststeiermark are the two principal districts in the Steiermark. Southern Styria surrounds its capital city of Leibnitz. This district is the most conducive to white wine-growing in the region and cultivates Muskat-Sylvaner (Sauvignon Blanc), Riesling, Weisser Burgunder, and Welschriesling vines for the most part. Klöch-Oststeiermark, like the Southern Styria district, is located on the border of Yugoslavia and begins about 15 miles east of the Mur River. The soil of the Klöch-Oststeiermark is volcanic and yields smoky white wines grown primarily from Gewürztraminer and Ruländer vines.

SWITZERLAND

The State of California is about ten times the size of Switzerland. Yet the 30,000 acres of vineyards cultivated within this comparatively small nation exhibit a great deal of character and surprising diversity.

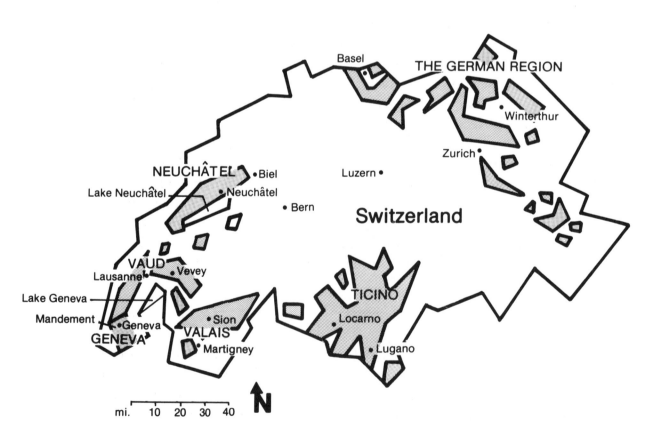

Switzerland is a nation of three cultures, each of which maintains its own language. In the eastern portion of the country is the German region, in the west the French, in the extreme south is the Italian sector. The country is politically divided into twenty-nine autonomous *Cantons,* each with its own customs, regulations, traditions, and life-styles. The same sort of distinctions and contrasts can be found in the vineyard topography from one region to another.

From the mountains of Switzerland rise three of Europe's most important rivers—the Rhein, which flows northward through the German region to the northernmost reaches of the country; the Rhône, which flows westward through the French Valais region located in the southwest portion of the nation and on into France; and the Po, which runs southward through the Italian sector and into Italy itself. The vines in these mountain districts are planted at higher elevations than in most other vineyards in Europe—the very highest being at Visperterminen, some 3,700 feet above sea level.

Virtually all of the 23 million gallons of wine made annually in Switzerland is dry and, as in the other nations in central Europe, most of it is white. In recent years, however, much more attention has been given to the planting of red wine-grape varieties. Nevertheless, it is the white *Chasselas* variety that is most widely planted in the country, along with Müller-Thurgau—the latter often called "Riesling-Sylvaner." *Amigne* and *Completer* are other white wine-grape varieties grown in Swiss vineyards. The principal reds are *Blauburgunder,* or *Klevener,* both of which refer to Pinot Noir. Also to be found are Gamay and Merlot, among others.

As in Germany, Austria, and other Western European wine-growing nations, the ancient Romans and the Roman Catholic church had the greatest influence on the origins of Swiss wine, particularly in the Vaud and Neuchâtel Cantons. The oldest monastery in Switzerland is the Abbey of St. Maurice, located near Monthey. The monks of St. Maurice owned many vineyards near the eastern shores of Lake Geneva. The White Monks are credited with introducing the vine into the area just east of the city of Lausanne, on the northern shore of the lake. These vineyards are now secularized. The Clos des Abbayes and Clos des Moines are the best known of these and both continue to produce superior wines from Chasselas vines.

Switzerland served as a battleground for Germanic tribes and Romans for centuries during and following the days of the Roman Empire. In the ninth century, however, Switzerland became a portion of the German Empire. Later in the same century, in 888, the French Burgundians invaded the Rhône Valley to the southeast of Lake Geneva in the region now known as the Valais. The Burgundians contributed a great deal to the art and craft of viniculture in that area, and the Burgundian character remains unmistakable in the wines of the region, even in modern times. The white *Pinot Gris* and the *Traminer* (the "Gewürz" prefix came centuries later in the Alsace) are varieties still cultivated in the region though they are known locally as *Malvoisie* and *Païen,* respectively. The Burgundian King Rodolphe gave the vineyards at Bevais, north of the Valais, near Neuchâtel, to the grand Burgundian Abbey of Cluny in the latter part of the tenth century during the time when the great Abbot Mayeul was the Benedictine primate.

Switzerland continued to remain under foreign subjugation until 1291, when the first three cantons of Schwyz, Unterwalden, and Uri were established in order to resist the Hapsburgs. During the next two centuries another ten cantons entered the Swiss confederation. The thirteen cantons remained self-governing and, despite their differences and quarrels, were still unified enough to raise some of the finest national infantry in all of Europe, defeating Charles the Bold of Burgundy repeatedly in the latter portion of the fifteenth century. By 1648 the Swiss achieved total political independence from the Holy Roman Empire—which was guaranteed by the Treaty of Westphalia.

Despite its fiercely guarded independence, Switzerland continued to be influenced by its neighbors. The Duc de Rohan, who commanded the French forces at Maienfeld, introduced the grape variety Pinot Noir into the Grisons Canton during the 1630s. The loose federation of Swiss cantons gave way to the Helvetic Republic in 1798 modeled on the Republic established after the French Revolution. It was comparatively short-lived, however, and the Swiss, inspired by America's success in federating her states, which were similar in some ways to the cantons, resumed the earlier form of government. In 1848, the new federal constitution was drawn and adopted.

No set of political instruments, however, could unify the essentially tripartite nature of Swiss culture and history. And Swiss wine growing, like Swiss society, continued to reflect its distinctive Roman-Italian, German, and French extraction. There is no true "Swiss" style.

Interpreting Swiss wine labels today can be difficult because the information on the labels varies depending upon the canton in which the wine was grown. Each has its own traditions and regulations. In general, wines are named either for the places in which they were grown, the grape variety used to make them, or by the name of the wine type. From the point of view of the American consumer, the most essential information printed upon most labels becomes the vintner's name, a statement that is equally true in nearly every vinicultural area in the world. The following Swiss terms should be noted:

Avec Sucre Residuel	labeling term that means that the wine has some residual sweetness; the wine is not dry

Dôle	government-tested red wine made from Gamay and Pinot Noir grapes grown in the Valais region
Johannisberg	white wine grown from Sylvaner grapes in the Valais region
Légèrement Doux	labeling term that means the wine has some sweetness; same as "Avec Sucre Residuel"
Premier Cru	wine grown upon the vintner's vineyard estate; the equivalent of "estate bottled"
Oeil de Perdrix	labeling term used for rosé wines made from Pinot Noir grapes
Salvagnin	government-tested red wine made from Pinot Noir grapes grown in the Vaud region

The Valais

This is the largest wine-growing region in Switzerland, cultivating more than 10,000 acres of vineyards and producing nearly 10 million gallons of wine annually. The Valais is a long, wide valley situated on both sides of the Rhône River in its western passage through the French sector at the southwestern reaches of the country. The climate of the Valais is one of the warmest and driest in Switzerland, and many of the mountain vineyards must be irrigated from thaws of the upper glaciers. The most noteworthy towns and villages of the region are Ardon, Chamason, Conthey, Leytron and Vétroz—all centered on the capital city of Sion.

The most famous wine of the Valais is the light, refreshing *Fendant*, named for the grape variety that is grown in abundance there. The Swiss cultivate the Sylvaner grape in the region, too, and perversely call the resulting wine "Johannisberg." This is generally a wine with good body and fine bouquet, often found in Geneva wine outlets. The true Johannisberg Riesling is also grown in the Valais and is reminiscent of the crisper, drier, Riesling wines grown in the French Alsace. Other white wines of the region are grown from *Malvoisie* (Pinot Gris) and the old Roman *Humagne* varieties. *Amigne* and *Arvine* are varieties cultivated for the production of strong, ordinary white wines and are sometimes made into dessert-wine types. *Ermitage* is a rather neutral dry white wine made from Marsanne grapes grown in the Valais.

One of the best-known red wines made in Switzerland is *Dôle*—a government-tested wine made from Pinot Noir grapes. It has neither the deep red color or coffeelike bouquet of French Côte d'Or wines from Pinot Noir but is distinctively light and fruity. Gamay vines are cultivated in the Valais, as well, and produce wines of a strawberry bouquet and flavor.

The Vaud

The greater portion of Vaud vineyards are situated in a crescent along the entire north shore of Lake Geneva. The region also includes some vineyards on both sides of the portion of the Rhône River between the Valais and the lake.

The Vaud, generally considered to be a French region, has three subdistricts: the Chablais, the Lavaux, and La Côte. The Chablais is the Rhône River sector, centered by the town of Aigle. Chasselas grapes grown in this area yield light

Vineyards in the Vaud region of Switzerland. (Source: Max F. Chiffelle, Office des Vins Vaudois.)

white wines of good quality, but not usually the equal of the whites of neighboring Lavaux. The lakeside villages on the eastern shores of Lake Geneva are "travel-poster" picturesque and many acres of beautifully terraced vineyards grow up the Lavaux mountainsides behind them. Some experts consider the epitome of Swiss wine growing to be the famed Dézaley slope, situated above the villages of Rivaz and Treytorrens in the Lavaux district. Here, light crops of the Chasselas grapes are grown to full ripeness, yielding very fragrant and rich white wine. Wines from these vineyards have their own government-approved appellation of origin. Other notable wine-growing towns in the Lavaux district are Chardonne, Cully, Epesses, St.-Saphorin, and the very famous Vevey, where the huge annual Fête des Vignerons has been held every year since 1651, when it was first started by the monks of the Abbey of St. Urban. The wines from these lower villages are almost always dry and austere products of the Chasselas grape. The most common and ordinary of these are labeled simply "Dorin."

The La Côte district extends westerly from Lausanne to the borders of the Geneva region. The wines of this locale are generally less flavorful and less distinctive than those from the Lavaux, but good-quality vineyards can be found in the vicinity of La Bonne Côte: Fechy, Luins, Perroy, and Vinzel.

Chasselas is grown for more than three-fourths of the wine produced in the Vaud. Gamay is the other principal grape variety grown there, and it is used alone or blended with a small percentage of Pinot Noir to make *Salvagnin*—a government-tested red that is similar, but rarely the equal, of Dôle in the Valais.

Geneva

Bordering the western end of the Vaud, surrounding the western tip of Lake Geneva, and following both sides of the Rhône River once it flows out of the lake, is the French Geneva region. This is one of the smallest wine-growing divisions in Switzerland, cultivating only 2,500 acres of vineyards and producing just a bit more than 2 million gallons of wine each year.

The Chasselas vine is grown abundantly in this canton and yields dry white table wines called *Perlan*, which resemble those of neighboring La Côte, but are often finished with a "spritz" of residual effervescence. In more recent years new plantings of the Gamay grape variety have significantly increased production of red wines in the region. Most of them are consumed locally, as is the Perlan.

Geneva is much less mountainous than most of Switzerland's wine regions—a factor that has permitted mechanization in the vineyards, and, in turn, reduced costs. This is reflected in the lower general price levels of the wines.

The Mandement, to the north of the Rhône River, is the largest of three Geneva wine-growing districts. A deed dated in the year 912 gave the Mandement vineyard to the Old Priory of Satigny, now the center village of the district. South of the city of Geneva are the districts of Arve-et-Rhône and Arve-et-Lac, the former located, as the name suggests, on the Rhône River and the latter on Lake Geneva. Both of these districts are small in comparison to the Mandement.

Neuchâtel

The region of Neuchâtel is the smallest vinicultural area in Switzerland. Its 1,300-odd acres actually begin in the Canton of Vaud and stretch northeastward along the northern shores of Lake Neuchâtel to the city of Biel. The French-style wines from this tiny locale are considered by most experts to be Switzerland's finest. Without question, the wines of Neuchâtel are the best-known Swiss wines in American wine markets.

Virtually all of the white wines produced in the region are made from Chasselas, which is 75 percent of the total regional output. It is common for these whites to be bottled very young while still containing some of the effervescence from primary fermentation: "to make the star" is a local term denoting a slight sparkle in the wine. The other 25 percent of Neuchâtel wine production is devoted to red and rosé wines vinified from the Burgundian Pinot Noir grape. The most notable rosé is the legendary *Oeil-de-Perdrix*, or "eye of the partridge," which is also grown in the Valais. A light red wine from Pinot Noir is known as *Cortaillod*, named for the village where it is grown.

The German Region

The vineyards of the German region, diverse in both character and geography, are scattered across the Rhein Valley that makes up the entire northern portion of Switzerland. The Swiss Rhein flows northward through the Grisons Canton, or Graübunden, which borders Liechtenstein, and continues north to the Bodensee and then westward to the historic city of Basel.

Vineyards in this part of the country, often referred to as "Eastern Switzerland," are scattered among 300 villages within eight cantons. The most noteworthy of the communities are Hallau, Wädenswil (where a large vinicultural research center is located), Winterthur, and world-renowned Zurich. Despite this large geographical expanse, the German region cultivates only about 4,000 acres of vines and comparatively little of its 2 million gallons of annual wine production finds its way to U.S. wine shops or restaurants.

While Chasselas (called *Gutedel* in this region) still reigns as the predominant white grape variety, it seems reasonable to expect that Müller-Thurgau will be gaining in popularity for it is in this region that Professor Müller developed the hybrid variety. The local wine growers and merchants still refer to the Müller-Thurgau as "Riesling-Sylvaner"—the names of the two components of the hybrid vine. Pinot Gris and Completer vines are also cultivated in the German region, but to a much lesser extent comparatively. The predominant red grape in the area is the Pinot Noir, called the *Blauburgunder* by the region's winegrowers.

Ticino

Ticino, the Italian sector of Switzerland, cultivates several hundred more acres of vines than the Geneva region, but it produces several hundred thousand gallons less wine. This is due primarily to the shy-bearing characteristic of the Merlot—the red wine grape grown most widely in the region. The wine that results is commonly labeled "Merlot di Ticino," but if the wine passes a government test for superior bouquet, flavor, and body, it may be labeled "VITI." The best of the VITI may be labeled "Riserva" after further aging in the Italian manner.

The Italian region is situated upon the Alpine foothills surrounding Lake Lucarno and Lake Lugano in the Ticino Canton. The area is somewhat subtropical in climate, with palm trees and other vegetation that one normally expects to find far to the south.

In addition to the dominant Merlot, small vineyard plantings of Bondala, Freisa, Gamay, and Pinot Noir can be found. Blends of these are made into an ordinary wine called "Nostrano," which is consumed locally. The native American *Isabella* vine still lingers in the Ticino—a holdover from the latter 1800s when it was used as a resistant rootstock for grafting during the *Phylloxera* epidemic.

BELGIUM

The Belgians drink more Burgundy wine than any other nation in the world except France. Yet few wines are grown in Belgium in modern times, certainly in comparison to the great wine production carried on by the Catholic church 1,000 years ago. During the Middle Ages there were wine-growing abbeys and monasteries in the vicinities of Bruges, Brussels, Ghent, Liège, Louvain, and Namur.

Nevertheless, the Belgians persist in their attempts at wine growing in an unfavorable climate and forbidding geography. Many of the most successful wineries are cooperative ventures that have amassed the capital to build large coal-fired (and more recently solar- and nuclear-powered) greenhouses in order to maintain optimal temperatures for the vines cultivated inside. One of the largest of these, located at Isca, produces more than 100,000 gallons per year.

LIECHTENSTEIN

More than half of the wine produced in this tiny principality is a red called *Vaduzer*, named after the capital city of Vaduz. It is made from the Pinot Noir variety, which the Liechtensteiners, like most Austrians and Swiss, call *Blauburgunder*. Most experts generally agree that the best vineyard for Vaduzer is that of Abtwingert.

LUXEMBOURG

The Grand Duchy of Luxembourg grows its wines from about 2,000 acres situated in German fashion on the north side of the upper Mosel Valley. As might be expected, these highlands provide an even shorter growing season than most of the marginal viticultural districts of the lower Mosel in Germany, and, hence, the wines, mostly grown from Riesling, generally exhibit a biting tartness from lack of full ripening. With superior cellar techniques, the best of these are made with a residual "spritz," or pétillant—and they can be very refreshing for a light summer meal when chilled. The most noteworthy districts are Ahn, Ehnen, Grechen, Grevenmacher, Remich, Wintringen, and Wasserbillig.

LAUSANNE · JUBLJANA 1977
1964

Maison fondée en 1796

NEUCHATEL
SUISSE

Samuel Châtenay s.a.

Propriétaire Encaveur

Neuchâtel (Suisse)

Mis en bouteille en nos caves

ALC. 11% BY VOL.

SEPPELT

1980   *1980*

*Produced from a blend of Cabernet Sauvignon grapes
grown at Great Western and Coonawarra, together
with Shiraz grapes from Keppoch and Barossa Valley.
This wine shows excellent fruit flavour
and oak character.*

AUSTRALIAN STILL RED WINE

Cabernet · Shiraz

IMPORTED BY SEPPELT WINES LIMITED LOS ANGELES CALIF.
PRODUCED & BOTTLED BY B. SEPPELT & SONS LIMITED · PRODUCE OF AUSTRALIA
ALCOHOL BY VOLUME 12·2% 750ML

11

THE WINES OF AUSTRALIA, NEW ZEALAND, CANADA, AND ENGLAND

The bonds of the British Commonwealth that link Australia, New Zealand, and Canada with Great Britain have also created close ties between the wine industries of these four nations. Aside from a common language and cultural heritage, there are the ties of politics and trade. Canada and England, for example, are the largest importers of Australian wines; and Australia, in turn, is a major importer of Canadian forest products and minerals.

On the other hand, each of these three Commonwealth nations also shows the unmistakable influence of European wine-growing traditions and practices. In the important wine-growing Barossa Valley of Australia the effects of a rich German heritage are still quite evident. The German language remains widely spoken there, and the wines grown throughout the southern states of Australia display a pronounced Teutonic character. The Australian wine industry has assimilated both its British and German influences and is now proceeding, with the help of the latest technology and progressive ideas, to develop its own unique quality.

Most of the vines cultivated in New Zealand are also of German origin, along with a good sprinkling of vines from France, Italy, Portugal, and Spain. New

Zealand wines rely heavily on these same countries for their style and for packaging concepts, but this is true in most of the New World wine-growing nations.

The French-speaking people who dwell in the Province of Quebec produce a comparatively small portion of Canada's wines, but the French influence, so deeply rooted and so deeply associated with wine, spills over into Canada's other wine-growing areas. Canada's rather rigorous climate restricts most of the wine growing to the southern sectors of the country. Canada's wine industry also has grown up in close proximity to that of the northern United States, and there is a particularly close kinship between wine growing in the Province of Ontario and New York State based on shared cold-weather technologies. The Italians, however, have had a significant impact on the wines of British Columbia.

Wine growing in England has a long and colorful past rooted in the history of wine in Western Europe. The industry, which all but died out during the nineteenth and early twentieth centuries, is currently undergoing a rebirth.

AUSTRALIA

While Australia is only the seventeenth-largest producer of wine in the world, it is, nevertheless, one of the most progressive. Wine production has increased more than five-fold there during the two decades that span the 1960s and 1970s. Most of this output is consumed within the country, but wine exports, now shipped to more than seventy nations, have grown to become a trade factor of national economic significance. Australian wine consumption has advanced to more than 5 gallons per capita annually, which is about twice the U.S. rate. There are more than fifteen times as many people in the United States as there are in Australia, yet U.S. wine production is only about four times as large. There can be no question that wine has become an important industry in modern-day Australia and is advancing to levels of commercial intensity approaching that in Europe.

The continent of Australia is only slightly smaller in square mileage than the mainland of the United States. Of the more than 180,000 acres of vineyards cultivated in the nation, approximately 60 percent are located in the South Australia region. The southeastern state of New South Wales contains 24 percent, while Victoria, directly south, has about 13 percent of the total Australian vine acreage. Western Australia contributes less than 2 percent of the total vineyards under cultivation, and less than 1 percent is located in Queensland and Tasmania.

Most of the notable wine-growing regions of Australia are situated in the southeastern coastal countryside, a bit closer to the equator than those of Europe.

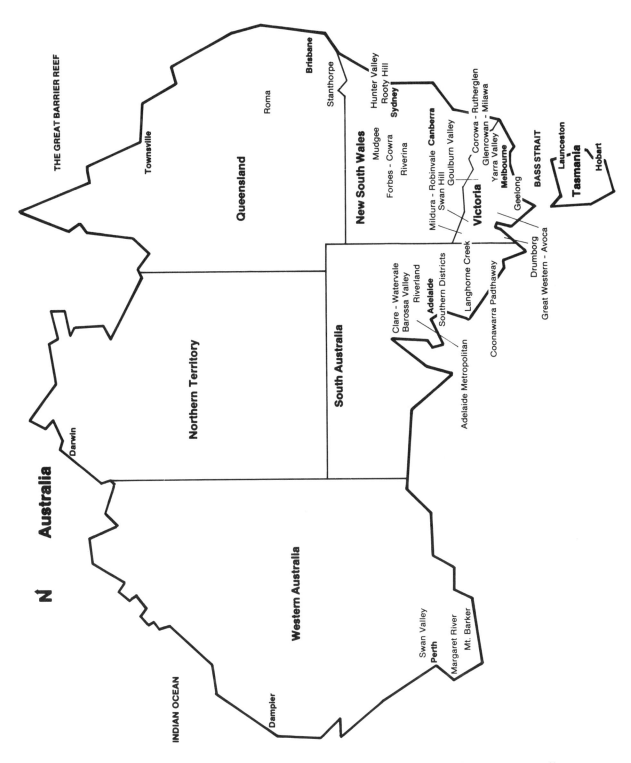

Such a location provides Australian vines with abundant sunshine—normally sufficient to fully ripen the grapes in most of the regions virtually every year. These same locales are generally also rather dry, and a large share of the vineyards located in the States of South Australia, New South Wales, and Victoria require irrigation. Heavier productivity is generally achieved from the irrigated vineyards—resulting in wines of comparatively lighter bouquet and flavor, but of higher strength, than the products of the higher and cooler nonirrigated districts in the same regions. Soils in the lower levels are often alluvial flatlands, with sandy loams and rather deep sands, somewhat lighter in consistency in South Australia and Victoria than in New South Wales. The soils at higher elevations are mixtures of limestone, sandstone, ironstone, and heavier sand in varying blends of brownish red and gray earths. While Australia's vineyards may not display the diversity of some other major wine-growing nations, there is quite enough variety to offer an interesting breadth of character and style.

The Australian government maintains no national guarantees of wine authenticity or appellation of origin, leaving those functions to the self-regulation of the wine industry. In recent years, several of the most prestigious wine-growing regions in the country have inaugurated programs to guarantee the regional identity of their wines. In addition, each regional capital city holds competitions in which the local vintners may show off their superior products. While there is no national wine regulation, state governments do, however, enforce strict labeling laws. A bottle of wine must contain at least 80 percent of the grape variety stated on the label. Many Australian wines exhibit two varietal names, such as "Cabernet Sauvignon-Shiraz"—in which case each constituent must account for at least 40 percent of the blend. Vintage content must be 100 percent of the vintage date displayed.

Captain Arthur Phillip brought the first vines to Australia in 1788. Phillip had ordered the stocks from Rio de Janeiro on his way from England to New South Wales, where he had been directed by the Crown to establish a penal farm. By 1791, Phillip, by then governor of the colony, had an experimental vineyard that had grown to about 3 acres. Phillip became ill and returned to England shortly thereafter, but his work with vines had shown considerable promise, enough so that two French prisoners were released from the penal farm to manage the vinicultural experiments. This, however, proved unsuccessful as the two Frenchmen knew little about wine growing.

The next figure upon the early Australian wine scene was explorer Gregory Blaxland, who established a vineyard in 1816 upon his Brush Farm on the banks of the Parramatta River near Sydney. Six years later Blaxland won the Silver Medal for his red wine entry in a London competition administered by what is now the Royal Society of Arts. When his red won the Gold in 1827, wine authorities in England began to look favorably on Australia's potential for commercial wine production.

Many Australians, however, consider John MacArthur to be the true father of their wine industry. MacArthur, the first importer of Merino sheep to Australia, had been exiled from Australia from 1809 to 1817—the result of a bitter argument with the infamous Captain Bligh, then governor of New South Wales. During exile, MacArthur toured some of the better wine-growing regions of France in order to gather vine stocks and information about their cultivation. He established his first vineyard plot at Camden in 1820, but later moved to the alluvial banks of the Nepean River near Penrith, where the first Australian commercial winery was constructed. By 1827, his production had grown to exceed 20,000 gallons per year.

There are still others in Australia who consider James Busby to be the patriarch of their wine industry. Busby came to the new colony from Scotland in 1824 and was appointed the headmaster of an orphanage. One of his topics of study was viticulture. He taught this with special enthusiasm since he was authorized to supplement his meager salary with one-third of the income from the school vineyards. Busby took wine samples with him on a journey back to England in 1830. Those wines were so highly regarded that he was commissioned at the government's expense to tour Spain and France for the purpose of selecting the finest vine stocks for propagation in Hunter Valley in New South Wales, Australia. By 1832 Busby had secured about 20,000 cuttings of prime pedigree and returned with them to the Hunter Valley in New South Wales. Starting with these original plant materials, the Hunter Valley has grown and flourished. Its success is a monument to Busby's dedication to wine quality.

Around 1838 Richard Hamilton and John Reynell had planted vines in their newly purchased land near Adelaide in South Australia. Several years later George Anstey propagated vines of Rhine Riesling (Johannisberg Riesling), Cabernet Sauvignon, and Shiraz (Syrah), among other varieties, from MacArthur's Camden vineyard and planted in the Southern Vales.

In 1837, Colonel William Light was the first Britisher to explore the vast Barossa Valley of South Australia. A later explorer in that locale, Johann Menge, came out with a prophecy of remarkable accuracy:

> I am certain that we shall see the place flourish, and vineyards and orchards and immense fields of corn throughout. It will furnish huge quantities of wine; it will yield timber for our towns, and superior stone and marble abounds for buildings.

It was in 1842 that non-British immigrants were first permitted to settle in Australia, paving the way for the employment of trained vineyard and winery workers from the European continent. Subsequently, many German winegrowers came to the new colony—and, as mentioned previously, the German influence has since become an integral part of the rich wine heritage of the nation.

Johann Gramp planted the first vineyards in the Barossa Valley, at Jacob's Creek in 1847. Soon afterward the legendary Joseph Seppelt came to the valley from Germany with a dream of growing tobacco. When he saw how very well the vine

The Barons of Barossa—an Australian fraternity founded by German immigrants—celebrate the vintage. (Source: Douglas McNaughton, Australian information Service.)

adapted to the beautiful Barossa, his interests quickly changed to wine growing—and thus the internationally famous House of Seppelt was born.

Gold fever gripped Australia at about the same time and with the same violence that it gripped the American West. Just as with the 1849 gold rush in the United States, prospectors flocked to Victoria in 1850 frantically searching for the precious metal. In similar fashion, most of those ventures also failed—leaving many native European entrepreneurs with few means of earning a living other than wine growing. Two of the most important villages to emerge from the gold rush days were Great Western and Rutherglen, names that have since become classic viticultural districts in Australia.

Samuel Sidney wrote of the 1852 viniculture scene in his *Three Colonies of Australia*:

> Men who have been previously slaves to spirit-drinking, on going to work at a vineyard, have sobered down to two bottles of Australian wine daily, to the infinite benefit of their health and finances.

It was Edward Henty and William Ryrie who were among the first to take the vine into Victoria, near Melbourne. By the mid-1860s their wines had won so many awards and medals in European competitions that some wine experts talked of Victoria becoming a world-class vineyard region. The British generally preferred heavier and sweeter wines, however, and Victorian wines, made, for the most part, by French and Swiss immigrants who labored in the vineyards and cellars, were usually light and dry. This, along with the invasion of the *Phylloxera* blight, dashed the hopes for Victorian wine greatness in the latter portion of the nineteenth century.

During this time it was also found that much of the vineyard lands of South Australia needed to be irrigated for optimal production. Two Canadian brothers, Ben and George Chaffey, had established irrigation systems in California, and, in 1887, were invited to Australia to engineer similar projects. They set up their first irrigation system in South Australia at Renmark and a second in Victoria at Mildura. News of the success of the Chaffey irrigation spread throughout upper Murray River in South Australia, fostering the establishment of vineyard plots and wineries that have since become huge operations. Later, the advancing technology of irrigation spread to Griffith in New South Wales and other now-important Australian wine-growing districts.

The Parliament of South Australia enforced a strict quarantine in order to avoid the ravages of *Phylloxera*, but they could not avert an economic wine recession similar to those that plagued the United States during the 1870s and 1880s. By the turn of the century, the state became the leading commercial winegrower of the Australian Commonwealth—a position it has never relinquished.

Wine commerce with England was greatly curtailed following the outbreak of World War I. The attending politics also gave rise to prejudices against the Teutonic people who had settled in Australia. The Armistice brought renewed activity in the wine-export trade, but some of the social tensions between the British and German cultures remained.

The Australian Great Depression preceeded that in the United States by a few years, but U.S. winegrowers had to face the Great Depression coming right on the heels of Prohibition. Australian and U.S. wine-growing history diverges even more during World War II. In the United States many of the manufacturing resources for wine were diverted to the Victory movement. Production and exports of wine were reduced in Australia, too, but domestic per capita consumption more than doubled from 1939 to 1945. Wines, sold by the carafe and by the glass, were consumed without any particular regard for vineyard region or producer. In the latter 1940s the profile of wine marketing changed in Australia, and more and more wine was sold in bottles labeled with pertinent source information. As a result, even more interest was generated among Australian wine consumers for the wines from their own country—and, as interest grew, the wines themselves improved greatly due to advances in wine technology and art. Improvements in quality continue today to win Australian wines more and more admirers both at home and abroad.

South Australia

The great Barossa Valley is perhaps the best-known wine-growing district in all of Australia, certainly the most notable in the region of South Australia. It is situated approximately 35 miles northeast of metropolitan Adelaide at an altitude of about 1000 feet above sea level. At its widest points, the Barossa spans 7 miles or so, and, from the towns of Kalimna and Bilyara at the north to Williamstown at the south, the valley measures 20 miles in length. Principal communities in the district are Angaston, Nuriootpa, and Tanunda, and there are many smaller villages, especially along the central portion of the valley where the Sturt Highway serves as the principal commercial thoroughfare.

As may be expected, the temperatures of the Barossa Range hills are generally cooler than those in the valley floor. Soils range from light sandy loams to the richer loams on clay subsoils, the latter known as *red-brown earth*. The combination of cooler temperatures and richer soils yields some of the finest wines of the region.

The most famous winegrower in the Barossa is undoubtedly B. Seppelt & Sons, Ltd.—certainly this is the firm best known to U.S. wine enthusiasts. Joseph Ernst Seppelt emigrated from Silesia in 1849, accompanied by his family and other families associated with his tobacco and spirits business in Wustewaltersdorf. Since its first plantings, the House of Seppelt has grown to be one of the largest wineries in the nation. Of particular note is the locally famous 1879 port made at "Seppeltsfield"—the firm's large wine production complex. That vintage year marked the first reserve held from the finest port wine made at Seppelt, a tradition that continues each year. Bottles of the 1879 and other early vintages are very rare—often selling for several thousands of dollars each. In modern times Seppelt has adjusted its product portfolio to reflect the increasing demand for varietal table wines in Australia. Most of the varietals are produced in the firm's impressive "Château Tanunda" winery complex. Consistent award winners are Chardonnay from Rutherglen vineyards, along with Cabernet Sauvignon and Shiraz (Syrah) grapes from Great Western vineyards, both districts located east across the border in Victoria (see below).

Another of the large Barossa wineries is Kaiser Stuhl, or "seat of the emperor" as translated from the German. The firm is perhaps better known by some of the locals as the Barossa Co-operative Winery, Ltd. From a rather difficult start and virtual failure during the Great Depression, it has prospered since World War II. The firm adopted the name *Kaiser Stuhl* (from a nearby hilltop) for wine labeling in 1958. The cooperative structure of Kaiser Stuhl carries over into its marketing functions also. Many of the wines are made entirely from one individual grower's grapes and labeled appropriately with each specific vineyard source. Among the most noteworthy of these are Materne's Dolce Domo vineyard at Greenock and Eric Stephen's Wyncroft in the Eden Valley, actually located about 15 miles east of the main Barossa Valley.

One of the newer names in the district is that of Wolfgang Blass. The first of the Wolf Blass wines were released in 1966, and a year later the first of many awards and medals for excellence was won. Demand continues to build for the wines of this progressive operation. Blass collected a staff of talented business and production experts, and their success has now engendered growth of remarkable proportions.

Other Barossa names of note are Château Leonay; Château Yaldara; G. Gramp & Sons, descendants of Johann Gramp who planted the area's first vineyards in 1847; Thomas Hardy & Sons; C. A. Henschke; Penfolds; St. Hallett's; W. Salter and Company; S. Smith & Son; and Tolley, Scott and Tolley, Ltd.

The South Australian Department of Agriculture operates one of the finest research facilities for viticulture in the nation just 2 miles east of Nuriootpa. Considerable acreage is devoted to working out solutions to the area's viticultural problems and to the advancement of the state of the art of wine.

The most northern of the South Australian vineyards are situated in the areas of Clare and Watervale, located about 90 miles north of the Barossa Valley. Elevation is about twice as high as in the Barossa, and the limestone soils in tandem with cooler weather yield wines of distinctive quality.

The Quelltaler name, of particular significance in the Clare-Watervale district, has a wine-making heritage that reaches back to 1865, when Francis Treloar first planted vines at the foot of Mount Horrocks. The family persisted in their quest for top quality, often using trial-and-error methods, and their success is best exemplified today in the Quelltaler Rhine Riesling wine, still referred to locally as "hock." Other important producers in the district are Manresa (the Sevenhill Winery operated by the Jesuit Brothers at St. Aloysius College), St. Francis Winery, and the Stanley Wine Company.

From its first vintage in 1895 Stanley has grown to a large concern that was taken over by the American H. J. Heinz Company, of catsup fame, in 1971.

Most of the vineyards that once graced the environs of Adelaide with the production of some excellent white table wines and rich dessert wines have long since given way to the expansion of the city. A few vineyards remain in Burnside,

Glenelg, and Magill, but these are sure to fall to further metropolitan Adelaide development in the near future.

The Southern Vales district in the South Australian region commences at the southern suburbs of Adelaide, extending south along the Gulf of St. Vincent coast through the cities of Reynella and McLaren Vale to Willunga. The Southern Vales is particularly well suited for wine growing as it has a consistently temperate climate and soils that vary from sand, sandy loam, and limestone to rich alluvial earth—all of which offer ideal support for vine cultivation.

One of the most famous names in the district is that of Reynell. Walter Reynell and Sons Wines, Ltd., has a colorful heritage going back to the very beginnings of wine growing in the Southern Vales to John Reynell, mentioned earlier, who planted the first vineyards in the area around 1838, and for whom the city of Reynella is named. In modern times the firm has been operated by Rothmans of Pall Mall, Ltd., a division of International Cellars Australia. The Reynell traditions carry on, however, and fine wines from Chardonnay, Traminer (Gewürztraminer), Rhine Riesling, Sémillon, Cabernet Sauvignon, Merlot, and Shiraz, among other fine varietals, are produced by the firm.

Other important vintners of the Southern Vales district are McLaren Park, Thomas Hardy and Sons, Ltd. (a giant firm with wineries in every major wine-growing region of Australia), F. E. Osborn and Sons, Ltd., Ryecroft, Seaview Winery, and the Southern Vales Co-operative Winery.

As the Reynell product line demonstrates, Southern Vales wine growing leans heavily toward varietal table wines, particularly reds from an abundance of Cabernet Sauvignon that is cultivated in the district. Crisp, dry whites from Sauvignon Blanc and Sémillon grapes are also becoming recognized as distinctively superior products grown there.

Situated near the extreme southwestern border with Victoria is the small wine district of Coonawarra, the "wild honeysuckle" in the language of the Australian aborigines. Located more than 250 miles to the southeast of Adelaide, the isolated Coonawarra is the most southern wine-growing locale in the South Australia region. Only 50 miles from the cold ocean waters to the southwest, the Coonawarra is also the coolest vineyard site in the state.

When full ripening is achievable, the wines of the Coonawarra can be some of the finest grown in the nation. While the more northerly and warmer regions yield fruit of rather uniform quality each vintage, the Coonawarra is subject to widely varying vintages. Frosts are always a jeopardy following the spring bud break and during the maturing season in autumn. The harvest season in April is usually more than a month later than that in the Barossa Valley—sometimes extending into the colder autumn rains that can ruin immature fruit. As one might expect, the cold-hardy German Rhine Riesling is widely cultivated in the red and black limestone soils that are typical of the area. It is, however, surprising that the fair-weather Cabernet Sauvignon and Shiraz should do so well in yielding heavy, rich red wines in such forbidding environs.

Shortly after the turn of the century, John Redman moved his family to the Coonawarra. His son, William, the sixth of ten children, left grade school and secured a job working in the cellars at Riddoch's Winery. Learning the trade there, he set out with his father and his brother, Robert, to start a winery of their own. With little capital, the struggling firm produced bulk-blending wines that were sold to other local wineries. The Redman Winery never became a large concern, and most of what was built up has since been sold, but the second- and third-generation members of the Redman family keep up the tradition of dedication and ambition in the new Redbank Winery they now operate.

The largest vintner in the Coonawarra district of South Australia is Wynn's, which is well-known in some U.S. circles. Other important firms are Lindemans (who purchased the Redman estate), Mildara, and Penfolds. The Penfolds firm is one of the very large companies in Australia that operate wine-producing facilities in each of the principal vinicultural states.

Some 40 miles northward from Coonawarra, and offering a distinct contrast, is the comparatively new Keppoch subdistrict, a virtual desert of red and gray sandy loam soils. Seppelt's planted the first vines there, all top-grade Old World varieties. The resulting fruit is now vinified in the firm's Great Western and Château Tanunda wineries. Lindemans, Thomas Hardy and Sons, and Wynn's each maintain vineyard plots in the Keppoch as well.

In the early 1840s Alfred Langhorne drove his cattle herd from New South Wales to the Bremer River just 25 miles east of Adelaide and settled there, giving his name to the site now known as Langhorne Creek. The soil is a rich alluvial loam, but rainfall is scant, requiring irrigation for grape growing. Most of the modern-day vineyards there are planted with Muscat de Frontignan, Palomino, Cabernet Sauvignon, Grenache, and Verdelho. The Bleasdale and Metala winery firms buy some of the Langhorne Creek grape production each year, but large quantities are sold to other vintners outside of the district as well.

The most important institution in Australia for the research and teaching of viticulture and enology is Roseworthy Agricultural and Oenological College. That school, located near the city of Adelaide, operates a large plot of vineyards and also a winery where students have an opportunity to study wine marketing as well as grape growing and winemaking.

New South Wales

The State of New South Wales, to the north of Victoria, is fringed by the southeastern coastline of Australia, at the center of which is the beautiful city of Sydney.

About 135 miles north of Sydney, near the coastal city of Newcastle, is the renowned Hunter Valley, the Australian viticultural district that is well known internationally for exceptionally high quality wines. The general regard that Australians hold for the Hunter Valley may be compared to U.S. devotion for the Napa Valley. Both have colorful histories and certain similarities in their backgrounds. Busby was the founding hero of the Hunter Valley, playing a role rather like that of George Yount, the father of Napa. Both regions struggled with lack of respect and recognition until more recent years, when they have finally received the high accolades they deserve as world-class wine producers. Yet, despite their renown, each contributes proportionately only a minor share of their respective national wine output.

The Hunter Valley may be divided into two main vineyard locales. The older, more traditional vineyard sites are located in the parishes of Pokolbin and Rothbury. West of Muswellbrook, in the upper reaches of the valley, are situated many of the newer vineyards established in the district since the end of World War II.

The soils of the Hunter Valley range from alluvial river flatlands to podzolic loams, sandstone, and shales. Temperatures are moderate, but rainfall is erratic from year to year—both in timing and volume. Frost and hail are frequent hazards, as is mildew. Each year can be distinctly different. There are very good, even great, growing years, as well as miserable ones that yield only common fruit.

Hunter Valley winegrowers continue to cultivate the traditional varieties of Sémillon and Shiraz, but the newer plantings in the valley have included Chardonnay, Gewürztraminer, Cabernet Sauvignon, and Merlot, among others.

Several of the larger Australian vintners have wineries in the Hunter Valley, principally Lindeman's, McWilliams, and Penfolds. A listing of the estate vintners include:

Arrowfield	Pokolbin Estate
Brokenwood	Roberts Rothbury
Château Douglas	Rothbury Estate
Château François	Saxonvale
Drayton	Saxonvale Pokolbin
Elliott	Sobels Queldinburg
Hermitage	Tamburlaine
Hollydene	Tulloch
Hungerford Hill	Tyrrell
Lakes Folly	Wollundry
Murray Robson	Wyndham
Oakdale	

The largest wine-growing district in the New South Wales region is the Murrumbidgee, centered principally on the towns of Griffith and Yenda, located about 350 miles west of Sydney.

Comparatively heavy crops of grapes devoted principally to making dessert wines are the traditional production of the Murrumbidgee Irrigation Area, or MIA as it is better known to the local wine trade. This region is undergoing a dynamic transformation, however, with new plantings of the finer Old World grape varieties producing higher-quality table wines through the use of new vinicultural technologies. The transformed district even has a new name—the *Riverina*.

Principal names among the larger vintners of the Riverina are the familiar McWilliams, Penfolds and Seppelt's, along with a relative newcomer, Wynn's.

Other wineries of note in the district are Calabria, De Bortoli, Fairefield, McManus, San Bernadino, Sergi, and Toorak.

More than 100 miles south of the Riverina, the Corowa district has been established upon the north bank of the Murray River, which marks the border between New South Wales and Victoria. This locale is best known for dessert wine production, particularly from the large Lindeman's firm.

Approximately 140 miles west of the Hunter Valley is the Mudgee district, which exhibits nearly the same growing conditions as the famous Hunter Valley. Some of the most important winegrowers in Mudgee are Augustine, Botolbar, Craigmoor, Huntingdon, Miramar, Montrose, and the Mudgee Winery.

Penfolds operates their "Minchinbury" winery, famous for sparkling wine, just west of Sydney in a subdistrict known as Rooty Hill. Other vineyard locales of interest in New South Wales are Buronga, Cobbitty, Cowra, the Harden-Murrumburrah area, and the Namoi Valley.

Victoria

The Victoria region is bordered by South Australia to the west, by New South Wales to the north, and by the Bass Strait to the south. It is situated at the extreme southeastern tip of the Australian continent, and its hub is the port city of Melbourne.

The State of Victoria is usually divided into two viticultural subregions—the Northeast and the Northwest. In between these subregions are the districts of Goulburn and Great Western.

The northeast portion of Victoria surrounds the town of Rutherglen, which was a gold rush boomtown. The prosperity of the vicinity diminished with the decline of gold strikes. The European prospectors-turned-winegrowers fostered renewed economic growth in the several decades that followed the gold rush, but the scourge of *Phylloxera* brought desperation and poverty to the area once more.

Southeast of Rutherglen, near Chiltern, the Viticultural Research Station continues to function as the teaching and research center for the region. It was founded in 1896 as a training facility for young people interested in growing grapes. During the *Phylloxera* blight interest in viticulture declined, and the school became a government center for the propagation and distribution of grafted vine stocks. The reestablished vineyards began to prosper and, by the mid-1960s, Northeast Victoria once again began to show renewed vinicultural interest and vitality. The lead was taken by the House of Seppelt, which had endured the hard times of blight, the Great Depression, and two world wars and remained steadfast in the continued cultivation of Rutherglen vineyards. Despite the area's ever-improving reputation for high-quality wine output, Seppelt is still the only large Australian winery with holdings in the district. Smaller vintners in Rutherglen, such as Buller, Morris, and All Saints, produce some of Australia's finest port-type wines. These wines typically show intense body and flavor.

More recently, through newly developed technology, vintners have been able to restrain some of this intensity for the production of Rutherglen table wines, principally reds from Cabernet Sauvignon and Shiraz. Some of the most noted vintners of these are A. D. Campbell, W. H. Chambers and Sons, G. T. Gehrig, L. Jones, and the Markwood Estate.

Seppelt's Great Western Champagne Winery. (Source: B. Seppelt & Sons, Ltd.)

John Purbrick, general
manager of Château Tahbilk
in the Victoria region.
(Source: John McKinnon,
Australian Information
Service.)

Approximately 80 miles north of Melbourne and 100 miles to the southwest of
Rutherglen is the Goulburn Valley. Sandy loam and gray alluvial soils, coupled
with long, hot growing seasons, typically yield very sweet grapes in the
Goulburn, and the wines that result are, as would be expected, comparatively
thin but strong.

The Goulburn Valley is the site of one of the loveliest winery estates in all of
Australia—the remarkable Château Tahbilk, which has a rich history dating back
to 1845. Several families have owned Château Tahbilk through the years, and the
property is now in the very caring hands of Eric Purbrick. A line of French winery
managers have brought a distinctly continental flair to the winery, and Château
Tahbilk has evolved into a true French château situated in a most attractive
Australian landscape. The wines of Château Tahbilk, especially those from Rhine
Riesling, Cabernet Sauvignon, and Shiraz, are in great demand, both in domestic
and export markets.

Some of the other highly regarded vintners in the Goulburn Valley are the
Darveniza Brothers, Mitchelton Vintners, and the large, new Rosebercon wine-
growing project.

The town of Great Western is situated in the eastern foothills of the Grampian mountains and near the town of Ararat, about 135 miles west of Melbourne. It is an unlikely place to find commercial winegrowing, with poor soils, an insufficiency of rainfall, and rather common frosts—all contributing to generally shy yields. Such adverse conditions, however, afflict some of the world's finest quality wine-growing locales, and some vintages of sparkling wines grown in the vicinity of Great Western offer a genuine challenge to the finer growths of Champagne in France.

The best-known wines in the district, the region, and the nation are those from Seppelt's Great Western—a facility whose history dates back to the 1830s, but whose fame came in the twentieth century through the enological genius of Colin Preece. There is no connection, other than an understandable rivalry, between the Seppelt's Great Western and New York State's Great Western, although both are famous for the production of award-winning champagne.

Another long-time vintner in Great Western is the Best Winery, which has grown Rhine Riesling, Pinot Meunier, and Shiraz, among other varietal table wines, for more than a century.

Further east, in the town of Avoca, the Nathan and Wyeth winery produces high-quality table and sparkling wines, as does the Robb family in their Redbank Winery.

The Victorian Northwest is a desert and had no viticultural use until it was developed through irrigation settlements on the Murray River for the repatriation of returning war veterans. It is a district of lowlands, most less than 400 feet above sea level, centered on the town of Mildura. A good share of the viticultural output in the Northwest is seedless table grapes although quantities of Sémillon and Shiraz are also cultivated for wine production.

Mildara Wines, Ltd., has been in business at Merbein, just north of Mildura, since 1891, and is nationally famous for its production of fine sherry-type wines from the traditional Spanish sherry grape varieties Palomino and Pedro Ximénez. Other prominent vintners in the Northwest district of Victoria are Bonnonee, Bullers, McWilliams, and St. Andrew.

One may need to do a bit of searching in order to locate the tiny Yarra Valley just east of Melbourne. But, while it is dwarfed by some of the larger commercial vineyard districts in Victoria, the Yarra has an outstanding and growing reputation for its truly fine table wines. The important grape varieties cultivated in the Yarra Valley are the classic Chardonnay, Riesling, Traminer, Cabernet Sauvignon, Merlot, and Pinot Noir. Soils are generally rich and well drained, ranging from red sands to grey podzolic loams. The district has typically cool temperatures compared to most other Australian wine-growing districts, which allows for near-perfect ripening during the vintage season.

Many of the wines grown in the Yarra district exhibit a Swiss character, due principally to the families de Castella and de Pury, who emigrated to the gorgeously landscaped valley during the late 1840s. Today, some of the most important commercial vintners there are Fergusson's, Mount Mary, Seville, St. Hubert's, Wantirna Estate, Yarra Yering, and Yeringberg, the last has remained in the hands of the founding de Pury family for nearly one and a half centuries.

About 50 miles west, across Port Phillip Bay, is the port city of Geelong, for which the historic Geelong vineyard district is named. This, too, was a site settled by the Swiss, principally by the Breguet and Pettavell families who planted the Neuchâtel vineyard there in the early 1840s. Later, the area became attractive to German emigrants, but shortly thereafter the Geelong was invaded by *Phylloxera*, and its popularity in the early 1870s as a premium table wine supplier fell off rather abruptly.

Today the Geelong is undergoing a rebirth in wine growing. The finest European red and white wine varieties are being planted, some upon sites that require irrigation, but all in a generally cool climate that is optimal for fruit maturation. The leader of this renaissance in the Geelong is the Sefton family, whose vines planted on the hillsides near the Moorabool River during the mid-1960s now yield grapes for their Idyll winery. Other important names in the district are Bannockburn, Hickinbotham, Prince Albert Vineyard, and Tarcoola.

Western Australia

There are three principal vinicultural districts in Western Australia: the Swan Valley, the Mount Barker-Frankland River vicinity, and Margaret River.

The Swan Valley is located about 15 miles north of Perth along the Swan River. Some of the first vines planted in the area were for table grape production, a portion of which was shipped in trade to Singapore. Clay subsoils support very fertile sandy topsoils which, coupled with dry, hot growing seasons, consistently provide bountiful yields of very sweet grapes. Some of the best-known producers in the Swan Valley area are Evans and Tate, Houghton, Sandalford, and Valencia—all of which vinify prime Old World varieties to wines with a distinctive Western Australian character.

About 200 miles to the southeast of Perth is the Mount Barker-Frankland River district. This is a much less developed, and, therefore, less well known, vinicultural area than the Swan Valley, but its cooler climate and less fertile soils are attracting new wine-growing interests. Wine producers in the district are Alkoomi, Château Barker, Forest Hill, Plantagenet, and Sheldon Park.

Leeuwin Vineyards is a new wine-producing venture in the Margaret River locale, and is a consortium that originally included famous Napa Valley vintner Robert Mondavi. The Leeuwin project was planted with Chardonnay, Rhine Riesling, Cabernet Sauvignon, and Shiraz, among other classic varieties, during the mid-1970s.

Two Busselton-vicinity physicians have each embarked upon commercial wine ventures in the Margaret River area. Dr. Cullen's Willyabrup wines and Dr. Bill Pannell's wines have both won awards for their Riesling and Cabernet Sauvignon selections.

Queensland

As mentioned at the beginning of this section, comparatively little wine is made in Queensland, the forbidding climate continues to discourage many vintners from risking fame and fortune there. One notable exception is the Bassett family of Roma, who have had success at their winery that is more than 300 miles west of Brisbane. Samuel Bassett planted the first Rhine Riesling and Muscat vines there in 1863, and his son carried on the legacy until 1973, when the firm was taken over by the Wall family. Other fine wine-grape varieties have since been planted, and production continues to advance under the capable direction of David Wall.

Tasmania

Despite the fact that Tasmania only produces a very small volume of wine commercially, the island, situated south of the Australian continent, does have some wine history. As long ago as 1827 Bartholomew Broughton made wine there, and in the 1830s William Lawrence cultivated vineyards near the city of Launceston. In modern times, commercial wine growing must contend with insufficient temperatures, although several entrepreneurs have been brave enough to make significant investments in Tasmania. Among these are C. Alcorso, Château Legana, J. F. Miguet, and Pipers Brook.

NEW ZEALAND

The islands that are New Zealand total a bit more than 103,000 square miles, just slightly smaller than the State of Colorado. Despite this comparatively small size,

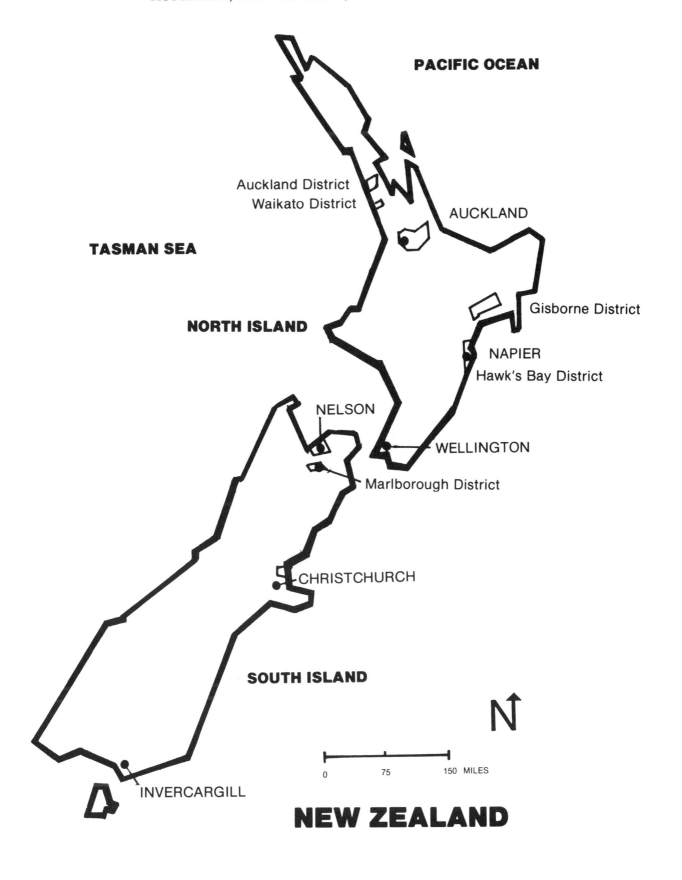

PACIFIC OCEAN

Auckland District
Waikato District

AUCKLAND

TASMAN SEA

Gisborne District

NORTH ISLAND

NAPIER
Hawk's Bay District

NELSON

WELLINGTON

Marlborough District

CHRISTCHURCH

SOUTH ISLAND

N

0   75   150 MILES

INVERCARGILL

NEW ZEALAND

New Zealand has a long north-south profile that spans latitudes comparable to the finest temperate wine-growing zones in Europe. New Zealand, with its wide variance of soils and microclimates, offers some of the most ideal viticultural conditions in the world.

Across the central regions of Marlborough and Nelson, long, cool growing seasons slowly ripen grapes to high intensities of flavor and light to medium strength. The Canterbury region to the south is colder and yields wines of strong acidity and flavor. The Auckland districts to the north are generally warmer, resulting in soft, heady wines.

The Reverend Samuel Marsden was the first to plant vines in New Zealand, in the early 1800s. James Busby was also an important early figure there during the early 1800s. But, other than some isolated vineyard plots, there was no viable commercial wine industry in the nation prior to the twentieth century. During the early 1900s, immigrant "gum diggers" from eastern Europe and Lebanon planted *Phylloxera*-resistant French-American hybrid grapes. Much of the resulting production was vinified into dessert wines that were of poor general quality and poorly received in the New Zealand wine marketplace, still traditionally Victorian in its attitudes.

During the past several decades, government and commercial commitments to vinicultural research have succeeded in matching Old World vine selections and special hybrid cultivars to the ideal locales across the nation. Presently, there are approximately 15,000 acres of commercial vineyards in New Zealand, double the number just ten or so years ago.

It is now the twenty-sixth-largest wine-producing nation in the world. Much of this remarkable increase in acreage is due to the New Zealand government's policy of strictly limiting wine imports into the country, a policy justified by a very delicate balance-of-payments position. But the major reason for the dynamic vinicultural expansion in New Zealand is the growth of acceptance of domestic wines. As vineyard technology has advanced, so has winemaking technology, and the result is that New Zealanders are increasingly aware of the improvements in quality and value of wines grown in their own homeland. Since World War II, wine consumption there has risen more than tenfold, and nowadays it is at a level in excess of 3 gallons per person annually.

Auckland

The Auckland region is the northernmost, the warmest, and the most humid of New Zealand's wine-growing areas. It includes the Kumeu/Huapai district located to the northwest of the city and the Henderson vineyard area to the immediate west of Auckland. A relatively new district south of Auckland is also becoming a significant vineyard locale. Auckland's strong port- and sherry-type wines made by the Lebanese and Yugoslavian immigrants during the 1930s, 1940s, and 1950s were once considered the typical New Zealand wines. Since then, many vineyards have been uprooted, some because of replanting programs directed toward the European *Vitis vinifera* varieties. The net result has been an Auckland region reborn to fewer, but better, vineyards. New estate vintners are joining the older established firms in the production of truly fine table wines. Sauvignon Blanc and Sémillon head the list of white wine varieties cultivated, while Cabernet Sauvignon and Pinot Noir are the most widely planted reds, the latter of which is building a fine reputation.

Henderson winegrowers include Babich's, Balic, Collard Brothers, Corban's, Delegats's, Lincoln, Mazurans, Montana, Nova, Pacific Vineyards, Panorama, Penfolds, Pleasant Valley, Robard and Butler, Soljan's, and Windy Hill. Kumeu/ Haupai vintners are Abel, Cooper's, Matua Valley, Nobilo, San Marino, and Selak's.

The vineyards to the south of Auckland are located on the Ihumatao Peninsula that juts out into Manakau Harbor. Growers here supply Villa-Maria, a wine-producing firm that, in less than twenty-five years, has become one of New Zealand's largest.

Bay of Plenty

Despite the fact that the Bay of Plenty has very fine natural growing conditions for fine wine grapes, it has never emerged as a popular wine-growing locale. As table wines supplanted dessert wines across most of New Zealand's larger vineyard regions, this region failed to attract the special expertise necessary to plant and maintain Old World vines. With land prices driven up by the continuing growth of suburbia, interest in renewed commercial wine-growing ventures in the Bay of Plenty region have not been forthcoming. One notable exception to this is the Morton Estate Winery, which celebrated its premier vintage in 1983. Wines from Morton are made from Chardonnay, Sémillon, and Cabernet Sauvignon.

The Waikato

About 50 miles south of Auckland, and perhaps twice that distance west of the Bay of Plenty, is the Waikato wine region of New Zealand. The region's center is the city of Hamilton. Karamea is a small winery that produces Müller-Thurgau,

Cabernet Sauvignon, and Pinot Noir wines a few miles to the southwest of Hamilton, but most of the wine production is to the north of the city, primarily by the vintner firms Cook's, De Redcliffe, and Totara. Cook's specializes in Chardonnay and Cabernet Sauvignon varietal table wine production, while De Redcliffe concentrates upon Chardonnay/Sémillon and Cabernet Sauvignon/ Merlot blends. Totara is a firm owned by the Chan family, originally from China, and makes a wine labeled "Fu Gai," a blend of Chenin Blanc, Golden Chasselas, Johannisberg Riesling, and Muscat.

The New Zealand Ministry of Agriculture and Fisheries operates a viticultural research station near Te Kauwhata under the direction of Dr. Richard Smart.

Gisborne and Hawke's Bay

The Gisborne and Hawke's Bay wine-growing region is the largest in New Zealand, producing about two-thirds of all the wine grapes grown in the entire nation. Müller-Thurgau is the major variety cultivated there, but a recent upsurge of *Phylloxera* has brought about a five-year replanting program in the region, and classic European grape varieties, among them Chardonnay, Chenin Blanc, and Cabernet Sauvignon, have been used widely for grafting scion stock upon louse-resistant root stock.

This region, surrounding the city of Napier, is located along the southeastern coast of North Island. The historic wineries and widespread fruit and vegetable production of the region draw a considerable tourist traffic. There is a stark contrast between the subtropical climate and heavy clay soils of the Auckland region and the more temperate, rather dry ripening season and rich, well-drained loam soils of the Gisborne and Hawke's Bay region. Many of the wines produced by the Auckland wineries are made from, or supplemented with, high-quality grapes grown in the Gisborne and/or Hawke's Bay districts.

The oldest winery in New Zealand is the Te Mata Estate Winery, located just north of Havelock North and east of Hastings. Te Mata has been producing wine since 1896 and presently offers award-winning selections of Chardonnay, Cabernet Sauvignon, and other fine Old World wines. Other producers in the region are Brookfield's, Eskdale, Glenvale, Lombardi, Matawhero, McWilliams, Mission, Ngatarawa, and Vidal (the last has no known connection to the famous French vine hybridizer).

Further south, just north of Wellington, Dr. Peter Heginbotham operates a small winery. His Pierre Winery produces limited quantities of Chardonnay, Chenin Blanc, and Cabernet Sauvignon, as well as some blended wines.

Marlborough and Nelson

These two districts make up the uppermost wine-growing region of South Island. Marlborough is located west of the city of Blenheim, and most of the vineyards of the district, situated on the south side of the Wairau River, are relatively new. Johannisberg Riesling and Müller-Thurgau are the principal varieties cultivated there; some Sauvignon Blanc and Cabernet Sauvignon are also found. Long, dry summers (sometimes excessively dry) are coupled with cool autumn temperatures to ripen very fine quality fruit. The vintners of Marlborough are Corbans, Hunter's, Montana, Penfolds, and Te Whare Ra, the last translates as "health in the sun."

Nelson is yet another relatively new viticultural district in New Zealand. It is located near the southwestern shores of Ruby Bay. The climate of Nelson is very similar to that of Marlborough, and the scant rain during some summer seasons has convinced some growers to install irrigation systems. The Nelson wine producers are Korepo, Neudorf, Ranzau, Victory, and Weingut Seifried. Most of these firms offer products made from Johannisberg Riesling, Müller-Thurgau, and Cabernet Sauvignon.

Canterbury

The vineyards of Canterbury, located just north of the city of Christchurch, are the southernmost commercial plantings in New Zealand. Summers can be rather dry and temperatures are generally cooler than Nelson or Marlborough. Most of the vineyards in Canterbury are very new, as is the region's only winery, St. Helena, which opened in 1981 with wines from Gewürztraminer, Johannisberg Riesling, and Müller-Thurgau.

CANADA

Canada has a bit more than 3.6 million square miles of land, just a fraction larger than the combined area of all fifty states in the United States. Canada's coast-to-coast topography is very similar to that of the United States. It has rolling hills and lesser mountain ranges in the east, flatland plains at the center of the nation, and the great mountain ranges that continue the continental divide northwestward from Colorado. Most of the commercial wine-growing activity is in the east and west, with comparatively little in the Prairie Provinces of Manitoba, Saskatchewan, and Alberta; again, similar to the overall profile across the United States.

Despite the rigors of short growing seasons and cold winters, Canada is the twenty-fifth-largest wine-producing nation in the world, often achieving more than 13 million gallons annually. Much of this production has emerged just during the past decade or so, a time span in which per capita consumption has more than doubled to reach about the same 2-gallon level annually as in the United States. The close parallel between Canada and the United States continues further: Both are nations that were "brought up on beer and whiskey," but continue to move toward a preference for wine. Both are nations that endured and survived Prohibition (although the effects were much more devastating for the U.S. wine industry), and both passed through eras when dessert wines and pop wines were popular.

The Vineland described by Leif Eriksson at about the year 1,000 is thought by some geographers and historians to actually have been the southeastern coast of Canada, not northeastern America. In any event, the first documented explorer of Canada was John Cabot who, in the commissioned service of British King Henry VII, anchored off the North American coast in 1497. During the next century voyages were made to Canada by three other nations in search of a new western passage to Asia. The first expedition was made by Portugal and headed by navigator Gaspar Corte-Real. The next was by Giovanni da Verrazano of Italy. Later, a series of explorations were made by the Frenchman, Jacques Cartier.

Between 1595 and 1605, French interest in the new western land grew rapidly. While some called the territory "New France," a more popular name was *Canada*—an Indian word misconstrued as meaning "country," though it actually signifies "town." Fur trading attracted French settlers into the St. Lawrence River region during the earliest years of the seventeenth century, the region that is today the French-speaking Province of Quebec. These French colonists were probably the first winegrowers in Canadian history.

The Roman Catholic church was an early influence in the development of commercial Canadian wine growing as in the United States and most European countries. In 1615, Franciscan missionaries arrived in Quebec and cultivated native *Vitis labrusca* vines for both sacramental and secular needs.

Canada's fledgling wine industry may have become much more developed had it not been for the Thirty Years War, during which the British seized Acadia and Quebec. The Acadians were banished from Canada, and some settled in southern Louisiana where "Cajuns" still speak French but grow very little wine. In 1758

Louisburg, in Arcadia, fell to English soldiers, and Quebec became occupied by Britain. There was little encouragement from England to grow wine in Canada, and the forbidding climate dampened such interest as remained.

The next fifty years was a period of political unrest in Canada, especially in the Quebec region. Nevertheless, emigrants from Europe continued to settle in Canada. One of these was a German, Johann Schiller, who started a small winery just south of Toronto in 1811.

Following Prohibition and the Great Depression, Canada instituted provincial control of wine distribution. In some provinces the government assumed monopoly control of all wines bought and sold at wholesale within provincial borders, similar to the system still practiced in Pennsylvania and a few other states. This served to discourage smaller vintners from entering the industry as "listings" were difficult to obtain unless comparatively large quantities of each wine lot offered were available. At the same time the provincial control allowed the established firms to grow in oligopolistic fashion until the late 1960s, when "cottage" vintners were given the opportunity to retail their wines to winery visitors. The provincial wine-marketing control authorities also changed several other regulations in order to give the smaller firms a chance to succeed.

Many cottage wineries emerged during the late 1960s and throughout the 1970s, but the wine boom of Canada has included continued growth of the large wineries as well, most of which now have production facilities in each of the more important wine-consuming provinces.

Ontario

The largest wine-growing region in Canada is in Ontario, principally in the southern tier from the southwestern shores of Lake Ontario and along the northern coast area of Lake Erie. More than 20,000 acres of vineyards are cultivated in the region. Most are in the Niagara Peninsula district that separates Niagara Falls from the city of Hamilton.

The rich but shallow, well-drained soils of the Niagara Peninsula are protected from cold north and west winds by an escarpment that surrounds the entire district except for the Lake Ontario side. The tempering effects of the cold lake waters help to deter the occurrence of false springs, when extended periods of warm March and April weather can cause bud break in the vineyards and result in burned shoots when winter temperatures resume. Sudden spring frosts can also be a problem. Summers are consistently warm, with adequate rainfall, and autumns usually sufficient in duration to ripen most varieties of wine grapes grown there.

The first vineyard plantings in the Niagara frontier were devoted to the native *Vitis labrusca* vines, but now more than half of the commercial vineyards in the locale are planted to Old World varieties and French-American hybrids. A significant share of vineyard acreage is also dedicated to hybrid cultivars developed by Vineland Station, the highly respected vinicultural research facility operated in the Niagara Peninsula by the Ontario Provincial Government.

Andrés Wines, Ltd., is one of the largest wine-producing firms in Canada, with facilities in Ontario, Alberta, British Columbia, Manitoba, Nova Scotia, and Quebec. The combined capacities of all the Andrés wineries exceeds 11 million gallons of bulk-wine storage and nearly 19,000 cases per day of bottling capability, which puts Andrés in the same league with the largest California wine producers.

The firm was founded in British Columbia by Andrew Peller in 1961 and expanded relatively quickly to other provinces. Headquarters for the firm were moved to Ontario after Peller acquired the Beau Chatel winery at Winona. The vast Andrés product portfolio is especially strong in table and sparkling wines. The best of these are the "Richelieu" selections, which are the top of the line.

Barnes Wines, Ltd., is the oldest operating winery in Canada. It was founded by George Barnes on the banks of the Welland Canal at St. Catharines in 1873. This firm also has a number of facilities, but all of these are situated within the Province of Ontario. While the magnitude of production at Barnes does not compare with some of the giant Canadian wineries, Barnes does offer a wide selection of wines, mostly table, but some sparkling, and dessert wines made from native and hybrid grapes. Their "Heritage Estates" label is reserved for their best Canadian-grown wines.

T. G. Bright and Co., Ltd., was established in 1910 when the Bright family acquired F. A. Shirriff's interest in a Niagara Falls winery they had started together in 1890. The firm can actually be traced even further back, to 1874, when Bright and Shirriff first began commercial winemaking in Toronto. The firm was purchased by Harry C. Hatch in the early 1930s and is still operated by the Hatch family. Bright's is another of the huge Canadian wineries, claiming to be the nation's largest. Nearly all production takes place in Ontario, with a comparatively small satellite winery operating in St.-Hyacinthe, Quebec. Despite the large size of the firm, it is a consistent award winner for its "Bright's President" line of premium sparkling and table wines, many of which are vinified from *Vitis vinifera* and hybrid selections.

Château-Gai was originally known as the Stamford Park Winery, founded just north of Niagara Falls by the Marsh family in 1890, the same year that Bright and Shirriff started their wine-making operations there. Late in the 1920s the firm became Canadian Wineries, Ltd., and started marketing a patented Charmat (bulk process) sparkling wine called "Château-Gai"—a brand that became so popular that the company has taken the same name. The firm is now a division of Ridout Wines, Ltd., itself owned by the famous John Labatt, Ltd., brewery empire. The Château-Gai winery premises are operated in Alberta, British Columbia, and New Brunswick, as well as in the main facilities in Ontario. A broad product line is headed by table wines made from several Old World *Vitis vinifera* varieties. A Gamay rosé is particularly well made.

Archie Haines of Jordan, Ontario, gave Jordan & Ste.-Michelle Cellars its humble start in 1921 in a small, stone building. Originally known as Canadian Grape Products, the firm was sold several years later to William B. Cleland, who changed its name to Jordan Wines and expanded production facilities into a vacated Welch Grape Juice plant that he had also acquired. Following Cleland's death, Jordan Wines was sold to Samuel Bronfman, patriarch of the giant Seagram's distilling empire. Jordan became managed by the Torno family, who owned and operated the Danforth Wine Company. Carling O'Keefe Breweries purchased controlling interest of Jordan Wines in 1972, and four years later amalgamated it and Ste.-Michelle Wines of Victoria, British Columbia, into the present-day Jordan & Ste.-Michelle Wines, Ltd. Jordan & Ste.-Michelle Wines have grown to include another wine production facility in Alberta: its total capacity rivals that of Andrés and Bright's. But the bulk of the firm's vineyard expansion has been in British Columbia, where Johannisberg Riesling and other European vine selections have been widely planted. Grapes grown there are used for the full spectrum of wines that bear the attractive Jordan & Ste.-Michelle labels. In 1986 Jordan & Ste.-Michelle Wines, Ltd., was sold to T. G. Bright and Co., Ltd.—making the Bright firm the largest wine producer in Canada.

The quaint summer resort community of Niagara-on-the-Lake is beautifully situated at the mouth of the Niagara River. Most of Ontario's cottage winery activity has developed in this area during the past decade or so.

In 1974 Donald Ziraldo founded Inniskillin, at first a very modest wine-producing facility, but success quickly spurred expansion. Today the Ziraldo philosophy is applied in a very attractive Niagara-on-the-Lake winery that offers fine table wines made from Chardonnay, Johannisberg Riesling, Seyval Blanc, Vidal Blanc, and Gamay.

Château des Charmes commenced winery operations in 1978 and is headed by Paul Bosc. It has already grown to a capacity of more than 100,000 gallons, with production totally devoted to premium table and sparkling wines.

Newark Wines, founded in 1979, and the Reif Winery, in 1982, are the most recent wineries to establish operations in the Niagara-on-the-Lake locale. Both make only table wines.

Moving westward from the Niagara Peninsula, one comes upon Montravin Cellars, Ltd., located in Beamsville, Ontario, a producer of both table and sparkling wines.

The London Winery, Ltd., was founded in 1925, in the Ontario city of the same name. This firm operates more than a dozen wine retail stores in the province and offers a full range of grape, fruit, and honey wines. The pride of London Winery is their solera dessert wines blended in the same manner as the famous solera sherry wines in Spain.

Enzo DeLuca is head of Colio Wines of Canada, Ltd., located in Harrow, Ontario. Colio was founded in 1980 and has achieved remarkable growth in its dedication to producing only table wines.

Last, but by no means least, is the Charal Winery, the most western of Ontario's wineries, located near Chatham in Kent County. Charal was established in 1975 by Charlotte and Alan Eastman, who are justifiably proud of the fine table wines they grow from their deep, rich soil. The Eastmans insist that their microclimate— situated at the most southern latitude in the nation—is the most conducive to fine wine growing in all of Canada. Their results would appear to confirm their convictions as Charal has won more than a dozen coveted awards in its comparatively short existence. The greatest achievement has been a rare gold medal for Chardonnay won at the tough "Wineries Unlimited" competition held annually in New York State.

British Columbia

In stark contrast to the thundering Niagara and rich flatlands of southern Ontario, British Columbia is characterized by a serene, austere terrain with stunning mountains, valleys, and lakes. One of these valley regions, the Okanagan, located about 250 miles east of Vancouver, is the heart of wine growing in British Columbia.

The Okanagan Valley is referred to as "Napa North" by some Canadians, but the Okanagan, with a north-south length exceeding 100 miles, is several times larger than California's Napa. And their climates have distinct differences. Spring frosts following bud break are more frequent in the Napa Valley, while frosts occurring during the September and early October ripening season are more feared in the Okanagan. Very harsh winter temperatures, sometimes below zero degrees Fahrenheit, are a perennial threat to vines cultivated in the Okanagan, as is the lack of rainfall, which often measures less than 10 inches annually. Thus the Okanagan and the Napa really have little in common aside from their natural splendor. Yet, despite certain environmental limitations in some microclimates, the light loam soils of the Okanagan can yield some truly fine table wines from Old World and hybrid vines.

The very first commercial winery in the province was Grower's Wines, Ltd., established in 1923 at Victoria, the capital of British Columbia. Eventually, Grower's became Ste.-Michelle and part of the Jordan & Ste.-Michelle amalgamation discussed above.

Perhaps the most famous winery in Canada, certainly in British Columbia, is the Calona Wines, Ltd., facility, which commenced operations during the early Great Depression years in the town of Kelowna in the Okanagan Valley. An Italian immigrant grocer, Pasquale Capozzi, and W. A. C. Bennett, owner of a neighboring hardware store, started the original Domestic Wines and By-Products, Ltd., in order to manufacture wines and associated products to assist impoverished local fruit growers. Under the most difficult of circumstances, Capozzi and Bennett parlayed several thousand shares, sold to locals at $1 apiece, and a great deal of employee dedication into one of the largest and most fully automated wine-producing firms in the nation. Calona Wines is owned today by Nabisco Brands, Ltd., and offers a full line of table, sparkling, and dessert wines, as well as some of the fruits and berry wine-types with which the colorful firm got started.

In 1978 Robert Claremont began operations at his Claremont Wines facility in Peachland, British Columbia. Production capacity has already reached nearly 100,000 gallons and is totally devoted to Okanagan-grown table wines.

In 1982 the Gray Monk Cellars, Ltd., Estate Winery was established by Trudy and George Heiss, who make only table wines, most of which are grown in their own Okanagan Valley vineyards.

High upon Mission Hill, overlooking the Okanagan Lake and Valley from the west, is the aptly named Mission Hill Vineyards winery. Founded in 1966, Mission Hill did not succeed until it was bought by Anthony Von Mandl. Now it is one of British Columbia's largest and most attractive wine-producing facilities. Mission Hill offers only table wines, some of which are vinified from Chenin Blanc, Gewürztraminer, Johannisberg Riesling, Cabernet Sauvignon, and Pinot Noir.

The Sumac Ridge Estate Winery of Summerland, British Columbia, was founded in 1980 by Harry McWatters and Lloyd Schmidt. Divino Estate Winery was started in Oliver, British Columbia, in 1983, by Barbara and Joe Busnardo. Both of these new winery firms produce only table wines.

Casabello Wines, another of the Ontario-based Ridout wineries, is located in Penticton, at the southern tip of Lake Okanagan. The Casabello firm has experimented a good deal with the cultivation of *Vitis vinifera* varieties in their locale and continues to devote its 3 million-gallon production facility entirely to table wines. The Ontario-headquartered firms Andrés and Jordan & Ste.-Michelle, also operate wineries in British Columbia.

Quebec

Perhaps the best indication of the rigors of cold weather in Quebec is the number of wineries that produce cider and/or other fruit and berry wines. Les Enterprises Verdi, Inc., of Montreal and Les Vignobles Chantecler, of Rougemont, are two of the largest of these operations in the province. Lubec, Inc., is located in St.-Antoine Abbé, and offers Kir in addition to apple cider, table, and aperitif wines. Julac, Inc., situated in Dolbeau, makes table and blueberry wines.

La Maison Secrestat, Ltd., is owned by Seagram's and makes table, dessert, and aperitif wines in its Dorval, Quebec, winery.
The oldest operating winery in the Province of Quebec is Vin Geloso, Inc., of Laval, founded in 1965. Today the large winery offers a full line of table, sparkling, dessert, and aperitif wines.

Les Vignobles du Quebec, of Hemmingford, was established in 1972 and makes table wines. The firm also operates another winery in Downsview, Ontario.

Andrés and Bright's also operate divisions in Quebec.

Alberta and Nova Scotia

The Andrew Wolf Cellars, Ltd., was founded in 1977 at Cochrane, Alberta. Wolf is both president and winemaker of his small winery, which is devoted entirely to table wine production.

Andrés, Château-Gai, and Jordan & Ste.-Michelle are Ontario firms that also operate wineries in Alberta.

Grand Pré Wines Company, Ltd., was founded in 1979 at Grand Pré, Nova Scotia, by Roger Dial. As president and winemaker, Dial has dedicated his winery to the pursuit of estate table-wine production.

ENGLAND

There is no natural reason that England's commercial wine industry should not be larger and more highly regarded than it is. Soils are generally suitable for viticulture in much of the nation, and microclimates exist in some of the more southern reaches of the country that are at least as favorable as those in northern Champagne and the upper Rheinland. The 2-gallon annual per capita consumption of wine in England indicates a reasonable demand for wine. The major obstacle to a domestic wine industry has been the ease with which the esteemed wines of the Continent can be obtained. The close geographical proximity of England to France and Germany has made the shipping of wines from the classic European vineyards a rather simple task for centuries. The relatively recent economic ties that bind European countries have served to facilitate the wine trade even more. Further, the bonds of the Commonwealth have made Australian wines readily available as well. There has simply been no dire need for British wines in Britain.

English wines have also suffered repression. Powerful brewing interests traditionally have discouraged wine drinking, and Britishers have generally regarded their climate as forbidding for viniculture. In addition, British governments have, like the U.S., depended heavily on alcoholic beverages as a major source of tax revenue, a constraint perhaps second only to the fact that most British wine writers, of which there have been many, tend to ignore their own wine industry.

Nevertheless, in the last several decades, increases in English wine consumption have kept pace with those of other Commonwealth countries. This has given rise to new commercial wine-growing interests in England, perhaps best exemplified by the founding in the mid-1970s of the English Vineyards Association, which has nearly 1,000 members who cultivate some 2,000 acres of vineyards both under cloches (greenhouses) and in the open air.

Despite the poor contemporary economic and market record of commercial wine growing in England, the country's new wine producers have a rich legacy of wine history to draw on in rebuilding their industry.

The first-century edict of Roman Emperor Domitian, which forbade wine growing outside of Italy, was enforced in Britain in the same manner as it was on the Continent. Evidence of this restriction are the many amphorae used in shipping wine from Rome that have been excavated in England, some of the best examples of which may be seen at the Verulamium museum at St. Albans. Following repeal of this law by Emperor Probus, many vineyards were planted in England and the new industry seems to have progressed, but very slowly.

After the early fifth-century withdrawal of the Romans from England, monks advanced the state of the art, both in quality and quantity. Wine emerged as an occasional beverage in Anglo-Saxon England. In *Beowulf* we find the following passage: "As mirth renewed, and laughter rang out, cup bearers poured wine from wonderfully made flagons."

In the *Ecclesiastical History of the English Nation,* Bede wrote of seventh-century vineyards in both England and Ireland. King Alfred promulgated laws in the ninth century that required just compensation be paid by those who damaged another's vineyard. The eleventh-century *Domesday Book* makes reference to more than thirty vineyard districts under cultivation in Norman England.

Also, the laity was not given wine by the clergy at Mass, a policy that inhibited potential growth of the monastic wine industry. Viniculture, however, had become an important part of British life in pre-Renaissance England. The Cellar Master of St. Albans, and presumably at other monasteries as well, was second only to the Abbot in authority. With potable water difficult to obtain because of pollution, the production of wine was understandably a high priority. Wine had evolved as an essential diet staple.

The importance of British wine growing peaked during the twelfth, thirteenth, and fourteenth centuries, when Bordeaux became part of England's royal holdings. Those coveted vineyard lands in France were part of a dowry given to Henry II when he married Eleanor of Aquitaine in 1152. (See chapter 4.)

Bordeaux wines became one of the favorites of British wine drinkers and the loss of the wine-rich province to France in 1453 was traumatic to both consumers and tradesmen in England.

Henry VIII dissolved the monasteries in the sixteenth century and ordered that God's cup be liberated among the people, a decree that served to significantly increase both the King's popularity and the number of vines cultivated in his realm. Despite this turn of events, the established dominance of the fine Aquitaine clarets in the British marketplace had long since overshadowed domestic wine production, and many of the finest English vineyards were gone by the end of the sixteenth century. Some survived, such as the five vineyard plots maintained by the Canterbury Cathedral. Some English viticultural locales even managed to grow, such as Winchester, which some historians argue was so named due to the wealth of vineyards that had been established there.

Interest in wine growing began to return to England in the seventeenth century, evidenced principally by the dozen or more books on the viticultural arts that were published. The best of these was John Rose's *Prince of Plants,* a definitive work addressed to cultivating several specific vine varieties in England. Vinicultural literature continued to emerge in Great Britain during the eighteenth century as well. Among the best-known books was *The Gardener's Dictionary* by Phillip Miller. The *Dictionary* was a huge work, published in eight editions during the early and middle 1700s. Only a portion was devoted to grape culture, but that segment was well respected by many contemporary viticulturists.

Charles Hamilton planted the first vines at Pain's Hill in Surrey during the early part of the eighteenth century. Having failed to make drinkable red wines from his Pinot Noir, he turned to making whites. He remarked of his sparkling wines that

> the first running was as clear as spirits, the second running was *Oeil de Perdrix,* and both of them sparkled and creamed in the glass like *Champaign.* It would be endless to mention how many good judges of Wine were deceived by my Wine, and thought it superior to any *Champaign.*

The English boycotted French wines during the Napoleonic Wars that were fought early in the nineteenth century. But widespread smuggling kept the British wine market well supplied and prevented the domestic wine industry from gaining any meaningful share increase.

Imports of sugar from the West Indies commenced after Waterloo, and English winemakers used this sugar to ferment their wines to higher alcohol percentages and also to retain much greater sweetness levels—both of which ultimately served to lower the general reputation of British wine quality.

But the most severe blow of all to commercialized viniculture in England was the introduction of the two American vine mildews, plus the *Phylloxera* blight during the mid-1800s. These organisms succeeded in slowly devastating both indoor and outdoor vines throughout the nation.

Shortly after World War II, Ray Barrington-Brock established the Viticultural Research Station at Oxted in Surrey. Workers at the station undertook the task of sifting through the wine-growing literature that had been amassed during the previous several hundred years in England, separating the factual from the false. Barrington-Brock's station also served to identify vine plant materials, dividing authentic varieties from imposters and grading stocks for propagation.

Another of the early pioneers in the resurrection of British wine growing was Edward Hyams, who also planted vines in the late 1940s, in East Kent. Modestly, Hyams has remarked that: "English wine growing will never be a great industry, but there is no reason why it should be an insignificant one." There can be no question that the resurgence of grape growing and winemaking in England would have taken much longer to occur were it not for the unselfish dedication of Barrington-Brock and Hyams.

The first commercial vineyard and winery in the rebirth was opened in Hampshire in 1952 by Major General Sir Guy Salisbury-Jones. His vineyards include Chardonnay and Pinot Noir vines, as well as some French-American hybrid selections. Production peaked in 1973, when output exceeded 1,000 cases. A larger winery was later constructed in Hampshire by A. M. Gore-Browne. M. J. Ward, of cider fame in the Kent and Sussex locales, was also an early vintner in the British commercial wine rebirth.

Perhaps much of the future fortune of the British wine industry will depend on the research work now under way at Pangbourne College, Wye College, and the English Vineyard Association's experimental vineyard. This work may reveal new varieties and/or clones that are more cold hardy, more disease resistant, and earlier ripening.

One thing to be sure, the British vintners are determined to produce wines that are capable of earning the esteem of their country—and, they hope, a good share of their growing market. As their technology develops, their wines should gain more and more recognition, not only in England, but also in other major wine markets.

CONCHA y TORO®

SPECIAL RESERVE

Casillero del Diablo®

100% CABERNET SAUVIGNON

MAIPO RED TABLE WINE

PIRQUE VINEYARD

ESTATE BOTTLED

GRAN VINO

PRODUCED AND BOTTLED IN MAIPO CHILE BY VIÑA CONCHA y TORO S.A.
CONTENTS 750 ML.   ALCOHOL 12.5% BY VOL.
IMPORTED BY EXCELSIOR WINE & SPIRITS CORP. NEW YORK, N.Y. 10016

12

THE WINES OF
SOUTH AMERICA
AND
MEXICO

The Spanish Jesuits that followed Columbus cultivated the first vines in the New World. In the 1520s, Mexican land grants were made with the proviso that settlers would plant ten vines for every person living on that land. In Mexico, the first mission was established by Franciscan monks at Loreto, the starting point of El Camino Real—the great mission trail ending in Sonoma, California. In South America, Spanish monks established vineyards at their missions during the mid-1500s, following the invasions of Pizarro and the conquistadores. Another three centuries passed, however, before commercial wine growing was first undertaken by Italian immigrants in Argentina. Chile was next to grow wine, modeling its industry on the French wine system. Brazilian viniculture emerged in the early twentieth century under Portuguese influence. Uruguay was settled by people who emigrated from all four of these European nations, and the comparatively small amount of commercial wine produced in Uruguay reflects these diverse traditions. Today there is more wine produced and consumed in South America than in North America.

Traditionally, few wines have been imported into the United States from South America or Mexico. This is due in part to the unstable economic and political situations that have plagued these nations, and in part to a history of rather poor-quality wines. In the last several decades, however, there has been some change,

VENEZUELA

GUYANA

COLUMBIA

ECUADOR

PERU

● Lima

BRAZIL

● La Paz

BOLIVIA

Rio de Janeiro ●

Sao Paulo ●

PARAGUAY

Santa Catarina

CHILE

Rio Grande Do Sul

Huasco
Vallenar

● Tucuman

Parana

Coquimbo

● Catamarca

● La Rioja

Cordoba

Aconcagua Region

URUGUAY

Valparaiso

● San Juan

Montevideo ●

SANTIAGO

Mendoza

Maipo Region

● San Raphael

Talco

BUENOS AIRES ●

Nuble

● Colonia Alvear Oeste

Linares

ARGENTINA

Maule Region

Talcahuano

Neuquen

Concepcion

Los Angeles

Rio Negro

South America

0 ├────────┤ 400   Miles

0 ├────────┤ 400   Kilometers

and North Americans can now get good values from the wines made by their neighbors to the south.

ARGENTINA

There is about 650 million gallons of wine made in Argentina per year from some 750,000 acres of vineyards, ranking it fifth among the world's wine-growing nations. In fact, Argentina produces more wine than all of the other South American countries combined. Argentines consume approximately 20 gallons per capita annually, or about ten times more than Americans, and very near the consumption levels in France and Italy.

The extreme western limits of Argentina are guarded by the Andes, the great chain of mountains that form the South American continental divide and a natural border between much of Argentina and Chile. To the east are the Argentine plains, mostly flatlands, which gently slope from about 2,000 feet to sea level in the province of Buenos Aires. It is upon these plains where many of the wines of the nation are grown.

Most of the vineyards of Argentina are cultivated in the Mendoza Province. This region was first irrigated by Italian immigrants from the Piedmont who employed Swiss technology to channel melted snow from the mountains to the vineyards. As in many other large wine-growing nations, *Phylloxera* has become a major threat. In some Argentine vineyards irrigation water is allowed to flood the vines, serving to drown a percentage of the pest and washing others out and downstream. Some viticulturists criticize this practice as crude and harmful to the vines, but the results cannot be disputed—grape quality and quantity continue to increase there.

Approximately two-thirds of the wine grown in Argentina is red table wine. Most of the balance is white and rosé table wines, although some dessert and sparkling wines are also made. Industry regulations are promulgated and enforced by the military through the Instituto Nacional Viniviticola. Inspectors monitor all phases of wine growing, from planting and cultivation to production, transportation, and marketing. Yet, despite this policing, there is little real regulation or standards. Label information is not generally informative, and brand names usually are the most reliable indicators of authenticity and/or quality and value. Both generic and estate names from other wine-growing countries are widely used, resulting in Argentine wines labeled "Margaux" and "Rioja," as well as "Burgundy," "Chablis," "Champagne," and "Rhine" (a practice still employed in the United States as well).

The best wines of Argentina are generally considered to be those grown in the Río Negro and Neuquén regions to the south of Mendoza. Other important regions are the Norte and Occidente, both of which are located in the northwestern part of the country on the eastern Andean plains. Córdoba is situated in the central part of Argentina, while Entre Ríos and Litoral are regions found in the eastern sector.

The principal grape varieties cultivated are Criolla, Sémillon, Malbec, and Tempranillo, as well as the traditional Italian varieties, Barbera, Nebbiolo, and Sangiovese. Among the more than 2,000 wineries operating in Argentina are several huge firms that continue to produce good, but ordinary, wines that are quaffed daily as diet staples throughout the nation. A few of the large operations, and many of the smaller firms, have also committed themselves to planting classic European vines. New Argentine vineyards of Chardonnay, Gewürztraminer, Johannisberg Riesling, Palomino, Cabernet Sauvignon, Pinot Noir, and Syrah bring to mind the wine renaissance that has taken place in the United States during the past several decades.

Many of the wineries in Argentina are very modern, with state-of-the-art production facilities directed by professional personnel who command respect internationally. These operations are producing increasing quantities of very good white and red table wines for the export trade, and some of these wines are gaining rather wide distribution in the United States.

Most of the important vintners operating in Argentina are situated in the Mendoza region. Among these are Bianchi, Crillon, and Suter, all of which are owned by the giant Seagram distilling firm. Peñaflor makes the locally well-known "Trapiche" brand, as well as the "Andean" label that is distributed in the United States. Viñedos Giol is a large state-operated cooperative winery, while Proviar is a firm owned by the French Champagne producer, Moët & Chandon.

BRAZIL

There was virtually no commercial wine grown in Brazil prior to 1900. Most Brazilians relied upon wines imported from Europe and other South American countries. But since the turn of the century the wine industry in Brazil has achieved remarkable growth, producing more than 70 million gallons annually since 1978. It is now the eighteenth-largest wine-growing nation in the world.

Most of Brazil's 175,000 acres of vineyards are located in the state of Rio Grande do Sul at the extreme southern tip of the country, bordering northeastern Uruguay. The balance is produced in the regions of Minas Gerais, Rio de Janeiro, Santa Catarina, and São Paulo. Considerable research has been directed toward growing grapes in the warmer and more humid regions of northern Brazil near the equator. By forcing vine dormancy through restriction of irrigation water, some growers have reported raising two grape crops per year.

The principal white wines grown in Brazil are now made from Malvasia, Johannisberg Riesling, and Trebbiano, while good reds are made from Barbera, Cabernet Sauvignon, and Merlot vines. Previously, the native American Isabella vine was the most widely cultivated variety in Brazil.

The most noteworthy wine producers are Vinicola Riograndense, Profivin, Viamao, and Dreher (the latter owned by the Heublein Corporation). Other American and European firms have also made relatively recent investments in Brazilian wine growing.

Nearly all of the wine made in Brazil is consumed there although some of the locally renowned sparkling wine called *espumante* is exported to the United States and other countries.

CHILE

While Argentina indisputably makes the largest quantity of wine of the South American wine-growing nations, most wine experts award Chile the honor of highest quality producer. Without question, viniculture in Chile is the most reminiscent of that in Europe.

Spain discovered Chile in 1536, and, by 1548, a Spanish priest named Carabantes had brought the first vines to the new nation. These early stocks were of the Pais variety—very similar to the traditional Criolla of Argentina and the Mission grape of California. The classic varieties of France, Germany, and Spain were not introduced into Chile until 1851, when Silvestre Ochagavia, a progressive winemaker of Spanish descent, planted the first Chardonnay, Johannisberg Riesling, Cabernet Sauvignon, and Cot (Malbec) vines, along with other selections. These vines adapted very well and continue to flourish as Chile is the only major wine-growing nation to have totally escaped the ravages of *Phylloxera*. The giant Andes peaks to the east, the desert to the north, and the cold polar Humboldt current from the west are thought to provide a natural barrier against the pest. Consequently, vines there continue to be grown on their own roots,

Ther vintage season in Chile. (Source: Viña Concha y Toro S.A.)

without needing to be grafted to *Phylloxera*-resistant rootstocks. However, another root insect was found in Chile, one called *Margarodes vitium*, which causes stunting of the vines and their eventual death.

By 1875, the commercial wine industry in Chile had grown to a production level of more than 13 million gallons annually, and by 1883 to near 30 million. In modern times output has leveled off at approximately 150 million gallons per year, occasionally surpassing 160 million during the heavier vintages. Chile is the thirteenth-largest wine-growing nation. All but about 3 percent of this production is also consumed by Chileans, their per capita consumption rate of 15 gallons per year ranks sixth in the world.

There are four official viticultural regions in Chile, each having the following subregions:

Bio Bio
  Coelemu
  Yumbel

Maipo
  Isla de Maipo
  Llano de Maipo
  Pirque
  Santiago

Santa Ana
Buin

Maule
  Cauquenes
  Chillán
  Curicó
  Linares
  Lontué

Molina
Parral
Quillón
Sagrada Familia
San Clemente
San Javier
Talca
Villa Alegre

Colchagua
Chimbarongo
Nancagua
Peumo
Rancagua
Rengo
San Fernando
Santa Cruz
Tinguiririca

Rapel
Cachapoal

The Ministry of Agriculture controls the use of appellations of origin in Chile, and only wine produced in the above subregions are permitted to be AOC-labeled.

The volume of wine output is also controlled by the Chilean government, surplus wine is distilled to brandy or industrial alcohol. White table wines for export must reach an alcohol strength of at least 12 percent, 11.5 percent for reds. Export wines labeled as "Courant" are one year old, "Special" are two or three years old, while "Reserve" wines are four or five years of age, and "Gran Vino" Chilean table wines are at least six years old.

The Andes mountains, with some peaks higher than 20,000 feet, dominate the topography of Chile and form a natural barrier of only 150 miles between the Argentine Mendoza and Chilean vineyards. Rainfall in Chile, as in neighboring Argentina and Bolivia, is scant. Irrigation water flows from mountain rivers to west-facing slopes of clay, limestone, and gravel soil upon which most of the Chilean vines are cultivated. Along with certain regions of Europe, the United States, Australia, and New Zealand, Chile has some environs of near-perfect natural land and weather conditions for viticulture.

One severe problem is earthquakes and tremors, which plague vintners in both Chile and Argentina. New wineries are built with massive reinforcement in order to withstand the frequent shocks.

Perhaps the finest wines in Chile are grown in the Maipo region located just south of Santiago, although superb growths are also found in the Maule region south of the capital city. Maipo valley firms that export wine to the United States include Concha y Toro, the largest operation and very successful with Cabernet and Merlot, Santa Rita, and Viña Linderos. The Aconcagua region, north of both Santiago and Valparaiso, contains some exceptional vineyards as well.

Technological advances are enabling Chileans to realize the superb potential of their red table wines grown from Cabernet Sauvignon, Malbec, and Merlot vines. Vintners such as Concha y Toro are building good reputations throughout the United States and in other countries. Other important producers include:

Viña Canepa
Viña Carmen
Casona
Viña Cousiño-Macul
Don Gabriel
Viña Errazuriz Panquehue
Viña Linderos
Los Robles
Miguel Torres
Viña Ochagavia
Portal Del Alto

Rabat
Viña San Pedro
Viña Santa Carolina
Santa Elisa
Santa Helena
Subercaseaux
Viña Tarapacá Ex Zavala
Viña Undurraga
Valdivieso
Vinos Exposicion

The new government of Chile, which came to power in 1973, has provided incentives for further advances in wine quality and has fostered the expansion into international markets as well.

URUGUAY

There are four small provinces in Uruguay that grow wine commercially: Canelones, Colonia, San José, and Soriano. All of these are adjacent to the capital city of Montevideo.

This general area is predominantly low, humid flatlands, somewhat comparable to some of the more southern vineyard locales in Italy. About 50,000 acres of vines are cultivated in Uruguay, and annual wine production is generally about 20 million gallons, ranking it twenty-third among the world's wine-growing nations. Little of the Uruguayan wine output has earned a quality reputation. The best grapes harvested from French and Italian vine varieties are made into ordinary table wines. Inferior white and red wines are generally either distilled into brandy or blended to make *Vino Seco,* a maderized fortified wine well known locally. Nearly all of the wine production of Uruguay is also consumed there, at a rate of about 7 gallons per capita per year.

MEXICO

Mexican viniculture has been very slow to develop despite the fact that the colonists who followed Cortés into Mexico planted the first vines in the New World.

The greater portion of Mexico is a large elevated plateau bordered by two mountain ranges: the Sierra Madre Oriental to the east and the Sierra Madre Occidental to the west, both of which fall off sharply to form narrow coastal plains. These ranges meet at La Junta, where mountain elevations rival all but the very highest Andean peaks in South America. In general, Mexico is not suited to viniculture. Where rainfall is sufficient it is too hot to grow fine-wine grapevines, and where the climate is more temperate, there is an insufficiency of water.

There are exceptions to this along the northern border of the country, especially in the San Solano Valley near Ensenada, where the old Santo Tomás de Aquino Mission produces good red table wines on the Pacific side of the Baja California Peninsula. Santo Tomás was founded in the early 1790s by Padre José Loriente, a Dominican monk who recognized that the rich loam soils and abundant sunshine were valuable vinicultural resources. Loriente found that the gentle ocean breezes tempered the Baja climate and mountain water provided ample irrigation to supplement the generally scant rainfall. The vineyards of Santo Tomás expanded for the next three decades until the Mexican government took control of all the missions in 1825. The twentieth-century renaissance of Santo Tomás derived in part from the expertise of Dmitri Tchelistcheff, son of the famous Napa Valley wine master, André. Tchelistcheff's recommendation that the mission vineyards be replanted with classic European vine varieties was a major factor in upgrading the wines from the region.

The Guadalupe Valley is also situated in the Baja near Ensenada, and it is here that the Domecq winery operates under the direction of its internationally famous parent facility, the Bodegas Pedro Domecq sherry winery of Spain. Industrias Vinicolas Domecq is best known in Mexico for the production of "Los Reyes" table wines, which enjoy a good reputation. Formex-Ybarra produces the locally distinguished "Terrasola" table wines, also grown in the Guadalupe Valley.

Another Mexican winery of note is Casa Madero, located near Monterrey at the base of the Yucatán Peninsula. Casa Madero, the second-oldest commercial winery in the Americas, was founded by Don Lorenzo Garcia, who secured the original land grant from King Philip II of Spain in the 1600s. Garcia constructed his winery near the ancient Mission of Santa Maria de las Parras, translated as "St. Mary of the Vineyards," and named after the profusion of native vines found growing there in the wild. Casa Madero continues its great heritage, now producing and marketing a large line of table wines, including the varietals Chenin Blanc, Pinot Blanc, Barbara, Cabernet Sauvignon, and Zinfandel.

The first commercial vineyard in the Americas was planted at Parras as well, established also in the 1600s, by Don Francisco de Urdiñola. This site is still operated as a producing vineyard by the Marqués de Aguayo winery located nearby. Other important Mexican vintners located in the Monterrey vicinity are Delfin, Perote, Rosario, and Vesubio.

Bodega at Mexico's Casa Madero, the oldest commercial winery on the North American continent. (Source: Casa Madero, S.A.)

Mexican wines are also grown in Chihuahua and Aguascalientes, with production in the regions led by the firms Delicias and Compañía Vinícola de Saltillo, respectively. The Cavas de San Juan, in Querataro, has the highest elevation of any winery in the nation, at more than 6,000 feet, and produces table wines from Chardonnay and Cabernet Sauvignon vines, among others.

Mexico's annual production of 5 million gallons of wine ranks it only thirty-second among the world's wine producers. However, new investments of resources have spurred gains in both quality and quantity in the Mexican vinicultural industry.

CONCHA y TORO

ESTATE   BOTTLED

75 %   25 %

Cabernet Sauvignon / Merlot

RAPEL RED TABLE WINE

*The classic blend of many fine Chateaux of Bordeaux.
Cabernet Sauvignon for complexity and longevity,
Merlot for softness and elegance.*

1984

PRODUCED AND BOTTLED IN RAPEL CHILE BY VIÑA CONCHA y TORO S.A.

ALCOHOL 12 % BY VOL.   CONTENTS 750 ML.

IMPORTED BY EXCELSIOR WINE & SPIRITS CORP. NEW YORK, N.Y. 10016

A MONSIEUR HENRI SELECTION

ALCOHOL 12%
BY VOLUME

NET CONTENTS
750ML

VINTAGE
1979

ESTATE
BOTTLED

TRAKIA™

MERLOT

DRY RED WINE FROM THE HASKOVO REGION OF BULGARIA

PRODUCED AND BOTTLED IN BULGARIA BY VINIMPEX, SOFIA
IMPORTED BY MONSIEUR HENRI WINES, LTD., WHITE PLAINS, NEW YORK 10604

13

THE WINES OF THE SOVIET BLOC COUNTRIES

The strong political bond is, of course, the prime reason for considering Bulgaria, Czechoslovakia, Hungary, Romania, the Soviet Union, and Yugoslavia in this single chapter. Most of these nations, however, also share a similar wine-growing heritage—Roman and/or Greek influence in the early development of vines and wines, then a decline in vinicultural activity due to centuries of barbaric invasions, and, finally, a recent resurgence of wine growing undertaken to meet a rapidly growing wine demand.

The placement of these nations this far back in the book should not be taken as a sign of their relative importance as winegrowers in the world. The combined annual wine output of the Soviet Bloc nations rivals that of France and Italy. Relegation to chapter 13 is due to the relative lack of available information and the restrictions on gathering new material about the wine industry in these countries. Finally, comparatively few Soviet Bloc wines ever reach U.S. markets, rendering in-depth discussion somewhat academic. Perhaps someday, however, the economic and political situation will shift, and these wines, some of which are quite good, may join the already abundant offerings of wines from around the world available to U.S. wine lovers.

BULGARIA

Although the Romans are given credit for growing the first vines in Bulgaria, it was, in fact, the Greeks who made the first wines there. Bulgaria, like Greece, was a part of the Roman Empire, and it is likely that emigrants from the neighboring Greek province of Thrace influenced the first wines of Bulgaria.

Slavic tribes migrated into Bulgaria following the fall of the Roman Empire and wine growing went into decline. In the seventh century, warring pagan tribes called Bulgars invaded the northern reaches of the territory, and the region has been known as Bulgaria ever since. Despite numerous attempts by Byzantine armies to drive the Bulgars out of the area, they held their ground and gradually became integrated into the Slavic culture. But the vinicultural arts under both the Bulgars and Slavs regressed, falling to its lowest point during the Dark Ages, when only very small peasant vineyards were cultivated. During the Ottoman rule of Bulgaria, from 1396 to 1879, commercial wine growing became virtually extinct.

The peasant Bulgarians continued to make wine in defiance of the Ottoman Moslem prohibition, but it wasn't until just following World War II that the wine industry of Bulgaria regained national political support. During the next three decades, Bulgarian viniculture—supported by the Soviet Union with modern machinery and the latest technology—has grown tremendously. In modern times Bulgaria has more than 400,000 acres of commercial vineyards and its 120 million-gallon annual output ranks it sixteenth among the world's wine producers. Bulgarians now consume about 6 gallons of wine per person annually, more than twice the rate in the United States. Perhaps most impressive of all is the penetration of Bulgarian wines into the highly competitive international markets as well as in the Communist Bloc nations.

Bulgaria's area is approximately 42,800 square miles, just a bit larger than the State of Virginia. The larger share of this area is not conducive to growing wine, principally because of two very picturesque but cold mountain ranges. The southwest frontiers of the country are formed by the Rhodope mountains, with elevations exceeding 9,500 feet. The Rhodope ranges extend across the Bulgarian border into Greece to the south and Yugoslavia to the west. The main east-west spine of Bulgaria is formed by the Stara range of the Balkan mountains. To the north of this traverse are gently sloping fertile flatlands bordered on the north by the romantic Danube River that separates Bulgaria from Romania. To the south of the Stara range is the Maritsa River that, along with the tributary rivers Arda and Tundzha, forms the very rich Maritsa agricultural basin. Generally, the northern sector of Bulgaria has more severe winters and a shorter growing season than the

BULGARIA

N

0   50   100 MILES

more temperate south. Rainfall varies widely from one microclimate locale to another, but usually measures from within 20 to 50 inches per year.

There are four major wine-growing regions that are distinguished by Vinprom—the national wine-growing control authority located in the city of Sofia. These are most often designated simply as the northern, southern, eastern, and southwestern quarters. Another state organization, Vinimpex, is the authority that controls the nation's export of wines and spirits.

The northern sector, located north of the Balkan spine, is one of the larger regions. Red wines are grown almost exclusively there, principally in the districts of Kramolin, Pavlikeni, Pleven, and Sukhindol. Traditionally, Gamza has been the major vine variety cultivated in the region, generally yielding wine that is light and brisk, but ordinary. In more recent times, Cabernet Sauvignon, Gamay, and Pinot Noir are being given the most attention by wine-growing officials there.

Scattered through the entire eastern sector of Bulgaria are small, remote white wine districts, ranging geographically from the port cities of Burgas, Pomorie, and

Varna on the Black Sea to Silistra and Ruse on the Danube. The most widely cultivated vines are Chardonnay, Dimiat, Rkatziteli, Rizling (Italian Riesling or Wälschriesling), and Sylvaner. In the northern reaches of the region are grown some truly fine white table wines, heavy in body, with rich varietal character. Typically, the southeastern whites are strong, deficient of good acid balance, and thin in body.

The other two regions are situated in south-central Bulgaria and produce primarily red wine. Principal subregions are found near the cities of Stara, Plovdiv, and Melnik. The variety Pamid is grown there to make a rather fruity and light red table wine. Mavrud, perhaps a distant relative of the fabled Greek *Mavrodaphne,* yields a very dark and heavy berrylike red wine. The wine grown nearer Melnik is reputed to be even heavier. A white wine region is located near Kyustendil in the far west of the nation.

The majority of Bulgarian wines for domestic consumption and Communist Bloc export are labeled according to the locale in which they are grown. Wines intended for West Germany—the most important export market outside of the Soviet Bloc—are labeled with such Teutonic names as "Klosterkeller" and "Sonnenküste." The "Pinot" Chardonnay and Cabernet Sauvignon now exported to the United States under the "Trakia" label are both well-made Bulgarian wines. Though each has a distinctive varietal character, neither displays the finesse expected from most French or U.S. wines made from the same classic varieties. Nevertheless, the Trakia wines remain exceptional values as they are currently sold in most U.S. markets for less than four dollars per bottle.

CZECHOSLOVAKIA

The strategic routes that reach across the land that is now Czechoslovakia have linked the Slavic and Teutonic cultures for centuries. Czechoslovakia itself, a country created by the division of the Austro-Hungarian Empire in 1918, contains a diverse range of ethnic groups, each with its own distinct customs and history. The nation's name is a contraction of the names of its two principal groups—the Czechs and the Slovaks—but a complete history of its peoples would have to include Austrians, Germans, Hungarians, Poles, Romanians, Ruthenians, and Slavs. Wine production in Czechoslovakia exhibits the same type of "melting pot" character.

There are approximately 130,000 acres of vineyard in Czechoslovakia, and annual wine production is generally about 40 million gallons. Czechoslovakian production is small compared with other Soviet Bloc countries, but it nevertheless ranks nineteenth among the world's wine-producing nations. Consumption of wine there is at a per capita rate of 3 gallons per year, also the lowest level of the Soviet Bloc countries. Classic Western varieties such as Gewürztraminer and Johannisberg Riesling are awarded the top grade in the Czechoslovakian varietal ranking system, and these vines account for about one-fifth of the nation's vineyards. Another 50 percent or so are devoted to second-class vines such as Grüner Veltliner and Müller-Thurgau. Yet another one-fifth of the vines in Czechoslovakia are red, primarily Cabernet Sauvignon and Frankovka (same as the Austrian Limberger).

Most Czechoslovakian wine is made in the region of Slovakia, a 200-mile rolling strip of beautiful countryside situated at the extreme southeastern end of the country along the Hungarian border. The principal city of the region is Bratislava, a Danube River port that is virtually surrounded by the Little Carpathian mountains. Much of the wine produced in Slovakia is so reminiscent of that made in neighboring Hungary that it is termed "Czechoslovakian Tokay." This is grown from Furmint and Muscat vines cultivated in that portion of the Hungarian Tokay vineyard that runs across into Czechoslovakia.

To the immediate northwest of Slovakia is the Moravian wine region of Czechoslovakia, which shares its southwestern border with Austria. The influence of the famous Austrian "Wine Quarter," or *Weinwiertel*, extends into this region, and its stamp is apparent on the character of the wines. Light, dry whites are produced in this region from the Austrian Grüner Veltliner as well as Riesling grapes.

At the extreme northwestern reaches of Czechoslovakia, north of Prague, is the tiny Bohemian vineyard region located along the East German border. As may be expected, this region takes much of its wine heritage from the Germans.

HUNGARY

While the Phoenicians and Greeks were establishing colonies and settlements in the western Mediterranean, nomadic tribes moved over the Caucasus mountains and through the Ukraine into what eventually became the Balkan colonies of the Roman Empire. The Romans organized Hungary into a province called Pannonia, and it is probable that the first vines were cultivated for wine production in that locale during the Roman occupation.

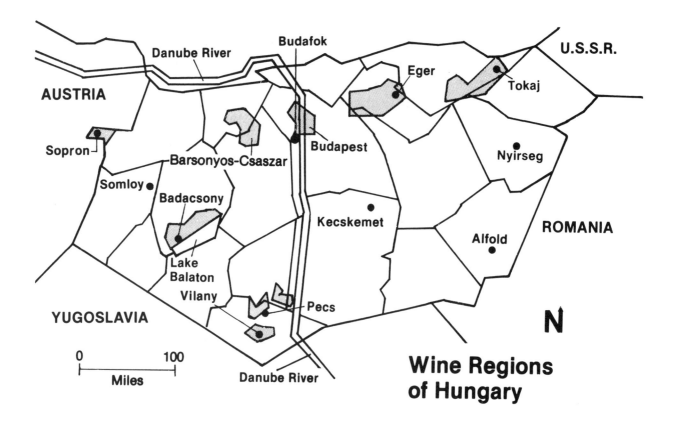

**Wine Regions
of Hungary**

During the fall of the Roman Empire, Pannonia was invaded by Germanic tribes that were later driven out of the province by the Huns. During the centuries following the death of Attila, king of the Huns, a series of other tribes occupied Hungary. Among these were once again Germanic tribes, then, in succession, the Asiatic Avars, the Slavic Moravians, and the Franks under Charlemagne. In the late 800s Hungary fell to the Magyars, and, in 955, Magyar rule fell, in turn, to Emperor Otto I of the Holy Roman Empire although the Magyars continued to live there in vassalage.

The first Hungarian monarch, King Stephen, founded several Benedictine monasteries during the early eleventh century and the culture of western Europe civilized the nation.

Despite the advancement of civilization in Hungary, political stability was not attained. Consecutively, Hungary endured conquest by Mongolia, Turkey, and the Hapsburgs. After World War II, in 1919, Hungary was declared an independent republic, but the Communist dictatorship of Béla Kun was formed, and the country was promptly invaded by the Romanians. Following World War II, the Hungarian People's Republic was founded, but economic and political instability have continued to plague Hungary to some extent into the present.

Despite this painful history, the Hungarians seem always to have been a joyful people—an attitude that is reflected in the attractiveness of their wines. They drink about 7.5 gallons per person annually, more than any other Communist Bloc nation, and rank eleventh in world per capita wine consumption.

There are approximately 400,000 acres of vineyards cultivated commercially in Hungary. These yield about 150 million gallons of wine each year, making Hungary the twelfth-largest wine-producing nation in the world. Nearly all of this output is made by seven very large government-owned estate vineyard-wineries called *combinats*. Some of these facilities cultivate more than 50,000 acres at a single site. There are only a few remaining private vintners. All Hungarian wine exports are handled by the state-operated marketing agency called Monimpex, which is headquartered in Budapest.

There are nearly 36,000 square miles of area in Hungary, about the same as the State of Indiana. The Alps form much of the western reaches of the country, and the Carpathian mountains dominate the east. The Danube River forms a natural border between Hungary and Czechoslovakia to the north.

Soils range from a volcanic rock in the northeastern highlands to an alluvial consistency in the east-central quarter. The central belt of Hungary is a desert. Superior winelands are made up of rich brown or grey humus soils that are plentiful in the western portion of the nation. Four distinct seasons exist; winters are rather harsh and summers dry and hot. Rainfall usually measures between 25and 40 inches annually. Most of the vineyards in Hungary are cultivated at elevations of less than 1,000 feet.

Four wine-growing regions are designated in Hungary, two on each side of the Danube River, which turns south at Esztergom to divide the nation virtually in half. To the west are the Northern Transdanubia and Southern Transdanubia wine-growing regions, while the Great Plain and the Northern Massif are situated in the eastern sector.

There are six subregions located in the Northern Transdanubia. Three of these, Balatonfüred-Csopak, Mount Badacsonyi, and Balaton, border the northern coastline of Lake Balaton. In this locale some of the finest Hungarian white table wines are grown. The most commonly planted vines are Furmint, Olaszrizling (Wälschriesling), Kéknyelü and Szürkebarát, the last a clone of Pinot Gris. Most of the Lake Balaton wines are somewhat reminiscent of the residually sweet white wines grown in the upper Rheinland of West Germany and northern Switzerland. The other three districts are Somló, Mór, and Sopron. Somló is located just a few miles north of Lake Balaton and is best known for light and rather thin white wines grown from Furmint and Olaszrizling. Thirty miles farther to the northeast is the Mór, which produces crisp, dry white wines from native Hungarian Ezerjó vines. Another 50 miles or so to the west, on the Austrian border, is Sopron, the only major red wine-producing locale in the Northern Transdanubia. Kékfrankos, a clone of Gamay, and Tramini are the principal Sopron varieties cultivated, both of which yield good, but ordinary, dry red table wines there.

The Southern Transdanubia has three subregions: Mecsék, Szekszárd and Vilány. Rather common white table wines are grown in all of the districts, principally from Furmint and Olaszrizling. The dry red from native Hungarian Kadarka vines is generally light and flavorful. Cabernet Sauvignon and Pinot Noir vines are finding more acceptance from the winegrowers in the region, perhaps indicating that consumers are looking for more complexity in their red wines.

The Great Plain region is located directly east of the Danube and is a 50-mile band that stretches across nearly the entire nation. The region is truly a great plain. Much of it consists of either wind-blown sand or alkali wasteland upon which even vines sometimes have difficulty surviving. The Great Plain, sometimes called the "Alföld," is where the everyday quaffing wines of Hungary are grown, primarily from Ezerjó, Olaszrizling, and Kadarka vines. The Great Plains vineyards account for more than half of the land in Hungary devoted to viniculture.

Beyond the Great Plain, at the foothills of the Carpathian mountains, is the Northern Massif wine-growing region where the most famous wines of Hungary are made, the *Tokaj* and *Egri Bikavér.*

Tokaj, or "Tokay," as it is known by many Westerners, is made from Furmint and Hárslevelü grapes infected by the noble rot, *Botrytis cinerea.* With a method similar to the one the Germans use to make Beerenauslese, Hungarian vintners take select berries called *aszú* and press them in vats from which the free-run Tokay Aszú juice is collected in special wooden casks. The remaining pomace (skins and seeds left in the press) is then pulverized into a mash and added back to the juice in amounts required to achieve the desired flavor and quality in the final product. After several days of fermentation, the new wine is filtered into other casks to age for up to six years. The aging cellars for Tokay are caves carved into the volcanic hillsides in which the rows of casks are maintained at naturally cool temperatures. The casks are filled not quite to the top to leave some *ullage,* or "air space," so that oxidation can maderize the wine in the same manner as in Madeira.

In addition to the famed Tokay *Aszú* there is Tokay *Aszú Essencia,* Tokay *Essence,* and Tokay *Szamorodni.* Tokay Aszú Essencia is distinguished by a higher required sugar content in the must. Tokay Essence is juice naturally pressed from Aszú grapes through the action of the weight of the grapes themselves, the free-run juice, as it is known in the West. Tokay Szamorodni, a lesser type, is a common white wine made from Tokay grapes that have been infected with the noble mold.

Tokay wines require long periods of time for the maderization process to take place, and subsequent secondary aging may go on for many years before full maturation is achieved. Some believe that these long-aged wines are one reason why some of the people in the Northern Massif live to be so old.

The end result of the Tokay process is a naturally sweet dessert wine with alcohol content rarely in excess of 10 percent by volume. At its best it is rather like Sauternes—a rich, golden elixir. At one time, there was a great demand for Tokay in the West, but the taste for sweet wines has diminished considerably in modern times and is far less today even than just a decade ago.

The legendary Egri Bikavér is believed to have been originated by French Benedictine Monks of the eleventh century. It derives its name, translated as "Bull's Blood of Eger," from a sixteenth-century Turkish war legend. The Turks, who were laying siege to Eger, observed that the defenders were taking refreshment from jugs containing a dark red beverage. A rumor swept the Turkish camp that the beverage being consumed by the Magyars was actually bull's blood. The Turks promptly fled the scene and the red wine has been called Egri Bikavér ever since.

Eger is an old agricultural town situated about 125 miles to the northeast of Budapest. It is sheltered by the Bukk and Mátra ranges of the Carpathian mountains. The blend of the wine is approximately 70 percent Kadarka, 20 percent Pinot Noir, and the balance Cabernet Sauvignon. Though at its best, Egri Bikavér is only a good dry red table wine, it is one of the wines from the Soviet Bloc most commonly found in contemporary U.S. markets.

ROMANIA

Romania derives its name as well as its earliest wine history from the Romans. The territory that eventually became Romania was conquered by Emperor Trajan in the first decade of the second century A.D. The colony was populated by people called the Daci by the Romans, and the Greeks, along with the Romans, introduced and developed the wine-growing arts there.

Battles were fought almost continually in the Daci colony for the next several centuries, with invasions from the Goths, Huns, Slavs, and Bulgars. Out of the "melting pot" of peoples in the region there evolved an ethnic group of non-wine-drinking Roman-Slavic warlike nomads called Walachians or Vlachs. The Vlachs were converted to Orthodox Christianity in the eleventh century and, two centuries later, led by Rudolph the Black, migrated to the rich agricultural plain between the Danube River and the southern Carpathian foothills. It was there that the country's wine-growing arts were reestablished, but not for very long. In 1411 the Walachian territory became a vassal state of the Ottoman Empire and, although the Vlachs resisted Turkish rule fiercely, their wine-growing activities were greatly impaired.

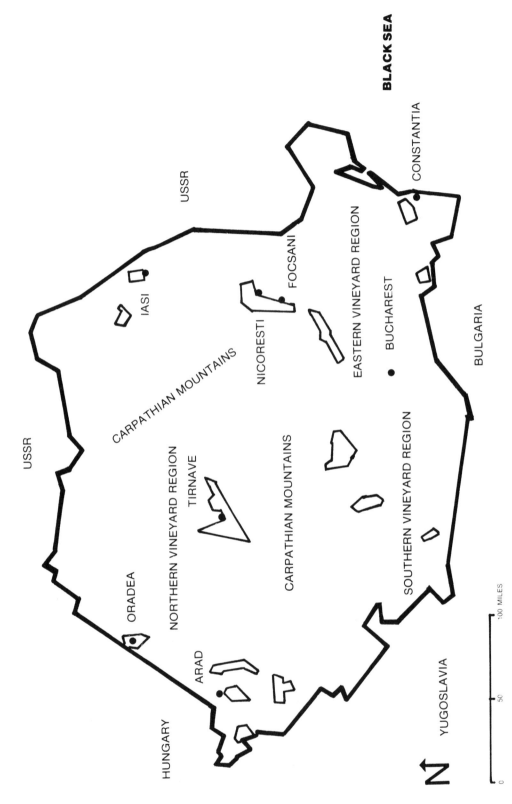

BLACK SEA

USSR

USSR

CARPATHIAN MOUNTAINS

IASI

NICORESTI

FOCSANI

EASTERN VINEYARD REGION

CONSTANTIA

BUCHAREST

BULGARIA

NORTHERN VINEYARD REGION

TIRNAVE

CARPATHIAN MOUNTAINS

SOUTHERN VINEYARD REGION

ORADEA

ARAD

HUNGARY

YUGOSLAVIA

N

0   50   100 MILES

ROMANIA

Under a proclamation made by the Sultan of Turkey in 1862 Walachia and Moldavia were joined as the principality of Romania. Sixteen years later, following the Russo-Turkish War, Romania was recognized as an independent nation.

Romania is still a country with a diversity of ethnic groups, each with its own customs, heritage, and language. Curiously, the wine-growing methods of Romania resemble those of Germany and northern France. Perhaps this is due to the demands of the cold Romanian climate.

While Romania is politically a Soviet satellite and is surrounded on all borders by sister countries of the Communist Bloc, it nevertheless shows more independence than any other nation behind the Iron Curtain. Its languages, based upon Latin, are written in the Latin alphabet rather than the Cyrillic alphabet used in the Soviet Union and some of the other Soviet Bloc nations. Only about 20 percent of Romania's wineries are state facilities. Another 50 percent or so are large cooperatives, and the balance is privately owned. Romania, the largest and northernmost of the Balkan states, carries on extensive trade both with Soviet Bloc countries and with the West.

Wine growing in Romania is controlled by the Intreprinderile Agricole de Stat (IAS), and wine exports are supervised by the state-operated Vinexport agency, both headquartered in the capital city of Bucharest. Since the 1960s a concentrated vineyard-planting program has increased Romanian vineyard acreage significantly, bringing annual wine output to more than 220 million gallons annually and ranking it tenth among the world's wine-growing nations. About 15 percent of this is exported, primarily to Czechoslovakia, East Germany, and Poland, as well as to Belgium, France, Sweden, the Netherlands, and the United Kingdom. The average Romanian drinks more than 7 gallons of wine each year, ranking Romania twelfth in the world in per capita consumption.

Yet despite these impressive statistics, Romanian wine quality has not progressed significantly during its century under the Russian sphere of influence. Romania is a country rich in natural resources, particularly oil and minerals, and these have gradually shifted the national emphasis from agricultural to industrial pursuits. It is rather common to find vineyards being cultivated in, or near, oil fields.

Romania, consisting of 91,600 square miles of rugged topography, is just a bit smaller in size than the State of Oregon. Typically, soils are poor and rainfall slight across most of Romania, in many areas the vine struggles for survival.

The Carpathian mountains, sweeping in a huge curve across the nation, divide Romania into distinct eastern, southern, and northwestern geographical sectors. The upper and lower ranges of the mountains are joined by the Transylvania plateau highlands.

The most internationally famous wine grown in Romania is *Cotnari*—the fabled "Pearl of Moldavia" that once rather commonly appeared with other sweet white dessert wines on many prestigious wine lists in both Eastern and Western Europe. In more recent years the Western taste for Cotnari and other heavy natural dessert wines, such as the Hungarian Tokay and French Sauternes, has markedly diminished. Nevertheless, Cotnari remains one of Romania's most distinctive white wines. It is grown from Grasă, Fetească Albă, and Tămîioasă vines in the northeastern portion of the country, near the Russian border.

Grasă, Fetească Albă, and Tămîioasă vines, as well as Muscat Ottonel, Pinot Gris, Sauvignon Blanc, and Wälschriesling, are also cultivated in the famous Transylvanian plateau region of Tîrnăve. Some of these grapes are made into fruity, well-balanced, varietal-labeled wines. *Perlă de Tîrnave* is a generic blend that is pleasant, residually sweet, but ordinary.

To the far west, in the Banat region, near the Hungarian border, white table wines are grown from Fetească Regală and Wälschriesling. Banat reds are made from Cabernet Sauvignon, Cadarca (the native Hungarian Kadarka), and Merlot. Few of the Banat wines are characteristically Romanian; perhaps they are closer in style to the wines of neighboring Hungary.

Situated along the great curve of the southeastern Carpathian foothills are the Drăgăşani, Arges, Dealul Mare, and Focşani wine-growing regions of Romania. It is in these regions that the greatest share of the nation's commercial wine growing takes place. The white table wines are made from Fetească Regală, Muscat Ottonel, Pinot Gris, Sauvignon Blanc, and Walschriesling, while reds are grown from Băbească Fatească Neagră, Cabernet Sauvignon, Merlot, and Pinot Noir. Soils in the Focşani region are very sandy and generally suitable only for viniculture. The vines grown on these sandy soils, however, yield wines that are usually rich in body, color, and flavor, yet with a light, pleasing acidity. Unfortunately, many of the wines grown in the other three regions in the foothills sector are sweet and without distinction. The Segarcea region along the Danube River Delta, at the southern border of Romania, also produces undistinguished, rather sweet, white and red table wines.

The chief city of the coastal lowlands of the Black Sea in Romania is Constanţa, built upon the ancient Greek port city of Tomis. Several miles inland, upon the Dobrogea Plateau, and among the Murfatlar hills, the variety Muscat Ottonel continues to be cultivated as it has been since the ancient Greco-Roman occupation. Nowadays Murfatlar Muscats are heavy, sweet, golden white wines that truly reflect the character of this southeasternmost portion of Romania. Modern-day vineyards of the Murfatlar region also include Chardonnay and other classic Western European vines, most of which are vinified into strong table wines with a recognizable Turkish character.

Experimental vineyard at the Murfatlar Research Station near the Black Sea in Romania. (Source: Philip Hiaring *Wines and Vines.* University of California, Davis.)

THE SOVIET UNION

The USSR, as it exists today, is a nation of many peoples and many histories. Prior to the rise of the Roman Empire, the great land expanse that was to become Russia was a wilderness in which only a few nomadic, barbaric tribes managed to scratch out a meager existence. Some of these tribes are described in the writings of ancient Greek and Roman historians. Later, another group of forest-dwelling tribes, equally barbaric, evolved in the northern reaches of the territory. These were the first Slavs, the ancestors of the Russian people.

However, little wine, at least from grapes, was ever made by the northern Slavs. The wine history of the Soviet Union properly belongs to Moldavia, Crimea, the Ukraine, and Georgia in the far more temperate south.

After World War II, the Soviet Union took over part of Moldavia from Romania; nonetheless, the background of the Moldavian people really forms a chapter in the history of Romania, and Moldavian wines are considered in the Romanian section above.

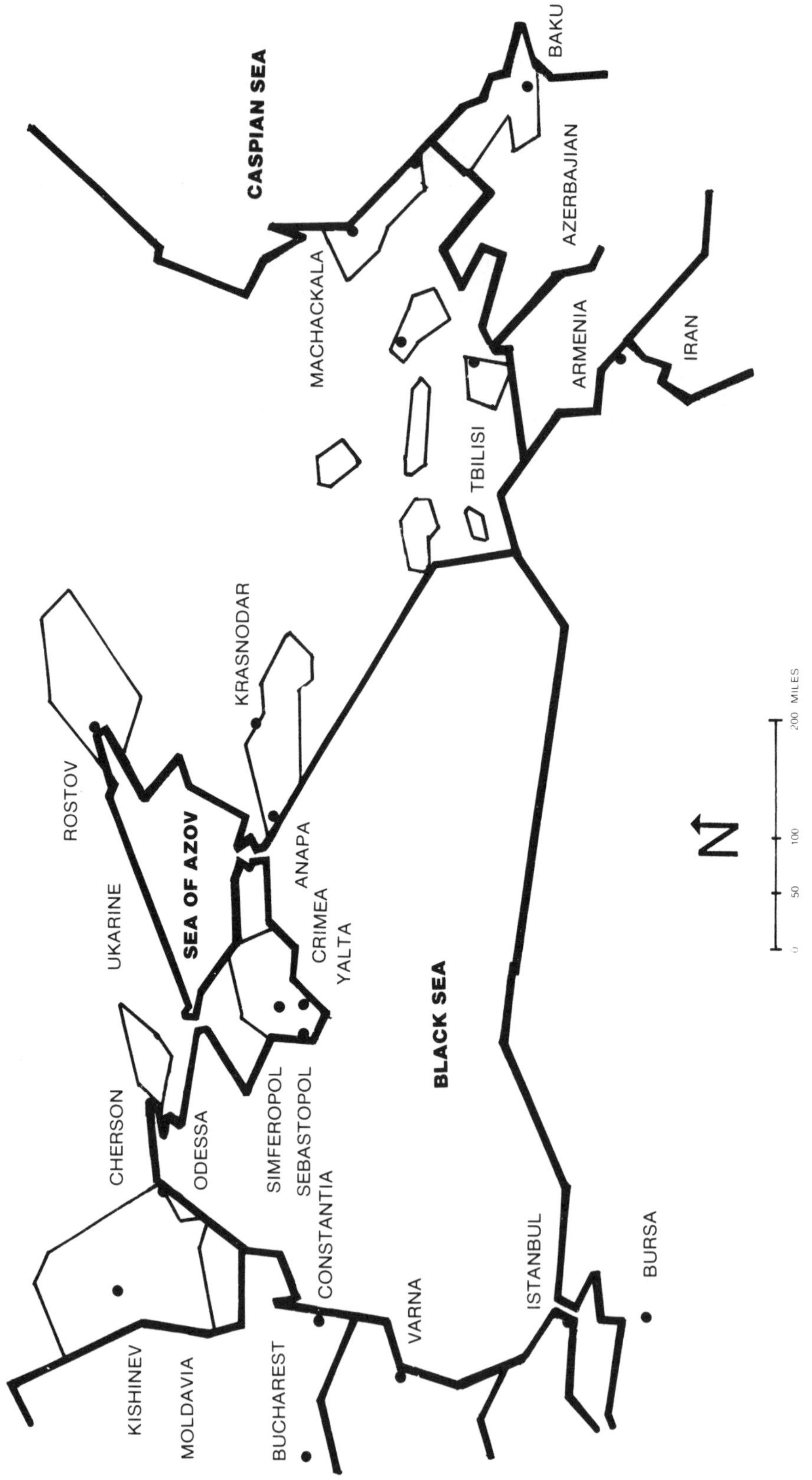

CASPIAN SEA

BAKU

AZERBAJIAN

MACHACKALA

ARMENIA

IRAN

TBILISI

STALINGRAD

KRASNODAR

ROSTOV

SEA OF AZOV

UKARINE

ANAPA

CRIMEA

YALTA

BLACK SEA

CHERSON

ODESSA

SIMFEROPOL

SEBASTOPOL

CONSTANTIA

ISTANBUL

BURSA

KISHINEV

MOLDAVIA

BUCHAREST

VARNA

N

0   50   100   200 MILES

MAJOR USSR WINE REGIONS

New vineyard planting near Kishnev in the Moldavia reigon of the USSR. (Source: Philip Hiaring, *Wines and Vines*, University of California, Davis.)

Crimea was known to the ancients as Cheronesus Taurica, a name taken from a mountain tribe called the Tauri that had descended from the Cimmerians during the seventh and fifth centuries B.C. The territory was colonized by the Greeks of Miletus, who built a number of ports there. Later it became a Roman colony, and the Romans introduced wine growing to the region as they did in so many of the territories they conquered. Crimea was invaded by the Goths during the middle of the third century and endured successive invasions by the Huns, Khazars, Byzantine Greeks, Kipchaks, Mongols, and Genovese over the following ten centuries. In the fifteenth century Crimea was invaded by Turks who managed to occupy the region for the next 300 years. Following the Russian victory over the Turks in 1777, the Crimean territory became part of the Russian Empire. At the end of the Crimean War in 1856 an autonomous republic was created for the citizens of Crimea. In World War II it was invaded by the Nazis, but following the Allied victories, Crimea became a part of the Russian Ukraine in 1954, and remains so today.

The earliest origins of the Ukrainians are more obscure. It is known that in the eleventh and twelfth centuries, the Ukraine gained the lofty title of "Mother Russia," owing chiefly to the fact that Kiev, the capital city of the region, was generally considered the center of Rus culture.

Some Georgians believe that they are direct descendents of the Biblical Noah, and, because Noah planted and tended a vineyard on Mount Ararat near where his ark came to rest, the Georgians claim that their region is the "motherland of wine." Their claims could well be justified as Mount Ararat is located less than 150 miles to the south of Tbilisi, the capital city of Georgia. There is also evidence that Georgia's first inhabitants migrated from the Lake Van region, which is situated in the same direction.

These regions have for many centuries not only grown wine, but their inhabitants have been heavy consumers both of their native-grown products and of wines imported from other lands through the many ports of the northern Black Sea. Interest in wine in the northern sections of the Soviet Union is a relatively recent phenomenon, and one that has arisen, at least in part, as a kind of government-sponsored alternative to vodka. During the years directly following the end of World War II, the Kremlin recognized overindulgence in vodka as a national problem. In the early 1950s the Soviet-state wine development organization began to increase the wine vineyard acreage along the northern Black Sea coastal territories. The project became nothing short of monumental in its proportions. By 1981 the Soviet Union had become the fourth-largest wine-producing nation in the world, with more than 909 million gallons made per year—trailing behind only Italy, France, and Spain.

The Russian consumer response was even more phenomenal. From an insignificant national rate, consumption of wine increased to more than 3 gallons per capita in 1970, 3.5 gallons in 1975, and more than 3.75 gallons in 1980. Despite the huge vineyard and winery expansion program, however, the Soviet Union became a net importer of wine. Unfortunately, the vodka problem was not solved in the meantime.

The Soviet Union's traditional wine-growing regions—the Moldavia-Crimea-Ukraine crescent, on the uppermost shores of the Black Sea, and Georgia, which separates the eastern Black Sea from the western Caspian Sea—continue to be the prime wine regions in contemporary times.

Moldavia still cultivates some of the traditional Romanian wine-grape varieties that were grown when it was part of that country. The district is bounded on the west by the Carpathian mountains and the Ukraine on the east. A large producer of agricultural crops, it is also rich in lignite, gypsum, and phosphorus.

Most of the new vines planted in Moldavia as a result of the great Soviet Union vineyard-expansion project undertaken more than thirty years ago have been classic Western varieties such as Gewürztraminer, Johannisberg Riesling, Cabernet Sauvignon, Merlot, and Pinot Noir. Modern Moldavian winemakers blend a number of varieties in order to achieve their desired finished products, most of which are sweet.

The Ukraine was once the granary of Russia and remains one of the most important agricultural regions in the Soviet Union. However, it is also rich in other resources, principally coal, oil, and minerals. Both the Ukraine and Moldavia are gradually becoming industrialized as the cities of Kiev, Khar'kov, and Odessa expand their manufacturing industries to take advantage of the plentiful regional resources. This has significantly diminished the overall importance of agriculture there during the past several decades and doubtlessly has also aggravated the Russian shortages of grain.

Nevertheless, the Ukraine remains a huge vineyard locale, cultivating such varieties as Perlina Stepu (Aligoté), Naddniprjanske (Johannisberg Riesling), and Oksamit Ukraine (Cabernet Sauvignon). Again, most of the production is sweet table and dessert wines.

The Crimean Peninsula is bordered to the north, west, and south by the Black Sea and to the east by the Sea of Azov. It is an area of extremes, blustery cold in winter, yet arid in summer. The southeastern coast below the Crimean capital city of Simferopol' is much more mild, however, and is known as the "Russian Riviera." It is a very fertile subtropical locale where cork oaks and olive groves are cultivated as well as vineyards. The district is approximately 100 miles long, and its center is the historic resort city of Yalta. Almost all of the wines made in the south of Crimea are of the dessert type, principally from Aligoté, Johannisberg Riesling, Pinot Gris, and Sylvaner vines. A Muscat is grown for the locally celebrated *Massandra*, named for an estate that once belonged to a beloved Crimean prince. Reportedly, Massandra is complex as well as sweet.

A hundred miles or so east of Yalta, across the Black Sea into Russia, is another wine district surrounding the city of Krasnodar. Classic Western white varieties are grown to make table wines that often reach distinction. More famous is the *Chyorniye Glaza*, or "Black Eyes," a portlike dessert wine of national repute, which is also made in this locale. One hundred and fifty miles north of Krasnodar is the Don basin, situated at the extreme northeastern end of the Sea of Azov. Its center is the city of Rostov. The primary products of this district are sparkling wine made from traditional Crimean vines, along with Johannisberg Riesling and Sylvaner. A sweet red "sparkling Burgundy" type, called *Tsimlyanskoye*, is made there and enjoys a reputation for particularly good quality. *Donski* and *Nazdorovya* are whites, the latter available in some U.S. markets.

In Georgia, the Caucasus mountains descend steeply southward toward the Kura and Rion river valleys that join the Armenian Plateau. Mount El'bruz, at 18,481 feet, is the highest peak in the Caucasus chain and also the highest peak on the European continent. Most of Georgia's wine is grown in the valley of the Rion River that flows westward to the Black Sea—forming the Tiflis (Tbilisi) district. To the east, in Armenia and Azerbaijan on the Caspian coast, most of the production is dessert wines. The region is extremely cold in the Caucasus highlands, but subtropical in the warmest lower reaches of the valleys. The Georgian region is even richer in natural resources than the Moldavian-Crimea-Ukraine crescent. Coal, manganese, gold, mercury, iron, copper, and oil are among the most important—and their presence, as in the north, has served to shift the economic emphasis from agricultural to industrial activity. Nevertheless, the Research Institute in Tbilisi continues to be the largest facility in the world devoted to grape and wine research and development.

The late Soviet premier Joseph Stalin was born to a poor Georgian shoemaker. The news media would often depict Stalin drinking a "light" Georgian wine. Most of the wines grown there are far from light, however, as grapes ripen to high levels of sweetness in the abundant Georgian sunshine. The typical products are heavy, golden-colored table wines such as *Gurdzhanni* and *Tsinandali*, which often exceed fourteen percent alcohol by volume. Some of the reds prominent in the Rion Valley are *Mukuzani, Napareuli,* and *Saperavi.*

YUGOSLAVIA

The earliest Slavs were barbaric tribes that emerged from the sparse woodlands of ancient Sarmatia, a vast primitive frontier that is now the central and western portions of the Soviet Union. It is improbable that these people ever heard of grape wine, let alone drank any. Though these pre-Roman Slavs were for the most part non-nomadic, some nevertheless migrated to the south and west, across the Danube River, and found more temperate environs in what is now Eastern Europe. A few settled along the eastern Adriatic coast, to the northwest of Macedonia. The first of these Slavic pioneers became known as Istrians, some of whom found a place in history circa sixth century B.C. as the infamous Illyrian thieves.

The Illyrian territory was invaded and occupied by the Roman legions during the second century B.C., and the Romans attempted to bring civilization to the Slavic tribes. Instruction in the wine-growing arts was a part of this civilizing process, but three centuries of Roman influence had little apparent impact.

For the next 2,000 years the region was almost constantly torn by strife. During this long, unstable period, the land that was to become Yugoslavia was settled by a number of ethnic groups, all of whom shared a heritage of war and poverty. A reasonably complete history of their background would touch on the histories of all the other peoples mentioned in this chapter.

Despite the deep cultural and religious differences in this complex heritage, the Slavic factions achieved political solidarity in 1918. After yet another political division of the country, Marshal Tito united Yugoslavia under his leadership after World War II, and it remains a single nation encompassing many diverse groups. Today Yugoslavia is a nation of six republics, two self-governed provinces, four languages, and two alphabets. Many of its citizens still reject the notion that Yugoslavia falls within the sphere of the Kremlin's influence.

Yugoslavia is a nation of great wealth in natural resources, perhaps richer than any other Soviet Bloc country. The nation remains largely agrarian, however, with much of this activity devoted to wine growing. The contemporary vineyards and wineries are less than forty years old and were established primarily due to the influence of the Kremlin and the example of the huge recent vinicultural advancement in other Soviet Bloc countries. The Yugoslavian wine industry is controlled by the socialist government, and about 50 percent of the facilities are also owned by the state. The other half consists primarily of individual *vignerons* who supply cooperative wineries. With an annual production of about 200 million gallons, Yugoslavia ranks eleventh among the world's wine-growing nations. Per capita consumption exceeds 7 gallons per year and has increased more than 20 percent since 1965.

The topography of Yugoslavia is as diversified as its people. To the north the Julian Alpine range extends from Austria toward the city of Ljubljana in Slovenia, where some of the nation's best white table wines are grown. The Dinaric Alps are situated along the entire western coast of Yugoslavia, to scenic Montenegro and on to the Albanian and Greek borders. Off the coastal lowlands of Dalmatia beneath these mountains are many islands upon which vineyards are cultivated. Across the Alps to the east is Hercegovina, Vojvodina, and, most important for commercial viniculture, Serbia. The Balkan highland vineyards of Macedonia, immediately north of Thessalonian Greece, are devoted, virtually entirely, to red table wine production.

Soils in the Drava and Mura river valleys of Slovenia consist principally of limestone and marl, which, coupled with a rather mild climate, yield Germanic-type white wines. These are perhaps the finest wines made in Yugoslavia. The best-known vineyard in the region is called *Jerusalem,* situated near the Hungarian border. It is named for one of the Crusades centuries ago. A few red wines are grown in the extreme western reaches of Slovenia, near the Italian border.

The Dalmatian and Istrian coastline has a very mild climate, one that produces grapes that are very sweet and makes wines that are strong. The Istrian Peninsula cultivates Cabernet Sauvignon, Merlot, and Pinot Noir, among other Western varieties, for the production of red wines. The Malvasia (from Crete), Pinot Blanc (from France), Ranina (the Austrian Bouvier), and Šipon (the Hungarian Furmint) are the principal white wine varieties of Istria. Viniculture in Dalmatia is considerably more original. It is here that many of the smaller Yugoslavian vintners make a broad range of white, red, amber, dry and sweet table and dessert wines. *Maraština* and *Pošip* are probably the most notable whites, *Opolo* the best rosé, *Plavač* and *Plavina* the best reds. *Dingač* and *Postup* are heavy sweet reds, the latter made in a rather Greek style. *Grk* is a maderized sherry-type.

The Vojvodina region of Yugoslavia is located in the east-central portion of the country, along the western borders of Hungary and Romania. One of the principal wines grown there is *Bermet*, made by the addition of herbs in much the same manner as some of the ancient Etruscan wines. Red wines grown from the Hungarian Kadarka vine, as well as the French Pinot Noir, are also important products of Vojvodina. However, the overwhelming majority of wine growing in the region is devoted to rather common, strong whites made from vines of Austrian, French, German, and Hungarian extraction.

To the south of Vojvodina and the Romanian Banat are the regions of Serbia and Macedonia, where more than half of the wine grown in Yugoslavia originates. Most of it is ordinary. The principal whites are grown from Smederevka and Wälschriesling vines, but the greater share of production is red table wine. Prokupac remains the most widely cultivated red variety in both regions, although Cabernet Franc, Gamay, and other Western reds are gaining popularity among winegrowers there.

IMPORTED BY INTERNATIONAL VINTAGE WINE CO., HARTFORD, CT

HUNGARIAN LIGHT WINE

DEBRÖI
Hårslevelü
WINE OF THE LINDEN LEAF GRAPE

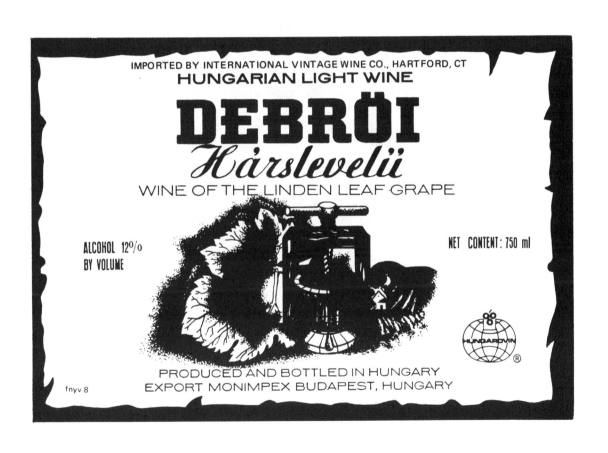

ALCOHOL 12%
BY VOLUME

NET CONTENT: 750 ml

PRODUCED AND BOTTLED IN HUNGARY
EXPORT MONIMPEX BUDAPEST, HUNGARY

fnyv 8

LA CONCORDE

KWV
CHENIN BLANC

SEMI-SWEET WHITE TABLE WINE

COASTAL REGION WINE OF ORIGIN

NET CONTENTS 750 ml (25,4 fl oz) ALCOHOL 11% BY VOLUME

SUGAR CONTENT AT HARVEST 20% BY WT

SUGAR CONTENT AT BOTTLING 0,8% BY WT

PRODUCED AND BOTTLED IN THE REPUBLIC OF SOUTH AFRICA

IMPORTED BY GLOBAL DISTRIBUTORS INC.,
LEEDS, ALABAMA, USA

A100

SA LITHO CO LTD

14

THE WINES OF
AFRICA,
SOUTHWEST ASIA,
AND THE EASTERN
MEDITERRANEAN

The wines from Africa are some of the most important in the world, with those from South Africa leading in quality and those from North Africa in quantity. Political and economic unrest continue to plague both the northern and southern reaches of the continent—difficulties that have no doubt stymied the efforts of African winegrowers. Nevertheless, Africa remains a significant region in the commercial wine world as this chapter attempts to show.

Finally, it is perhaps fitting that this book should end where the history of wine began, among the countries of Southwest Asia and the Eastern Mediterranean, where the earliest records of human involvement with wine can be traced. Thus the final pages concern the wines of Iran, Turkey, Lebanon, Israel, Egypt, Cyprus, and Greece.

A special note should be made of how heavily this chapter relies on the works of Hugh Johnson, particularly the latest edition of his *World Atlas of Wine* and his new *Modern Encyclopedia of Wine* (both published by Simon and Schuster, 1981 and 1983, respectively). These are essential works for the library of any wine aficionado.

SOUTH AFRICA

Wine has been grown in South Africa for some 300 years—a relatively brief period compared to the several thousands of years of wine history of certain locales in North Africa. The first South African vines were planted by Jan van Riebeeck in the early 1650s, soon after the Cape colony was founded. Van Riebeeck wrote in his diary on February 2, 1659:

> Today, praise be to God, wine was made for the first time from Cape grapes, namely from the new must fresh from the vat. The grapes were mostly Muscadel and other white, round grapes, very fragrant and tasty. The Spanish grapes are still quite green, though they hang reasonably thickly on several vines and give promise of a first class crop. These grapes, from three young vines planted two years ago, have yielded about 12 quarts of must, and we shall soon discover how it will be affected by maturing.

Van Riebeeck planted more vines on his Boschheuvel farm, but few others in the colony followed up on his success as row crops and grain were more in demand and provided a more immediate cash return.

Simon van der Stel became governor of the Cape of Good Hope in 1679, and, being a wine lover, planted many vines on his picturesque Groot Constantia farm. Van der Stel encouraged growers to plant vines throughout the colony and, helped along by the expertise of some French Huguenot immigrants, vineyard plantings increased by more than 500 acres by 1687. Besides Constantia, vineyards were established in the communities of Franschhoek, Paarl, and Stel's namesake, Stellenbosch. The vine seemed to thrive immediately in South Africa. Captain William Dampier entered the following passage in his log in 1691: "The country is of later years so well stocked with vineyards that they make abundance of wine. This wine is like a French High Country white wine."

The Napoleonic Wars forced a major reduction in wine trade between England and France. Britain, which had annexed South Africa in 1795, relied heavily on the wines from this country to fill the void and passed a preferential tariff to discourage French imports.

For the next half century, South African wine growing expanded widely in order to satisfy the thirst of the British. Some of the wines earned the praises of Alexandre Dumas and Frederick the Great, king of Prussia, but for the most part South African winegrowers concentrated on increasing quantity, rather than improving quality. Nevertheless, success continued until 1861, when Gladstone, who was then chancellor of the excequer in England, abolished the preferential tariff. That event, along with the invasion of the *Phylloxera* blight some twenty years later, all but destroyed the wine industry in South Africa.

Resistant graftings were employed by the South African growers, and the project of replenishing their vineyards progressed very quickly, resulting in sufficient wine production to satisfy domestic demand in just several years. But the growers overplanted, resulting in overabundant production and low prices. By the start of the twentieth century the South African wine industry was in desperate need of moderation and regulation.

One answer to the economic problem was to reduce production costs, which was achieved by the formation of cooperatives during the early 1900s. A truly effective method of stabilization, however, did not arrive until 1918, when Die Kooperatiewe Wijnbouwers Vereniging van Zuid Afrika (KWV), or "The Co-operative Winefarmers' Association of South Africa," was founded by several leaders from the cooperatives. Today the KWV is governed by twelve directors, all winegrowers elected from among the rank and file of more than 5,000 members. The Paarl, Robertson, Stellenbosch, and Worcester vineyard regions are each represented by two directors, while Malmesbury, Montagu, Olifants River, and Orange River regions supply one director each.

The directorate keeps supply in balance with demand for South African wines by the administration of production quotas and price floors for all members of the KWV. In addition, buffer stocks are maintained and bonus payments made in lean vintage years in order to insure stability in the wine industry. The KWV controls every major aspect of production and marketing for South African vintners. There is no doubt that the KWV is the most powerful self-imposed regulatory organization in any of the principal wine-producing nations in the world.

In 1973 the South African government enacted additional rules for wine labeling, including a complex appellation-of-origin system, along with specific requirements for varietal, vintage, and other information. Enforcement is maintained by the Wine and Spirit Board, an official body with membership from government and the wine industry. Chairmanship of the board is held by the Director of the Viticultural and Oenological Research Institute (VORI) at Stellenbosch. This institution has been very active in vinicultural research during the past several decades, contributing much to the state of the art of wine growing.

There are more than 275,000 acres of vineyard in modern-day South Africa, ranking it ninth among wine-growing nations. Per capita consumption stands at about 2.5 gallons annually, just slightly more than the rate in the United States.

The climate, and especially levels of seasonal rainfall, is the primary factor determining vineyard locale in South Africa. Limited rainfall confines most of the commercial wine growing to the southwestern reaches of the country, in a narrow section connected to the north and east by Cape Town. Most of the regions are situated among the beautiful mountain ranges and foothills where rainfall can vary from 30 to more than 300 inches per year. Soils are typically sandstone in the west and granitic in the east, shales are found in the valleys, and there are alluvial sandy loams in the river valleys. Overall the climate is mild, with heavier rainfall in the coastal areas and irrigation required among some of the interior vineyard locales.

The Coastal Region embraces the vineyards surrounding the cities of Constantia, Durbanville, Paarl, Stellenbosch, and Tulbagh—each designated as official Wines Of Origin districts by the Wine and Spirit Board. This region produces the most, as well as the finest quality, wines in all of South Africa.

Historically, the vintners of Paarl have been noted for their fine "sherry" and "port" wines. These are generally superb products grown from the same Palomino and Souzão vine selections, and made by the same methods, that are traditional in Spain and Portugal. Paarl is the largest single vineyard district in South Africa, with more than 50,000 acres under cultivation. Table wines are grown in Paarl, but they still have not gained the international reputation that the district's dessert wines have attained. Important producer names are Backsberg, Boschendal, Fairview, Landskroon, L'Ormarins, and Nederburg. It is at Nederburg that an annual auction is held during the vintage season each March. The event has been successful in drawing wine buyers from many countries, and it continues to enhance the reputation of both Nederburg and the entire Paarl district.

Tulbagh is situated about 30 miles north of Paarl, in the highlands. Most of its 10,000 acres are devoted to white table wine production—principally Teutonic-type wines from Gewürztraminer and various clones of Riesling. Vintners of particular note are Montpellier, Theuniskraal, and Twee Jongegezellen.

Stellenbosch, unquestionably the most prestigious South African wine district, is also a large producer, with more than 35,000 acres of vineyards. Most of the production in Stellenbosch is table wine. Whites, distinctive for good balance and exceptional varietal character, are made from Chenin Blanc, Colombard, and Johannisberg Riesling. Sauvignon Blanc and Steen, a clone of Chenin Blanc believed to be derived from the Loire Valley in France, are also grown in Stellenbosch for white table wines. Rapidly gaining popularity is the red Pinotage, a hybrid of Cinsaut and Pinot Noir developed by the VORI in Stellenbosch. Cinsaut and Pinot Noir continue to be widely planted, as does Shiraz (Syrah). Chardonnay, Gewürztraminer, and Cabernet Sauvignon are also planted in significant acreages, with vintners in more recent times demonstrating increasing interest in these varieties.

The Stellenbosch Farmers' Winery bottles under several different brand names. Those most commonly found in U.S. markets are "La Gratitude," "Lanzerac," "Libertas," "Tasheimer," and "Zonnebloem." "La Gratitude" is a dry white blend, first introduced in 1937 by an American, Dr. Charles Winshaw, one of the founders of the large cooperative. "Lanzerac" rosé is semidry, with a very appealing floral freshness in both nose and taste. There are two types of "Libertas" on the market: "Château Libertas" and "Oude Libertas." The former is a blend of Cabernet Sauvignon and other reds made in the Bordeaux style, but it lacks enough tannin for long periods of bottle aging. Dry Steen, Cabernet Sauvignon, and Pinotage are bottled under the "Oude Libertas" brand. Each "Libertas" is very popular in South African markets. "Tasheimer" is a semidry white table wine reminiscent of some of the strong, fruity wines grown in the warmer regions of Germany. "Zonnebloem" is another brand name used for several wine types. The "Zonnebloem" Cabernet Sauvignon, which is exported to the United States, is very rich in body, color, "berry-fruitiness," and tannin.

Bergkelder is one of the largest vintners in the Stellenbosch region, with distribution to major markets in the United States. The principal brands of the firm are "Fleur du Cap" and "Grünberger." Some experts consider the "Fleur du Cap" Pinotage to be the best example of the variety; perhaps it is closer in character to Rhône/Cinsaut than to the Pinot Noir side of its parentage. Other important Stellenbosch wineries are Le Bonheur, Gilbey's, Kanonkop, Montagne, Simonsig, Spier, and Uitkyk.

Historic Constantia is the southernmost, the coolest, and the smallest vineyard locale in South Africa—located just south of the city of Cape Town. However, the 1,000 acres that make up the Constantia district are devoted to very high quality wines, most made from Muscat grapes. One notable exception to the concentration on Muscat vines is the old Groot Constantia winery, founded in the 1670s by pioneer vintner and governor Simon van der Stel and still operating. Today the facility cultivates table wines from many of the classic European vine varieties, including Chenin Blanc, Johannisberg Riesling, Sauvignon Blanc, Cabernet Sauvignon, and Shiraz.

One of the larger wine regions of South Africa is Worcester. It is located about 20 miles east of Paarl in the Breede and Hex river valleys. Worcester is known primarily for the production of dessert wines and brandy, although some white table wines are made there, too. Muscadel and Hanepoot (Muscat of Alexandria) are the principal varieties cultivated.

Other South African districts that produce large amounts of dessert wines and brandy are Malmesbury, Piquetberg, and Olifants River, each farther north of Paarl. East of the Cape are Robertson, Montagu, and Swellendam, principally dessert wine and brandy producers, as well. Some of the more recent wines grown from classic European varieties in the Robertson district, primarily by the De Wetshof and Zandvliet wine producers, have won for Robertson a new reputation as a quality wine district.

Vineyards in the Worcester region of South Africa. (Source: Cooperative Winegrowers Association of South Africa, Ltd.)

NORTH AFRICA

During the last several thousand years of history, the present-day North African nations of Algeria, Tunisia, and Morocco have been occupied by the Phoenicians, Greeks, Romans, Moors, and the French. The vine was probably introduced to the territory by the Phoenicians although most of the development of early North African viniculture was no doubt due to the Greek and Roman influences that followed. Under the Moors, the North African wine industries suffered because of the Islamic prohibition of alcohol, but in more recent times, wine growing in North Africa has resurged, principally encouraged by France.

The French colonies of North Africa were developed to produce huge volumes of strong, mostly ordinary, table wines. Algeria at one time was one of the largest wine-producing nations in the world. These wines were generally exported in bulk to France, where they were blended with the common lower-alcohol wines grown in the Midi. Rumors flourished that North African wines went to Bordeaux and Burgundy, where secret blends were supposedly made; wags dubbed such products "Clos de Carthage" and "Château Mystère." Though probably only a few of such covert marriages ever really took place, a couple of scandals were uncovered and ran their course.

In 1962 independence was granted to Algeria, and the great French market diminished sharply, a situation aggravated further by untimely new European Economic Community (EEC) regulations that forbade previous blending practices. Very quickly there ensued an international glut of ordinary wine, which threatened the economic stability of wine throughout the world. However, new markets began to emerge, some in other African countries, such as Chad and the Ivory Coast, which switched from imported French wines following the EEC rulings. The Soviet Union also began to import North African wines.

Today the wine industries of Algeria, Tunisia, and Morocco are still undergoing the very long-term adjustments necessitated by such a monumental loss of market share and economic support. To quality-minded consumers of North African wines, this has been, in part at least, a blessing in disguise, as the surviving producers have been pressured into abandoning many of their marginal vineyards in favor of more distinctive growths.

Algeria

Comparatively little wine was grown in Algeria prior to the middle of the nineteenth century. The *Phylloxera* blight convinced many French *vignerons* to emigrate to Algeria in the 1870s and 1880s, and it was during this period when Algerian vineyard plantings became widespread. The resulting vinicultural industry grew to immense proportions and had an enormous impact on the nation's economy: at one time more than one-third of the nation's labor force worked in the vineyards (and this did not include those who worked in the wineries and the wine markets). Vineyards were planted nearly continuously along the coastal lowlands stretching nearly 500 miles between the port cities of Annaba and Oran. By the latter 1950s Algeria's total vineyards exceeded 900,000 acres, more than any North African nation by far and, at that time, about twice the acreage of the United States. While most of the production was devoted to blending wine, some of the Algerian vineyards were given distinction. The coveted French VDQS (Vins Délimités de Qualité Supérieure) had been awarded to twelve growths there prior to the 1962 decree of political independence.

Today, following the loss of the once-great blending-wine markets in Europe, many of the great plains vineyards of Algeria no longer exist. Most of the vines have been removed, leaving land now used for growing grains. Some vineyards have been established upon the hillsides further south, mostly in the provinces of Algiers and Oran, in the western portion of the country. Among the world's wine-growing nations, Algeria ranks twenty-first in volume of production.

Algerian wine growing is governed by the Office Nationale de Commercialization des Produits Viticoles (ONCV) that recognizes seven regions of superior wine-growing quality, all located in Algiers and Oran. The ONCV only authorizes labels that identify regional origin, however, and not specific vineyards. Consequently, consistency of wine quality and value can vary considerably under the same labels.

The principal varieties of the great plains in Algeria were Alicante-Bouschet and Aramon, and these are still the main grape types in the remaining vineyards. Aramon, in particular, is a very heavy-yielding variety, bearing bunches that often weigh several pounds. However, with the demise of the ordinary-wine vineyards and the planting of more prestigious locales, many of the better-known European vine varieties have become popular. The best reds are grown from Cabernet Sauvignon and Pinot Noir, with rosés made from Carignan, Cinsaut, and Grenache. While white table wine quality continues to improve in Algeria, whites currently made from Aligoté and Ugni Blanc are rarely on a par with the red and rosé offerings.

Most of the wines grown in Oran are generally relegated to blending stock, yet the higher vineyard elevations in the province, some of which are as high as 2,000 feet, yield strong and more distinctive wines. The most highly regarded of these is the Coteaux de Mascara. Mascara is powerful red wine and is sometimes compared to Burgundy, although Mascara may be heavier bodied and more spicy in character. The Coteaux de Tlemcen is another distinctive vineyard locale in Oran, a producer of good quality white, rosé, and red table wines; its wines are typically lighter and softer textured than those from Mascara. Situated between Mascara and Tlemcen are the vineyards of Monts du Tessalah at Sidi-bel-Abbés, primarily blending-wine sources. Ordinary wine is also the principal yield of the vineyards in the immediate vicinity of the city of Oran.

To the east of Oran in the locale of Dahra are the former French VDQS vineyards of Aïn Merane, Mazouna, Mostaganem, and Taughrite. Good-quality reds that are dark and heavy, yet with a soft acidity, are the distinctive product of the Dahra. Also of note are the rosé wines of the Dahra, which are very fruity and light.

Further east is the Coteaux du Zaccar, a large wine-growing district surrounded by Algiers, the old port city that is the capital of the Algiers vineyard region. The best wines in the province are generally acknowledged to be grown in the Media hills, some of which reach 4,000 feet in elevation. Reds and rosés from Media and nearby Aïn Bessem Bouira have won the most attention primarily for their good balance of fruitiness and acidity, which results in more finesse than the heavy richness of some of the Dahra wines.

Tunisia

Nearly all of the vinicultural activity in Tunisia takes place in the land area immediately surrounding the historic cities of Tunis and Carthage. Some 400 years before the birth of Christ, a manual for Tunisian viniculture was written by Mago, a native of Carthage. This suggests that wine growing had become an important commercial industry there at least by then.

Despite the fact that the most widely planted vines are the white Muscats, the wines of highest repute in Tunisia are red—primarily from Carignan, Cinsaut, Grenache, and Syrah grapes. Soil quality and rainfall quantity are adequate for viticulture, and sunshine is abundant—summer temperatures in excess of 105 degrees Fahrenheit are the rule rather than the exception. As in all of the North African wine-growing countries, there is not much variation in vintage quality due to the consistency of the climate. The climate of the coastal areas is moderated by the Mediterranean Sea, while inland more intense heat and humidity settle upon the plains beneath the mountain ranges.

The *Phylloxera* blight did not invade Tunisia until 1936, but, even so, the industry managed to continue expanding vineyard acreage until the country attained independence twenty years later. Following independence, vineyard acreage decreased by nearly 50 percent, from more than 120,000 acres to less than 65,000 acres. Today, fewer than forty wineries remain, most of which are either cooperatives or government-owned facilities.

The Medjerdah River Valley, west of Tunis, and the Mornag hills, on the opposite side of the city, yield particularly good red table wines grown from Cinsaut and Mourvèdre vines. The Union des Cooperatives Viticoles de Tunisie is Tunisia's largest wine operation and produces a "Château Mornag," as well as a "Magon" from the Medjerdah—both of high repute. Further west in the Medjerdah Valley is the Terres Domaniales winery, a state-owned facility that offers Château Thibar, a soft, heavy, red estate wine that compares with good Bordeaux. North of Tunis, near Carthage, Château Feriani and Société Lomblot produce fine reds from the Coteaux d'Utique vineyards. Other noteworthy operations are the Société des Vins Tardi and Héritiers René Lavau. Comparatively few Tunisian wines make their way to American markets.

Morocco

The Romans probably planted the very first vines in Morocco some 2,000 years ago. A commercial wine industry never grew from these vineyards, however, due primarily to the Moslem wine prohibition. The vineyards that survived were typically small enterprises, cultivated for table grape and raisin production, often situated among groves of fruit and olive trees.

The French entered Morocco in 1912 and, following the end of World War I, established the first wine vineyards—plantings that grew to exceed 100,000 acres during the next three decades. With the attainment of independence in 1956, Morocco lost its European markets, just as Algeria and Tunisia did when they became independent. Today about 60,000 acres of commercial vineyards remain in Morocco, some of which, according to certain experts, produce the very finest wines in North Africa.

Modern Moroccan vineyards are generally large plantations and are usually cultivated with the same types of mechanized equipment that are commonly found in Europe and the United States. Moroccan wineries are also large and operated with modern machines and technology.

Wine growing is very tightly controlled and monitored in Morocco by the Appellation d'Origine Garantie (AOG). The AOG is closely patterned after the French Appellation d'Origine Contrôlée (AOC) and enforces the strictest set of government wine-producing regulations of any North African country. About half of the wines grown in Morocco are consumed there, although the per capita consumption rate is less than 1 gallon annually.

Most of the wine vineyards of Morocco are situated in the vicinity of the capital city of Rabat. In the northern foothills of the Atlas mountains, about 75 miles southeast of Rabat, is the Fez-Meknès region, the largest and perhaps the finest quality vineyard area in the nation. The AOG growths in the Fez-Meknès include Beni M'Tir, Beni Sadden, Guerrouane and Sais, all of which have won acclaim for their soft, but heavy-bodied red table wines grown from Carignan, Cinsaut, and Grenache vines.

Another 150 miles or so further east, near the Algerian border, are the Oujda vineyards, noted primarily for ordinary blending-wine production. South of Rabat are the vineyards of the Casablanca region, best known for light, fruity reds from AOG Doukkala, Sahel, and Zennata. Further west is the Boulaouane region, where Gris de Boulaouane, a very pale, soft, and light-bodied rosé, is produced from Criolla vines thought by some locals to have been initially planted in the Doukkala by the Portuguese in the fifteenth century. Gris de Boulaouane is very popular in Moroccan wine markets, as are lower-priced reds from Doukkala, Sahel, and Zennata.

Fifty miles to the southeast of the Boulaouane is a comparatively small wine-growing area located on the slopes surrounding the legendary city of Marrakesh. The typical products of this region are pleasant red and rosé wines of light texture.

Egypt

The earliest known records of wine appreciation come from Egypt. The many scenes of grape growing and winemaking, as well as wine serving, depicted in the ancient Egyptian hieroglyphics and works of art provide unquestionable proof that wine was an integral part of their civilization. Some of the Pharaohs personally owned large vineyards, often situated nearby their palaces so that wine-growing operations could be readily observed. In the more arid locales, their vines were irrigated from large reservoirs constructed inside the walls that protected the vineyard gardens.

The ancient Egyptians consumed great quantities of wine. The region of Aaa, located in Tennu, was said to have used more wine than water during the Twelfth Dynasty. The huge wine presses of Tsaha yielded wine in waves, according to Thutmoe III. Yet even this was often insufficient, as Egyptians regularly imported additional wine from Greece and Phoenicia. When the Romans occupied Egypt, such Roman writers as Horace, Pliny the Elder, and Virgil spread the fame of the finer wines found there. The many political, social, and economic upheavals that followed the fall of the Roman Empire (c. 300 A.D.) made wine growing a virtually defunct industry in Egypt.

Today the majority of the people in Egypt are Islamic Arabs, subject to this religion's prohibition of alcohol; one would expect only marginal consumption statistics. A commercial wine industry continues to grow, however.

Nestor Gianaclis, an Egyptian wine enthusiast possessed of a remarkable determination, began a search in the early 1900s for the original locale where the finest wines were grown in dynastic Egypt. Gianaclis's energy was rewarded—he eventually succeeded in locating the highly acclaimed Mareotis vineyard site at Abu Hummus, on the northwestern portion of the Nile Delta near Alexandria. Today the Gianaclis vineyards total more than 15,000 acres, from which about half the production is distilled. "Cru des Ptolémées," "Reine Cléopatre," and "Nefertiti" are among the best-known white table wines made there, and a rather amber-colored wine called "Gianaclis Village" is also exported to the United States. The most noteworthy red is labeled as "Omar Khayam."

SOUTHWEST ASIA AND THE EASTERN MEDITERRANEAN

Mount Ararat reaches 16,946 feet in elevation in the area where Iran, Turkey, and the Soviet Union converge. The ninth chapter of Genesis recounts the planting of a vineyard there by Noah and his sons soon after the landing of the ark. To some wine historians, this marks the beginnings of Western winemaking—although there is evidence that wine was made in China and Egypt prior to Noah's time. Ararat's climate is little suited to viticulture, and one can easily understand why Noah's successors in wine growing sought more promising locales in which to establish new vineyards.

One likely region was the Tigris-Euphrates river valleys that gave rise to the ancient civilization of Mesopotamia. This region offered a much more favorable climate for the vine than Ararat, and many historians feel that the arts of wine growing as practiced in the Western world were first developed here.

The Tigris-Euphrates basin was inherited by the Persians, who were gifted winegrowers and heavy imbibers for centuries. It wasn't until the coming of Mohammed and the Islamic religion in the seventh century A.D. that wine drinking went into a decline in this area. The Koran preaches against both the production and consumption of wine, and as the influence of Islam spread through the Mideast, winemaking and marketing became relegated to the Jews.

The viticultural arts, perhaps first nurtured in Mesopotamia some 2,000 years before Christ, probably migrated west to Phoenicia (present-day Lebanon), and then south to Palestine, and on to the Nile Delta and Alexandria. It was in this Eastern Mediterranean region that wine technology and appreciation flourished for millennia prior to the birth of Christ.

Iran

The Azerbaijan viticultural region, located at the extreme northwestern tip of Iran, less than 50 miles from Mount Ararat, remains one of the most important grape-growing areas in the nation.

In modern times the Iranians consume annually only about one-thirtieth of a gallon of wine per capita. Actually, the Islamic Iranians may consume virtually no wine at all since this statistic reflects the consumption by Iranian wine imbibers of Armenian and Jewish extraction.

There is no encouragement from the Iranian government to grow or consume wine. Iranian vintners often negotiate with third-party intermediaries so that grape suppliers will have no direct knowledge that their crop has been used to produce an alcoholic beverage. Some growers cultivate their vineyards in "succotash" style, employing many different vine varieties, some of which may be direct descendents from the vines of Noah. The wine producer of Iran must thus contend with "blends" made even before the wine is fermented.

One of the most important viticultural areas in Iran is at Shiraz, located in the south-central portion of the country. Shiraz is the original name of the variety, Syrah, thought to have been brought from Iran to the Rhône Valley of France in the Middle Ages by returning Crusaders. In Australia and South Africa the original Shiraz vine name has been preserved.

A wide range of wines are made in Iran. Some of those made in the style of Bordeaux and Rheinland products have won awards for quality in European competitions. The leading winery is Iran-Ararat, located near Teheran. With more than 200,000 acres of vines under cultivation, Iran is an important grape producer, though most of the harvest is devoted to table grape and raisin production. Iran does not have a significant ranking among the world's wine-producing nations.

Turkey

There are more vineyards cultivated in Turkey than in the United States, and the history of Turkish viniculture, like that of Iran, reaches back to Noah's plantings on the hillsides of Mount Ararat.

Despite these credentials, Turkey clings to the dictates of the Moslem prohibition and produces only about 10 million gallons of wine per year, less than 2 percent of the annual production volume in the United States. Most of the Turkish wine made commercially nowadays is a result of the encouragement of the late Kemal Atatürk. Atatürk was a heroic Turkish soldier in the 1920s and became the nation's beloved leader and a patron of modern arts, letters, and government. His landmark decree of 1928, which abolished the Islamic religion as the national faith, has yet, however, to gain significant compliance among the Turkish populace.

There are three principal wine-growing regions in Turkey: one in the vicinity of Ankara, the capital city; another along the western coastal area near the city of Izmir; and the other in Trakya, northwest of Istanbul near the Grecian border. Other vineyard locales can be found in the Dardanelles, associated with the legend of Paris and Helen of Troy. The communities of Malatya and Elâziğ, in eastern Turkey, along with ancient Bursa and Izmit in northern Turkey, also produce white and red table wines. There are many smaller vineyard areas scattered through the mountains and the plains across virtually the entire country.

More than one hundred commercial wineries operate in Turkey although twenty-one are operated by Tekel, a government-owned monopoly organization. The most widely planted white wine varieties are Johannisberg Riesling, Muscat, Sémillon and Sultanye—the last related to the famous Thompson Seedless, or

Vitis sultana, of central California table grape fame. Red wines are made from Cabernet Sauvignon, Calkarasi, Carignan, Cinsaut, Gamay, and Merlot.

Perhaps the best-known wine of Turkey in international markets is *Buzbag* (pronounced as "boorswahr"), a dry red made from Bogazkarasi vines grown by the large Tekel government facilities at Elâziğ.

Cyprus

The island of Cyprus has throughout its colorful history been a pivotal point in the eastern Mediterranean. Its central geographical location made it a logical port in the trade routes between the Middle East, southern Europe and North Africa. Cyprus in one way or another became associated with nearly every Western culture. The Greek goddess of love, Aphrodite, according to legend, was born there, Kings Solomon and Richard Lion-Heart imported Cypriot wines, and the entire island was, under Roman rule, given to Cleopatra by Mark Antony.

The wine industry of modern Cyprus is crucial to the nation's economy: wine growing provides the largest single share of employment, and wine is the nation's chief export. Excluding the "tail" of the country, Cyprus is scarcely 100 miles long, within which about 100,000 acres of vineyards are cultivated. Despite attempts to introduce European vines to the island, local growers continue to prefer traditional varieties, principally the white Xynisteri and Muscat of Alexandria, along with the red Ophthalmo and black Mavron.

The oldest winery in Cyprus is Etko/Haggipavlu, established in 1844. It is perhaps best known for a dark, dry red called *Ambrosia,* which can be found in some U.S. markets. Etko also produces a dry white *Nefeli,* named for the sister of Dionysus. *Emva* from Etko is reminiscent of an Oloroso sherry from Spain.

The Keo winery offers a crisp, dry white table wine named *Aphrodite,* as well as a full-bodied red called *Othello.* The *Palomino* white from the Loel winery on Cyprus is a clean, but rather neutral white. Sodap, a cooperative wine producer, vinifies *Arsinoe* white and *Afames* red, both of which are reminiscent of the more common growths of central Italy.

One of the most intriguing wines of Cyprus is *Commanderia,* a sherry-type product that may be the world's oldest recognized wine type. Circa 800 B.C., the Greek poet Hesiod praised wine of the same name made from sun-dried grapes, as Commanderia continues to be today.

Under British rule Cypriot viniculture enjoyed the benefit of English production and markets. Much of this ended in 1960, however, when Cyprus was granted independence and formed its own republic. Subsequently, new markets were cultivated in some of the Scandinavian and Oriental countries, as well as the

United States. Britain remained an important market, too, but to a much lesser degree than it had been prior to 1960. The 1974 Turkish invasion of Cyprus aroused a great deal of uncertainty among the producers and workers in the Cypriot wine industry. This unrest continues.

Lebanon

It was in Lebanon, at the eastern end of the Mediterranean Sea, that the Phoenicians, perhaps as early as 1250 B.C., became the world's first great international wine traders. Later, the people of this narrow strip of land between Jordan and the sea were the Canaanites. Baal, their primary deity, was god of soil, agriculture, and fertility and a very powerful adversary to the Hebrew God during Old Testament times, as the chapters of Judges and Kings in the Bible relate.

The land of the Canaanites included the Bekáa Valley, situated beneath Mount Lebanon. This is the site of the vast subterranean winery at Ksara, which was established in the late nineteenth century by the Jesuits. Some authorities give high praise to the wines grown in the Bekáa, especially the reds from Cabernet Sauvignon and Syrah vines. The most important wineries are Château Musar, located just north of Beirut, as well as Kefraga, Naquad, and Domaine de Tournelles.

Israel

Moses sent Joshua and Caleb out to investigate the Promised Land, and, according to chapter 13 of Numbers in the Old Testament:

> Then they came to what is now known as the Valley of Eschol where they cut down a single cluster of grapes so large that it took two of them to carry it on a pole between them . . . The Israelis named the valley "Eschol" (meaning "cluster") at that time because of the cluster of grapes they found! (Num. 13: 23-24)

Following the Exodus from Egypt, the Jews planted vineyards in the Holy Land, and some of the resulting wines fulfilled the promise of Eschol, evidenced by the renown these wines gained throughout the Western world as it then existed. Not all of these wines were fine, however, as their usual character was probably rather reminiscent of light vinegar. Nevertheless, it was during this period in the Holy Land that winemakers first recognized the need for wine-production standards and research. This recognition may have been an early forerunner of the Jewish kosher law, rules that spell out precise standards and controls for the production and consumption of all food and drink—including wine. In any event, it was in Israel that wine may have first become a diet staple and a religious symbol of life.

The history of the wine industry of Israel parallels in many ways the Jews' own history of tragedy and endurance. Vineyards and wineries have been established, destroyed, and established again. The latest rebirth occurred in the late nineteenth century when European vines were planted at Mikveh, near Carmel, by Jewish pioneer scientists assigned to a newly founded school of agriculture there. Bordeaux winegrower Baron Edmond de Rothschild, of French Bordeaux wine and banking fame and himself of Jewish extraction, funded further viticultural research in Israel following World War II. Rothschild built two wineries as well, one at Richon-le-Zion, near Tel Aviv, and the other at Zikhron-Ya'agov, on Mount Carmel near Haifa. Eventually both became the property of local grape growers. In 1957 the Israeli Wine Institute was founded, and this organization has served to further develop vinicultural technology there.

Today Israel cultivates about 25,000 acres of vineyards and is the smallest commercial grower of vines in the Middle East. The major wine-growing districts are found in the hills of upper Galilee and lower Galilee, where vineyards are tended near the cities of Jerusalem, Judea, Nazareth, and Samaria, as well as in the coastal area between Haifa and Tel Aviv. Although there is about twice as much rain in the hills as the lowlands, Israeli viticulture still requires irrigation for the dry, hot summers. Soils range from shallow and stony to deep, calcareous topsoils. The best-known vintners are Carmel and the Société Cooperative Vigneronne des Grandes Caves. Israel grows such traditional European grape varieties as Cabernet Sauvignon (for reds), and Sémillon, Sauvignon Blanc, and Chenin Blanc (for whites), along with other varieties suited to its hot, dry climate. All Israeli wines are kosher and thus acceptable for religious use as well as regular consumption as table wines.

Greece

The earliest "vineyards" of Greece were often just a few vines cultivated where conditions permitted, often among olive trees or in some other dual-purpose locale. The parallel rows of vines that we identify as vineyards today were not established until about the seventh century B.C., perhaps due to the influence of Phoenician traders. It was during the next several centuries that the Greeks brought their vineyards to the highest point that they were to reach prior to the Roman occupation. At that time the Greeks were active in grape selection, endeavoring to develop strains of higher quality and hardier resistance to the ravages of disease, insects, and cold weather. Homer wrote that Odysseus' vineyard had fifty varieties of vines, each in a separate row, each situated so as to ripen fruit in sequence throughout the vintage season. The techniques of pruning, cultivation, and the importance of soil moisture were among the many items of concern to the winegrowers of Homer's Greece.

Long before the Romans invaded the Grecian peninsula, Greek wines were slowly aged and mellowed in nonporous jars, the celebrated amphorae. Plugs and stoppers of many types, often laced with resin and/or wax, were employed with care to achieve the best possible closure. Of course, these early wine masters had no idea that their closures were keeping air from entering their amphorae and therefore denying vinegar bacteria the oxygen necessary for spoilage. What those winemakers did know, though, was that the better their amphorae were sealed, the better quality was the resulting wine. Consequently, the Greeks mastered the art of pottery making, using the superb clays available there. Today we can admire their skill, both in the construction and decoration of the amphorae, in the many examples of these superb artifacts on display in museums around the world.

The importance of wine in Greek culture is perhaps most vividly demonstrated in the myths and cults of Dionysus, the Greek god of fertility and wine. Today the mention of Dionysus probably first brings to mind orgiastic celebrations led by maenads—women driven mad by the intoxicating power of the god; but we should remember that the wine god also had a much tamer aspect. The wild Dionysian revels eventually gave way to a civilized festival known as the *Greater Dionysia*, a celebration that included not only wine and music but dramatic performances. The performances at the Greater Dionysia were the origin of Greek drama, and thus of all Western drama as we know it.

Wine also enters significantly into the writing and art of ancient Greece. Herodotus, the Greek historian, held wine growing as a major concern and gave it a good measure of attention during his travels. There are many references to wine in the poems of Hesiod and Homer. Greek sculpture and vase painting is replete with scenes and symbols of grapes and wine. Hippocrates, the father of medicine, taught that "wine is wonderfully wholesome for man in sickness and in health," and to the god of medicine, Asclepius, a quote is attributed that "the power of the gods is only just equal to the uses of wine."

The Greeks took their wine expertise to their Italian colonies more than six centuries before Greece fell to the expanding Roman Empire. Though the Romans thought highly of their Italian wines, especially those from Campania, the most sought-after at Roman tables were those imported from Greece. Consequently, the Romans encouraged the growth of vines, vinicultural research, and commercial winemaking in occupied Greece. The Romans were quick to build on Greek advances in the arts of growing and making wines, and it was essentially Greek wine lore that Rome carried to the far corners of Europe.

The Turks, who followed the Romans in occupying Greece, were Islamic, and therefore prohibited wine and wine growing. This severely hampered the advancement of viniculture in Greece, a condition from which the country never really recovered. In all truth, the wines of Greece are today not among the world's best, but recent developments in technology hold promise for the future.

Today there are about 400,000 acres of vineyards cultivated in Greece, of which about half are devoted to wine production and the balance to table grapes and raisins. Annual wine yield is generally about 140 million gallons, ranking Greece fourteenth among the world's wine-producing nations. Per capita consumption is more than 11 gallons per year, ninth among principal wine-consuming countries.

Most of the Greek vineyards of today are cultivated upon rocky topsoils, principally of limestone constituencies, upon chalky or tufa subsoils. Over many centuries of development, vineyards have been moved from the coastal lowlands up to the hillsides, some now existing at altitudes exceeding 3,000 feet. The peninsula of Greece has the advantage of the surrounding sea in tempering the climate, and the temperatures and rainfall are very similar to those in neighboring southern Italy. The principal grape varieties grown in Greece are red and white Muscats.

It was in Greece that the first notions of "appellation of origin" were conceived. The ancient sweet wines of Crete and Thera, the perfumed wines of Carystos, Lesbos, Oenoia, and Pitania, and the tonic wines of Chios, Cnide, and Thásos, were all identified by region of origin more than 1,000 years before the birth of Christ. Today the Minister of Agriculture in Greece governs the labeling of wines from specific regional departments throughout the country. Qualifying wines are sold with a serial-numbered band sealing the capsule and cork in each bottle. However, until recently, enforcement of regulations in Greece was lax, and even today less than 15 percent of the wine grown in the nation qualifies for the seal.

At the extreme northern reaches of Greece is the region of Macedonia-Thrace, the fourth-largest wine-growing locale in the country. Up until the *Phylloxera* blight destroyed most of the vineyards in northern Greece during the early 1900s, wines from this region were reputed to be among the highest quality in the country. Today, wines are grown from grape varieties native to Western Europe that are grafted upon resistant rootstocks. But the resulting wines are much less distinctive than the pre-*Phylloxera* products.

Central Greece, third-largest district, is divided into three separate regions: Attica, Boeotia, and Euboea. Nearly all of the wine production in central Greece is white table wines grown from Savatiano vines—most of which is consumed locally or in metropolitan Athens. Separating Macedonia-Thrace and central Greece is the Thessaly region, in which two white varieties, Rhoditis and Savatino, as well as the red Sykiotis are cultivated to make ordinary table wines. Though the wines are common, Thessalian vineyards are uncommonly beautiful. The vineyards of the foothills of legendary Mount Olympus form some of the most stunning landscapes found in all of Greece.

To the east are the historic Aegean islands, including Lemnos, Lésvos, and Samos. Chios vines did not survive the *Phylloxera* blight, and the island no longer grows wine.

To the southwest is Peloponnese, the largest of the Grecian wine-growing regions. The best-known vineyards in this scenic and austere locale are at the town of Nemea; here is produced a very heavy-bodied and strong red table wine called the "Blood of Hercules." While Nemea is situated near Corinth at sea level, Mantinia, the "Pearl of Arcadia" is located in the center of the Peloponnese, surrounding the ancient ruins at Mantinea. Dry white wines are made from Moschofilero vines cultivated in these highland vineyards.

Crete is the second-largest producer of wines in Greece. Red wines grown from Kotsifali and Mandilari vines in the Archanes and Peza appellations of origin are often exported to Europe. Liatiko vines are grown in the Daphnes and Sitia regions, yielding white wines that are believed to be the original "Malvasia," or "Malmsey" sack. These wines, very popular in international markets during the Middle Ages, caught the attention of Prince Henry of Portugal. He purchased some vine cuttings and established what eventually became the famous Malmsey vineyards upon the Island of Madeira.

To the north and northeast of Crete are, respectively, the very picturesque and romantic Cyclades and Dodecanese islands. The earliest of all Greek wines are thought to have been grown in the Cyclades. Nowadays this area is famous for white wines grown from Assyrtiko vines on the isle of Thera. The white wines of Rhodes, in the Dodecanese, are grown from Athiri and Muscat vines, red from Amorgiano. Wines from Rhodes were exported in ancient times in amphorae branded with the particular name of the wine followed by a bunch of grapes. "Rhodos" is still a popular appellation of origin in the export trade.

More than half of the wine grown in Greece is resinated. In ancient times the Greeks added crude resins to their wines to inhibit deterioration and spoilage. The resin floated on top of the wines, acting as a barrier to oxygen and vinegar bacteria infection. Over the years the Greeks acquired a taste for the resin flavors, eventually adding resins with varying strengths and tastes. Today these types of resinated white and rosé table wines are famous as *retsina.* The specific resin used is taken from the Aleppo pine, and the best of these resins are thought to come from trees grown in Attica.

Another fabled wine of Greece is *Mavrodaphne*—a sweet red dessert wine of high alcohol content. Some wine historians consider Mavrodaphne to be one of the original sources for the once-popular Malmsey in England.

And He took the cup, and gave thanks, and gave it to them, saying, "Drink ye all of it . . . Do this, as oft as ye shall drink it, in remembrance of me . . . (Matt. 26:27)

BIBLIOGRAPHY

Adams, Leon D. *The Wines of America*. 3rd ed. New York: McGraw-Hill, 1985.

Adlum, John. *A Memoir on the Cultivation of the Vine in America and the Best Mode of Making Wine*. Duff Green, Washington, 1828.

Allen, H. Warner. *A History of Wine*. London: Faber and Faber, 1961.
———. *The Wines of Portugal*. New York: McGraw-Hill, 1963.

Amerine, M. A., and E. B. Roessler. *Wines: Their Sensory Evaluation*. Rev. ed. San Francisco: Freeman, 1983.

Amerine, M. A. et al. *Technology of Wine Making*. 4th ed. Westport, Conn.: Avi, 1980.

Anderson, Burton. *Vino*. Boston: Atlantic Monthly Press-Little, Brown, 1980.

Australian Wine Board. *Wine Australia*. Adelaide: The Australian Wine Board, 1979.

Balzer, Robert Lawrence. *Adventures in Wine*. Edited by Anna Marie Peterson. Los Angeles: Ward Ritchie, 1969.

Berry, Charles Walter. *Viniana*. London: Constable, 1934.

Bespaloff, Alexis. "Gemütlichkeit by the Glass." *Food and Wine*, (November 1980).
———. *Guide to Inexpensive Wines*. New York: Simon and Schuster, 1973.
———. *The Signet Book of Wine*. New York: New American Library, 1971.

Botwin, Michael. "The Regional Wines of Switzerland." *American Wine Society Journal* (Winter 1974).

Brenner, Gary. *The Naked Grape*. Indianapolis, Ind.: Bobbs-Merrill, 1975.

Broadbent, J. M. *Wine Tasting*. London: Wine and Spirit Publications, 1970.

Burroughs, David, and Norman Bezzant. *Wine Regions of the World*. London: Heinemann, 1979.

Butler, Frank Hedges. *Wine and the Wine Lands of the World*. New York: Brentano's, n.d.

Cattell, Hudson, and Lee Stauffer Miller. *Wine East of the Rockies*. Lancaster, Penn.: L & H Photojournalism, 1982.

———. *The Wines of the East, Native American Grapes.* Lancaster, Penn.: L & H Photojournalism, 1980.

———. *The Wines of the East, The Hybrids.* Lancaster, Penn.: L & H Photojournalism, 1978.

———. *The Wines of the East, The Vinifera.* Lancaster, Penn.: L & H Photojournalism, 1979.

Chilean Traditional Wine Exporter Committee. *ProChile.* Santiago: Chilean Traditional Wine Exporter Committee, Larrain & Asociados Editores, 1983.

Chile Export Promotion Office. *Chilean Wines: A Tradition.* Santiago: Chile Export Promotion Office, August 1983.

Chroman, Nathan. *The Treasury of American Wines.* New York: Rutledge-Crown, 1973.

Church, Ruth Ellen. *Entertaining with Wine.* Chicago: Rand-McNally, 1976.

———. *Wines of the Midwest.* Chicago: Swallow Press, 1982.

Churchill, Creighton. *The Great Wine Rivers.* New York: MacMillan, 1971.

———. *The World of Wines.* New York: MacMillan, 1964.

Cooper, Rosalind. *The Wine Book.* Tucson, Ariz.: HP Books, 1981.

Curry, Kristine N. "South African Wines: A Secret Worth Sharing." *Chicago Tribune,* August 24-25, 1983.

Domaine Chandon. *A User's Guide to Sparkling Wine.* Yountville, Calif.: Domaine Chandon, 1984.

de Isasi, Enrique. *Con Una Copa de Jerez.* Madrid: Hauser y Memet, S.A., n.d.

Dorozynski, Alexander, and Bibiane Bell. *The Wine Book.* New York: Golden Press, 1969.

Eastern Grape Grower & Winery News Directory. N.Y.: Watkins Glen, 1984.

Edita Lausanne. *The Great Book of Wine.* Lausanne: Edita Lausanne, 1970.

Egyptian Vineyards & Distilleries Co. *Egyptian Wines and Spirits.* Alexandria: Egyptian Vineyards & Distilleries Co., n.d.

Emerson, Edward R. *Beverages, Past and Present.* New York: Knickerbocker Press, 1908.

Evans, Len. *Complete Book of Australian Wine.* Sydney: Hamlyn, 1978.

Fadiman, Clifton, and Sam Aaron. *The Joys of Wine.* New York: Abrams, 1975.

Fisher, M. F. K. *Wine in California.* Berkeley: University of California Press, 1962.

Fluchère, Henri. *Wines.* New York: Golden Press, 1974.

Fried, Eunice. "Cyprus: Ancient Secrets of Wine." *The Friends of Wine* (May-June 1981).

———. "The Wines of Bulgaria." *The Friends of Wine* (July-August 1982).

Fuller, Andrew S. *Grape Culturist.* New York: Orange Judd, 1867.

Giordano, Frank. *Texas Wines & Wineries.* Austin: Texas Monthly Press, 1984.

Gohdes, Clarence. *Scuppernong.* Durham, N.C.: Duke University Press, 1982.

Gold, Alec, ed. *Wines and Spirits of the World*. Chicago: Follett, 1973.

Grossman, Harold J. *Grossman's Guide to Wines, Spirits and Beers*. 4th ed. New York: Scribner, 1964.

Hallgarten, S. F. *Vineyards, Estates and Wines of Germany*. Dallas: Publivin, 1974.

Hallgarten, S. F., and F. L. Hallgarten. *The Wines and Wine Gardens of Austria*. Herts, England: Argus, Watford, 1979.

Halliday, James. *Wines & Wineries of South Australia*. St. Lucia: University of Queensland Press, 1981.
———. *Wines & Wineries of Victoria*. St. Lucia: University of Queensland Press, 1982.
———. *Wines & Wineries of Western Australia*. St. Lucia: University of Queensland Press, 1982.

Hasler, G. F. *Wine Service in the Restaurant*. London: Wine & Spirit Publications, 1973.

Hayes, C. J. H., Baldwin, M. W., and C. W. Cole. *History of Western Civilization*. New York: MacMillan, 1962.

Hellenic Export Promotion Organisation. *Wine in Greece*. Athens: Hellenic Export Promotion Organisation, n.d.

Hiaring, Anne. "Winegrowing in Islamic Iran." *"Wines and Vines* (December 1976).

Hiaring, Philip. "The Editor Finds the Latch-String Out in Austria's Wine-land." *Wines and Vines* (January 1980).
———. "On the Scene at the Fête des Vignerons." *Wines and Vines* (December 1978).

———. "A Vinous Tour of Yugoslavia." *Wines and Vines* (October 1979).
———. "A Visit to the Argentine Wine Industry." *Wines and Vines* (June 1975).
———. "Wine Grapes in England? Quite So." *Wines and Vines* (September 1974).
———. "Wines & Vines in Hungary and Rumania." *Wines and Vines* (October and November 1978).

Hungarian Foreign Trading Company. *Monimpex*. Budapest: Hungarian Foreign Trading Company, 1976.

Husmann, George. *The Native Grape*. New York: Woodward, 1868.

Hyams, Edward. *Grapes under Cloches*. London: Faber and Faber, n.d.

Jacobs, Julius L. "The Greeks' Word Was 'Oinos.'" *Wines and Vines* (December 1974).

Johnson, Hugh. *Modern Encyclopedia of Wine*. New York: Simon and Schuster, 1983.
———. *The World Atlas of Wine*. 2nd ed. New York: Simon and Schuster, 1978.

Kaufman, William I. *Encyclopedia of American Wine*. San Francisco: The Wine Appreciation Guild, 1984.
———. *The Traveler's Guide to the Vineyards of North America*. New York: Penguin Books, 1980.

Keehn, Karen. *Structure of Wine and Its Interaction with Flood*. Hopland, Calif.: McDowell Vineyards, 1986.

Kressman, Edouard. *The Wonder of Wine*. New York: Hastings House, 1968.

Lallemand Editeur. *Champagne Wine of France*. Paris: Lallemand Editeur, 1968.

Lamb, Richard B., and Ernest G. Mittelberger. *In Celebration of Wine and Life*. San Francisco: The Wine Appreciation Guild, 1980.

Lawrence, R. de Treville, Sr. *Jefferson and Wine*. The Plains, Va.: Vinifera Wine Growers Association, 1976.

Layton, T. A. *Wines of Italy*. London: Harper Trade Journals, 1961.

Lesko, Leonard H. *King Tut's Wine Cellar*. Berkeley, Calif.: Scribe Publications, 1977.

Lichine, Alexis. *Guide to the Wines and Vineyards of France*. Rev. ed. New York: Knopf, 1982.

Loubere, Leo A. *The Red and the White*. Albany: State University of New York Press, 1978.

Lucia, Salvatore P., M.D. *Wine and Your Well-Being*. San Francisco: Popular Library, 1971.

Massee, William E. *Wine-Food Index*. New York: McGraw-Hill, 1962.

Meredith, Ted. *Northwest Wine*. 2nd ed. Kirkland, Wash.: Nexus Press, 1983.

Milam, James R., and Katherine Ketcham. *Under the Influence*. Seattle: Madrona, 1981.

Moore, Bernard. *Wines of North America*. Secaucus, N.J.: Winchmore Publishing, 1983.

Morris, Roger. *The Genie in the Bottle*. New York: A & W Publishers, 1981.

Morse, Joseph Laffan, ed. *Universal Standard Encyclopedia*. New York: Unicorn, 1954.

Muir, Augustus. *How to Choose and Enjoy Wine*. New York: Bonanza, 1972.

Netter, Frank H., M.D. *Nervous System, The Ciba Collection of Medical Illustrations*. Vol. I. New York: CIBA Pharmaceutical Company, 1968.

Ordish, George. *Vineyards in England and Wales*. London: Faber and Faber, 1977.

Palmer, R. R., and J. Colton. *A History of the Modern World*. 2nd ed. New York: Knopf, 1963.

Paronetto, Lamberto. *Chianti*. London: Wine and Spirit Publications, 1970.

Pellegrini, Angelo M. *Wine and the Good Life*. New York: Knopf, 1965.

Quimme, Peter. *The Signet Book of American Wine*. New York: New American Library, 1975.

Ray, Cyril. *Lafite*. New York: Stein and Day, 1969.
———. *The Wines of Italy*. New York: McGraw-Hill, 1966.

Read, Jan. *Guide to the Wines of Spain and Portugal*. New York: Monarch, 1977.

Robertson, George. *Port*. London: Faber and Faber, 1978.

Roux, M. P. *Vineyards and Châteaux of Bordeaux*. Dallas: Publivin, 1972.

Roux, M. P., P. Poupon, and P. Forgeot. *Vineyards and Domains of Burgundy*. Dallas: Publivin, 1973.

Sandeman Sons & Company. *Port and Sherry*. London: Sandeman Sons & Company, 1955.

Schoenman, Theodore. *The Father of California Wine, Agoston Haraszthy.* Santa Barbara, Calif.: Capra, 1979.

Schoonmaker, Frank. *Encyclopedia of Wine.* 5th ed. New York: Hastings House, 1973.

Schoonmaker, Frank, and Tom Marvel. *American Wines.* New York: Duell, Sloan and Pearch, 1941.

Seelig, R. A., ed. *Fruit & Vegetable Facts & Pointers.* Alexandria, Va.: United Fresh Fruit and Vegetable Association, September 1968.

Seward, Desmond. *Monks and Wines.* New York: Crown, 1979.

Simon, André L. *The Blood of the Grape.* London: Duckworth, 1920.
———. *Champagne.* New York: McGraw-Hill, 1962.
———. *A Dictionary of Wines, Spirits and Liqueurs.* New York: Citadel, 1963.
———. *The Commonsense of Wine.* Cleveland, Ohio: World, 1966.
———. *The Noble Grapes and the Great Wines of France.* New York: McGraw-Hill, 1968.

Simon, André L., ed. *Wines of the World.* New York, McGraw-Hill, 1969.

Simon, André L., and Elizabeth Craig. *Madeira.* London: Constable, 1933.

Simon, André L., and S. F. Hallgarten. *The Great Wines of Germany.* New York: McGraw-Hill, 1963.

Sincomar-Parlier et Fermau. *The Fine Wines of Morocco.* Casablanca: Sincomar-Parlier et Fermau, n.d.

Smets, Paul. *Kloster Eberbach.* Mainz: Rheingold-Verlan, 1964.

Stauss, Hans Karl, M.D. "Romania and Its Wines." Jackson, Miss., 1982. Mimeo.

Stone, Dee. "The Cape Winelands." *The Friends of Wine* (May-June 1983).

Stone, Frank H. *Aids and Resources.* Salt Lake City, Utah: Society of Wine Educators, 1983.

Thompson, Bob, and Hugh Johnson. *The California Wine Book.* New York: Morrow, 1976.

University of California at San Francisco, the Society of Medical Friends of Wine, and the Wine Institute. *Wine, Health & Society.* Symposium proceedings, jointly sponsored by the University of California at San Francisco, the Society of Medical Friends of Wine, and the Wine Institute. Oakland, Calif.: GRT Book Printing, 1981.

Valaer, Peter. *Wines of the World.* New York: Abelard, 1950.

Velardi, Cathy. "Wine: A Top Export Item for Yugoslavia." *Wines and Vines* (November 1981).

Veronelli. *The Wines of Italy.* Rome: Canesi Editore, n.d.

Vine, Richard P. *Commercial Winemaking.* Westport, Conn.: Avi, 1981.

Viticultural and Oenological Research Institute. *Vines and Wines in South Africa.* Viticultural and Oenological Research Institute, n.d.

Wagner, Philip M. *American Wines and Wine-Making.* 5th ed. New York: Knopf, 1972.
———. *A Wine-Grower's Guide.* 2nd ed. New York: Knopf, 1972.

Waugh, Alec. *In Praise of Wine*. New York: Sloane, 1959.

Waugh, Harry. *The Changing Face of Wine*. London: Wine and Spirit Publications, 1970.
———. *Pick of the Bunch*. London: Wine and Spirit Publications, 1970.

Warner, Charles K. *The Winegrowers of France and the Government since 1875*. New York: Columbia University Press, 1960.

Wasserman, Sheldon. *The Wines of the Côtes du Rhône*. New York: Stein and Day, 1977.

Wine Institute of New Zealand. *New Zealand Wine Annual*. Auckland: Wine Institute of New Zealand, Burnham House, 1983.

Wine Institute of New Zealand. *New Zealand Wine & Food Annual*. Auckland: Wine Institute of New Zealand, Burnham House, 1984.

Wine Institute. *Wine and Medical Practice*. 10th ed. San Francisco: The Wine Institute, 1981.

Wines and Vines. "New Zealand's Wine Industry Is Growing." *Wines and Vines* (December 1979).

Wines and Vines Directory. San Rafael, Calif., 1986.

Winkler, A. J. et al. *General Viticulture*. Berkeley: University of California Press, 1974.

Younger, W. *Gods, Men and Wine*. Cleveland, Ohio: World, 1966.

Yoxall. *The Wines of Burgundy*. 2nd ed. New York: Stein and Day, 1978.

APPENDIX

GLOSSARY

ABBOCCATO. Italian term referring to level of sweetness; semidry.

ACERBE. French term referring to wines made from acidic, harsh-tasting grapes.

ACETIC ACID. Colorless, pungent substance commonly known as vinegar; CH_3CO_2H.

ACETIFICATION. The process by which acetic acid is formed; the oxidation of ethanol (alcohol) into acetic acid by bacteria called *acetobacter*.

ACID. Compounds in wine that, in proper balance, contribute a tart freshness to taste and help a wine age. Sometimes used in reference to the harshness of grapes and wine.

ACIDITY. Term used to indicate tartness or sharpness on the palate; does not relate to astringency or dryness.

AEROBIC. Term used to describe microorganisms requiring oxygen in order to grow.

AFTERTASTE. Term used to refer to the flavor that remains in the mouth after a wine has been swallowed; an olfactory function of sensory receptors located in the mouth and nose.

AGE. Length of time a wine has existed, often taken as a sign of quality. However, "old" wines are not always "good" wines.

AGED. Wine kept in storage (either in bulk or in bottle) under a condition designed to improve its qualities.

AGING. The maturation of wine; the oxidation (reaction of one or more wine constituents with oxygen) process in which wines become mellowed.

AHR. Wine-growing region of Germany on the banks of the Ahr River.

ALCOHOL. One of the chemicals resulting from the fermentation of grape juice or MUST. When fermentation is complete, the natural alcohol content will have reached about 12 percent by volume. In making dessert and aperitif wines, additional alcohol (ethanol) is added in the form of grape brandy (usually at about 190 degrees proof or approximately 95% pure ethanol) that increases the total alcohol content to about 20 percent by volume.

ALEXANDER VALLEY. Wine-growing region located between the Napa and Sonoma valleys of California.

ALICANTE. Wine-growing region located on the southeastern coast of Spain.

ALOXE-CORTON. Important wine-growing town located in the Côte de Beaune section of the Côte d'Or district of the Burgundy region of France.

ALSACE. Wine-growing region located in northeastern France that is comprised of the Haut-Rhin and Bas-Rhin. Alsatian wines often show their Teutonic heritage in type, style, and packaging, but do not usually equal the finer German growths.

AMABILE. Term often used to refer to level of sweetness; sweeter than ABBOCCATO.

AMARO. Term often used to refer to bitterness.

AMELIORATION. Addition of water and/or sugar to juice or wine. In most European countries, when natural sugar levels are insufficient in a given vintage, sugar is allowed to be added to grape juice and MUST prior to fermentation. California juice and MUST may not be ameliorated at all; juice and MUST in other states may be ameliorated in accordance with U.S. Bureau of Alcohol, Tobacco and Firearms regulations.

AMERICAN WINES. Production is from three main sources: American vines (*Vitis labrusca*) grown predominantly east of the Rocky mountains; European vines (*Vitis vinifera*) grown mostly in California, but increasingly in other states; and hybrids of these two species, grown mostly in the eastern and central areas of the United States.

AMONTILLADO. Popular type of Spanish sherry; may be dry but is usually noticeably sweet.

AMOROSO. Spanish sherry that is darker and sweeter than AMONTILLADO.

AMPHORAE. Ancient Greek jars, vases, or jugs with oval bodies and narrow necks.

ANAEROBIC. Term used to describe a microorganism able to grow in an environment lacking in oxygen.

ANJOU. Wine-growing district in the central Loire Valley of France.

ANTHOCYANINS. Color pigments found in the skins of grapes from which the color of wines originates.

APERITIF WINE. Wine that contains added essences and flavors of spices, herbs, roots, etc.; for example, vermouths.

APPEARANCE. The visual aspect of wine evaluation, concerned with color and clarity.

APPELLATION D'ORIGINE CONTRÔLÉE (AOC). Translated from the French as "authenticity guaranteed"—the highest level of wine quality authorized by the French government as regulated and enforced by the l'Institut National des

Appellations d'Origine. The nature of the specific regulations regarding wine production methods, grape varieties, maximum production levels, geographic borders, alcoholic strength, and other such criteria varies by region.

ÂPRE. French term used to refer to wines that are very harsh.

ARBOIS. Wine-growing district in the Jura region of eastern France.

ARGENTINA. Fifth-largest wine-growing nation in the world. One of its principal wine regions is Mendoza.

ARKANSAS. Eighth-largest wine-growing state in the United States.

AROMA. Term used to refer to the fragrance of a juice, MUST, or wine. Aroma is contributed by the fruit and is one part of the BOUQUET.

AROMATIZED WINES. Generally regarded as the same as APERITIF WINES.

AROME SPIRITUEUX. French term used to refer to the bouquet of a wine at the time of serving; usually a bouquet that lasts longer than the flavor. *See* SÈVE.

ASTI. Capital city of the Piedmont region of northern Italy. Asti Spumante is a white sparkling wine that is usually rather sweet and very fruity.

ASTRINGENCY. Term used to refer to the response of the palate to tannin, a response similar to that produced by aspirin.

AUSLESE. Famous German wine made from specially selected bunches of overripened grapes that may or may not be infected with EDELFÄULE.

AUSONE. Ancient St.-Émilion château in the Bordeaux region of France once owned and named for Ausonius, a Roman consul.

AUSTERE. Term used to describe strong wines. *See* HEADY.

AUSTRALIA. The seventeenth-largest wine-growing nation in the world, and one showing rapid growth. Most of the vineyards of Australia are cultivated in the State of South Australia; New South Wales and Victoria are also important regions. Many of Australia's wine-growing techniques resemble those of California, as do some of the high-quality wines that result.

AUSTRIA. Important wine-growing nation that produces mostly light, delicate white wines in the German style. Fifteenth-largest producer of wines in the world.

BACTERIA. One-celled microscopic plants. The bacteria called *acetobacter* are responsible for turning wine into vinegar.

BALANCE. Term used in describing the proportions of dryness (or sweetness) and acidity in wine.

BALLING. Graduated VISCOSITY scale that shows the simultaneous impacts of alcohol and dissolved solids in a HYDROMETER.

BARDOLINO. Red wine grown in the Piedmont region of northern Italy.

BAROLO. Red wine grown in the Piedmont region of northern Italy.

BARRIQUE. Wine cask used principally in the Bordeaux region of France. It contains approximately 60 U.S. gallons. Similar-sized casks of the same name are found in other regions of France and in Algeria.

BARSAC. Wine-growing *commune* located in the Sauternes district of Bordeaux, France.

BAUMÉ. Scale measuring sugar content in grapes.

BEAUJOLAIS. Important wine-growing district in the southern portion of the Burgundy region of France.

BEAUJOLAIS NOUVEAU. Newly made, or very young, BEAUJOLAIS wines that are meant to be consumed within several months following harvest.

BEAUJOLAIS-VILLAGES. Wines grown from the locales of thirty-five villages in the Beaujolais district of Burgundy; generally considered superior to wines labeled only as "Beaujolais."

BEAUNE. Wine-growing capital city of the Burgundy region of France.

BEERENAUSLESE. German wine made from individually selected grape berries of specially selected bunches of overripe grapes infected with EDELFÄULE.

BENTONITE. A montmorillonite clay compound used in winemaking (usually in younger wines) as a clarification agent. Its great adsorptive capacity will precipitate suspended solids and colloids; may also tend to diminish color intensity of the wine as a side effect.

BEREICH. German for *area*. Used to refer to vineyard origins; for example, "Bereich Bernkastel" (from vineyards located within the legal bounds of the Bernkastel District).

BERNKASTEL. River-port wine-growing center of the middle Mosel region in Germany.

BIANCO. Italian for "white."

BIG. Term generally used to describe wines that exhibit an abundance of positive qualities.

BIKAVÉR. Red wine grown in Hungary, known as the "Bull's Blood," or *Egri Bikavér*.

BINNING. Storage of bottled wines in bins, usually for the purpose of aging.

BITE. Term used to refer to an unpleasant taste value that generally results from high acidity.

BLANC DE BLANC. French for "white from white"; denoting a white wine made entirely from white grape varieties.

BLANC DE NOIR. French for "white from black"; denoting a white wine made entirely from black grape varieties.

BLAND. Term used to describe wines lacking in acidity and/or overall character.

BLENDED WINE. Two or more wines mixed together, generally in an effort to improve the overall character through melding individual attributes.

BOCKSBEUTEL. The short, squat flagon-type "ram's-head" bottle generally associated with the Franken wine-growing region of Germany.

BODEGA. Spanish for "wine cellar," usually constructed above ground. The term also refers to a Spanish "wine house."

BODY. Term used to describe how wine feels in the mouth. This feeling is caused by dissolved solids. A wine may be "light-bodied," or thin, as opposed to "heavy-bodied," or thick.

BONDED. A term used by the U.S. Bureau of Alcohol, Tobacco and Firearms (BATF) in reference to wines upon which the federal excise taxes have not yet been paid. A "bonded area" denotes the borders within which wine may be made and stored. A "bond" is a financial document that guarantees payment of excise taxes. Both a "bond" and a "bonded area" must be applied for and approved by the BATF as part of a vintner's operating permit in the United States.

BONNES MARES. Important vineyard in the Côte de Nuits section of the Côte d'Or district of the Burgundy region of France.

BORDEAUX. Important wine-growing region in southwest France. Its center is the port city of the same name. "Claret" is the English term for red Bordeaux wines.

BOTRYTIS. *See* POURRITURE NOBLE or EDELFÄULE.

BOTTLE. Glass container in any U.S. government-approved size used for wine packaging and marketing.

BOTTLE AGING. Designed program of improving wine quality through periods of storage in bottles.

BOTTLE FERMENTATION. Secondary fermentation of wine in bottles to capture carbon dioxide gas in the production of sparkling wines.

BOTTLE SICKNESS. Term in wine production usually referring to a temporary loss of bouquet and flavor in wines just bottled—often due to the addition of preservatives and the rigors of cask-to-bottle cellar treatment.

BOTTOMS. Sediment in wine tanks after fermentation, racking, clarification, etc. More often called LEES.

BOUQUET. Term used to describe the fragrance of a wine. The bouquet consists of the fruit aroma and the volatile constituents that result from the cellaring techniques used to make the wine.

BRANDY. Distilled wine; the "spirits" of wine.

BRAZIL. Eighteenth-largest producer of wine in the world.

BREATHING. Practice of uncorking a wine bottle well in advance of serving in order to allow the wine to expel head-space gases. The usefulness of letting a wine breathe is questionable.

BRIGHT. *See* BRILLIANT.

BRILLIANT. Term used to describe wines that have a flawless clarity.

BRIX. Graduated HYDROMETER scale used to measure dissolved solids in grape juice; not to be confused with BALLING, which is influenced by alcohol in solution along with dissolved solids.

BRUT. French for "raw" or "natural" unsweetened wines (usually champagne); the very driest.

BUAL. Grape variety cultivated on the isle of Madeira. Also, a type of Madeira wine that is generally heavy-bodied and sweet.

BUCELAS. Vineyard region nc :h of Lisbon, Portugal.

BULGARIA. Eastern European country; sixteenth-largest wine-growing nation in the world.

BULK PROCESS. Production of sparkling wine in special tanks rather than through the traditional *méthode champenoise* of fermenting sparkling wine in individual bottles. CHARMAT is another name for the bulk process.

BUNG. Stopper, usually made of wood or glass, used to seal a keg, barrel, or some other bulk wine-storage vessel.

BUNGHOLE. Opening at the top of a bulk wine-storage vessel in which the bung is placed as a seal.

BURGUNDY. Important wine-growing region in central France. The finest wines are generally considered to be grown in the Côte d'Or (comprised by the subdistricts Côte de Beaune and Côte de Nuits) districts. "Burgundy" is also a generic term used indiscriminately on the labels of red wines that have no resemblance to true Burgundy.

BUTT. English term for Spanish cooperage. Each butt contains approximately 126 Imperial gallons (about 151 U.S. gallons).

CABERNET. Short for Cabernet Sauvignon, the premier red wine grape of the Médoc in Bordeaux, France, as well as the Napa and Sonoma Valley regions of northern California. Also used incorrectly to refer to the hybrid RUBY CABERNET.

CABERNET FRANC. Important red wine grape variety cultivated in the St.-Émilion district of Bordeaux, France.

CABERNET SAUVIGNON. See CABERNET.

CABINETT-WEIN. See KABINETT.

CALIFORNIA. Largest wine-growing state in the United States. The principal regions are the North Coast counties (Napa, Sonoma, Alexander, and Mendocino valleys); Alameda; Contra Costa; Santa Clara;

Central Valley; and Southern California. The principal grape varieties are from the Old World *Vitis vinifera* species.

CANDLING. Process of judging clarity in a bottle of wine by holding it in front of a filament bulb or lighted candle.

CANTINA. Italian for "cellar" or "winery."

CANTINA SOCIALE. Cooperative winery of Italian grape growers.

CAPITEAUX. French term meaning "warmly rich in alcohol."

CAPSULE. Seal over the closure of a wine bottle used to protect the neck and closure and improve bottle-packaging appearance.

CARBOHYDRATE. Carbon, hydrogen, and oxygen chemically bonded as a compound. Sugar is a carbohydrate.

CARBONATED WINES. Wines injected with carbon dioxide gas, rendering the wine effervescent.

CARBON DIOXIDE. The gas produced by fermentation; CO_2.

CARBONIC MACERATION. Method by which whole grapes are fermented in a closed container during which the carbon dioxide gas (CO_2) generated from fermentation permeates the grapes. A process employed heavily in the Beaujolais district of the Burgundy region in France.

CARBOY. Glass bottle, usually with a capacity of 5 gallons.

CARIGNAN. Common red wine grape grown in southern France and Central California.

CASA VINICOLA. Italian for "winery."

CASE. Container in which bottled wine is held, usually made of heavy paperboard, wood, or plastic, and normally with a capacity of 12 bottles (24 half-bottles, 6 magnums).

CASK. Wooden container for bulk wine-storage and aging, usually made of some species of white oak and containing at least 200 U.S. gallons; generally built with bulging sides. Not to be confused with the smaller butts, hogsheads, pipes, barrels, or puncheons or the larger tuns.

CASKINESS. Term generally used to refer to wines that may have been aged in casks that were not cleaned or treated properly beforehand.

CASSE. Term used to describe the haze that develops in wines as a result of an excessive metal content.

CASSIS. Wine-growing seaport village near Marseilles in Provence, France.

CASTELLI ROMANI. Wine-growing locale near Rome in the Latium region of Italy.

CATAWBA. Important native American grape variety cultivated principally in New York State and Ohio. Often made into "Pink Catawba," a sweet rosé wine.

CAVE. French for wine "cellar."

CELLAR. Any building, either above ground level or below, used in the various phases of the wine-making process.

CELLARED AND BOTTLED BY . . . *See* MADE AND BOTTLED BY.

CELLAR TREATMENT. The materials and methods used in the various phases of the wine-making process.

CÉPAGE. French for "grape cultivar."

CERASUOLO. Italian for "light red."

CHABLIS. Important wine-growing village and district in the Burgundy region of France; produces some of the finest white wines from the Chardonnay variety. *Petit Chablis* is a lesser grade grown within the district. *Chablis* is used as a generic term indiscriminately for other dry white wines bearing little or no resemblance to true Chablis.

CHAGNY. Important wine-growing village in the Côte de Beaune section of the Côte d'Or district of the Burgundy region in France.

CHAMBERTIN. Important wine-growing township in the Côte de Nuits section of the northern Côte d'Or district of the Burgundy region in France.

CHAMBOLLE-MUSIGNY. Important wine-growing township in the Côte de Nuits section of the Côte d'Or district of the Burgundy region in France.

CHAMBRER. The act of bringing a wine, usually red, carefully to cool room temperature.

CHAMPAGNE. Important sparkling wine-producing region northeast of Paris, France. *Champagne* is used as a generic term for sparkling wines bearing little resemblance to true Champagne.

CHAMPAGNE ROUGE. Misnomer; such a wine properly does not exist. It refers to red sparkling wines often labeled "Sparkling Burgundy."

CHAPTALIZATION. Addition of sugar to juice or MUST in order to increase the resultant alcohol strength from fermentation (note that the term AMELIORATION denotes the addition of *water and/or sugar*).

CHARACTER. The sum of the qualities that distinguishes a wine: thecolor, taste, and bouquet of a particular wine type.

CHARDONNAY. One of the most important white wine grape varieties in the world. The grape grown for all of the great white Burgundies and the premier dry white wine variety grown in California.

CHARMAT. Bulk or tank method of producing sparkling wines, usually a much faster process (and generally less respected) than the traditional French *méthode champenoise* bottle-fermentation technique.

CHARNU. French term generally used to refer to wines that have body, but not much strength.

CHARPENTE. French term used to describe wines that have been well made.

CHASSAGNE-MONTRACHET. Important red and white wine-growing locale in the Côte de Beaune section of the Côte d'Or district of the Burgundy region in France. Contains a section of the fabled Montrachet Grand Cru white wine vineyards.

CHASSELAS. Common grape used for both eating and winemaking in Europe. The variety is called *Gutedel* in Germany and the Alsace, and *Fendant* in Switzerland.

CHÂTEAU. French for "castle." The wine estate comprising vineyards and winery in France, usually in Bordeaux.

CHÂTEAUNEUF-DU-PAPE. Literally means "new home of the pope." A famous red wine grown in the southern Rhône Valley, near Avignon, France.

CHÉNAS. Important vineyard region in the Beaujolais district of Burgundy, France.

CHEVAL-BLANC. Outstanding St.-Émilion château in the Bordeaux region of France.

CHIANTI. Red wines grown in large volumes primarily from Sangiovese grapes cultivated in the Tuscany region of Italy. Chianti Classico wines are from superior, centrally located vineyards.

CHIARETTO. Italian for "light red."

CHILE. South American country that is the thirteenth-largest producer of wines in the world. Some of the most notable vineyards are Concha y Toro, Tarapacá, Undurraga, and Vial.

CHINON. Important wine-growing town in the Loire region of France.

CHIROUBLES. Important vineyard region in the Beaujolais district of Burgundy, France.

CLARET. Term used by the English for red wines grown in the Bordeaux region of France, rarely used as a generic term by U.S. vintners.

CLARETE. Spanish term denoting a red wine that is light in body and color; generally refers to wines from the Rioja.

CLARIFY. To make a wine clear by adding refining agents (such as BENTONITE) in order to precipitate suspended solids.

CLASSICO. Inner zone of an Italian DOC. Generally refers to superior growths.

CLASSIFIED GROWTH. A particular vineyard estate or château in Bordeaux that was classified during the Paris Exposition of 1855. There are only six first-growths, but many second-, third-, fourth-, and fifth-growth châteaux.

CLEAN. Term used to describe a wine free from the detrimental effects of unsanitary cellar treatment or overprocessing. When the palate experiences the full varietal character and detects no interference from other varieties blended in, the wine is called *clean*.

CLEAR. Wine having been clarified and/or filtered successfully from visible solids, but not BRILLIANT.

CLOS. French for "walled vineyard." Generally found in Burgundy.

CLOUDY. A rather heavy presence of suspended solids in a wine.

CLOYING. Excessively sweet.

COARSE. Harsh and overpowering in taste; may refer to young wines not allowed to mellow through sufficient cellar treatment and aging.

COLARES. Wine-growing district near Lisbon, Portugal.

COLLOIDAL SUSPENSION. Hazy or cloudy suspensions of semisolid particles in wine; not to be confused with metal CASSE.

COLMAR. Capital city of the Alsace wine-growing region in northeastern France.

COLOR. The hue of a wine. Usually refers to recognized values such as "light straw," "ruby," "tawny," etc.

COMPLEX. A term used to describe a wine in which bouquet and/or flavors are composed of many different constituents that may be difficult to separate and classify.

CONCENTRATE. Dehydrated grape juice, either red or white, used for sweetening grape juice and wines that are deficient in natural grape sugar.

CONCORD. Important native American grape cultivar developed by Ephraim Bull of Concord, Massachusetts. The Concord, very popular as a juice grape, also finds acceptance as a table grape and wine grape, most notably for kosher wines produced in the northeastern United States.

CONEGLIANO. Important wine-growing district north of Venice in the Veneto region of Italy.

CONSORZIO. Association of growers in Italy who generally identify the wines grown within their region by affixing a seal on bottle necks. Originally intended to authorize vineyard and winery inspections to assure compliance with regulations and guarantee the integrity of DOC guidelines, but this has yet to be realized.

COOKED. Term used to describe a "baked" character or an oxidized bouquet and flavor. Generally used positively in reference to maderized wines and negatively in regard to wines that have endured excessive heat in shipping and/or storage.

COOPERAGE. Term that traditionally refers to wine containers made from wood. The word derives from *cooper*, a British sailing term for the ship's barrel maker. In modern times *cooperage* refers to any container used for wine, whether of wood, steel, glass, or any other material.

COOPERATIVE. Winery owned by more than one grape grower, generally formed to share the cost of winery establishment and operation among members.

CORK. Bark of the cork oak, grown in large acreages in Mediterranean countries, harvested and processed into stoppers for both still and sparkling wine bottles.

CORKSCREW. Spiral metal device with a sharp tip used to remove corks from wine bottles.

CORKINESS. Term used to describe an unpleasant flavor and bouquet in a wine that was bottled with a defective cork. Usually spoilage results because there was an incomplete seal, and outside air was able to enter the bottle.

CORPS, VIN QUI A DU CORPS; VIN CORSÉ (body, wine with body, full-bodied wine). French terms used to describe wines that possess substance, pronounced taste, and vinous strength, and that "fill the mouth"; the opposite of a light, dry, cold, or watery wine.

COTEAUX DU LAYON. Important wine-growing subdistrict in the Anjou district of the Loire region in France.

COTEAUX DU LOIRE. Important wine-growing subdistrict north of Tours, in the Loire region of France.

CÔTE DE BEAUNE. Important wine-growing section of the Côte d'Or district in the Burgundy region of France.

CÔTE D'OR. "Golden slope" of northern Burgundy where the finest red wines of the region are grown. In the opinion of some experts, in certain years the finest red wines of the world are grown there.

CÔTE-RÔTIE. Wine-growing district in the extreme north of the Rhône Valley region of France famous for the "blond" and "brunette" vineyards.

CÔTES DU RHÔNE. *See* RHÔNE.

COURT. French term used to describe wines that are deficient in taste and flavor.

CRADLE. Device, usually made of wicker in one or another basket weave, in which a wine bottle is placed at an angle for serving.

CRAMANT. Important wine-growing *commune* in the Champagne region of France, which produces BLANC DE BLANC (not to be confused with CRÉMANT).

CREAM OF TARTAR. Colorless crystalline deposit of potassium bitartrate that will precipitate from unstable wines during refrigeration. *See* TARTARIC ACID.

CRÉMANT. Sparkling wine that has a reduced level of effervescence.

CRESCENZ. German labeling term sometimes used to denote estate bottling, the same as *Erzeugerabfüllung*.

CRU. French for a specified vineyard "growth," classified for a specific echelon of quality, such as a *premier cru classe* or a *grand cru classe*.

CRU, CRUDITÉ. French term meaning "rawness." Applied to wines that are too young, and thus retain a disagreeable greenness. *See* VERT.

CRUST. Sediment of unstable solids from wine that have collected and solidified on the surface of the bottle; common in red wines. Most often associated with very old wines, especially ports.

CRYSTALLINE DEPOSITS. Crystal deposits composed primarily of tasteless potassium bitartrate that accumulate either at the bottom of the bottle or at the bottom of the cork. They are often the result of white wine's exposure to low temperature. *See* TARTARIC ACID.

CUVÉE. Literally means "tub full" or "vat full"; in the winemaking sense refers to the quantity of production from a vineyard. The first pressing of grapes yields the *première cuvée*, the second pressing yields the *deuxième cuvée*, and so forth, each succeeding pressing yielding a lesser quality of wine than the former. The term *cuvée* is often synonymous with CRU. The most common use of the term is in identifying blends of base wines fermented a second time for sparkling wines.

CZECHOSLOVAKIA. Eastern European country; nineteenth-largest wine-growing nation in the world.

DÃO. Important wine-growing region in Portugal.

DECANT. Operation of delicately transferring wine from a bottle to a decanter so as to separate any sediment that may have formed in the bottle during aging.

DÉGORGEMENT. French for "disgorge." The technique of removing the frozen plug of sediment from a bottle of sparkling wine after the REMUAGE (riddling), but prior to the addition of DOSAGE.

DEGREES BALLING. Divisions for dissolved solids upon the Balling HYDROMETER scale when used as a measurement of VISCOSITY in solutions containing ethanol (ethyl alcohol), such as wine.

DEGREES BRIX. Divisions for dissolved solids upon the Brix HYDROMETER scale when used as a measurement of

VISCOSITY in solutions that do not contain ethanol (alcohol), such as grape juice or MUST.

DEIDESHEIM. Important wine-growing district in the Rheinpfalz region of Germany.

DELAWARE. Important native American grape variety discovered growing wild in Delaware County, Ohio, during the early 1900s. The fruit is light red in color, but yields white wines that are important constituents of many New York State "champagne" cuvées.

DÉLICAT or DÉLICATESSE. French term meaning "delicate." Refers to a wine that has very little acidity and color. Though the wine may have one or more coarse constituents, it has been blended to mask that imbalance. Often used synonymously with *élégant*.

DELICATE. Term used to describe wines with subtle bouquet and flavor values.

DEMIJOHN. Small glass containers for wine; usually wicker-covered. A common misnomer for CARBOYS (5-gallon jugs).

DEMI-SEC. French for "nearly dry" or "semidry." Most often used in the description of sparkling wines.

DENOMINAZIONE DI ORIGINE CONTOLLATA. Instituted by the Italian government in 1963 as the official regulatory system for wine quality and origin control. Usually referred to by the acronym "DOC." It specifies the regulations and requirements for each wine name or title prescribed by the Italian Ministry of Agriculture.

DESSERT WINE. In the United States, this is a wine that has received an addition of brandy, or has been "fortified," usually resulting in a sweet port- or sherry-type wine. The term may also refer to any sweet wine that is served with dessert courses.

DEVELOPED. Degree of wine maturity; a measurement of aging.

DINNER WINE. *See* TABLE WINE.

DISGORGING. English form of the French sparkling wine term *dégorgement*, meaning to expel the frozen plug of sediment in the neck of a sparkling wine bottle with the carbon dioxide gas pressure that has developed during secondary fermentation.

DISTINCTIVE. Term for a wine with finesse and the qualities that distinguish its special character from that of lesser wines.

DOLCE. Italian for "sweet."

DOMAINE. French for "vineyard estate" or "wine estate"; most commonly used in Burgundy.

DOM PÉRIGNON. Famous wine-master monk at the Abbey of Hautvillers in the Champagne region of France who is given credit for inventing sparkling wines during the seventeenth century. In modern times, "Dom Pérignon" is a brand name for a very fine Champagne produced by Moët & Chandon in Épernay, France.

DOSAGE. Addition of a rather high-alcohol, very sweet syrup to sparkling wines directly after *dégorgement* to sweeten the wine slightly. The *dosage* usually contains a preservative to prevent a third fermentation.

DOURO. Important wine-growing region of Portugal where port wine is made. It is named for the Douro River that flows through the valley to the city of Oporto.

DOUX. French for "sweet"; most often used in the description of sparkling wines.

DREGS. Precipitated sediment in wine; more commonly referred to as LEES (bulk wines) or SEDIMENT (bottled wines).

DRY. Absence of fermentable sugar; opposite of sweet.

DULL. *See* FLAT.

DUR or DURETÉ. French term meaning "hard." Used for coarse wines that affect the palate in a disagreeable manner.

EARTHY. Term relating to the contribution to the bouquet and/or flavor of a wine of the soil upon which grapes are grown. The "chalk" of Champagne and "flint" of Chablis are good examples.

ÉCHÉZEAUX. Important wine-growing *commune* of the Côte de Nuits section of the Côte d'Or in the Burgundy region of France.

EDELFÄULE. Fungus *Botrytis cinerea*, or "noble mold," that permeates the skins of grape berries, allowing moisture to evaporate and concentrating sugar and flavors that remain. Edelfäule is the German term for *Botrytis* and is associated with BEERENAUSLESE and TROCKENBEERENAUSLESE wines. *See also* POURRITURE NOBLE.

ÉGRAPPAGE. French for the "destemming" of grapes.

ÉLÉGANT. *See* DÉLICAT.

ENOLOGY. Art, science, and study of making wine; the same as OENOLOGY.

ENTRE-DEUX-MERS. Important wine-growing district located between the Dordogne and Garonne rivers in the Bordeaux region of France.

ÉPERNAY. Important wine-producing city in the Champagne region of France.

ÉPLUCHAGE. Removal of poor-quality berries from bunches of grapes; performed in the Champagne region of France.

ESSENTIAL OILS. Organic oils generated in grapes that are distinctive in aroma and taste; the ORGANOLEPTIC profile of a particular grape.

EST! EST!! EST!!! Legendary wine grown in the Montefiascone district of the Latium region of Italy.

ESTATE BOTTLED. Labeling statement that generally signifies that the same authority who vinified the wine also grew the grapes that made the wine. Because often misused, it may not always be the indication of a superior wine that it is intended to be.

ESTERS. Volatile (evaporative) organic compounds that comprise the bouquet or the "nose" of a wine. Some esters are contributed by the grapes, while others arise due to specific vinification procedures, such as aging in oak barrels.

ETHYL ALCOHOL. See ALCOHOL.

ÉVENT, GOÛT D'. French for "flat" or seemingly lifeless. A condition that may arise when wines are overaged or have been stored in containers not properly sealed.

EXTRACT. Term for total dissolved solids in wine, including sugar, color pigments, glycerols, etc.

EXTRA DRY. "Bone" dry or totally lacking in residual sugar; the absolute opposite of sweet. Sometimes used incorrectly in labeling sparkling wines that are really slightly sweet, but not as dry as BRUT or SEC.

FAIBLE. French for "weak." Generally associated with wines that exhibit thin-bodiedness and little alcoholic strength, but may also be used for wines having little flavor—a characteristic preferred by some.

FALSE WINES. Wines made from sources other than grapes.

FATTORIA. Italian for "wine producer."

FERME or FERMETÉ. French for "firm." A term used to describe strong and vigorous wines exhibiting heavy-bodiedness. Also may refer to young green wines. Generally a fault in finished wines, but may be a positive attribute in blending wines meant to add character to weaker wines.

FERMENTATION. Generally signifies the transformation of sugar to alcohol (ethanol), carbon dioxide, and energy through the action of yeasts, although bacterial fermentations also occur in wines.

FERMENTATION LOCK. Device on fermenting vessels that allows gases to escape out of the FERMENTER, but keeps outside elements from entering.

FERMENTERS. Containers, generally constructed of glass-lined steel, stainless steel, or wood, in which the fermentation process of wine takes place.

FILTERING. Passing a wine through filter media in order to clarify it.

FILTRATION. Forcing a wine through media in which suspended solids are extracted; frequently for the purpose of removing yeast and bacteria cells.

FIN or FINESSE. French for "light" and "delicate" wines.

FINE. Superior wines; also a term meaning "to clarify a wine."

FINGER LAKES. Important wine-growing region in central New York State.

FINING. *See* CLARIFY.

FINIR or VINS QUI FINISSENT BIEN. French for "wines that finish well." A term that may be used in evaluations of wines that have an agreeable AFTERTASTE. Also used for wines that improve with age. VINS DE GARDE are wines that keep well in cellar storage.

FINISH. Term that refers to the last impression of the wine before, during, and after swallowing; includes the AFTERTASTE as well.

FINO. Lightest and driest of the Spanish sherries.

FIRM. Term usually referring to wines that exhibit an aftertaste of tannin.

FIXED ACIDITY. Organic acids in wines that are nonvolatile, such as tartaric, malic, and lactic acids.

FLAGEY-ÉCHÉZEAUX. *See* ECHÉZEAUX.

FLAT. Term for a wine devoid of interesting qualities; lacking finesse or polish. Also, sparkling wine that has lost its effervescence.

FLAVORED WINES. Wines that have values of taste and aroma added to the natural fermented grape juice used to make the wine, such as vermouth and some pop wines.

FLAVOROUS. Term used to describe full or extra-full flavor values.

FLAVORS. Term used to describe distinct tastes as experienced by the palate.

FLEURIE. Important wine-growing district in the Beaujolais region of France.

FLINTY. Term used to describe the stony or rocky flavors found in some white wines such as Chablis.

FLOR. Spanish for "flower." Generally refers to the surface-growing yeasts that synthesize acetaldehyde, the compound that contributes the nutty flavor common to sherry-type wines.

FLOWERS OF WINE. Development of a white film on the surface of wine that denotes the growth of ACETOBACTER. The acetification process in progress (the development of vinegar).

FLOWERY. Term used to describe the aroma and bouquet of wine that smells like flowers in blossom; an example is the white wine made properly from the variety JOHANNISBERG RIESLING.

FORST. Important vineyard located in the Rheinpfalz region of Germany.

FORT. French for "strong." Wines that exhibit a superior alcoholic strength and, perhaps, a very pronounced flavor.

FORTIFIED WINE. Wine that has been increased in alcohol content by the addition of brandy; good examples are SHERRY and PORT (DESSERT WINE).

FORTIFY. Act of adding brandy to wine to increase the alcohol content.

FOXINESS. Aroma and flavor generally attributed to grapes from the *Vitis labrusca* species, among others.

FRANC DE GOÛT. French for "natural taste," referring to wines that have no flavor other than that of the grape itself. Does not include wines of natural earthy or herbal flavors.

FRANCE. Second-largest wine-growing nation in the world, regarded by many wine enthusiasts as the most important producer. Major wine regions include Bordeaux, Burgundy, Champagne, Rhône, Alsace Loire, Midi, and Provence.

FRANKEN. Important wine-growing region in Germany.

FRANKEN RIESLING. Same as SYLVANER.

FRASCATI. White table wine grown in the Latium region near Rome, Italy.

FREE RUN. Juice or wine that flows freely from the press without the exertion of pressure.

FREISA. Red wine, sometimes FRIZZANTE, produced in the Piedmont region of Italy.

FRESH. Term used to describe a lively bouquet and flavor.

FRIZZANTE. Italian for PÉTILLANT or "slightly sparkling"; fizzy.

FRONSAC. Wine-growing district in the Bordeaux region of France.

FRONTIGNAN. Important wine-growing district in the Midi region of southern France. Also may refer to the grape variety Muscat de Frontignan.

FRUIT WINES. Wines made from fruits or fruit essences, or fruit concentrates other than grapes. Not to be confused with true fruit wines that must be made entirely from fresh fruit other than grapes.

FRUITY. Term applied to wines having high values of bouquet and flavor captured from the grape (or whatever fruit from which it was made). Often used in evaluating wines made from *Vitis labrusca* and *Vitis rotundifolia*.

FULL. Term for wines that are heavy-bodied or strong in values of bouquet and flavor, or both.

FULL-BODIED. Term used to describe wine that feels thick, rich, and heavy in the mouth, such as port, as opposed to thin and light, such as Chablis.

FUMÉ. *See* SAUVIGNON.

FUMEAUX. French for "heady." A term for wines with such high alcohol strength that they evaporate excessively, perhaps irritating the membranes of the nose.

FUNCHAL. Important seaport on the isle of Madeira from which Madeira wines are shipped.

FURMINT. Important wine grape variety cultivated in Hungary from which Tokay wines are made. The Flame Tokay of California is a different variety altogether.

GAMAY. Important red wine grape variety grown in the Beaujolais district of the Burgundy region of France.

GEISENHEIM. Important wine-growing town in the Rheingau region of Germany. Also the location of the Geisenheim Institute, which pursues research in enology and viticulture.

GÉNÉREUX. French for "generous." A term used to describe wines that offer abundant bouquet and flavor; wines that tend to warm and soothe the palate.

GENERIC. Labeling term that describes wines from or characteristic to a particular geographical region or political boundary such as BURGUNDY or CHAMPAGNE in France. This can be contrasted with varietal labeling, which takes the name of the principal grape variety used in making the wine, such as PINOT NOIR, which is the most important red grape variety grown in Burgundy. Some countries, such as the United States, are permitted to use some of the more common generic terms originating in Europe, such as "California Burgundy," or "New York State Champagne."

GERMANY. Seventh-largest wine-growing nation in the world. Most notable areas include the Rheingau, Mosel, Nahe, Rheinhessen, Rheinpfalz, Franken, and Baden.

GEVREY-CHAMBERTIN.   *See* CHAMBERTIN.

GEWÜRZTRAMINER. Important grape variety grown principally in the Alsace region of France, but native to northern Italy.

GRAACH. Important village in the middle Mosel region of Germany.

GRAIN. Term denoting a distinct but not excessive roughness or harshness, especially apparent in many young wines. Not necessarily a negative attribute.

GRAND CRU. French for "great growth." Used primarily to classify vineyards in France, it has a different significance from one wine region to another, but is uniform within regions.

GRAPE. Fruit grown from the vine, of which more than fifty species are now known. The majority of wine grapes grown in the world are from the species *Vitis vinifera*, or Old World grapes. Other important species in U.S. wine growing are *Vitis labrusca* and *Vitis rotundifolia*, "native"

and "muscadine" grapes, respectively. Crosses between varieties either within or across species result in hybrids, such as the "French-American" hybrids.

GRAVES. Important wine-growing district in the Bordeaux region of France.

GRAY RIESLING. Important grape variety in California, especially in the Livermore Valley. Some claim it is identical with the Chauché Gris grape of the Arbois district in the Jura region of France.

GREECE. Fourteenth-largest wine-growing nation in the world and an ancient site of much vinicultural history.

GREEN. Term used to describe undeveloped wines; also wines that display a grassy or herbaceous bouquet and flavor.

GREEN HUNGARIAN. Common grape variety grown widely in California.

GRENACHE. Important red and rosé wine grape grown widely in the Rhône Valley region of France and in California.

GRIGNOLINO. Red table wine grown in the Piedmont region of Italy. Also the name of a grape variety cultivated in southern California.

GRINZING. Vienna, Austria, suburb made famous for its *Heurige*, or "new wine," each year.

GROSSIER. French term used to express coarseness.

GUMPOLDSKIRCHNER. Delicate white wine grown in Austria; some claim it is that country's finest growth.

GUTEDEL. *See* CHASSELAS.

HALLGARTEN. Important wine-growing village in the Rheingau region of Germany.

HAMMONDSPORT. Wine-growing center of the Finger Lakes district of upstate New York.

HARD. Term used to describe wines that affect the palate as coarse and/or harsh. The opposite of delicate and soft.

HATTENHEIM. Important wine-growing village in the Rheingau region of Germany.

HAUT. French for "high," but more often taken in wine terminology to mean "higher than" or "farther away from" or "better than," such as "Haut-Médoc," the superior section of the Médoc district of Bordeaux.

HAUT-BRION. Graves chateau of high repute located in the Bordeaux region of France. One of the original "First Growths" of the Paris Exposition of 1855 Classification.

HAUTVILLERS. Important wine-growing village in the Champagne region of France. It was in the abbey of this village that the monk, DOM PÉRIGNON, is credited with inventing Champagne.

HEADY. Term usually referring to wines with excessive alcohol content. Roughly equivalent to "strong" wines. Also, used loosely as a term for sparkling wines that show a persistent foam on their surfaces.

HEAVY. Refers to heady or strong wines that are not necessarily equally strong in bouquet and flavor. Also used in describing the VISCOSITY of wines, especially sweet dessert wines.

HERMITAGE. Important wine-growing district in the northern Rhône region of France.

HEURIGE. See GRINZING.

HIPPOCRAS. Ancient medicinal elixir made from blending wine, spices, and honey or sugar.

HOCHHEIM. Important wine-growing village in the Rheingau region of Germany. The origin of the term HOCK.

HOCK. English term for German wines in general. Thought to have originated from HOCHHEIM, once a port city from which many German wines were shipped to the British Isles.

HOGSHEAD. Small wine cask, usually found in Bordeaux, containing approximately 225 liters, or about 59.5 U.S. gallons.

HOSPICES DE BEAUNE. Old hospital located in the city of Beaune, capital of the Burgundy region of France. The hospital has become famous for an annual auction sale of wines grown on vineyards it has acquired over the years through charitable donation.

HUNGARY. Twelfth-largest wine-growing nation, located in Asia Minor. Perhaps most famous for a dark red table wine called Egri Bikavér, or "Bull's Blood." Hungary is also well known as the producer of Tokay, Badacsony, Villány, and Szekszárd wines.

HYBRID. Result of a crossbreeding of two different varieties of vines. New cultivars may exhibit in varying proportions the properties contributed by each parent.

HYDROMETER. Floating instrument used to measure the density, specific gravity, or VISCOSITY of liquids, such as grape juice or wine.

ICE BUCKET. Device used to chill wines

prior to serving. Should be large enough to hold at least a 3/4-liter bottle along with cracked ice.

ITALY. Important European wine-growing nation that produces more wine annually than any other country, and Italians consume more wine on a yearly per capita basis than any other nationality. Most important regions include Lombardy, Piedmont, Tuscany, and Veneto. The United States imports more wine from Italy than from any other nation.

JEREZ. *See* SHERRY.

JEROBOAM. Large wine bottle that usually has a capacity of three liters, or four times the capacity of a common, standard wine bottle. Four-liter jeroboams also exist.

JEROPIGA. Concentrated grape juice, or grape syrup, made by boilingdown that is used for sweetening some wines produced in Portugal and Spain; *See* MISTELA.

JOHANNISBERG. Important wine-growing town in the Rheingau region of Germany; often used to refer to "Schloss Johannisberg," which is located nearby. Also a name given to some Swiss white wines grown from the variety JOHANNISBERG RIESLING.

JOHANNISBERG RIESLING. *See* RIESLING.

JOSEPHSHOF. Important vineyard in the Mosel region of Germany.

JULIÉNAS. Important wine-growing subdistrict of the Beaujolais district in the Burgundy region of France.

JURA. Wine-growing region in eastern France near the Swiss border.

JURANÇON. Wine-growing region in southern France near the Spanish border.

KABINETT. German wine made without the addition of sugar, generally considered the driest and lowest grade of *Qualitätswein mit Prädikat*.

KEG. Very small wooden container used to store wine. Usually less than 30 U.S. gallons in capacity.

KELLAR. German for "cellar"; often short for "wine cellar."

KELTER. German for "press." Often short for "grape press" or "wine press."

KEUKA LAKE. The "thumb" of the Finger Lakes region in upstate New York. Site of the largest New York State wineries.

KNIPPERLE. White wine grape variety cultivated in the Alsace region of France.

KOSHER WINE. Jewish sacramental wine made under rabbinical law and supervision.

KREUZNACH. Important wine-growing district in the Nahe region of Germany.

LABRUSCA. Short for *Vitis labrusca*, the native grape species indigenous to the northeastern part of the United States and the southernmost reaches of Canada.

LACRYMA CHRISTI. Legendary white wine grown upon the slopes of Mt. Vesuvius in the Campania region of Italy.

LACTIC ACID. Important acid constituent of grapes and wine that accounts for a cheeselike flavor. It is lactic acid that is fermented from malic acid during a MALOLACTIC FERMENTATION.

LAFITE-ROTHSCHILD. Famous Pauillac château in the Mádoc district of the Bordeaux region in France. One of the original "First-Growth" châteaux classified in the Paris Exposition of 1855.

LAGE. German for "locale." Generally used to describe a specific vineyard site.

LAGRIMA. Type of Málaga wine made from overripe grapes grown in Spain.

LAMBRUSCO. Very popular, rather sweet red wine grown in the Emilia-Romagna region of Italy. Popular in U.S. markets.

LATE HARVEST. Wines made from grapes purposely left past peak ripeness. A practice heavily employed in many of the winegrowing regions of Germany.

LATOUR. Famous Pauillac château located in the Mádoc district of the Bordeaux region of France. One of the original "First-Growth" châteaux classified in the Paris Exposition of 1855.

LEES. Sediment that precipitates from young wines during and after fermentation that is composed primarily of grape pulp, yeasts, color pigments, acid salts, etc. In clarification procedures, the "fining lees" denotes the precipitation of the fining agents.

LÉGER. French for "light." Wines that are *léger* have little body and/or color, sometimes because of a higher-than-normal alcohol content.

LEGS. Term used to describe the condensation of alcohol and other volatile compounds, including glycerol, on the inner surface of the wineglass above the surface of the wine. Not necessarily an indication of any particular positive or negative attribute of a wine.

LÉOGNAN. Important wine-growing *commune* in the Graves district of the Bordeaux region of France.

LIEBFRAUENSTIFT. Legendary vineyard that surrounds the Liebfrauenkirche (the "loving wife's church" that refers to Mary, the virgin mother of Jesus Christ) in the city of Worms, at the southern extremity of the Rheinhessen region of Germany; the birthplace of LIEBFRAUMILCH.

LIEBFRAUMILCH. Multiregional wine grown in the Rhineland of Germany. First produced by monks centuries ago from the LIEBFRAUENSTIFT vineyard; a very popular wine in U.S. markets.

LIGHT. Term used to describe a low value of VISCOSITY or body; the "mouth feel" of wines, usually dry white wines; also may be properly used to describe a wine lacking in values of bouquet or flavor.

LIQUOREUX. Term used to describe wines that are sweet and soft and taste as though they had been treated with a liqueur.

LIQUOROSO. Italian for "strong"; generally used for fortified wines.

LIVERMORE VALLEY. Important wine-growing region in California just east of San Francisco.

LOIRE. Important wine-growing region in the west-central portion of France.

LOMBARDY. Important wine-growing region of northern Italy.

LONG. Term used to describe wines that have flavors that linger in the mouth; abundant aftertaste. Also may refer to wines that are consistent over a number of vintages.

LUXEMBOURG. Small European wine-growing nation with approximately 2,000 acres of vineyards situated along the upper Mosel. It produces wines similar to those of Germany.

MÂCHE. French for "mash"; a term used to describe a very heavy-bodied wine, somewhat thick or pasty.

MÂCON. Important wine-growing capital city of the MÂCONNAIS district in the Burgundy region of France.

MADE AND BOTTLED BY. Labeling statement on U.S.-produced wines that indicates that at least 10 percent of the wine has been produced by the bottler.

MADEIRA. Important wine-growing island belonging to Portugal; famous for *Malmsey* and *Sercial* wines.

MADERIZATION. The oxidation of ethyl alcohol and acetic acid into aldehydes, considered a benefit in the making of *Madeira* or sherry but a detriment in white table wines.

MAGNUM. Wine bottle usually with twice the capacity of a normal 750 ml bottle.

MÁLAGA. Important wine-growing region in southern Spain; produces wines somewhat similar to sherry.

MALBEC. Important grape variety grown for red wines in the Bordeaux region of France; also becoming popular in California.

MALIC ACID. Acid constituent of grapes and wine that accounts for an applelike flavor. It is malic acid that is fermented into lactic acid during a MALOLACTIC FERMENTATION.

MALOLACTIC FERMENTATION. The transformation of malic acid to lactic acid, carbon dioxide gas, and energy by the action of bacteria.

MALMSEY. Legendary wine made from MALVASIA grapes grown on the Portuguese island of MADEIRA.

MALVASIA. Important grape variety cultivated on the Portuguese island of MADEIRA for the making of MALMSEY wines; also widely planted in other southern European locales. Known as *Malvoisie* in France.

MANZANILLA. Very dry, pale wine produced near the sherry region of Spain, not, however, a sherry.

MARCOBRUNNER. Famous white wine produced in the village of Erbach in the Rheingau region of Germany.

MARGAUX. Important wine-growing subdistrict of the Médoc district in the Bordeaux region of France. Also a famous château of the same name located in the same subdistrict that is one of the original "First-Growth" châteaux classified in the Paris Exposition of 1855.

MARQUE. French for "mark"; usually used to designate a trademark, such as *marque deposée*.

MARSALA. Sweet dessert wine made in a similar manner to sherry.

MARTILLAC. Important wine-growing *commune* in the Graves district of the Bordeaux region in France.

MASCARA. Important vineyard region of Algeria in North Africa.

MATURE. Term used to describe a wine that has been properly cellared and aged so as to have reached full development of all ORGANOLEPTIC qualities.

MATURITY. Level at which a wine has become MATURE. Also, full ripeness, a state in which grapes have developed upon the vine for the use intended by the wine master.

MAVRODAPHNE. Popular red dessert wine produced in Greece.

MAY WINE. Wines made in Germany in which the very aromatic leaves of the woodruff (the herb called *Waldmeister* in Germany) have been infused. Most often served cold in a *Bowle* with strawberries or some other fruit floating in it.

MEAD. Wine made from honey; traditional in England.

MÉDOC. Most important wine-growing district of the Bordeaux region in France. Important subdistricts in the more prestigeous Haut-Médoc include Margaux, Pauillac, St.-Julien and St.-Estèphe. Three of the original five "First-Growth" châteaux of the 1855 Paris Exposition Classification are in the Médoc.

MELLOW. General term usually referring to a wine that is not biting or harsh and/or has benefited from cellar treatments that have softened it. May also loosely refer to lower levels of sweetness.

MENDOCINO. Wine-growing locale in the North Coast region of California.

MERCUREY. Wine-growing subdistrict of the Chalonnais district in the Burgundy region of France.

METHUSELAH. Very large wine bottle, most often used in the Champagne region of France; generally eight times the size of a normal 750 ml wine bottle.

MEURSAULT. Important wine-growing subdistrict in the Côte de Beaune section of the Côte d'Or district of the Burgundy region in France.

MICHIGAN. Sixth-largest wine-growing state in the United States.

MILDEW. Fungal disease of vines that cripples both green tissue and the fruit. Two noteworthy types are commonly known as *downy* mildew (occurs when there is an excess of rainfall) and *powdery* mildew (occurs when there is a deficiency of rainfall).

MILLÉSIME. French for "vintage"; used in identifying the year in which the grapes that made a specific wine were grown.

MIS EN BOUTEILLES AU CHÂTEAU. French for "bottled at the winery estate"; used as an indication of authenticity of origin and quality.

MIS EN BOUTEILLES AU DOMAINE. French for "bottled at the vineyard estate"; used as an indication of guaranteed origin and quality.

MISSOURI. Seventh-largest wine-growing state in the United States.
See JEROPIGA.

MISTELLA. *See* JEROPIGA.

MOELLE. French for "marrow"; a term referring to oily wines, a bit sweet and heavy, but not as a result of sugar or of being LIQUOREUX.

MOELLEUX. French for "mellow."

MOLDY. Term referring to "off" values of bouquet and flavor, usually applied to wines that have been made from grapes stored or aged in cooperage that has harbored mold.

MONTANT. French for "rising"; a term used to describe wines that are pleasantly HEADY and spiritous.

MONTEFIASCONE. *See* EST! EST!! EST!!!

MONTHÉLIE. Important wine-growing *commune* in the Côte de Beaune section of the Côte d'Or district of the Burgundy region of France.

MONTRACHET. Important white wine-growing subdistrict of the Côte de Beaune section of the Côte d'Or district in the Burgundy region of France.

MORDANT. French for "biting"; a term used primarily to describe overpowering wines or blending wines that dominate the other constituents in a given blend.

MOREY. Important wine-growing *commune* in the Côte de Nuits section of the Côte d'Or district of the Burgundy region of France. Perhaps more often referred to as *Morey-St.-Denis*.

MORGON. Important wine-growing subdistrict in the Beaujolais district of the Burgundy region in France.

MOSCATEL. Dessert wines made from Muscat grapes in Portugal.

MOSCATO. Italian for "Muscat." The term may refer to any specific variety of Muscat grape cultivated in Italy; also refers to many different wines produced from Muscat grapes in that country.

MOSEL. Important wine-growing region along both banks of the Mosel River in Germany. Upriver, the Mosel flows through wine-growing regions in Luxembourg and France.

MOSELBLÜMCHEN. Name given to blends of wines grown in the Mosel region of Germany. Primarily fanciful, it carries no significance regarding specific origin or vinification controls.

MOU. French for "flabby." A term used to describe wines that lack body and acid balance.

MOULIN-À-VENT. Important wine-growing subdistrict in the Beaujolais district of the Burgundy region of France.

MOUSSEUX. French for "foaming." A term used to describe sparkling wines produced by the French *méthode champenoise* process, but not in the Champagne region, such as the sparkling Loire wine "Vouvray Mousseux." Sparkling wines not produced in the Champagne region may not be labeled "Champagne" in France. The Italian equivalent is *mussante*.

MOUTON-ROTHSCHILD. Famous Pauillac château in the Médoc district of the Bordeaux region of France. Recognized as a "First Growth" in 1973, the only modification ever made to the Paris Exposition of 1855 Classification.

MULLED WINE. Sweetened and spiced wine served hot, sometimes with a bit of lemon juice.

MUSCADELLE. White grape variety cultivated in the Bordeaux region of France.

MUSCADINE. Common name for *Vitis rotundifolia*—the grape species indigenous to the southeastern United States.

MUSCADET. Important wine-growing region in the western portion of the Loire Valley of France.

MUSCAT. Family of very aromatic grape varieties that spans several species. Muscats may be white, red, or black, but the most famous Muscat wines are white, such as *Muscat de Frontignan*.

MUSCATEL. Dessert wine grown from MUSCAT grapes. In the United States, the term generally refers to "cheap" California wine, but it does not necessarily have this negative connotation in European countries.

MUSIGNY. Important vineyard located in the *commune* of Chambolle- Musigny in the Côte de Nuits section of the Côte d'Or of Burgundy, France.

MUST. Crushed grapes that have been destemmed.

MUSTY. Term often used interchangeable with MOLDY or *mousey*; the distinction may be that musty wines can result from aging in decayed or waterlogged cooperage.

MUTAGE. Process of adding brandy to fermenting juice or MUST to arrest fermentation and retain some of the natural grape sugar.

MYCELIA. Concentration of fungus filaments.

NAHE. Important wine-growing region along the banks of the Nahe River in Germany.

NAPA. Refers to the important Napa Valley wine-growing region north of San Francisco, California. Some of the finest U.S. wines are grown in this locale.

NATURAL FERMENTATION. Fermentation taking place with natural, rather than cultured yeast cells.

NATURAL WINES. Wines resulting from NATURAL FERMENTATION; wines produced without the addition of sugar. Also, wines that have not been fortified with added brandy.

NATUREL. French for "natural"; generally refers to wines made without added sugar.

NATURWEIN. German term used to denote wines that have been fermented with only their natural grape sugar.

NEBBIOLO. Important red wine grape variety grown widely in northern Italy.

NÉGOCIANT. French for "shipper." The term refers to wine buyers in France who "negotiate" annually for the purchase of each vintage of wine produced by certain vintners. Négocians age the wines and bottle them under their labels and then ship them to markets through their distribution networks.

NERO. Italian for "very dark red."

NERVEUX. French for "vigorous"; a term for wines of strength and spirit, or with high alcohol and flavor, perhaps coupled with high TANNIC ACID content.

NEUCHÂTEL. Swiss wines grown in vineyards along the shores of the Neuchâtel Lake.

NEW YORK STATE. Second only to California in wine production in the United States. Most of the grapes cultivated for wine are varieties of native *Vitis labrusca*, although French-American hybrid vineyards have increased dramatically over the past several decades. In more recent times, small "boutique" wine estates have commenced, growing Old World *Vitis vinifera* varieties in modest acreages. Principal region is the Finger Lakes, although Chautauqua, the Hudson River Valley, and Long Island locales also have significant production.

NIAGARA. Important white native grape grown in the northeastern portion of the United States and the NIAGARA PENINSULA of Ontario, Canada.

NIAGARA PENINSULA. Southernmost portion of Ontario, Canada, situated between Lake Erie and Lake Ontario; one of the largest wine-growing regions of Canada.

NIERSTEIN. Important wine-growing town in the Rheinhessen region of Germany.

NOBLE ROT. *See* EDELFÄULE or POURRITURE NOBLE.

NOSE. Term relating to the reaction of the senses to a wine's odor; often used in describing the bouquet of a wine or the aroma of grapes, grape juice, and grape MUST.

NOUVEAU. Term for new or unaged wine that generally has a very fruity bouquet and flavor. Perhaps best exemplified by the annual production of BEAUJOLAIS NOUVEAU.

NUITS, CÔTE DE. Northern portion of the famous Côte d'Or district in the Burgundy region of France; famous for its superb reds.

NUITS-ST.-GEORGES. Important wine-growing town in the Côte de Nuits portion of the Côte d'Or district of the Burgundy region in France.

NUTTY. Descriptive term for a wine with a rather nutlike bouquet and/or flavor, usually derived from one or another process of MADERIZATION, such as in the making of *Madeira, Marsala,* or sherry.

ODOR. Term that most wine judges use to describe a fault in a wine's aroma and bouquet.

OEIL DE PERDRIX. "Eye of the Partridge"; rather pinkish gray tint observed in the color of some wines, most often whites made from black grapes, such as Blanc de Noir sparkling wines.

OENOLOGY. British spelling of ENOLOGY.

OHIO. Fifth-largest wine-growing state in the United States. The principal regions are in the Bass Islands-Sandusky area and along the Ohio River.

OIDIUM. *See* MILDEW.

OILY. Term used to describe noticeable levels of grape stem and/or seed oil found in a wine; generally an indication of poor winemaking.

OLOROSO. Darkest and sweetest of the Spanish sherries.

OPORTO. Important port wine trade center in northern Portugal.

OREGON. Wine-growing state that is presently increasing production rapidly; has the strictest labeling laws of any state in the United States.

ORGANOLEPTIC. Term referring to the impression a wine makes on the sensory organs of sight, smell, and taste.

ORIGINALABFÜLLUNG. German for

"bottled by the grower"; more strictly defined than "estate bottled," but recently discontinued under new German wine-labeling laws.

ORVIETO. White wine grown in the Umbria region of Italy.

OXIDATION. A reaction of wine constituents with oxygen, resulting, for example, in a browning of color and the formation of acetaldehyde from ethanol (alcohol). Wine aging is a form of controlled oxidation.

PALATINATE. Archaic name for the Rheinpfalz wine-growing region of Germany.

PALOMINO. Principal grape variety cultivated for sherry wine production in Spain; may also be found in limited acreages in California.

PASSE-TOUT-GRAINS. Blends of Pinot Noir and Gamay wines grown in the Burgundy region of France.

PASTEURIZATION. Process of inhibiting harmful microorganisms by the application of heat, in wine at temperatures ranging from 140 degrees to about 180 degrees Fahrenheit; may also be termed *flash* pasteurization when the desired temperature is held for only a short time, perhaps less than 30 seconds, then the wine is cooled back down to storage temperature. Both generally considered detrimental to wine quality.

PÂTEUX. French for "pasty." *See* MÂCHE.

PAUILLAC. Important *commune* in the Médoc district of the Bordeaux region of France.

PEDRO XIMÉNEZ. Important grape variety cultivated in Spain for the production of sherry and *Montilla*.

PENNSYLVANIA. Fourth-largest wine-growing state in the United States. The principal regions are located in the vicinity of the Lake Erie shoreline and the southeastern portion of the state.

PÉTILLANT. French for "slightly sparkling"; CRÉMANT is another term used in France to describe this quality in wines.

pH. Scale used to measure acidity from the strongest acidity at pH 1, to neutrality at pH 7, to the strongest alkalinity at pH 14.

PHYLLOXERA. Root louse (some airborne, leaf-galling types also exist), more precisely known as *Phylloxera vastatrix*. A parasite that attacks grapevines. The great *Phylloxera* epidemic of the mid-1800s killed most European vineyards, which were restored by grafting the vines onto U.S. rootstocks.

PIERCE'S DISEASE. Bacterial malady, especially prevalent in the southeastern United States, which often kills grapevines.

PIESPORT. Important wine-growing town in the middle Mosel region of Germany.

PINARD. French slang term used for ordinary red wine.

PINEAU DE LA LOIRE. Same as the grape variety Chenin Blanc. Of importance in the Loire Valley region of France; an increasingly popular variety in California and other U.S. regions.

PINOT NOIR. Refers to the great red wine grape variety, the source of the classic red wines of the Côte d'Or district (and Côte de Beaune subdistrict) in the Burgundy region in France. Pinot Noir has been grown with limited success in California. In recent times other states, principally Oregon, have achieved superior results from the variety. Pinot is often used incorrectly in combination with Chardonnay.

PIPE. Wine container equal to 2 hogsheads, or about 81 U.S. gallons.

PIQUANT. French term for a sharpness, or high level of acidity in a wine.

PIQUETTE. Secondary wine of very low quality made by the addition of water to grape POMACE. Generally, a wine made for consumption by winery workers at certain establishments in France.

PLAT. French for "dull"; a term for wines that have little body, flavor, or spirituousness.

POMACE. The pressed seeds, skins, and pulp that remain in the press after the juice or wine has been extracted.

POMEROL. Important wine-growing district in the Bordeaux region of France.

POMMARD. Important wine-growing *commune* in the Côte de Beaune section of the Côte d'Or district of the Burgundy region in France.

POP WINE. Usually refers to wines of rather low alcohol content that have been infused with fruit flavors.

POROSITY. Size limitation of foreign particles or suspended solids that may pass through a media used in wine filtration.

PORT. Sweet dessert wine produced in the Douro region of Portugal; also used as a generic term for similar wines produced elsewhere.

PORTUGAL. Eighth-largest wine-growing nation in Western Europe. Some of the more well-known regions are the Douro, Dao, Madeira, Minho, and Setúbal.

POUILLY. Important vineyard locale in the eastern portion of the Loire Valley region of France.

POUILLY-FUISSÉ. Important white wine locale embracing two neighboring villages, Pouilly and Fuissé, in the Mâconnais district of the Burgundy region of France.

POUILLY-FUMÉ. Superior wine type made of Sauvignon Blanc grapes grown near the village of Pouilly-sur-Loire of the Loire Valley region of France.

POURRITURE NOBLE. French for "noble rot"; *Botrytis cinerea*—a fungus that permeates the skins of grape berries, allowing moisture to evaporate and concentrating sugar and flavors. *Pourriture Noble* is associated with the classic Sauternes wines grown in the Bordeaux region of France. *See also* EDELFÄULE.

POUSSÉ. Strong fresh fruity bouquet and taste found particularly in wines that have fermented too long in contact with the skins of the grapes.

PPM. Abbreviation for "parts per million." An expression of the number of units of a given substance, such as sulfur dioxide (a wine preservative and antioxidant) found in a total of one million; roughly equivalent to "milligrams per liter."

PRÉCOCE. French for "precocious"; a term for wines that mature quickly.

PREMIER CRU. French for "First Growth." In the Bordeaux region the term applies to the five First Growths awarded this status in the Paris Exposition of 1855 Classification, plus Château Mouton-Rothschild so classified in 1973. In Burgundy, the term applies to a great number of the finest vineyards, but is secondary to GRAND CRU.

PRESS WINE. Wine that is extracted from a fermented MUST after the FREE RUN has been collected, generally considered somewhat inferior to the free run.

PRICKED. Term used to describe the odor of ethyl acetate (like paint thinner) in wines (not acetic acid or vinegar).

PRODUCED AND BOTTLED BY. Labeling statement on U.S.-produced wines that indicates at least 51 percent of the wine has been actually produced from grapes grown by the producer.

PROOF. Measure of alcoholic strength usually used for distilled spirits, seldom for wine. One degree of proof is approximately equal to one-half of one percent of alcohol by volume.

PROPRIÉTAIRE. Proprietor; owner.

PULIGNY-MONTRACHET. Important white wine *commune* containing a section of the fabled MONTRACHET vineyard in the Côte de Beaune section of the Côte d'Or district of the Burgundy region in France.

PUNCHEON. British wine-container measure equal to 56 Imperial gallons or 70 U.S. gallons.

PUNT. Indentation in the bottom of a wine bottle, originally intended to provide added strength to the container. In modern times it is being dispensed with as a result of technological advancement and production efficiency.

QUALITÄTSWEIN. German for "quality wine" and short for *Qualitätswein bestimmter Anbaugebiete* (often designated as QbA). Signifies that the wine has been grown and produced in one of eleven specific German wine districts as identified on the label.

QUALITÄTSWEIN MIT PRÄDIKAT. German for "quality wine with special properties" (QmP). A step above QbA because no sugar is allowed to be added in the production processes. The *Prädikat* categories, in ascending order, are KABINETT, SPÄTLESE, AUSLESE, BEERENAUSLESE, and TROCKEN-BEERENAUSLESE.

QUINTA. Vineyard estates in the Douro port wine region of Portugal.

RABOSO. Red table wine grown in the Veneto region of Italy.

RACKING. Transferring wines from one vessel to another to separate out the LEES.

RANCIO. Term used to describe the bouquet of some sweet oxidized wines; has no connection to the term *rancid*.

RAYA. Lower grade of Spanish sherry that is usually distilled into brandy or sold for modest prices.

RÉCOLTE. French for "vintage season" or "harvest."

RED TABLE WINE. Wines, usually made by the process of including the skins during fermentation in order to leach out red color pigments (although some are made by heating the MUST prior to pressing and fermentation), that are predominantly dry. Typical reds are the French wines of the Médoc, St-Émilion, and the Pomorol districts in the Bordeaux region and the wines of the Burgundy region that are made from the cultivars Pinot Noir and Gamay.

REGIONAL. Wines originating from a general area rather than from a specific village or vineyard are termed *regional*. Generally denotes lesser quality.

REHOBOAM. Large wine bottle, generally found in Champagne; the equivalent of about six normal-sized 750 ml bottles.

REIMS. Important wine-producing city in the Champagne region of France.

REMUAGE. *See* RIDDLING.

RESERVA. Spanish for "reserve"; wines selected for special aging and/or usage.

RESIDUAL SUGAR. Generally refers to the amount of sweetness left in a finished wine; wines that are not fermented dry have residual sugar.

RETSINA. Greek wine that has been infused with pine resin to produce a rather turpentine-like bouquet.

RHEINGAU. Important wine-growing region in the Rhineland of Germany.

RHEINHESSEN. Important wine-growing region in the Rhineland of Germany.

RHINE WINE. Wine grown from vineyards in the Rhineland of Germany; also loosely applied to any white wine made in the German styles or from grapes indigenous to Germany.

RHÔNE. Important wine-growing region located on both sides of the Rhone River in southern France. Upriver the Rhône also serves as a wine-growing locale in Switzerland.

RICH. Term used to describe wines that are heavy-bodied or with abundant and robust bouquet and flavor values.

RICHEBOURG. Important vineyard in the Côte de Nuits section of the Côte d'Or district of the Burgundy region in France.

RIDDLING. The French REMUAGE. The process of working the sediment in bottle-fermented sparkling wine into the neck of the bottle, usually performed on a rack or table that holds the bottles inverted. The riddling method is generally to raise each bottle slightly and, with a quarter-turn, to firmly reinsert the bottle back to its resting place so as to jar the sediment loose from the sides of the bottle. After several weeks of thrice-daily riddling, all the sediment has been made to spiral downward into the bottle neck.

RIESLING. Principal grape variety cultivated for the finest of German wines; also properly referred to as JOHANNISBERG RIESLING or, in California, as White Riesling; not to be confused with Gray Riesling or Missouri Riesling, which are not true Riesling grapes. The Emerald Riesling is a California-developed hybrid from Johannisberg Riesling parentage.

RIOJA. Important wine-growing region in northern Spain.

RIPE. Term generally used to describe wines that have reached their full term of aging or have achieved a proper state of bouquet and flavor development.

RISERVA. Italian for "reserve"; the same as the Spanish RESERVA.

ROMANÉE, LA. Important red wine vineyard in the Côte de Nuits section of the Côte d'Or district of the Burgundy region in France.

ROMANÉE-CONTI. Important vineyard in the Côte de Nuits section of the Côte d'Or district of the Burgundy region in

France. Produces some of the most expensive red wine in the world during superior vintages.

ROMANIA. Eastern European country; the tenth-largest wine-growing nation in the world.

ROSATO. Italian for "rosé."

ROSÉ. Generic name for pink table wines made in the same manner as red wines but with less skin contact time during fermentation. Can be dry, near-dry, or rather sweet. Examples are *Anjou* and *Tavel.*

ROTTEN EGGS. Term used to describe wines that have degenerated because of the formation of hydrogen sulfide (H_2S).

ROUND. Term referring to a wine with a good balance of all characteristics; a wine that has been blended harmoniously.

RUBY CABERNET. California-developed hybrid from CABERNET SAUVIGNON parentage.

RUSSIAN RIVER. Important wine-growing valley in the Sonoma region of northern California.

SAAR. Important wine-growing district situated upon the banks of the Saar River which, like the wine river Ruwer, is a tributary to Germany's Mosel River. The Mosel-Saar-Ruwer are often grouped together as a single region.

SACK. Usually refers to a dry, or somewhat dry, Spanish sherry. This was a favorite wine of Shakespeare. The name *sack* is thought to be a Spanish derivation of the French *sec*, meaning "dry."

ST.-ÉMILION. Important wine-growing district in the Bordeaux region of France.

ST.-ESTEPHE. Important wine-growing subdistrict in the Médoc district of the Bordeaux region in France.

ST.-JULIEN. Important wine-growing subdistrict in the Médoc district of the Bordeaux region of France.

ST.-PÉRAY. Important wine-growing *commune* in the Rhône Valley region of France.

SALMANAZAR. Largest commercially available wine bottle; the equivalent of twelve normal-sized 750 ml bottles. Generally found only in the Champagne region of France.

SAMOS. Important wine-growing island of Greece.

SANCERRE. Important wine-growing locale near Pouilly in the Loire Valley region of France.

SANGIOVESE. Red grape variety cultivated widely in the Tuscany region of Italy.

SANGUE DI GIUDA. Italian for "the blood of Judas"—a red wine grown in the Lombardy region of Italy.

SAN JOAQUIN. Huge wine-growing region in California; also known as the *Central Valley* region.

SANTA CLARA. Important wine-growing region south of San Francisco, California.

SANTA CRUZ. Important wine-growing region south of San Francisco, California.

SANTENAY. Important wine-growing *commune* in the Côte de Beaune section of the Côte d'Or district of the Burgundy region of France.

SANTORIN. Important wine-growing island of Greece.

SARDINIA. Important wine-growing island of Italy.

SAUMUR. Important wine-growing district near Anjou in the central portion of the Loire Valley region of France.

SAUTERNES. Important wine-growing district in the Bordeaux region of France. Some U.S. wines are generically labeled "Sauternes" or "Sauterne," as well as "Haut Sauternes." Most of them, however, bear little resemblance to the very expensive true Sauternes of France.

SAUVIGNON. Generally refers to the Sauvignon Blanc grape cultivated widely in the Sauternes district of Bordeaux and in the Pouilly district of Loire. The *fumé* wines of Pouilly are the inspiration for the *fumé* wines now being made in northern California; these California wines are labeled either "Sauvignon Blanc" or "Fumé Blanc." May also refer to the renowned red Cabernet Sauvignon grape variety.

SAVOIE. Wine-growing region located in eastern France near the Swiss border.

SCHAUMWEIN. German term used to denote sparkling wines. *See* SEKT.

SCHLOSS JOHANNISBERG. Historic monastic vineyard in the RHEINGAU region of Germany.

SCHLOSS VOLLRADS. Important vineyard near SCHLOSS JOHANNISBERG in the Rheingau region of Germany.

SCUD. Slang term used to describe mold that may develop on wines that are low in alcohol content.

SCUPPERNONG. Variety of southeastern U.S. Muscadine grape; often used to refer to any white variety of MUSCADINE grape, though this is technically incorrect.

SEC. French for "dry" or "without sweetness." Also used to describe sparkling wines that may have some residual sweetness, but are not as sweet as DOUX. Dry sparkling wines are generally referred to as BRUT or NATUREL.

SECCO. Italian for "dry"; although the term is often used to describe wines that are not totally dry.

SÈCHE. French term used to describe flat wines that have become bitter.

SEDIMENT. The precipitated solids formed as a result of fermentation, clarification, or some other cellar process, referred to in the wine trade as LEES. The sediment in wine bottles, however, is properly termed *sediment*, not *lees*.

SEIBEL, ALBERT. Important hybridizer of grapes in southern France during the latter part of the nineteenth century and the early portion of the twentieth century. Some of his most popular hybrids are Seibel 5279 (Aurora Blanc), Seibel 5898 (Rougeon), Seibel 9110 (Vignoles), and Seibel 10878 (Chelois). Most of the Seibel hybrids are now grown commercially in the central and eastern portions of the United States.

SEKT. German term for sparkling wines, not necessarily made by the traditional French *méthode champenoise* process.

SÉMILLON. Important grape variety grown in the Sauternes district of the Bordeaux region of France. Cultivated in limited acreages in California and other areas of the United States.

SERCIAL. Important grape variety cultivated on the Portuguese island of Madeira.

SEVE. The perfuming of the palate that lingers after the wine has been swallowed.

SEYVE-VILLARD. Important grape hybridizer who developed, among others, the widely cultivated Seyval Blanc (Seyve-Villard 5276) in France.

SHERRY. English name for the fortified wine of the Jerez district of southern Spain, sherry is characterized by a nutlike bouquet and flavor. More loosely used as the generic name for any wine that has a high aldehyde content deliberately generated in order to make a sherry-style wine.

SICILY. Import wine-growing island of Italy.

SOAVE. Popular white wine grown in the Veneto region of northern Italy.

SOFT. Term usually referring to white or rosé table wines that are low in both acidity and astringency; much the same as *smooth*.

SOLERA. The Spanish fractional blending system used to age sherry wines. Wines are blended in tiers of casks, with each successive tier containing blends of older wines. After a set period, wines are partially drawn from younger tiers and blended into the older tiers. The last solera contains the wines that are drawn off for bottling.

SONOMA. Important wine-growing valley north of San Francisco, California. Some of the finest U.S. wines are grown here.

SOUR. Term often used incorrectly in the United States to describe the acidity or astringency of a wine.

SOUTH AFRICA. Important wine-growing nation, the ninth-largest wine producer in the world. Some of the most notable vineyard regions in the country are Constantia, Overberg, Paarl, Robertson, Stellenbosch, Tulbagh, and Worcester.

SOUTIRAGE. French for "racking." *See* RACKING.

SOVIET UNION. Important wine-growing nation; the fourth-largest wine producer in the world, with about twice the output of the United States. Nearly all of the wine in the Soviet Union is grown along the northern shores of the Black Sea and the western shores of the Caspian Sea. The most notable vineyard regions are in Moldavia, the Ukraine, Georgia, and Armenia.

SOYEUX. French for "silky"; a term used to describe wines with no roughness or harshness that produce a very agreeable sensation on the palate.

SPAIN. Important wine-growing nation; the third-largest wine producer in the world. The most important vineyard regions are Jerez de la Frontera (sherry), Málaga, Rioja, Catalonia, and La Mancha.

SPARKLING BURGUNDY. Originally a U.S. term for sparkling red wine, it has caught on in France, and some "Sparkling Burgundy" wines are now produced in the Burgundy region of France.

SPARKLING WINE. Wine, usually white or rosé, in which carbon dioxide gas is captured during secondary fermentation in a closed container. The traditional French method of bottle-fermentation is called *méthode champenoise*. The bulk, or tank, method is called the CHARMAT process. The most famous sparkling wine is Champagne.

SPÄTBURGUNDER. German term for the French Pinot Noir grape variety.

SPÄTLESE. German for "late picked"; refers to grapes left on the vine for several days or weeks after ripening to dehydrate the grapes berries of some of their natural water, yielding high sugar concentrations.

SPECIFIC GRAVITY. Ratio of the weight of a given volume of liquid compared to an equal volume of water.

SPICY. Term for bouquet and flavor reminiscent of spices; such as cinnamon or nutmeg. The best example would be wine properly made from Gewürztraminer, which is indigenous to the Alsace in France.

SPRITZIG. German term for slight effervescence; used to describe very young wines that have not fully fermented and produce a prickling sensation upon the palate. Such wines are quaffed during the fall wine festivals in Germany.

SPUMANTE. Sparkling wines made in Italy; the same as *mussante* wines. Produced either by the traditional French *méthode champenoise* or CHARMAT (bulk) process.

STALKY. Term used to describe wines that have become oily due to excessive contact with grape stalks (stems).

STEINBERG. Important vineyard in the Rheingau region of Germany.

STEMMY. *See* STALKY.

SULFUR DIOXIDE. A compound of sulfur and oxygen (SO_2) used in winemaking as an antioxidant, bactericide, and yeasticide. Also used in winery cleaning procedures as a disinfectant and preservative.

SUPERIORE. Italian DOC term relating to a wine of superior grade, usually a result of further aging, either in bottle or cask.

SUPPLE. *See* ROUND.

SWEETNESS. Taste sensation directly opposite to sour; in wine, sweetness results from added or residual sugar content. Wines with sweetness levels that are barely detectable may be properly termed *near-dry*; wines described as *sweet*, such as port and Sauternes, have a noticeable sweet taste.

SWITZERLAND. Important wine-growing nation in Europe; the twentieth-largest wine-producing country in the world. The most notable vineyard regions are Valais, Vaud, and Neuchâtel.

SYLVANER. Important white grape variety cultivated in most wine-growing regions in Germany; also grown in Italy and the Alsace region of France. There are only very limited plantings of Sylvaner in the United States. Spelled as "Silvaner" in Germany.

SYRAH. Important red grape variety cultivated in the Rhône Valley region of France; increasingly planted in the vineyards of California and other U.S. regions. Not to be confused with Petit Sirah, which is a different variety. Spelled as "Shirz" in its native Iran.

TABLE WINE. In the United States, is any wine having less than 14 percent alcohol content that qualifies for the $.17 per gallon tax category, but generally refers to any wine consumed at the table with food.

TÂCHE, LA. Important vineyard in the Côte de Nuits section of the Côte d'Or district of the Burgundy region of France.

TAFELWEIN. Wine without any specific quality classification in Germany, but if labeled "Deutsche Tafelwein," it must be German in origin. "Landwein" is a Tafelwein with even stricter requirements.

TANNIC. Term generally used for wines that are astringent or stemmy (grape stems contain astringent flavor values).

TANNIC ACID. Astringent acid with a leathery taste, normally added to increase the life span of a wine by slowing down the aging process.

TANNIN. Special phenolic compounds found in grape stems, seeds, and skins that contribute to astringency, particularly in young red wines. Tannins are also introduced in wines from the wood of aging vessels and may lengthen the life of wines by slowing oxidation reactions.

TART. Term used to describe wines that are high in fixed or total acidity.

TARTARIC ACID. Natural acid of grapes. Tartaric acid is unstable in wine at cold temperatures, and it will precipitate out as the acid salt potassium bitartrate (CREAM OF TARTAR).

TASTE. Sensations produced on the palate, which detects acidity, bitterness, and sweetness, as well as the VISCOSITY of wine.

TASTEVIN. Small tasting cup; the best are made of silver; used for tasting wines. Used predominantly in Burgundy.

TAVEL. Important rosé wine-growing district in the lower Rhône Valley region of France.

TAWNY. Amber hue taken on by red wines that have been exposed to high tempera-ture and/or aging terms; Tawny Port is a good example.

TEINTURIER. Very heavily pigmented black grape generally used for blending to enhance color intensity.

TENUTA. Italian for "estate"; usually denotes a wine and/or vineyard estate; may also be seen expressed as *tenementi*.

TERLANO. Important wine-growing locale in the Alto Adige region of Italy.

TEROLDEGO. Important wine-growing locale in the Alto Adige region of Italy.

TEXAS. Wine-growing state that is rapidly increasing its wine production.

TINTO. Portuguese or Spanish for "red."

TIRAGE. Laying of bottles on their sides in piles for secondary fermentation in the production of sparkling wines.

TOKAY. Dessert wine produced in Hungary.

TONNEAU. Traditional Bordeaux wine cask measuring 900 liters or about 238 U.S. gallons.

TOPPING UP. Refilling of casks in order to replace the wine that has been lost in the space known as the *ullage. See* ULLAGE.

TOTAL ACIDITY. Aggregate of all acids measured in a given wine; the sum of *fixed* and *volatile* acids.

TOURAINE. Important wine-growing district in the central Loire Valley region of France.

TOURNER. French for "turned"; a term used to describe wines that have turned into vinegar or decomposed in some other way.

TRABEN-TRARBACH. Important wine-growing community in the middle Mosel region of Germany.

TRAMINER. *See* GEWÜRZTRAMINER.

TREBBIANO. Important grape variety cultivated in central and northern Italy.

TRENTINO. Important wine-growing region in northern Italy.

TRIER. Ancient Roman wine-growing settlement, now the capital city of the upper Mosel region of Germany.

TROCKENBEERENAUSLESE. German for "dry berry special selection"; the separation of those berries on each bunch of grapes that have been *raisinized* by the noble mold, *BOTRYTIS cinerea*. The juice is highly concentrated in sugar content and may have a rather caramel-like flavor. Slowly fermented with a very sweet finish, Trockenbeerenauslese is one of the most expensive wines made in the world.

TUSCANY. Important wine-growing region in central Italy.

UGNI BLANC. Same variety as the Trebbiano of Italy.

ULLAGE. Air space in a wooden aging vessel generated by seepage, evaporation, and assimilation of the wine in the pores. The ullage should be refilled at least weekly in order to keep the wine from exposure to oxygen. *See* TOPPING UP.

UMBRIA. Important wine-growing region in central Italy.

UNITED STATES. Sixth-largest wine-growing nation in the world. The principal states are California, New York, Washington, Oregon, Texas, Pennsylvania, Ohio, Michigan, Missouri, Arkansas, and Virginia.

ÜRZIG. Important vineyard in the middle Mosel region of Germany.

USÉ. French term used to describe wines that have not matured properly; a faulty maturation due to some other cause than a leaking cork.

VALDEPEÑAS. Red wine grown in the La Mancha region of Spain.

VALPOLICELLA. Red wine grown in the Veneto region of Italy.

VALTELLINA. Red wine grown in the Lombardy region of Italy.

VARIETAL WINE. Wine labeled for the variety of grape from which it was predominantly or entirely made. Good examples would be California "Cabernet Sauvignon" and New York State "Seyval Blanc."

VARIETY. Individual strain or cultivar within a group of closely related plants. Though each variety has its own unique characteristics, it will still be recognizable as a member of its species.

VAT. Tub or some other wine container constructed to rest in a vertical position, as opposed to a cask, which rests in a horizontal position.

VELOUTÉ. French for "velvety"; a term used to describe wines with no harshness or bitterness that are nonetheless dry, full-bodied, and well balanced.

VELTLINER. White grape variety

cultivated principally in Austria and Switzerland. Sometimes referred to as Grüner Veltliner.

VELVET. Term used to describe the softness and delicacy of wines of perfect balance that have reached peak maturity.

VENDANGE. French for "grape harvest"; used to refer to the harvesting of the grapes and the making of new wines.

VENDEMMIA. Italian for "grape harvest"; the same as VENDANGE.

VENETO. Important wine-growing region located in northern Italy.

VÉRAISON. French viticultural term used to describe the point in the growing season when grapes start to ripen, become soft, and begin to change color.

VERDICCHIO. White wine grown in the Marches region of central Italy.

VERMOUTH. Wine that contains aromatic essences derived from herbs, roots, spices, etc. Dry vermouth is generally known as the French type and is white. Sweet vermouth, often referred to as the Italian type, is normally very dark from the addition of caramel color.

VERT. French for "green"; a term for young wines containing high acidity levels.

VERZENAY. Important wine-growing village in the Champagne region of France.

VIGNE. French for "vine."

VIGNOBLE. French for "vineyard."

VILA NOVA DE GAIA. Important port wine center located opposite the city of Oporto on the Douro River in Portugal.

VIN. French for "wine."

VIÑA. Spanish for "vineyard."

VIN DE PAILLE. French term for wine made from grapes dried upon straw (paille) mats in order to enrich sugar and flavor content prior to being made into wine.

VIN DE PAYS. French for "wine of the area"; the wine is usually consumed in the locale where it is grown and rarely found outside this locale.

VINEUX. French for "vinous"; a term used to characterize wines according to the soil and climate in which they were grown, as opposed to their fruit flavor attributes.

VIN GRIS. French term used to describe wines having only a faint hue of pinkish color. See OEIL DE PERDRIX.

VINHO VERDE. "Green" wine grown in the Minho region of Portugal.

VINIFERA. Short for *Vitis vinifera*, the most prolific species of wine grape grown on earth. Also known as the *Old World* vine, generally considered to be the finest wine-grape species. The cultivars CHARDONNAY, PINOT NOIR, CABERNET SAUVIGNON, and JOHANNISBERG RIESLING are classic examples of *Vitis vinifera*.

VINICULTURE. Art, science, and study of both grape growing and winemaking as related disciplines.

VINIFICATION. Process of making grapes into wine.

VINO. Italian and Spanish for "wine."

VINO COTTO. Concentration of grape juice by heating or boiling down. The "cooking" evaporates the water from the natural juice and enriches sugar and flavor content.

VINO DE PASTO. Pale dry sherry type, perhaps a bit softer than a *fino*.

VINO PASSITO. Wine made from grapes dried in raisinlike fashion to enrich their sugar and flavor content prior to being made into a wine; an Italian term.

VINO SANTO. Same as VINO PASSITO.

VINOSITY. Term that refers to the *vinous* (soil and/or vegetative flavors) as opposed to *fruity* (grape ester flavors) bouquet and taste.

VIN ROSÉ. *See* ROSÉ.

VIN SEC. French for "dry wine."

VINTAGE. Crop of grapes being harvested; the wine from a crop of grapes from a particular year. A *vintage* year is often construed as a good or great growing season that has resulted in a distinguished wine.

VINTNER. Wine maker; usually refers to the ownership and/or management of a wine-making facility.

VIRGINIA. Wine-growing state that is presently increasing production rapidly.

VISCIDITY. Lack of tannic acid that causes a wine to age prematurely.

VISCOSITY. Resistance of a gas or liquid to flow; a measure of adhesion and cohesion.

VITICULTURE. Art, science, and study of grape growing.

VITIS. Taxonomic name of the grapevine species, of which there are more than fifty known so far. The most important wine species is the Old World *Vitis vinifera*. *See* VINIFERA.

VOLATILE ACIDITY. Organic acids in wines that are evaporative or distillable. The chief one is ACETIC ACID.

VOLNAY. Important red wine-growing *commune* located in the Côte de Beaune section of the Côte d'Or district of the Burgundy region of France.

VOSNE-ROMANÉE. Important wine-growing *commune* in the Côte de Nuits section of the Côte d'Or district of the Burgundy region of France; reds are primarily produced, but there are some whites.

VOUGEOT. Important wine-growing *commune* located in the Côte de Nuits section of the Côte d'Or district of the Burgundy region of France; reds are produced here primarily, but there are some whites also.

VOUVRAY. White wine grown in the Touraine district of the Loire Valley region of France.

WASHINGTON. Third-largest wine-growing state in America. The most notable regions are located in the Seattle-Tacoma bay area, the Port Angeles shoreline, and the Columbia-Yakima river valleys in the southeastern portion of the state.

WEIN. German for "wine."

WEINGUT. German for "wine estate" or "vineyard and winery estate."

WEINKELLEREI. German for "wine cellar."

WHITE TABLE WINES. Wines made dry, or nearly dry, from the juice of either white or red grapes, usually with an alcohol content of less than 14 percent by volume. The French wines from Chablis typify vinous or flinty dry whites. Flowery white wines are common to Germany, and fruity white wines are found in New York State and are made chiefly from the Niagara grape cultivar. Sauternes from Bordeaux in France are legally taxed as white table wines, but are so sweet as to be used primarily for dessert courses.

WINE. Product resulting from the fermentation of grape juice or grape MUST. The five main categories of wine are TABLE WINE, SPARKLING WINE, DESSERT WINE, APERITIF WINE, and POP WINE.

WINE GROWING. Art and science of growing grapes and making wine commercially.

WINERY. Building, cave, room, vault, etc., in which grapes are made into wine.

WINZER. German for "vintner" or "winegrower."

WINZERGENOSSENSCHAFT. German for "winegrowers cooperative association."

WINZERVEREIN. German for "winegrowers cooperative."

WOODY. Term that refers to wines that have a bouquet and flavor characteristic of wet wood, usually as a result of overraging.

WORMS. Ancient city located on the Rhine River of Germany that marks the boundary between the Rheinhessen and Rheinpfalz wine-growing regions; also the location of the legendary Liebfrauenkirche, the birthplace of LIEBFRAUMILCH.

WÜRZBURG. Important wine-growing town located in the Franken region of Germany; not to be confused with Würzberg, which is located in the Saar district of the Mosel region of Germany.

XERES. Archaic spelling of Spain's *Jerez* or Sherry.

YEASTS. One-celled plants, about one micron in diameter, that secrete enzymes that convert sugar(s) into ethyl alcohol, carbon dioxide gas, and energy.

YEASTY. Term used in a negative sense when describing the characteristic bouquet and flavor of yeast in wines, usually caused by excessive contact with the LEES; used in a positive sense for Champagne or other bottle-fermented sparkling wines in which a good dissolution of yeast has occurred in TIRAGE aging.

YQUEM. Famous Sauternes château and the only producer of white wines to be classified with the five "First Growths" in the Paris Exposition of 1855 Classification; located in the Bordeaux region of France.

YUGOSLAVIA. Eastern European country; the eleventh-largest wine-growing nation in the world.

ZELL. Important wine-growing town in the Mosel region of Germany.

ZINFANDEL. Red grape variety grown primarily in California.

ZUCCO. White wine grown on the Italian island of Sicily.

ZWICKER. Random blend of white wines grown in the Alsace region of France, primarily for local consumption.

ZYMASE. Enzymes produced by wine yeasts that are essential for fermentation. *See* YEASTS.

INDEX

669